THOMAS BETTERTON

studio of Kneller

A
BIOGRAPHICAL
DICTIONARY

OF

ACTORS, ACTRESSES, MUSICIANS, DANCERS,
MANAGERS & OTHER STAGE PERSONNEL
IN LONDON, 1660 - 1800

Volume 2: Belfort *to* Byzand

by

PHILIP H. HIGHFILL, JR., KALMAN A. BURNIM
and
EDWARD A. LANGHANS

SOUTHERN ILLINOIS UNIVERSITY PRESS
CARBONDALE AND EDWARDSVILLE

List of Illustrations

THEATRE EXTERIORS AND INTERIORS

	page
Goodman's Fields Theatre, c. 1730s	465
Haymarket Theatre, Mid-Eighteenth Century	466
Drury Lane Theatre, 1775	467
Drury Lane Theatre Proscenium Arch, 1793	468
Drury Lane Theatre After 1797 Alterations	469
Drury Lane Theatre, 1791–94	470
Bagnigge Wells, 1788	471
Surrey Theatre, 1828	472
Lincoln's Inn Fields Theatre After It Became a Warehouse	473
Sadler's Wells, 1792	474
Wren's Section View of a Restoration Playhouse, c. 1672–74	475
Front of Astley's Amphitheatre, c. 1780(?)	476
Arena of Astley's Amphitheatre, c. 1780(?)	477
Covent Garden Theatre, before 1794	478
Covent Garden Theatre, 1808	479
Dorset Garden Theatre, 1673	480
Stage of Dorset Garden Theatre, 1673	481
King's Theatre in the Haymarket, c. 1780	482
Pantheon Theatre, 1795	483
Orchard Street Theatre in Bath	484
King's Theatre in the Haymarket, 1780s(?)	485
A Country Fair Booth	486
A Provincial Theatre, 1788	487

Volume 2

Belfort *to* Byzand

Belfort, Mrs *(fl. 1760–1761)*, *dancer.*
Mrs Belfort (or Belfont) appeared as one of the followers of Ceres in *The Rape of Proserpine* at Covent Garden on 20 October 1760; she danced in the several winter performances of the work up to 12 January 1761 when she was replaced by Miss Daw.

Belguard. *See* BELLGUARD.

Belingham. *See* BELLINGHAM.

Bell, Mr *(fl. 1750–1751)*, *singer, actor?*
A Mr Bell sang, with Hemskirk, Mrs Yates, and Mrs Hooper, at "a Concert of Vocal and Instrumental Music" at Sadler's Wells on 22 April 1751. This Bell was heard no more in London; but there is a chance that he was the Bell who joined the Hallam company in New York to make his American debut on 17 September 1753 at the Nassau Street Theatre as Sir John Bevil in *The Conscious Lovers.*

The name of the American Bell occurs once in the fragmentary records of the Philadelphia stage in the eighteenth century. His first appearance there was at Hallam's New Theatre in Water Street, for Adcock's benefit on 12 June 1754, playing Axalla, in *Tamerlane.*

Bell, Mr *(fl. 1785–1791)*, *equestrian, dancer, tumbler.*
A Mr Bell was noticed with seven others in *A New Dance, the Country Wake* at Astley's Circus on 24 July 1786. The bills for the performances at this amphitheatre are incomplete, and he was probably with the company earlier, inasmuch as a "Master Bell," presumably his son, was noticed on 13 June 1786 when, according to an affidavit signed by Philip Astley the proprietor, he "threw . . . 18 flip-flaps, and a somerset."

Mr Bell was on the company list in 1788, and in May 1791 was involved in a tumbling act and a dance called *The Irish Fair* with Mrs Bell; in July he displayed "equestrian skill" and shared in two comic dances, *The Merry Sailors* and *The Happy Negroes.* Later the same month, a diversion called *The Metamorphose* was performed, on "two horses by Mr Bell." Nothing further is known of the Bell family's activities.

Bell, Mrs *(fl. 1791)*, *dancer. See* BELL, MR *(fl. 1785–1791)*.

Bell, Master *(fl. 1785–1786)*, *tumbler. See* BELL, MR *(fl. 1785–1791)*.

Bell, Miss. *See* FARREN, MRS WILLIAM.

Bell, Christopher *(fl. 1628–1661)*, *flutist, sackbut player.*
Christopher Bell's musical career was nearly over before the Restoration, but he was one of the musicians from pre-Commonwealth days who lived to serve under Charles II. He was first mentioned as a royal employee on 15 July 1628, and his name appeared periodically on warrants through 1641, one being a petition of Bell's against Walter Gray (apparently not a musician) for using abusive language against him. All of Bell's service during these early years was in the wind music under the mastership of Nicholas Lanier.

Though there is no record of his interregnum activity, Bell was appointed on 1 January 1661 as a musician in ordinary for flute and sackbut to Charles II at a salary of £40 yearly plus an annual livery fee of £16 2s. 6d. The last mention of him that is specifically dated is a warrant of 3 August 1661. Sometime shortly after this he must have died; a list of musicians dated 1660 has a later but undated note to the effect that Phillip Beckett replaced the deceased Mr Bell.

Bell, Richard *d. 1672, actor.*
Richard Bell may have been a member of the King's Company at their Bridges

Street playhouse in March 1668 when he was twice involved with the law, but no roles are known for him until a year later. On 20 March 1668 a warrant was issued to arrest some overly eager bailiffs who had apprehended Bell illegally, and the next day another warrant stated that William Davis had a case against Bell; nothing more is known of these matters. The following theatrical season Bell was performing, his first role of record being Christophero in *The Island Princess* on 6 November 1668; sometime during the season he also played the medium-sized comic part of Frapolo in *The Sisters*. He was active with the King's troupe for the next two seasons, but his roles were usually secondary ones: the Duke of Arcos in *The Conquest of Granada* in December 1670, Vincent in *Love in a Wood* in March 1671, and Julius Caesar sometime during the season. His last recorded role, about January 1672, was again Caesar. Summers, citing no evidence, states that Bell was homosexual.

On 25 January 1672 the Bridges Street Theatre burned and Bell was killed in the fire. The parish registers of St Paul, Covent Garden, list a double burial on 27 January for Richard Bell and Frances, daughter of Richard Chace—apparently another victim of the disaster.

Bell, Thomas *d. 1743, singer.*

Thomas Bell, a countertenor, was paid £11 10*s.* per quarter for performing at the Cannons concerts sometime during the period 1717–20. He may have been the Bell who fought a duel at Epsom in 1689 with dramatist and song writer Thomas D'Urfey which Tom Brown satirized in verse:

> *I Sing of a Duel in Epsom befel,*
> *'Twixt fa-so-la Durfey, and so-la-mi Bell:*
> *But why do I mention the scribbling Brother?*
> *For naming the one, you may guess at the other.*
> *Betwixt them there happen'd a horrible Clutter,*

> Bell *set up the loud Pipes, and* Durfey *did splutter.*
> *Draw,* Bell, *wer't thou Dragon, I'll spoil thy soft Note,*
> *Thy squeaking, said t'other, for I'll cut thy Throat.*
> *With a Scratch on the Finger the Duel's dispatch'd,*
> *Thy Clineas (Oh Sidney!) was never so match'd.*

If Bell squabbled in his youth, he was serious in his maturity. After his engagement at Cannons he was sworn a Gentleman of the Chapel Royal in ordinary on 14 March 1720, replacing the deceased Daniel Williams; and though details are missing, he also held posts at St George's Chapel at Windsor, and at Eton.

He wrote his will on 27 April 1743, describing himself as of Datch, Buckinghamshire, and one of the "Singing men" of the Chapel Royal in London. The will was proved on 20 May 1743 by his son and executor Herbert. Thomas Bell had two other sons, James and Robert, and a daughter Ann. To his wife Elizabeth he left the bulk of his estate, which consisted of some furniture, insurance, and arrears due him from the Chapel Royal, Windsor Chapel, and Eton. After his death his widow received—or was supposed to receive—a pension from St George's Chapel, Windsor.

Bell, Thomas *d. 1815, actor, dancer.*

Thomas Bell made his first verifiable theatrical attempt as a member of an irregular company at the Haymarket Theatre on 24 March 1778. He played Blunt in Cibber's alteration of *Richard III*.

Bell was in a few minor unnamed parts in out-of-season performances at the Haymarket in 1784–85, but after this he was probably not seen in London again. He apparently toured and was the Bell who was at Edinburgh in all the winter seasons between 1782–83 and 1793–94. He was also there in June 1795. According to the *Hi-*

bernian Journal, he made his Irish debut at Dublin on 13 April 1796.

There is a possibility that our subject was the Thomas Bell who was executor of the will of the actor William Hamilton, which was signed on 30 November 1801. That Thomas Bell was then living in Dean Street, Soho. But the Edinburgh Bell died in Scotland in 1815 and was buried in Coupar-Angus churchyard.

Bellam, [Mr?] [*fl. 1730*], *dancer.*

One Bellam was the second Ethiopian in a *Dance of Six Ethiopians* given at Lincoln's Inn Fields Theatre on 24 April 1730.

Bellamy, Mr. *See* **Digges, West Dudley.**

Bellamy, Mr [*fl. 1761*], *singer.*

A Mr Bellamy was paid 5*s.* on 13 November 1761 for singing in the chorus of *The Coronation* at Covent Garden. Perhaps he was Richard Bellamy.

Bellamy, Mrs, later Mrs Walter, née Seal *d. 1771, actress.*

Mrs Bellamy, best known as the mother of the famous actress George Anne Bellamy (1731?–1788), was the daughter of a rich Quaker named Seal who had a farm at Maidstone. The authority for the early events of Miss Seal's life is George Anne Bellamy's *Apology*, a five-volume "autobiography" published in 1785, which is by no means reliable and was really written by Alexander Bicknell, the author of several historical works. According to this memoir, Miss Seal's father prospered sufficiently to purchase an estate near Tunbridge Wells, called Mount Sion. After some years of comfortable living, he died of a fever. Having neglected to make a will, he left all to his wife, with no provision for Miss Seal, who was then about four years old. The mother disposed of all the property at Maidstone and moved to Tunbridge Wells, where she let out elegantly furnished houses during the season to people of distinction and quality. Soon she married a builder "of some eminence" named Busby, without reserving to Miss Seal "the least part of her fortune" which was in hand from her first husband. Busby, contrary to expectations, was heavily in debt, and soon his creditors seized the new Mrs Busby's properties, leaving her and Miss Seal destitute of support.

At this point, according to George Anne Bellamy's memoir, Mrs Godfrey, mistress of the Jewel House and sister to the Duke of Marlborough, befriended them and sent Miss Seal off to a fashionable boarding school in Queen's Square, London. While there, at the age of 14, Miss Seal attracted the attention of the profligate James O'Hara, the second Baron of Tyrawley, previously Baron of Kilmaine, of whom Walpole reported that he had once returned from an extended diplomatic mission abroad with "three wives and fourteen children." Lord Tyrawley housed Miss Seal in his apartments at Somerset House, but soon finding it necessary to make an alliance with a lady of fortune in order to extricate himself from his distressed financial affairs, he married Lady Mary Stewart, the only surviving daughter of William Stewart, Earl of Blessington and second Viscount Mountjoy. Lady Mary was reputedly ugly and foolish—a deliberate choice by Lord Tyrawley to persuade Miss Seal of his continuing devotion to her—but the lady had a fortune of £30,000. Lord Tyrawley's scheme was thwarted, however, when Viscount Mountjoy heard of Miss Seal's presence in Somerset House and arranged a separation between his daughter and the fortune-hunter.

Miss Seal, meanwhile, gave birth to a son by Lord Tyrawley; George Anne Bellamy provides no date in the *Apology* for her brother's birth, but it was probably sometime about 1726 or 1727. In 1728 Lord Tyrawley was sent off as ambassador to the Court of Lisbon, and Miss Seal, upon the encouragement of the actress Mrs Butler, became an actress on the Dublin stage.

Tyrawley soon sent for Miss Seal, who, upon her arrival in Portugal, discovered that he had already taken up a local mistress. Miss Seal, it is said, married out of jealousy a Captain Bellamy, master of a trading vessel and an acquaintance of Lord Tyrawley. Soon after, she gave birth to a daughter, George Anne Bellamy, whose paternity was acknowledged by Tyrawley, and Captain Bellamy disappeared, apparently forever.

There is reason to accept the above account by George Anne Bellamy with reservation if not suspicion. To begin with, a Miss Seal acted on the London stage as early as 1718 and as late as 1730, during or after which period her placement at boarding school would have been most unlikely even for one with so bizarre a life. It is possible, of course, that Mrs Bellamy was not the Miss (sometimes Mrs) Seal who acted at London between 1718 and 1730, but circumstantial evidence suggests she was. A Miss Seal also played at Dublin in 1729; and according to George Ann Bellamy, her mother had acted at Dublin "for several years" before going to Portugal. When "Mrs" Seal played Selima in *Tamerlane* at the Haymarket on 2 May 1729, she was announced as "lately arrived from Ireland." The date of George Anne Bellamy's birth is obscured by some confusion and contradiction, but it probably was 1731 (see the entry for BELLAMY, George Anne). It should be noted, however, that in his book *Enchanting Bellamy* (1956), Cyril Hartmann suggests that George Anne Bellamy was born in 1728, that Miss Seal was already pregnant when Tyrawley went off to Lisbon, and that George Anne fabricated the story of her mother's visit to Lisbon in order "to make her parentage creditable."

In any event, the name of Miss Seal first appeared in the bills on 1 August 1718 when she acted Dorinda in *The Tempest* at Drury Lane, no doubt for the second time, for earlier (on 11 July 1718) the same role was played "by a young Gentlewoman who never perform'd before." She also played Lucy in *Love in a Wood* on 15 August. Her roles at Drury Lane in the following season, 1719–20, included Euphemia in *The Spartan* on 11 December and Philadelphia in *The Amorous Widow* on 14 May. On 22 June 1720 she acted Louisa in Cibber's *Love Makes a Man* at Coignand's Great Room. She shared a benefit with Mrs Heron at Drury Lane on 26 May 1721, when Steele's *The Funeral* was played, but her role is unknown. Her other roles at Drury Lane during this earlier period included Leonora in *The Mourning Bride* (17 April 1722), Miss Prue in *Love for Love* (for her benefit shared with Wright on 22 May 1722), Dorinda again in *The Tempest* (7 January 1723), Arabella in *The Committee* (for her benefit shared with Thurmond, the dancing master, on 13 May 1723), Lady Grey in Theophilus Cibber's *Henry VI* (5 July 1723), and Widow Lackit in *The Scornful Lady* (for her benefit, shared with Mrs Heron on 8 May 1724).

According to *The London Stage*, Miss Seal was also at Drury Lane in 1725–26. Thereafter she went to Ireland, but not before giving birth to a son by Lord Tyrawley. At Dublin, according to George Anne Bellamy, Miss Seal was received with considerable applause, "more owing to the people of that kingdom not being accustomed to capital performers, than to the brilliancy of my mother's powers." After several years of playing first characters with success, a dispute with her manager caused her to leave Dublin and return to London, to play as mentioned above, the role of Selima in *Tamerlane* at the Haymarket on 2 May 1729. In the following season, as Mrs Seal, she was at Goodman's Fields Theatre, where on 10 April 1730 she acted Mrs Foresight in *Love for Love*. About this time her adventures in Portugal with Lord Tyrawley and Captain Bellamy must have transpired. George Anne Bellamy claimed she had been born at Fingal, Ireland, on 23 April 1733, although she afterwards substituted 1731 when supplying a copy of a birth certificate for a life insurance application. By 1734, Miss Seal was acting at the Aungier Street Theatre in Dublin as Mrs Bellamy; she took a benefit there on 14 February 1734.

Mrs Bellamy returned to London by the fall of 1736 to make her first appearance on the Covent Garden stage as Sylvia in *The Recruiting Officer* on 24 September 1736. In that season of 1736–37 she acted 17 other roles including among them Dorinda in *The Stratagem*, Narcissa in *Love's Last Shift*, Angelica in *The Constant Couple*, Belinda in *The Provok'd Wife*, Lady Grace in *The Provok'd Husband*, Belinda in *The Old Batchelor*, Lady Macduff in *Macbeth*, and Isabella in *Wit without Money*. Acting mainly in the line of sophisticated and provocative ladies in comedy, Mrs Bellamy remained at Covent Garden through 1741–42, adding numerous other roles to her repertory including Dorcas in *The Fair Quaker of Deal*, Nerissa in *The Jew of Venice*, Cynthia in *The Double Dealer*, Hero in *Much Ado About Nothing*, Lucinda in *The Conscious Lovers*, Bellemante in *The Emperor of the Moon*, Emilia in *The Man of Mode*, and Florinda in *The Rover*. In the last role, on 21 April 1741, she shared benefit receipts of £120 with Haughton. The evening before, her daughter George Anne, who supposedly had passed six years in a convent at Boulogne, made her first appearance on any stage, as a servant to Columbine in *Harlequin Barber*.

Sometime before 22 December 1742, Mrs Bellamy married a Mr Walter, a soldier, the son of Sir George Walter. On that date she was announced in the role of Florinda in *The Rover* as "Mrs Walter, formerly Mrs Bellamy." Walter, according to George Anne Bellamy, was young enough to be her mother's child rather than her husband. The union was founded "solely on passion." Walter's dissipation soon led him to an affair with another woman whom he took off to Gibraltar, where his regiment was stationed, but first decorating her with clothing he purloined from his wife's closet while she was away at the theatre. Now billed as Mrs Walter, the deserted actress played Lady No in *The London Cuckolds* on 27 December 1742 and Mrs Page in *The Merry Wives of Windsor* on 27 January 1743. She was at Covent Garden also in the next season, making her last appearance there on 16 May 1744 as Mrs Page. Her daughter George Anne had made her "official debut" at that theatre on 22 November 1744. Mrs Walter accompanied George Anne to Dublin in 1745–46, playing at Smock Alley in that season and the next. Her roles there included Elvira in *The Spanish Fryar* (2 December 1745), Mrs Sullen in *The Stratagem* (16 December 1745), Lavinia in *The Fair Penitent* (2 January 1746), and Melinda in *The Recruiting Officer* (16 January 1746). She then retired from acting, a circumstance hastened no doubt by a severe attack of rheumatism which kept her in bed for over four months.

Mrs Walter returned to London with her daughter in 1749, and soon took up residence in a house in Brewer Street, Golden Square, which was owned by John Calcraft, one of her daughter's lovers. Though she had more than sufficient to maintain her, by testimony of her daughter, Mrs Walter turned to the family's old occupation, the letting out of rooms to persons of quality. A warm relationship continued between Mrs Walter and her daughter. When George Anne gave birth to George Metham's son, Mrs Walter attended her daughter at York and then cared for the child through his case of small pox, "suffering him to sleep in the same bed with her . . . notwithstanding she had never had that dreadful disorder."

On 2 December 1771, Mrs Walter became afflicted with what the eminent Dr

Schonburg diagnosed as an incurable "lethargic palsy." She lingered for some ten days and died at her residence in Brewer Street on 14 December 1771, with George Anne Bellamy "kneeling by her bed-side, kissing her hand." Her daughter gave her an expensive funeral, costing 42 guineas, which at that point in her life George Anne could ill afford. In September 1776, The *Town and Country Magazine*, either unaware of Mrs Walter's earlier life or preferring to ignore it, described her as a person "who lived a very genteel life, and was the complete gentle-woman; she had a fine understanding, happily cultivated with a polite education."

Bellamy, B. P. *[fl. 1797], actor.*

Mr B. P. Bellamy, "from York," acted Juba in *Cato* at the Haymarket on 4 December 1797. He was probably related to the R. P. Bellamy who made his debut as Polonius at Covent Garden on 11 September 1815. The latter was from Norwich and perhaps was, in turn, related to the Bellamy who, with James Smith, managed the playhouse at Yarmouth for William Wilkins after it opened on 4 December 1778.

Bellamy, George Anne *1731?–1788, actress.*

The actress George Anne Bellamy was born, by her own account, at Fingal, Ireland, on 23 April 1733, St George's Day, a circumstance accounting for her Christian name, which was mistakenly given as Georgiana. Writing in 1749, Chetwood gave the year of birth as 1727, without comment or source, but he seems to have confused her birth with that of her brother, Captain O'Hara. George Anne herself later changed the year to 1731, when she produced an affidavit of her birth in connection with a life insurance application. In his book *Enchanting Bellamy* (1956) Cyril Hartmann argued for 1728; however, 1731 would appear more accurate as it corresponds well with the chronology of most

events leading up to her birth. Her mother was the actress Mrs Bellamy, later Mrs Walter, née Seal (in whose entry the story of George Anne's parentage will be found). Her birth was "legitimate" only in the sense that at that time her mother was married to a sea captain named Bellamy; the pregnancy resulted from Mrs Bellamy's liaison with James O'Hara, second Baron of Tyrawley.

As an infant George Anne was cared for by the wife of Captain Pye, Tyrawley's adjutant, who resided near Fingal. At the age of four she was supposedly placed in an Ursuline convent at Boulogne where she remained for five years while her mother resumed her acting career at Dublin and London. Then at the age of 11, according to *An Apology for the Life of George Anne Bellamy* (1785), she went to live at London, first under the care of a Mr DuVall, a peruke-maker in St James's Street and

Harvard Theatre Collection

GEORGE ANNE BELLAMY
as the Comic Muse

by Cotes

formerly in the service of Lord Tyrawley, and then with the family of a Mr Jones, an apothecary in St James's Street. Upon his return from his mission at Lisbon, about 1742, Lord Tyrawley took her to live at Bushy Park, showing some considerable paternal interest; "My Lord's fondness for me knew no bounds," wrote George Anne, "He not only thought he perceived in my features the perfect resemblance of his own, but he flattered himself that, with the aid of due cultivation, I should likewise inherit his wit, which was universally allowed to be really brilliant." Tyrawley introduced her to good company, including Lord Chesterfield, who took a liking to her, and Alexander Pope, who had no use for her. When her father left to become ambassador to Russia he settled an allowance of £100 a year upon her, which she forfeited by deciding to live with her mother, who was now at London. By her account, George Anne then made her appearance when she was "just fourteen," alluding to her supposed debut as Monimia in *The Orphan* at Covent Garden on 22 November 1744.

The fact of the matter, however, is that when just several days shy of the age of ten (if indeed she was born in 1731), George Anne made her first appearance on any stage, at Covent Garden on 20 April 1741, as the servant to Colombine in *Harlequin Barber*, a pantomime performed by the French family of dancers named Mechel. George Anne made no reference in her *Apology* to the performance, in which Polly Woffington, sister of the famous Peg Woffington, also made her first appearance. By this time no doubt George Anne was already living with her mother who was a regular member of the Covent Garden company in that season. George Anne's name appeared on no other bills in 1740–41, although she may well have played similar mute roles, but about a year later at the same theatre on 27 March 1742, again announced as her first time on any stage, she played Miss Prue in *Love for Love*, a role

which gives credence to the argument that she could not have been just barely ten years old at this time. Again no mention of this event appeared in the *Apology*. Apparently she made no other appearances for several years, remaining at London with her mother who (now as "Mrs Walter") was still engaged at Covent Garden. She did play, however, in a private performance of *The Distrest Mother* at Kingston in the spring of 1743 with no less a personage than Garrick himself.

The opportunity to meet and perform with Garrick occurred as the result of a visit by George Anne and her mother to the residence of Mrs Jackson, wife of the governor of the East Indies, at Montpelier Row, Twickenham. On an evening walk there, they met the actress Margaret Woffington, whom Mrs Bellamy knew from Dublin, and were invited to visit for some time at her home in Teddington, where they were introduced to the Irish actor Thomas Sheridan, then playing for a while at Covent Garden. Sheridan in turn invited the Bellamys to his apartments at Kingston, "which were generally crowded with Irish gentlemen from the College of Dublin." Garrick also visited frequently in order to meet unobtrusively with Mrs Woffington with whom he had lived intimately. Parlour conversations usually turned to theatrical affairs, which Miss Bellamy, without blinking, stated in her memoir she "was totally unacquainted with till I was introduced into this circle." The group hit upon the idea of getting up among themselves a performance of *The Distrest Mother*, in order to try the abilities of Mrs Woffington's sister, Polly. Garrick played Orestes, Mrs Woffington and Mrs Bellamy did the attendants, Polly did Hermione, and George Anne did Andromache. All the people of fashion, according to George Anne, flocked to a barn at Kingston to see this extraordinary event. Still persisting in her *Apology* to assert that this was her first theatrical venture, George Anne claimed that Garrick had been more impressed with her than he had been with Polly Woffington—"though I was inferior in beauty to my fair rival, and without the advantages of dress, which she enjoyed, yet the laurel was bestowed upon me."

What George Anne claimed to be her professional debut occurred on 22 November 1744 at Covent Garden—now billed as a "Young Gentlewoman" making her first appearance on any stage—when she played the capital role of Monimia in *The Orphan*, a part usually played at that theatre by the great Mrs Cibber or by the capable Mrs Giffard. The imposing interpreter of Chamont, James Quin, at first protested but the manager, John Rich, insisted that the young girl be allowed to appear. Describing herself as "just fourteen," and having "a figure not inelegant, a powerful voice, light as the gossamer, of inexhaustible spirits, and possessed of some humour," George Anne proved a considerable success, despite her stage fright for three acts. The delighted Quin lifted her in his arms, declared her "a divine creature," and swore his everlasting protection and friendship. "If you ever want anything in my power, which money can purchase, come to me . . . and my purse shall always be yours." Then, according to the *Apology* at least, he offered some good advice: "Do not let the love of finery, or other inducement, prevail upon you to commit an indiscretion. Men in general are rascals." Quin died before she had need for his money, but had she heeded his caution about men she might have spared herself some considerable grief in her private adventures.

On 6 December George Anne played Aspasia in *The Maid's Tragedy*, which she repeated on 8 December. On 11 February 1745 she acted Celia in *Volpone*, and Aspasia again on 28 February and 7 March, in each instance billed as a young gentlewoman except for the last night when finally she was identified as Miss Bellamy. She also acted Arsinoe in *Mariamne* on 11

and 12 March, and Anne Bullen in *Henry VIII* on 16 April 1745, sharing on the last date a benefit with Reinhold, Destrade, and Rawlings. It was an ambitious first year at a patent house for so young an actress.

In the fall of 1745 George Anne and her mother Mrs Walter engaged at the Smock Alley Theatre, Dublin, where she made her first appearance on 11 November as Monimia. Also acting in the Smock Alley company in 1745–46 were Thomas Sheridan (also the manager), the young Spranger Barry, who was already acclaimed "the Irish Roscius," and Garrick, who only a few years earlier had made his startling debut on the London stage. George Anne had good example and steady challenge. "I was obliged to appear almost every night, and sometimes in characters very unfit for me," she wrote. "The great applause that I received, however, spurred me on, and excited in me the strongest endeavours to deserve it." Her many roles in her first Dublin season, with dates of first performance, included Desdemona (18 November), Cleopatra in *All for Love* (28 November), the Queen in *The Spanish Fryar* (2 December), the "Queen" in *Richard III* (14 December), Cherry in *The Stratagem* (16 December), Calista in *The Fair Penitent* (2 January), Cordelia (13 January), Andromache in *Orestes* (3 February), Athenais in *Theodosius* (10 February), Imoinda in *Oroonoko* (24 February), Miss Prue in *Love for Love* (5 March), Almeyda in *Don Sebastian* (10 March), the title role in *Jane Shore* (7 April), Marcia in *Cato* (21 April), and Leonora in *The Revenge* (28 April).

As busy as she was, George Anne had time to earn a reputation as a troublesome personality and a spirit to be reckoned with. She had a tiff with Garrick who objected to her being cast as Constance in *King John*, a role she especially hoped to play. When Mrs Furnival was awarded the role instead, George Anne contrived through the influence of her patroness Mrs Butler to

Harvard Theatre Collection

GEORGE ANNE BELLAMY at the age of 30
artist unknown

Jane Shore for Garrick's benefit on 26 April 1746, so apparently they were reconciled by the time Garrick left for London at the end of the season.

In this same first season at Dublin she had an explosive encounter with Mrs Furnival over a costume. (George Anne mistakenly placed this event in 1746–47, when Mrs Furnival was not in the company.) George Anne was critical of the costuming conditions which prevailed during the first half of the eighteenth century, writing in the *Apology*:

The dress of the gentlemen, both of the sock and buskin was full as absurd as that of the ladies. Whilst the empresses and queens appeared in black velvet, and, upon extraordinary occasions, with the additional finery of an embroidered or tissue petticoat; and the younger part of the females, in cast gowns of persons of quality, or altered habits rather soiled; the male part of the dramatis personae strutted in tarnished laced coats and waistcoats, full bottom or tye wigs, and black worsted stockings.

In a prologue, George Anne, dressed in boy's clothes, had derided the poverty of the dresses at the rival Dublin theatre in Rainsford Street. She then took steps to assure the "brilliancy of her ornaments," by having a dress formerly belonging to the Princess of Wales made into a rich costume in which she intended to play Cleopatra in *All for Love* (28 November, 1745), "and as the ground of it was silver tissue, my mother thought that turning the body of it in, it would be a no unbecoming addition to my waiste, which was remarkably small." Her maid-servant, the dresser and a mantua maker were set to work in sewing on a number of diamonds which had been loaned by Mrs Butler and her friends. Whereupon, Mrs Furnival—"who owed me a grudge"—happened to pass by the open dressing room, and seeing the completed costume unattended appropriated it to adorn herself in the character of Octavia.

keep the house very thin, less than £40, thereby humiliating Garrick. George Anne claimed that the next time *King John* was given she played Constance to Sheridan's King and Garrick's Bastard, and "more people were turned away than could get places." The whole story is somewhat deflated by the fact that *King John* was played only once at Smock Alley in 1745–46, on 5 February, indeed with Mrs Furnival as Constance, and George Anne did not play the role until her third season at Smock Alley, on 3 March 1748, with Sheridan as Bastard; and Garrick had gone to London. Continuing with her story, George Anne stated that she had spitefully refused to play Jane Shore for Garrick's early-season benefit. Hoping to persuade her, Garrick had written an epistle to her—a "*silly goody goody*"—that somehow found its way into the press. She did, in fact, play and would not give it up despite a heated physical confrontation with George Anne's maid. Cleopatra was obliged to appear in a plain white satin dress ornamented by a single diadem. Sheridan was so confounded when Mrs Furnival, as the matronly Octavia, appeared on the stage, "the jay in all her borrowed plumes," that he forgot his lines, and Mrs Butler exclaimed aloud from the boxes, "Good Heaven, the woman has got on my diamonds!" thereby causing the audience to believe Mrs Furnival had stolen them and causing a great stir in the house. "No more Furnival!" they cried out, and thus hooted from the stage for her impropriety Mrs Furnival had to give up the role to Mrs Elmy who finished the performance. When Sheridan read in the *Apology* this story about Mrs Furnival stealing the dress he called it a fabrication of George Anne's brain.

During her second season at Smock Alley, 1746–47, George Anne played Arpasia in *Tamerlane* (4 November), Indiana in *The Conscious Lovers* (11 November), Portia in *The Merchant of Venice* (1 December), Doris in *Aesop* (15 January), Lady Townly in *The Provok'd Husband* (20 January), Sigismunda in *Tancred and Sigismunda* (19 February), Miss Biddy in *Miss in Her Teens* (9 March), Belvidera in *Venice Preserv'd* (25 May), Clarinda in *The Suspicious Husband* (29 June), and Lady Macbeth (13 July). Her claim that Garrick offered her an engagement at Drury Lane in 1747–48 at £10 per week is exaggerated, for when she later went to Drury Lane (in 1749–50) he paid her only £7 per week and even at the height of her career (in 1757–58) she was paid only £10 10s. per week. In any event, George Anne's refusal, she said, so offended the great actor-manager that he vowed never to engage her upon any terms. She stayed on at Smock Alley in 1747–48, adding to her repertory the roles of Amanda in *Love's Last Shift* (5 October), Flippanta in *The Confederacy* (8 October), Mrs Sullen

in *The Stratagem* (18 November), Lady Sadlife in *The Double Gallant* (11 January), Lady Betty Modish in *The Careless Husband* (9 February), Alinda in The *Loyal Subject* (29 February), Constance in *King John* (3 March), Almeria in *The Mourning Bride* (8 March), Laetitia in *The Old Batchelor* (10 March), Lady Froth in *The Double Dealer* (21 March), and Millamant in *The Way of the World* (25 March). In this season George Anne became a secondary victim in an assault upon Mrs Dyer in her dressing room by a drunken brute named Kelley, an event leading to another outburst from the volatile Irish audience. Sheridan beat off the attacker and apologized to the audience for the interruption in the play. But the next night a band of Kelley's ruffian friends created a turmoil in the theatre when they accused Sheridan of having insulted the public by declaring he was a better bred gentleman than any of them.

Harvard Theatre Collection

GEORGE ANNE BELLAMY, as Clarinda
artist unknown

A dispute with Sheridan over her account due for ticket orders led Miss Bellamy to quit Smock Alley at the close of the 1747–48 season, despite the offer of Benjamin Victor, the treasurer, to pay the £75 if she would re-engage. In consequence of her three years of experience at Dublin, George Anne was now accounted as "one of the most rising actresses in the three kingdoms," especially in tragedy. Chetwood, who was taken by her youth and amiability, considered her to be an "admirable improving genius" who would soon reach "the Top of Perfection." Describing her as a person of liberal heart "to feel and ease the Distresses of the Wretched," he credited her—despite her reputation to the contrary —"with every moral Virtue," and in a verse dubbed her with the name—"Inchanting Bellamy!"—by which audiences and critics of her time came to call her:

> *The Maid, in Action just, in Judgment*
> *strong,*
> *Exacts our Wonder, and inspires our*
> *Song;*
> *From slavish Rules, mechanic Forms,*
> *unty'd,*
> *She soars, with sacred Nature for her*
> *Guide. . . .*
> *Each magic Charm, lamented Oldfield*
> *knew,*
> *Inchanting Bellamy! revives in you.*

Returning to England in the fall of 1748, Miss Bellamy engaged with Rich at Covent Garden, where she made her first appearance in three years on 22 October, as Belvidera in *Venice Preserv'd*. Her reception was warm, said George Anne, although the house was thin. Her story that "Mr Town" enthusiastically cried out, "The same! The same!" for the next night and the audience joined in the demand, causing *Venice Preserv'd* to be performed four successive nights to crowded houses, and that the play was one of the "most drawing" in the repertory throughout the season, again is somewhat exaggerated. Actually, according to the bills, *Venice Preserv'd* was performed once more on 7 November, and not again that season. George Anne then played another favorite role, Monimia in *The Orphan*, on 24 October, and during the rest of the 1748–49 season appeared regularly in at least 15 other roles: Marcia in *Cato*, Imoinda in *Oroonoko*, Indiana in *The Conscious Lovers*, Leonora in *The Revenge,* Athenais in *Theodosius,* Elaria in *Emperor of the Moon*, Almeyda in *Don Sebastian*, Volumnia in *Coriolanus*, Lady Fanciful in *The Provok'd Wife*, Eudocia in *The Siege of Damascus*, Statira in *The Rival Queens*, Harriet in *The Man of Mode*, Lady Froth in *The Double Dealer*, Lady Percy in *Henry IV*, and Anne Bullen in *Henry VIII*.

By now George Anne Bellamy was fast becoming the rage both on and off the stage. The saga of her gambling and extravagance, supported by her string of lovers, is difficult to sort out in the *Apology* because of her cavalier attitude toward specific dates, yet her progress with various rakes can be followed in some broad outline. Soon after her return from Dublin to play at Covent Garden according to her story, she was abducted and carried off in a carriage by a young swain, William, Fifth Lord Byron. George Anne's account of the abduction and an abortive rescue by her brother Captain O'Hara strikes one as a preposterous concoction. In any event the experience so unsettled her that she fell ill and went to the country to convalesce at the home of a Mrs Clarke, her mother's relative, at Braintree, Essex. Mrs Clarke's sister had recently left a £300 legacy to George Anne, provided she should not go on the stage. The story in the *Apology* of George Anne being exposed as an actress by a Mr Moore and her subsequent ejection from the Clarke house also has its incredible aspects.

George Anne's affair with George Montgomery Metham began soon after. She claimed that his enthusiasm and devotion caused him to carry her off the Covent

Garden stage just before the beginning of the fifth act of *The Provok'd Wife*. Genest suggests 20 April 1749 as the date for this dramatic event. George Anne was, indeed, in the bills as Lady Fanciful in *The Provok'd Wife* for that night. She was also in the bills, however, for Harriet in *The Man of Mode* on 22 April, for Imoinda in *Oroonoko* on 3 May, and for Anne Bullen in *Henry VIII* on 4 May. She and Metham eloped to Yorkshire where on 17 December 1749 she gave birth to his son George, a circumstance which delayed her appearance at Covent Garden until 23 January 1750, when she played Belvidera. Now settled in a house in Lisle Street, Leicester Fields, provided by Metham—although he constantly put off marrying her —she played but sparingly for the balance of the season, adding Juliet, Octavia in *All for Love*, and Calista in *The Fair Penitent* to her repertory, taking only £37. 10s. 6d. at her benefit in the latter role on 20 March 1750.

When Barry, Macklin, and Mrs Cibber left Drury Lane at the end of 1749–50, Garrick determined, despite his resolution to the contrary ("the resolutions of managers are seldom considered binding," wrote George Anne, "when opposed by their self interest") to engage Miss Bellamy in an attempt to patch up his broken fortunes. On 27 July 1750 he wrote to his partner Lacy, "If Bellamy agrees with us, she may open with *Juliet*." She engaged at £7 per week, and indeed when the season opened on 28 September 1750 she appeared as Juliet to Garrick's Romeo. On the same night at Covent Garden Barry and Mrs Cibber opened in the same roles, and one of the most famous theatrical rivalries of the century had begun. The duel lasted for 12 consecutive nights, at first capturing the imagination of the Town, but when the potential audience exhausted itself, both theatres began to lose money. A brief poem in the *Daily Advertiser* bespoke the final boredom and irritation of the public:

'Well, what's today,' says angry Ned,
As up from bed he rouses.
'Romeo, again!' and shakes his head,
'Ah, pox on both your houses.'

When Mrs Cibber weakened on 21 October, Covent Garden capitulated, and Drury Lane triumphantly added a thirteenth performance. Both productions, each of the first rank, stirred a controversy which raged for days in the coffee houses over the relative merits of the male performers (see BARRY, Spranger, for discussion). A less fevered debate was waged over the contending Juliets. Generally Mrs Cibber's grander beauty and forceful tragic expression at Covent Garden finally defeated Miss Bellamy's amorous rapture and natural loveliness. "Miss *Bellamy*, if she possesses not Mrs *Cibber's* softness, she makes a larger compensation by her variety," wrote a critic in the *Gentleman's Magazine* for October 1750; "For my own part, I shed more tears in seeing Mrs *Cibber*, but I am more delighted in seeing Miss *Bellamy*."

Miss Bellamy's other roles in that first season with Garrick included Cordelia, Almeria in *The Mourning Bride,* Amanda in *Love's Last Shift*, Mrs Sullen in *The Stratagem*, Calista, Eltruda in *Alfred*, and Monimia. For her benefit as Belvidera on 18 March 1751, at which time she was residing in a house in King Street, St James's Square, she received about £40. By now, her amorous private life was becoming matter for gossip in the press, and in *A Guide to the Stage* (1751), "little Bel Juliet" was spoken of as a great favorite with the town gallants. She also continued to be plagued by ill health, and rumors flew about. On 18 May 1751 the *General Advertiser* advised that "Miss Bellamy . . . is not dead as mentioned one of the Papers yesterday."

She passed two more years under Garrick's management, adding such roles as Ismena in *Phaedra and Hippolitus* (with an original prologue, by desire, on 3 December 1751), Andromache in *The Dis-*

trest Mother (with an original epilogue on 10 December 1751), Sigismunda in *Tancred and Sigismunda* (taking £200 at her benefit on 14 March 1752), Rutland (a breeches role) in *The Earl of Essex*, and the title roles in *Lady Jane Grey* and *Eugenia*. In 1751–52 and 1752–53 she resided at her house in Thrift Street, Soho. By now she was also earning a reputation for placing puffs in the press; on 9 April 1752 the *Drury Lane Journal* suggested she was almost as skilled a practitioner in that art as Garrick himself. The critics often spoke of her more raptuously as a woman than as an actress. "No woman ever equalled Miss Bellamy in the requisites from nature," wrote John Hill in *The Inspector* (1753),

Harvard Theatre Collection

GEORGE ANNE BELLAMY, as Cleone
artist unknown

"and were but her love to her profession, her application to its necessary studies, and her patience in going through the difficulties that lie in the road to eminence in it, equal to her abilities, she would have few equals." The author of *The Present State of the Stage* (1753) found her "diffident of her own abilities" and in need of instruction to achieve a less pompous diction and to eliminate too many "periodical cadences and elevations of voice."

The vicissitudes of living as Metham's mistress now becoming oppressive to her, and convinced he would not marry her, she took up with one of his friends, John Calcraft of Grantham (1726–1772), an eminent politician. In a letter dated 22 January 1752, Calcraft bound himself to her for £50,000 in a marriage contract, one he never kept. About the same time she made another professional alteration by leaving Drury Lane in the fall of 1753 and again engaging at Covent Garden, where she would remain for six years. But just as the 1753–54 season began, George Anne ran off again with Metham. Richard Cross, the Drury Lane prompter, wrote in his diary on 24 October that John Calcraft, "who kept her, swears to kick Rich etc. Great noise about it in ye. Bedford Coffee House." She was back, however, by 20 November to make her first appearance at Covent Garden in four years, as Athanais in *Theodosius*, and Cross, who kept a sharp eye on the other theatre, wrote "Miss Bellamy play'd Athenais. Sad House." She followed with Monimia, Eudocia, Celia in *Volpone*, and Andromache. On 23 February 1754 she played the Empress Fulvia in Francis's new tragedy of *Constantine*, almost to empty benches. The day after the fourth performance on 28 February, she gave birth to a daughter by Calcraft, Caroline Elizabeth. Under the circumstances, thought Tate Wilkinson, Athanais, and Monimia were "very improper" characters for her to have acted that season. Not fully recuperated, she had to defer her benefit scheduled for 23 March. She was ready by 26 March to act Indiana, and on 28 March did Jane Shore for her benefit. When the season concluded, she showed some discretion by changing her appellation of Miss to Mrs Bellamy.

On 10 January 1755 she played Eurydice in a revival of *Oedipus*, not acted in 12 years, and "was so overcome by the horror of the piece," according to Genest, "that she was carried off in a state of insensibility." Her name appeared for the role again on the eleventh, but by the third performance on the fifteenth the manager had replaced her with Mrs Vincent, an actress perhaps with less delicate nerves. The following season Mrs Bellamy acted the title role in *Zara*, for the first time, on 30 October, 1755. A revival of *The Rival Queens* on 15 January 1756 (last acted at Covent Garden on 14 March 1749) led to a near catastrophe in consequence of the animosity between Mrs Woffington as Roxana and Mrs Bellamy as Statira, when the former stage queen, incensed by two superb dresses which the latter had imported from Paris, in the quarrel scene "fairly drove Statira off the stage, and stabbed her almost behind the scenes." Many of the audience having seen the off-stage tussle, expressed their displeasure. The battle, now limited to words, continued in the Green Room. The next summer at the Haymarket Foote ridiculed the affair with an entertainment called *The Green-room Squabble; or, a Battle Royal between the Queen of Babylon and the Daughter of Darius.*

During the 1750's, George Anne's personal life became more complicated and the tide of fortune began to turn against her. She did not love Calcraft, but used him to further her social standing through his contacts with such people as Henry Fox, the Marquess of Granby, and General Hervey. Calcraft amassed a huge fortune and settled George Anne in a palatial house in Parliament Square, with £2500 a year for housekeeping. When she discovered that he really had been married for some years to a woman at Grantham, still alive, George Anne claimed she fell perilously ill, to the point where she gave confession. But she recovered and the medical bills cost Calcraft £900. This event probably occurred in 1756–57, a season in which she gave only one performance, as Almeria in *The Mourning Bride* on 31 March. It perhaps was also about the time she gave birth to Calcraft's eldest son, Henry.

By 5 December 1757 she was sufficiently well to make her first appearance of the season as Cordelia—she was received "with universal satisfaction"—to Barry's Lear. With Barry as her leading man, she proceeded on a very heavy schedule of performances which included Juliet, Athanais, Statira, Calista, Eudocia, Indiana, Constance in *King John*, the Queen in *Richard III*, Lady Randolph in *Douglas*, and the title roles in *Alzira*, *Mariamne*, and *Anna Bullen*. Her salary was £10 10s. per week; for her benefit on 9 March 1758, when she acted Cleopatra in *All for Love*, she took a profit of £202 10s. That season she also attempted Lady Macbeth for the first time in London on 10 December 1757, to Barry's Macbeth, causing the *Theatrical Review* to take umbrage at what it regarded as gross miscasting, at the same time providing an informative assessment of Mrs Bellamy's powers and charms at this point in her career:

Her talents lie chiefly to the pathetic; she has strong sensations of the tender; habit has not yet steeled her heart, nor dried her eyes of the precious fluid. . . . She has besides in her looks, in the scenes of distress, a soft wildness, which commands pity; but her action is not clear of affectation; her motions are too much prepared and studied; they favour too much of the looking-glass.

Her voice is pleasing, not unmanageable, and follows pretty well her sense of each situation; but its strength is very limited; and when she forces it out of those narrow bounds which nature has set to it, it becomes hoarse, harsh, and untuneable; this defect of her voice excludes her from any hopes of succeeding in parts where rage, jealousy, etc. are to be exhibited . . .

Who but a fool, or an enemy, could have suffered or obliged her to undertake the part of lady Macbeth, the most cruel female character, perhaps, ever ventured on any stage? Her performance of it, I own, was not uncooth, but her every look was so out of character, that one might have without impropriety addressed in those words of Lear, to trusty Kent in the stocks; *who is't that has so thy place mistook, to set thee here?*

Still continuing at Covent Garden in 1758–59 at a salary of £10 10s. a week, she offered her usual line of characters. John Calcraft began to balk at her extravagance and her utter disregard for the value of money. But confident that he would pay off the substantial debts she had amassed, she planned a holiday in Holland at the end of the 1758–59 season. Calcraft disappointed her, and she was obliged to borrow £2000 on her jewels from Bibby, the pawnbroker in Stanhope Street, Clare Market. Reserving £200 for her trip, she paid off her creditors as far as the money would go, and visited for some weeks at the Hague and Amsterdam. Upon her return she decided not to reengage with Rich in 1759–60; she toyed with the idea of acting at Dublin but decided to remain idle. She continued to live with Calcraft, but uneasily, seldom seeing him. When she discovered him *in flagrante delicto* with one of her intimate friends, she determined to leave him—as soon as he would pay off her remaining debts. His promised settlement never came, but he did agree to give her £2000 for the jewels she had pledged, whereupon she departed for Bristol. Both Woodward and Mossop, contending managers at Dublin, vied for her services, and she settled upon Mossop at Smock Alley for 1760–61 at a salary of 2000 guineas (she claimed). Woodward felt she had been shabby in her dealings with him,

apparently having first promised to join him, but several years later they were to make it up.

Wilkinson reported that Smock Alley audiences who remembered her from those halcyon days in the 1740's with Barry, Sheridan, and Garrick were shocked by the change in her appearance. At the age of 31, "the roses were fled, the young, once lovely Bellamy was turned haggard! and her eyes that used to charm all hearts, appeared sunk, large, hollow, and ghastly." In *The Meretriciad* (1761), a verse treatise on notorious actresses and women of the town, Edward Thompson took her to task for resuming her career and confirmed that by now her physical attractions had somewhat diminished:

> *But here observe the Juliet of her days,*
> *Fall'n from the pinnacle of public*
>   *praise . . .*
> *. . . How did the Town applaud thy*
>   *happy choice,*
> *Altho' in thee she lost the sweetest voice?*
> . . . .
> *But since Old Time has worn the dimple*
>   *sleek,*
> *And furrow'd wrinkles o'er the blushing*
>   *cheek,*
> *Who would imagine you would play the*
>   *whore,*
> *And fly in raptures to the* Irish *shore?*
> *If e'er these lines should reach thy flinty*
>   *heart,*
> *Fly to thy babes—and act the mother's*
>   *part . . .*

Mrs Bellamy returned to Covent Garden for 1761–62, at a salary of £10 10s. per week, approximately £272 for the season, appearing on that stage for the first time in two years (as Juliet) on 25 September. In 1762 she settled for a three-year engagement with the theatre at Edinburgh. There she took up her affair with the actor West Digges which had begun the previous year when they were both acting at Smock Alley. Despite his reputation for vanity and irascibility, George Anne found him to be "really the accomplished gentleman and an entertaining companion." The fact that Digges was already married did not prevent her from offering comfort during his illness at Dublin—"love for me was the cause of it"—and then agreeing to enter into a "*serious* connection" with him. Indeed they supposedly went through a ceremony of marriage in Scotland in 1763. For a while Digges, in an odd reversal of custom, took her surname and appeared as Mr Bellamy, playing Macbeth under that name to Mrs Bellamy's Lady Macbeth at Edinburgh on 27 November 1762. They lived together in a cottage in Bonnington near the toll-gate on the Newhaven Road, often dining by candlelight in the middle of the summer and generally gaining reputations as foolish eccentrics. Mrs Bellamy was regarded as "the most extravagant fool possible; so that she hired porters to carry her canary birds from Edinburgh to Glasgow." But the relationship was marred by frequent disputes which ran so high that in one instance Digges in a violent rage stripped off his clothes and ran out into the winter midnight air to drown himself in the pond near the cottage. Mrs Bellamy, unmoved, locked him out, refusing to readmit him until the cold air had cooled his resolution and he was ready to accept her severe terms. In George Anne's words, they were "mutually unhappy" during the several years they lived together.

She made her first appearance at Edinburgh on 5 May 1762 as Sigismunda, with a prologue spoken by Digges. On the next three nights she acted Estifania in *Rule a Wife*, Jane Shore, and Lady Townly, to great success. "The expectation of the public was never so highly raised, nor its pleasures so truly gratified," reported the *Courant* (8 May), "as they have been for some nights at the Theatre. The house has been generously filled by five o'clock, and crowds turned away for want of room." More performances were added beyond the four originally planned, and she offered in addition Monimia, Juliet, and Lady Mac-

beth. She played Cleone for her benefit on 22 May.

Among her adventures in Scotland was a ride from Edinburgh into Glasgow in the spring of 1764 to act at the new Argyle Street Theatre under the management of Beatt and Love. A fanatical religious mob burnt part of the stage and all her costumes. Undaunted, George Anne sent for Bates, the stage manager, and told him to announce at "the Cross at Trongate . . . Mrs Bellamy will appear and act to-night." She dressed at the Black Bull Tavern, and was conveyed in a chair to the theatre, where the stage had been quickly repaired. Her courage and gallantry, it was reported, was rewarded by a very large turnout of the *ton*.

The last time she was advertised to appear on the Edinburgh stage was for 30 June 1764, when she delivered an occasional prologue to *The Miser*. According to her own statement, Mrs Bellamy severed her connection at Edinburgh because Thomas Sheridan arrived sometime in July. On 25 July 1764 the *Courant* announced: "As Mrs Bellamy is not to appear any more on the Edinburgh stage, she begs leave to return her thanks to the public in general, and to those friends who have done her the honour to patronise her in particular, for the favours she has received during her residence in Scotland, of which she will ever retain the most grateful sense." She remained in Edinburgh for a while at a "small English house in New Street." The above grateful notice did not appear every day for a month (despite her statement to the contrary in her *Apology*) nor do the newspaper records support her assertion that she also advertised that any creditors should deliver their accounts to her at her house, "opposite Lord Milton's in the Canongate."

Mrs Bellamy then returned to Covent Garden in 1764–65, making her first appearance in three years, as Cleone on 7 December 1764, with an original prologue. That season she also played Constance,

Cordelia, Desdemona, Juliet, Veturia in *Coriolanus*, Cleopatra in *All for Love*, Lady Fanciful, and Eudocia in *The Siege of Damascus*. She continued at Covent Garden for six years. By 1767–68 her salary had been reduced to about £8 or £9 per week, with a benefit. Her wardrobe in 1769 was valued at £106, the highest figure for any person in the company. In 1769–70, her last full season in London, she acted Juliet, Alicia in *Jane Shore*, Arpasia in *Tamerlane*, Isabella in *Measure for Measure*, Berinthia in *The Relapse*, Roxana in *The Rival Queens*, and on 31 March 1770, the title role in *Isabella*, for her benefit at which she took £166 10s.

She was not re-engaged at Covent Garden for the following season, no doubt because of failing health and rapidly declining beauty. Instead she lived quietly with her new paramour, Henry Woodward, with whom she set up house in 1767. They had acted together at Dublin back in 1747–48, and many times since; George Anne claimed to have refused his offer of marriage when they played at Covent Garden in earlier years. The ten years they passed together—in what she asserted was a platonic relationship—were probably the most peaceful of her life. After her retirement, her lodgings in Leicester Street being too expensive, she moved to Strand-on-the-Green, a riverside village near Kew, where Woodward often came. Some 26 years her senior, Woodward died on 17 April 1777 after a long illness, probably cancer, through the last years of which George Anne apparently nursed him with exemplary tenderness. By his will dated 20 January 1777 and proved 18 April 1777, Woodward left her his gold watch, chain, and seals, all his plate, jewels, linen, china, and the whole of the furniture in his house in Chapel Street. He also left the interest of £700 in three per cent consolidated bank annuities to his brother, John Woodward, tallow-chandler of Cripplegate, during his life, the principal after his death to be laid out in the purchase of an annuity for

the natural life of George Anne Bellamy, to be paid personally to her quarterly and not liable to her debts or to possible future depredations by husbands. All the residue of his property not otherwise bequeathed was to be sold to purchase additional annuities for her. George Anne complained in her *Apology* that she had received only £50 from Woodward's legacy. In *Letters addressed to Mrs Bellamy, occasioned by her Apology*, Edward Willet, a solicitor acting for the executors, called her *Mrs Duplicity* and produced letters addressed to her proving she had received £619 from the estate by 1785. Actually there had been only £400 in stocks in the estate, and not the £700 Woodward had bequeathed.

Whatever amount she had received from Woodward's will, Mrs Bellamy seems afterwards to have lived in some privation, although its degree may well have been exaggerated by sentimentalists and moralists. After her mother's death she moved into her home in Brewer Street, having given her parent an expensive funeral (42 guineas) which she apparently could ill afford. Calcraft, who died in August 1772, left her not a penny of his £250,000 fortune, not even mentioning her in his will. To his children by her, Henry and Caroline Elizabeth, he left £5000 apiece. (He did leave, however, £3000 and annuities of £1500 to Miss Bride, another actress, by whom he had four children.) The annuity Calcraft had earlier granted to George Anne had long since lapsed, and not even a suit in court could regain it. Neither did George Anne's father Lord Tyrawley leave her anything. Her children were little comfort. Henry Calcraft was a gambler and wastrel in his youth though eventually he had a distinguished career as a Lieutenant General in the East India Company. George Metham also followed a military career but settled in Jamaica. George Anne lived off loans and gifts, often being victimized by creditors' suits and foreclosures. In a letter to Jane Pope on 26 February 1779, the former actress Kitty Clive, by then so amiably situated at Strawberry Hill, re-membered that Mrs Bellamy used "to have 22 new different changes of mourning for the late prince of Wales and who I suppose has not one rag of them left to mourn her own sins. I say I do not feel pleasure at her misfortunes but I certainly can not feel any sorrow tho'. Thank God my heart can melt at the distresses of the good and virtuous."

Mrs Bellamy made a single appearance at a special night given for her after the season ended at Covent Garden, playing Alicia in *Jane Shore*, on 1 June 1780. Not having acted in some ten years, she was so frightened, according to her own account, that Miss Catley had to push her onto the stage. The performance proved to be her last. The receipts of the benefit are not known, but on 30 June 1780 she paid Covent Garden £8 15s. for oil and candles burnt on her night.

The authority for the details of the birth and early life of George Anne Bellamy is her six-volume "autobiography," *An Apology for the Life of George Anne Bellamy, late of Covent Garden Theatre, written by herself,* published in 1785, three years before her death. The actual writing of the *Apology* is credited to Alexander Bicknell, author of several historical works including a *Life of Alexander the Great.* No doubt George Anne provided many of the materials. The work is idealized, with many fulsome moralizations, and it is suspect because of many omissions of fact now established. It suffers from a vague retrospection over many years which diminishes its credibility in individual instances. Horace Walpole, in disparagement of another author's work, wrote: "I read such books as I do Mrs Bellamy's, and I believe in them no more." Nevertheless, the *Apology* remains a useful work, if only because there is none more accurate covering the same period of Mrs Bellamy's life.

To the *Apology* was appended an "original letter" to John Calcraft, which George

Anne had intended to publish in 1767 but had been dissuaded from doing by Colman. Obviously the *Apology* had been announced some months in advance, for in February 1784, Mrs Clive wrote to Jane Pope about it, "I think this is the most impudent part of it—for it can have no other subject than how many different men she has been a strumpet to—she ought to dedicate it to the Constable." Society read the work with avidity, but professional critics were not kind, pointing out, as had Walpole, the many falsifications and anachronisms. The *European Magazine* decided that she was about five or six years older than she professed, and she indignantly produced the certificate from the Insurance Office, issued in 1764, which stated 1731 as her year of birth. She acknowledged a slight mistake of a year or so—"it is a matter of little consequence, when a woman is turned of fifty, what her age may be," she added.

On 12 April 1785, Mrs Bellamy wrote to Tate Wilkinson that she was heavily afflicted by rheumatism in her right arm and could not work on the sixth volume of her life. But it was published in May of that year, at which time her address was No 10, Charles Street, St James's. On Tuesday evening, 24 May 1785, she was offered a special benefit at Drury Lane, which she accepted despite her proud public protestations of being comfortably situated. The play was *Braganza*; she did not act in it, the role of the Duchess being taken by Mrs Yates, which as it turned out was that actress's last performance. Charles Stuart had written an address, but Mrs Bellamy "was too much frightened" to speak it. At the end of the play, reported the *European Magazine* of June 1785, Miss Farren came before the curtain to speak a verse by Alexander Bicknell which ended with:

But see, oppress'd with gratitude and
  tears,
To pay her dutious tribute she appears.

Whereupon the curtain rose to reveal Mrs Bellamy, in an armchair, who succeeded "in muttering a few words, expressive of her gratitude," to a house reported to be "extremely full." The number of tickets out is not known, but on that date Drury Lane paid her £88 10*s.* 2*d.* for "Bt Balance." Kitty Clive asked Jane Pope in a letter dated 30 May 1785 to send her a report "how it really was," and with feline spite suggested that Miss Pope ought to begin to be wicked and then write an apology —*"That* seems at present to get at riches the quickest way." But her curiosity got the better of her and Kitty asked for the sixth volume of Mrs Bellamy's *Apology*: "I suppose she intends going on like Tristram Shandy and give us a vol every year then perhaps we may have the humours of a convent for I have persuaded her to retire to one as the only sensible resource she has left." Six months later, no doubt not realizing the true opinion which Mrs Clive held of her, Mrs Bellamy requested the loan of £25 from her until Christmas. Mrs Clive replied curtly, "I can't comply with your request," and then wrote to Jane Pope in November 1785, "I really would not give her so many farthings to save her from that Destruction she must certainly come to and which she so truly deserves." Whatever George Anne had gained by her *Apology* and benefit was soon gobbled up by creditors. Her landlady served a writ for £14, and only the intercession of a Mr Batten, of Hare Court, Temple, a friend of the Woodward family, saved her from the sponging house. By 4 May 1786 she was fairly destitute, living in Eliot's Row, St George's Fields, under the rules of the King's Bench Prison. A broken ankle which could not be reset correctly made her lame, and for the rest of her distressed years she needed help to walk. She died on 16 February 1788.

In person George Anne Bellamy was a middle-sized woman and quite lovely in her younger years. Her complexion was very fair, her eyes were a pretty blue, and her hair was dark, as verified by the Lindo portrait of her. Her face and figure gave great delight, her voice was powerful, yet plaintive when she wished, and she trod the stage, according to Mrs Ward, "always like a woman of rank." Although a great favorite, she was below the rank of the great actresses of her day, such as Mrs Cibber, Mrs Pritchard, or later Mrs Siddons. She was, however, a serious rival in roles of pathos and grief, such as Monimia, with tears at her command, not like an actress who, according to the *Theatrical Review* (1758), is "reduced to the poor shift of hiding her face, when her situation demands that her eyes should overflow with grief." She possessed, in the words of Thomas Wilkes, "All the softness of her sex, and that sweet sensibility which gives the most affecting pathos to tender parts in Tragedy." Her Cordelia and Juliet were engaging by virtue of her beauty and assumed innocence. But roles of violence and rage were less suited to her talents. During her 29 active years on the stage she played quite regularly some 96 roles.

The following portraits and prints of George Anne Bellamy are known: 1. An oil portrait by F. Lindo, in the Garrick Club. 2. A profile "taken at the age of 30," an anonymous process print in the Harvard Theatre Collection. 3. A mezzotint portrait by A. Van Haecken, after J. Van Haecken, in the Harvard Theatre Collection 4. As "The Comic Muse," a portrait by F. Cotes and Ramberg, engraved by F. Bartolozzi as a plate to *Bell's British Theatre*, 1785. A copy was engraved by Sands, and another by Mackenzie, the latter as a plate to *Eccentric Biography*, 1803. A version, in reverse, was engraved by F. Maradan, after Benoist, and published in France by various copiers. 5. A crude profile engraving, published in *Town and Country Magazine*, September 1776. 6. As Clarinda in *The Suspicious Husband*, an anonymous engraving published by Smith and Sayer. 7. As Cleone in *Cleone*, an anonymous engraving published by Harrison, 1781. 8. As Juliet in *Romeo and Juliet*, with Garrick as Romeo, by Benjamin Wilson, engraved by R. Laurie, published by R. Sayer. Another engraving by Ravenet was published by Boydell, 1765; Stayer also did an engraving of it. 9. As Juliet, an engraving by S. Harding, published by A. Molten, 1784. 10. As Erixene in *The Brothers*, with Garrick as Demetrius, an engraving by J. Collyer, after D. Dodd, published as a plate to *New English Theatre*, 1777. 11. "Elopement from Covent Garden Theatre," in the arms of a young man, engraved by Newham, after Ramberg, as a plate to *Bell's British Library*, 1786; several other versions of this incident, anonymously engraved, are in the Harvard Theatre Collection. 12. Seated in a room, with others, anonymously engraved, in the Harvard Theatre Collection. 13. In a bedchamber with companion, anonymously engraved, in the Harvard Theatre Collection. 14. Seated on steps of Westminster Bridge in despair, engraved by Maradan, after Benoist.

Bellamy, Richard   *d. 1813, singer, chorus master, composer.*

Richard Bellamy, Bachelor of Music and one of the leading bass singers of his day, was appointed a Gentleman of the Chapel Royal on 28 March 1771 and a lay vicar of Westminster Abbey on 1 January 1773. He also became a vicar choral of St Paul's Cathedral in 1777 and was almoner and master of the choristers there from 1783 to 1800. Perhaps he was the Mr Bellamy, who, as a young man, received 5*s*. for singing in the chorus for a production of *The Coronation* at Covent Garden of 13 November 1761.

In May and June 1784, Richard Bellamy sang as one of the principal basses in the Handel Memorial Concerts at Westminster Abbey and the Pantheon, and in 1786 he sang in the Drury Lane oratorios, appearing in the *Messiah* on 3 and 24 March. On the latter date the song "The trumpet shall sound" was sung by him. Bellamy also sang in Salomon's Concerts at the Hanover Square Rooms in 1790. In 1794 Doane gave his address as No 6, Crane Court, Fleet Street.

Entries in the Drury Lane account books indicate that on occasion Bellamy provided Drury Lane Theatre with the use of his choir boys, probably for the oratorios. On 5 May 1794 he received £25 4*s*. "for St Paul's Boys," in 1797 £8 8*s*., in March 1798 a total of £54 15*s*., and on 4 November 1800, £10. Although he supposedly relinquished his appointments in 1801, Bellamy received £10 10*s*. on 12 May 1802, through Shaw, an attorney, again for "St Paul's Boys." Among Richard Bellamy's students were the nineteenth-century singer John C. Clifton, to whom he was related, and William Edward Heather. According to Mee, Bellamy "seems to have sung at Oxford in most years" after 1800 in the concerts at the Oxford Music Room.

In 1788 Bellamy published a *Te Deum* for full orchestra, which had been performed at the installation of the Knights of Bath in May of that year, and a set of anthems. He also published several sonatas and a collection of glees.

Some time before 1770 Richard Bellamy married Miss Elizabeth Ludford, the daughter of Thomas Ludford (1709–1776) and Anne Ludford (d. 1748). Elizabeth's mother Anne Ludford was the only daughter of the Reverend Edward Taylor, rector of Finningley, Nottinghamshire, and his wife Rachel, and she had previously been the widow of Thomas Bold, a distiller of London, before marrying Ludford. Elizabeth's father, Thomas Ludford, was a nephew of Mrs Ann Playford, the wife of Henry Playford, a celebrated music publisher in London. By Thomas Ludford's will, dated 12 January 1776 and proved on 28 June 1776, Mrs Elizabeth Ludford Bellamy received in trust for herself and her children—"but in no ways for the control of her present or future husband, but left entirely to her own direction and good management"—a freehold house and land at Hayes, a leasehold house in Marsham Street, Westminster, for the remainder of a term of 61 years which commenced in 1767, and the leasehold of houses and lands under the Earl of Donegal in Ireland for a remainder of a term of 61 years which commenced in 1761. Ludford bequeathed directly to Miss Elizabeth Maria Bellamy, but under the direction and care of Mrs Bellamy, her mother, the house in Hayes with all its belongings, £120 for her sole use, a bond of a Richard Williams for £280, and a silver tea kettle and lamp. To the Bellamys' son and his godson, Thomas Bellamy, then six years old, Ludford gave a silver tankard, a silver watch and £10 annually to assist in his education. Ludford requested that a Thomas Bellamy, perhaps another relative but possibly a scribal error for Richard Bellamy, pay up his note of ten guineas immediately, which he directed was then to be given to his godson.

It seems that Richard Bellamy profited little by his father-in-law's will although he outlived Elizabeth Bellamy, whose death-date is unknown. (The registration of the marriage of a Richard Bellamy to Eliza Mary Randall at St George, Hanover Square, on 14 May 1794 may pertain to a second marriage. Bellamy apparently had no namesake son.) On 3 March 1811 Richard Bellamy, apparently ill, petitioned the Royal Society of Musicians for assistance, but although the request was properly signed, it was not accompanied by his certificate of marriage, a certificate of the "birth of his child" (suggesting he still had a minor child?), or a satisfactory account of his property. Bellamy presented the proper certificates (which are lost) to the Governors of the Fund on 7 April 1811 and was granted an unspecified allowance.

Richard Bellamy died two years later at Edmonton, Middlesex, at the end of August or the beginning of September 1813 (and not on 11 September as conjectured by Grove); for, on 5 September 1813 his widow asked for funeral costs from the Royal Society of Musicians and was told that her son T. L. Bellamy had already paid the expense and would not take money from the Governors. In his will, dated 2 August 1813, Richard left all his estate and effects (unspecified) to his wife and sole executrix, Dorothy Bellamy, indicating that after the death of Elizabeth Bellamy he had remarried at least once. Bellamy mentioned no children. The will was proved by oath of his widow on 10 November 1813. On 7 November 1813, Dorothy Bellamy was granted the usual widow's allowance from the Royal Society of Musicians. She lived for at least another 27 years. During the 1830's she received annual gifts from the Society, for which she dutifully sent letters of gratitude. On 5 January 1840 the Governors granted her £6 6s. per month for medical relief; presumably she died soon thereafter.

Bellamy, Thomas Ludford *1771–1843, singer, proprietor, choir master.*

Thomas Ludford Bellamy was born in St John's parish, Westminster, on 15 September 1771, according to his "Brief Memoir" in the *Monthly Mirror* of March 1808 (and not in 1770 as stated in *Grove* and the *Dictionary of National Biography*). He was the son of the celebrated singer and vicar choral of St Paul's, Richard Bellamy, and Elizabeth Ludford Bellamy. He was educated in the choir of Westminster Abbey under Dr Benjamin Cooke and also in the choir of St Paul's School under the direction of his father. In May and June 1784, as Master Bellamy, he sang among the trebles in the Handel Memorial Concerts at Westminster Abbey. After his voice broke—"settling to a tenor bass"—he took lessons from Signor Tasca, a celebrated bass singer.

Bellamy was employed as a principal

bass in the choirs of the Chapel Royal, Westminster, and St Paul's, serving as his father's deputy at the latter place, and from time to time in the concerts of the Academy of Ancient Music. According to Sainsbury, he was particularly noticed at a concert at the Academy by Joah Bates, who volunteered to tutor him in the singing of ancient music. "In consequence of such instruction, Bellamy's performance at those concerts was soon crowned with the most flattering success."

Billed as "Bellamy Jun," Thomas made his first appearance at Drury Lane on 11 March 1791 singing "Honour and Arms" from *Samson*, in an oratorio selection of works of Handel. In the oratorios at the King's Theatre in 1793 he performed a principal vocal part in the *Messiah* on 20 February, when he sang three songs, "Thus saith the Lord," "But who may abide," and "Why do the Nations." On 22 February in *Redemption* he sang "He layeth the beams" (*Samson*) and "The Lord is a Man of War" (*Israel in Egypt*), the latter song with Dignum. Doane listed Bellamy's address in 1794 as No 6, Crane Court, Fleet Street.

In 1794, finding little prospect of professional advancement at London until important musical positions should be vacated by deaths, Bellamy went to Ireland, by some accounts to manage a nobleman's estate, but more probably to attend to the property left to him there by his grandfather Thomas Ludford. By his will, proved on 28 June 1776, Ludford had bequeathed to his grandson, through Ludford's daughter Elizabeth Bellamy, a leasehold of houses and lands under the Earl of Donegal for a remainder of a term of 61 years which commenced in 1761. (Ludford had also left his grandson, who was also his godson, a silver tankard, a silver watch, and £10 annually to assist in his education.)

At Dublin, Bellamy sang in concerts at Fishamble Street in 1795. About 1797 he became stage manager at the Crow Street

Harvard Theatre Collection

THOMAS LUDFORD BELLAMY
by Allingham

Theatre, where he also made his singing debut on 9 February 1798. He sang at Cork in September 1798 and at Limerick in October 1798 and August 1799. He was doubtless the Bellamy who was proposed as a professional member of the Irish Musical Fund on 5 March 1798 but preferred to become an honorary member. Ill health obliged Bellamy to give up his post as stage manager after 18 months, but he remained as a principal singer at Crow Street until September 1800, when he purchased John Banks's shares in the theatres at Manchester, Chester, Shrewsbury, and Litchfield. As joint manager with Thomas Ward he devoted himself to this venture for five years.

Most of Bellamy's activities in the management were centered at Manchester, where he enjoyed mixed success. There seems to have been no doubt about his talents as a singer, but the press often commented on his disagreements with Ward over managerial polices. The *Monthly Mirror* of January 1801 proclaimed that Bellamy "certainly yields the palm to no stage singer, Incledon excepted"; the *Theatrical Inquisitor* pronounced him to be "undoubtedly one of the best singers in any country theatre, his voice is good, and his knowledge of music perfectly scientific." Among his best roles at Manchester were Signor Arionelli in *The Son-in-Law* and the Italian singer in *The Critic*. In *The Marriage Promise* on 23 December 1803, Bellamy was "loudly encored" in the song of "The Thorn," which he introduced "and gave in a very exquisite manner." While *The Townsman* alleged that Bellamy was the best singer who ever trod the Manchester stage, it found his acting to be, at best, indifferent. When he played Montenero in *The Wife of Two Husbands* on 28 February 1804, *The Townsman* wrote that "Mr Bellamy's Montenero had nothing to recommend it for its acting," though he gave the songs with his usual skill; and when he acted Arviragus in *Cymbeline* on 3 March 1804, the same paper begged him "never to attempt Tragedy."

Most of the criticism of the management of the Manchester Theatre was directed at Ward. Contrary to Bellamy's wishes, Ward, it was reported, conducted the theatre on a "niggardly plan," with the result that the personnel of the company changed too often, the plays were mutilated by cutting and the performances marred by excessive doubling of roles. Neglectful management had led to very low salaries and poor discipline among the actors. Good new plays from London, it was charged, were slow to be produced, but the bad ones managed to arrive quickly. The same music was played, perpetually, night after night, the blame for which was laid on Bellamy by *The Townsman*, as that department was under his supervision. On 16 March 1805 *The Townsman* announced that Bellamy had sold his interest in the theatre and would leave after the expiration of that season.

The columnist expressed fears for the theatre's future, acknowledging that it was certainly in a better state than when Bellamy came to it: "and I must be allowed to regret that his haughty demeanor, which his friends attribute entirely to a natural warmth of temper and an unfortunate manner, and not to an inherent offensiveness of disposition, should have lost him that favour, to which he was, on other accounts, well entitled." In the *Theatric Tourist*, Winston had remarked that Bellamy was "by no means a favourite with the people."

Apparently Bellamy had wanted to dissolve his partnership with Ward several years before he finally did. On 16 September 1803 he had written a letter to A. Graham of Drury Lane in which he dignifiedly bargained for an engagement there. He wanted Graham to understand that he had received many inquiries from Mr Sheridan and other London managers, but he would never accept without Mrs Bellamy getting a situation also and without articles for less than three years. The Drury Lane management evidently had found his terms unacceptable.

When Bellamy finally left Manchester in 1805, he purchased from Michael Atkins the theatrical rights of the Arthur Street theatre at Belfast and of the theatres at Newry and Londonderry. After two postponements caused by the delay of vessels carrying actors and scenery, Bellamy opened the Belfast theatre on 15 January 1806 with a company which included Mrs Bellamy and a number of actors from provincial theatres in England. Belfast proved to be "a ruinous speculation." According to the *Monthly Mirror*, Bellamy still was sole proprietor of these Irish theatres in March 1808, but by then he was already in London, finally having been engaged for five years by Harris at Covent Garden, where in October 1807 he made his first appearance in the title role of *Robin Hood*.

In 1812 Bellamy was engaged at Drury Lane at a salary of £10 per week for his first season, 1812–13, and then £11 per week for another four seasons. On 27 May 1817 he received a note from Ward, on behalf of the management, easing him out: "I have laid your application for a renewal of your engagement before the sub-Committee, & they direct me to express their sincere regret at being under the necessity of making a great reduction in the Opera department of the Company." Among the roles he had played in London were Don Caesar in *The Castle of Andalusia*, Captain Wilson in *The Flitch of Bacon*, Baldwin in *Godolphin*, Charles in *The Haunted Tower*, Hecate in *Macbeth*, Fitzwater in *The English Fleet*, and Artabanes in *Artaxerxes*.

Upon his dismissal from Drury Lane, Bellamy took up engagements in various concerts and oratorios. In 1817 he was one of the principal singers "for the Choral Music" at the Music Room in Oxford and for the Grand Musical Festival at Norwich. In 1819 he was appointed master of the choir at the Spanish Chapel, and in 1821, upon the death of his friend James Bartleman, he was appointed principal bass at the Concert of Ancient Music. He was also a member of the Catch Club, the Glee Club, the Melodists' Club, and several Masonic lodges.

On 7 January 1818 Bellamy, with his relative, John Clifton, announced a musical academy based on Logier's system which would open on 3 February at No 48, Albemarle Street, Piccadilly. In order to oblige his neighbors in Chelsea, Bellamy also operated the academy on Wednesdays and Saturdays at his home, "the Vale, King's-road, Chelsea." The academy was running at the same address in Albemarle Street in May 1819, but by 12 November 1826 it was at No 19, Upper Berkeley Street, Portman Square.

Bellamy had married the popular actress Mrs Berry at Dublin in May 1799. She had been born Harriet Grist, the daughter of Thomas Grist, a provincial actor who had played at London in 1775–77. From an undated letter by Bellamy to Elliston, it is apparent that he had at least two daughters, and possibly three, since "the infant daughter of Mr Bellamy of Drury-lane Theatre" died in March 1816.

After a professional career of almost 60 years, Thomas Ludford Bellamy died on 3 January 1843. An obituary described him as having been "gentlemanly in his address and manners, and very like the Duke of Wellington in person." In his will, which was drawn up on 24 February 1837, when he lived at No 15, Compton Street, East Brunswick Square, he left all his funds and stocks (amounts unspecified), furniture, and personal estate to his wife Harriet Bellamy. The will was proved on 29 March 1843 (at which time Bellamy was described as formerly of Compton Street, but late of No 50, Judd Street, Brunswick Square), and administration was granted to

Harvard Theatre Collection

THOMAS LUDFORD BELLAMY, as Dr Pangloss

by R. Jean

"Harriet Bellamy widow the relict & universal legatee," a grant which refutes Winston's notation in a Folger manuscript that Harriet Bellamy died in February 1833.

A portrait of Bellamy, done by Allingham and engraved by S. Freeman, was published by Vernor, Hood, and Sharpe in 1808. Another portrait by S. Drummond and engraved by I. Purden was published by Earle and Hemet in 1800. A vignette in stipple of Bellamy as Dr Pangloss by R. Jean was engraved by H. R. Cook and published by J. King in 1814.

Bellamy, Mrs Thomas Ludford. *See* **GRIST, MISS HARRIET.**

"Belle Espagnole, La." *See* **REDIGÉ, MME PAULO.**

Bellguard, Mr *fl. 1738*, *actor.*
Mr Bellguard played one of the Bridesmen in *The Mad Lovers* at Fielding and Hallam's booth in Tottenham Court on 7 August 1738 and repeated this role in the same work under its variant title, *The Man's Bewitch'd*, at Hallam's booth at Southwark Fair on 5 September. On 23 August, between these two engagements, a piece also called *The Man's Bewitch'd* was done at Pinkethman's booth at Bartholomew Fair, and Bellguard acted one of the friends of Don Furioso.

Bellicourt. *See* **BALICOURT.**

Bellin, Mr *fl. 1794*, *bass viol player.*
Doane's *Musical Directory* of 1794 lists Mr Bellin, of No 12, Bennett's Hill, Thames Street, as a participant in performances by the Cecilian Society.

Bellingham, Mr *fl. 1775*, *actor.*
A Mr Bellingham made his first appearance as Roger in *The Gentle Shepherd* at the Haymarket Theatre on 20 November

1775, but his name does not appear on any later bills.

Bellmotte. *See* **BALMAT.**

Belloli, Marianna *fl. 1793*, *singer.*
Signora Marianna Belloli sang at the King's Theatre in the Haymarket from February through June 1793. Her first role was Egesta in *I giuochi d'Agrigento* on 5 February, after which she appeared as La Contessa in *Le nozze di Dorina* starting 26 February (but her role was omitted on 23 April), Ermellinda in *Teodolinda* on 19 March, Stellidaura in *I zingari in fiera* starting 14 May (but her role was omitted on 8 June), and Delmirena in *Odenato and Zenobia* on 11 June. She sang in both serious and comic works, but her roles were not always important.

"Belly." *See* **AICKIN, JAMES.**

Belmont, Mr *fl. 1792*, *actor.*
Mr Belmont played Sparkish in *The Country Girl* at the Haymarket Theatre on 15 October 1792.

Belon. *See* **BALON.**

Belsill or **BELVILLE.** *See* **BELFILLE.**

Beltazar. *See* **BALTHAZAR.**

Ben, Miss *fl. 1720*, *actress.*
Miss Ben, possibly an amateur, played Elvira in *Love Makes a Man* on 22 June 1720 at Coignand's Great Room.

Benard. *See* **BERNARD.**

Bence, Mr *fl. 1750–1757*, *fair booth operator.*
Mr Bence ran a booth on Bowling Green at Southwark Fair on 8 September 1750, presenting *Love and Empire* and *The Rival Beaux*. Though 1751 is unaccounted for, he was back at the same place on 22 Sep-

tember 1752 offering *The Intriguing Chambermaid* and *Harlequin Triumphant.* His activity in 1753 is also unknown, but he returned to his old stand on 20 September 1754 with Mrs Midnight's (Christopher Smart's) *The Old Woman's Oratory* and *The Birth of Harlequin.* On 6 September 1755 he advertised his productions of *The Happy Gallant* and *The Fairy* as being presented at Bence's Room, Swan Yard, West Smithfield, during Southwark Fair. In 1756, on 20 September, he gave *The Intriguing Captains* at his booth at the upper end of the Bowling Green at Southwark Fair, and on 5 September 1757 at Bartholomew Fair he did *A School for a Wife* at his room in Swan Tavern.

This Mr Bence may have been the William who was cited in the baptismal registers of St Paul, Covent Garden. Priscilla, a daughter of William and Beatrix Bence, was christened on 18 December 1746, and their son William was baptised on 18 January 1748. John, son of William and Elizabeth Bence (the same William but a second wife, perhaps), was christened on 30 May 1752.

Bencki, Mr [*fl.* 1751], *violoncellist.*

At a benefit recital for the aging Signora Cuzzoni at Hickford's on 23 May 1751, Mr Bencki played the violoncello, contributing his services free to help her make enough to pay her debts before leaving England.

Bencraft, James *d. 1765, actor, dancer, singer.*

James Bencraft (or Bancroft, Bencroft), who was to become a patentee of Covent Garden, started his career acting Lockit and Nimming Ned in *The Beggar's Opera* as part of the Lilliputian Company at the Lincoln's Inn Fields Theatre on 1 January 1729. Though billed as James Bencraft at this first appearance, he was Young Bencraft when he played at the fairs in the summers of 1730, 1731, and 1732. At Fielding and Oates's booth at Southwark

Fair on 9 September 1730 he was Doodle in *The Generous Free-Mason*; on 26 August 1731 at the Mills-Miller-Oates booth at Bartholomew Fair he danced (or possibly sang) and played Gudgeon in *The Banished General*; and on 23 August 1732 at the same booth and fair he acted Lack Brains in the droll, *Henry VIII.* On 23 August 1733, when he made his next appearance at the same fair and booth, he was billed simply as Bencraft and played Dick Dreary in the droll, *Jane Shore*, and the Shepherd in *The Gardens of Venus.* He had grown up, and we may guess that he was now in his early twenties and thus born about 1710–15.

Though *The London Stage* records Bencraft as a member of the Covent Garden company in 1733–34, no roles are noted for him, so he was probably assigned only bit parts. In the summer of 1734 he again played at Bartholomew Fair, this time at two different booths: on 24 August he was a Sailor in a pantomime dance called *The Force of Inclination* at the Fielding-Oates booth, and on 2 September he played Scaramouch in *The Farrier Nicked* at the Ryan-Legar-Chapman-Hall booth. During the 1734–35 season with John Rich's troupe he played John in *Don Quixote in England* on 1 October 1734 at Lincoln's Inn Fields and a Countryman in *The Rape of Proserpine* on 30 December at Covent Garden.

Rich's contract with Bencraft for the 1735–36 season specified 3s. 4d. daily for a total of £28 13s. 4d. for 172 days and no benefit. During the season he continued appearing in pantomimes: Scaramouch in *Apollo and Daphne* on 17 October 1735 and Pierrot in *The Chymical Counterfeits* on 1 July 1736 were typical. But he was also granted some roles in straight plays, such as Tatter in *The Funeral* on 9 January 1736, Hotman in *Oroonoko* on 2 April, and Francesco in *Hamlet* on 16 April—and on 4 June, despite the original contract, he was allowed to share a benefit with two others. Rich must have recognized that Bencraft was a performer with a considerable range who was worth encouraging.

Bencraft played at Bartholomew Fair again in the summer and then returned to Covent Garden in the fall to add such new parts to his repertory as a Lass in *The Rape of Proserpine* (comic female impersonation was another side of his talent), Pearmain in *The Recruiting Officer*, and Hildebrand in *The Woman Captain*. The bills do not show a benefit for him in the spring of 1737, nor did he play at the fairs in the summer. He was back in stride in 1737–38, however, and in a burst of activity after the turn of the year he added such parts as Gadshill in *1 Henry IV*, Shadow in *2 Henry IV*, Vernon in *1 Henry VI*, the Mad Taylor in *The Pilgrim*, and, for the benefit he shared with three others on 3 May 1738, Cant in *The Beggar's Wedding*. During the summer and early fall he also made up for his disappearance from the fairs the year before: on 7 August he danced and played Squire Graygoose in *The Mad Lovers* at Fielding and Hallam's Tottenham Court booth; on the twenty-third he was Don Furioso in *The Man's Bewitched* at Pinkethman's Bartholomew Fair booth; on the twenty-ninth he acted Rigadoon in *Love and a Bottle* at Covent Garden; and on 5 September he danced and played Squire Graygoose again at Hallam's Southwark Fair booth.

Before the end of the decade the industrious Bencraft added to his repertory at Covent Garden such roles as the Miller in *The Necromancer*, the Hussar in *Perseus and Andromeda*, Simple in *The Merry Wives of Windsor*, Shoemaker in *The Relapse*, Alonzo in *Rule a Wife and Have a Wife*, the Dragon in *The Dragon of Wantley* (on 12 September 1739, billed as "Signor Bencraftini"), Barnaby in *The Old Bachelor*, the Giantess in *The Opera of Operas* (which suggest he was probably a big man), and, in *The Rehearsal*, he sang a song. He was busy, too, at Bartholomew Fair in both 1739 and 1740.

By 1740–41 he was paid 6*s.* 8*d.* daily and given a solo benefit. Among his new parts this season were Cogdie in *The Gamester*, Burgundy in *King Lear*, and Richard in *The Provoked Husband*. His benefit was on 11 April 1741 for the entertainment of the Free Masons (to which he probably belonged); he sang for his friends and made a profit of £54 11*s.* He topped off the season acting and dancing at Bartholomew Fair.

During the 1740's Bencraft's pattern changed little; he continued in many of his old roles, added a few new ones, avoided high comedies but took lighter roles in serious plays, appeared regularly in pantomimes, and usually spent his summers at one of the fairs or at such suburban theatres as Richmond or Twickenham. He seems to have reached a plateau in his career, and perhaps what prevented him from making further progress was the competition he faced within the Covent Garden troupe: during these years Rosco, Hippisley, Woodward, and Ray played similar roles and had as much skill as Bencraft. The additions to his repertory, then, present few surprises: the third Witch and the second murderer in *Macbeth*, Abhorson in *Measure for Measure*, Petulant in *The Plain Dealer*, Haly in *Tamerlane*, Ben Budge in *The Beggar's Opera*, the Duke of Florence in *All's Well That Ends Well*, the title role in *The Jealous Husband* and a Cyclop in *The Loves of Mars and Venus*.

Woodward and Hippisley were not at Covent Garden starting in 1747–48, and Rosco was not there the following season; in consequence Bencraft's repertory expanded considerably near the end of the decade to include Rosencrantz in *Hamlet*, Longbottom in *The Country Lasses*, the Burgomaster in *Apollo and Daphne*, Fourbin in *The Soldier's Fortune*, Hairbrain in *Wit Without Money*, a Recruit in *The Recruiting Officer*, Setter in *The Old Bachelor*, Cornwall in *King Lear* (a surprise), Lory in *The Relapse*, Mouldy in *2 Henry IV*,

Petulant in *The Way of the World*, Gibbett in *The Stratagem*, and Meleager in *The Rival Queens*. Almost all of these roles he kept in the ensuing decade. The "obliging and humorous Jemmy" Bencraft, as Smollett called him, was also elected, on 17 December 1748, to the Sublime Society of Beefsteaks.

During the 1750's Bencraft relaxed his pace, took on fewer new parts, reduced his summer activity and perhaps spent more time at his home at the corner of the Piazza, Covent Garden. His 1758 season was his last fully active one, and in 1759–60, for very good reasons, he performed infrequently. On 23 January 1760, when he was probably nearing 50, Bencraft resigned his bachelorhood, choosing for his wife Henrietta Rich, the daughter of the famous harlequin and Covent Garden manager, John. They were married at their parish church, St Paul, Covent Garden. By this time Bencraft had become a patentee of Covent Garden; when John Rich died in 1761 he left his daughter Henrietta a fifth of the profits from the sale of his share.

He had relinquished a good many of his roles starting in 1759–60, reclaimed a few in 1760–61, and in 1761–62 had his last season as a performer. He played Gibbett in *The Stratagem* on 9 September 1761, Pantaloon in *The Fair* on 13 October, a Recruit in *The Recruiting Officer* on 2 November, and probably the Dragon in *The Dragon of Wantley* (billed as "the Giant") starting 30 April 1762. This last work was acted for his benefit and, on 4 May when it was last performed, he probably made his last stage appearance.

Bencraft raised a small family in the early 1760's. A daughter Harriet was born probably in 1761, Charlotte was baptized on 27 November 1762 and apparently died before 1783, and Mary was baptized on 6 October 1764. But James Bencraft himself died shortly afterward, on 10 January 1765 at his house in Covent Garden, and on the twentieth he was buried at his parish church, St Paul, Covent Garden.

He had made his will on 3 December 1764, and it was proved by his widow on 24 January 1765. To her James left all the moveables in his house, and to Richard Hewetson and Theodosius Forest he bequeathed the rest of his estate. The two men, probably lawyers, were to retain 20 guineas each for mourning rings and then sell the remainder of the estate and invest the proceeds in public stocks or government securities in trust for his widow Henrietta. After her death the dividends were to be given to the children. On 4 August 1767 Henrietta received a dividend from Covent Garden of £1065 18*s.* 6½*d.*, and she may well have received similar dividends in other years. When John Rich's widow Priscilla died in 1783 Henrietta was living in Hillingdon, Middlesex; to her Mrs Rich left £100, and to her daughters Harriet and Mary she gave £400 each, to be given them when they reached 21 if they obeyed their mother in selecting husbands. Since the third Bencraft girl, Charlotte, was not mentioned, perhaps she had died by this time; the eldest daughter, Harriet, was probably already past 21 when Priscilla Rich died. Mrs Bencraft died at Uxbridge at the age of 86.

Though contemporary documents yield little information about James Bencraft's theatrical talent, they have much to say of his character. On 21 January 1765, the day after his funeral, the *Gazetteer* called him "that truly honest amiable and benevolent man, whose perpetual pleasantry and delectable vein of humour cannot more aptly be described than in the word of Hamlet— 'That fellow of infinite jest &c—alas poor Jemmy." And Bencraft's friend William Havard wrote a most generous tribute:

A Person, who, in his lowest circumstances of Life, felt for Distress, & to the utmost of his Pow'r, reliev'd it; when in a superior Situation he exercis'd ye same beneficent Quality, with the additional one, of never forgetting an old friend. He was Master of a peculiar (indeed an original) vein of Humour, wh rendered him irresistably agreeable, for it was so happily constituted, that no satyrical Turn, or ill-natur'd supposition ever mingled in his Conversation.

This chastity of Mirth (if I may be allowed ye Expression) endear'd him to Many, and render'd him acceptable to All.—Yet these accomplishments, however rare, were exceeded by ye Virtues of his Heart—For, his Promise was ever unshaken, & his Integrity firm—

To sum up the Whole of his Character, he was an unalterable friend, a most affectionate Husband, and a fond Parent.

Benda, Mme [fl. 1790–1792], singer.

Madame Benda made her first appearance on 6 May 1790 at the Pantheon, and Fanny Burney fortunately was there to record her impressions:

This being the last Pantheon, I put in my long-intended claim; and it was greatly facilitated by the circumstance of a new singer, Madame Benda, making her first appearance. She is just arrived from Germany, and has been humbly recommended to the notice of Her Majesty: it was on this account my father engaged her to try her powers at the Pantheon; and the Queen was herself interested I should hear her success . . .

Poor Madame Benda pleased neither friend nor foe: she has a prodigious voice, great powers of execution, but a manner of singing so vehemently boisterous, that a boatswain might entreat her to moderate it.

Perhaps the German singer brought her voice under control as time went on, for in 1792 when Haydn was in London he included Madame Benda in his list of musical people there.

Bendler, Salomon 1683–1724, singer.

Salomon Bendler (or Bendeler, Blender) was born at Quedlinburg, Germany, in 1683, the son of the musical theorist Johann Philipp Bendeler [sic]. Salomon was "newly arriv'd" in London when he sang the bass roles of Argantes in *Rinaldo* on 23 January 1712 and Fengon in Zeno and Gasparini's *Ambleto* on 27 February at the Queen's Theatre in the Haymarket.

Shortly after this brief London engagement the basso sang at the Hamburg opera, at Leipzig, and at Brunswick with great success. Bendler died in 1724.

Bene, Signora del. *See* FERRARESE, SIGNORA.

Benedetti. *See* BALDASSARI.

Benelli, Antonio Peregrino 1771–1830, singer, composer.

The Italian tenor singer and composer Antonio Peregrino Benelli was born at Forli on 5 September 1771. As Grove points out, early biographers have confused the name of his teacher in counterpoint, Padre Mattei, with that of Padre Martini, the latter having died when Benelli was only 12. Benelli made his first appearance at the Teatro San Carlo at Naples in 1790. He was engaged by the King's Theatre at London in 1798, where he made his debut, announced as from Naples, on 21 April 1798, singing the role of Paolino in *Il matrimonio segreto*. *The Morning Chronicle*, 23 April, found his voice to be "fine and flexible, strong, at the same time melodious," and observed further that he was "a good actor" with "rapid and neat" execution. William Parke, the musician, commented that although Benelli managed the most difficult passages with brilliancy and ease, his style was "rather too florid."

On 26 April Benelli offered his second role, Egardo in *Elfrida*. Mistakenly calling him Binetti, the *Monthly Mirror* (April 1798), reviewing this production, remarked, "We have not heard so clear a tenor voice for a number of years." That season, Benelli also sang a principal character in *Il barbiere di Siviglia* and Emone in *Antigona*. In 1798–99, between 8 December and 30 July, he sang Egardo again, Alfonso in *Ines de Castro*, the title role in *Medonte*, and Iarba in *Didone*. The last piece, which opened on 30 May 1799, contained additions to Paisiello's music by Benelli, specifically a new air in the second act composed and sung by him. After completing his second season at the King's, Benelli apparently intended to return to Italy. However, in consequence of a contract dispute with the singer Signor Damiani in August 1799, the management engaged Benelli, "who was then upon the eve of his departure," for the next season. In 1799–1800 he sang Alfonso again, Alessandro in *Alessandro e Timotes* (by Sarti, the first performance in England on 15 April 1800), and Evandro in *Alceste*, making his final appearance in the latter role on 2 August 1800.

In the following year Benelli was engaged at Dresden, where he remained until 1823, at which time he retired with a pension at the age of 51 because his voice failed. He then obtained a professorship of singing at the Berlin Opera House and became a contributing critic to the *Allegemeine musikalische Zeitung* of Leipzig. In this paper, he severely attacked Spontini's opera, *Olympia*, in 1828. When Spontini in retaliation printed this attack side by side with a very favorable review which Benelli had previously written about the same piece, the professor was discredited, left his position in Berlin, went first to Dresden, and then to Börnichen in Saxony, where he died in poverty on 16 August 1830.

Grove describes Benelli as a "clever composer," particularly of church music. He also published *Gesangslehre* (1819), which first appeared in Italian as *Regole per il canto figurato*, and "Bermerkungen über die Stimme" (1824) in the *Allegemeine musikalische Zeitung*.

Benety. *See* BINETY.

Benford, Austin [*fl.* 1674–1685], *singer.*
Austin (or Augustine) Benford (or Benfold) began his singing career with the King's Musick as a boy under the tutelage of John Blow, the first notice of him being on 7 November 1674 when he accompanied

the King to Windsor. By 10 July 1676 his voice had changed, and he had left the Chapel Royal but remained under the care of Blow; on 12 January 1680 he was still in Blow's care and thought of as a former Chapel boy. This special consideration may have been given him because he continued singing and was destined for a place among the adult singers at court. At the coronation of James II on 23 April 1685 he supplied the place of John Abell as a Gentleman of the Chapel Royal, which suggests that Benford may, like Abell, have been a countertenor or alto.

Benge, Mr [*fl.* 1794], *equestrian?*
Frost's *Circus Life and Circus Celebrities* mentions a Mr Benge connected with the Royal Circus in 1794; he was possibly an equestrian.

Benico. *See* SEBENICO.

Benigni, Giuseppe [*fl.* 1790–1791], *singer.*
A male soprano, Giuseppe Benigni first sang in London on 6 April 1790 with the King's Theatre opera company at the Haymarket Theatre after the loss of their own, larger house; he was Cherinto in *L'usurpator innocente*. On 29 April he sang Candarte in *La generosità d'Alessandro*; on 28 May he sang Pilade in *Andromaca*; and on 3 June he concluded the season as Giovinetto in Paisiello's *Il barbiere di Siviglia*. The next spring he was active with the troupe at the Pantheon, where he sang Idrano in *Armida* on 17 February 1791; this opening night was roundly criticized by the journalists, who found the acoustics of the remodeled house as poor as the production. Benigni completed the season singing Ataliba in *Idalide* on 14 April and Volunnio in *Quinto Fabio* on 2 June.

Benini, Anna [Signora Bernardo Mengozzi] [*fl.* 1784–*c.* 1791], *singer.*
Anna Benini and Bernardo Mengozzi sang at Naples in 1784 and were either

married by that time or wed the next year (their independent entries in Grove contain conflicting information). The soprano seems not to have used her married name on the stage in London, where she and her husband came in 1786. At the King's Theatre in the Haymarket on 9 January 1787 she sang Giannina in *Giannina e Bernardone* for what was probably her first London appearance. In the premiere of *Il tutor burlato* on 17 February her husband made his first English appearance as Don Leandro, while she sang Rosina. When Madame Mara was indisposed and could not sing the title role in *Virginia* on 22 March, Signora Benini replaced her, though only temporarily. The Grove article notes that she also sang Jephtha's daughter in Handel's *Jephtha*, but no specifics are given; the oratorio was not done in London while Signora Benini was there, though she may have sung in it elsewhere.

After their season in England the couple went to Paris, where Signor Mengozzi taught and composed and both sang. The libretto of *La sposa in equivoco*, published at Venice in 1791, names Anna Benini, so perhaps by then she was active there. She is said to have had a pleasant figure and a voice that was sweet, but not powerful; her style and sober personality are said to have been better suited to serious than comic operas, though in London only her role in *Virginia* was a serious one.

Benion, John ₁*fl. 1661–1677*₁, *actor.*

John Benion (or Binion, Bynion, Dynion) was a minor actor in the King's Company and played an unspecified role in *The Royall King* at the Vere Street Theatre about 1661–62; on 15 April 1667 he probably played the Captain in *The Change of Crownes* at the Bridges Street playhouse. He was included in a list of King's Company members dated 7 February 1677, but there seems to be no later record of him. The information on Benion's participation in the two plays just cited comes from promptbooks; he seems not to have acted any roles large enough to warrant having his name in a printed cast.

Benisford. *See* BERRISFORD.

Bennald, Mr ₁*fl. 1736*₁, *actor.*

Mr Bennald played George Barnwell in *The London Merchant* and Jobson in *The Devil to Pay* at York Buildings on 26 April 1736.

Bennell, Peter *d. c. 1775, musician.*

Peter Bennell was the son of John Bennell of the parish of St George, Hanover Square. A letter of attorney to his father was entered in the office of the Clerk of the Great Wardrobe on 1 July 1762. Peter Bennell was a musician in ordinary to George III and was succeeded on 9 December 1775 by Luffman Atterbury; Bennell had probably died shortly before this date.

Bennet. *See also* BENNETT.

Bennet, Mr ₁*fl. 1749–1751*₁, *house servant.*

A house servant named Bennet, capacity unknown, was on the roster at Covent Garden Theatre in the seasons of 1749–50 and 1750–51.

Bennet, Mr ₁*fl. 1784–1789*₁, *actor.*

The Mr Bennet who was with the Hughes family's theatrical company at Exeter in the winter of 1784–85 is probably the Bennet who was in the Richmond Theatre for a few performances in July of 1789. His roles are not known.

Bennet, Mrs ₁*fl. 1783–1785*₁, *dresser.*

A Mrs Bennet was a dresser at the King's Theatre in 1783–84 and 1784–85.

Bennet, Master ₁*fl. 1748*₁, *actor.*

A Master Bennet was a member of the dramatic company at Richmond, Surrey, in the summer of 1748. His roles are not known.

Bennet, Elizabeth *1714–1791, actress, singer.*

Miss Elizabeth Bennet was designated alternately "Mrs" and "Miss" in several theatrical seasons. But in her will she carefully called herself "spinster."

A "Miss Bennet" was first noticed in London at the Haymarket Theatre on 4 June 1733, playing Mustacha in *The Opera of Operas.* As "Mrs Bennet" she played an unspecified role in *The Amorous Lady* and sang a song at the Haymarket on 26 July following. She was on the bills of the Mills-Miller-Oates booth at Bartholomew Fair on 23 August 1733, playing Mrs Blake in *Jane Shore* and Thalia in *The Gardens of Venus.*

Where or how this actress was employed the following winter is not known, and she made only one recorded appearance, as "Mrs Bennet," in the summer of 1734, at the Fielding-Oates booth at Bartholomew Fair on 24 August, playing Silvia in *The Barren Island.* Evidently she also acted in a program or two at the Ryan-Laguerre-Chapman-Hall booth at the Fair that August. She again disappeared but was Rose in *The Recruiting Officer* at the Great Booth on the Bowling Green in Southwark on 7 April 1735. From 16 July to 5 September she was with a summer company at Lincoln's Inn Fields, playing Lady Grace in *The Provok'd Husband,* Mrs Basinghall in *Squire Basinghall,* Angelina in *Love Makes a Man,* and Fidelia in *The Carnival,* Dollalolla in *The Tragedy of Tragedies,* Mrs Overdo in *Bartholomew Fair,* and Dolly in *The Beggar's Opera.* But she also found time (as "Miss Bennet") to go to York Buildings in July to play Berinthia in *The Relapse.*

Miss Bennet (as she will be called uniformly now) was on the lists at Drury Lane as a dancer in the 1735–36 season, dancing with "The French Company" in *Harlequin Restor'd* on 7 October and 20 November and as Comedy in the same pantomime on 12 January 1736. On 28 February she was the Lodging Woman in the pantomime *The Fall of Phaeton* and on 7 May the Nurse in *Love for Love.*

Her employment was more regular but her roles scarcely better in the season of 1736–37, when, from 14 September through 17 May, she played Mrs Chat in *The Committee,* Aunt in *The What D'Ye Call It,* Beggar in *Phebe,* Mrs Centaure in *The Silent Woman,* Situp in *The Double Gallant,* Terror in *The Fall of Phaeton,* Lucy in *The Recruiting Officer,* Mrs Vixen in *The Beggar's Opera,* and Lettice in *The Eunuch.*

In the following season Miss Bennet was absent from Drury Lane bills between 16 November 1737 and 5 January 1738 but was still named in 19 parts, 7 of them new: Hortensia in *Aesop,* Margery in *The King and the Miller of Mansfield,* Araminta in *The Confederacy,* Trusty in *The Provok'd Husband,* Prudence in *The Amorous Widow,* Lady Woodville in *The Man of Mode,* and Foible in *The Way of the World.*

In the season of 1738–39 Miss Bennet danced, sang, and solidified her position as an important actress of some of the livelier and more appealing smaller comic parts. Her name appeared in the bills some 25 times, and she added the following characters: Scentwell in *The Busy Body,* Lady of Pleasure in *The Harlot's Progress,* Gypsy in *The Stratagem,* Mrs Artichoke in *Robin Goodfellow,* Mrs Wisely in *The Miser,* Hortensia in *Aesop,* Lucy in *Oroonoko,* Jenny in *The Tender Husband,* Maid in *Columbine Courtezan,* Betty in *Bold Stroke for a Wife,* Honoria in *Love Makes a Man,* Dame Pliant in *The Alchemist,* Night in *Amphitryon,* Haymaker in *Harlequin Shipwreck'd,* Lady Loverule in *The Devil to Pay,* Lamorce in *The Inconstant,* Dorothea in *The Man of Taste,* and Mrs Vixen in *The Beggar's Opera.*

It would be tedious to name all of Elizabeth Bennet's parts over the next 26 years, when she kept a tight hold on her minor roles like those above and steadily expanded her repertoire in her general line of gossips, flirts, pert maidservants, cast mistresses, and secondary heroines in comedy. She must have committed to her capacious memory well over a hundred roles. Some, like Flareit in *Love's Last Shift*, were quite substantial. Most were modest. She also continued to dance, for several years, and to sing until the end of her career.

Drury Lane furnished her winter employment, but at least once, in the summer of 1741, she ventured to Bristol from 8 June until 2 September, and occasionally she was to be found in the little nonce companies which gathered at the fairs in the London area to earn enough to keep off the bailiffs during the recess of the patent theatres. A letter from Garrick to Jane Pope in Liverpool, dated 18 July (1763?), sent an epilogue of Roscius's making and gave Miss Pope permission to speak it at Miss Bennet's benefit at that theatre.

By February 1765 Elizabeth Bennet was listed as making £2 10s. per week. Contrasted with the same sum earned each day by Mrs Cibber in the same company, the amount was not munificent, but it was over twice as much as that earned by some other actors; and her humble competency at least assured her of a place season after season.

James Winston's transcripts of the records of the Drury Lane retirement fund show her leaving the stage after 1766. She died on 15 September 1791 and was buried in St Paul, Covent Garden, churchyard on 24 September.

According to several accounts, Elizabeth Bennet lived for many years with William Gibson, the Covent Garden actor and Liverpool manager who died in 1771. He left everything "belonging to me to my dear and much beloved ffriend Mrs Elizabeth Bennet, formerly of the Theatre Royal in Drury Lane London and [I] do hereby appoint her the sole Executrix of this my will." One of Winston's newspaper cuttings in the Folger Library yields up the information, however, that they lived together "in no criminal way. They paid their housekeeping share and share alike."

Miss Bennet, who began her will "I Elizabeth Bennett of Hart Street in the Parish of St Paul, Covent Garden . . . Spinster," left "all the Books I now have which were the property of the late Mr William Gibson at the time of his decease to be equally divided among" William ("Gentleman") Smith, Thomas King, and Richard Wroughton, all eminent actors. To her long-time servant Sarah England she bequeathed £800 in East India annuities and all her household goods. She divided £1000 of the annuities among Richard Morris of "the County of Salop Grocer Mr Edward Wynne of the same place Mercer Mr Edward Pryce of Blackmore Street Clare Market Linen Draper [and] May Pryce Spinster and Hannah Little (wife of William Little) late of Chiswell Street Moorfields Hatter (sisters of the said Edward Pryce)." The Liverpool Infirmary was to have £400 in annuities.

Elizabeth left £200 each to the retirement funds of Covent Garden and Drury Lane Theatres. Smaller bequests went to: Thomas King, £100; Maria King his wife, £100; Mrs Isabella Poustin, wife of Joseph Poustin, Tavistock Street, 10 guineas; the Liverpool Dispensary, £20; the Charity Schools of St Paul, Covent Garden, £20. Ten guineas each went to Jane Pope and Elizabeth Hopkins, the actresses, and Susanna Davies, the widow of Tom Davies the actor and bookseller, and Joanna Wroughton, wife of Richard Wroughton. A mixed bag of actors, managers, and theatrical tradespeople also received 10 guineas apiece: Susannah Pope, Theodosia Mills, Sophia Baker, John Pearce, Richard Wroughton, James Wild, John Hayman Packer, and Dorothy Townley. "[A]lso," she added, "I give and bequeath unto Mary Robinson the reputed Daughter of my late Nephew Frederick Robinson deceased the Sum of Twenty Pounds." The will was signed on 24 August 1791 and proved on 20 September following.

Thus, it seems, Elizabeth Bennet was a good example of a kind of inhabitant of the theatre of the English eighteenth century, humbly respectable, with varied but limited talents, who were dependably assistant to the more spectacular players, and who saved money and had solid connections to the middle classes.

Jane Pope, in a manuscript now in the British Museum, left an extensive necrology for the summer of 1791, which deprived the stage of many people. She summed up:

lastly Mrs Bennett who had been many years a useful and commendable actress at D.L. Parts (though not in the first line) not to be excell'd & who in her . . . Philanthropy . . . & Integrity deserv'd all the regard she met with

Miss Elizabeth Bennet has often been confused with the novelist and Edinburgh manager Agnes Maria Bennett (c. 1768–1868), the mother of Mrs Harriet Pye Esten.

Bennet, Harriet Pye. *See* ESTEN, MRS JAMES.

Bennet, John [*fl. 1744?–1772?*], *instrumentalist.*

A Mr Bennet, instrumentalist, played in August 1744 at the Mulberry Garden, Clerkenwell. He may have been the Bennet alluded to by Charles Burney in a manuscript memoir in the British museum as a member (c. 1748) of the Drury Lane pit band. This Bennet was "an *eleve* of Dr Pepusch, played the Tenor, & occasionally was a chorus singer & figurante in processions. He knew the laws of counterpoint very well."

A John Bennet is listed in Mortimer's *London Directory* (1763) as a "Tenor [horn player] to the Queen's Band, Organist, and Teacher on the Harpsichord."

According to Grove, "A Mr Bennett [*sic*] appears to have been the first bandmaster"

of the Band of the Royal Regiment of Artillery. The band was formed in 1762, and Bennet(t) was supplanted in the leadership by Antony Rocca in 1772.

Bennet, Julia. *See* HUGHES, JULIA.

Bennett. *See also* BENNET.

Bennett, Mr [*fl. 1795–1816?*], *boxkeeper.*

A Mr Bennett was carried on the pay list at Drury Lane Theatre from the beginning of the 1795–96 season until June 1800 before being identified in the account books as a boxkeeper. In the latter year he earned 15*s.* per week. By 1812–13 his salary for a work-week of six days was £1 5*s.*

In 1812–13 a second Bennett, also a boxkeeper, came to the house, at 18*s.* per six-day week; and in the next season a chorus singer of the name was earning £1 5*s.* per week. Whether the singer was one of the boxkeepers converted to or doubling in song, or a third Bennett, is not known. He (or one) earned £2 per week in 1815–16.

Bennett, James [*or Ellis?*] [*fl. 1799*], *boxkeeper.*

A James Bennett (*Morning Post* 17 May 1799) or Ellis Bennett (*Morning Chronicle*) gave evidence at a London trial and identified himself as a boxkeeper at Drury Lane Theatre. He may have been the James Bennett (from the "workhouse") who was buried at St Paul, Covent Garden, on 6 January 1832.

Bennett, John [*fl. 1665*], *scenekeeper.*

John Bennett served as a scenekeeper at court starting 10 April 1665, but the end of his tenure was not noted in the Lord Chamberlain's accounts.

Bennett, Maria [*fl. 1752*], *singer.*
Twelve Songs by Lewis Granom as Sung at Cuper's Gardens by Miss Maria Bennett

and *Sylvia Bright Nymph, Sung by Miss Bennett at Cuper's Gardens* were published in November 1752. As principal singer she was from June through September the vocal counterpoint to Clitherow's displays of fireworks at "Concerts of Vocal and Instrumental Music" at the Gardens. But the proprietor, the Widow Evans, had her license revoked because of dissolute behavior by patrons of the Gardens, which were not opened again until 1755. There is no other record of Maria Bennett.

Bennett, Warner ₍*fl. 1741–1768?*₎, *dancer, singer, actor.*

Warner Bennett began his long career dancing, and possibly singing, at Goodman's Fields Theatre on 9 October 1741 as one of three Priests in *The Imprisonment, Release, Stratagems and Marriage of Harlequin*, repeated many times that season. He went over to Covent Garden on 15 March 1742 to sing with Salway, Leveridge, and others for the benefit of Ryan. He may have been the "Bennet" who played Rodolpho in *Amelia* for the benefit of Mrs Lampe at the Haymarket on 24 March 1743, though the part was somewhat out of his line at the time.

Bennett was in the small but good ballet corps at Drury Lane in 1743–44. In 1744–45 "Bennett" was listed as an actor in the company. A card from him, with the signature identifying him as Warner Bennett, and deferring his benefit performance, was published in the *Daily Advertiser* for 17 October 1745.

A "Bennett" was acting in Hussey's booth in the George Inn Yard in Smithfield at the time of Bartholomew Fair, 23 August 1746 and following. On 7 November 1746 he, or another of the name, was listed as one of the vocalists who furnished incidental music to *Macbeth* at Drury Lane. Around 25 August 1747 he was joint proprietor with Yeates Sr of a booth "facing the hospital gate," according to a bill describing attractions at Bartholomew Fair.

Bennett played the trifling part of a drawer in *The Beggar's Opera* at Covent Garden on 26 September and repeated it at least six times more that season. From the beginning of the season of 1748–49 through that of 1767–68 he was playing practically continuously at Covent Garden in the winters. He was with Bencraft, Dunstall, and other Covent Garden actors in the summer company at Richmond and Twickenham in 1749. By the spring of 1760 he was being paid £1 10s. for a six-day week. At his disappearance from the bills in 1767–68 he was earning £2.

Bennett gradually abandoned harlequin parts as he aged. He exhibited a growing competency but was never really important. He must have been adolescent when he began, with such parts as Donalbain in *Macbeth*, and Snap, the youthful beggar in *The Royal Merchant*. Quite early, however, he began taking on mature parts. Some of them were: Gibbet in *The Stratagem*, Sylvius in *As You Like It*, Mago in *A Duke and No Duke*, Stephano in *The Rover*, Burgundy in *King Lear*, Gregory in *Romeo and Juliet*, Obadiah in *The Committee*, Slender in *The Merry Wives of Windsor*, Young Clencher in *The Constant Couple*, the Beggar in *The Beggar's Opera*, Trapland in *Love for Love*, Tybalt in *Romeo and Juliet*, Thrifty in *The Cheats of Scapin*, Lopez in *The Wonder*, Ratcliff in *Richard III*, and Sir William in *Love in a Village*.

Benning, Ragny. *See* RAGOIS, BENIGNE.

Benonville, Mr ₍*fl. 1774*₎, *machinist?*

A Mr Benonville, possibly an employee at the Drury Lane Theatre, was paid £10 10s. for models of machinery, according to the theatre's accounts.

Benser, John Daniel *d. 1785, instrumentalist, composer.*

John Daniel Benser was the teacher of Johann Cramer from 1774, when Cramer arrived in London, until about 1777. He was primarily a pianist, and for that instrument he wrote several sonatas, but if he was the Mr Benser who played the tenor at the Handel Memorial Concerts at Westminster Abbey and the Pantheon in late May and early June of 1784, he was certainly proficient on stringed instruments as well. A Mr Benser, probably John Daniel, was recorded as a visitor at the Royal Society of Musicians on 6 March 1785, perhaps requesting financial aid; on 3 December 1785 he died, and it was reported that his widow was in great distress for want of necessities.

Bensley, Robert *1742–1817, actor.*

Robert Bensley was a principal actor in the London theatres for 31 years during the eighteenth century. Despite his prominent and lengthy career the details of his life have often been confused or the object of conjecture by early biographers. He was always described in the playbills only as Mr Bensley. Knowing that Sir William Bensley, a director of the East India Company, had left the actor, who was his nephew, the bulk of his property when he died in 1809, some historians have bestowed the name of William upon him gratuitously. The mistake was compounded by the fact that both Robert and a William Bensley, printer and perhaps a relative, died at Stanmore in the same year, 1817.

In a catalog of Mathews's Gallery of theatrical pictures which were exhibited in 1833 at the Queen's Bazaar in Oxford Street, several portraits of him, one by Mortimer (as Hubert in *King John*) and two by De Wilde (as Oakley in *The Jealous Wife* and Harold in *The Battle of Hastings*), are listed as of Richard Bensley. The name of Robert, however, is firmly settled upon him by an autographed letter from him to Garrick, by a letter from the Committee of the Theatrical Fund to George Colman on 25 October 1773 signed by him, by his will, and by the memorial tablet in Stanmore Church. The inscription on

Harvard Theatre Collection

ROBERT BENSLEY

by Dance

the tablet, which states that Robert Bensley was aged 75 at the time of his death in 1817, consequently determines his year of birth to have been 1742.

The events of Bensley's early life are found in several contemporary memoirs which are not always in agreement. When a very young man, Bensley was engaged both in the strolling companies of Stanton at Staffordshire and of Roger Kemble. According to *The Secret History of the Green Room*, "his youth and inexperience made his exertions be treated with ridicule by his associates" in the provinces. The *European Magazine* (May 1796), on the other hand, asserts that he had been educated at Westminster and at the influence of his relations appointed an officer (a lieutenant in the Marines, according to Farington, and a captain in the Army, according to Oxberry). The account states that he served in the War against the French and Indians. While in North America he reportedly acted Chamont in *The Orphan* and other characters in military theatricals. When peace came, as the story goes, he was discharged as a half-pay officer (at a pension which Oxberry grossly overstated to be £1000 a year) and was then warmly recommended to David Garrick as a promising actor.

By whatever route, Bensley, announced as a "Gentleman," arrived for his first appearance at Drury Lane on 2 October 1765 as Pierre in *Venice Preserv'd*. The event, according to Gilliland, was attended by a large body of his former military brothers. He had been drilled in the role by George Colman, who seems to have been an early friend. Bensley next played Hamet in *The Orphan of China* on 25 October 1765. Other roles that season included Standard in *The Constant Couple* on 29 January and Polydore in *The Orphan* on 4 February.

This was the same season in which Samuel Cautherley, Garrick's protégé, also made his debut. Hugh Kelley, writing in *Thespis*, was not impressed by either but would form no premature opinion about these "two raw young striplings on the stage." Satisfying Garrick was a more crucial test, however, and on 20 April 1766 the great actor-manager wrote to Colman that "Bensley's success pleases me." Bensley was re-engaged for the following season. On 28 August 1766 Garrick wrote to him at length, as he was inclined to do with his young talents, commending him on his "fiery trial" of that summer, in which Bensley had gone to Liverpool to assume eight different characters. The manager expressed his pleasure that Bensley had taken on so arduous a task and admitted some previous doubts—"as you are naturally inclined to indolence I had some fears for you." Garrick asked him to study the roles of Theodosius, the Bastard in *King Lear*, Aboan in *Oroonoko*, and Buckingham in *Richard III* for the coming season. *Theodosius* was not played until the following season, with Reddish in the title role and with Bensley then at the rival theatre. But Bensley did

play the other three in 1766–67 on 29 October, 2 December, and 11 April. Despite Garrick's fears of laziness, Bensley was obviously extremely diligent, for in that same season, 1766–67, he also played for the first time Constant in *The Provok'd Wife* (10 October), the title role in *The Guardian* (21 March), Lysimachus in *The Rival Queens* (30 March) and Horatio in *The Fair Penitent* (28 April).

Bensley had spent the summer of 1767 again at Liverpool under Thomas King's management. King wrote to Garrick on 8 July 1767 of Bensley's determination—"which I find he now makes no secret of"—to switch allegiance to the service of Covent Garden. The young actor no doubt had been persuaded by his warm friendship with Powell, who with Colman had become co-patentee of the rival house. Bensley's salary had been set by Powell for 1767–68 at 16s. 8d. per day, an apparent advance over his former wages at Drury Lane. He made his first appearance at Covent Garden again as Pierre in *Venice Preserv'd* on 16 September 1767 and then played Hubert in *King John* on 23 September. Among other roles that season, he played Shore in *Jane Shore*, for the first time, on 16 October.

According to testimony given in a law suit against Colman in 1770, after this season Bensley articled for four more years at Covent Garden, at 19s. 8d. per night for 1768–69 and 1769–70 and at £1 3s. per night for 1770–71 and 1771–72. He stayed there for eight consecutive seasons, through 1774–75, at first playing mostly a line of second characters in tragedy and then advancing to some first-line parts upon the deaths of Powell and Holland. Among his many roles during this period were (with the date of his first time in each at Covent Garden): Leontine in *The Good-Natured Man* (the first performance of Goldsmith's play) on 29 January 1768, the Ghost in *Hamlet* on 25 April 1768, Carlos in *Love Makes a Man* on 16 December 1768, Cha-

Harvard Theatre Collection

ROBERT BENSLEY, as Harold
by De Wilde

mont in *The Orphan* on 18 October 1769, Tamerlane in *Tamerlane* on 4 November 1769, Macbeth on 19 December 1769, the father in *The Roman Father* on 29 March 1770, Posthumus in *Cymbeline* on 18 April 1770, Barnwell in *The London Merchant* on 1 October 1770, Young Belfield in *The Brothers* on 9 January 1771, Iago on 28 January 1771, Barbarossa in *Barbarossa* on 11 October 1771 (*Theatrical Review*: "if the Managers were not absolutely lost to every sense of their duty . . . they would not think of continuing him in this character"), Julius Caesar on 4 May 1773, Bevil in *The Conscious Lovers* on 22 May 1773, Oakly in *The Jealous Wife* on 21 October 1774, and Jachimo in *Cymbeline* on 20 May 1775.

Bensley returned to Drury Lane in 1775–76 (Garrick's last year of management), making his first appearance there in eight

years on 28 September 1775, again in the familiar role of Pierre. His engagement was at £8 10s. per week, providing him with about the fifth highest salary among the men in the company. From this time until his retirement in 1796 he remained loyally at Drury Lane, but sometimes playing at the Haymarket during the summer. He also acted at Bristol in 1771, 1772, and 1779. Although his salary did not increase very much over these years (it was at £10 per week in 1790–91), he did receive annual benefit sums which averaged between £120 and £140 per season.

According to a manuscript list of "Mr Bensley's cast" in the Forster Collection, in 1774–75 he was prepared to play at least 51 roles in 42 plays. Over the next 20 years, he added at least 25 more roles. Few were parts in newly written plays, but rather were roles representative of the plays to be found in regular rotation in the familiar eighteenth-century repertory. As Joseph Knight pointed out, the fact that Bensley attempted few new roles perhaps may be attributed to the dearth of any important tragedies during the latter half of his career. In addition to the roles already mentioned, the following incomplete list is representative (with the date of his first time in each at Drury Lane): Evander in *The Grecian Daughter* on 10 October 1775, Heartfree in *The Provok'd Wife* on 31 October 1775, Manly in *The Plain Dealer* on 11 December 1775, Malvolio on 10 April 1776, Strictland in *The Suspicious Husband* on 10 May 1779, Manly in *The Provok'd Husband* on 20 January 1780, Cassius on 15 February 1780, and Lusignan in *Zara* on 15 December 1780. With the performance for his benefit on 6 May 1796, in which he played his familiar role of Evander in *The Grecian Daughter* to the Euphrasia of Mrs Siddons, Bensley retired from the stage. The public sent him off with benefit receipts of £362 1s. 6d.

Perhaps Bensley's retirement from the stage at the age of 54 had been hastened by ailing health. In January of 1789 he had become so ill that he had had to recuperate in Bath for several months and it was supposed that he would never return to the theatre. But he had played for six more years, and after his retirement from the stage he lived on for 20 more, serving for some years, according to Gilliland, as barrackmaster at Knightsbridge Barracks. A Robert Bensley was mentioned in *The Gazette* on 12 April 1798 as having been appointed paymaster (not barrack-master), a post which the same source indicates he resigned by 27 November of the same year. As mentioned above, the death of his relative Sir William Bensley, in 1809, was reported to have made him financially independent.

In private life Bensley seems to have been a man of intelligence and good nature (although there are some anecdotes about his quick temper), and in the words of O'Keeffe, "an exceedingly well-informed sensible man." For some time he represented his fellow actors as a member of the Committee of the Covent Garden Theatrical Fund. He was also an official deputy from Drury Lane at Garrick's funeral. There existed the story about an early amour with the singer Isabella Mattocks, gossip with perhaps some truth to it.

When working at Bristol, having purchased Holland's share of the Bristol playhouse in 1772, Bensley fell in love with a Miss Francina Augustina Cheston of Queen

By Permission of the Huntington Library

ROBERT BENSLEY, with MISS FARREN in *The Fair Circassian*
artist unknown

Square, after he had been the "accidental cause of her being thrown from her horse." They married at St Stephen's, Bristol, on 8 September 1772. Maria Macklin wrote to her father at the time that Miss Cheston brought Bensley a thousand pounds. There is no evidence that Mrs Bensley ever appeared on the stage. From 1777 at least until 1796, the Bensleys lived at their house at No 21, Charlotte Street, Bedford Square, Bloomsbury. Perhaps the Elizabeth Bensley who married Charles Bowen at St George, Hanover Square, on 24 May 1802, was their daughter.

Bensley died at Stanmore on 12 November 1817. In his will, drawn on 23 December 1809 and proved on 5 December 1817, he left all his real and personal estate to his wife. She died seven years later, on 9 August 1825.

Many critics of his day reported Robert Bensley to be a respectable and sound actor, who by his diligence and devotion to his craft overcame some serious physical deficiencies. Others were harsh and unfavorable to him. The assessment by William Hawkins in *Miscellanies in Prose and Verse* (1775) sums up much of the objective critical comment about him:

Though as an actor, I must confess Mr. Bensley adds very little to this science; yet from the cast of parts he is in receipt with, somewhat entitles him to a place among the principal performers. Though to enter critically upon this gentleman, he has neither face, voice, manner, or scarce any theatrical requisite; his person to be looked at, is tolerable; but as soon as set in motion, it becomes contemptible; or, at least, as much intolerable; there however is one principal requisite in this actors' favour, which deserves notice; this is, his being more generally correct in his parts than the rest of his professors, together with a willingness to please, as he appears to study his parts with unremitted diligence and care; which, from a pretty good education, and his knowledge of the dramatic authors, carries him through his cast of characters with a tolerable good grace. I cannot

quit this gentleman, without doing him the justice to say, that human nature never produced a more amiable character in private life.

To some, Bensley's physical defects were distracting. There appeared to be a certain "mechanism in his acting"—as the *Gentleman's Magazine* (January 1774) put it, "B for Bensley, as stiff as you please"—which made an unfavourable impression upon those seeing him for the first time. There were peculiarities in his gait and tone which made possible some unkind parodies of him. When John Bannister came on at the Haymarket in August 1778 playing the role of Dick in Murphy's *The Apprentice*, he imitated Bensley in a light-hearted respectful way. Bensley's person was slight and according to Francis Gentleman, his features were "contracted and peevish." Waldron considered him to be an overrated actor who enjoyed the favor of an audience more partial to him as a man than as a performer. In all his roles, Waldron claimed, "we can trace the same *measured step*, the *goggling eye*, and *redundancy of extravagant and awkward action*." His debut on the London stage, he thought, was creditable but promised no great degree of success, mainly because of a countenance "expressive of only one sentiment," and that not likely to catch the sympathy of an audience. The *Monthly Mirror* described his eyes as "glassy and protuberant" and his action as ungraceful and "not far removed from that of an Automaton."

Bensley's voice tended to be monotonous and sepulchral, with a nasal quality that was frequently harsh and fatiguing to the ear. These deficiencies worked apparently to his disadvantage in such roles as Pierre, in which he was accounted much too boisterous, and Alzuma, in which "He roar'd so loud, and look'd so wond'rous grim, / That his very shadow durst not follow him" (*Covent Garden Magazine*, February 1773). As King Henry in *Richard III* his lack of tender tone apparently made the role "totally unsuited to his powers" (*Public Advertiser*, 19 February 1788). His playing of the Ghost in *Hamlet* was almost universally discounted: "can Bensley play a ghost? / O yes,—his eye is fix'd as in a frost! / But then he bellows!"

Yet his sourness, nasal tones, and bluntness of manner, worked to enormous advantage in roles such as Eustace in *The Surrender of Calais*. Among his most successful portrayals was that of Malvolio, in which Boaden claimed he was perfection, and which Colman declared was beyond competition. Charles Lamb in his *Essays of Elia* provided a description of Bensley's interpretation of Malvolio which is probably more revealing of Lamb's point of view about the nature of the role than it is about Bensleys protrayal. According to Lamb, Bensley's Malvolio raised a "kind of tragic interest'":

Bensley had most of the swell of soul, was greatest in the delivery of heroic conceptions, the emotions consequent upon the presentment of a great idea to the fancy. He had the true poetical enthusiasm—the rarest faculty among players. . . . The part of Malvolio . . . was performed by Bensley with a richness and a dignity, of which (to judge from some recent castings of that character) the very tradition must be worn out from the stage. . . . Bensley, accordingly, threw over the part an air of Spanish loftiness. He looked, spake, and moved like an old Castilian. He was starch, spruce, opinionated, but his superstructure of pride seemed bottomed upon a sense of worth. There was something in it beyond the coxcomb. It was big and swelling, but you could not be sure that it was hollow. He was magnificent from the outset; but when the decent sobrieties of the character began to give way, and the poison of self-love, in his conceit of the Countess's affection, gradually to work, you would have thought that the hero of La Mancha in person stood before you . . . you had no room for laughter! if an unseasonable reflection of morality obtruded itself, it was a deep sense of the pitiable infirmity of man's nature, that can lay him open to such frenzies,—but in truth you rather admired than pitied the lunacy while it lasted,—you felt an hour of such mistake was worth an age with the eyes open.

An examination of other contemporary comments on Bensley's Malvolio finds that nobody else agreed with Lamb's somewhat sentimental sense of his acting. Lamb had high praise as well for Bensley's Iago—"the only endurable one which I remember to have seen"—and his Hotspur, especially in the fine madness of his rant about glory.

Bensley was obviously a better actor than the unfriendly critic of *Theatrical Biography* (1772)—who found him *"no actor at all"*—would have us believe. In many roles, such as Old Norval in *Douglas*, he fell short, but these failures must be balanced against such successes as Alcanor in *Mahomet*, a role in which he could display his reported impressive qualities of good sense and sensibility to advantage. "Mr Bensley played it naturally, and was deservedly much applauded." Henry Bate found his Morose in *Epicoene*, a role he played in a controversial production at Drury Lane in 1776, to be capital, even though now and then "he forgot the surly old man, and sunk into the superannuated driveller." On the other hand, the *Westminster Magazine*, reviewing the same performance, called him "the worst Old Man we ever saw. He presents the countenance of a sickly old Woman, and the uniform goggle of his eyes, by which he means to express infirmity and distress, is the look of a man in anguish from the colic."

Garrick reputedly had bestowed the nickname of "Roaring Bob" upon Bensley, who, it seems, did try to perpetuate a school of acting which Garrick had striven to subvert. John Bernard allied Bensley with the style of Quin—"the system to which he belonged considered dignity to consist a good deal in cutting the stage at right angles, with the head up, and brows down; a coldly cor-

rect enunciation, and a full-flowing wig!"
For many years, however, Bensley served his
managers well in the stock roles of the
fond parent, the considerate guardian, the
reserved noble, and the austere moralist.
As a leading man he had less success. His
Pierre in *Venice Preserv'd*, a role he played
for some 30 years, was at best "perfectly
correct" and spirited. Many roles for which
he was unsuited were probably thrust upon
him by the exigencies of the demanding
repertory. Most testimony indicates he was
a diligent and cooperative person who could
be relied upon to provide a steadying influence in the company. He possessed a substantial general knowledge of the dramatists, whose words, it is said, he always
learned and delivered to perfection. In his
later years on the stage he managed to retain his full vigor. At his retirement in
1796, the *Monthly Mirror*, expressing the
sentiments of most of the press, considered
the departure of Bensley as a public loss, for
"with all his imperfections upon his head,"

he was nevertheless accounted "a good actor," and by many, one of the first tragedi-
ans upon the stage.

The following illustrations of Robert
Bensley are known: 1. As Harold in *The
Battle of Hastings*, small canvas by Samuel
De Wilde, in the Garrick Club. Engraved
by P. Audinet and published as a plate to
Bell's British Library, 1793. 2. As Oakly
in *The Jealous Wife*, small canvas by Samuel De Wilde, in the Garrick Club. Engraved by P. Audinet and published as a
plate to *Bell's British Library*, 1792; an
anonymous engraving of the same picture
was printed for C. Cooke, 1808, and published in *British Drama*, 1817. 3. As
Prospero in *The Tempest*, water-color
drawing by Robert Dighton, in the Garrick
Club. 4. As Hubert in *King John*, with
William Powell as King John and William
Smith (as the Bastard?), medium canvas
by J. H. Mortimer, in the Garrick Club. Exhibited at the Society of Artists in 1768.
Many engraved copies. 5. Head, small
pencil drawing by J. Roberts, in the Garrick
Club. 6. As Howard in *Sir Walter Raleigh*, small water-color by W. Loftis, in the
Folger Library. 7. As Banquo in *Macbeth*,
small water-color by W. Loftis, in the Folger Library. 8. As Hubert in *King John*
(with J. P. Kemble as John), small water-
color by W. Loftis, in Folger Library. 9.
As Henry VI in *Richard II*, small water-
color by W. Loftis, in the Folger Library.
10. As Prospero in *The Tempest*, small
water-color by W. Loftis, in the Folger
Library. 11. Portrait, profile vignette by
George Dance, engraved by William Dan-
iell and published by him, 1814. 12. As
Bajazet, anonymous engraving. 13. As
Busiris in *Busiris*, by J. Roberts, and engraved by Thornthwaite and published as
a plate for *Bell's British Theatre*, 1777.
14. As Busiris, anonymous vignette, published by Harrison and Company, 1781.
15. As Iago in *Othello*, by J. Roberts, engraved by C. Grignion and published as a
plate for *Bell's Shakespeare*, 1775. 16. As

Harvard Theatre Collection

ROBERT BENSLEY, as Mahomet
by Edwards

Mahomet in *Mahomet*, by E. Edwards, engraved by J. Collyer, and published by T. Lowndes as a plate for the *New English Theatre*, 1777. 17. As Mahomet, by J. Roberts, engraved by Thornthwaite and published as a plate for *Bell's British Theatre*, 1776. 18. As Antony in *Julius Caesar*, anonymous, published as a plate to edition of the play by J. Harrison, 1780. 19. As Pierre in *Venice Preserv'd*, by E. Edwards, engraved by J. Collyer and published by T. Lowndes as a plate for the *New English Theatre*, 1776. 20. As Barbarossa in *Barbarossa*, with Maria Macklin as Irene, by E. Edwards, engraved by J. Caldwall and published by T. Lowndes as a plate for the *New English Theatre*. 21. (?) As Bassanio in *The Merchant of Venice*, with Charles Macklin as Shylock, Maria Macklin as Portia, and many others, large oil canvas by John Zoffany, in the Tate Gallery. Reproduced by R. Mander and J. Mitchenson in *The Artist and the Theatre* (1955), with explanation. 22. As Omar in *The Fair Circassian*, with Miss Farren as Almeida, large steel engraving signed "J.P.," a caricature (in Huntington Library), with following title and verse as caption:

> *A Moving Scene in the Fair Circassian*
> *a woeful Tragedy written by Mr Pratt*
>
> *Lo Bensley stared with all his might*
> *E'en till his Eye-ball started.*
> *Lo Farren flew to meet his Sight*
> *But she had laced her self so tight*
> *Her Top and Bottom parted.*

23. As one of the actors at "The Apotheosis of Garrick," a large canvas by George Carter, c. 1782, in the Stratford Art Gallery of the Shakespeare Memorial Theatre, Stratford-on-Avon. 24. In the character of Mahomet on a Delftware wall tile, in the City of Manchester Art Gallery. 25. In a painting by Joseph Highmore, showing a man and a woman seated in a castle hall, possibly a scene from *Cymon* as played by Robert Bensley and Mrs Abington.

Benson. *See also* **BANSON.**

Benson, Mr [*fl.* 1735], *actor.*

The Mr Benson who played Morelove in *The Careless Husband* on 19 June 1735 at Lincoln's Inn Fields may possibly be related to one of the later eighteenth-century Bensons.

Benson, Mr [*fl.* 1776–1786], *actor.*

A Mr Benson, almost certainly the father of the well-known London actor Robert Benson, played in a number of unconnected out-of-season performances at the Haymarket Theatre. He usually performed for the benefit of fellow players, in the winters of 1776 through 1778, in the spring of 1781, and in the winter of 1784–85. He was a member of a troupe which occupied the Hammersmith Theatre in the summers of 1785 and 1786. Here he seems to have been given the best parts.

Benson's roles were mainly comic, ranging widely, however, from Marmoset in *The Prejudice of Fashion* to Squire Mockmode in *Love in a Bottle*. Among others of his parts were: Don Julio in *A Bold Stroke for a Wife*, Dumps in *The Natural Son*, Thomas in *The Agreeable Surprise*, Sneak in *The Country Lasses*, Peeping Tom in *Tom of Coventry*, Whittle in *The Irish Widow*, and Bagatelle in *The Poor Soldier*.

Benson's wife, who was with him in performances in 1784 through 1786, played such parts as Kitty Pry in *The Lying Valet* and Mrs Bruin in *The Mayor of Garratt*. On the occasion of Benson's benefit at Hammersmith on 24 July 1786 she played Miss Jenny in *The Provok'd Husband* "with songs in character." A Master Benson, almost certainly their son, and identified by Hogan as Robert Benson, made his "first appearance on any stage" as the Prince of Wales in *Richard III* at the Haymarket on 24 March 1778, for West's benefit. He then played a page in *The Orphan* for Freeman's benefit at the same theatre, 9 April, a night on which the elder Benson performed in the afterpiece. Robert Benson was on the London stage until his death in 1796. But his parents are not recorded as having played in a winter patent theatre.

Benson, Mrs *[fl. 1675]*, *singer*.
A Mrs Benson, possibly an amateur, sang in the court masque *Calisto* for Charles II on 15 February 1675.

Benson, Mrs *[fl. 1728–1731]*, *actress*.
Mrs Benson, the widow of "Mr Secretary Benson," was announced in the newspapers early in the 1728–29 theatrical season as soon coming on the stage; this, doubtless, was the Mrs Benson who played Lady Percy in *1 Henry IV* at Lincoln's Inn Fields on 19 November 1728, a peasant in *Apollo and Daphne* on 23 November, and Lady Macduff in *Macbeth* (for her shared benefit) on 28 April 1729. During the next season she acted Mrs Page in *The Merry Wives of Windsor* on 15 May 1730 for her shared benefit. Whether or not she completed the 1730–31 season is not known; on 25 September she was in *Apollo and Daphne* again, and though she was presumably in subsequent performances of it, her name did not again appear in the playbills.

Benson, Mrs *[fl. 1784–1786]*, *actress, singer. See* **BENSON, MR** *[fl. 1776–1786]*.

Benson, Miss *[fl. 1797–1806?]*, *actress. See* **BENSON, ROBERT**.

Benson, Robert *1765–1796, actor*.
Robert Benson was evidently the son of the minor players Mr Benson (fl. 1776–1786) and Mrs Benson (fl. 1784–1786). Unlike his parents, who never really got a foothold in London, he was an actor of some consequence in secondary roles at various theatres, including Drury Lane, until he was overtaken by the madness which ended his existence when he was 31.

By Permission of the Trustees of the British Museum

ROBERT BENSON, as Timurkan

by Graham

Benson's debut was on the stage of the Haymarket Theatre on 24 March 1778, in a special performance licensed by the Lord Chamberlain for the benefit of the actor West. He played the Prince of Wales in *Richard III*, a part usually reserved for the debut of young children. Robert's second opportunity came in another such out-of-season performance on 9 April, when he was a page in *The Orphan*. On that night the elder Benson played in the afterpiece.

Young Benson was not named in the bills again until 7 April 1779, being too old for pages and finding few parts available for adolescent youths. On that night he played Donalbain in *Macbeth*; and he was entrusted with Gloster in *2 Henry IV* on 1 June, the last night of the season. The following season he was probably in the company for the entire campaign, hidden in crowds and choruses, but he acted only twice in named parts from 20 December through 23 May: Prince John in *1 Henry IV*, repeated, and Donalbain again. He was even more obscurely noted in 1780–81, though he was allowed on 18 May to speak an epilogue.

Benson was not in the roster of any London company in the seasons from 1781–82 through 1785–86. Gilliland placed him vaguely during some part of that time first as chief actor under the management of Francis Godolphin Waldron, of a barn-theatre at the "bottom of Peascod-street" in Windsor, then as manager there himself. *The Secret History of the Green Room* (1792) says that he played at several of the small towns surrounding London but that the realization that "twenty-five shillings per week as a servant, was better than eight or nine shillings . . . as a Hero" made him seek London, where he was taken on at 30*s.* per week.

But when Benson returned to Drury Lane on 13 November 1786—no longer "Master" Benson—his salary was £1 5*s.* per week, according to the treasurer's book. His first part was the conspirator Spinosa in *Venice Preserved.* It was atypical, except in its unimportance, of his service in the next few seasons. Gradually he ascended in two secondary lines of character, comic eccentrics and smooth young gentlemen and noblemen, and seemed to balance them very well. A selection might include: Silvius in *As You Like It,* Clip in *The Confederacy,* Medium in *Inkle and Yarico,* Arviragus in *Cymbeline,* Stukely in *The West Indian,* Marcellus in *Hamlet,* Leicester in *Henry II,* Burgundy in *King Lear,* Hortensio in *Catherine and Petruchio,* Kite in *The Recruiting Officer,* Charles Ratcliffe in *The Jew,* the Baron of Oakland in *The Haunted Tower,* Endless in *No Song, No Supper,* William in *The Fugitive,* an Officer in *The Count of Narbonne,* one of the Brothers in

Comus, Harry in *All the World's a Stage,* and Montano in *Othello.*

For the summer of 1791 only, Benson took on the management of the Richmond theatre in partnership with Thompson and the elder Charles Macready, but they did not prosper. In the winters he remained at £3 to £4 per week in the Drury Lane company. In one summer (1786) he acted at Hammersmith and in others (1794 and 1795) at the Haymarket. A news clipping of 1793 asserted that "Mr Benson of the Haymarket Theatre, succeeds the late Mr Wrighten as prompter of the New Drury Company, at a salary of five pounds a week," but this was an error. William Powell was given the post.

Benson also tried his hand at play-writing. His operatic farce *Britain's Glory; or, a Trip to Portsmouth,* in which he played the part of Cabin, achieved three performances at the Haymarket on and after 20 August 1794 and was published soon after by John Barker. His only other dramatic attempt, also a musical farce, came out at the Haymarket on 29 August 1795 and was given seven evenings, with the author playing the role of Drowsy. It was published by J. Wallis in 1798. Samuel Arnold furnished the music for both efforts.

In 1783 Benson married Susanna Satchell (1758–1814), third daughter of a maker of musical instruments and a sister of Elizabeth Satchell, who had married Stephen George Kemble. This connection did Benson no harm, of course, at Drury Lane. Mrs Benson had come to the stage for the first time (as Miss S. Satchell) at Covent Garden on 17 May 1783 in the part of Floretta in *The Quaker,* an afterpiece. She had followed that, on 24 May, in the leading part of Statira in *Alexander the Great.* She did not attain such eminence again. Along with her husband she played out-of-season and summers at Hammersmith, Banbury, Richmond, Windsor, and the Haymarket, and also at Drury Lane. She continued to act very small parts off and on at the patent theatre until at least 1811 (at £1 per week until at least 1800).

Robert Benson came to his death suddenly after a brief illness, on 20 May 1796. He had been supposed to play that night the part of Escalus in *Romeo and Juliet* but did not do so. The account of his end in *The Gentleman's Magazine* for May 1796 agrees in its vital particulars with several others:

About three o'clock in the morning he flung himself from the top of a house in Bridges-street, Covent-garden, where he lodged, and his head pitching on the kirb-stone, his brains were dashed in the high road. This lamentable circumstance is to be attributed to his having been afflicted with the brain fever, from which he was supposed to have recovered. He had not the least article of cloaths on; and he attempted to get out of the two pair of stairs window, by breaking a square of glass; but not being able to open the window, he got out of the garret-window. He has left a widow (sister to Mrs. Stephen Kemble, who was expected in town from Edinburgh the day after the melancholy event happened), and four young children. He was an industrious, useful, and meritorious performer; and by his death an aged father and mother are deprived of support.

The *Theatrical Telegraph* of 1796 added that

He had been confined for some days in his bed; but finding himself getting well, went to the Theatre on Thursday evening, and agreed to perform in the play on Friday evening. His going out too soon caused a relapse, which produced the . . . shocking event.

Benson was buried at St Paul, Covent Garden, on 24 May. The burial register gives his death date as 19 May and his age as 31.

The widow and her children received a benefit from the Drury Lane management on 9 June and the house was full, but the charge was made that they got nothing because Sheridan carried off the proceeds.

Benson was never a principal player, but his diligence and versatility were often commended. The censorious *Secret History of the Green Room* (1792) called him a very "quick study," who "avoids the dissipation too incident to his brethren." And the *Thespian Magazine* (June 1793) recounted how on 26 April 1793 Benson, having played the first two scenes of *The Chapter of Accidents* in one role, surprised the audience by the efficiency with which he "at a few minutes' notice" switched to the part abandoned by Robert Palmer, who was suddenly taken ill. Benson finished without one mistake.

On the other hand, Waldron, who had managed him and acted with him, published the opinion (but anonymously) that Benson was "The worst actor that, perhaps, ever insulted an audience in the respectable line of playing in which he has been of late thrust upon the town. . . . In the course of our theatrical experience, we never met with a more complete mutilator of blank verse than the gentleman before us."

Mrs Benson, continuing to act until at least 1811, died, aged 56, in the summer of 1814 and was buried on 13 August at St Andrew's, Bristol.

At least two of the four children of the Bensons were on the stage. The two principals of *The Children in the Wood*, an afterpiece at the Haymarket on 21 August 1797, were Master Menage and Miss Benson. The afterpiece was repeated several times. Miss Benson was at the Haymarket again the following summer, this time with her mother. She did *The Babes in the Wood*, now with Master Tokley, and her mother sang Dolly Trull in *The Beggar's Opera* and was also in several choruses. They were not, however, much employed.

In the winter seasons of 1797–98 through 1799–1800, Miss Benson was with her mother acting at Drury Lane, and she continued there for some time after 1800. At the end of the season of 1804–5, there were apparently two Misses Benson in the company, one of whom was earning £1 5s. Presumably she was an actress. The other, for whom no salary was given, was called a dancer.

There was a William Benson acting post –1806 at the Sunderland Theatre; and a Master then Mister Benson was at the Edinburgh Theatre Royal from 1800 through 1819. It is very probable they were children or near relatives of Robert Benson.

Robert Benson's portrait as Timurkan in *The Orphan of China*, drawn by Graham and engraved by Reading, was published by G. Cawthorn in 1797.

Benson, Mrs Robert, Susanna, née Satchell *1758–1814, actress. See* **BENSON, ROBERT.**

Bensor. *See* **BENSER.**

Bent, Mr [*fl.* 1793–1805], *gallery doorkeeper.*

Mr Bent was gallery doorkeeper at Covent Garden beginning at least as early as 1793–94, at which time he was being paid 12s. weekly. He was regularly cited in the accounts through 11 June 1799; after this the references to him are infrequent and ambiguous, for his name either changed to Blay in 1805 or he was replaced by a Mr Blay that year. He seems, however, to have worked through 28 September 1805 at least, receiving the same salary over the years.

Bentham, Samuel *c. 1653–c. 1730, singer.*

Samuel Bentham the younger was the son of Rev Samuel Bentham, Rector of Knebworth, by his first wife, Edith. He was born at Knebworth about 1653 and baptized there on 19 January 1654. While the younger Samuel was still a boy his mother died and his father remarried; his stepmother had been Elizabeth Fawcet, daughter of Elizabeth Fawcet of St Martin-in-the-Fields. Through Elizabeth Fawcet Bentham, young Samuel became related legally to the Harris and Richardson families, some or all of whom were musical. Either by his first or second wife the elder Bentham had other children who were still alive when Elizabeth Bentham made her will in 1708: James, John, Mary Burton, Frances Bentham, Ursula Berry, Edith Hutton, and Elizabeth Richardson (The various wills from which this list was compiled are sometimes obscure, and some of these may have been Elizabeth Bentham's siblings rather than her children or step-children.) The second Mrs Bentham apparently treated young Samuel as her own, and her will made no reference to his being born of an earlier marriage.

Samuel Bentham the younger, the subject of this entry, received his A.B. from St John's College, Cambridge, in 1674 and his A.M. in 1678. A marriage license was issued to Samuel Bentham of Ely, Gentleman, bachelor, about 25, and Ruth Allestry of St Mary-le-Bow of London, spinster, about 24, at her own disposal, on 29 May 1678; they married at St Sepulchre the next day. Bentham's first position seems to have been as a minor canon of Ely Cathedral, a post he held for 36 years while concurrently serving in London. Bentham was sworn a Gentleman of the Chapel Royal extraordinary (without fee, waiting for a vacancy) on 24 July 1683, was admitted in ordinary on 10 November 1684 on the death of John Harding, and advanced to a full place on 24 February 1694. In the Chapel he served as a clerk, as one of the ministers, and as a bass singer. On 9 November 1716, upon the death of John Radcliffe, Bentham became Confessor to the Royal household. It may have been about this time that he was made a minor canon of Westminster, a post he certainly held by 10 June 1725; he was also a minor canon at St Paul's, but when he was appointed to this post is not certain.

About Bentham's personal life we know more. Samuel and Ruth Bentham had a daughter, Ann Elizabeth, who was baptized at Holy Trinity on 21 February 1687; she grew up to marry one Smith, probably Jonathan Smith the Serjeant of the Vestry of the Chapel Royal. The Benthams also had two sons, Samuel and William, and Rimbault notes that Bentham's grandsons were, in later years, Dr Edward Bentham, Regius Professor of Divinity at Oxford, and Rev James Bentham, historian of Ely. When the will made by Samuel Bentham's stepmother was proved on 14 October 1708 by her daughters, Samuel's family figured in the bequests. Elizabeth Bentham left some interest in her estate to Samuel's wife Ruth, after whose death the principal was to be divided in four parts, two parts to go to their son Samuel "by reason he has had but little from his father," one part to their daughter Ann Elizabeth, and one part toward the education of their youngest son William. She made no bequest to her step-son Samuel; in fact, the wording of the will implies that he was no longer living. It may be that she and Samuel had been estranged, perhaps over his neglect of his eldest son, or she may have felt he was not in need of a bequest.

Deaths in the Bentham family followed hard upon one another in 1729 and 1730. Samuel Bentham's wife Ruth died at 76 on 20 January and was buried on 22 January 1729 at Westminster Abbey; Samuel died on 27 February 1730 at 77 and was buried in the South Cloister of the Abbey on the fifth; and their daughter Ann Elizabeth Smith was buried at the Abbey on 22 August 1730.

Benton, Charles d. 1758, musician.

On 17 July 1758 the *Scot's Magazine* recorded Charles Benton's death: "At London, aged near 100, Mr. Charles Benton.

He was a midshipman on board the navy in the reign of Charles II but for several years before his death professed music, and played till lately in Drury Lane theatre. He enjoyed his senses to the last."

Benucci, Francesco [or **Pietro?**] c. 1745–1824, singer.

The basso singer Benucci is given the name Francesco by Grove but Pietro by the *Enciclopedia dello spettacolo*. Born about 1745 in Florence, Benucci sang at Pistoia in 1769, at Venice in 1778–79, and at Vienna beginning in 1783. When Mozart's *Le nozze di Figaro* was first presented on 1 May 1786 in Vienna, Benucci was the Figaro, and on 26 January 1790 he created the role of Guglielmo in the premiere of *Così fan tutte*. He contracted to sing from 9 May through 11 July 1789 at the King's Theatre in the Haymarket in London for an unspecified sum and a free benefit.

Benucci's first English appearance was on 9 May as Il Conte Zefiro in *La vendemmia*, into which he and Anna Storace introduced what may have been the first segment of a Mozart opera ever heard in London: "Crudel perchè finora," the duet between the Count and Susanna from *Le nozze di Figaro*. The audience was delighted and demanded an encore. On 28 May 1789 Benucci sang a principal role in *La buona figliuola*, and on 11 June he was Don Bartolo in Paisiello's *Il barbiere di Siviglia*. On 17 June the King's Theatre burned to the ground, and the company had to complete the season at Covent Garden. The Oxford Musical Society gave concerts at the Oxford Music Room on 24, 25, and 26 June 1789; Benucci volunteered his services and "the enthusiasm of the audience led to many encores." After this successful yet ill-fated season, Benucci returned to the Continent. He died in Florence on 5 April 1824.

Beozzi. *See* BESOZZI.

Beralta. *See* PERALTA.

Berardi, Signor [fl. 1763–1765],
dancer.

Signor Berardi (or Bernardi) danced at
Drury Lane for two seasons, 1763–64 and
1764–65. During his initial season he was
frequently named in the bills as participating in such specialty dances as a *Terzetto*
with Duval and Miss Tetley on 10 March
1764 or, with the same pair, *The Turkish
Coffee House* on 20 March. In 1764–65
his daily salary was 6s. 8d. (or £2 per
week), which ranked him fairly high on
the theatre's pay scale for dancers but below such stars as Miss Baker and Mr Al-
dridge. During this second season, in addition to specialties, he was in the dance se-
quences in *The Genii* on 13 November
1764, did a dance number in *The Winter's
Tale* on 26 March 1765, and played one
of the "Cheerokees" in *The Witches* on 11
May.

Berchenshaw. *See* BIRCHENSHA.

Bercher, Jean. *See* D'AUBERVAL, JEAN.

Berecloth, Mr [fl. 1788–1814], *doorkeeper.*

Mr Berecloth (or Berclotte, Berricloth)
was cited regularly in the Covent Garden accounts from 1788 through 1805 and again
in 1813–14, and he may have worked as
well during the years unaccounted for. He
was a doorkeeper, according to an entry in
1794–95, but his weekly salary was variously recorded. In most seasons he was paid
12s., but entries in 1800 and 1805 list him
at 6s. In 1794–95 a Mrs "Brerecloth"
(probably a misspelling) served as a Covent Garden dresser; she was doubtless the
doorkeeper's wife.

Berecloth, Mrs [fl. 1794–1795],
dresser. See BERECLOTH, MR.

Bereford. *See* BERRISFORD.

Berenstadt, Gaetano [fl. 1717–1724],
singer.

Gaetano Berenstadt (or Berenstatt, Bar-
renstadt), who may have been of German-
Italian birth, first appeared in London,
billed as lately arrived, on 5 January 1717
at the King's Theatre in the Haymarket under Heidegger; he sang the bass role of
Argante in Handel's *Rinaldo* which the
composer altered for Berenstadt's *alto* voice.
The only other role he seems to have sung
this season was Mario in *Pirro e Demetrio*
on 2 February 1717, but he performed at
concerts at Hickford's music room on 13
and 27 March and at York Buildings on 14
June. *Rinaldo* was repeated for his benefit
on 18 May, the receipts for the performance
being almost the highest recorded for the
season: £130. The charges, £82 6s., were
also rather high, so Berenstadt's profit was
not abnormal. After this season he returned
to the Continent.

In 1719–20 Handel found Berenstadt
singing at Dresden in the service of Friedrich Augustus I, Elector of Saxony, and it
may have been then that the composer
persuaded Berenstadt to return to England
in the fall of 1722. Back in London at the
King's Theatre, Berenstadt sang Adelberto
in *Otho* on 12 January 1723, Sicino in
Coriolano on 19 February, Niso in *Erminia*
on 30 March, and the title role in *Flavio*
on 14 May. During July some of the company went to Paris where they were ad-
vertized to give "12 Representations at the
Theatre of the Palace Royal: In Consideration which 35000 Livres will be given to
the Principal Actors and their Charges de-
fray'd." Berenstadt and Senesino, the two
castrati in the King's Theatre troupe, were
among the five who made the trip. In the
fall they were back in London, and Berenstadt sang Osmano in *Farnace* on 27 November 1723, Sergio in *Vespasiano* on 14
January 1724, Tolomeo in *Giulio Cesare*
on 20 February, and Lucio in *Calfurnia* on
18 April.

In May 1724 *The Session of Musicians,*

a satirical poem, was published, describing a mock court trial at which Apollo judged the musicians of London and chose his favorite. Singers Berenstadt and Boschi, "(who peep'd in for sport) / Were pitch'd upon for Criers to the Court." They were needed, too, for upon hearing about the trial, mobs of musicians rushed in to declare themselves candidates.

> In vain tall B[eren]s[tad]t, gaping o'er
>   the Crowd,
> With hideous Jaws, bawl's Silence out
>   aloud!
> Till from his Throne the anger'd God
>   arose,
> Whose awful Nod the Tempest did
>   compose . . .

The nod went, of course, to Handel.

After the 1723–24 season, Berenstadt apparently returned to the Continent. A satirical print by Hogarth is said to represent Berenstadt, Senesino, and Cuzzoni.

Beresford. *See* BERRISFORD.

Berg, George [*fl. 1753–1771*], *instrumentalist, composer.*

George Berg was born in Germany but settled in London and studied with John Christopher Pepusch. When Pepusch died in 1753 he left his former pupil a five-guinea piece of gold. By about 1763, when *Mortimer's London Directory* was published, Berg was living in Lincoln's Inn Fields, near Great Turnstile, and known as a composer and harpsichord teacher. In 1763 the Catch Club awarded Berg first prize for a glee, "On softest beds at leisure laid." He won further awards in later years. On 13 February 1764 at the Great Room, Spring Gardens, St James's, his opera *Antigono* was produced, and songs of his composition were sung frequently enough at Marylebone Gardens to warrant a collection being published. He was organist of St Mary at Hill, near Billingsgate, in 1771. As a composer he wrote works for flute, horn, organ, and harpsichord as well as numerous songs.

Bergman, Benedict [*fl. 1792–1794*], *violinist.*

Doane's *Musical Directory* of 1794 listed violinist Benedict Bergman of No 22, Litchfield Street, Soho, as participating in concerts for the New Musical Fund. This was very likely the B. Benedict who played violin in the King's Theatre band until 1792, when he went to America. A Mr Bergman, possibly this same musician, was a member of the American Company playing at the Hartford theatre in 1794.

Berisford. *See* BERRISFORD.

Berkeley, Mrs [*fl. 1765*], *house servant? See* BERKELEY, MISS.

Berkeley, Miss [*fl. 1761–1776*], *house servant.*

A "Miss Berkeley" profited from the distribution of tickets for joint benefit performances at Drury Lane every May from 1762 through 1776. In addition, she was several times permitted to borrow sizeable sums from the funds of the theatre. In a list of salaries of servants of the house dated 9 February 1765, preserved by Fanny Kemble and purportedly in the hand of David Garrick, a Mrs and Miss Berkeley are listed under the heading "Proprietors." This surely does not mean part owners of the patent. It probably signifies that the £1 10s. and 10s. 6d. per week listed as their respective salaries came to them for presiding over some sort of dispensary of refreshments for the audiences.

Berkely, Mr [*fl. 1766–1767*], *property man.*

A "Berkely Jr" is given, under the heading "Properties," in a Drury Lane pay list of 24 January 1767. He was paid £1 per week.

Berkely, Miss ₍fl. 1776–1777₎, actress.

A "Berkely Junr" is listed among the actresses in the manuscript account books of Drury Lane Theatre at a salary of 10s. 6d. per week for the season of 1776–77.

Berkenshaw. See BIRCHENSHA.

Berkley. See BARCLAY.

Bernacchi, Antonio Maria 1685–1756, singer.

Born in Bologna on 23 June 1685, Antonio Maria Bernacchi became one of the most important, if not one of the best, male sopranos of the early eighteenth century. He studied under Pistocchi and Ricieri and had gained enough fame by the age of 16 for the Elector Palatine to want his services. Bernacchi sang at Mannheim, Vienna, and Venice in 1709–10 and 1712, and at Bologna in 1710 and 1712–13. His first appearance in England was as Demetrio in *Pirro e Demetrio* on 10 March 1716 at the King's Theatre in the Haymarket. On 18 April he sang Arsace in *Clearte*, and for his benefit on 2 June he chose *Pirro e Demetrio* again but with a special scene added for himself. During the next season he sang Goffredo in *Rinaldo* on 5 January 1717, Dardanus in *Amadigi di Gaula* on 16 February, concerts at Hickford's music room in March, a role in *Venceslao* for his 13 May benefit, and a concert at York Buildings on 14 June. Though he was in London for two successive seasons, he did not make a great impression on the English.

Bernacchi spent most of his time in Venice from 1717 to 1729, but during these years he was extremely popular and also sang in Bologna, Pesaro, Milan, Turin, Naples, and Munich. In 1727 at Bologna he had a contest with the famous Farinelli in a performance of *La fedeltà* (the later title of Orlandini's *Antigona*); though the younger Farinelli dazzled the audience with an elaborate cadenza, Bernacchi sang an even more highly embellished and polished aria that carried the day. The two *castrati* were rivals, yet they became good friends and sang together frequently; Bernacchi taught some of his secrets to Farinelli, and the latter arranged a fine memorial service for his colleague after his death.

It may have been the unpleasant year in Naples in 1728, when Bernacchi became embroiled in a bitter competition with Carestini, that led to his accepting Handel's invitation to return to England for the 1729–30 season, but the proffered salary of £1200 must have been irresistible. Back at the King's Theatre Bernacchi sang the title role in the premier performance of *Lotario* on 2 December 1729, Arsace in *Partenope* on 24 February 1730, Cosroe in *Ormisda* on 4 April, and the title role in a revival of *Tolomeo* on 19 May. By this time, however, Bernacchi was past his prime, and though some critics had a little praise for him ("a vast compass, his voice mellow and clear, but not so sweet as Senesino, his manner better; his person not so good, for he is as big as a Spanish friar"), the comments of the librettist Paolo Rolli reflected the general disappointment:

Bernacchi failed to please on the first night [of *Lotario*], but at the second performance he changed his method and scored a success. In person and voice he does not please as much as Senesino, but his great reputation as an artist silences those who cannot find it in them to applaud him. The truth is that he has only one aria in which he can shine, because . . . he has blundered in the opera as a whole.

As one opera patron commented, he "does not suit the English ears."

After this unfortunate season in London he returned to Italy where his fame was undiminished, and he continued singing with success until 1736; before his retirement he performed in Venice, Modena, Milan, and his native Bologna, and even after 1736 he occasionally sang in private. Upon leaving the stage he settled in Bologna and established a singing school that gained a splendid reputation and turned out such notable singers as Guarducci, Raaff, Amadori, and Vittoria Tesi. It was perhaps as a teacher that Bernacchi ultimately made his greatest contribution to music. The singer had been a member of the Accademia Filarmonica in Bologna since 1722, and after his retirement from the stage he was able to devote more time to its activities. He served as its president in 1748–49 yet also found time to do some composing of both secular and religious music. Bernacchi died at Bologna in 1 March 1756.

Though famous in his day, he was criticized by many musicians for debasing his art by, as Heriot puts it, "introducing *instrumental* execution into his cadenzas, imitating flutes and oboes and other agile but inhuman agencies such as the song of birds." His teacher Pistocchi was disappointed upon hearing Bernacchi in later years and gave the unkindest cut of all: "I taught you to sing," he said, "and now you play."

Bernacchi was pictured in a painting by Antonio Fedi of a large group of musicians, an engraving of which was made between 1801 and 1807.

Bernal, Mr (fl. 1796), *puppeteer.*

Mr Bernal presented a puppet show at a booth at Bartholomew Fair in 1796.

Bernard, Mr (fl. 1750), *actor.*

A Mr Bernard played the small comic part of Clump in *The Funeral* at Covent Garden on 3 May 1750.

Bernard, Mons (fl. 1790–1793), *machinist.*

A Bernard, machinist from the Paris Opéra, first appeared on the lists of the King's Theatre in London in the season of 1790–91. He was commended in the *Morning Post* of 21 March 1791 for devising the ocular delights of the "Grand Heroic Ballet . . . Telemachus in the Island of Calypso" by D'Auberval:

The machinery in this Ballet is highly deserving of praise. Calypso's Grotto, which is formed by the wings and a flat scene rising suddenly from the earth, had a surprising effect. The Mechanism by which this change is produced, we apprehend, is wholly new in this country.

Bernard's name does not occur in the bills or accounts surviving for the 1791–92 season, but he was perhaps at the theatre, for he was listed again in 1792–93, as "Benard." He also created the machinery for the production of the opera *La bella pescatrice* at the Pantheon on 9 May 1791.

Bernard, John 1756–1828, *actor, manager, author.*

John Bernard the actor was born at Portsmouth naval station in 1756, the son of John Bernard, an Irish lieutenant in the British naval service, and his wife Ann, the daughter of a naval post captain.

According to his own account he was irreversibly dedicated to the stage by the age of 10. He remembered that the London and provincial actor George Mattocks, who occasionally came to Portsmouth, was his "beau ideal of a hero and fine gentleman" and a "stimulant" to his "inclination" to be on the stage, despite his mother's puritanical horror at the idea. His family sent him to a Latin grammar school near Chichester, where he remained until his sixteenth year, occasionally acting in school productions. Shortly after leaving school he presented himself to the veteran strolling manager Jackson, whose company was at Farnham and who gave him an opportunity to try out as Jaffeir in *Venice Preserved*. His mother got wind of the performance and brought him home in humiliation.

But John's dream was not to be denied. His ambition was freshly inflamed at Chichester by the acting of the young George Frederick Cooke, and although his father tried to place John in the Navy and then to article him to an attorney, nothing would serve but the stage. On 5 May 1773 "about five o'clock in the morning" John left home. "I attired myself in my best blue suit of clothes," he recalled, "had a watch in my fob; about five pounds in my pocket . . . two shirts and two pairs of stockings in a bundle, with a light heart, a burning brain, a slim, genteel figure, and a weak ladylike voice." These assets he offered to Bensley at Bristol, who was not impressed. He next turned to the eccentric country manager "Mr Thornton, who governed a band of dramatic desperadoes at the village of Chew Magna," where John made his first uninterrupted professional appearance, again as Jaffeir, in a theatre "fitted up in the interior of a malthouse." The receipts were a gratifying nine pounds, and, he says, "I was immediately engaged to sustain the 'juvenile tragedy' and 'genteel comedy,' and my name was inserted in the bill . . . as 'Mr. Budd,' a young gentleman only seventeen years of age." His share of the first two nights, brought gratefully and personally to his room by the manager, was "eight shillings of the King's current coin, and three tallow-candles of British manufacture." It may have been shortly after this time that Bernard dropped "Budd" and assumed for his country campaigns the *nom de guerre* of "Barnett," which he retained until about 1782. His father had used the name when he had joined the Navy as a young man.

Thornton's group strolled on, to Kainsome and Glastonbury; but after playing at that place, Bernard went to an even smaller company at Castle Cary, under the management of a Mr Taylor, on the strength of Taylor's promise that he could play Hamlet. The association lasted as far as Westbury-under-the-Plain, where he fell into debt. He crept back to Thornton at Chard, who rehired him at 2s. 6d. per week and took him to a sixteen-week stand at Taunton. Tiring of this bargain, John decamped with his friend Hill the singer, walking the 48

JOHN BERNARD
by S. Harris

miles to Weymouth, where they were taken on by the manager Williams for a guinea a week. Here what Bernard called his "hegira" was once again interrupted, this time by a magistrate with an order to return home, procured by his mother. At this point his father returned from a voyage, tired over the dissension, and reluctantly consented to a stage career for the boy, and John set off, well-provisioned, for London.

Ironically, Bernard had to come to London to gain a permanent footing in the provinces. John Scott, an acquaintance from Taunton, called one day at John's lodgings in Tavistock Street, Covent Garden, and persuaded him to go down to Brentwood, Essex, to watch Penchard's company perform. There John again met Thornton, who offered him a place, which he refused. He did, however, join David Osborn on the Braintree-Needham-Dedham circuit, and there he was seen by some alderman from

Norwich who preferred him to a position with Griffith at Norwich at 30 shillings a week "in the theatre which ranked with Bath, out of the metropolis."

At Norwich he met a Mrs Cooper, *nèe* Roberts, six years older than John and an experienced actress: "To do her justice, she was one of the most versatile women out of London—a kind of Garrick in petticoats," he wrote, "having played in the course of one season Lady Macbeth, Juliet, Violante, Nell (in the 'Devil to Pay'), Macheath, and Mandane, and all with a degree of merit which is not invariably witnessed in the metropolis." John married her in 1774.

At the end of the Norwich season, billed still as the "Barnetts," the pair joined Hughes, the Exeter manager, who wanted them at Weymouth in the ensuing spring. Hughes gave them a two-year contract, a generous proposition, but one which kept them from accepting a sudden tempting offer from Palmer at Bath. They played at Barnstaple, then wintered in the season of 1775–76 at Plymouth Dock, where they had good custom because of "the detention of an outward bound fleet by bad winds, and the arrival of a squadron from the Straits."

Tate Wilkinson saw them at Taunton and offered them sixty guineas to spend the summer of 1776 at York, Halifax, and Wakefield, a proposal which they accepted. They were allowed by the benevolent Wilkinson to cut short their engagement to rejoin Hughes, who had abruptly decided to begin the winter season of 1776–77 several weeks early. But in the spring of that season Mrs Bernard fell ill, and they were prevented playing at all during the summer of 1777.

Mr and Mrs Bernard made their first appearance at Palmer's fashionable theatre in Bath in the 1777–78 season, as Portia and Gratiano to Henderson's Shylock, and secured several other excellent roles. They were there under the acting management of Keasberry, who then engaged them at Rich-

mond for the following summer. During their stay at Bath, Bernard studied music under Herschel, later renowned for his astronomical discoveries. They were at Weymouth and Exeter with Hughes again in 1778–79, at Barnstaple and Taunton in the summer of 1779, and thereafter at Exeter in winter and at Weymouth in summer until an offer came from Daly in Ireland in 1782.

The Bernards joined the Cork company when both John and Stephen Kemble were present in it, along with West Digges, Jack Kane, Miss Young, Mrs Barsanti, Mrs Melmoth, and the Miss Phillips who afterwards was Mrs Crouch. They held their own with this experienced troupe, despite a protracted illness suffered by Mrs Bernard, until a dispute over parts with the difficult Daly led them to accept an offer from Truby and Watts at Capel Street, Dublin, at a joint £8 per week. They journeyed to Limerick to play during the assizes (and to make the acquaintance of John's uncle Robert Bernard). An excellent benefit at the end of the Cork season discharged their debts and repaid John Kemble for a large and kind loan.

The season of 1782–83 opened well at the Capel Street house in Dublin in a company containing Stephen Kemble, Vandermere, O'Reilly, O'Neil, Ryder, Macready, and Mrs Gardner. "We had," wrote Bernard, "the smallest but most comfortable theatre, with the best patronage." But their felicity did not last, for Truby and Watts were using the performances as a front for a gambling enterprise at the rear of the house. Exposed, the managers absconded, leaving a company disorganized but kept afloat for a time by Mrs Bernard's recovery of health and the arrival of Mrs Sparks the singer from Edinburgh. With the group disintegrating, however, the Bernards answered the overtures of Michael Atkins at Belfast.

Despite his relative inexperience, Bernard was chosen by Atkins to lead the com-

pany to Londonderry and Sligo while Atkins supervised the preparation of a new
theatre at Belfast. At Sligo Bernard fell
seriously ill, but he recovered in time to
help open the new house. The following
summer Mr and Mrs Bernard were engaged
by Vandermere at Waterford.

The Bernards left Ireland for Bristol in
the summer of 1784 and joined the Bath
company which was playing there. John
struck up friendships with the new-come
Tom Blanchard and John Jackson, as well
as with the older hands Edwin and Weston.
Staying at the Bush tavern, he also made
the acquaintaince of Covent Garden's tragedian David Ross.

The Bath company of 1784–85 was a
brilliant one, including Dimond, Murray,
Brunton, Blanchard, Keasberry, Blissett,
Miss Cleland, and others. The Bernards
were high on the list of favorites and, indeed, the season opened with John and his
wife in two of their best characters, Lord
Sparkle and Lady Bell Bloomer in *Which
Is the Man.* In the frenetic social whirly-gig
of "the Bath," Bernard's gregarious nature
blossomed. At the house of the influential
Dr Harrington he met the Earl Conyng-
ham, Lord Cork, Sir Charles Bampfylde, the
poet Meyler, the musicians Loder and Rauzzini, the beau Sir John Oldmixon and the
celebrated eccentric Sir John Danvers. Bernard, with some of these, founded the Bath
Catch Club at the White Lion Inn.

Bernard's recollection was that he was
"the ruling favourite of the theatre" at Bath
in the 1785–86 season, so much so that
Harris of Covent Garden sent Charles Dibdin to look him over. The Bernards are said
to have refused Harris's offer of £6 per week
for John and £4 for his wife. The couple
spent the summer of 1786 with Fox at
Brighton, principally because John was
"severely debiliated" and Dr Harrington
had recommended sea-bathing. There the
Prince of Wales patronized their performances and invited John to the Royal revels
at the Pavilion.

The season of 1786–87 was the third and
final season for the Bernards at Bath. During it, John made his debut as dramatic
author with a farce called *The Whimsical
Ladies,* the music composed by Boyton:
"This production did some good to the
treasury, and Mr Palmer gave Boyton and
myself a clear joint night at Bristol, by
which I cleared forty pounds." John also
penned and staged a "musical interlude" in
two acts called *The British Sailor.* Near the
end of the season the Bernards signed articles with Harris to go to Covent Garden
for four years on what Bernard remembered
as ascending salary scales, he for £10
through £13, Mrs Bernard for £5 through
£8 per week. (But the surviving accounts
for the theatre show that John and his wife
each received £4 for 1787–88, the same for
the following two seasons, and only £5 each
in 1790–91. Bernard did not achieve £6
until his final season in London, that of
1795–96.)

Bernard was thrown from a gig and injured his leg on an excursion near the end
of summer and hence missed the first
month or so of the Covent Garden season
of 1787–88. He and Mrs Bernard finally
appeared on 19 October, he as Archer in
The Beaux' Stratagem and Kecksy in *The
Irish Widow,* she as Mrs Sullen and the
Widow in the same pieces. Bernard recalled
that "My engagement with Mr Harris was
to sustain the business of Lee Lewis, which
was very extensive, including all the fops
and eccentric gentlemen with smart servants and feeble old men *ad infinitum.*"

The playbills certainly show that during
their first season at Covent Garden the
Bernards saw frequent service. His parts included: Flutter in *The Belle's Stratagem,*
Slender in *The Merry Wives of Windsor*
(as a sudden substitute for Cubitt), Razor
in *The Provok'd Wife,* Jack Meggot in
The Suspicious Husband, Antipholus of
Ephesus in *The Comedy of Errors,* Gratiano
in *The Merchant of Venice,* Count Basset
in *The Provok'd Husband,* Welford in *The*

Capricious Lady, Young Marlow in *She Stoops to Conquer*, Pink in *The Ton*, and Captain Absolute in *The Rivals*. He was, however, not above going on as one of the Recruits in *The Recruiting Officer*.

Mrs Bernard was equally useful as Mrs Page in *The Merry Wives of Windsor*, Fairlove in *The Tender Husband*, Oriana in *The Inconstant*, Spaconia in *A King and No King,* Charlotte in *Love à la Mode*, Adriana in *The Comedy of Errors*, Louisa in *Love Makes a Man*, Lady Freelove in *The Jealous Wife*, Zelida in *Romance of an Hour*, Florinda in *Tit for Tat* and Charlotte Weldon in *Oroonoko*. The pair lived that year at No 19, Bedford Street, Covent Garden.

Almost at once Bernard was elected to the Beefsteak Club, where his convivial nature was met in jollification by such kindred spirits as R. B. Sheridan, G. A. Stevens, Robert Merry, the Lord Say and Sele, Lord Townshend, George Saville Carey, Charles Bannister, and Lord Cavan. During the winter Bernard purchased half of Jefferson's two-thirds share of the Plymouth circuit for £400, Jefferson and a Mr Wolf each retaining one third. Both Bernards acted at Plymouth during the summer of 1788.

The Bernards' second season in London was professionally nearly a duplicate of the first. For their benefit on 22 May 1789 Bernard was allowed to revive his "musical interlude" *The British Sailor*. During the season he was elected to the secretaryship of the Beefsteak Club, was made an honorary member of the Anacreontic Society, and founded the comedians' club called "The Strangers at Home," which embraced in its merry membership Charles Bannister, Jack Johnson, Blanchard, Suett, Incledon, Kelly, Dignum, Sedgwick, and O'Keeffe, and met at the Garrick's Head in Bow Street, Covent Garden.

The Bernards were at Covent Garden Theatre, playing substantially the same variegated lines of parts, through 1790–91,

and living at No 35, Bow Street. For the two seasons following, Bernard forsook London summer and winter for the country. Bernard himself testified in his memoirs that the lady known as Mrs Bernard died suddenly on tour at Lostwithiel in 1792. But a manuscript letter in the Harvard Theatre Collection from Benjamin Strett the antiquary to an unknown correspondent claims that she was alive c. 1805 and married to a man named Tellure or Taileure. There are also two gossipy letters in the Harvard Theatre Collection from the actor-printer Thomas Woodfall to the manager and stage historian James Winston about Bernard and his affairs. The first raises doubts as to whether or not the lady Mrs Tayleure had ever actually been married to Bernard. The second reports having recently seen Bernard who "informed me he *was* [married to her] and spoke of it as one of the weaknesses of his youth."

John's Plymouth enterprise had gone fairly well, but a dispute among the partners in 1793 threatened disruption, and for a few weeks Bernard played with a secessionary company in a wooden theatre he erected in George Street.

During the winter seasons of 1793–94 and 1794–95 John returned to Covent Garden to play his usual series of roles at £6 per week. His afterpiece, *The Poor Sailor* (with music by Thomas Attwood), came out at Covent Garden on 29 May 1795. It received five performances that season and 15 before the end of the century. Bernard signed for 1795–96 but was in the theatre only from 14 September through 2 November 1795, on which latter date he made his last London appearance, as Osric in *Hamlet*. During his last few years in London he had lived at No 12, Kirby Street, Hatton Garden.

Bernard had been appointed manager at Brighton for 1795 but because of an illness had resigned control to Hull. He had also obtained an interest in a theatre at Dover and one on Guernsey, as well as continuing to share in the Plymouth concern. Apparently he suffered large financial losses in one or all of these speculations in 1795 and 1796, and so in the latter year he readily accepted an offer of £1,000 for the first year from Wignell the Philadelphia manager.

Bernard arrived in America in 1797 accompanied by his second wife, who had been Miss Fisher of the Guernsey company and whom he had married in 1796. His American debut was at the Greenwich Street Theatre in New York as Goldfinch in *The Road to Ruin*. He went then to Philadelphia where he played for six years in a variety of roles both in comedy and tragedy. From 1803 to 1805 he was, according to Dunlap, at the Federal Street Theatre in Boston. His second wife, who also acted in America, died in 1806.

In 1806 also he went back to England to recruit, returning with a third wife, who had been Miss Wright, and also with Cipriani from Sadler's Wells, Caulfield from Drury Lane, Mrs Stanley (the Hon Mrs Twistleton) from Covent Garden, and Vining the singer. From 1806 through 1811 Bernard managed the Federal Street Theatre jointly with Snelling Powell and James A. Dickson. He toured widely and is known to have played in points as widely separated as Baltimore, Canada, and Kentucky. For one brief period he seems to have managed the Green Street Theatre in Albany, New York. By the summer of 1819 he was manager of the Washington Gardens, a new ampitheatre in Boston. Soon afterward he returned finally to England.

A letter from Thomas Woodfall in the Harvard Theatre Collection alludes to Bernard's illness and his poverty: "Poor fellow —recollecting him in the heyday of life and witnessing him now as the slippered Pantaloon—distressed, surrounded by a young family and neglected . . . He is really very miserably situated." He died in destitute circumstances on 29 November 1828.

Bernard's theatrical abilities have some-

times been exaggerated by historians of the American stage because he shone with some luster in the cruder settings of Philadelphia, New York, and Boston. In England, indeed, he was perhaps more noted among notables for his clubbable, gregarious nature than for his acting. Nevertheless, he owned sufficient talent to discharge ably his responsibilities to the variety of secondary characters he learned.

The *Biographical and Imperial Magazine* for January 1790 thought him "much too stiff" in Murphy's comedy *The Way to Keep Him* and commented that he "did ample justice" to Cornwall's sturdy servant in *King Lear* "only that he carried his buffoonery too far. Let us ask Mr. B. whether he supposes the most pert and frivolous coxcomb when slain by an unexpected blow would by an unnatural quaintness of voice and gesture make his death a matter of merriment?"

The *Candid and Impartial Strictures* of 1795 thought him "A performer of merit in many parts. His coxcombs are tolerable, but not so good as a London audience ought to expect. He has been too long accustomed to a strolling life for us to think he would be ever able to rid himself of the many bad habits he has about him, so we shall not begin the tedious task of enumerating them." The "candid and impartial"—and anonymous—author of these strictures was, however, a rival actor, Francis Godolphin Waldron.

The pseudonymous "Anthony Pasquin" (John Williams) in the third part of *The Children of Thespis* (1788) was even harsher, but then he was harsh to most of his subjects:

Agile BERNARD, thro' GEORGE's three nations well known,
In ARCHER's disguise, made his bow to the town;
But who gave him the part prov'd in fact but his foe,
As no bulwark he rais'd—twixt the groom and the beau;

A vile shrug *that's repellant, was common to either,*
*But his limbs seem'd dependants belong-
ing—to neither.*

The American manager Wood spoke of
Bernard's imitativeness in the part of Shylock, but at least the model was splendid:

Bernard was far from thinking humbly of his
own Shylock, which, I may add, acted originally as a comic part (perhaps for the purpose of depreciating the poor persecuted
Jew,) was frequently found in the cast of
professed comedians, as King, Dowton, and
many others. The usage long prevailed of ex-
hibiting Shylock with a shaggy red beard, and
enormous hooked nose. In obedience to this
custom, Bernard fabricated by means of wax
an artificial nose, which gave him a strong
resemblance to the prints of Macklin, whose
matchless performance in this play he dilated
upon with vast pleasure. He enjoyed every
advantage of studying Macklin, having in
London, as well as in the Irish theatres, invariably appeared as the Gratiano. His performance of this part detracted nothing from
his popularity.

Whatever critics thought of Bernard, he
was popular with his audiences. James
Winston in his *Theatric Tourist* (1805)
left two characteristic anecdotes illustrating
Bernard's influence with the pit and gallery:

When John Kemble, in performing Hamlet,
repeated his entreaty to his schoolfellow
[Guildenstern] to play upon the pipe, Bernard who performed the part, replied 'Well,
if I must, I must;' and played the air of the
Black Joke: a joke by far too black for the
occasion. The Gentleman who supplied us
with this article (a man of strict veracity)
declared that he was present. In 1794, the
song of *The Little Farthing Rushlight,* being
very popular with the gallery, Incledon [the
great tenor] was not suffered to proceed with
his character of Lubin in the Quaker, till
Bernard had complied with the wishes of the
audience, by singing it.

Bernard had a long and rather exact
memory and he also seems to have journal-

ized extensively. His two-volume *Retro-
spections of the Stage*, which in great part
has been employed for this entry, was
brought out in 1830 by his son Bayle Bernard. Further selections from his memoirs,
relative to his American experiences, were
published by Laurence Hutton and Brander
Matthews in the *Manhattan and New York
Magazine* in 1884, and Bernard's son selected further matter for Tallis's *Dramatic
Magazine* in 1850–51. The whole of the
American matter has appeared as *Retro-
spections of the American Stage*. Though
the style of both books is digressive, Bernard had a ready wit, an excellent eye for
character, and an almost universal acquaintance among theatrical figures of the later
eighteenth century; thus the volumes are
valuable chronicles of theatrical life and re-
positories of amusing anecdote.

John Bernard was painted for the Beefsteak Club by P. Marshall. The likeness
was presented to the Garrick Club in 1900
by John's daughter-in-law Mrs Bayle Bernard. The Garrick Club also owns the
painting by Samuel DeWilde of Bernard
as Jack Meggot. A line engraving of this
picture was made by Corner for *Bell's British Library* in 1791. Barry drew and Ridley
engraved Bernard's likeness in 1794. In
the Folger Library's manuscript volume entitled "Portraits of Eminent Actors Taken
from Life by W. Loftis 1787–1815" is a
fine water-color of Bernard in costume.

Bernard, Mrs John the first, formerly Mrs Cooper, née Roberts, *1750–1792, actress. See* **BERNARD, JOHN.**

Bernardi, Signor. *See* **BERARDI, SIG-NOR.**

Bernardi, Signora [*fl.* 1770], *singer.*

Signora Bernardi sang Gianetta in the
premiere of *Il disertore* at the King's Theatre in the Haymarket on 19 May 1770; the
opera was not repeated, and this seems to
be her only appearance during the season

that was considered worth noting in the bills. *The London Stage* incorrectly lists her as a male in the summary for the 1769–70 season.

Bernardi, Master ₁*fl. 1783–1785*₁, *call boy.*

One Bernardi was the *buttafuóri,* or call-boy, at the King's Theatre in the Haymarket in 1783 and 1784–85.

Bernardi, Francesco. *See* SENESINO.

Bernardo, ₁**Mr?**₁ ₁*fl. 1688*₁, *musician.*

In a list of members of the King's Musick who were paid on 20 October 1688 for attending the King at Windsor is the name Bernardo; since this is the only such reference, it may be some musician's first, rather than last, name.

Bernasconi, Antonia *b. c. 1740, singer.*

The German soprano Antonia Bernasconi was born in Stuttgart about 1740, the daughter of a valet to the Duke of Württemberg. Her mother's second marriage was to the Italian composer Andrea Bernasconi, who gave Antonia her early musical training in Munich. On 26 December 1767 in Vienna she sang the title role in Gluck's *Alceste,* which the composer is said to have written especially for her. In Milan on 26 December 1770 she sang Aspasia in Mozart's *Mitridate, rè di Ponto.* She sang frequently in Naples and other Italian towns in the 1770's and came to England in 1778 for a two-season stay at the King's Theatre in the Haymarket.

Her first London appearance was as Dircea in the premier performance of *Demofoonte* on 28 November 1778, when the noted Pacchierotti also made his London debut. On 23 January 1779 she sang Mandane in the Bertoni-Metastasio *Artaserse;* on 25 March she was Lavinia in the first performance of *Enea e Lavinia;* and on 29 May she had a principal part in *L'Olimpiade.* During the 1779–80 season she sang a leading role in *La contadina in corte* on 14 December 1779, Ottavia in *L'amore soldato* on 8 February 1780, a major role in *La schiava* at her benefit on 13 April, Gionchiglia in *Il duca d'Atene* on 9 May, and a major part in *La buona figliuola* on 25 May. During her London stay she lived at No 5, Dover Street, Piccadilly. While her first London season had featured her in serious operas, her second displayed her *buffa* talent. Burney, though full of praise for her frequent partner Pacchierotti, was less than enthusiastic about Signora Bernasconi: "she had a neat and elegant manner of singing, though with a voice that was feeble and in decay." After her seasons in London she went back to Vienna, where she sang for several years. She died sometime after 1783.

Bernet, Mr ₁*fl. 1797*₁, *scene painter.*

A Mr Bernet was listed as a painter at Covent Garden Theatre on 21 May 1797, in an account-book entry coupling him with the well-known scene painter Wilkins. Jointly they received £4 9s. 3d. for an unspecified amount of work.

Berneyoski, Hans ₁*fl. 1661–1668*₁, *drummer.*

The exact spelling of Hans Berneyoski's name is uncertain, for in contemporary records it hardly ever appears the same way twice. By a warrant dated 23 December 1661 he was to be paid £60 as a kettledrummer in the King's Musick. He was listed again on 12 November 1663 and in 1668. His name usually appeared at the end of the list of trumpeters, and his master was the sergeant trumpeter, Gervase Price.

Berond. *See* BAYZAND.

Berrecloth or **Berricloth.** *See* BERECLOTH.

Berridge, Mr [fl. 1794], bass viol player.

Doane's *Musical Directory* of 1794 lists Mr Berridge, of Southwall, as playing the bass viol in the Handel memorial concerts at Westminster Abbey, but the years of his activity are not specified.

Berriman, Joseph d. 1730, actor.

Joseph Berriman was a minor member of the Lincoln's Inn Fields company under John Rich from about 1726 to 1729. Sometime before 1726 he married Anne Parker, a singer and actress in Rich's troupe who, after Berriman's death, became Mrs William Hallam. The Berrimans were regularly cited on the free list for the theatre during the period 1726–1729, and beginning in April 1727 the playbills named Joseph Berriman in casts. His first mentioned role was Gratiano in *The Jew of Venice* at Lincoln's Inn Fields on 17 April 1727. His name was not printed in the bills again until the summer of 1728, when he played, among other roles, Maherbal in *Sophonisba* on 5 July and Obadiah Prim in *A Bold Stroke for a Wife* on 12 July. He acted Shallow in *The Merry Wives of Windsor* on 28 December 1728, and his last recorded role was Anhalt in *Frederick* when it opened on 4 March 1729. Berriman died in February 1730.

Berriman, Mrs Joseph. *See* HALLAM, MRS WILLIAM.

Berrington. *See* BARRINGTON.

Berrisford, [Robert?] [fl. 1745–1777], house servant.

A Mr "Barrisford" appeared among Drury Lane house servants sharing a benefit on 14 May 1746. On 8 May 1747 he also shared, but as "Berrisford." On 9 May 1748 he was identified for the first time as a "Boxkeeper." He continued to hold this position and to share benefits at the theatre through the season of 1776–77, when his salary was 12s. per week. On 28 May 1774 he appeared in the benefit bill as "Bereford," and on 5 Oct 1775 (when he was called "Front or Side Boxkeeper") he was "Beneford."

He may very well have been the "Robert Berriford" who was buried at St Paul, Covent Garden, on 13 March 1778; and this was probably the same man ("Robert Berrisford") whose daughter Anne, by Abigail his wife, had been baptized at that church on 5 June 1748.

(There is no evidence to connect Berrisford with the Ebenezer Barresford who married Mrs George Bulkley, née Mary Wilford, the Covent Garden dancer and actress.)

Berroughs, Miss. *See* PALMER, MRS JOHN.

Berry. *See also* BARRY.

Berry, [Ann?] [fl. 1749], actress.

A Miss Berry, possibly Ann, the daughter of Drury Lane actor Edward Berry, played the Maid in *The Harlot's Progress* at Phillips's booth at Bartholomew Fair on 23, 24, 25, 26 August 1749; when Phillips moved his production to Southwark Fair, Mrs Peters took the maid's role. There is no certainty that this young woman was Edward Berry's daughter, yet she would seem to have been about the age of Ann Berry at this time; in Edward Berry's will, dated 28 April 1749, the references to her make it clear that she is still quite young, and she certainly might have had theatrical interests. Ann Berry, sometime before her father's will was proved on 15 January 1760, became Mrs James Hyde.

Berry, Catherine. *See* D'EGVILLE, MRS JAMES HARVEY.

Berry, C[hristopher?] [fl. 1776–1781], actor.

Mr C. Berry, described by Reed as being from Norwich, was hired by the Covent

Garden Theatre for the 1780–81 season at £2 per week. He appears to have played first at Richmond before making his Irish debut at the Crow Street Theatre on 23 September 1776. From 25 August to 18 November 1778 he was probably the Mr Berry acting with Joseph Austin's troupe at Chester, and sometime before his arrival in London he seems to have performed at Norwich. There was a Christopher Berry of Norwich who, in 1790, was a subscriber to Tate Wilkinson's *Memoirs*, so perhaps Mr C. Berry was the same person. For his first appearance on the London stage he played Clodio in *Love Makes a Man* on 13 October 1780 at Covent Garden, billed as "A Young Gentleman." During the rest of the season he acted Osric in *Hamlet* (26 October), Lovelace in *Three Weeks after Marriage* (8 December), and the Gentleman Usher in *King Lear* (27 December), and he probably played smaller roles not cited in the bills. Though his contract was to have run only until 22 May 1781, he was paid on 29 May £2 13s. 4d. for eight days, which suggests that he completed the season, which had ended on 28 May.

Berry is said to have become a Captain in Lord Cork's regiment after 1781, but the Army List does not mention him. Joseph Austin said Berry, "a lively Performer in Fops and airy Gentlemen, was with me some time at Chester, Newcastle, and came to Covent Garden."

Berry, Edward 1706–1760, *actor, singer, dancer.*

Edward Berry was born in 1706 and made his first recorded stage appearance as Hobinal in *The Village Opera* on 6 February 1729 at Drury Lane. His roles for the first few years of his career were mostly comic, involving some singing and dancing, and he was in numerous afterpieces and pantomimes. His second appearance, for instance, was as Squire Clodpole in *The Lover's Opera* on 14 May 1729; on 13 June he was Grig in *Phebe*; on 27 June he played

Vulture in *The Country Lasses*; and on 18 July he was Ply in *The Country Wedding*. These and other roles from his initial season he repeated in 1729–30, adding, among other parts, Symon in *Patie and Peggy*, Richard in *The Clown's Stratagem*, and Jolt in *The Stage Coach Opera*. In August and September 1730 he acted at the Fielding-Oates booths at Bartholomew and Southwark Fairs, playing Squire Noodle in *The Generous Free Mason* at both.

Berry's 1730–31 season was similar, some of his new roles being a Sailor in *The Fair Quaker of Deal*, a Forester in *Cephalus and Procris*, and Young Heartfree in *The Sailor's Opera*. On 12 May 1731 when he shared his first benefit with three others, however, in addition to being in the afterpiece, he played his first recorded serious role: the young Orbellan in *The Indian Emperor*. On 7 June he was Antonio in *The Tempest*, and though he finished the season in lighter pieces and acted again at Bartholomew Fair in August, the beginnings of his career as a tragic actor were visible. In 1731–32 he had no opportunity to play in serious works, but his standing in the Drury Lane company was rising, for at his 8 May 1732 benefit he shared the profits with only two others.

The 1732–33 season found Berry playing Mortimer in *1 Henry IV*, the Chamberlain in *Henry VIII*, and Kent in *King Lear*, though the rest of his roles were more typical of previous years: Fanciful in *The Imaginary Cuckolds*, Cimon in *Damon and Phillida*, Merlin in *The Tragedy of Tragedies*, Phaon in *Damon and Daphne*, and Sparkle in *The Miser*. He also played Falstaff, which he was to make part of his repertory later, but this first essay was in droll form: *The Comical Humours of Sir John Falstaff* at Bartholomew Fair on 23 August 1733.

When Berry followed Theophilus Cibber and other Drury Lane seceders to the Haymarket Theatre in the fall of 1733, a number of new roles were assigned him, including several Shakespearean ones: Worcester in *1 Henry IV*, Mowbray in *2 Henry IV*, Marcellus in *Hamlet*, and Lodovico in *Othello*. In this remarkably busy season he also played, for the first time, a number of roles in comedies of some substance, such as Cacafogo and later the Duke in *Rule a Wife and Have a Wife*, Corvino in *Volpone*, Story in *The Committee* and Macheath in *The Beggar's Opera*. Among non-Shakespearean serious characters he acted Bedamar in *Venice Preserv'd*, the Governor in *Oroonoko,* Marcus in *Cato,* Barnwell Senior in *The London Merchant*, Cecil in *The Albion Queens*, and Bellmour in *Jane Shore*. When he returned to Drury Lane in March 1734 he was allowed to keep a good many of these new parts.

During the rest of the 1730's the industrious Berry kept building his repertory, gradually adding heavier characters in comedies as well as tragedies, and slowly relinquishing his participation in farces and pantomimes. A sampling might include: Page in *The Merry Wives of Windsor*, Raleigh in *The Unhappy Favorite*, Seyton in *Macbeth*, Lysippus in *The Maid's Tragedy*, Pylades in *The Distrest Mother*, Manly in *The Provok'd Husband*, the Elder Worthy in *Love's Last Shift*, Lucius and Sempronius in *Cato*, Sir John in *The Conscious Lovers*, Gloucester in *King Lear*, the King in *1 Henry IV*, York in *2 Henry IV*, the title role and Casca in *Julius Caesar*, Prospero in *The Tempest* (his first Shakespearean lead, on 10 February 1737), Escalus in *Measure for Measure*, Acasto in *The Orphan*, Gonzalez in *The Mourning Bride*, Claudius in *Hamlet*, Renault in *Venice Preserv'd*, and Kite in *The Recruiting Officer*. Though he dropped several farcical roles, he stayed with Jobson in the ballad opera *The Devil to Pay* and the Miller in the sentimental *The King and the Miller of Mansfield*. Indicative of his importance in the troupe, on 7 May 1737 he received his first solo benefit, at which he entertained his fellow Masons with some Masonic songs.

Harvard Theatre Collection

EDWARD BERRY, as Dominic
by T. Worlidge

He advertised this year that tickets would be available from him at his lodgings in Crown Court, Russell Street.

After this vigorous activity and steadily growing influence he left the stage for two years, perhaps by choice but possibly by force. On 30 August 1737 he and his fellow actors Oates and Shepherd created a disturbance in the pit at Drury Lane, demanding the restoring of Oates, who had just been discharged after 21 years of service. Berry was gone from Drury Lane after this, and on 4 January 1738 he announced the opening of a coffee house "opposite Playhouse Passage in Bridges-street," an establishment which he seems to have kept even after returning to acting.

On 15 May 1739 Berry returned to Drury Lane for a single performance, a benefit for himself to entertain his brother Masons, tickets for which he made available at his coffee house. In the fall he went back to the theatre full-time, opening with his old part of Jobson on 4 September 1739 and billed as not having performed at Drury Lane for two years—a slight error in view of his benefit the previous May, but the bills sometimes lied. His 1739–40 roles were remarkably like those he had been doing before he left in 1737, so he was apparently restored to Drury Lane as though nothing had happened.

In the 1740's Berry added, among other roles, Sealand in *The Conscious Lovers*, Tiresias in *Oedipus*, Adam in *As You Like It*, Solanio and Antonio in *The Merchant of Venice*, Thorogood in *The London Merchant*, Brabantio in *Othello*, Bonniface in *The Stratagem*, Sir Epicure Mammon in *The Alchemist*, Sir Toby Belch in *Twelfth Night*, Hecate in *Macbeth*, the Ghost in *Hamlet*, Strictland in *The Suspicious Husband*, Horatio and Sciolto in *The Fair Penitent*, Leonato in *Much Ado About Nothing*, Capulet in *Romeo and Juliet*, and the Duke in *Measure for Measure*. He was clearly one of the most useful performers in the troupe, willing to carry a heavy load of large—though rarely leading—roles. In addition to his Drury Lane work, in 1742 and continuing each summer through 1748, he acted at the Jacob's Well Theatre at Bristol; at almost the same time he gave up his fair-booth appearances in London, his last being on 23 August 1743 at Bartholomew Fair when he played Simon in the droll *The French Doctor Outwitted*.

Perhaps it was over-exertion which led to an illness in April 1743; one report had it that "no body expected his Life," though the callous Drury Lane manager Fleetwood sent word to the ailing actor that he would not open the doors for Berry's benefit unless the whole charge of the benefit was paid. Berry's health improved, and he was able to act during the summer, but how he settled with Fleetwood is not recorded.

During this busy decade of the 1740's Berry moved several times. In 1742 he was in Crown Court, Russell Street, where he had been for some years; by 1748 he used Little Bridges Street, Covent Garden, as his address; and the next year he was living at Mr Pope's (the peruke maker) in Russell Street—where he stayed until his death. At some point in his career Berry married, but whether or not his wife was alive and with him in the 1740's is not known. He had a daughter Anne, and perhaps she was the Miss Berry who appeared at Bartholomew Fair in August 1749.

In the last decade of his life Berry continued at Drury Lane, as busy as ever and still playing most of the roles of earlier years. In addition, though he had stopped acting in the summers at Bristol, he went to Edinburgh to play a Bacchanal in the elaborate production of *Comus* which Lampe produced on 14 January 1751. Back in London his life was made more exciting on 16 January 1752 when he was on his way home from Temple Bar and "was stopt at the end of Arundel Street by three Fellows one with a short Pistol and the other with a Hanger, who robb'd him of his Watch, some Silver, and his neckcloth and then walk'd off with their Booty."

At Drury Lane in the 1750's Berry played, in addition to his old parts, Old Knowell in *Every Man in His Humour*, Jaques in *As You Like It*, Aboan in *Oroonoko*, Duncan in *Macbeth*, Menenius in *Coriolanus*, Sir Sampson in *Love for Love*, Falstaff in *The Merry Wives of Windsor*, and Dominic in *The Spanish Friar*. Though he was now in his decline, his last season on stage, 1758–59, was practically a summary of his career since 1733 when his line turned definitely toward heavier parts. The list also shows how busy Berry remained right to the end: Jaques in *As You Like It* on 16 September 1758, King in *The Mourning Bride* on 19 September, Leonato in *Much Ado* on 23 September, Ghost in *Hamlet* on 25 September, Capulet in *Romeo and Juliet* on 28 September, King Henry in *Richard III* on 12 October, Strictland in *The Suspicious Husband* on 20 October, Caliban in *The Tempest* on 24 October, Gloucester in *King Lear* on 25 October, Heartwell in *The Old Bachelor* on 27 October, Duncan in *Macbeth* on 30 October, Sir Epicure Mammon in *The Alchemist* on 7 November, Dominic in *The Spanish Friar* on 14 November, Baldwin in *The Fatal Marriage* on 15 November, Cacafogo in *Rule a Wife* on 23 November, Surly in *Sir Courtly Nice* on 24 November, Sir Jealous in *The Busy Body* on 2 December, Narbas in *Merope* on 13 December.

On 16 December 1758 Phillips replaced him in *The Busy Body*, and after this Berry seldom acted. Yet he was well enough to act on 29 and 30 December, and on 3 January 1759 he played his only new role of the season, Enobarbus in *Antony and Cleopatra*. He performed twice more in January and once in February, and on 15 March he made his last appearance, as Sir Epicure Mammon. On 16 April he was given a benefit, but the bill noted that he had been "for some time past" confined by a severe illness.

On 8 January 1760 Edward Berry died at the age of 53. He was buried at St Martin-in-the-Fields on 13 January. To his only daughter, Anne, he left his estate of £1000. His will had been written on 28 April 1749; in it he referred to Anne as his dear child, suggesting that at that time she was still fairly young. He asked Thomas Fletcher of Gutter Lane, Cheapside, to assist Anne and see that she received what was rightly hers. By the time Berry died, Anne had grown up and had married James Hyde, and on 15 January 1760 she was granted administration of her father's estate. With some of the money he left her she set up a monument to Berry's memory:

> Here lie the Remains
> of
> Edward Berry
> Who lived with
> Public Applause, Private Esteem;
> The former he acquired as

> An excellent Comedian
> the latter as
> An Honest Man

> Obiit 8 Jan 1760 Ætat 53
> Light lie the 'Turf. What tho' no breathing Bust
> Of mimic marble dignifies thy Dust?
> Yet filial sorrow pays the duteious tear
> And heart-warm Friendship heaves a sigh sincere;
> Pleas'd may thy shade these humble rites receive
> The last sad Tribute Gratitude can give.

Genest wrote later that "Berry's figure was well adapted to Sciolto, Acasto and characters of that cast; No man had more feeling than he, and it generally had its proper effect, but by being too fond of aiming at tenderness, he grated upon the ear of an auditor." Hill, in *The Actor*, also noted Berry's sensitivity when playing Sciolto; Berry, he said, "actually feels the shock the author represents him under, when his daughter is prov'd to be a prostitute: It ought to be allow'd him, that we even see in his countenance the anguish, rage and despair," and his eyes are "big with real tears." Yet, paradoxically, Hill remarked that Berry was "little able to give expression to that feeling."

The *Theatrical Examiner* in 1757 wrote: "Mr. B———y, with a huge body and voice,—roars out a howl . . . upon almost all occasions! . . . I remember some years ago he was less guilty of this crime, which I presume an injudicious applause gave birth to." *An Essay upon the Present State of the Theatre* (1760) was blunt about it: "Mr. Berry is an actor of some merit in comedy, but his performance in tragedy is very indifferent."

Poor Berry would not have been happy to hear that he developed the wrong line, but the critics were in general agreement on his excesses in serious roles; Davies found Berry "a very good general actor in tragedy and comedy" but he "wanted dignity of behaviour, and elevation of mind to represent Philip [in *The Brothers*]." Davies agreed that the actor's chief fault was in shedding too many tears, too loudly and too ungracefully.

In certain characters, however, Berry apparently did well. *A General View of the Stage* counted Sciolto, Acasto, Capulet, and King Henry (in *Richard III*) among Berry's most suitable serious characters.

He keeps nature generally in view, in the expression of paternal fondness, but sometimes does more than she requires in his excessive grief. He has the art, known but by few on the stage, of diversifying his old men: his Adam in As You Like It, is genuine nature in a low sphere. . . . I have seen him also in Comedy acquit himself to general satisfaction, principally in Boniface, Caliban, and Serjeant Kite in the Recruiting Officer . . . We may say, that if Mr. Berry is not the greatest actor, he is at least a very useful one.

This may have been damning with faint praise, but it was probably a sound evaluation of hard-working Edward Berry's talent.

Berry was painted by Thomas Worlidge, as Dominic in *The Spanish Friar*; this painting, from the Charles J. M. Eaton collection in Baltimore, is on loan to the Walters Art Gallery from the Peabody Institute. An engraving of the Worlidge painting was made by R. Houston.

Berry, Harriet. *See* GRIST, HARRIET.

Berry, John *d. 1821, actor.*

John Berry may have been the "Young Gentleman" who acted Patie in *The Gentle Shepherd* at the Haymarket Theatre on 26 September 1791, for at that playhouse on 24 October Berry played Lady Pentweazel in *Taste* and was billed as making his second appearance on any stage. *Taste* was done for his benefit, and tickets were to be had of him at the George in the Haymarket. It was presumably this same actor who played again at the Haymarket on 23 April

1798, appearing as Glenalvon in a production of *Douglas*.

Berry left London after this and was mentioned in the Tunbridge Wells bills in 1800. By 1803 he had settled in Edinburgh, and it was probably there that he married. A benefit bill dated 10 April 1811 indicated that the Berrys were living at No 4, James's Street. Berry acted at Edinburgh at least through the 1815–16 season, but his career as an actor of some ability gradually gave way to his reputation as a drinker. On 15 May 1816 Berry shared a benefit with his wife, but he was given the benefit out of charity; he had earlier been dismissed for drinking and had strolled for a time. On the promise that he would reform, the Edinburgh manager Murray gave him this second chance. Berry did not take advantage of the opportunity, and the rest of his life was a continual degeneration. He died on 11 July 1821. Wemyss, writing in 1847, filled in the details:

It was in Cumnock I heard of the death of poor Berry, one of my first theatrical acquaintance, once the idol of the Edinburgh audiences, and, beyond doubt, the best low comedian of his day. Liston, Matthews, and Emery, combined, would not have formed a better actor than Jack Berry; but dissipation and repeated acts of neglect of his profession, through dissipation, at length so exhausted the kindness and patience of Mr. Henry Siddons, that he was reluctantly compelled to abandon him; and, in leaving the Edinburgh theatre, the last restraint upon his unhappy failing, was lost in Dumbarton, where he and his wife had been giving an entertainment of a theatrical nature. He fell in a state of intoxication against a glass door, lacerating his arm in so dreadful a manner as to produce lockjaw, from which, by the care and attention of his physician, he recovered, but was never the same man again. He became a member of a travelling company, performing in the open air, at fairs: and thus the man whose talents had delighted the most enlightened audience in the British Empire, was converted into the low buffoon of a mountebank's caravan. He died in abject misery, almost shunned by his pot-house companions.

Berry, Thomas d. 1701?, actor.

Thomas Berry, apparently the elder of two actors of the same name, was a member of Thomas Betterton's company at the Lincoln's Inn Fields Theatre where he was first mentioned as playing the King in Betterton's version of *Henry IV* on 9 January 1700. He acted Bosman in *The Czar of Muscovy* about March 1701, another elderly role, after which his name was no longer cited in the bills. He may have been the Thomas Berry who was buried at St Martin-in-the-Fields on 4 April 1701.

Berry, Thomas [fl. 1737], actor.

A Thomas Berry, probably not the same as the actor of that name who performed elderly roles at the turn of the century, was reported as having left the Drury Lane company in 1737.

Berryman. *See* BERRIMAN.

Berselli, Matteo [fl. 1719–1721], singer.

A *castrato*, Matteo Berselli sang at Dresden with the troupe belonging to Friedrich Augustus I, Elector of Saxony, before coming to England. At Dresden he was paid 7000 thalers annually as second sopranist and received free food, lodging, utilities, and a carriage. In September 1719 he and the more famous Senesino renewed their contracts at Dresden but agreed with Handel to come to London the following season. The pair arrived on 19 September 1720 along with soprano Maddalena Salvai and, apparently, Senesino's brother. The librettist Paolo Rolli found lodgings for Senesino and Berselli in a large house in Leicester Street which they shared with an *abbé*. During the 1720–21 season at the King's Theatre in the Haymarket Berselli sang Sidonia in *Astarto* on 19 November 1720, Tigranes in *Radamisto* on 28 De-

cember, Megabise in *Arsace* on 1 February 1721, Orazio in *Muzio Scevola* on 15 April, and Arbace in *Ciro* on 20 May. He apparently left England after this season.

Bert, Miss. *See* BIRT, MISS S.

Berteau, Mons [fl. 1675], dancer.

Monsieur Berteau (or Berto) was one of the dancers in the court masque *Calisto* on 15 February 1675.

Bertholdi. *See* BERTOLLI.

Bertie, Mr [fl. 1708], manager?

On 24 February 1708 Sir John Vanbrugh wrote the Earl of Manchester saying that Owen Swiney had been bought out as an "Undertaker" of the opera at the Queen's Theatre in the Haymarket by Vanbrugh and a Mr Bertie. Summers identifies this partner as probably Peregrine Bertie (1686–1742), later Duke of Ancaster, son of the Earl of Lindsey and Vice Chamberlain of the Household—one who might, indeed, have had funds to invest in the theatre and might have been interested in management. A second possibility which Summers does not suggest is Montague Bertie, second Earl of Abingdon (c. 1673–1743). Another Vanbrugh letter, dated 14 May 1708, confuses the issue by referring to a Signor Bertie; and, whoever this Bertie was, it is not known whether he became actively involved in the management of the theatre or remained Vanbrugh's silent partner.

Another or possibly the same Bertie appeared in a different theatrical connection, but again there is a veil over the true facts. An alleged daughter of actress Anne Oldfield, nicknamed "Dye" (probably for Diana), had the last name of Bertie; she was placed in Mademoiselle Puelle's school for girls in 1706, and after leaving she became a fashionable lady and married nobly. There is great doubt whether or not the girl was actually Anne Oldfield's daughter, but she might have been; if Mrs Oldfield was the mother, there is just as much doubt about who might have been the father. The most likely candidates are two of her lovers: Peregrine Bertie and Montague Bertie (who, incidentally, was related to Charles Churchill, Anne's next lover). These two Berties seem to have moved in theatrical circles, and perhaps one of them joined with Vanbrugh in his Queen's Theatre venture.

Bertin, Mr (fl. 1793), pianist.
Gerber's *Neues historisch-biographisches Lexikon* of 1812–14 mentions one Bertin, a pianist, who appeared in London in 1793. He may have been related to Pierrot Bertin, the French violinist.

Bertles, Miss. *See* DIGHTON, MRS ROBERT.

Berto. *See* BERTEAU.

Bertolli, Francesca (fl. 1729–1737), singer.
Early eighteenth-century commentators had a great deal of trouble with Francesca Bertolli's name; it was variously spelled (Bartholdi, Bartoldi, Bertholdi, Bertoldi, and Bertoli) and her first name was sometimes even set down as Francesco—perhaps because she was a specialist in male roles. A contralto, she was perhaps more famous for her beauty than for her vocal excellence, though her advance billing was very complimentary; the *Daily Journal* of 2 July 1729 reported that she had been hired by Handel for his 1729–30 season at the King's Theatre in the Haymarket and was said to have a "fine Treble Voice; she is also a very genteel Actress, both in Men and Womens Parts." She probably arrived in London in late September 1729. According to a letter from the librettist Rolli to his friend Riva on 6 November 1729, she

was to be paid "450 Lira in all" and was "pretty, they say, but I have not yet seen her. Poor thing, what with travelling and living expenses, she will not take ten guineas back home. You ought to come and protect her and help her and be pleasant to her without Partiality."

Signora Bertolli's first London role was Idelberto in *Lotario* on 2 December 1729. Mrs Pendarves saw a rehearsal of the opera a few days before it opened and wrote her sister that the singer

has neither voice, ear, nor manner to recommend her; but she is a perfect beauty, quite a Cleopatra, that sort of complexion with regular features, fine teeth, and when she sings has a smile about her mouth which is extremely pretty, and I believe has practised to sing before a glass, for she has never any distortion in her face.

By the middle of December Rolli had seen *Lotario* and had written whimsically to Riva, confirming the singer's beauty: "There is a certain Bertolli, a Roman girl, who plays men's parts. Oh! my dear Riva, if you could only see her perspiring under her helmet—I am sure you would fall in love with her in your most Modenese fashion! She is a pretty one!" During this season Signora Bertolli also sang Armindo in *Partenope* (24 February 1730), Arsace in *Ormisda* (4 April), and Alessandro in *Tolomeo* (19 May).

In 1730–31 she was C. Lelio in *Scipio*, Gandarte in *Poro*, Argante in *Rinaldo*, and Eduigi in *Rodelinda*. Her 1731–32 season began with a revival of *Poro* on 23 November 1731 in which she switched to the role of Erissena. This season she also sang Onoria in *Aetius* (Richelet's translation of Metastasio's *Ezio*), Melo in *Sosarme*, Claudio in *Coriolano*, probably Vitige in *Flavio*, and Rutilia in *Lucio Papirio*. In May 1732 Handel produced his oratorio *Esther*, and a satirical letter entitled *See and Seem Blind* commented on Signora Bertolli's first attempt to sing in English: *"Sene-*

sino and *Bertolli* made rare work with the *English* Tongue you would have sworn it had been *Welch*; I would have wish'd it *Italian,* that they might have sung with more ease to themselves, but for the Name of *English*, it might as well have been *Hebrew*."

During the 1732–33 season Signora Bertolli sang Arbace in *Cato*, Tassile in *Alessandro*, Alessandro in *Tolomeo* again, and Medoro in *Orlando*—all in Italian—but she tested her English once again in Handel's *Deborah* on 17 March 1733. Whether or not she mangled the language this time is not known. Her pronunciation apparently did not deter the Prince of Wales; on 11 July 1733 Viscount Percival wrote in his diary that he "heard this day that the Prince attempted to gain the favors of Mrs Bartholdi, the Italian singer . . . but . . . in vain."

For the next two seasons Signora Bertolli, along with the famous Senesino, left Handel's company to sing with the rival Porpora troupe. At Lincoln's Inn Fields in 1733–34 she appeared as Il Dido Libero in *Arianna in Naxo*, Nino in *Astarto*, and Amata in *Enea nel Lazio*. In addition, since she had formed useful contacts in elegant circles, she participated in private musicales at the home of the Earl of Egmont in January, February, and March of 1734. When the fall opera season began, the Porpora group moved to the King's Theatre where they ultimately triumphed over Handel's company at Covent Garden. During this 1734–35 season the Italian beauty sang Semira in *Artaserse*, Calipso in *Polifemo*, Eurinome in *Issipile*, and Clitemnestra in *Ifigenia in Aulide*. The following season she was Sabina in *Adriano in Sira*, Farnace in *Mitridate*, and Ormonte in *Onorio*, after which she rejoined Handel's troupe. During her last season in London, 1736–37 at Covent Garden, she sang Ramise in *Arminio* (12 January 1737), Leocasta in *Giustino* (16 February), and Selene in *Berenice* (18 May). Her last appearance was probably

at the closing performance of *Berenice* on 15 June 1737.

Berton. *See* BURTON.

Bertoni, Ferdinando Giuseppe *1725–1813, composer.*

Ferdinando Giuseppe Bertoni was born at Salò, Lake Garda, on 15 August 1725 and had his early musical training at Brescia and Bologna. In 1745 at Florence his first opera, *La vedova accorta*, was performed, and two years later his first oratorio was sung at Venice. He was made organist at St Mark's in Venice in 1752, and five years later he was appointed choirmaster at the Ospedale San Lazzaro dei Mendicanti there. Beginning in 1752, when he wrote the music for *Le pescatrici*, with a libretto by Goldoni, he began turning out operas annually and with good success for most of the major Italian theatres, while for the girls' choir at the Mendicanti he composed oratorios. Despite his admiration for Gluck, Bertoni attempted his own version of *Orfeo* in 1776. One of his greatest successes was *Quinto Fabio*, first presented at Milan in January 1778, the title role being sung by the accomplished Pacchierotti. This led to the engagement of both the singer and the composer at the King's Theatre in the Haymarket for the 1778–79 season.

Bertoni was not unknown to Londoners, for on 28 April 1761 his *Le pescatrici* had been performed, but that was the only opera of his done in London before he was hired as house composer at the King's Theatre; before he left in 1783, however, the English were treated to a sizeable percentage of his output. On 28 November 1778 his *Demofoonte* was given its first performance, with Pacchierotti also making his London debut. Following this, Bertoni saw a number of his works either given premier performances or revived at the King's: *Artaserse* on 23 January 1779 (first given at Forlì in 1776), *La governante* on 15 May, *L'Olimpiade* on 29 May (a *pasticcio* first given at Venice in

1765); during the next season *Alessandro nell'Indie* was performed on 27 November 1779 (a *pasticcio* first heard at Venice in 1770 and in London chiefly directed, rather than composed, by Bertoni), the *pasticcio Il soldano generoso* on 14 December, *Quinto Fabio* on 22 January 1780 (first given at Milan in 1778), *Il duca d'Atene* on 9 May, and *Orfeo* on 31 May (first given in 1776 and performed in London in the form of an oratorio). In May 1780, and perhaps throughout these first two seasons in London, Bertoni was living at No 20, Queen Anne Street, Westminster.

After the 1779–80 season Bertoni returned to Venice for a year, wrote two operas there, and returned to England for the 1781–82 and 1782–83 seasons, again as house composer. His *Ezio* was sung on 17 November 1781 (a *pasticcio* first assembled for Venice in 1767), *Giunio Bruto* on 12 January 1782 (made up of music by a number of composers and directed by Bertoni), *Quinto Fabio* revived on 7 March, and *Ifigenia in Aulide* on 25 May (first staged at Turin in 1762). Sometime in 1782 Lady Craven produced an "Arcadian Pastoral" for which Bertoni wrote about 12 airs and choruses "in a very good stile." The next season his *Il convito* was brought out on 2 November 1782, *Medonte* on 14 November (based on Sarti's opera, partly set by Bertoni and directed by him), *Cimene* on 7 January 1783, and *L'Olimpiade* revived with some alterations on 6 March. After giving London this sampling of his talent, Bertoni left his position at the King's Theatre and returned to Italy.

He succeeded the deceased Galuppi as choirmaster at St Mark's in Venice in 1785 and continued composing. His total output included 48 operas, 12 scenic cantatas, 11 oratorios, and a number of chamber works. Burney found Bertoni's music too languid and lacking in the "enthusiastic turbulence" that could excite audiences. He was, nevertheless, very popular with London audiences. Bertoni retired in 1810 and went back to Lake Garda where, on 1 December 1813, he died.

Bertram, Charles *[fl. 1794], horn player.*
Doane's *Musical Directory* of 1794 lists Charles Bertram, of York House, Piccadilly, as a horn player at concerts given by the New Musical Fund.

Berwick, Mrs *[fl. 1765], dresser.*
According to a schedule of salary payments for Drury Lane Theatre dated 9 February 1765, Mrs Berwick was one of the women's dressers receiving 1s. 6d. daily or 9s. per week.

Berwillibald. *See* **GIACOMO, GIORGIO.**

Besand. *See* **BAYZAND.**

Besford, Mr *[fl. 1759], messenger.*
A Mr Besford, messenger, was earning 12s. per week at Covent Garden in September 1759.

Besford, Mr *[1766–1768], actor.*
A minor actor named Besford played Shadow in *2 Henry IV* at Covent Garden on 9 October 1766 on the same night that Master Besford played Falstaff's page. He was acting at Covent Garden in 1767–68 and may also have been one of the house servants mentioned in the entry of Joseph Besford.

Besford, Mr *[1767–1788], lamp man. See* **BESFORD, JOSEPH.**

Besford, Esther *b. c. 1757, actress, dancer.*
Esther Besford was born about 1757, the daughter of Joseph Besford, the Covent Garden property man. Her mother probably was the Mrs Besford who danced at Covent Garden in 1767–68. As a child Miss Bes-

ford made her first appearance on the stage at Covent Garden on 1 April 1766 in the role of Princess Elizabeth in *Virtue Betrayed, or, Anna Bullen*. In the next season, on 20 October 1766, she played the little Duke of York (a role often filled by young girls) in *Richard III*. Announced as an apprentice to Fishar, and then only ten years old, she made her first appearance as a dancer in a *New Pantomime Ballet* on 20 April 1767. Several weeks later on 10 May she was paid £4 4s. for eight nights. On 16 April 1768 she danced with Master Blurton in a new pantomime dance called *The Spanish Coal-Heaver* and on 25 May 1768 she performed a hornpipe for the first time. Miss Besford made her first appearance as a speaking adult actress on 19 May 1773 in the title role of *Polly Honeycombe*.

She remained at Covent Garden through the season 1785–86 as a minor actress and dancer. Her few named roles included Margaret in *A New Way to Pay Old Debts* on 18 May 1775 and Miss Aubrey in *The Fashionable Lover* on 17 May 1786. In 1776–77 her salary was £1 per week, which was raised to £2 in 1777–78 and remained at that figure until 1782–83, when it was raised to £4 per week. She also danced at Bristol in 1777 and 1784–85. Administration of her father's will was granted to her on 1 September 1789. No more was heard of her after that date.

Besford, Joseph *d. 1789, property man.*

In a *per diem* pay-list of the Covent Garden company for 1767–68 provided by Arthur Murphy (in connection with a case brought against the manager James Harris) are found four people by the name of Besford: a property man, a lampman, and a messenger, each at 2s. per day, and a dancer, Mrs Besford, at 3s. 4d. per day. Not listed by Murphy was another Besford who acted there that season. Presumably they were all related. Payments to more than one Besford continue to be made regularly each year in

the account books from then through 1789, and it becomes almost impossible to discriminate among them.

The property man in Murphy's list was Joseph Besford who served in that capacity at Covent Garden from at least 1766–67 through 1788–89. Occasionally he appeared on the stage as a supernumerary or to attend the various properties he built. On 2 June 1766, for example, he was paid 5s. for riding the horse in the pantomime *Perseus and Andromeda*. By 1785–86 he was being paid £5 14s. 6d. per week. Perhaps he was the Besford who worked as an extra at the Bristol theatre in the summer of 1778.

Joseph Besford died in Bow Street on 8 July 1789 and was buried at St Paul, Covent Garden, on 12 July. Probably the dancer Mrs Besford was his wife and she apparently died before he did, for administration of his will was left to his daughter Esther Besford, spinster, on 1 September 1789.

Besford, Mrs [Joseph?] [fl. 1767–1768], *dancer.*

Mrs Besford was a dancer at Covent Garden in 1767–68 earning 3s. 4d. per week. She probably was the wife of Joseph Besford.

Besford, Samuel [fl. 1763–1791], *actor, dancer.*

Samuel Besford was doubtless the young performer who was in the Covent Garden bills as Master Besford from 1764–65 to 1766–67, playing such parts as Falstaff's page in 2 *Henry IV*. He also shared in tickets on 12 May 1764, at which time he played a page in *Romeo and Juliet*. A payment of £2 2s. was recorded on 10 May 1767 to "Master Besford for his performance in The Fairy Favour."

A Mr Besford acted small parts, usually unnamed, and danced in the chorus at Covent Garden in 1776–78, 1780–82, and 1783–85; he was also dancing and acting at the Haymarket in the summers of 1777, 1785, and 1788 at a usual salary of £2 per week. On 11 March 1784 he was identified as playing the female role of the maid in *Rule a Wife and Have a Wife* at Covent Garden. Samuel Besford was buried at St Paul, Covent Garden, on 15 December 1791.

Besozzi, Antonio *1714–1781, oboist.*
Antonio Besozzi was born in Parma in 1714, the son of Giuseppe and brother of Gaetano, both oboists. From 8 October 1727 to 1731 he was a member of the Campagnia at Parma, after which he travelled; he was at Naples about 1738 when his son Carlo was born. In 1739 Antonio accepted the first oboe chair in the Dresden court orchestra, and in 1754 he was joined by his son Carlo, who had already, at 16, become an accomplished oboist. In early 1757 the pair came to England where, on 25 March, they played an oboe concerto at Drury Lane; it was probably shortly after this that they had a benefit at the Great Room in Dean Street, Soho. While in England they were described as the Signori Besozzi, and since they were of a sizeable family of instrumentalists, almost all of whom played the oboe, they have been sometimes incorrectly identified either as brothers or as Gaetano Besozzi and his son Girolamo.

By the winter of 1757 Antonio and Carlo had gone to Paris, and in December of that year they appeared at the Concert Spirituel there. In 1758 and 1759 they both played in the Stuttgart court orchestra, after which they returned to Dresden, where Antonio remained unil 1774 and Carlo until 1792. Antonio went to Turin, where he died in 1781. Carlo, while at Dresden in 1772, made a favorable impression on visitor Charles Burney, and when he played at Salzburg in May 1778, Leopold Mozart was equally taken with his talent. In addition to his playing, Carlo Besozzi composed several oboe *concerti* and a number of quintets (which he called *sonatas*) for two oboes, two horns, and a bassoon.

Besozzi, Carlo *b. c. 1738, oboist. See* **BESOZZI, ANTONIO.**

Besozzi, Gaetano *1727–1798, oboist.*
Gaetano Besozzi (or, incorrectly, Beozzi) was born in Parma in 1727, the son of oboist Giuseppe Besozzi and member of a musical family that went yet another generation back and would continue into the late nineteenth century; nearly all the Besozzis were either oboists or bassoonists or both. Gaetano played at the court of Naples until 1765 when he joined the royal chapel in Paris, where Burney heard him with great satisfaction. In 1793 he came to England and helped inaugurate the concerts of the Oxford Musical Society on 1 May 1793. According to Doane's *Musical Directory* of 1794, Besozzi played oboe for the King's Theatre in the Haymarket and lived at No 13, Poland Street. His older brother Antonio and his nephew Carlo had performed in London in 1757. Gaetano Besozzi died in London in 1798.

Best, Mr [fl. 1779–1785], *actor.*
Mr Best played Harlequin to Miss Dudley's Columbine in *entr'acte* vaudeville at the Haymarket Theatre on 15 March 1779. In 1780 he was acting in Belfast, and there, shortly before 1 June 1785, he married Miss Mary Russell, an actress who played at the Haymarket in 1777–78.

Best, Mrs. *See* **RUSSELL, MARY.**

Beswick, Mrs [fl. 1787], *dancer.*

A Mrs Beswick was advertised as a principal dancer with the company of Charles Hughes at the Royal Circus in the spring and summer of 1787. A Miss Beswick also danced in the company. Mrs Beswick may have been a relative of the J. Beswick who acted sometime after 1806 at Sunderland.

Beswick, Miss [fl. 1726], *house servant?*
A Miss Beswick shared a benefit with a Mr Gilbert at the Haymarket Theatre on 12

April 1726; they may both have been house servants at the theatre, working with the French players who were performing there at this time.

Beswick, Miss [fl. 1787], *dancer. See* **BESWICK, MRS.**

Besworth, [Mr?] [fl. 1761], *wardrobe assistant.*

One Besworth—unless this is an error for Besford—was paid £6 18s. on 7 February 1761 at Covent Garden for making a costume for the Ghost in *Hamlet*; Besworth was presumably on the theatre staff.

Betenham. *See* **BETTENHAM.**

Bethal. *See* **BETHELL.**

Bethan. *See* **BETHUN.**

Bethell, William [fl. 1784–c. 1794], *singer.*

William Bethell (or Bethal) sang tenor in the Handel Memorial Concerts at Westminster Abbey and the Pantheon on 26, 27, 29 May and 3, 5 June 1784. Doane's *Musical Directory* of 1794 listed Bethell, of No 13, Great Shire Lane, Temple Bar, as a tenor who participated in performances by the Choral Fund and the Handelian Society. He also sang in oratorios at Drury Lane Theatre.

It is possible that the singer was the William Bethell who was buried at the age of 54 at St Paul, Covent Garden, on 1 June 1797. His wife Ann had been buried there on 15 January 1786. They had a daughter Elizabeth who was baptized on 9 September 1773 and a son William who may have been born early in the same year.

Bethun, Mr [fl. 1733–1738], *dancer.*

Mr Bethun (or Bethan, Bethen, Bethum) was first mentioned in the bills when he was given a benefit on 27 March 1733 at the Haymarket Theatre. On the following

14 August he danced the *Irish Trot* at Covent Garden, and on 15 October he was one of the countrymen in *Harlequin Dr Faustus* at Drury Lane. His other roles at Drury Lane this season were a Chinese Guard in *Cephalus and Procris* on 13 November and a Satyr in *Cupid and Psyche* on 4 February 1734.

Though the bills mentioned no roles for him, Mr Bethun was a member of the Drury Lane company again in 1736–37. His last notice was on 24 January 1738 when he danced as a Chinese Guard in *Harlequin Grand Volgi*, an indication that he was probably with Drury Lane for the full 1737–38 season. Bethun may have been (or been related to) the Mr Bethune who worked at Covent Garden in 1746.

Bethune, Mr [fl. 1746], *house servant?*

Mr Bethune was entered in the Covent Garden Theatre accounts on 17 October 1746 for 1s. 6d. per day, and his name remained on the house list until 29 November. He may have been a house servant, and perhaps he was (or was related to) the Drury Lane dancer Mr Bethun who was active in the 1730's.

Beton, Miss [fl. 1798], *actress.*

On 24 March 1798 at Drury Lane, Miss Beton played the Stranger's Daughter in *The Stranger*; on the fifth of June she was in *The Eleventh of June* when that interlude was given its premiere. She may well have been related to the Master Beton who acted walk-ons at Drury Lane in 1800–1801.

"Bette." *See* **DAVENPORT, ELIZABETH.**

Bettenham, George d. 1694, *singer.*

George Bettenham (or Bettenhave), a *basso*, was a member of the Chapel Royal and participated in the coronations of Charles II on 23 April 1661, James II on 23 April 1685, and William and Mary on

11 April 1689. Despite his long service, the records seldom mention him. He died on 19 September 1694.

Betterton, John *d. 1816, actor. See* BETTERTON, THOMAS WILLIAM.

Betterton, Julia. *See* GLOVER, MRS SAMUEL.

Betterton, Thomas *1635–1710, actor, manager, author.*

The greatest English actor between Burbage and Garrick and by some authorities considered better than either, Thomas Betterton played an astounding range of characters with consummate skill and sensitivity and at the same time was deeply immersed in playwriting, theatre management, the training of actors, and the staging of plays for most of his fifty-year career.

Matthew Betterton, the father of the actor, was probably an under-cook to Charles I, though he styled himself a gentleman of Westminster. He lived in Tothill (or Tuttle) Street, Westminster, in a house which had been bequeathed him on 18 September 1637 by his second wife's father, Thomas Flowerdew of St Margaret, Westminster. Though nothing is known of Matthew's first wife, he married his second, Frances, about 14 October 1630 and by her apparently had four sons and two daughters. Of the sons, three are known by name: Thomas (c. August 1635–28 April 1710), William (4 September 1644–1661), and Charles (baptized 10 June 1647—buried 20 December 1678). Since Thomas was described as a younger son of Matthew but the eldest son surviving in 1663, there must have been a fourth son, born sometime before Thomas and possibly a child of Matthew's first wife. The dates of the two daughters in the family have not been found, but their names were Frances and Mary.

Thomas was baptized at St Margaret, Westminster, on 12 (or possibly 11) August 1635. He was given a "polite" educa-
tion, but Gildon was later to observe that Betterton had "not had the Benefit of such an Education in the learned Languages, as some may have had" but that he read much in French and English, "by the Assistance of which Languages all Knowledge may now be obtain'd." This interest in reading manifested itself at an early age, and it was presumably at his own choice that young Thomas was bound apprentice to the bookseller John Holden, friend of Sir William Davenant and father of the Restoration actress. (Thomas was not, according to his own statement to Pope, apprenticed to the bookseller John Rhodes, as some early biographies stated.) The theatrical connections during his apprenticeship were even more complete: Edward Kynaston, later to become a famous player, was probably Betterton's under-apprentice.

Curll, whose trustworthiness as to facts varies almost from page to page, in *A History of the English Stage* (1741, authorship questionable), stated that Thomas volunteered for the King's service during the civil war and was in the battle of Edgehill along with the Caroline actors Hart, Mohun, and Smith; this is pure fiction, unless Thomas went to battle at the age of seven. He surely would have missed most of the excitement of the Interregnum, and if his apprenticeship to Holden was normal, he would have served from about 1649 to 1656, concluding his term at the age of 21. Though a different Thomas Betterton may have been involved, at least two volumes appeared with that name as author: *A Mixt Poem . . . upon the Happy Return of His Sacred Majesty Charles the Second* (1660) and *The Muses Joy For the Recovery of that weeping Vine, Henrietta Maria* (1661). Considering his training, the future actor may well have done some publishing, though his indifference in later years about the publication of his own plays would suggest otherwise.

After completing his apprenticeship Betterton may have picked up some acting ex-

Courtesy of the Public Record Office

Theatre regulations governing Betterton's new company, 16 April 1695 perience (Curll supposed that he started acting in Davenant's early productions at Rutland House in 1656), but there are no records of his theatrical activity before 1659–60 when he was a member of John Rhodes's company. Rhodes, formerly wardrobe keeper at the old Blackfriars and sometime bookseller, formed a troupe just before the Restoration and was probably acting at the Cockpit in Drury Lane by 24 March 1660. Though the titles of several plays which Rhodes produced have been recorded, specific dates are missing, so Betterton's first appearance has not been established. His roles during the few months before he joined Davenant's new Duke's Company were most impressive: the Bondman, Deflores in *The Changeling*, Pericles, Archas in *The Loyal Subject*, and Memnon in *The Mad Lover*—and he was doubtless in other revivals. The prompter Downes later cited these parts and noted that Betterton was "but 22 Years Old [*recte*, 24] . . . his Voice being then as Audibly strong, full and Articulate, as in the Prime of his Acting" and he was "highly Applauded."

By October 1660 Thomas Killigrew and Sir William Davenant were close to opening their officially sanctioned patent houses. On 8 October the King's men, under Killigrew but with Davenant sharing in the profits, were acting at the Cockpit, which they rented from Rhodes. The company consisted of a combination of actors drawn from the earlier Rhodes troupe, from the Red Bull company, and from a third group which William Beeston had organized; thus Betterton, for a brief period, was a member of the King's Company and played with several actors, including Charles Hart and Michael Mohun, who would be his rivals for the next 22 years. How long he remained with this group is not clear; accounts as late as 17 December 1661—a whole year later—still list him as a member, though it is certain that he had joined Davenant's company by January 1661. Perhaps he remained with the Killigrew troupe for

only four weeks and joined the Duke's Company when it opened Salisbury Court on 5 November 1660, or perhaps, because of restrictions announced in mid-December against players changing companies, he had to wait until the beginning of the year to switch his allegiance. Though no roles are listed for him and he was probably one of the lowest-ranking members of this rather brilliant troupe, this training with older actors may have been a useful experience.

Betterton purchased a share in the Duke's Company in 1660, so from the beginning he was involved in theatrical finances. When he joined the troupe he, James Nokes, and Thomas Sheppey were made overseers of the accounts, and these three, as deputies, held Davenant's four shares in the company. But Betterton's primary duty was acting.

His first listed role with the Duke's players was Deflores, on 23 February 1661 at Salisbury Court, and a week later he played the title role in *The Bondman*. On 28 and 29 June he acted what may have been his first role in a Restoration play, Solyman in the two parts of Davenant's *The Siege of Rhodes* at the opening of the converted tennis court in Lincoln's Inn Fields, complete with the novelty of changeable scenery. On 24 August, less than a year and a half after he began his professional acting career, he played Hamlet. For a beginning actor, these months must have been a heady experience, and one wonders how different Betterton's career might have been had he stayed with the rival company. The Duke's troupe was a youthful one, with better opportunities for a young actor of talent plus the chance to help guide the destiny of the group. Most important, in Davenant the actors had a first-rate teacher of long experience. Downes, in commenting on Betterton's fine Hamlet, noted that Davenant, "(having seen *Mr. Taylor* of the *Black-Fryars* Company Act it, who being Instructed by the Author *Mr. Shakespeur*) taught Mr. *Betterton* in every Particle of it;

which by his exact Performance of it, gain'd him Esteem and Reputation, Superlative to all other Plays." Even granting Downes a degree of exaggeration, Davenant's training of the highly responsive Betterton must have contributed greatly to the actor's remarkable achievements in the years to come and must also have made Betterton, in turn, a good teacher of fledgling performers.

Downes was not Betterton's only admirer; another was the inveterate playgoer Samuel Pepys. On 1 March 1661 at a performance of *The Bondman* Pepys made his first report on the young actor (though he must have seen him in action before this): "But above all that I ever saw, Betterton do the Bondman the best." Pepys probably never saw anyone else play the role, of course, but it would be uncharitable to dampen his enthusiasm, for it was quite sincere. On 19 March he saw the play again and recorded that he was "every time more and more pleased with Bettertin's action." Then, at *Hamlet* on 24 August 1661: ". . . but above all, Betterton did the prince's part beyond imagination."

While he was playing Hamlet onstage Betterton was acting Romeo off. He had probably known the actress Mary Saunderson from the beginning of his theatrical career, for she was one of the first women Davenant hired, and she, with three others, boarded with Sir William and Lady Mary. Though she may have acted earlier, her first recorded appearance was in June 1661 in *The Siege of Rhodes*, with Betterton. She was about 24 at this time; he was almost 26. Neither could have had much stage experience, and both were thrust from the beginning into sizeable roles. A romance developed, and on 16 December 1661 when she appeared as Aurelia in *The Cutter of Coleman Street*, with Betterton playing Colonel Jolly, she was called by the prompter, Downes, "Mrs Betterton"—and so, too, in subsequent roles.

It was probably sometime between the following March and June 1662 that Betterton was chosen both as Davenant's dep-

uty and an official agent of Charles II to journey to France and investigate the Parisian theatre. He acted Mercutio in *Romeo and Juliet* on 1 March, and since there is then a blank in the records he probably left for France soon after that performance. Betterton's mission was to bring back ideas that would advance the techniques of the English stage, for Davenant and the King both knew how far behind the Continent England had fallen during the 18 years of virtual theatrical silence that followed the closing of the playhouses in 1642. Just where Betterton went, how long he stayed, what he saw, whom he met, and what ideas he brought back have not come to light, but he must surely have seen the work of Molière and *commedia dell'arte* troupes, the plays of the new school of French playwrights, the accomplishments of the skilled Italian designers and machinists, and the more advanced playhouses in Paris.

If his mission was to return with ideas on improving English stage spectacle, the rival King's Company may have gained more from his trip than Davenant's troupe, for their new theatre in Bridges Street was to open a year later, whereas the Duke's players would not be able to build a theatre from the ground up for almost ten years. Since Betterton went as an emissary of the King, he probably shared his experience with both London houses, but it is not possible to tell just what trends in the English theatre during the following years he may have influenced.

If his trip was made in the spring, he was back by July and involved in what would appear to be a rather dirty piece of business. Sir Henry Herbert, the aggressive Master of the Revels, who had fought doggedly against Davenant and Killigrew in 1660 and 1661 to retain his control over English theatricals, was still vigorous in his opposition to the patent companies—not because he wanted them silenced, but because he wanted more control over their activities and a share of their profits. On 4 July 1662 he tried to stop the Duke's Company from acting by sending a messenger from his office, Edward Thomas, with a warrant to the players. Betterton and at least eleven other actors assaulted the messenger, beat him up, and held him prisoner for two hours. At the trial, held on 18 July, all the actors confessed their guilt and were fined 3s. 4d. each. Who was in the right and how bloody the affair actually was is not known, nor is it clear how deeply Betterton was involved. That he was connected with the incident at all seems inconsistent with reports from contemporaries that he was a well-behaved gentleman.

The actor was busy again at Lincoln's Inn Fields by 30 September 1662 when he played Bosola in *The Duchess of Malfi*, with Mrs Betterton as the Duchess, and on 18 October he was Monsieur Brisac in *The Villain*, with Mrs Betterton as Bellmont. On 22 October Pepys chatted with one Benier, "who being acquainted with all the players, do tell me that Betterton is not married to Ianthe [Pepys's pet name for Mary], as they say; but also that he is a very sober, serious man, and studious and humble, following his studies, and is rich already with what he gets and saves." The couple had been masquerading as man and wife, but they finally obtained a marriage license on 24 December 1662, at which time Betterton was recorded as a bachelor from Westminster, about 30 (he was actually 27), and Mary a spinster from St Giles, Cripplegate, about 25, marrying with the consent of her widowed mother; they were to marry at Islington. Later biographers chose to ignore or failed to notice the facts concerning Betterton's belated marriage and instead lauded the pair for having maintained unspotted reputations in an age of licentiousness. Though we may never know the full story behind the facts, they somehow make Mary and Thomas Betterton more human, and they may, indeed, have a bearing on the couple's later behavior.

Thomas's father Matthew died soon after this marriage. He made his will on 10 June 1663, and it was proved by his widow and executrix Frances on 28 June. By this time only two of Matthew's sons were still alive, Thomas and Charles. Matthew bequeathed to his daughters Frances and Mary all the money due him from the days of Charles I plus half the moveables of his estate. Young Charles, still a minor in 1663, had been placed in the King's kitchen and was directed to give his mother the profits of his work there until he reached his majority, in return for which she was to provide his maintenance. Matthew left Thomas a seal ring of gold that had belonged to Matthew's grandfather; the rest of his estate, including the house in Westminster, he left to his wife.

These personal matters did not disturb the careers of Thomas and Mary Betterton. On 6 January Thomas played Sir Toby Belch in *Twelfth Night*; on the eighth he was Don Henrique and Mary Portia in the successful *The Adventures of Five Hours*; and on 23 February he acted Iberio and she Pyramena in *The Slighted Maid*. When he played Hamlet on 28 May, Pepys was there and was given "fresh reason never to think enough of Betterton." On 22 December 1663 Thomas was given the title role in Davenant's version of *Henry VIII*. Though by now a seasoned performer and the talk of the town, Betterton still submitted willingly to the instructions of his manager and mentor, Davenant, who had learned from "old Mr *Lowen*, that had his Instructions from Mr *Shakespear* himself." Downes thought the part of Henry "so rightly and justly done" by Betterton that "none can, or will come near him in the Age." Before the death of Davenant in 1668, Betterton continued profiting from his master's counsel, playing such roles as Lord Beauford in *The Comical Revenge* (March 1664), Owen Tudor in Boyle's *Henry V* (13 August 1664; Betterton wore King Charles's coronation suit), Macbeth (5 November 1664), Solyman in *Mustapha* (3 April 1665), and Richard III in *The English Princess* (7 March 1667).

Rarely did Betterton disappoint Pepys, as on 4 September 1667 in *Mustapha* when "both Betterton and Harris could not contain from laughing in the midst of a most serious part, from the ridiculous mistake of one of the men upon the stage; which I did not like." But a month later Pepys started fretting because Betterton was sick and could not perform; by 6 November 1667 when he saw *Macbeth* with John Young as Macbeth instead of his hero, Pepys felt the role was "mighty short of the content we used to have when Betterton acted, who is still sick." When Thomas was well again, Pepys faithfully gathered a company to go and see him in Boyle's *Henry V* on 6 July 1668, and on 31 August at *Hamlet*, the diarist was "mightily pleased with it; but above all, with Betterton, the best part, I believe, that ever man acted."

When Sir William Davenant died on 7 April 1668 the government of the Duke's Company fell into the hands of his widow, Lady Mary, and her son Charles, then only 12. Betterton and Henry Harris, the two leading actors of the troupe, were made managers of acting, and Betterton was appointed co-manager of the company generally. Much of the responsibility Davenant had carried in the preparation of productions and the care and feeding of young performers—especially the young women in the company—now fell to Betterton. Indeed, it may have been about this time that the Bettertons took into their home a young girl who was destined to become one of Thomas's leading ladies: Anne Bracegirdle. Anne's father had suffered economic losses, and the childless Bettertons were apparently happy to do for her what the Davenants had done for Mrs Betterton.

For his added duty as one of the trainers of the younger actors Betterton paid himself an extra 20s. out of the public receipts each week. Davenant had, more sensibly, taken his managerial profits from his shares in the company rather than cut into the daily income from which the troupe's expenses had to be paid; Betterton should have seen that his new system was selfish and economically unsound, but perhaps his new position of power and his growing wealth blinded him. By now he held two and three-quarters shares in the company, and within the next six years he would increase this to three and a quarter shares—more than any of the other eleven investors. He was thus earning money as an actor, a manager, and a company sharer, to which he added income from his investment in the theatre building.

The Duke's Company had occupied the little converted tennis court in Lincoln's Inn Fields during the 1660's, but now they contracted for an elegant new playhouse in Dorset Garden. Betterton's contribution to the planning of the building is not known, but we have some details of his curious financial investment in it. Using half of his shares in the company as collateral, Betterton put £225 toward the building of the new house; £102 10s. he paid in cash, and the remaining £122 10s. he put on a promissory note. This remainder was to come from his share in the rent of the new theatre after it was built and from his share of several debts owed the company. The scheme for his investment was planned to yield him 25 percent interest, though it came to 15½ percent in the final analysis, partly because the sharers made a gross error in estimating the cost of the new theatre. They anticipated a total cost of £3000 and raised that amount; the final cost was three times that, and one wonders how they could have been so far off. But what is most baffling is the vicious circle Betterton and his fellow sharers set up in connection with their own and the company's finances. Betterton, for example, as a company sharer, paid rent on the theatre to Betterton the building sharer, who had borrowed money against his company shares to invest in his building shares.

Meanwhile, without reducing his performing schedule, Betterton turned his hand to playwriting—or, more properly, play adapting, again following in the steps of his deceased master. His first effort was upon Webster's *Appius and Virginia*, altered to *The Roman Virgin*; it was performed on 12 May 1669 with Betterton as *Virginius* but not published until 10 years later. After this, or possibly before it, he wrote *The Amorous Widow*, partly based on Molière's *Georges Dandin* and perhaps done with the help of Aphra Behn; when it was first produced, probably during 1668–69, he acted Lovemore, but again he was negligent about publishing, and it did not appear in print until 1706. Hard upon this came *The Woman Made a Justice*, produced on 19 February 1670 but never printed; whether or not it, too, was an adaptation is not known. Of the three, *The Amorous Widow* was the most successful, and it held the stage deep into the following century.

Why Betterton did not care to publish his works when they were performed is a mystery. It became a joke among his contemporaries, and when the 1676 *A Session of Poets* came out, one section dealt specifically with the actor's plays:

Apollo quite tir'd with their tedious harangue,
Finds at last Tom Betterton's face in the gang,
And since poets without the kind players may hang,
By his own sacred light he solemnly swore,
That in search of a laureate he'd look out no more.
A general murmur ran quite through the hall,
To think that the bays to an actor should fall;
But Apollo, to quiet and pacify all,
E'en told 'em, to put his desert to the test,
That he had made plays as well as the best,
And was the great'st wonder the age ever bore,
For of all the play scribblers that e'er writ before

His wit had most worth and most modesty in't,
For he had writ plays, yet ne'er came in print.

Because he failed to publish his plays with clear ascriptions of authorship, some of his pieces were attributed to Mrs Behn, and since all her plays during this period were done by the Duke's Company, perhaps she did have a hand in some of Betterton's work.

Sometime in 1671, perhaps during the summer but certainly before the new Dorset Garden Theatre opened in November, Betterton went again to France at the request of the King; with him went Joe Haines, the King's Company comedian. His mission was to investigate French opera productions, and at the elaborately equipped but acoustically poor *Salle des Machines* he saw the Lully-Molière comedy-ballet *Psyché*. It is likely that Betterton's experience contributed to such English productions of the 1670's as *The Empress of Morocco*, the Shadwell version of *The Tempest*, the court masque *Calisto*, and Shadwell's *Psyche*, for he was frequently complimented for his expertise in the staging of spectacles.

The new theatre in Dorset Garden opened on 9 November 1671 with Dryden's *Feigned Innocence; or, Sir Martin Marall*, but the cast was not listed and Betterton's participation is not known; he seems not to have played in this popular work when it first came out and perhaps did not act at the theatre's opening. His first certain role there was the title part in *Charles VIII* in late November. Thomas and Mary Betterton moved, rent free, into one of the two apartments overhanging the theatre's porch, facing the Thames. According to testimony he presented in 1691 "his vigilancy and great care" preserved the playhouse through the years and several times kept it from burning down; he also said that he spent a great deal from his own pocket to improve the building.

During the next few years Betterton acted such roles as Bevil in *Epsom Wells* (2 December 1672) and Grimalhaz in *The Empress of Morocco* (3 July 1673, but it had been done earlier at court) in addition to his old parts. In December 1674 and January and February 1675 he and his wife were called upon to help train the performers for the last of the great court masques, *Calisto*. While Mary instructed the young princesses Mary and Anne, Thomas taught the male performers, many of whom were courtly amateurs, and, according to Curll, Thomas also ended by serving as prompter. The elaborate spectacle was done on 15, 16, and 22 February 1675. At almost the same time Betterton was engaged in preparations for the Dorset Garden opening of Shadwell's semi-opera *Psyche*. It was given on 27 February 1675, and in the printed edition the author said, "In those things that concern the Ornament or Decoration of the Play, the great industry and care of Mr. Betterton ought to be remember'd, at whose desire I wrote upon this Subject."

On 12 June 1675 Betterton played the leading role in another Shadwell work, *The Libertine* ("Mr Betterton Crown'd the Play," said Downes); at the end of September 1675 he acted his first part in an Otway play, the title role in *Alcibiades*; he was Dorimant in *The Man of Mode* on 11 March 1676 ("all the world was charm'd with Dorimant," wrote Dennis later); he was Philip II in Otway's *Don Carlos* on 8 June 1676 and Titus in his *Titus and Vespasian* in December 1676; and he played Antony in Sedley's *Antony and Cleopatra* on 12 February 1677, Belville in *The Rover* on 22 March, and Orestes in Charles Davenant's operatic *Circe* on 12 May. In September 1677 *The Counterfeit Bridegroom* was done; it appeared shortly thereafter with no ascription of authorship and has been attributed to both Betterton and Aphra Behn. Shortly after this, in January 1678, Betterton played the title role in Shadwell's version of *Timon of Athens*;

in June he was Welford in *Squire Oldsapp*; in September he had the title part in Lee and Dryden's *Oedipus*; in April 1679 he was Troilus in Dryden's *Troilus and Cressida*; he took the title role in *Caius Marius* in October 1679, Castalio in *The Orphan* in late February 1680, Torrismond in *The Spanish Friar* on 1 November 1680, the lead in Tate's version of *King Lear* in March 1681, and Jaffeir in *Venice Preserved* on 9 February 1682 — not to mention many less familiar roles he is known to have acted, plus the many that the incomplete records may not have revealed. In addition, he was a popular speaker of prologues and epilogues, having delivered them for at least nine plays by 1682 (by 1700 he spoke for 20 more, and between then and 1707 he similarly served still another 15). Cibber said that in delivering prologues Betterton "had a natural Gravity that gave Strength to good Sense, a temper'd Spirit that gave Life to Wit, and a dry Reserve in his Smile that threw Ridicule into its brightest Colours." In addition to his prologue speaking, the actor may have turned out another play before 1682: *The Revenge* (also called *The Vintner Tricked*), done in late June 1680, printed that year anonymously, and again sometimes attributed to Aphra Behn.

Despite his heavy acting, writing, and managing schedule, Betterton found time to be a good counsellor and friend of young playwrights, and most especially of the troubled and talented Thomas Otway. *A Satyr upon the Poets* (1680's) commented that

> He had of's many wants much earlier
>   dy'd
> Had not kind Betterton supply'd
> And took for pawn the embryo of a play,
> Till he could pay himself the next Third
>   Day.

Indeed, Otway was foolish with his finances and often in need of money. When *Venice Preserved* was performed he was so

poor that the Duchess of Portsmouth presented him with 20 guineas, and his constant friend Betterton (with others) gave
him another 20 and urged him to retire to
Hampshire where he could live cheaply
and work on a new play. Otway pretended
to take the advice, but he was noticed a
few months later on the outskirts of London in poor garb. Aphra Behn loaned him
£5, read the four finished acts of his new
tragedy based on the Iphigenia legend, and
advised him to show it to Betterton. He
failed to do so, and when Betterton heard
of it and sought him out, the playwright
was dead and his play had been stolen by
an unknown thief.

Keeping the body and soul of a poet like
Otway together was perhaps less difficult
though more rewarding than trying to save

Harvard Theatre Collection

THOMAS BETTERTON, as Hamlet
artist unknown

the body and soul of the Duke's Company.
Curll said later that Betterton "employed
himself in visiting, and overlooking their
Actions as a Guardian, or Father," but
though the players and the playing may
have prospered under his tutelage, his
troupe's finances had deteriorated. London
could no longer support two companies,
and though the rival King's players were in
more serious trouble than the Duke's, Betterton probably realized that unless a merger could be arranged, both might collapse.
He might have considered biding his time
until the rival company foundered, hoping
to hold the Duke's players together until
then, but time was probably against him,
and as early as 14 October 1681 he, Charles
Davenant, and William Smith took the ini-
tiative—and a rather underhanded move it
was, too.

They signed an agreement with Charles
Hart and Edward Kynaston, two pillars of
the King's Company, under which they
would desert their troupe and play for 5s.
daily at Dorset Garden. In the case of Kynaston, the 5s. fee would jump to a 10s.
daily salary as soon as he could free himself
from the King's players. On top of this,
Hart and Kynaston agreed to make over
their King's Company stock to the Duke's
Company and promote a union of the rival
troupes. This was simple sabotage. If nothing finally came of it, it was only because
the King's Company manager, Charles Killigrew, also recognized the necessity of a
union and approached the Duke's players
with such a proposal. An agreement to
unite was signed on 4 May 1682, and during
the ensuing months the details were worked
out, with Betterton, Smith, and Davenant
negotiating for their group and Killigrew
(in virtual disregard of his players) acting
for the King's Company. Since the merger
was in actuality the absorption of the King's
troupe by the Duke's, Betterton and his
colleagues became the leaders of the new
United Company.

Betterton and Smith were made co-managers, though the titular heads were members of the Davenant and Killigrew families, few of whom had much interest in theatrical affairs beyond making money. The managers, in addition to coping with the Davenants and Killigrews, had to face the absurdity of paying rent on two playhouses when the United Company could barely afford to operate one. Drury Lane became the troupe's headquarters, but since the actors had to pay for Dorset Garden anyway, they occasionally did their spectacle productions there. Under these circumstances, it is a wonder that the United Company survived as long as it did.

When the new group was formed in 1682 Betterton was a vigorous 47; he still had 28 more productive years ahead of him in the theatre, so despite his age he should perhaps be pictured as being in his prime in the 1680's. He was unrivalled now (Hart and Mohun of the King's Company had retired at the union) and his reputation as an actor was enormous. From his contemporaries came nothing but praise for the great care he took in preparing his roles. He was noted for the "exact" and "just" quality of his work on stage, for his rigid self-discipline, and for his willing response to criticism or direction. Gildon later quoted Betterton as saying, "[I]t has always been mine and Mrs. *Barry*'s Practice to consult e'en the most indifferent Poet in any Part we have thought fit to accept of." And Davies told a story of Betterton at a rehearsal of *The Rival Queens*, searching his memory for a reading of a particular line as Charles Hart had delivered it; at last "one of the lowest of the company repeated the line exactly in Hart's key. Betterton thanked him heartily, and put a piece of money in his hand as a reward for so acceptable a service."

A whole new world of parts opened for Betterton when the companies merged, for many plays that had been the exclusive property of the King's troupe were now available to him. During the life of the United Company, from 1682 to 1695, he was able to add to his repertory such characters as Brutus in *Julius Caesar*, Othello, Arbaces in *A King and No King*, Manly in *The Plain Dealer*, the title role in *The Duke of Guise*, Doctor Faustus, Jupiter in *Amphitryon*, the title role in *King Arthur*, Alexander in *The Rival Queens*, Heartwell in *The Old Bachelor*, Maskwell in *The Double Dealer*, and probably Antony in *All for Love*.

But much of Betterton's professional time between 1682 and 1695 was spent handling the affairs of the United Company. In August 1683 at the King's request he made another journey to France to "fetch ye design" for an opera and bring back a company of dancers for the entertainment of the court. A letter dated 22 September 1683 from Lord Preston in Paris to the Duke of York in London tells part of the story:

I should not have presumed to give your Highness the trouble of this if something of charity had not induced me to it. I do it at the instance of a poor servant of his Majesty's, who some time since was obliged by a misfortune to leave England. It is Mr Grahme [probably Louis Grabu, the musician], sir, whom perhaps your Highness may remember. Mr Betterton coming hither some weeks since by his Majesty's command, to endeavour to carry over the Opera, and finding that impracticable, did treat with Monsr Grahme to go over with him to endeavour to represent something at least like an Opera in England for his Majesty's diversion. He hath also assured him of a pension from the House [probably Drury Lane], and finds him very willing and ready to go over. He only desireth his Majesty's protection when he is there, and what encouragement his Majesty shall be pleased to give him if he finds that he deserves it.

The situation in Paris was unfavorable for Betterton's plans; the active troupes there were already committed and would not risk a trip to England; all Betterton came back with, apparently, was Grabu, who would have done better to stay in France.

Having made a commitment to the Frenchman, Betterton drew him into a collaboration with Dryden in an opera, *Albion and Albanius*, for which Betterton arranged the scenes and machines. It opened on 3 June 1685 at Dorset Garden and was a disaster. Roger North called it the first full opera made and prepared for the stage in England "but of a French genius." In addition to the death of Grabu's hoped-for patron Charles II in the previous February, the opera opened, as Downes noted, "on a very Unlucky Day, being the Day the Duke of Monmouth, Landed in the West: The Nation being in a great Consternation, it was perform'd but Six times, which not Answering half the Charge they were at, Involv'd the Company very much in Debt." It might have fared no better under ideal circumstances, for, as Moore puts it, Grabu's "talent for setting English verse to music left almost everything to be desired." One contemporary poem blasted practically everyone connected with the production, especially poor Louis Grabu but also Betterton:

Betterton, Betterton, *thy decorations,*
　And the machines were well written
　　we knew;
But all the words were such stuff, we
　want patience,
And little better is Monsieur Grabu.

Damme, says Underhill, [*the actor*], *I'm*
　out of two hundred,
Hoping that Rainbows and Peacocks
　would do;
Who thought infallible Tom *could have*
　blunder'd,
A plague upon him and Monsieur
　Grabu.

The poem goes on in this vein, drubbing Grabu at the ends of the verses. The peacock referred to was an elaborate machine that moved forward on the stage and opened its tail to fill the entire proscenium opening. It is sometimes difficult to reconcile the studious Betterton who was so splendid a Hamlet with the Betterton who catered to the gaudiest tastes in town.

Robert North, looking back from the vantage point of about 1726 at Betterton's operatic productions of earlier years, said:

Mr Betterton who was the chief ingineer of the stage, contrived a sort of plays, which were called Opcras but had bin more properly styled Semioperas, for they consisted of half Musick, and half Drama. . . . Mr Betterton whose talent was speaking and not singing) was pleased to say, that 2 good dishes were better than one, which is a fond mistake, for few care to see 2 at a time of equall choice. . . . His better reason had bin the true one, that the towne had not will or pallate enough to know and relish what's good, or that they had not voices to performe it.

This did not prevent Betterton from producing, during his years with the United Company, his own and Dryden's *The Prophetess* (altered from Massinger and Fletcher, published in 1690), *Amphitryon*, a revival of *Circe, King Arthur,* and *The Fairy Queen*—all with music by that other Restoration genius, Henry Purcell.

Hard upon the calamitous production of *Albion and Albanius* Betterton went again to France. A pass was issued to him on 25 July 1685, but what his mission was this time—other than fleeing from the jibes of the moment—is not known.

Meanwhile, the Davenants, chiefly Alexander and Charles, the clever ones, had been manipulating the shares in the company. Alexander began secret negotiations with lawyer Christopher Rich who, within a few years, was to gain virtually complete control of the United Company. On 5 November 1687, apparently as part of this move, Betterton and Smith were deposed as managers by Alexander Davenant; in their place Alexander put another Davenant, Thomas, whose knowledge of theatrical affairs seems to have been minimal. In the orders from the Lord Chamberlain to the company over the next few years Betterton was still mentioned, but after 1690 his name was dropped. It is noteworthy that from 1690 to 1694 the actor performed more frequently and was able to spend more time helping other playwrights with their scripts. In 1689, for instance, he helped Dryden cut *Don Sebastian* (for which Dryden thanked him in his preface), and in 1690 Settle also thanked him for "several extraordinary Hints to the heightening of my best Characters" in *Distressed Innocence*.

Little is known of the Bettertons' home life during these (or indeed any other) years, though we may gain a hint from a letter which Sir George Etherege wrote to Betterton on 16/26 May 1687 from his isolated diplomatic post at Ratisbon:

A poor man, who has lost the enjoyment of his friends and the pleasures of London, ought to have all the means he can to divert his chagrin and pass away the time as easy as is possible; in order to [do] this I am often forced to trouble my acquaintance in England, and I do not doubt you will forgive me making bold with you among the rest. I have three in my family who now and then give me a litle music; they play very well and at sight, and we have all the operas, and I have a correspondent at Paris, who sends me what is new there. If you could do me the favour to procure me some of the best compositions with the several parts, and let them be given to Dr. Wynne at my Lord Middleton's office, he will take care to send them to me. I shall esteem myself much obliged to you for this courtesy, and your kindness will be the greater if now and then you give me an account of the stage, and of other matters which (you shall judge) I will be glad to hear of.

Betterton probably responded to these requests, and we would be most fortunate if his letters could be discovered. That Etherege should have asked these favors reflects pleasantly on Betterton and on his musical knowledge. Presumably Mary and Thomas had a circle of cultured friends and were convivial hosts at musical evenings.

Vulgar satirists of the day left few public figures alone, and perhaps it was simply because he was the foremost actor of his time that Betterton was attacked in the anonymous *Satyr on the Players* (c. 1684):

> For who can hold to see the Foppish
>   Town
> Admire so bad a Wretch as Betterton?
> Is't for his Legs, his Shoulders, or his face
> His formal Stiffness, or his awkward
>   grace
> A Shop for him had been the fittest place
> But Brawn Tom the Playhouse needs
>   must chuse
> The villains Refuge, and Whores Rendezvouse:
> When being Chief, each playing Drab to
>   swive,
> He takes it as his cheif Prerogative.

What grains of truth there may have been in any of this is anyone's guess, but there may have been a few.

Over the years Betterton must have built up a reasonable fortune, but in 1692 he lost it. He and Sir Francis Watson had invested in a commercial venture in the East Indies, the actor putting up £2000 "which was his all." The ship with their cargo worth £120,000 was captured by the French between Ireland and England. Watson and Betterton were ruined, yet the Bettertons took into their home Watson's daughter, Elizabeth, and the actor "educated [her] with all the Care and Tenderness of a Parent, til she thought fit to marry herself to Mr. *Bowman* the Player." Elizabeth Watson, like Anne Bracegirdle before her, was adopted by the Bettertons and introduced to the stage.

After this disaster, Betterton had good reason to consider afresh his position in the United Company and his future there. He had been divested of his managerial position, and though he was the troupe's leading actor he no longer had control over the company's destiny nor a secure financial situation for himself. Christopher Rich, as he gained control, introduced changes that put Betterton's acting career in jeopardy; in an effort to put the company on a sounder financial footing, he cut salaries and redistributed some of the roles. His notion—economically sound—was to give roles which had belonged to some of the old and highly paid actors to younger members of the troupe who would gladly act for less. Faced with the curtailment of their power, their salaries, and their roles, the older actors in the troupe quite naturally rebelled. Near the end of 1694 Betterton drew up a list of complaints against Rich and his silent partner Sir Thomas Skipwith. A sizeable group of players, mostly the older ones but some of the promising younger ones, signed the complaint and started, with Betterton, a move to secede and form their own company. Faced with the loss of most of his best actors, Rich presented a reply to the complaints which was cleverly off the point on almost every count. The confrontation was hopeless from the start, for neither side was interested in listening to the other, and a split was inevitable.

Betterton, Elizabeth Barry, and Anne Bracegirdle, the leaders of the rebels, negotiated with King William himself and were successful in getting a license to lease and reconvert the old Lincoln's Inn Fields tennis court into a playhouse (Rich held both royal patents from the old King's and Duke's companies, so all that was available to the seceders was a license). Betterton, though now 60, was still as energetic as ever, and he maneuvered his followers through the secession and into their new playhouse by 30 April 1695, less than six months after the legal fight with Rich began. On that date the brilliant new-old company presented for the first time Congreve's *Love for Love*, with great success.

The first few years of the new company may have been the most harried in Betterton's life, but he was in charge now, and they may also have been his happiest. Certainly the phenomenal success of *Love for Love* must have overjoyed him, yet it was clouded over by a managerial mistake. The role of Valentine had apparently been written by Congreve for Joseph Williams (Betterton had evidently decided not to act but only to speak the prologue), but Williams and Susanna Verbruggen deserted to Drury Lane when Betterton refused to include them as sharers in the company. As a result, he lost two fine performers and had to cast himself as Valentine, a role for which he was certainly too old. The following year, in July 1696 he made what turned out to be another error, though it must have seemed like a good idea at the time; he negotiated with the French dancer Sorin to join the company, and this was the beginning of a series of disastrously expensive contracts which he made with foreign performers who, though they proved extremely popular, cost the company far more than it could afford.

On the other hand, as an actor Betterton shone as brightly as ever and dazzled the town even when he attempted roles unsuited to his age; to all parts he brought a maturity of interpretation that apparently made them memorable. He played Osmyn in *The Mourning Bride* on 20 February 1697, for instance, and Sir John Brute in *The Provoked Wife* in the middle of the following April. On 11 July 1698 *The Maid's Tragedy* was performed, and Betterton very likely acted Melantius, a role he played with such dignity that later when Robert Wilks played opposite him as the young prince Wilks was virtually struck dumb and could hardly get his words out. On 9 January 1700 Betterton played Falstaff in his own version of *Henry IV* (published that year), about which Villiers Bathurst said on 28 January, "the criticks allow that Mr Betterton has hit the humour of Falstaff better than any that have aimed at it before." The next month he acted Angelo in Gildon's version of *Measure for Measure*, and on 5 March he played Fainall (the right part for him) in *The Way of the World.*

He seems to have been as correct in his acting as he was wrong in his management of the company during these years, and he may well have wished for the help of his old fellow-manager William Smith. But Smith had died in 1696, leaving £100 to his "friend and oldest acquaintance" Betterton plus £6 more for mourning, and the request that Thomas oversee the education of his son. Smith had probably been the more sensible of the pair when it came to finances and the touchy problems of human relations in the theatre, for he was, as his delightful will demonstrates, a most amiable man. Betterton, on the other hand, was stolid and sometimes tyrannical. In 1697–98 the volatile actor John Verbruggen complained that the company was being mismanaged and that Betterton was showing favoritism—which he apparently was—to himself, Mrs Barry, and Mrs Bracegirdle.

The playwright Crauford complained in his preface to *Courtship à la Mode* in 1700 of the reception his play received when he submitted it to the Lincoln's Inn Fields company:

Mr Betterton did me all the justice I could indeed reasonably hope for. But that example he gave was not, it seems, to be followed by the whole company, since 'tis known that Mr Bowman . . . kept the first character of my play six weeks and then could hardly read six lines on't. How far that way of management makes of late for the interest and honor of that house, is easy to be judged. Some who valued their reputations more were indeed rarely or never absent. To these I gave my thinks; but finding that six or seven people could not perform what was designed for fifteen, I was obliged to remove it after so many sham rehearsals, and in two days it got footing upon the other stage.

Even if only half true, the comment suggests an appalling lack of discipline in the troupe, for which Betterton was responsible.

He seems to have been most obliging personally, for Crauford paid him thanks, as had others before him (Dryden, Settle, Mrs Manley, Boyer), yet he did not instill a sense of obligation in his players. Barton Booth later told Colley Cibber "How impracticable [Betterton] found it to keep their Body to that Common Order which was necessary for their Support; of their relying too much upon their intrinsick Merit."

Some of the problem stemmed from the aging actors, a few of whom became negligent, or diligent only for themselves and their benefits, Booth noted, and the influx of highly paid foreign novelties like L'Abbé, Mlle Subligny, and Balon did not help company morale. Gould's *The Play-House, A Satyr* (c. 1700) made Betterton sound wily indeed:

> *Here one who lately, as an Author notes,*
> *Hawk'd thro' the Town, and cry'd Ga-*
>   *zettes and Votes,*
> *Is grown a Man of such Accomplish'd*
>   *Parts,*
> *He thinks all Praise beneath his just*
>   *Deserts:*
> *Rich as a Jew, yet tho' so wealthy known,*
> *He rasps the Under-Actors to the Bone.*
> *Not Lewis more Tyrannically Rules,*
> *Than He among this Herd of Knaves and*
>   *Fools.*
> *Among his other Vertues, ne'er was Elf*
> *So very much Enamor'd of Himself;*
> *But let Him if he pleases think the best*
> *Upon that Head; and we'll Supply the*
>   *rest.*
> *What if some Scribblers to his Sense*
>   *submit?*
> *He is not therefore only Judge of Wit:*
> *Approving such, betrays a Vitious Tast:*
> *For few can tell what will for ever last,*
> *If all cou'd Judge of Wit that think they*
>   *can,*
> *The Vilest Ass wou'd be the Wittiest*
>   *Man.*
> *In Company, with either Youth or Age,*
> *H'has al the Gum and Stiffness of the*
>   *Stage:*

Dotard! and thinks his haughty Move-
    ments there,
A Rule for his Behaviour ev'ry where.
To this we'll add his Lucre, Lust and
    Pride,
And Knav'ry, which in vain He strives
    to hide,
For thro' the thin Disguise the Canker'd
    Heart is spy'd.
'Tis true, his Action *Merits just Ap-*
    plause;
But lies the Fame most in th' Effect *or*
    Cause?
If from good Instruments fine Musick
    springs,
The Credit's chiefly his that tun'd the
    Strings:
Thus, tho' they Speak, they speak An-
    other's Thought;
As Monkey's *Grin, and Parrots learn by*
    Rote.

There must have been some truth in Gould's accusations (even granting that he was a crank), for Tom Brown in his *Amusements* (c. 1695) had roasted Betterton and Mrs Barry on similar grounds:

Now for that majestical man and woman there; stand off, there is no coming within a hundred yards of their high mightiness. They have revolted, like the Dutch, from their once lords and masters, and are now set up for sovereigns themselves. See what a deference is paid 'em by the rest of the cringing fraternity, from fifty down to ten shillings a-week; you must needs have a more than ordinary opinion of their abilities. . . . His gravity will not permit him to give you audience till the stateliness of his countenance is rightly adjusted, and all his high-swelling words are got in readiness.

These satirical jabs at Betterton's money, methods, and manner were supported shortly after the turn of the century by specific examples.

About the summer of 1703 one of the French performers Betterton had lured to England, the dancer L'Abbé, complained to the Lord Chamberlain that he had "every reason in the world to be unhappy at Mr. Betterton's management in my case. I humbly ask you to be persuaded that I left Mr. Betterton not out of caprice or ill feeling but as a matter of honor." Precisely what Betterton had done is not known. We have details, however, for a second case, concerning Betterton's cavalier treatment of actor Thomas Doggett. On 8 November 1703 Doggett explained to the Lord Chamberlain that his contract with Betterton provided him with the option of not acting during the summers. On 24 May he had received word from Betterton and Mrs Barry that the company wanted him to perform with them at Oxford, and he agreed to come for £20 or a share. When he arrived at Oxford, Betterton proposed less lucrative terms, and, when Doggett refused, the manager gave his parts to others. About 6 November 1703 Doggett wrote Betterton, "The Company has bin so very free to tell me they thought theire bargin with me very hard. I must confess theire stopping part of my mony and the trouble they have given me to gett [a] part is sufficient proof they spoke theire opinion." This punishment for having refused at Oxford to alter his terms forced Doggett to appeal for a discharge.

After the turn of the century Betterton continued playing with vigor, sometimes in leading roles, but sometimes in interesting small ones—all, presumably, of his own choice. He played the title role in *Tamerlane*, Bassanio in *The Jew of Venice*, Horatio in *The Fair Penitent*, and Falstaff in *The Merry Wives of Windsor*, along with numerous others less familiar. And when *A Comparison of the Two Stages* came out in 1702, damning practically everyone, Betterton and his leading lady were praised instead. Critick, one of the characters, rhapsodizes, "Who knows not the effect of *Batterton*'s fine Action? Who is not charm'd with Mrs. *Barry?* What Beauty do they not give every thing they represent? . . . how many an indifferent Play has had good success when these Persons have been concern'd in it." Ramble soon agrees: "Well, of all the Men and Women upon Earth, commend me to the immortal Pair, *Batt.* and *Barry.*" Sullen then joins the chorus: "They are indeed excellent, and what is stranger, never to be worn out." A sad note had to be struck somewhere, and Critick says, "I doubt you're mistaken there, for *Batt.* wears away apace; his Activity is at an end, and his Memory begins to die." Betterton may well have been declining physically by this time, and perhaps that could account for the seemingly contradictory reports of his good acting, bad management, obliging behavior, tyrannical rule, and lax discipline. He was, after all, only a human being, and he was getting old.

He was not old or rich enough to quit, however. He still kept to a full acting schedule, shepherded his troupe (whether well or ill), guided the mounting of plays, and dabbled in play doctoring. In 1703 an edition of *Hamlet* was printed which may have been his version, and since he had devoted part of his career to playwriting, *A Comparison Between the Two Stages* also contained some comments on Betterton the author:

CRIT. Betterton is a very honest Fellow, and has all along been bred on the Stage; he's not only a good Actor, but in the number of wretched Poets now a Days, he may pass, at least for a good Judge of Poetry; and I shou'd not ha' scrupled him my particular Favour, if he had not play'd the Fool, and writ himself.

RAMB. How? has *B.* writ any thing?

CRIT. He has not only frequently been dabbling among other Men's Works, but he has given us something of his own; that is, he own's 'em to the Stage by all manner of ways, but indeed, they are but alterations of other Men's Plays new dipt, and christen'd with other Names.

RAMB. Pray name one.

CRIT. The *Vintner trick'd*: Or, a *Match in Newgate*. I take it to be Marston's *Dutch Curtezan* by the Title; another is, *The Amo-*

rous Widow: or, *The wanton Wife*, lately brought on, and often acted.

SULL. I never saw either of 'em in Print.

CRI. No, he has more Wit than to print 'em; but the Stage has been dishonoured with 'em many a time.

With the 1703 quarto of *Hamlet*—if, indeed, Betterton had anything to do with it—the actor's play-adapting may have ended; no other works attributed to him came out until after his death. In 1712 *Miscellaneous Poems and Translations by Several Hands* was published, containing "Chaucer's *Characters, or the Introduction to the* Canterbury *Tales*," freely paraphrased in verse by Betterton; his contribution included his version of the Reeve's Tale, titled *"The Miller of* Trompington." These poems were reprinted in *The Canterbury Tales of Chaucer Moderniz'd* (1741), which also contained similar efforts by Dryden and Pope, among others. *The Bond-Man* was published anonymously in 1719 and has sometimes been listed as Betterton's work, but this is questionable. In 1720 *The Sequel of Henry the Fourth* came out, the title page assuring us that the play was "Alter'd from Shakespear by the late Mr. Betterton," but Hazleton Spencer in *Shakespeare Improved* doubted that the actor had anything to do with it. A 1722 adaptation of Massinger's *The Roman Actor* has likewise been attributed to Betterton and doubted. *A History of the English Stage* (1741), according to the *Cambridge Bibliography of English Literature*, was a compilation by Oldys and Curll, based on Betterton's papers. But it is likely that by 1703 Betterton had done most of his writing, and the early years of the eighteenth century show him gradually divesting himself of his secondary tasks.

At the end of 1704 Sir John Vanbrugh proposed to Betterton that the Lincoln's Inn Fields troupe move into the new Queen's Theatre in the Haymarket upon its opening the following spring. Betterton, perhaps recognizing this as the proper time to relinquish his managerial duties, transferred his license to Vanbrugh. The actor's critics were quick to pounce on this new opportunity to ridicule Betterton and his two leading ladies, Mrs Barry and Mrs Bracegirdle, who with him had shared the spoils at Lincoln's Inn Fields. The dedication to *The Lunatick* (1705), signed by "Franck Telltroth," reminded the "three Ruling B—s" that now

There will be no more Clandestine Sharing betwixt You without the rest; no more private Accounts, and Double Books; no more paying Debts half a score times over out of the Publick Stock, yet never paying them in reality at all. There will be no more sinking Three Hundred and fifty Pounds at a time in the Money repaid on a famous Singer's Account, but never accounted for it to the rest of the Sharers; no Stopping all the Pay of the Under Actors on Subscription-Nights, when You were allow'd forty or fifty Pound a Night for the House, besides the Benefit of the Galleries; no more sinking Court-Money into Your own Pockets, and letting the Sallary People and Under Sharers starve without Pay; no more taking Benefit-Days in the best season of the Year, and Dunning the Quality for Guinea-Tickets to help out the Defects of all the other above named Perquisites; no fifty Shillings per Week for scowring Old Lace, nor burning it, and selling the Product for private Advantage; no Twenty Shillings a Day House-Rent; no sharing Profits with the Poetasters; nor Eating and Drinking out the other half before the Performance; no saving Coals at Home, by Working, Eating and Drinking, &c. by the Stock-Fire; nor, in short, any Advantage to be made but by stated Sallaries, or the best Improvement of Natural Gifts, as far as Age, Ugliness and Gout will permit.

Though exaggerated and perhaps written out of jealousy, the attack is too full of specific details to be taken lightly, and complaints of a similar nature during Betterton's Lincoln's Inn Fields years support this final blast at the actor's managerial misbehavior.

Betterton was wise to accept the new opportunity at the Queen's Theatre, and the rest of his stage career was devoted to the two things he did best: acting and teaching. The new theatre opened on 9 April 1705, and despite the building's poor acoustics for straight plays, Betterton acted there through December 1707, playing many of his old roles and adding such new ones as Morose in *The Silent Woman*, Montezuma in *The Indian Emperor*, and Theseus in *Phaedra and Hippolitus*. He was probably being paid about £200 yearly, £50 of which was for his training of the younger players; Mary Betterton, though virtually retired now, served only as an instructor of acting, probably at £80 annually.

In January 1708 the actors moved to Drury Lane, leaving the Queen's to singers. The following year Zachary Baggs, the Drury Lane treasurer, published a report to prove to the public that manager Christopher Rich was not underpaying his actors; he may have distorted the figures to make his point, but even so, the report provides us with some notion of Betterton's financial situation at the end of his career. According to Baggs, Betterton was earning 41*s.* weekly, and his wife, who did not act, 11*s.* This added up to £112 10*s.* annually, plus £76 4*s.* 5*d.* at his yearly benefit. Baggs observed that this did not include gifts the actor may have received, and that gifts plus extra prices at Betterton's benefit must have cleared him £450, so that the player's total income from 12 October 1708 to 4 June 1709 must have been, said Baggs, £638 14*s.* 5*d.* Though this suggests that Betterton was well off at this time, the destitute situation of Mary Betterton after his death indicates that he may well have used up his earnings paying debts that had accumulated over the years since his disastrous financial loss in 1692.

If Baggs was correct about Betterton's income, the actor probably deserved all he received, for during his last years he carried what for a man in his seventies was a very heavy schedule, summing up his career by acting many of the roles which had made him famous. On 7 April 1709 a special benefit for him was given (the one Baggs spoke of), for which Elizabeth Barry and Anne Bracegirdle came out of retirement so that they might act with him once again in *Love for Love*. Congreve wrote a special prologue which Mrs Bracegirdle spoke as the two actresses stood, one on each side of the venerable old man:

> *So we, to former Leagues of Friendship true,*
> *Have bid once more our peaceful Homes Adieu,*
> *To aid old THOMAS, and to pleasure you.*
> . . . .
> *Time was, when this good Man no Help did lack,*
> *And scorn'd that any* She *should hold his Back;*
> *But now, so Age and Frailty have or-dain'd,*
> *By two at once he's forc'd to be sustain'd.*
> . . . .
> *Be true to Merit, and still own his Cause*
> *Find something for him more than bare Applause;*
> *In just Remembrance, of your Pleasures past,*
> *Be Kind, and give him a Discharge at last.*
> . . . .
> *In Peace and Ease, Life's Remnant let him wear,*
> *And hang his consecrated Buskin here.*

The scene onstage during the prologue was strikingly like the description John Downes the prompter had given a year earlier at the end of his *Roscius Anglicanus*: Betterton, "like an old Stately Spreading Oak now stands fixt, Environ'd round with brave Young Growing, Flourishing Plants." Then, "to speak his fame" Downes listed Betterton's most successful parts; had he

noted them all, the list would have numbered at least 120. Then, again anticipating the sentimental benefit of 1709, Downes closed his book with Dryden's lines:

> *He like the setting Sun, still shoots a Glimmery Ray,*
> *Like Antient ROME Majestick in decay.*

The benefit drew a packed house of great splendor, with many patrons pressing to sit on the stage to watch Betterton play Valentine for the last time. It was a moving occasion, even if the old man could hardly do justice to the role now, and everyone must have supposed that this would be the end of Betterton's career. Steele certainly wrote of it in such a tone:

[A]ll have shown a great respect for Mr. Betterton: and the very gaming part of this house have been so touched with a sense of the uncertainty of human affairs (which alter with themselves every moment) that in this gentleman they pitied Mark Anthony of Rome, Hamlet of Denmark, Mithridates of Pontus, Theodosius of Greece, and Henry the Eighth of England. It is well known, he has been in the condition of each of those illustrious personages for several hours together, and behaved himself in those high stations, in all the changes of the scene, with suitable dignity. For these reasons, we intend to repeat this favour to him on a proper occasion, lest he, who can instruct us so well in personating feigned sorrows, should be lost to us by suffering under real ones.

But London was still to see a good bit more of Betterton during the following season. He went back to the Queen's Theatre in the fall of 1709, and his company improved the acoustics with some remodelling. On 15 September he played Othello to open the season. Sir John Perceval wrote to Elizabeth Southwell after seeing it, "I declare that they who cannot be moved at Othello's story so artfully worked up by Shakespeare, and justly played by Betterton, are capable of marrying again before their husbands are cold, of trampling on a lover when dying at their feet, and are fit to converse with tigers only." Five days later Betterton played *Hamlet; The Tatler* recorded Mr Greenhat's reactions to the performance:

[H]ad you been to-night at the play-house, you had seen the force of action in perfection: your admired Mr. Betterton behaved himself so well, that, though now about seventy [*recte*, 74], he acted youth; and by the prevalent power of proper manner, gesture, and voice, appeared through the whole drama a young man of great expectation, vivacity, and enterprise. The soliloquy, where he began the celebrated sentence of, 'to be, or not to be!' the expostulation, where he explains with his mother in her closet; the noble ardour, after seeing his father's ghost; and his generous distress for the death of Ophelia, are each of them circumstances which dwell strongly upon the minds of the audience, and would certainly affect their behaviour on any parallel occasions in their own lives.

Though the bills for this season at the Queen's did not always list full casts, it is probable that Betterton's next appearance was on 3 December 1709 when he played Montezuma in *The Indian Emperor*. On the eighth he acted the title part in *The Old Bachelor*; on the tenth he repeated Montezuma; and on the seventeenth he played Macbeth. When *Macbeth* was repeated on 27 December, the title role, believe it or not, was omitted. On 4 February 1710 Betterton offered playgoers their last opportunity to see his King Lear; on 9 March he was in *The Old Bachelor* again; on 13 March he may have played Montezuma once more at Mrs Barry's benefit (but no cast was listed on the bill); and on 13 April he made his last appearance, playing Melantius in *The Maid's Tragedy*, with Wilks as Amintor and Mrs Barry as Evadne. Cibber later wrote about Betterton's final performance:

The last Part this great Master of his Profession acted was Melantius in the *Maid's Tragedy,* for his own Benefit; when being suddenly seiz'd by the Gout, he submitted, by extraordinary Applications, to have his Foot so far reliev'd that he might be able to walk on the Stage in a Slipper, rather than wholly disappoint his Auditors. He was observ'd that Day to have exerted a more than ordinary Spirit, and met with suitable Applause; but the unhappy Consequence of tampering with his Distemper was, that it flew into his Head, and kill'd him in three Days.

Cibber was a bit melodramatic; Betterton was still alive on 27 April when Wycherley reported to Pope: "All the news I have to send you is that poor Mr Betterton is going to make his Exit from the Stage of this World, the Gout being gotten up into his Head, and (as the Physicians say) will certainly carry him of[f] suddenly." The next day, 28 April 1710, Thomas Betterton died, and on 2 May he was buried at the south end of the East Cloister in Westminster Abbey.

On the day of the funeral Steele set down his thoughts in *The Tatler*:

I was resolved to walk thither; and see the last office done to a man whom I had always very much admired, and from whose action I had received more strong impressions of what is great and noble in human nature, than from the arguments of the most solid philosophers, or the descriptions of the most charming poets I had read. As the rude and untaught multitude are no way wrought upon more effectually, than by seeing public punishments and executions; so men of letters and education feel their humanity most forcibly exercised, when they attend the obsequies of men who had arrived at any perfection in liberal accomplishments. Theatrical action is to be esteemed as such, except it be objected that we cannot call that an art which cannot be attained by art. Voice, stature, motion, and other gifts, must be very bountifully bestowed by nature, or labour and industry will but push the unhappy endeavourer in that way the further off his wishes.

Roscius, Steele noted, said that "The perfection of an actor is only to become what he is doing," and this was Betterton's greatest talent.

Steele had heart-breaking news to tell of Betterton's widow, Mary: "His wife, after a cohabitation of forty years in the strictest amity, has long pined away with a sense of his decay, as well in his person as his little fortune; and, in proportion to that she has herself decayed both in her health and reason." Mary Betterton had lost her reason before the actor's death, and the pair had for some time been poverty-stricken; Betterton's last years must have been tragic indeed, and he was forced by circumstances to keep acting to the very end.

Almost exactly two years after her husband's death, Mary Betterton died, having regained her reason shortly before. A pension granted her by Queen Anne was apparently never paid. Betterton had died intestate – or at least no will has been discovered; it seems probable that the poor man had little to leave. Some "Books, Prints, drawings, etc." which had been his were sold on 24 August 1710 at his house in Russell Street, Covent Garden, and on 20 June 1719 Mary (Mrs Martin) Kelly was granted administration of the estate of her late brother, Thomas Betterton. In the administration, the actor was described as of St Bridget's, alias St Bride's, late of St Paul, Covent Garden.

Much of what was written about Betterton came out after his death and described the actor in his later years, so we can only guess what he must have been like in his prime. Gildon was one of the player's greatest admirers, and in 1709 he visited Betterton at his country house at Reading and recorded what he claimed to be the actor's own comments on his profession. How much Gildon fabricated is impossible to tell, but what he reported Betterton as saying may serve here as a framework for the comments by others on Betterton and his work.

According to Gildon, Betterton thought an actor "should not be too tall, nor too low and dwarfish, but of a moderate Size; neither over-fleshy, which is prodigious, nor over-lean, like a Skeleton. Tho this is a thing so little regarded by our Managers or Audience . . . A Player, therefore, should be of an active, pliant and compacted Body, which may be improv'd by learning to dance, fence and vault." How well Betterton measured up to his own qualifications in his prime cannot be known, but by the 1690's he fell short. Cibber was kind:

The Person of this excellent Actor was suitable to his Voice, more manly than sweet, not exceeding the middle Stature, inclining to the corpulent; of a serious and penetrating Aspect; his Limbs nearer the athletick than the delicate Proportion; yet however form'd, there arose from the harmony of the whole a commanding Mien of Majesty, which the fairer-fac'd or (as *Shakespear* calls 'em) the curled Darlings of his Time ever wanted something to be equal Masters of.

Anthony Aston was as candid as ever, probably accurate, and certainly detailed; Betterton, he said, though a superlative actor,

labour'd under an ill Figure, being clumsily made, having a great Head, a short thick Neck, stoop'd Shoulders, and had fat short Arms, which he rarely lifted higher than his Stomach. – His Left Hand frequently lodg'd in his Breast, between his Coat and Waistcoat, while, with his Right, he prepar'd his Speech. – His Actions were few, but just. – He had little Eyes, and a broad Face, a little Pock-fretten, a corpulent Body, and thick Legs, with large Feet. – He was better to meet, than to follow; for his Aspect was serious, venerable, and majestic; in his later Time a little paralytic. . . . He was incapable of dancing, even in a Country-Dance.

The Kneller portrait of Betterton confirms some of this, and it is likely that the actor, like other great ones before and after, had to make up for physical deficiences in other ways.

Of an actor's use of his body, Betterton said that "*Action* is *Motion*, and Motion is the Support of Nature, which without it would again sink into the sluggish Mass of Chaos. . . . [Words] receive almost their whole Force from a most moving and pathetic Action, in which [an actor's] Eyes, Hands, and Voice join'd in a most lively Expression." He recommended practising in front of a mirror, focusing on fellow actors yet opening up sufficiently to the audience, and avoiding frequent changes of place and posture. The comments of Aston and Cibber confirm the control he exercised over his own movements, yet at times he may have been extravagant; the anonymous *The Female Wits* (1696) pokes fun at Betterton and others by having little William Pinkethman instructed to imitate Betterton and to "Fetch long Strides; walk thus; your Arms strutting, your voice big, and your Eyes terrible."

But though Betterton thought action "superiour to all other Qualities," playgoers, as Pepys regularly revealed, went to hear a play, not just see it. Gildon quoted Betterton quoting "a learned Country-man of ours" on the subject: "The Operation of Speech is strong, not only for the Reason or Wit therein contained, but by its Sound. For in all good Speech there is a sort of Music, with Respect to its Measure, Time and Tune." Betterton also, as one might expect, cited Hamlet's speech to the players and urged actors to develop distinct and articulate voices and "vigorous Pronunciation." To achieve proper climaxes, "the Voice must with the Sentence climb up by several Degrees of the Sentence to the Period." And Betterton advised that in preparing a speech, "you ought first with Care to consider the Nature of the Thing of which you are to speak, and fix a very deep Impression of it in your own Mind, before you can be thoroughly touch'd with it your self, or able by any agreeable Sympathy to convey the same Passion to another."

Cibber noted that "Betterton had a Voice of that kind which gave more Spirit to Terror than to the softer Passions; of more Strength than Melody. The Rage and Jealousy of *Othello* became him better than the Sighs and Tenderness of *Castalio*." Then, forgetting himself, he commented that Betterton was "the most affecting lover within my memory" and that he "had a resistless recommendation from the very tone of his voice, which gave his words such softness, that, as Dryden says, Like flakes of feather'd snow / They melted as they fell." Aston agreed that Betterton was grave ("His Voice was low and grumbling"), and he even thought Betterton sounded too much like a sage philosopher in *Hamlet*. But "he could Tune [his voice] by an artful *Climax,* which enforc'd universal Attention, even from the *Fops* and *Orange-Girls*."

Of characterization, Betterton said, rather traditionally, that "An Actor . . . must vary with his Argument, that is, carry the Person in all his Manners and Qualities with him in every Action and Passion; he must transform himself into every Person he represents, since he is to act all sorts of Actions and Passions." The clue to good characterizations was discrimination, the ability to "choose the Good, and reject the Ill" and "*to know what is fit, and to express it*." Betterton had this ability, and praise came from all sides for his vivid, clearly differentiated characterizations. Cibber said "he could vary his Spirit to the different Characters he acted. Those wild impatient Starts, that fierce and flashing Fire, which he threw into *Hotspur*, never came from the unruffled Temper of his *Brutus*." Rowe, in his introduction to his Shakespeare edition of 1709, said of Betterton's Shakespearean roles, "whatever part . . . he performs, he does it as if it had been written on purpose for him, and that the author had exactly conceived it as he plays it." And *The Laureate* of 1740, calling him "the compleatest Actor we ever could boast of," marvelled at his ability to "throw himself into many and quite opposite and different Shapes, from *Peircy* to *Falstaff*, from *Othello* to *Thersites*, from *Brutus* to *Sir Solomon Single*, &c."

Farquhar, in his *A Discourse upon Comedy* (1702) chose the actor's Alexander in *The Rival Queens* to comment on Betterton's remarkable ability to display what later would be called the dual personality of an actor:

We must suppose that we see the very Alexander . . . Yet the whole audience at the same time knows that this is Mr. Betterton who is strutting upon the stage and tearing his lungs for a livelihood. And that the same person should be Mr. Betterton and Alexander the Great at the same time is somewhat like an impossibility in my mind. Yet you must grand realities of eternity, heaven, and hell, if you hadn't power to raise the old hero from the grave to act his own part.

A story, sometimes told of our present subject and sometimes of Garrick, but probably applicable to both, supports Farquhar's comment. A clergyman once asked the actor how it was that he was so much more successful in his profession than the cleric was in preaching. "I think," replied the actor, "it is because you preach as if all the grand realities of eternity, heaven, and hell, were but fiction; whereas I play as if all I acted was real."

Tony Aston was greatly impressed by Betterton's ability to remain in character (he stayed in costume to the end of the play even if he was not in the concluding scenes), and Chetwood was struck by the actor's careful conservation of his artistic energy for the climactic point in a play. This self-discipline worked, too, in Betterton's handling of an audience. According to Cibber,

Betterton had so just a sense of what was true or false Applause, that I have heard him say, he never thought any kind of it equal to an attentive Silence; that there were many ways

of deceiving an Audience into a loud one; but to keep them husht and quiet was an Applause which only Truth and Merit could arrive at: Of which Art there never was an equal Master to himself.

Cibber used Betterton's Alexander as an example: "tho' *Betterton* never wanted Fire and Force when his Character demanded it; yet, where it was not demanded, he never prostituted his Power to the low Ambition of a false Applause." And, as Cibber noted, the role of Alexander invited extravagance, but Betterton would not let himself be trapped into such easy acting.

In critical comments on specific roles these multiple talents of Betterton become more apparent. In *Julius Caesar,* for example, Cibber noted that

when the *Betterton Brutus* was provok'd in his Dispute with *Cassius*, his Spirit flew only to his Eye; his steady Look alone supply'd that Terror which he disdain'd an Intemperance in his Voice should rise to. Thus, with a settled Dignity of Contempt, like an unheeding Rock he repelled upon himself the Foam of *Cassius*. . . . Not but in some part of the Scene, where he reproaches *Cassius*, his Temper is not under this Suppression, but open into that Warmth which becomes a Man of Virtue.

Of his Othello, Steele in *The Tatler* wrote:

I have hardly a notion that any performer of antiquity could surpass the action of Mr. Betterton in any of the occasions in which he has appeared on our stage. The wonderful agony which he appeared in, when he examined the circumstance of the handkerchief in Othello; the mixture of love that intruded upon his mind upon the innocent answers *Desdemona* makes, betrayed in his gesture such a variety and vicissitude of passions, as would admonish a man to be afraid of his own heart, and perfectly convince him, that it is to stab it, to admit that worst of daggers, jealousy. Whoever reads in his closet this admirable scene, will find that he cannot, except he has as warm an imagination as Shakespeare himself, find any but dry, incoherent, and broken sentences; but a reader that has seen Betterton act it, observes there could not be a word added; that longer speech had been unnatural, nay impossible, in *Othello's* circumstances. The charming passage in the same tragedy, where he tells the manner of winning the affection of his mistress, was urged with so moving and graceful an energy, that while I walked in the cloisters [of Westminster Abbey, at Betterton's funeral], I thought of him with the same concern as if I waited for the remains of a person who had in real life done all that I had seen him represent.

It was in *Hamlet* that Betterton, as Cibber would say, "outdid his own outdoing." The two confrontations with the Ghost seem to have been the scenes that most excited the audiences. Of the first, Cibber rhapsodized:

Betterton was an actor, as *Shakespear* was an Author, both without Competitors! form'd for the mutual Assistance and Illustration of each others Genius! [In Hamlet's encounter with the Ghost] the Passion never rises beyond an almost breathless Astonishment, or an Impatience, limited by filial Reverence . . . This was the Light into which *Betterton* threw this Scene; which open'd with a Pause of mute Amazement! then rising slowly to a solemn, trembling Voice, he made the Ghost equally terrible to the Spectator as to himself! and in the descriptive Part of the natural Emotions which the ghastly Vision gave him, the boldness of his Expostulation was still govern'd by Decency, manly, but not braving; his Voice never rising into that seeming Outrage or wild Defiance of what he naturally rever'd. . . . [T]o keep the Attention more pleasingly awake by a temper'd Spirit than by meer Vehemence of Voice, is of all the masterstrokes of an Actor the most difficult to reach. In this none yet have equall'd *Betterton*.

Having conserved his energy and not "set out at the strength of his speed" (as Betterton counselled Wilks, according to Chetwood), Betterton was able to make the second scene with the Ghost the climactic moment it should be. *The Laureate* (1740) reported how the actor handled it:

I have lately been told by a Gentleman who has frequently seen Mr *Betterton* perform this Part of *Hamlet*, that he has observ'd his Countenance (which was naturally ruddy and sanguin) in this Scene of the fourth Act, where his Father's Ghost appears, thro' the violent and sudden Emotions of Amazement and Horror, turn instantly on the Sight of his Father's Spirit, as pale as his Neckcloath, when every Article of his Body seem'd to be affected with a Tremor inexpressible; so that, had his Father's Ghost actually risen before him; he could not have been seized with more real Agonies; and this was felt so strongly by the Audience, that the Blood seemed to shudder in their Veins likewise, and they in some Measure partook of the Astonishment and Horror, with which they saw this excellent Actor affected. And when *Hamlet* utters this Line, upon the Ghost's leaving the Stage, (in Answer to his Mother's impatient Enquiry into the Occasion of his Disorder, and what he sees) *—See—where he goes—ev'n now— out at the Portal*: The whole Audience hath remain'd in a dead Silence for near a Minute, and then—as if recovering all at once from their Astonishment, have joined as one Man, in a Thunder of universal Applause.

This was the kind of acting—tightly controlled, startlingly real, yet stunningly theatrical—that audiences would not see again until Garrick's advent. Barton Booth, who emulated but could not match Betterton, said, "When I acted the Ghost with Betterton, instead of my awing him, he terrified me. But divinity hung round that man!"

Charles Gildon's *The Life of Mr. Thomas Betterton* (1710) was the earliest attempt at a biography, and though it is sketchy on his life and probably contains more Gildon than Betterton on acting, it has the virtue of being contemporary. Equally thin was the 1749 *An Account of the Life of that Celebrated Tragedian Mr. Thomas Betterton*, published anonymously. *The Life and Times of . . . Thomas Betterton* came out anonymously in 1888, but contained more about Restoration theatre history than about the actor; this was also true of Robert Lowe's *Thomas Betterton* of 1891, though his work has remained the standard reference on the player. As of 1972, no full-dress modern biography has been published.

The Garrick Club has a portrait of Betterton by Kneller or his studio, and two Knellers have been reported at Knole, one of them dated 1708 and showing the actor in his own hair. The National Portrait Gallery has a painting of Betterton from the studio of Kneller dating about 1690–1700. A copy of a Kneller, once attributed to Alexander Pope though possibly the work of Jervas, belongs to the Earl of Mansfield. R. Williams made a mezzotint after one of the Knellers (they are similar), and engravings of it were done by R. B. Parkes, W. Evans, J. Wooding, M. Van der Gucht, E. W. Alais, J. B. Allen, and Geoffrey. A pastel by Greenhill done about 1663, supposedly picturing Betterton as Bajazet (a role he is not known to have played), is in the Bankes collection, Kingston Lacy. Two other portraits of the actor were in the Betterton sale of 1710; one showed him with bayes on his head, and a second was willed by Mrs Betterton to Frances Williamson. The Victoria and Albert Museum has a small portrait of the actor which is a variant of the Kneller. A frontispiece in Rowe's *Shakespeare* of 1709 pictures Hamlet, Gertrude, and the Ghost, and supposedly represents Betterton, Mrs Barry, and possibly Barton Booth. Of all the portraits, the one in the National Portrait Gallery is perhaps the most telling and captures that piercing glance and commanding air that made Thomas Betterton the greatest actor of his time.

Betterton, Mrs Thomas, Mary, née Saunderson *c. 1637–1712, actress.*

Mary Saunderson's birthdate and parentage are somewhat obscure, but since she was a spinster of about 25 when she married in December 1662, she was probably born about 1637. Her origins may have been humble; her widowed mother's Christian name was not given on Mary's marriage allegation, and she had it attested by Enoch Darrack of St Pancras, Soper Lane, a grocer. Of her childhood, nothing is known.

She is said to have acted before her marriage at the Red Bull and reputedly was the first professional actress on the English stage, but this reputation cannot be corroborated. She was certainly one of the earliest, however, and her initial roles would suggest the possibility of some previous acting experience. At some point she joined Sir William Davenant's players, probably in 1660, and she was one of four actresses who boarded at Davenant's lodgings in a wing of the converted tennis court in Lincoln's Inn Fields that Sir William used as a playhouse.

Miss Saunderson's first recorded appearance was as Ianthe (which Pepys used as a pet name for her thereafter) in Davenant's *The Siege of Rhodes* when it was produced in its expanded two-part version by the Duke's Company on 28 and 29 June 1661. On 24 August she played Ophelia to Thomas Betterton's Hamlet, the first of several Shakespearean roles for which she became famous. The first role assigned her as Mrs Betterton, according to the prompter Downes, was Aurelia in *The Cutter of Coleman Street* on 16 December 1661 at Lincoln's Inn Fields. Though the records are woefully incomplete, during the following twelve months she played Juliet (1 March 1662), Cleora in *The Bondman* (2 April), the title role in *The Duchess of Malfi* (30 September), Bellmont in *The Villain* (18 October), and an unidentified role in *The Valiant Cid* (1 December) — before getting married. On 22 October 1662 Pepys recorded in his *Diary* that Benier (his barber?) "who being acquainted with all the players, do tell me that Betterton is not married to Ianthe, as they say; but also that he is a very sober, serious man, and studious and humble."

The sober and serious Thomas Betterton brought Mary Saunderson honestly to the altar in December 1662. Their marriage license described Betterton as a bachelor, about 30, from Westminster, and Mary as from St Giles, Cripplegate, a spinster, about 25. Interestingly, though Mary was certainly at her own disposal at that age, the license stated that the marriage was with the consent of her widowed mother. The license was dated 24 December 1662, and the couple married shortly thereafter in Islington. There is obviously more to the story, and it is odd that gossipy Pepys did not track it down. Perhaps we may never know why Mary chose to assume Betterton's name for a year or why the marriage was delayed or what part in it all the widow Saunderson may have played, but something happened—a false pregnancy is one possibility that comes to mind—and it may well have had a bearing on Mary's later life.

Mrs Betterton continued playing roles of importance during the years that followed: Queen Catherine in the Davenant version of *Henry VIII* (22 December 1663), Lady Macbeth (again, as altered by Davenant; 5 November 1664), and the title role in Betterton's *The Amorous Widow* (1668–69). When the Duke's players moved to their elegant new Dorset Garden Theatre in 1671 she continued as one of the leading actresses in the company. She was apparently well liked by audiences, and most especially by Pepys, though he seldom went beyond saying that she did a part very well (Cleora in *The Bondman*) or that his "Ianthe" had a sweet voice (apparently Catherine in *Henry VIII*). On the other hand, Mrs Betterton is only once recorded as having delivered an epilogue, at Dorset Garden in September 1677 after *The Siege of Babylon*, so though she may have done well in character, her own personality may not have been attractive

enough to warrant giving her such assignments.

She had a flair for teaching, however, and an interest in playing foster mother to young actresses. In December 1674 and January and February 1675 she and her husband trained the courtly performers for the production of the masque *Calisto*, done in March. Mrs Betterton's chief responsibility was teaching Princesses Mary and Anne (later Queen Anne) and Mrs Jennings. Anne was later to remember this kindness in a pension granted Mrs Betterton. In the late 1660's, probably, the childless Bettertons took young Anne Bracegirdle into their home when Anne's father fell on hard times; they apparently treated her as their own child and doubtless helped prepare her for her stage career. In 1692 they repeated this gesture with Elizabeth Watson, daughter of Sir Frederick Watson, who lost his own and Betterton's fortune in a commercial venture in the East Indies; the Bettertons generously adopted Elizabeth, who eventually married the actor John Boman. Mary Betterton's interest in helping others continued long after her own acting career ended, for after the turn of the century her chief function in the theatre was training the younger performers.

In the later 1670's Mrs Betterton played three more roles indicative of her talent. On 11 March 1676 she created Belinda in *The Man of Mode*; in January 1678 she was Evandra in Shadwell's version of *Timon of Athens*; and in April 1679 she was cast as Andromache in Dryden's *Troilus and Cressida*. These parts, like Ophelia and Juliet, suggest her penchant for playing the sweet young girl or good woman; yet at the other extreme stand Lady Macbeth and the Duchess of Malfi, dynamic and tormented females. In between was such a role as Elvira in *The Spanish Friar*, done 1 November 1680, which Dryden may have written with Mrs Betterton in mind. The playwright described Elvira as "of middle stature, dark-coloured hair, the most bewitching leer with her eyes, the most roguish cast! her cheeks are dimpled when she smiles, and her smiles would tempt a hermit." So the actress had a talent for coquette roles, too. As she grew older she moved into such parts as the Queen Mother in *The Massacre at Paris* (7 November 1689) and the Duchess of York in *Richard III* (1690–91).

Though she may have preferred playing good women or witty sophisticates, she was apparently best as Lady Macbeth. Colley Cibber, remembering her as she was in about 1690, made some very revealing comments about her in this role:

Mrs. *Betterton*, tho' far advanc'd in years [she would have been about 53], was so great a Mistress of Nature that even Mrs. *Barry*, who acted the Lady *Macbeth* after her, could not in that Part, with all her superior Strength and melody of Voice, throw out those quick and careless Strokes of Terror from the Disorder of a guilty Mind, which the other gave us with a Facility in her Manner that render'd them at once tremendous and delightful. Time could not impair her Skill, tho' he had brought her Person to decay. She was, to the last, the Admiration of all true Judges of Nature and Lovers of *Shakespear*, in whose Plays she chiefly excell'd, and without a Rival. When she quitted the Stage, several good Actresses were the better for her Instruction.

After the Duke's and King's companies joined in 1682, Mrs Betterton was apparently used less and less, and by December 1694 when Betterton started proceedings that led to his setting up a second company to rival Christopher Rich's at Drury Lane, she apparently stopped acting and assumed a semi-retired position in the troupe. Her last two recorded roles (though she may have played others that the sparse records do not show) were Wishwell in *The Maid's Last Prayer* at the end of February 1693 and Ximena in *Love Triumphant* in mid-January 1694. She signed the list of grievances her husband drew up against Rich,

though she registered no specific complaints herself; when the Drury Lane patentees replied to Betterton's protest, they noted that Mrs Betterton had been receiving £10 weekly for acting, £6 weekly as her share of the rent and 50s. weekly, apparently for training the younger actors. But, they complained, "She not appears in any pts to ye satisfaction of ye audience."

Mary Betterton's position in the United Company during its last years must have been awkward. She was apparently past her prime as an actress, yet she held major roles which some of the younger members of the troupe aspired to. As Betterton's wife she was the first lady of the company—and continued to be so listed even after she gave up acting—so her salary was indeed higher than she probably deserved. After Betterton formed his own company to act at Lincoln's Inn Fields and later at the new Queen's Theatre in the Haymarket, Mrs Betterton remained on the roster, apparently, but was gradually reduced in rank and salary; a Public Record Office document showing "An Establishm^t for ye Company," undated but probably about 1705–1707, shows her at the bottom of the list of women, designated as "Housekeep^r & to teach to act" at a fixed salary of £80 annually—about half what Mrs Bracegirdle and Mrs Barry were paid.

How all this may have affected Mrs Betterton can only be guessed. Davies, writing later in the century, described her as a woman "of a thoughtful and melancholy temper" who was "rather a prudent and constant than a fond and passionate wife," and Cibber noted that she "was a Woman of an unblemish'd and sober life." Her famous husband died on 28 April 1710, apparently intestate and poverty-stricken. On 2 May 1710 the *Tatler* revealed that she had

long pined away with a sense of [Betterton's] decay, as well in his person as his little fortune; and, in proportion to that she has herself decayed both in her health and reason. Her husband's death, added to her age and infirmities, would certainly have determined her life, but that the greatness of her distress has been her relief, by a present deprivation of her senses. This absence of reason is her best defence against age, sorrow, poverty, and sickness.

Queen Anne granted Mary Betterton a pension (though it was apparently not paid her before her death), and the players, in addition to having paid her £1 weekly over the years as a pension, gave her a salary of £25 during the 1710–11 season and a benefit on 4 June 1711 – but in her pitiful state she may have been unaware of these kindnesses. By 10 March 1712 she had regained her reason and she then wrote her will. In it she described herself as of the parish of St Martin-in-the-Fields, a widow, and "weak in body" (she was about 75). Among her bequests were £20 to her sister Mary Head, £5 each to her nephew John Williamson and her niece Mrs Anne Harrison, £5 to her husband's sister Mrs Mary Kelly (though she called Mrs Kelly her niece), and 20s. each for mourning rings to her friends Mrs Bracegirdle, Mrs Barry, Thomas Doggett, Robert Wilks, Mrs Anne Betterton and her niece Flint, to be paid out of the arrears of the pension from the Queen. Her niece Frances Williamson, wife of John, was named executrix and given the bulk of her estate, including her "dear husbands picture."

Soon after this, Mary Betterton died. She was buried on 13 April 1712 in Westminster Abbey, beside the body of her husband. In an age when lampooners castigated nearly every other performer, including her sober husband, she escaped unscathed; but the information we have about her personal life and stage career hint at wounds of a deeper sort. The odd circumstances surrounding her marriage, the adopted children and the interest in teaching, the qualities she brought to Lady Macbeth, her natural introversion in an age of extroverts, the later years of apparent uselessness and decay, the childless marriage, and her tragic madness – all suggest an inner life austere, possibly guilt-ridden, perhaps loveless, and truly pathetic.

Betterton, Thomas William   d. 1834, actor.

Thomas William Betterton was the son and grandson of sextons of St Andrew's Church, Dublin, named Butterton. For obvious professional reasons he changed his name to that of the great Restoration actor. He first came before the public in 1778 when he played in the company managed by Myrton Hamilton in the new Ann Street Theatre in Belfast. He must have been already in the company for several months when, on 21 December 1778, he married an actress of the troupe, for on 9 January 1779, while they were at Newry on the Belfast circuit, their daughter Julia was born. Betterton's bride was the "Widow Palmer," according to W. J. Lawrence. But W. S. Clark records no "Widow Palmer" in the Belfast company in this or any other year. It may be supposed that Lawrence meant Mrs James Parker, widow of the previous manager, who was an actress with the company. Parker had died in 1778.

Lawrence believed that the meaning of Tate Wilkinson's remark that Betterton "had squandered a little fortune at Newry and other towns in Ireland" was that he probably did so "in building the Hill Street theatre" in Newry in 1783. Lawrence does not suggest where the fortune was obtained. But the Bettertons were indeed again at Newry in 1784. They were engaged at Edinburgh in 1785–86 but left in March to join Wilkinson's organization on the York circuit. They were still, or again, at York in 1788–89. Betterton was a favorite there, praised extravagantly by the local press for his easy, manly deportment and good looks. The couple's son Peter, three months old, died in York and was buried at All Saints Pavement on 23 February 1788. (The church register called the father Thomas William Betterton.) In the summer of 1791 Betteron was at Liverpool, and in 1792 both Bettertons were back in Ireland, first at Newry, then at Drogheda.

Mrs Betterton died at some time in 1793, and her widower moved restlessly around among Irish provincial theatres that year: Wexford in March and April, Kilkenny in June, Galway in July and October. He was also at Waterford sometime in 1793, for a 10-year-old "theatric wonder," Miss Betterton with "great Powers of Voice and expression," is spoken of at that place and time in a Folger Library manuscript, and this was no doubt the celebrated Julia.

The Bettertons, father and daughter, had by 1794 crossed over to Watson's management in Hereford. Betterton was playing his line of fops and young rakes with W. W. Dimond and William Keasberry in Bath and Bristol in 1795–96 and 1796–97, more than half sustained by his daughter Julia, who at 15 had already begun to make her reputation.

Julia's growing talents and fame were well managed by her father to bring them and at least one young male Betterton to London in 1797. They were preceded by what several critics ridiculed as a "grand puff preparatory." Betterton wangled £7 10s. per week for his daughter and a like sum for himself from Harris at Covent Garden.

On 12 October Julia was introduced to the town as Elwina in a revival of *Percy* ("not acted these 12 years"). For his first appearance on 20 October Betterton chose Castalio in *The Orphan*. He followed this up on 21 October, with the elegant Belcour in *The West Indian*, and then awaited critical compliment for his efforts as young men in tearful tragedy and sentimental comedy. But the next *Monthly Mirror* delivered judgments to the effect that both father and daughter were too mechanical, and that she, at least, was possessed of an impudent confidence which in an actress of

17 was nothing short of unmaidenly. Julia's later history shows how the judgment was modified by the *Mirror* and other publications as her roles expanded and she matured into one of the leading actresses of early nineteenth-century London. But Betterton's treatment by the *Mirror* was in some ways worse, and the strictures on him were never withdrawn:

This gentleman has . . . all the defects of his daughter; his *tragedy* is without passion, and his *comedy* without humour; the consumptive monotony of his voice is also extremely unpleasant; and his countenance bears no variety of expression.

But as he speaks judiciously, possesses a handsome figure, treads the stage with confidence, and deports himself like a gentleman, we think in *secondary* characters, he is likely to prove useful.

But Betterton's gentility, alas, was a quality feigned for the stage. He had all along treated his daughter with a callousness bordering on brutality. He now seized her salary and denied her necessities. He was probably shrewd enough to stipulate good employment for himself in his daughter's articles as she became more desirable professionally and their careers were closely parallel until after her marriage in 1800. Their joint benefit at the end of the 1798–99 season at Covent Garden is said to have produced for them a clear £267. On this occasion there first appeared in London a "Master Betterton," dancing a hornpipe.

The Bettertons were at the Birmingham theatre in the summers of 1798 and 1800. There on 27 June, Master J. Betterton danced a hornpipe and accompanied the singing of the famous Mrs Mountain on the oboe. (On 10 September 1798, Thomas himself, now a metropolitan actor of dignity, had condescended to dance a "Hornpipe, on request, [but] for the last time on any stage.")

By 1799–1800 Betterton had risen at Covent Garden to £8 10s. per week; but the next year his daughter was making £9 and the year after that £10. He never again equalled her in salary or ability, though his versatility seems to have increased: for his benefit on 10 May 1800 he played Conolly in *The School for Wives* and performed "in vaudeville," doing a variety of characters.

Betterton is supposed by the gossip of the time to have sold his daughter to Samuel Glover for £1000, and probably both dealers saw it as a profitable financial transaction only. As Julia came more under the influence of her husband, Betterton apparently tried to bring forward his son John, but the boy's talent was pale beside that of his sister or even that of his father.

The bill for Betterton's benefit of 28 May 1801 celebrated the aging actor for the first time in the rather incongruous role of Hotspur, and also delivering an "Address to Britons in the Character of a British Tar," the whole "to conclude with a Hornpipe by Mr I[ohn] Betterton." The boy and his father were then living at No 263, High Holborn.

Thomas Dutton's strictures in his *Dramatic Censor* (1800) on Thomas Betterton's persistence in youthful rakes, fops, and heroes failed to deter the actor, and he went on playing these roles as long as he was in the patent theatre.

During the short seasons from April through November at Cross's Royal Circus in 1802, 1803, and 1804 Betterton turned his versatile hand—and feet—to several tasks: acting and dancing old rustic men in pantomime, marching in arena spectacles amid jostling horses on the tanbark, and engaging in stylized mass gladiatorial combats. But he continued to accept acting engagements in the country, where he was still a glamorous figure from London; and even the Manchester *Townsman* of 7 February 1804 spoke of him respectfully while abusing the local manager for not hiring better players, reporting that Betterton was "now performing at Stockport."

Betterton is unknown to fame for some years following 1805, though he was probably busy in provincial companies. The Lord Chamberlain's office granted either him or his son John a license to stage an entertainment at the Lyceum on 29 November 1813. In the summer of 1814 he bobbed up in Gosport.

By 1816 he had followed his uncertain fortunes to America, and he made his debut in New York at the Park Street Theatre on 24 April as Lord Ogleby in *The Clandestine Marriage*—perhaps his stint with the circus had reconciled him to playing comic old men. Reese James records only one performance for him in Philadelphia, 11 April 1818, though doubtless he played oftener there. From October 1818 through 19 April 1819 he was in the company at Halifax, Nova Scotia, and in the following summer was under John Bernard's banner at the Washington Gardens amphitheatre in Boston. By 4 April 1820 at the latest, however, Betterton had retreated from his sally into America and was back at Sadler's Wells—though under the management of an American, John Howard Payne.

Thomas William Betterton died in 1834 and was buried in the ground of St George the Martyr, Queen Square, Bloomsbury. His son John had died in May 1816, after an anemic career mostly as a dancer. His daughter Julia Glover died in 1850 after a substantial career.

(As late as April 1915 the partisans of William Glover, the veteran actor-manager, who was taking a benefit at the Royal Theatre in Glasgow, were claiming for him —quite falsely—that he was a direct descendant of Thomas Betterton, the Restoration actor. Glover's grandmother was Julia Butterton Glover.)

Betterton, William *1644–1661, actor.*

William Betterton was born on 4 September 1644 at Cromish (?), Berkshire, the third son of Matthew Betterton and younger brother of the famous actor Thomas. He was admitted to Merchant Taylors' School in 1656, and when John Rhodes formed a company of players to perform at the Cockpit in Drury Lane in 1659–60, William Betterton was one of the younger actors who played female roles. His only known role was Aminta in *The Maid in the Mill*, which he acted on 29 January 1661 at Salisbury Court as a member of Sir William Davenant's newly formed Duke's Company. According to Downes, he drowned while swimming at Wallingford, Berkshire, not long after this. Curll, writing in 1741, considered his death a "great Loss [to] our *English* Stage," but there is hardly enough evidence to judge William Betterton's talent.

Betti. *See* BITTI.

"Bettie, Mrs." *See* HALL, ELIZABETH.

Bettini, Signora [*fl.* 1744–1745], *dancer.*

On 14 December 1744 Signora Bettini and Signor Leonardi made their first appearance in London dancing a specialty number at Drury Lane. The pair performed frequently together during the season, though Signora Bettini also did solo dances and, for her shared benefit (with five others) on 9 May 1745, she danced a minuet with Baudouin. She did both serious and comic dances. In a Burney collection of clippings at the British Museum is an undated newspaper notice concerning the arrival of a Signora Bettina from Naples who was to dance at the King's Theatre in the Haymarket; it is with another clipping dated 13 November 1741.

Betts, Mr [*fl.* 1748], *actor.*

A Mr Betts played Gonzalo in *The Tempest* at Phillips's Booth on the Bowling Green at Southwark Fair on 7 September 1748 and four more times that month. (A Mr Betts acted at Bristol in the summer of 1763.)

Betts, Mr [*fl.* 1797–1799], *actor, singer.*

A Mr Betts played the role of Bob Bobstay in *A Naval Interlude* out-of-season at the Haymarket on 26 March 1798. Perhaps he was the Mr Betts who sang "Mad Tom" at Covent Garden on 18 May 1799, announced as his first appearance on the stage. No other performances by him are known, unless he was perhaps that Mr Betts, who, with his wife, acted in Cross's spectaculars at the Royal Circus in 1802 and 1804. A song called *General Elliott*, by W. P. R. Cope, was published about 1795 as "sung by Mr Betts," but where it was sung was not mentioned.

Betts, Arthur 1776–1847, *violinist, composer.*

According to the deposition of his brother Edward to the Royal Society of Musicians on 30 May 1797 Arthur Betts was born in January 1776 and was christened in May of the same year. In his autobiographical letter to Sainsbury about 1823, from which that biographer wrote his dictionary entry on him almost *verbatim*, Arthur Betts states his place of birth as Lincolnshire. His father, Edward Betts, was no doubt a musician who by 1790 was living in the Royal Exchange, London, where his other sons Edward and John Edward Betts had set up a musical instrument business. At the age of nine, Arthur Betts was placed under the care of his brother John, the violin maker, for his musical education, although he did not become formally bound to him until five years later when on 28 May 1790 he was entered into the apprentice register of the Worshipful Company of Musicians: "Arthur Betts son of Edward Betts of the Royal Exchange gentleman was this day bound apprentice to John Betts for seven years." He also received instruction on the violin from Hindmarsh and Viotti and in musical theory from Eley, Dussek, Russell, and Steibelt.

On 3 December 1797 Betts was recommended for membership in the Royal Society of Musicians by Martin Platts, who in his letter of support described him as a performer "on the Violin and Tenor, Violoncello and Piano Forte. Is engaged in the Opera and Opera Concert Covent Garden Oratorios; has scholars and other private engagements. Is a Married Man has no children [and is] 22 years of age." Betts was unanimously elected on 4 March 1798 and signed the membership book on 6 May. He was also admitted to livery as a freeman of the Worshipful Company of Musicians on 14 March 1799.

Either Arthur or one of his brothers, John or Edward, played the violin at the oratorios and concerts given at Covent Garden from 23 February to 30 March 1798, from 8 February to 15 March 1799, and from 28 February to 4 April 1800. One of them also played in a concert of Handelian music at the Haymarket on 8 February 1799. It was probably Arthur who was the Betts assigned by the Royal Society of Musicians to play the violin at their annual spring concerts at St Paul's for the benefit of the clergy regularly from 1798 to 1800, from 1802 to 1804, and in 1806. In 1794, according to Doane's *Musical Directory*, he was a member of the Amicable Society and lived in the North Piazza of the Royal Exchange. It was still his address in 1823.

Betts composed, according to his own list, three sonatas for *pianoforte* and violin, a duet for two performers on the *pianoforte*, a set of duets for violin and violoncello, a set of duets for violin and tenor, a sonata for *pianoforte* and violoncello, a *divertimento* for *pianoforte* and violin, and an *andante* for violin *obbligato* with second violin and bass. He also composed several songs and arranged pieces such as the "Overture to the Man of Prometheus," by Beethoven, as a quintet for two violins,

flute, alto, and violoncello. About 1825 he published Pyke's *Three Duets for Two Violins*. He died at London in September 1847.

Betts, Edward, *b. c. 1773?–d. c. 1806, musician, instrument maker.*

Edward Betts was the son of Edward Betts and the brother of Arthur and John Betts. In his deposition to the Royal Society of Musicians in behalf of his brother Arthur on 30 November 1797, he identified himself as an established instrument maker in the Royal Exchange and as having been old enough in 1776 to have recollections of his brother's christening that year. He may have been the Betts who performed at the Covent Garden oratorios between 1798 and 1800. He was dead by 1806, for on 28 May 1806, "Edward Betts, son of Edward Betts, late of Holborn Musical Instrument Maker deceased," was bound apprentice to John Betts. The son, who was a good violin maker in the first quarter of the nineteenth century, died about 1830.

Betts, John [Edward?] *1755–1823, violin maker, teacher, musician.*

The celebrated violin maker and connoisseur of Italian instruments John Betts was born, according to Grove, in 1755 at Stamford, Lincolnshire. He was the son of Edward Betts and brother of the musicians Arthur and Edward Betts. Probably his full name was John Edward Betts. He was taught music by Richard Duke. On 13 February 1782, described as a musical instrument maker of No 2, Royal Exchange, he was admitted to livery as a freeman of the Worshipful Company of Musicians. His music students included his brother Arthur Betts who was bound apprentice to him on 28 May 1790, his nephew Edward Betts who was bound apprentice to him on 28 May 1806, and A. D. Abbott who was bound to him on 11 July 1795 for instruction on the violin, tenor, bass harpsichord, and organ. He or one of his brothers played at the Covent Garden oratorios in 1798–1800 and at the Haymarket on 8 February 1799.

In 1794 Doane's *Musical Directory* described him as a violin and violoncello maker living in the North Piazza of the Royal Exchange, the Betts family location for many years. Although an expert violin maker in the tradition of Stainer and Amati, he was, in the words of Grove, "another of the many craftsmen who at that time failed to recognize the outstanding merits of Stradivari's work." He died at London in 1823.

Betts, Richard ₁*fl. 1669*₁, *musician?*

Richard Betts was one of seven men apprehended by a warrant dated 18 June 1669 for performing without a license; the warrant covered the keeping of playhouses, but the men named would appear to have been musicians playing for dumb shows.

Betty, Mrs. *See* PETTY, MRS.

Betz. *See* BETTS.

Beverly, John ₁*fl. 1794?*₁, *double-bass player.*

Doane's *Musical Directory* of 1794 lists John Beverly, of Cambridge, as a double-bass player in the Handelian concerts at Westminster Abbey, but no specific years of activity are mentioned. He could have been the John Beverley of St Pancras who was buried at the age of 84 on 2 April 1827 at St Paul, Covent Garden.

Bevil, Mr ₁*fl. 1729–1731*₁, *box-keeper.*

Mr Bevil was a boxkeeper at the Goodman's Fields Theatre during the 1729–30 and 1730–31 seasons (at least) and shared benefits on 18 June 1730 and 11 May 1731.

Bevon, Mrs. *See* KENNEDY, MRS MORGAN HUGH.

Bew, Charles ₁*fl. 1791–1837*₁, *actor.*

Charles Bew, according to a newspaper cutting, was the son of a bookseller in London, probably John Bew of No 28, Paternoster Row, who published popular and ephemeral literature, including some books on theatrical matters, in the 1770's. He was first noticed on 19 June 1791 when he was introduced at the Norwich Theatre as "a juvenile son of the buskin, whose name is Bew" in the character of George Barnwell. In the next month, on 19 July, he played Young Bevil in *The Conscious Lovers* at Edinburgh. He was probably the Mr Bew who played at Belfast in February 1792. After spending at least four years in the provinces, Charles Bew came to London to play an unnamed principal role in the after-piece of *Saint Andrew's Festival* at Drury Lane on 29 May 1795. The piece itself was damned and apparently Bew never again played in London. From 1796 to 1799 he was with the theatre at Edinburgh, where hampered by "his defect of speech" he experienced no great success. "Timothy Plain" called him lamentable as King Henry VII in *Richard III* and condemned him as Lothario in *The Fair Penitent* and Randolph in *Douglas*—"Where Nature had placed her decided negative, neither a bushy wig, nor a chalked chin, can give the deportment of a noble mind labouring under misfortunes."

In the early part of the nineteenth century Bew was involved as a patentee of the Brighton Theatre, and then he turned to the practice of dentistry, with some obvious success. On 22 October 1829 the Brighton paper announced that "Mr Bew, Surgeon Dentist to His Majesty, Their Royal Highnesses, the Duke and Duchess of Clarence, and the Royal Household" was moving from No 69, East Street, to No 12, Pavilion Parade, "where he may be consulted as usual from 10 till 4 each day on all diseases of the Teeth and Gums . . . and Impediments of Speech, arising from Dental Deformity." In the same notice his

"Treatise on Maladies incidental to the Teeth, Mouth, and Tic Douloureux" was advertised to be had of a bookseller named Taylor, in North Street. Bew was still alive in 1837.

His wife, Mrs Lois Mary Bew (née Searles?), also acted at Edinburgh between 1796 and 1799. A daughter named Jemima Marian Bew acted in the Drury Lane company at the Lyceum between 1810 and 1814. In a ceremony witnessed by Charles Bew and Lois Mary Bew, Jemima married the actor Frederick Vining at St Paul, Covent Garden, on 2 March 1814, and continued to act for a while under her married name. Some question exists about the legitimacy of this daughter. James Winston identifies Miss Bew as the daughter of John Henry Johnstone, the actor, by a Miss Searles, afterwards Mrs Bew, whose father kept a shop under the Piazza in Covent Garden. Winston had heard that when Johnstone left Miss Searles with child, Charles Bew married her. The 1814 edition of *Memoirs of the Green Room* insinuates some sort of "near" relationship between Johnstone and Miss Bew, both acting in the same Drury Lane company, and suggests that at several provincial theatres she acted as Miss Johnstone.

Bewford. *See* **BOWFORD.**

Bewley, Mr ₁*fl.* 1715₁, *housekeeper.*
Mr Bewley (or Bruley), a housekeeper at Lincoln's Inn Fields Theatre, had a benefit there on 25 November 1715—according to the playhouse accounts, but not the bills. If he was the husband of Widow (Elizabeth?) Bewley, he died sometime between 1719 when she was cited as Elizabeth and 29 May 1721 when she was styled a widow. A relationship certainly seems probable, and the John and William Bewley who worked at Lincoln's Inn Fields and then Covent Garden from 1724 to 1736 could be sons of this couple.

Bewley, Elizabeth ₁*fl.* 1716–1721₁, *house servant?*
An Elizabeth Bewley, apparently a house servant at Lincoln's Inn Fields, was active at the theatre from about 1716 to 1719 or later. On 29 May 1721 a Widow Bewley, possibly Elizabeth, shared a benefit, the total receipts being £115 13s. If these references are to the same person, she may have been the wife of the Mr Bewley who served at the theatre in 1715, and the benefit for her would have been a gesture toward the widow of a deceased employee.

Bewley, John ₁*fl.* 1724–1736₁, *stage doorkeeper.*
Starting with the 1724–25 season and continuing through 1735–36, the Lincoln's Inn Fields and Covent Garden records show two Bewleys at work, and it is not always possible to distinguish between them. John Bewley was a stage doorkeeper at a salary of 5s. per night, and William Bewley was the first gallery doorkeeper in 1724–25 at 2s. per night and probably the one who advanced to boxkeeper by 1731–32. A benefit on 25 May 1730 shared by a Bewley and at least three others probably concerned William; a benefit on 31 May 1736 with two others probably concerned John. It seems likely that the Mr Bewley and Elizabeth (Widow?) Bewley who preceded John and William at Lincoln's Inn Fields were their parents.

Bewley, William ₁*fl.* 1724–1736₁, *gallerykeeper, boxkeeper. See* **BEWLEY, JOHN.**

Bezand or Bezond. *See* **BAYZAND.**

Bezozzi. *See* **BESOZZI.**

Biaggini, Signor ₁*fl.* 1783₁, *exhibitor.*
In the winter of 1783 at the Lyceum, Signor Biaggini exhibited an air balloon

described as "an Aerostatical Globe of Ten Feet in diameter."

Biancardi, Signor *[fl. 1720], musician?*

One Biancardi, possibly a musician, was listed among those who performed at the Cannons Concerts in 1720; his salary was £7 10*s*. per quarter.

Bianchi, Signor *[fl. 1769–1770], singer.*

On 5 September 1769, the *Public Advertiser* announced that a Signor Bianchi, tenor, was among the new singers engaged at the King's Opera. The company gave 76 performances in 1769–70 of operas for which casts were not always given. Bianchi's first billed role was as Masino in *La contadini bizzare* on 7 November 1769. He also sang the title role in *Gioas Rè di Giuda* and no doubt appeared in most of the other operas. On 2 February he sang at a concert of vocal and instrumental music and on 1 March he sang one of the parts in the oratorio *La Passione.*

Bianchi, Francesco *[fl. 1748–1749], singer.*

Francesco Bianchi was a member of John Francis Croza's small opera company at the King's Theatre in the Haymarket during the 1748–49 season. He sang Marcion in *La comedia in comedia* on 8 November 1748, but, unfortunately, the casts for the rest of the operas done that season were not listed on the bills. Bianchi was probably related to the more famous composer of the same name who was active at the end of the century.

Bianchi, Francesco *c. 1751–1810, composer, musician.*

The Italian composer Francesco Bianchi was born at Cremona in 1751 or 1752. His first opera *Il gran Cidde* was produced at the Teatro della Pergola, Florence, in 1773. After his *Eurione* was performed at Pavia

in 1775 he went to Paris to write for the Comédie-Italienne, where he served as *maestro al cembalo* until 1778, after which time he returned to Italy. Between 1779 and 1794 he wrote nearly 50 operas which were produced at the important theatres of Italy. He became vice-conductor at Milan Cathedral in 1783, and from 1785 to 1793 he was the second organist at St Mark's in Venice.

Francesco Bianchi's opera *Semiramide* (*La vendetta di Nino*) was the vehicle for a tremendously successful engagement by Brigitta Giorgi-Banti at Naples in 1790. Banti then went to London in 1794 to make her debut at the King's Theatre in the same piece on 26 April. Bianchi himself arrived in London in 1795 to take up the position of composer to the King's Theatre. *Semiramide* was revived on 7 February 1795 under his direction and was followed soon by his *Aci e Galatea* on 21 March. Haydn, who heard the latter opera on 28 March, found the music "very rich in parts for the wind instrument" and thought that "one would hear the principal melody better if it were not so richly scored." Bianchi played at the harpsichord for the first three performances of each of these works. He was re-engaged as house composer in 1795–96 at a salary of £600 and remained in that capacity at least through the season 1798–99. In that latter season his revised version of *Ines de Castro* was performed 21 times. Contrary to the information given by earlier biographers, he did not go to Dublin to conduct at the Crow Street Theatre or at Astley's Amphitheatre from 1798 to 1800—that person was John Bianchi—but rather seems to have remained in London working at his profession. His operas *Alzira*, *La morte di Cleopatra*, and *Armida* were performed in 1801–2, and several years later Bianchi played at the harpsichord for a revival of his *Erfile* at the King's on 19 February 1805.

In 1800 Bianchi had married Miss Jane

Jackson, the daughter of John Jackson, an apothecary in Sloane Street, Chelsea. As Miss Jackson she had sung in 1798 at the Concerts of Ancient Music, and she later appeared as Mrs Bianchi at the King's Theatre. (After Bianchi's death she became best known as Mrs Bianchi Lacy, in consequence of her subsequent marriage to the singer John Lacy.) By her Bianchi had a daughter, Caroline Nelson Bianchi, who died at the age of five on 28 June 1807. Residing in Hammersmith, Bianchi taught music (a notable pupil was Henry Bishop) but with the loss of his child heavy on his heart he committed suicide on 27 November 1810 at the age of 59. He was buried with his daughter in Kensington Churchyard where a flat stone marks their grave. In his will, which was drawn up on 12 July 1808 and proved on 14 December 1810, Bianchi left his estate to his wife Jane who was also granted administration of the will as sole executrix. One of the witnesses to the will was a G. Bianchi, no doubt a relative.

In addition to about 60 operas Bianchi also composed oratorios and church music. He wrote a theoretical work, "Dell attrazione armonica," parts of which his widow published in the *Quarterly Music Review* (II–III, 1820–21). A list of his works is found in the *Enciclopedia dello spettacolo*. Bianchi was painted by Luigi Scotti in a large group of musicians; an engraving of this picture was printed between 1801 and 1807.

Bianchi, Mrs Francesco, Jane, née Jackson, later Mrs John Lacy *1776–1858, singer.*

Miss Jane Jackson was born in London in 1776, the daughter of an apothecary in Sloane Street, Chelsea, and made her first appearance as a soprano at the Concert of Ancient Music on 25 April 1798. She married the composer Francesco Bianchi in 1800 and under her married name appeared at the King's Theatre from 1809

to 1812. The *Morning Chronicle* of 26 June 1809 judged her to be a singer "of inferior merit; yet . . . not unpleasing from her unaffectedness, her propriety of action, and her good taste, which triumphs over the defects of a very bad voice." By Francesco Bianchi she had a daughter Caroline who died at the age of five on 28 June 1807. Her despondent husband killed himself in 1810 and left her the sole legatee and executrix of his estate. In 1812 she married the singer John Lacy, and it was as Mrs Bianchi Lacy that she became best known, at the King's Theatre between 1812 and 1815. She also sang often at Windsor before George III and Queen Charlotte. In addition to being regarded as one of the finest Handelian singers of her day, she was a good *pianoforte* player, painter, and linguist. She sang in concerts at Willis's Rooms on 1 March 1809, at the Vocal Concerts, Hanover Square Rooms on 2 March 1810, and at the Music Room at Oxford.

In 1818 she accompanied Lacy to Calcutta where they frequently performed at the court of the King of Ouda. After eight years there, they returned to England about 1826 to retire into private life. They also travelled to Florence and other continental cities. She died at Ealing on 19 March 1858.

Bianchi, Giovanni Battista *[fl. 1780–1782], conductor, composer.*

An Italian musician, Giovanni Battista Bianchi was apparently no kin to his better-known contemporary, Francesco Bianchi (1752–1810), with whom he was sometimes confused by early biographers. He was successor to Bertoni as director of musical performances at the King's Theatre in 1780–81 and 1781–82. He also was one of the house composers. On 25 November 1780 he contributed some music and arranged and conducted for a new comic opera, *L'Arcifanfano*. In celebration of George III's birthday he composed music for the first part of a *festa teatrale*, *L'omaggio*, performed at the King's on 5 June 1781.

Bianchi, John C. M. *1775–1802, violinist, composer.*

Although the *Monthly Mirror*, October 1802, described John C. M. Bianchi at the time of his death as a "celebrated performer on the violin" and "an accomplished Scholar, as well as an excellent theoretic and practical musician," the scarcity of notices about him might deny his celebrity. In 1794 a John Bianchi, violinist, was listed by Doane's *Musical Directory* as a participant in professional concerts living at No 75, King Street, Westminster. At this time he would have been about 19 years of age. (Possibly he was the son of Giovanni Battista Bianchi who was a conductor and composer at the King's Opera, 1780–82.)

It was John Bianchi, not the composer Francesco Bianchi as most biographers of the latter have assumed, who was conductor at the Crow Street Theatre and at Astley's, Dublin, from 1798 to 1801. An anonymous diary at the Royal Irish Academy identifies him as John, and musical conductor at Astley's Royal Amphitheatre, where he played the violin for his own benefit on 19 February 1801. No doubt he was the same Professor Bianchi who was admitted as an honorary member of the Irish Musical Fund on 5 March 1798. This society asked him to play for the annual Handel commemoration concert in the spring of 1800. Bianchi returned to London to perform at the Haymarket in the summer season of 1801. On 11 August 1801, announced as from the Theatre Royal, Dublin, and as making his first appearance in London in six years, he played a medley concerto, in which he introduced the favorite Irish air of "The Grinder." On 21 August he performed 'The Blue Bell of Scotland" and again offered "The Grinder."

Bianchi died at Neuilly, near Paris, "of a deep decline," in September 1802, at the age of 27. It was also reported at this time by the *Monthly Mirror* that his manuscripts, consisting of English canzonets and violin concertos, were to be edited and published by his friend J. Moorehead.

Bianchi Lacy, Mrs. *See* BIANCHI, MRS FRANCESCO.

Bianchini, Mr *[fl. 1743–1747], house servant.*

Mr Bianchini was a house servant at Covent Garden from at least 1743–44 through 1746–47, but his duties are not mentioned in the theatre accounts.

Bianci. *See* BIANCHI.

Bibby, Mr *[fl. 1746], actor, singer.*

Mr Bibby was first noticed in the bills on 3 March 1746 when he played Pope in *Harlequin Incendiary* at Drury Lane. He appeared again on 8 April as Aegeon in the pastoral opera, *Love and Friendship*; for his shared benefit on 25 April he played Spright in *The Amorous Goddess* and sang a specialty song; and on 1 May, his last notice in the bills, he again sang a solo. He may have been (or been related to) Thomas Bibby, the provincial manager active in the 1780's.

Bibson, Miss *[fl. 1781], actress.*

Miss Bibson was a member of the troupe that played from 15 March to 9 April 1781 at the Crown Inn, Islington; she was one of the mob of women in *The Recruiting Officer* on 15 March, but she was not named in the bills for the other plays done.

Bick, James *d. 1712?, ventriloquist, imitator.*

James Bick made a living in the reign of Queen Anne amusing tavern patrons with tricks of ventriloquism and quaint imitations, especially of a trumpet. He is supposed to have filled a vacant trumpet position in a band so correctly that the finest ear could not detect the difference. Clinch of Barnet, a more famous and successful imitator, succeeded Bick. Musgrave listed James Bick as deceased in 1712, though Caulfield's *Remarkable Persons* spoke of him as active toward the end of the reign of Queen Anne, which would suggest that he may

Harvard Theatre Collection

JAMES BICK
by R. Grave

have lived a year or two longer. Caulfield was not always accurate, however: he said that Bick was supposed to have been named after the Sergeant Trumpeter John Shore Bick, but this makes little sense, for Bick was named James, and John Shore was not named Bick.

J. Faber Sr made an engraving of Bick, and P. Grave made a copy of the Faber.

Bickall. *See* BICKNELL.

Bickerstaff, Miss *d. c. 1724, actress.*
Though she was not named in the play-bill, Miss Bickerstaff must have acted in *Virtue Betrayed* at Drury Lane on 9 June 1703, for on 3 July "the little Girl that play'd the Part of Queen Bess in *Anna Bullen* [the alternate title of *Virtue Betrayed*]" spoke a new epilogue, garbed in a Quaker's dress. Professor Emmett Avery has identified the "little Girl" as Miss Bickerstaff. It is likely that she was related to the actor John Bickerstaff, who made his first

recorded appearance on 23 June in *Vice Reclaimed.*

"Bickerstaff, Isaac." *See* STEELE, SIR RICHARD.

Bickerstaff, John *d. c. 1724, actor.*
John Bickerstaff (or Jonathan Biggerstaff) may have been the son of John Bickerstaff of Travis Inn, St Andrew, Holborn, a widower whose will was administered by his son John on 29 April 1710. The actor's first theatrical notice was on 23 June 1703 when he played Apish in *Vice Reclaimed* at Drury Lane two weeks after a Miss Bickerstaff made her first, and apparently her last, appearance on the stage, in *Virtue Betrayed* at the same playhouse—which suggests that the two may have been related. John Bickerstaff was given a benefit on 7 January 1704, shared with two others, and another on 5 July.

His name appeared only sporadically on the bills during the next few seasons, but he is known to have acted Hemskirk in *The Royal Merchant* on 12 June 1705, Burris in *The Loyal Subject* on 25 July of the same year, and Single in *Sir Solomon Single* on 11 March 1707. These roles suggest that Bickerstaff had a fairly wide range, for Hemskirk is noisy and middle-aged, Burris is "an honest Lord," and Single is a young man; none of the roles are major ones, however.

In the winter of 1707–8 Bickerstaff was one of the signers of a petition against uniting the Drury Lane and Queen's Theatre companies, and during that season and the one following he carried a full load of acting assignments, chiefly comic roles. At Drury Lane he played Plume on 18 October and then Brazen on 26 November 1707 in *The Recruiting Officer*, Petruchio in *The Chances* on 24 February 1708, Jeremy in *Love for Love* on 10 June, Busy in *Bartholomew Fair* on 31 August, the title role in *Amphitryon* on 16 September, Lorenzo in *The Spanish Friar* on 2 October, Seyton in *Macbeth* on 6 February 1709, Young Fashion in *The Relapse* on 2 February, Kastril in *The Alchemist* on 19 February, Peregrine in *Volpone* on 26 February, Marcellus in *Hamlet* on 7 May, and Aeneas in *Troilus and Cressida* on 2 June. He had apparently proved a useful secondary actor and an earnest worker. In 1709–10 Bickerstaff added to his growing repertory Ben in *Love for Love* on 3 December 1709, the title role in *2 Don Quixote* on 4 February 1710, and the Captain in *A Bickerstaff's Burying* –dedicated to "The Magnificent Company of Upholders," a curtain-raiser first given on 27 March.

Aaron Hill was at the helm at Drury Lane during the 1709–10 season, and Bickerstaff, George Powell, Barton Booth, Theophilus Keene, and Francis Leigh were all partly involved in the management of the troupe; these five, who made up the bulk of the managership, were at odds with Hill during the season, and in June 1710 the conflict came to a head. In a letter to Vice Chamberlain Coke dated 5 June 1710 Hill told his side of the story:

I had taken away the useless power of the seven Managers, that unexpected blow, was a great surprise to em, resented warmly by all; . . . Mr Bickerstaff & Mr Keen appeared most publickly disgusted, all the other actors in general, were pleased beyond expression & ever since the managers lost their power have shewn a double life & industry in their application to Business.

Hill made Pack the manager of rehearsals, but Pack gave up the position in a day or two and Hill offered it to Booth; Booth refused to accept it unless all seven managers were restored, whereupon Hill gave his brother the job. A few days later Hill was called to Essex, and while he was gone there was an uproar at the theatre. The actors, wrote Hill,

refused to act, threatened to take the cloaths out of the House etc. I came up to Town im-

mediately, found all this true, with this addition, that Bickerstaff had beaten a poor fellow blind, without any other provocation, than reproving him for abusing me, most scurilously y^t he had told Baggs [the Drury Lane treasurer] he would push my Brother off the stage by the shoulders & in short y^t he had with Kean endeavoured to disorder & disgrace the whole Company.

These & many Insolences more which I blush to remember I was confounded to see oblig'd to suspend Mr Bickerstaff & Mr Keen, to the former of whom I [wrote] a letter, containing the reasons for my Proceedings & Friendly advice not to be misled by villains who make him the cats paw to their designs; Instead of taking this as he should have done, he forc'd the Printer to put his name in the Bills, told me he neither valued you, me, nor any man alive, that himself was his own Master & he would come behind the scenes & see who durst hinder him.

Francis Leigh threatened to go and act with Pinkethman at Greenwich, and Booth hurled invectives at Hill and tried to tell him who would act and when. Hill heard that the actors were threatening to run off with the costumes, so he ordered the theatre locked up until a guard could be posted. Late that afternoon (apparently Friday, 2 June 1710) Hill was in the theatre office with his brother and the treasurer, Zachary Baggs, when they heard Booth, Powell, Keen, and the others, presumably including Bickerstaff, "breaking open the great Doors within"—the actress Mrs Bradshaw having let them in a private way from her lodgings beside the playhouse. The invaders burst into the office "with drawn Swords in their hands, with much ado I got out into the open passage had drawn my sword & while surrounded by a crowd some to Prevent & some to increase the Tumult Powell had shortened his sword to stab me in the Back & had cut a Gentlemans hand through who prevented the thrust." Leigh struck Hill's brother on the head from behind, and Hill himself managed to flee to St James's to find the Vice Chamberlain; not finding him, he returned to the theatre to find the regular doorkeeper dismissed and admission to him and his brother denied.

After all these garboils, the company still performed that evening, with apparently all five of the rioters except Keene in the cast. The company had but one more performance to give before the season ended, so Hill felt safe in requesting that Booth, Powell, and Leigh, the chief instigators, be arrested; he thought that Bickerstaff and Keene would, upon that action, "be easy [when] their inflamers are made such necessary examples." Vice Chamberlain Coke, after reading Hill's account of the events, dismissed Powell from the company and suspended the rest.

The suspended performers—and even Powell—were back on the Drury Lane roster for the 1710–11 season, with Wilks, Cibber, and Doggett as managers. Among Bickerstaff's new parts this season were Rakehell in *She Would If She Could* on 21 December 1710 and Kister Aga in *Abra Mule* on 20 March 1711. For the next few seasons his activity slackened somewhat, but without relinquishing his comic roles he began to try a few more serious ones: Banquo in *Macbeth*, the Poet in *Timon of Athens*, Claudius in *Hamlet*, Sullen in *The Beaux' Stratagem*, and Kent in *King Lear*. He also moved up to Voltore in *Volpone*, and played Heartwell in *The Old Bachelor*, Elder Worthy in *Love's Last Shift*, and Casca in *Julius Caesar*.

Just as he moved into more significant and heavier roles in the late 1710's, Bickerstaff was afflicted with gout, and the rest of his acting career was curtailed. For his benefit on 20 April 1719 he advertised that he had "not been able to wait on his Friends, by reason of his being lame"; and, indeed, *Love for Love* was done for him, but he was not in it. By the following November, after playing at least twice during the summer and early fall, he had improved enough to act more frequently, but it is notable that he never acted any of his roles in tragedies

again. He kept playing Ben, Sullen, Voltore, Busy, Heartwell, and one or two other parts, acting frequently in November but less and less as the season progressed. When his benefit came on 25 April 1720 he was again unable to attend because of his lameness. He played sporadically in 1720–21, apparently did not act for his benefit on 12 April 1721, but on 15 April acted Sullen in *The Beaux' Stratagem*, his last recorded role.

A year later, on 25 April 1722 at his benefit, the bill noted that Bickerstaff "by Lameness with the Gout, has not appeared on the Stage for above this Twelve Month"; he advertised plaintively that he hoped his friends would not forsake him and miss his benefit. The following season, on 3 May 1723, he again could not act at his benefit, and one of the notices that appeared was heart-breaking: "Mr. Bickerstaffe, being confined to his Bed by his lameness, & his wife lying now dead, has nobody to wait on the quality & his friends for him."

The once volatile young man was now, on 7 October 1723 when he wrote his will, "ill and indisposed of body." He described himself as of St Martin-in-the-Fields and asked that he be decently and quietly buried. To his kinswoman Margaret de Fountaine he left 20*s.* for a mourning ring, and the rest of his estate he bequeathed to his friend Mary Whitwood in trust for his daughter, Mary Sanders. Shortly after this, John Bickerstaff died; his will was proved on 12 December 1724.

Of Bickerstaff's acting ability very little is known beyond what can be surmised from the roles he played. In December 1758 the *London Chronicle* said of his Marplot in *The Busy Body*—a role for which he is otherwise not recorded—that he had "neither youth, person, voice, or countenance"; it was a very complete condemnation of him, if the comments did, in fact, apply to Bickerstaff. His roles, played in a company that had some strong performers, suggest that he certainly had a flair for comedy, and if it was his lameness rather than lack of talent which caused him to abandon his heavier roles, perhaps he was a sound actor in tragedy.

Bickham. *See also* BECKHAM.

Bickham, Mr (*fl.* 1733), *actor?*

One Bickham, possibly an error for Beckham, was given a benefit at the Haymarket Theatre on 20 August 1733 when *Cato* was performed; unfortunately, the playbill provides no cast, so it is impossible to tell whether Bickham acted or not. It would seem unlikely that Mr Beckham, who was active at this time, should receive a solo benefit, since he was only a minor actor.

Bickham, Mrs (*fl.* 1779), *candlewoman.*

A Drury Lane salary list dated 8 November 1779 describes Mrs Bickham as a candlewoman on the staff, but her salary is run in with other items and cannot be determined.

Bicknell, Mr (*fl.* 1794), *bassoonist.*

Doane's *Musical Directory* of 1794 lists Mr Bicknell, of Blackman Street, the Borough, as playing the bassoon at Handelian Society concerts.

Bicknell, Mrs (*fl.* 1755), *singer.*

A Mrs Bicknell sang at Widow Yeates's booth at Bartholomew Fair on 3 September 1755.

Bicknell, Margaret, née Younger *c. 1680–1723, actress, dancer.*

Margaret (sometimes, incorrectly, Mary) Bicknell (or Bickall, Bignall, Bignell) was the daughter of James and Margaret Younger, both born in Scotland. Since she was already married when she made her first stage appearance in 1702, the suggested birthdate of 1695 given in the *Dictionary of National Biography* cannot be correct, and a date closer to 1680–85 would be more reasonable. Her father rode with the third troop of Guards and served in Flanders under William III, and her mother was a Keith, nearly related to Keith, the Earl Marshal of Scotland. Margaret had a sister, Elizabeth, who also became a performer. Of Margaret's husband, all that seems to be known is that his name was Bicknell and that he predeceased her; they were married sometime before 20 August 1702 when, as Mrs Bicknell, the performer made her first appearance at Drury Lane doing a "Scotch dance."

She may have appeared on stage before this without being named in the bills, and the records for the first few years of the eighteenth century are so scanty that we cannot be certain how active she may have been at Drury Lane during the 1702–1703 season. She danced there several times at least, and she was given a benefit concert at York Buildings on 24 February 1703 and another on 1 July at the theatre. They suggest a standing higher than the few performance references would indicate. It was at her 1 July benefit at Drury Lane that she made her first recorded attempt as an actress, playing Hoyden in *The Relapse*, a role for which she seems to have been type-cast.

In the fall of 1703 she danced regularly at Drury Lane, and on 23 October she was billed as a singer; the spring and summer of 1704, however, found her inactive. After her nine-month absence, she returned on 27 October 1704, beginning her new season with a shared benefit (though *The London Stage* calendar does not show this). By November she may have been negotiating with the Queen's Theatre in the Haymarket which was preparing for its opening; Drury Lane manager Christopher Rich complained that month that she and some of his other actors were being wooed by Queen's managers Congreve and Vanbrugh. Though there is no clear evidence that Mrs Bicknell switched companies, it may be significant that her name disappeared from the Drury

Lane bills after 5 February 1705, so she may have joined the Queen's troupe for their April opening. She was certainly there for the 1705–6 season, chiefly serving as a specialty dancer, and about June 1706 she acted Lisset in *The Adventures in Madrid.*

Beginning with the 1706–7 season at the Queen's, Mrs Bicknell turned more of her attention to acting. Among other roles, she played Mrs Edging in *The Careless Husband* on 7 November 1706, Rose in *The Recruiting Officer* on 14 November, the title role in *The Northern Lass* on 13 January 1707, Pert in *The Man of Mode* on 18 January, Cherry in *The Stratagem* on 8 March, and, for her benefit, Juletta in *The Pilgrim* on 30 April. No dancing, other than what she might have done within the plays, was mentioned for her in the season's bills. During the following season she played Rachel in *The Jovial Crew* on 1 January 1708 just before the acting companies regrouped and the actors went back to Drury Lane, leaving the Queen's to the opera singers. Back at Drury Lane she was Phaedra in *Amphitryon* on 3 February, Prue in *Love for Love* on 7 February, Silvia in *The Old Bachelor* on 15 March, and, for her benefit, Melantha in *Marriage à la Mode* on 19 May. Again, the bills this season made no mention of her dancing.

For her benefit on 14 April 1709 she chose to play Margery Pinchwife in *The Country Wife*, and Steele, in the *Tatler* for 16 April reported on it:

Through the whole action she made a very pretty figure, and exactly entered into the nature of the part . . . Mrs. Bignell did her part very happily, and had a certain grace in her rusticity, which gave us hopes of seeing her a skilful player, and in some parts supply our loss of Mrs. Verbruggen.

Judging from her roles and later reports, she apparently supplied that loss very nicely.

Along with other performers, Mrs Bicknell was back at the Queen's for the 1709–10 season when the two houses again al-

tered their managerial and production arrangements. To her growing list of roles she added Hillaria in *Love's Last Shift*, Madame d'Epingle in *The Funeral*, and Martha in *The Scornful Lady*, and on 16 February 1710 she was billed once again as a dancer. In a list of performers working under Owen Swiney at the Queen's Theatre this season, she stood third among the women, behind Elizabeth Barry and Anne Oldfield; in less than a decade, she had become a star attraction.

The 1710–11 season saw another, but rather permanent, change in managerships, so that Mrs Bicknell played the first half of the season at the Queen's and, starting in January 1711, moved back to Drury Lane for the rest of her career. Her last role at the Queen's Theatre, on 29 December 1710, was Silvia in *The Recruiting Officer*, where before she had played the lesser role of Rose. At Drury Lane she added to her repertory, among other parts, Nerissa in *The Jew of Venice*, Dol Mavis in *The Silent Woman*, and Frolick in *Injured Love*. In 1711–12 she had to drop back to Rose in *The Recruiting Officer*, for she was again in a troupe with Anne Oldfield, to whom the part of Silvia belonged. But she added Mary Buxom in *Don Quixote*, danced more frequently, and received in the 5 May 1712 issue of the *Spectator* a handsome puff:

It would be a great improvement, as well as embellishment to the theatre, if dancing were more regarded, and taught to all the actors. One who has the advantage of such an agreeable girlish person as Mrs. Bicknell, joined with her capacity of imitation, could in proper gesture and motion represent all the decent characters of female life. An amiable modesty in one aspect of a dancer, and assumed confidence in another, a sudden joy in another, a falling off with an impatience of being beheld, and a return towards the audience with an unsteady resolution to approach them, and a well-acted solicitude to please, would revive in the company all the fine touches of mind raised in observing all the objects of affection or passion they had before beheld. Such elegant entertainments as these would polish the town into judgment in their gratifications, and delicacy in pleasure is the first step people of condition take in reformation from vice. Mrs. Bicknell has the only capacity for this sort of dancing of any on the stage; and I dare say all who see her performance tomorrow night [6 May], when sure the romp will do her best for her own benefit, will be of my mind.

After this praise it is odd that only once during the next three seasons (on 6 October 1714) did the bills announce dancing by Mrs Bicknell; but her activity generally seems to have slackened, and in those three years she also added relatively few important new roles to her line: Lady Sadlife in *The Double Gallant* on 27 December 1712, Mrs Clerimont in *The Tender Husband* on 28 January 1714, and Kitty in *What d'Ye Call It?* on 23 February 1715.

During these years she may have been busier with her social life than her theatrical career. She and her sister Elizabeth Younger had developed questionable reputations among the wits in town, and Pope, in *A Farewell to London. In the Year 1715* wrote:

> *My Friends, by Turns, my Friends confound,*
>   *Betray, and are betray'd:*
> *Poor Y———r's sold for Fifty Pound,*
>   *And B———ll is a Jade.*

The fact that, according to Gay, Mrs Bicknell moved in Pope's circle of friends may account for her faring better in the poet's barb than her sister. Through the 1717–18 season her career seems to have remained on a plateau, with hardly any new roles added to her repertory and only occasional appearances as a dancer and fewer as a singer.

Starting in the fall of 1718, however, and continuing until January 1723, a few

months before her death, her career picked up. She began dancing with great frequency (often with her sister), continued in most of her old roles, and occasionally added new ones. Silvia in *The Recruiting Officer* now became one of her parts; she played Belinda in *The Old Bachelor* rather than Silvia; and she added Hippolita in *The Tempest*, Columbine in *The Dumb Farce*, Lady Wrangle in *The Refusal*, Columbine in *The Escapes of Harlequin*, Florinda in *The Rover*, and Flora in *She Wou'd and She Wou'd Not*. Her dancing seems to have been chiefly what John Weaver would have designated as grotesque or scenical—that is, comic dances or roles in pantomimes. She frequently did *Tollet's Ground* with her sister, and on 5 May 1719 she and Birkhead were billed as *The Strippers*; this was no misprint, for on 12 April 1722 with Boval she performed "the Stripping Dance." Exactly what it was remains a mystery.

The roles Mrs Bicknell played most frequently over the years—Margery Pinchwife, Hoyden, Edging, Pert, and others—were comic, sprightly parts; rarely did she venture into serious roles. Her last recorded role, however, was Charlotte in *Oroonoko* on 21 May 1723 at Drury Lane, a part she had played frequently over the years. On the morning of 24 May she died of consumption. The *Daily Journal* was strangely abrupt in reporting her death: "Her parts will be very well supply'd by her Sister Mrs Younger, a Person of a very promising Genius."

Margaret Bicknell was buried on 27 May 1723 at St Paul, Covent Garden, though she was noted in the register there as being from the parish of St Margaret, Westminster. Her will, drawn on 4 May 1723 (which fact suggests that though she acted to the end, she was aware of her serious condition), described her as a widow living in Poland Street. To her sister and residuary legatee Elizabeth Younger she left £10 for mourning. To surgeon John Weymiss and his wife, of Great Poultry Street, she gave

£70; to her uncle Patrick Younger, his wife, and their daughter Mary, she bequeathed £5 each for mourning; to Joseph Ashton of Surrey Street she gave £10; and to her maid Mary Warren she left £10 above her wages. Her house in Poland Street she left in trust to four-year-old Charlotte, natural daughter of her sister Elizabeth Younger. Weymiss and Ashton were asked to be her executors, and they proved her will on 7 June 1723.

Biddiford. *See* **BIGFORD.**

Biddy, Miss *[fl. 1728–1729]*, *dancer.*
Miss Biddy danced during the 1727–28 and 1728–29 seasons at Drury Lane and acted (apparently for her debut) the Country Maid in *Acis and Galatea* on 30 March 1728; on 15 November she was Venus in *Perseus and Andromeda.* During her second season at the theatre she was listed as Mrs Biddy, suggesting that she was probably just out of her minority. She seems not to have continued her dancing career after the spring of 1729.

Bidotti, Mons *[fl. 1788–1794]*, *dancer, actor.*
Monsieur Bidotti's first appearance in London would seem to have been on 23 August 1788 when he, Madame Julien, Miss Blanchet, and others danced, so said the bill, a *pas de deux* at the Royal Circus. A month later, on 27 September, the Drury Lane account books show that Bidotti (or Bedotti) was employed there at 4s. 2d. per day. He returned to Drury Lane the next season, but worked only from 26 December 1789 to 1 March 1790, his first mention in the bills being on the former date, when he was a minor member of the cast of *Harlequin's Frolicks.* This season his salary was £1 5s. per week. In 1790–91 he was dropped to £1 weekly, and one of the rare times he was mentioned in the bills was on 26 October 1790 when he danced in the afterpiece, *Don Juan.* Bidotti remained with the Drury Lane company at this same salary through the spring of 1794, performing with them at the King's Theatre and at the Haymarket while their new Drury Lane was under construction. He was one of the Vintagers in *The Pirates* on 21 November 1792, but this was about the only time his participation was significant enough to be noticed in the bills. In 1793–94 he worked for the company only a brief time, from 16 to 30 May 1794, playing again in *The Pirates.*

Bidwell, Mr *[fl. 1778–1779]*, *actor.*
Mr Bidwell was paid £1 3s. 4d. for two weeks' work at Drury Lane on 3 October 1778, and though he was not mentioned in the bills until 28 April 1779 when he had an unspecified role in the premiere of *The Double Deception*, he appears to have been employed at the theatre the full season. He had contributed 11s. to the retirement fund, but the money was returned to him, so presumably he left the theatre at the end of the 1778–79 season.

Bielby. *See* **BEILBY.**

Bienfait, Mons *[fl. 1756]*, *dancer.*
Monsieur Bienfait may have been with the Covent Garden company throughout the 1755–56 season, but the only notice of him in the bills is on 22 April 1756 when he was in a new dance called *Les Paisans Iriquois*, danced a *pas de trois* with Guerin and Lucas, and was in *Les Savetiers.*

"Big Sam." *See* **MACDONALD, SAMUEL.**

Bigari, Francesco *[fl. 1766–1772]*, *scene painter, machinist.*
Francesco Bigari (or Bigar), sometimes billed as "Bigari Junior," was the son of Vincenzo Bigari of Bologna and brother of Angelo Maria Bigari. Francesco was a painter of historical events and landscapes who, beginning in 1766–67, was on the staff of the King's Theatre in the Hay-

market. During his first two seasons he worked with Conti, after which he was billed alone through 1771–72, his last London season. In 1766–67 Bigari and Conti provided scenes for *Gli stravaganti* and *La buona figliuola*, and in 1767–68 they painted scenes for *Carattaco, Il signor dottore, Sifare, Ifigenia in Aulide, Sesostri*, and *Il ratto della sposa*. For the production of *Le contadine bizarre* in 1768–69 Bigari prepared the scenes, and after the season was over he designed what was billed as "An elegant transparent Temple of Apollo" for *Love and Innocence* at Marylebone Gardens on 10 August 1769. At the King's Theatre in the 1769–70 season he provided the scenes for *Ezio, Il padre e il figlio rivali, Orfeo e Euridice*, and *Il disertore*. In 1770–71 he did scenes for *Le vincende della sorte, Gli 'uccellatori, Astarto rè di Tiro, Semiramide riconosciuta, Le pazzie d'Orlando*, and *La contadina in corte*. In his last season at the King's Theatre, 1771–72, Bigari designed *Il carnovale di Venezia*. His brother Angelo Maria probably went to Ireland about 1772 to work at the Smock Alley Theatre through 1784; since Francesco's departure from London and Angelo Maria's arrival in Ireland coincide, there may possibly have been some confusing of the two painters.

Bigford, Mary   [fl. 1727], candlewoman.

Mary Bigford (or Biddiford) was mentioned in the Lincoln's Inn Fields accounts on 8 and 27 February and 6 March 1726 (probably 1726/27) as a candlewoman at a salary of 1s. 2d. daily.

Bigg. *See also* BIGGS.

Bigg, John   *b. 1777, violinist, organist, bassoonist, teacher.*

John Bigg was born in the parish of St George, Hanover Square, on 24 March 1777. His mother, Mrs Keziah Balderston, gave a sworn deposition of those facts on 2 February 1799 "at the public office in Great Marlbro' Street" when Bigg was to be proposed for membership in the Royal Society of Musicians. He had "not been registered though christened privately at home by a Clergyman from St Georges, Hanover Square, and particular charge given to the Clerk to see it done, yet was shamefully neglected."

The eminent John James Ashley proposed him to the Society on 3 March, and he was elected on 2 June 1799 by 11 yeas to one nay. On 7 July he attended for the first time to sign the membership book. Ashley deposed that Bigg had "studied and practised music for a livelihood for upwards of seven years, is Organist of Benti[n]ck Chapel, has a number of scholars on the Piano Forte, and performs on the violin. Is a single man and will be twenty-two years of age the 24th of [March 1799]."

In May 1800 "Biggs" (a frequent mistake) was on the list to play bassoon at the annual benefit concert conducted by the Society at St Paul's Cathedral. He was there again in 1802 and 1804. On 6 September 1807 the Board decided that a fine imposed upon him for non-attendance as an elected Governor of the Society for the previous year should be remitted, on the receipt of his letter claiming ill health. On 5 March 1809 he wrote the Society enclosing a certificate from a physician, which obtained him £10 temporary medical relief. After further supplication from him a committee was sent to wait on him and report his true condition. On 1 October 1809, a Mr Foster reported to the Society that a consultation of Doctors Pemberton, Gower, and Nevison had reached the opinion that Mr Biggs was free of bodily disease but labored under a considerable degree of hypochondria. Nevertheless, on two later occasions, in November and December, he received £5, and was also awarded 5 guineas per month, plus provision for schooling his two children. His condition worsening, on

6 May 1810 he was granted £8 6s. 6d. per month.

He was listed again (as a violinist) to play in the St Paul's concerts in May 1811, although his allowance for illness continued. On 6 February 1814 he sent word that he was too unwell to attend the meeting to make his affidavit about his pension; the Board decided that he would be "sworn in the country." He acknowledged payments totalling £43 3s. in the course of the years preceding 6 March 1814. The last entry concerning this neurotic musician seems to have been on 3 January 1819, when his allowance was ordered continued.

Biggari. *See* **BIGARI.**

Biggs. *See also* **BIGG.**

Biggs, Mr　[*fl.* 1737],　*actor.*
Mr Biggs was listed as participating in *The Honest Yorkshireman* at Lincoln's Inn Fields on 7 May 1737, for his benefit and three others' in "Capt. Gulliver's Company of Lilliputians," but his role was not cited in the playbill.

Biggs, Mr　[*fl.* 1794–1797],　*singer.*
A Mr Biggs, with 22 others, sang some of the music of Matthew Locke in a "Chorus of Witches and Spirits," in performances of *Macbeth* at Drury Lane on 21, 22, and 23 April 1794. He was probably the Biggs who had a vocal part in *The Battle of Eddington* and was James in *The Romance of an Hour* at the Haymarket on 10 May 1797.

Biggs, Mrs　[*fl.* 1719–1720],　*actress.*
Mrs Biggs first appeared on stage at Lincoln's Inn Fields on 26 October 1719 playing Belinda in *Tunbridge Walks*. During November she was remarkably active and played some major roles, including Dorcas in *The Fair Quaker of Deal*, Angelica in *Love for Love*, Melinda in *The*

Recruiting Officer, and Isabella in *The Squire of Alsatia*. She acted Melinda again in December, but the calendar shows no further activity for her until 11 October 1720 when she played Arabella in *The Committee*, after which her name disappeared from the bills.

Biggs, Miss. *See* **BROWN, MRS** [*fl.* 1798].

Biggs, Anne, later Mrs Samuel Young *1775–1825, actress, singer.*
Anne Biggs was born in Debenham, Suffolk, in 1775 to James Biggs (d. 1808) and his wife Sarah (d. 1812), both of whom performed, but never in London. Her father was at various times manager at Lymington, Barnstaple, and Taunton and acted with his wife at Edinburgh in 1791. Anne's sister (perhaps her twin) Binney Smith Biggs (1775–1829), later Mrs David Grove, a second sister (later acting as Mrs Brown), and her brother James, all pursued careers in the theatre. Her paternal uncle, Edward Smith Biggs, was a composer of songs and canzonets.

Miss Biggs came on the stage with her father's company in 1788, when she was 13. After a seasoning period of several years in the rigorous round of the country comedian she went to the Bath and Bristol company under W. W. Dimond's management. She succeeded the popular Miss Wallis, making her first appearance at Bristol as Miss Alton in *The Heiress*, in April 1796.

She had not been long with Dimond's company when she suffered an odd misfortune while on circuit with the manager. His fear of some refractory horses caused him to order the occupants of his carriage to alight in a thunderstorm. Anne was drenched and as a consequence she was laid up for seven months with acute rheumatism, not able to move. It was the beginning of the ill health which plagued her all her life. When she finally was able to act, she and Dimond quarreled over salary, and she left the company.

At 22, Anne received a better gift from Fortune, for on 8 April 1797 Elizabeth Farren left the London stage to become Countess of Derby. Miss Farren's line of acting was exactly congenial to the developing art of Anne Biggs, who was invited to Drury Lane by Sheridan on a trial basis. After a first and successful appearance as the Widow Brady in *The Irish Widow* on 17 October 1797, she assumed most of Miss Farren's parts and soon also the sentimental characters left by Mrs Jordan. Within months she was a public favorite in London as she had been at Bath. She had evidently cured the "only fault" discerned in her action by the *True Briton* of 18 October: her "mode of turning away at the close of every speech and retiring toward the back of the stage, as if the character was of no consequence when the speech was ended." It was reported that she received a "handsome salary," and the account books do indeed show her receiving initially £8 per week. But, like others, she had a great deal of trouble collecting on Sheridan's lavish promises, and the books also show the theatre in arrears to her for several seasons, from 1800 through 1803.

At the beginning of her second season in London Anne was joined at Drury Lane by her older brother James, also from Bath. But he died suddenly on 9 December 1798. Her sister Mrs Brown came to the Haymarket in August 1798.

In the summer season of 1799 Anne was advertised at Birmingham as from Drury Lane. She was also at Edinburgh, Glasgow, Plymouth, and Liverpool (but had to decline a generous offer from York) in the following two summers, 1800 and 1801.

Anne Biggs married a surgeon, Samuel Young of North Audley Street, Bristol, on 3 February 1802, setting at naught the report that she was engaged to John Fawcett the younger. In 1800 she had been living at No 17, Charles Street, Covent

Harvard Theatre Collection

ANNE BIGGS, as Cora
artist unknown

Garden. In May 1804 she was said to be at No 4, Cecil Street, Strand.

Anne Biggs Young retired from the London stage after 1803–4. But in a letter to the Haymarket manager James Winston dated 2 September 1808, she asked for employment, proposing terms of £12 per week "and a benefit night at the usual charges." There is no evidence that Winston heard this with favor. She was reported to be in America in 1811 but whether acting or not is uncertain. In a memorandum of 11 June 1823 Winston noted "Terry shewed me a letter from Mrs Young of Brunswick St White Conduit House. stating her husb[d] was gone on board a ship as a surgeon having met with misfortunes she was going as companion to a Lady & begged assistance."

What happened to Samuel Young is

not known, but his wife was obviously alone and in need toward the end of her life. She died at a friend's house at Islington (or Hampstead) on 28 June 1825. An anonymous writer related that "either from carelessness of the future, or a disbelief in the possibility of needing its assistance, [she had] declined contributing to the stock [of the Drury Lane Theatrical Fund], whence all her cares might have been soothed."

The *Post* recalled in her obituary that

for some years past she had in vain endeavoured to procure a situation on the London boards. All ambition in her mind was subdued by misfortune, distress, and absolute poverty. She would willingly have descended to any lower class in her profession, and all she wanted was the decent support of life.

Miss Biggs at the height of her short career could have chosen almost any part she wanted. Her preference was cast about equally for the jilts, flirts, and hoydens of farce, for the soft young women of sentimental comedy, and the frightened heroines of Gothic melodrama. She was occasionally seen in the younger leads and secondary characters of Shakespeare, especially Ophelia, but otherwise generally eschewed heavy tragedy. Here is a partial but representative list of her longer roles:

Lady Teazle in *The School for Scandal*, Violante in *The Wonder*, Angelica in *Love for Love*, the Countess in *The Follies of a Day*, Eliza Ratcliffe in *The Jew*, Cora in *Pizarro*, Beatrice in *Much Ado About Nothing*, Letitia Hardy in *The Belle's Stratagem*, Lady Duberly in *Heir at Law*, and Matilda in *A Word for Nature*.

Miss Biggs was often the critics' darling, though she was not a stranger to stricture. The *Monthly Mirror* paternally praises and corrects her, as in the following remarks on her work in *The Castle Spectre*:

We are much pleased with some of the Angela of Miss Biggs; but we wish she would

not tragedize so much, or display so many fine attitudes, and throw her arms into such fantastic dispositions; and if she could communicate more ease and simplicity to her delivery it would be all the better. But why pronounce it *Osmyn* all through the play instead of *Osmond?* And why present to him the dagger as if it were a pistol, and she, like Estifania, were threatening to shoot the man through the head?

Thomas Dutton scolded her for the habits of "adjusting her dress, and fiddle-faddling . . . in the midst of a speech replete with interest and pathos" and "unseasonable attention to personal attractions," but he commended her for, "in addition to natural talents . . . [her] indefatigable diligence. Illness itself, unless it wears a serious aspect, is not capable of deterring her from the discharge of her professional duty."

Though the *Mirror* found that she "wants some of these airy captivations, and mirthful levities, which distinguish the woman of fashion" and that "Her comedy has frequently a *penseroso* cast," nevertheless

Miss Biggs is indebted to nature for an agreeable and expressive countenance, and a light and very elegant figure, which her peculiar taste in dress enables her to set off to the best advantage. In private society, her manners and conversation are particularly affable, sprightly, and engaging.

But the praise and the kindly censure, and she herself, were forgotten long before she reached her lonely end. A few pictures are left:

William Owen exhibited a portrait of her at the Royal Academy in 1799. An oval engraving by Ridley "from an Original Miniature," was published 31 March 1802 in the *Monthly Mirror*.

[B]iggs, James [fl. 1669], scenekeeper.

A James (B)iggs is said to have been a scenekeeper at the Bridges Street Theatre in

1699, but this is the only reference to him, and in view of the conjecture about the first letter of his last name, perhaps the citation is an error.

Biggs, James 1771–1798, *actor, singer.*

The London comic actor James Biggs was born in Suffolk, the son of the provincial manager James Biggs (d. 1808) and his wife the actress Sarah (d. 1812). He had three sisters on the stage: Anne Biggs, who became Mrs Samuel Young; Binney Smith Biggs, who married David Grove, the actor; and a Miss Biggs who became Mrs Brown.

James began acting, probably at Barnstaple, under his father's tutelage and in his company. He was certainly at Barnstable with his father, his sisters, and his wife in the summer season beginning 28 May 1782. He performed such characters as Scrub in *The Stratagem* and Tom in *Peeping Tom*, while she was given roles like Norah in *The Poor Soldier*. The *Monthly Mirror* thought him "a very pleasing performer," adding "we cannot say so much of his wife." From 1794 through the summer of 1798 he was acting major rustic roles in comedy, and sometimes singing, in the company at Bristol and Bath. He also portrayed eccentric characters at Weymouth in the summer of 1795.

The influence of his sister Anne, who was already settling into her London career, helped him convert his provincial success into an opportunity at Drury Lane, where he appeared for the first time on 27 September 1798, as Ralph in a revival after ten years of *The Maid of the Mill*. On 13 October he was Scrub in *The Stratagem*, and on 16 October Lingo in the afterpiece *The Agreeable Surprise*, after playing Don Alvarez in *The Outlaws*, which he repeated on 18 and 29 October. His acting career and a brief affair with Julia Betterton were cut short by his death on 9 December 1798. In the words of his friend John Cranch,

a fever, originating in a cold, taken on a shooting party, and which baffled the skill and most humane attention, of Mr. Donnelly, Doctor Mosely, and Doctor Reynolds, deprived the public of an excellent comedian, his particular acquaintaince of a most agreeable companion, and his relations of one who lived in . . . their tenderest affections.

Biggs died at his lodgings in Great Russell Street, Bloomsbury. He was buried near the grave of Lawrence Sterne in St George's New Ground, Bayswater.

The cash book of Drury Lane Theatre for 15 December 1798 laconically states his daily salary: "Mr Biggs dead—1 / 6 / 8 off list."

An administration of his property (which, sadly, amounted in valuation only to £100) was given to his Uncle Edward Smith Biggs, the composer, who was also the "Guardian lawfully assigned to James Biggs a Minor or natural lawful son & only Child." Biggs was said to be a widower. (There is some possibility that the actor's son was the subject of the following entry of 13 June 1800 in the baptismal register at St Paul, Covent Garden: "Lewis James, son of James & Elizabeth Biggs" who had been *born* "21 Decr 1791." Speculation as to why the christening was so long deferred is idle.)

Biggs, John [fl. 1667?–1689], *actor.*

There may have been two or more actors named Biggs during the Restoration period, but the scanty evidence suggests that there was possibly only one, named John, and that he may have been connected with the Nursery for young actors at Hatton Garden in London about 1667 and John Coysh's troupe at Norwich in 1672. In a promptbook for *The Wise Woman of Hogsdon* a J. Biggs was noted as playing Old Chartley, and the related promptbook for *The Comedy of Errors* has a Mr Biggs listed for Antipholus of Ephesus; both books pertain to Coysh's strollers or the Nursery, or possibly both. On 9 September 1689 a John Biggs was arrested for acting drolls illegally, and it is likely that he was the same person.

Biggs, John [fl. 1731–1739], violoncellist?

A John Biggs was given a benefit concert at Stationers' Hall on 12 March 1731; he was probably the Mr Biggs who played a violoncello solo at the Haymarket Theatre on 19 February 1736 for his benefit and shared a benefit with four others at Lincoln's Inn Fields on 7 May 1737. He had another benefit at the Haymarket on 1 March 1739, and on 28 August of that year became one of the original subscribers to the Royal Society of Musicians.

Bight. See BRIGHT.

Bigi, Giacinta [fl. 1791–1796], singer.

Signora Giacinta Bigi's name appeared in the cast of Scipione when it was published in Venice in 1791. She came to London to sing at the King's Theatre in the Haymarket from 16 February to 19 July 1796, her first appearance being as Rossolane in I traci amanti on the former date. Subsequently she appeared as Diana in the first English production of Gluck's Ifigenia in Aulide on 7 April 1796, Ninetta in La modista raggiatrice on 16 April, Ismene in Antigona on 24 May, and Dinna Zaveria in Il tesoro on 14 June.

Bignal, Mr [fl. 1732], actor.

On 4 August 1732 a Mr Bignal acted at Tottenham Court at the Great Theatrical Booth in the Cherry Tree Garden near the Mote. He was probably related to the Mrs Bignal who acted at the Haymarket in March 1732.

Bignal, Mrs [fl. 1732], actress.

Though the playbill for the 17 March 1732 performance of The Wanton Jest at the Haymarket Theatre has Miss Radnor playing La Batterelle, the 1731 edition of the play lists Mrs Bignal; since the work was in print before it was produced, perhaps the 1731 edition shows an intended, not an actual, cast. Mrs Bignal was probably related to the Mr Bignal who acted at Tottenham Court in August 1732.

Bignall or Bignell. See BIGNAL and BICKNELL.

Bigonzi, Signor [fl. 1724], singer.

Signor Bigonzi (or Bigonsi, Bigonzo), an alto singer and possibly a castrato, appeared in London for one season, singing Licinio in Vespasiano on 14 January 1724, Nireno in Giulio Cesare on 20 February, and T. Sicelio in Calfurnia on 18 April.

Biland. See BEELAND.

Bilingthon, Mme. See BILLINGTON, MRS JAMES.

Billington, James 1756–1794, double-bass player.

James Billington was a well-known woodwind player in the theatre pit bands of late eighteenth-century London and brother to Thomas Billington the composer. He was first employed at Drury Lane in the 1778–79 season at £1 15s. per week.

Billington married the young singer Elizabeth Weichsel on 13 October 1783 and was almost immediately involved in fame and unhappiness. The pair went to Ireland in 1784, she to act successfully and he to play in theatre bands at Smock Alley, Crow Street, and Capel Street, Dublin, and presumably also at the various provincial places where Mrs Billington acted over the next season and a half: Cork, Nenagh, and Waterford. She was soon unfaithful to him; they quarreled, were reconciled; a child was born and died; Elizabeth deserted him for Richard Daly the manager, who is said to have paid Billington for her favors —all in a confused progression of scandals and sorrows as recounted by James Ridgway's anonymous *Memoirs of Mrs Billington . . .* (1792). Less murky historical accounts tell us of Mrs Billington's theatrical coups in Ireland, her illness, the couple's return to London, the subsequent inevitable submergence of James Billington's personality and professional requirements in his wife's affairs, and his subservience to her success.

But Billington was a capable musician, and though Betsy Billington's high, if dubious, social connections and her professional leverage with managers no doubt insured him good fees, he would have had steady employment—and far less humiliation—without her. He had been proposed for membership in the Royal Society of Musicians by the great oboist John Parke on 4 November 1781 and admitted in 1782. It was said of him then that he had "practis'd Music for Seven Years, he plays the Double Bass is engag'd at Drury Lane Theatre and Vauxhall, is a single man (25 years of Age)." In 1787–88 he was employed by the Academy of Ancient Music for their concerts and paid £12 12*s*. He was sent by the Royal Society of Musicians in 1789, 1790, 1791, and 1792 to play in their annual charity concerts at St Paul's Cathedral, and in the latter two years he was engaged for the band at the Covent Garden oratorios. His address in 1794 was given by Doane as Walcot Place, Lambeth.

In 1794, perhaps embarrassed by the unfavorable publicity stirred by the publication in 1792 of Ridgway's *Memoirs,* but also probably eager for a wider European success, he and his wife and her brother Carl Weichsel left for Italy. He died suddenly of apoplexy in Naples in May 1794, the day after his wife's triumphant debut at the Teatro San Carlo.

Billington, Mrs James, Elizabeth, née Weichsel *1765 or 1768–1818, singer, actress, composer.*

Elizabeth Weichsel Billington was born in Litchfield Street, Soho, by some accounts in 1765, by others in 1768. Her father, Carl Weichsel, was a native of Freiberg in Saxony and principal oboist at the King's Theatre, Vauxhall, and elsewhere. Her mother, Fredericka Weichsel (née Weirman) had been a favorite pupil of Johann Christian Bach and was a singer at Vauxhall for 22 seasons. Elizabeth's brother, Carl, rose to some reputation as a violinist and led the band at the King's Theatre from 1802 through 1814. Brother and sister studied and practised together, and Elizabeth's brilliant voice tone was often attributed to the influence of the constant accompaniment of Carl's violin during those early years.

Elizabeth Weichsel's authentic genius began to manifest itself early in her rapid progress on the harpsichord, under the tutelage first of her father and later of J. C. Bach and J. S. Schröter. On 10 March 1774 she and Carl played in a concert at the Haymarket for their mother's benefit. On 20 May 1777 the pair played at Hickford's Rooms with Samuel Wesley, and on 18 March 1778 they joined as equals the excellent players Florio on the German flute and Stamitz on the viola, in a *quartetto* at Covent Garden, following a performance of an oratorio. The *Public Advertiser* of 13 March stated that she was 11 years old.

Elizabeth was also writing music for her masters' inspection, and she was reported to have published two sets of sonatas before she was 12. This cannot now be verified but is likely, considering the advanced excellence of her piano technique at that age. (Goulding published her *Three Sonatas for Violin and Pianoforte* in 1792.) She prided herself on her abilities at the keyboard as much as on her acting ability. In a letter to her mother from Dublin dated 22 June 1784, when she had been singing for at least five years, she ignored her voice, saying only "I assure [you] I am counted a very pretty actress, and every body that has heard me play on the piano

Beaverbrook Art Gallery, Fredericton, New Brunswick

ELIZABETH BILLINGTON, as Saint Cecilia

by Reynolds

forte, say that I am the greatest player in the world." It was neither as piano prodigy nor composer that Elizabeth was to be remembered, however, but as the greatest English soprano singer of all time.

After the death of her teacher J. C. Bach in 1782 Elizabeth began to take singing lessons from the voice teacher and double-bass player James Billington, and the intimacy soon resulted in marriage, against the stringent opposition of her family. On 13 October 1783 she signed the marriage register of Lambeth Church, assuming her mother's maiden name (and misspelling it: "Wierman").

The Billingtons may have left London soon after their wedding. For their colorful activities during the next two and a half seasons, until their return to London, we must rely upon James Ridgway's anonymous *Memoirs of Mrs Billington from her Birth* (1792), universally condemned as "scurrilous," but perhaps nevertheless containing much truth.

Late in November of 1783 the newly-weds arrived in Dublin, accompanied by her father and brother, and registered at the Marine Hotel. Shortly afterward the family took rooms with Mrs Gunstone at No 107, Capel Street, but did not stay long. Ridgway charged that Mrs Billington began there a series of liaisons which resulted in her being obliged to lodge alone at Mrs Partridge's in Parliament Street. Her husband soon inserted a notice in the newspapers stating that he would not pay debts incurred by his wife. He then broke into her room and seized her possessions, and she was left destitute in a miserable apartment in Little Strand Street. They were, however, shortly reunited when she began to succeed with the audiences.

Mrs Billington had engaged at Smock Alley (according to W. S. Clark; Grove, less authoritatively, says Crow Street) where she sang Polly in *The Beggar's Opera*, Eurydice in an adaptation of Gluck's *Orpheus*, and Mandane in *Artaxerxes*, all

"with some degree of applause." She also sang at the Rotunda and at the English opera house in Capel Street under Giordani's management. In midsummer of 1784 a girl was born to Mrs Billington, but she and her husband left their daughter in Dublin and went to perform at Waterford under Vandermere's management. While they were absent the child died.

After an engagement at Nenagh in Tipperary they returned to Dublin and Richard Daly's management. It did not take long for Mrs Billington to fall to the blandishments of that celebrated debaucher of actresses, and Billington was charged with profiting from his wife's meetings with the manager in their apartment on Upper Ormond Quay. Mrs Billington fell seriously ill in the middle of the 1785–86 season. She managed to collect £60 owed them by Daly, and she and her husband left Dublin and returned to London, moving into rooms at No 11, Great Newport Street, Long Acre.

At Covent Garden on 13 February 1786 Elizabeth Billington made her first appearance in a dramatic role in London, singing by royal command the part of Rosetta in *Love in a Village*. Harris, the manager, had offered an engagement for three nights only, but she had insisted on 12 nights and had asked to be paid £12 per week. The disagreement over terms was forgotten after the royal patronage and sensational popular success of her first performance, and she not only remained in the company for the season but was rehired at £12 per six-day week in 1786–87.

During that first season Elizabeth worked unremittingly with her husband and the voice coach Mortellari to improve her acting technique and the range and quality of a voice which her brother-in-law the composer Thomas Billington felt had been originally "very indifferent." During the summer following she went to Paris to pursue *bel canto* studies with the aging Sacchini, whose last pupil she was. She never relaxed her efforts to improve professionally, and during various stages in her career sought further instruction from Paer, Morelli, Himmel, and others, developing, according to a contemporary, a voice of great power combined with grace and sweetness to complement "a great deal of genuine beauty and very unaffected and charming manners." Her growing fame brought her a commission to sing at the third Chester Music Festival in 1786. The subscription concerts at the Oxford Music Room were postponed that year from November 20 to the next day to suit her, inasmuch as she was engaged in London. She returned to Oxford in June 1787 and on 8 November 1788, and many times again, well into the nineteenth century.

For the season of 1788–89 she received, for singing from 15 September through 18 June, 1000 guineas plus her benefit. She was well worth the sum, for she had become one of the first attractions of the British theatre. In 1789–90 she was earning £26 5s. per week from 13 October through 14 June, virtually the same as the season before for a month's shorter employment. In December 1790 she was reported at Dublin, and she engaged only as a principal performer for the oratorios at Covent Garden in the spring, from 11 March to 15 April. Her name was in two bills at Cork, on 11 August and 29 September, and on a September notice at Limerick. In the season of 1791–92 she was back at Covent Garden, receiving £15 5s. each night she sang; and she engaged for the oratorios as well, from 25 February through 30 March. At this time she was living at No 53, Poland Street, Oxford Road. By 1794 she was at Walcot Place, Lambeth.

In addition to her appearances at Covent Garden, Mrs Billington had busied herself at the successive Handel Commemorations, Vauxhall Gardens, and the Concerts of Ancient Music. She was singing at Edinburgh in February 1793.

The departure of Elizabeth, her husband, and her brother from London for the Continent in 1794 has been attributed to the gossip caused by the publication of Ridgway's *Memoirs* in 1792, several answering pamphlets, and an inconclusive libel suit instituted by the Billingtons. This explanation seems at least dubious. We may assume some desire on her part to test her abilities against continental competition. Still, the gossip at its height could not have been comfortable. Even her partisan and admirer Haydn retailed it (the translation is by H. C. R. Landon):

Today, 14th January 1792, the life of Madam Bilingthon was published in print. Her life is exposed in the most shameless detail. The publisher is said to have gotten hold of her own letters, and to have offered to return them to her for 10 guineas; otherwise he intended to print them publicly. But she didn't want to spend the 10 guineas, and demanded her letters through the courts; she was refused, whereupon she appealed, but in vain, for even though her opponent offered her £500, he nevertheless issued this treasure of hers today, and you couldn't get a single copy after 3 o'clock in the afternoon.

It is said that her character is the worst sort, but that she is a great genius, and all the women hate her because she is so beautiful. N.B. She is said, however, to have written the most scandalous letters, containing accounts of her amours, to her mother.

The Billingtons went first to Italy. When the King of Naples heard Mrs Billington sing at a party given by the British envoy Sir William Hamilton, he was easily successful in persuading her to appear at the Teatro San Carlo. Her debut there in May 1794 was not as casual, probably, as the accounts of the royal persuasion make it seem, since Bianchi created his opera *Inez de Castro* specially for the occasion.

The day after her triumphant first appearance James Billington, coming from a dinner with the Bishop of Winchester, died suddenly of an apoplexy. Mrs Billington stayed for 16 months longer in Naples, singing in operas composed for her by Paer, Himmel, and Paisiello, and founding a lasting friendship with a kindred spirit, Lady Hamilton, Nelson's "Emma."

In 1796 she and her brother Carl Weichsel began a highly successful operatic tour which took them to Florence, Leghorn, Trieste, Rome, and Milan. The *Monthly Mirror* of October 1797 noted: "Mrs Billington is at Venice. She proposes, after singing at the Carnival, to return to England." She did not. Instead she went on to Padua in 1798, then to Milan, where she was received kindly by Josephine Bonaparte and, in 1799, married her second husband, a young Frenchman named Felican or Felissent. They went to live on an estate at St Artien, between Venice and Treviso, but by 1801 she had been driven back to England by his brutal treatment. He followed her

but was arrested and expelled from the country.

Mrs Billington, so far from being forgotten in her own land, was the more frantically courted by the managers because of the notoriety generated by her continental adventures. She seems, with characteristic disregard of consequences, to have signed agreements with both her old employer Harris at Covent Garden and with Richard Brinsley Sheridan at Drury Lane. Sheridan, in a letter dated 3 June 1801, exulted "now I have *secured* her which I am truly delighted at." But by 20 July he was writing to the Reverend Mr Dudley that a "Dilemma has arisen," and asking him to "use your friendly offices to remove misunderstanding on either side and to preserve between Harris and me that confidence and mutual good-will in which we have so long lived." Mr Dudley was evidently the correct emollient, at least from Mrs Billington's point of view, for it was arranged that she should sing that season alternately at Covent Garden and Drury Lane for 3000 guineas and a benefit guaranteed to amount to £500 (it amounted in the event to £600 13s.). She stipulated in addition that her brother should lead the band when she appeared and be paid £500 for the season.

Her reappearance in London was in her tested part of Mandane in *Artaxerxes*. She also sang at the King's Theatre in the title part of Nasolini's *Merope*, sharing acclaim with her rival Signora Banti on 25 March 1802, on the occasion of Banti's benefit. Mount-Edgecumbe testified that

Harvard Theatre Collection

ELIZABETH BILLINGTON, as Mandane
by Gillray

The curiosity to hear these two celebrated singers together was so great, that the theatre overflowed, and even ladies were obliged to sit on the stage for want of places. The performance satisfied every expectation, and the applause bestowed equally on both, was as rapturous as it was well deserv'd.

The music had been composed by Nasolini expressly to give scope to Mrs Billington's abilities.

It embraces a great variety of movements from the highest and most rapid flights of the *bravura* to the most soft and simple measure. It would be difficult to decide in which of the two, she was most successful.

In the 1802–3 season she became the recognized *prima donna* at the Italian Opera. She repeated the triumph of *Merope*, sang in Portogallo's *Fernando in Messico*, and in another role written expressly for her, Winter's *La grotta di Calipso*. She continued to sing at the King's Theatre until 1806–7 and the coming of Madame Catalani. At her last benefit there on 27 March 1806 she sang Vitelli in Mozart's *La clemenza di Tito*, with Braham as Sesto. The *Daily Advertiser*'s critic was witness to her lasting favor with the public:

The Benefit of Billington, the Goddess of Song, was last night as numerously attended as on most former occasions, proving at once her great popularity . . . and Billington was as warmly applauded as ever. All the People of Fashion in Town were present.

Mrs Billington formally retired 3 May 1811 at the conclusion of a concert for her brother's benefit. She sang one final time, however, at Whitehall Chapel in 1814 in a benefit performance for "sufferers from the German war."

In 1817 her husband Felissent showed up suddenly at her opulent villa in Fulham, and for some reason she accompanied the blackguard to her property near Venice. There she died on 25 August 1818, according to some accounts as a result of a beating inflicted by her husband.

The child by James Billington (perhaps) who had died in Dublin was her only recorded offspring, but it has been conjectured that an adopted child, whom she placed in a convent in Brussels, was her own daughter. The will of Thomas Billington, her husband's brother, also provided for his nephew Henry Billington, conceivably Elizabeth's son.

Elizabeth Billington delighted audiences high and low wherever she went, but critics, while conceding her powers, were of two minds sometimes about her execution. She had been trained for concert in a tradition of *bravura* singing which encouraged full exercise of the singer's ingenuity. Her great contemporaries and immediate predecessors, like Mara and Braham, had succeeded splendidly with the more baroque ornamentation. But tastes and fashions were in rapid flux during the time in which Mrs Billington attained her maturity, and her insistent embellishment often encountered critical stricture even as it drew popular adulation. George III, often accounted a pretty critic of the vocal art, is supposed to have dispatched Lord Carmarthen to "get her to sing pathetic songs, and not to overgrace them." Yet the subscribers to the Ancient Music Concerts found her to be chaste and simple in her treatment of Purcell and Handel. Few who ever heard her, however, were less than charmed by the brilliance and sweetness of her magnificent soprano, though Lord Mount-Edgcumbe thought that she

possessed not the feeling to give touching expression, even when she sung with the utmost delicacy and consummate skill. Her face was handsome, and her countenance full of good humour, but it was incapable of change, and she was no actress.

Yet he had high praise for her flexibility, agility, and taste in all phases of opera.

As to Mrs Billington's singing in the more popular roles in the ballad operas and pastorals of the patent theatres and pleasure resorts of London, one contemporary testified that when she first appeared at Covent Garden she was immediately the toast of those who were accustomed to hearing opera, but that those who had been nurtured on the ballads of Miss Catley had never experienced anything like Mrs Billington's "cadences." However, her beauty and spirit soon won her the victory, from the pit to the highest galleries.

Her London debut part of Rosetta in

Love in a Village always stirred her audiences and remained one of her own sentimental favorites. Among her many other strikingly effective singing roles were Polly in *The Beggar's Opera*, Coraly in *The Peruvian*, Lorenza in *The Castle of Andalusia*, Berengaria in *Richard Coeur de Lion*, Rosina in *Rosina*, Rose in *Fontainbleau* and Lady Lucy in *The Lady of the Manor*.

All through her professional life she had kept up her practice on the piano. Salomon said that "she sang with her fingers." Toward the end of her career she gave several concerts on keyboard instruments. Writers of popular songs, like composers of operas, competed for the honor of writing for Mrs Billington, and several of the songs written into pastoral and comic operas especially to show off her vocal athleticism were published.

Betsy Billington can scarcely be said to have led a blameless life, much less an orderly one. Gossip about her sexual adventures, with partners from country actors up the social scale to and including the Duke of Sussex and even the Prince of Wales, was rife through her career. But she was probably the victim in most of her encounters with men. There is plentiful evidence that she was a thoughtful and warm-hearted person. She was generously available for benefit concerts, without fee. When Mrs Clendining was desperately seeking to resume her acting career while her husband was in debtor's jail and their children were unprovided for, Mrs Billington took the family under her roof. As late as 30 June 1819 the newspapers reported that attorneys for the "Count" de Florissent were moving for possession of "certain title deeds, leases and other documents" deposited for security on a loan of £6,500 which Mrs Billington had made to George Mattocks. She herself had never pressed Mattocks for the money.

Elizabeth Billington was often the subject of formal portraits and of likenesses in costume. The most famous picture of her is that by Sir Joshua Reynolds in which he painted her, surrounded by cherubs, as St Cecilia. Two anecdotes originated with this extravagant picture: Admirers of the singer complained that, as magnificent as the huge, life-size depiction of their idol was, it did not do her full justice. "Well of course," Reynolds is supposed to have replied, "but how could I help it? I could not paint her voice." Mrs Billington proudly took Haydn to Reynolds's house to see the painting. "It is like," said Haydn, "but there is a strange mistake. You have made her listening to the angels; you should have made the angels listening to her." The picture is now in the Beaverbrook Art Gallery, Fredericton, New Brunswick, Canada. It was engraved by an unknown engraver in 1802, James Ward in 1803, A. Cardon in 1812, J. Rogers in 1825, and S. W. Reynolds in 1838. The engraving by F. Bartolozzi is undated.

George Romney also painted her as St Cecilia, and the original is in the Boston Museum of Fine Arts. She also sat for five portraits by Sir Thomas Lawrence, one by John James Masquerier, and one by Adam Buck.

Cosway drew and Ridley engraved a portrait of Mrs Billington as Coraly in *The Peruvian* for the *Monthly Mirror* of October 1801. This was re-engraved in 1801 by H. Adlard and copied later by V. Matteini and engraved by Böttger. Downman painted a formal portrait which was engraved by J. C. Armytage. Hopwood engraved from an anonymous portrait, and an anonymous engraver copied Hopwood.

S. de Koster drew a bust of Mrs Billington, in profile, and it was engraved by T. Burke in 1802 and again later. An undated profile head in stipple, originator and engraver both anonymous, were published by R. Phillips. The *Memoirs* of 1792 contain a plate of a likeness of her by A. Van Assen. She was done as Clara in *The Duenna* by W. Hopwood, engraved by S. Noble; engraved by Barlow from an anonymous drawing of her as Constantine in *The Crusade*; and a picture by T. Stothard of her in costume as Mandane in *Artaxerxes* was engraved by J. Heath for the *New English Theatre* published by W. Lowndes in 1788. There are extant also engravings by J. G. Woo of her as Coraly in *The Peruvian*, by J. Alais of her as Mandane, and as Rosetta in *Love in a Village*. There are at least three states of the picture by R. Westall of her as Rosetta, the first engraved by Thornthwaite for *Bell's British Theatre* in 1790, the second also by him, and the third by Brocas. Prattent also drew and engraved her in the character for *The Lady's Magazine*; and Linsell drew her as Rosetta and Alais did the engraving, for J. Roach in 1802. There is a late portrait drawn by Kafter and engraved by Burke.

Mrs Billington's amours, travels, and theatrical politics were attractive themes for the caricaturists Rowlandson, Gilray, Woodward, and, especially Williams. (See Nos 9730, 9840, 9915, 9970, 10168, 19169, and 12309 in the British Museum's collection of satirical engravings.)

Billington, Thomas *c. 1754–1832, pianist, harpist, singer, teacher, composer.*

Thomas Billington was born in Exeter about 1754. He was the brother of the double-bass player James Billington (and consequently brother-in-law of the famous singer Elizabeth Weichsel Billington). Another brother, Horace (d. 1812), was a painter well known in his day.

According to Billington's recommendation for election to the Royal Society of Musicians, rendered on 2 February 1777, he had "studied Music upwards of Seven years and was brought up as a Chorister in the Cathedral of St Peter's Exeter, [and] is a single man." He was admitted to the Society on 6 April 1777.

Thomas was almost certainly the Billington among the tenors listed as singing at Westminster Abbey and the Pantheon in the first Handel Memorial Concerts in May and June of 1784. The Royal Society of Musicians detailed him to sing at the annual charity concerts for the clergy at St Paul's Cathedral in 1790, 1791, and 1792. He sang catches and glees with Rheinhold, Champness, and others at the end of a performance at Covent Garden Theatre on 6 May 1783.

During much of his professional career he lived and taught at his house at No 24, Charlotte Street, Rathbone Place. But in 1824 he moved to Sunbury, Middlesex.

Billington's will, signed 13 September 1827, was not witnessed, and it was necessary for his neighbors Stephen Oborn, surveyor, and John Bliss, carpenter, of Sunbury to come forward on 9 February 1832 "to swear acquaintance of the deceased formerly of Sunbury but late of Tours in the kingdom of France." He had probably died at Tours, not at Tunis, as Grove and the *Dictionary of National Biography* have it.

In the original will Billington left all estates real and personal to his friend and son-in-law Nehemiah Southwell Price, Esq, of Pond Street, Hampstead. In a codicil added 28 May 1828 but not found and proved until April 1832, Billington made other bequests: To his sister Sophia, widow of Joseph Price, Esq, of Stratton Street, Piccadilly, he left all monies then in his account with Coutts and Co., bankers, to his wife for her own use, confident that she would distribute according to their deserts to his sister Mary Billington and nephews Thomas Comins and Henry Billington.

Much of Thomas Billington's composition and compilation was of a peculiar nature. He was fond of selecting the more serious and gloomier passages in English verse and furnishing settings, combining selections from his own music and that of other composers. The more solemn side of Pope and Thomson, of sentimental novelists like Sterne, and especially some of the "Graveyard" poets—Gray, Shenstone,

Young—were much favored. A letter from Billington to the fashionable author Edward Jerningham thanks Jerningham for having selected him to set a poem, which is now returned: "Mr B will be very happy to play the airs and even to sing—if agreeable in Green Street any Evening." Billington was also considerably given to adapting the work of better composers.

Works by Billington to the number of 30 may be found in the British Museum's *Catalogue of Printed Music*. He also published *Some Observations on Singing* sometime toward the end of his life.

Billioni, Mons [fl. 1749–1751], *dancer*.

Monsieur Billioni made his first appearance in England at Covent Garden on 11 January 1749, dancing with Signora Desdechina (or Dedeschina). He apparently made little progress in London, and the following season found him in Dublin, making his first appearance in Ireland at the Smock Alley Theatre on 10 December 1750. He was billed there as being first dancer and ballet master to Count Saxe.

Billoe, Miss [fl. 1741], *actress*.
Miss Billoe played Dorinda in *The Stratagem* on 6 October 1741 at the converted tennis court theatre in James Street.

"Billy." *See* LEARNED HORSE, Little Military.

Bilsingham, Miss [fl. 1786], *dancer*.
At Astley's Amphitheatre on 4 September 1786 the new musical spectacle *Love from the Heart* was performed, and in it Miss Bilsingham danced one of the attendants on the Lord Mayor.

Bimolle, Arcangelo [fl. 1763], *violinist*.
A document purporting to be a translation of a letter of 18 March 1763 from "Signor Bimolle (a Florentine fidler) in London, to The Signora Chiara Aquilante (the famous Opera Broker) at Naples," was published in the *Theatrical Review* of 1763. The letter (after thanking the Signora for a parcel of *maccherone* and animadverting against British cookery) settles into a penetrating, if rather spleenful, denigration of the taste in opera of the London public and of Johann Christian Bach for pandering to its Handelian predilections. The letter sounds very knowledgeable about the King's Theatre, and it is probable that Bimolle was a member of the band there.

Bincks, Mrs [fl. 1735–c. 1740], *dresser*.
The Covent Garden accounts for 1735–36 list Mrs Bincks as a dresser at a salary of 1s. 6d. daily; she was paid £12 18s. for 172 days. By 13 November 1740 she had left her position, for on that date a note was entered in the books reading "Mrs. Bincks late a Dresser on acct 5 / 5 / 0." A duplicate entry was written on 12 February 1741. It seems likely that Mrs Bincks was related to Miss Bincks the actress who became Mrs Richard Vincent in 1738; if Mrs Bincks was the young woman's mother, her retirement from the theatre may well have come shortly after her daughter married.

Bincks, Miss. *See* VINCENT, MRS RICHARD.

Binetti. *See* BINETY and BENELLI.

Binety, Anna [fl. 1761–1763], *dancer. See* BINETY, GIORGIO.

Binety, Giorgio [fl. 1761–1763], *dancer*.
Giorgio and Anna Binety (or Benety, Binetti, Binneti) danced at the King's Theatre in the Haymarket for three seasons, 1760–61 through 1762–63, their first appearance being on 24 January 1761. They were possibly husband and wife, though the distinctive use of their first names in the

bills when they began to perform suggests they were brother and sister; they were not billed as Signor and Signora Binety, but separately.

Bingham, Mr [fl. 1778], actor.

Mr Bingham, billed as "A Young Gentleman" making his first appearance on any stage played Jaffeir in *Venice Preserv'd* at Drury Lane on 16 March 1778. Two newspapers the next day advised Bingham against pursuing a stage career, one noting that his "nature seems totally averse to his succeeding on the stage" and the other saying,

making every allowance for time and the habits of the stage to maturate his judgment and instruct his feelings, we fear there is but little prospect of Bingham's success. His face, person, and address, however, are not against him—but his *voice* and *judgment* seem insuperable barriers—the top of the former was inclining to a whine, which comedized some of the finest passages of the Play.

Apparently Bingham took their advice, for after this single appearance, he was not seen again.

Bingham, George [fl. 1689–1697], violinist?

George Bingham was apparently a violinist, for his name appeared regularly in the Lord Chamberlain's accounts with others who were members of the band of 24 violins serving William and Mary. He was appointed to the monarchs' private music on 5 July 1689, accompanied the King on his trip to Holland from 1 January to 13 April 1691, was petitioned against by trumpeter William Shore on 18 October 1695 in connection with a £10 bond, and on 4 April 1696 was replaced by William Gorton.

Bingis. *See* BINGNER.

Bingner, Mr [fl. 1766–1767], lobby doorkeeper.

Mr Bingner (misspelled Bingis in one account book entry) was a lobby doorkeeper at Covent Garden in 1766–67 at a salary of 2s. daily.

Binion. *See* BENION.

Binks, Miss. *See* VINCENT, MRS RICHARD.

Binley, [Mr?] [fl. 1792], singer.

One Binley, apparently a man, sang at Apollo Gardens in 1792, according to Wroth's *London Pleasure Gardens*.

Binnell. *See* BENNELL.

Binneti. *See* BINETY.

Birch, Mr [fl. 1737], actor.

Mr Birch made his first appearance at Norwich on 4 April 1737 and was billed as from the Theatre Royal London—but there is no other reference to his London activity.

Birch, Mr [fl. 1766], actor.

The Covent Garden accounts for 1766 list a Mr Birch, actor, at a daily salary of 5s.

Birch, Mr [fl. 1794], singer?

Doane's *Musical Directory* of 1794 lists Mr Birch of Litchfield as a bass (singer, presumably) in the Handelian Memorial performances at Westminster Abbey.

Birchall, Robert d. 1819, music publisher, impresario.

Robert Birchall was associated as a music publisher with T. Beardmore at No 129, New Bond Street in 1783, and in the following year he began a musical circulating library. From 1783 to 1789 Birchall and Hugh Andrews were music publishing partners, and from May 1789 to his death in 1819, Birchall was in business for himself at No 133, New Bond Street. In addition to his publishing efforts, Birchall was manager of the Ancient Concerts and most benefit concerts in London, but the years of his activity as an impresario are not clear.

Birchensha, John   *d. 1681, theorist, teacher, violist.*

As early as 1651 John Birchensha (frequently Berkenshaw) was listed as one of the prominent viola teachers in London, but his fame rests more on his theoretical writings. He was probably of the family which had one branch in Denbighshire and another in Flintshire. At some point he was in Dublin, living with the Earl of Kildare; he left there at the rebellion and was in London at the Restoration already set up as a composition and viola teacher. On 13 January 1662 Pepys wrote: "All the morning at home, with Mr. Berkenshaw (whom I have not seen a great while came to see me), who staid with me a great while talking of musique, and I am resolved to begin to learn of him to compose." The diarist started lessons the following day and by 24 February he was finishing a song of his own composition but concerned that he had to pay his teacher £5 for the instruction. By this time Birchensha had developed a system of composition which he reduced to a single card; Pepys ridiculed his "Great card of the body of musique which he cries up for a rare thing and I do believe it cost much pains but is not so useful as he would have it." The lessons continued, but on 27 February teacher and student parted:

This morning came Mr. Berkenshaw to me and in our discourse, I, finding that he cries up his rules for most perfect (though I do grant them to be very good, and the best I believe that ever yet were made), and that I could not persuade him to grant wherein they were somewhat lame, we fell to angry words, so that in a pet he flung out of my chamber, and I

never stopped him, having intended to put him off to-day, whether this had happened or no.

But crafty Pepys still used Birchensha's system, lame parts and all, and found it an effective device for amateur composition.

Evelyn gives the only evidence for public performance, writing on 3 August 1664 of going to "a concert of excellent musicians, especially one Mr. Berkenshaw, that rare artist, who invented a mathematical way of composure very extraordinary, true as to the exact rules of art, but without much harmony." During this year the theorist published his translation of Alstedius's *Templum Musicum*; Pepys dutifully read, but was probably not prepared to like, his ex-mentor's work: "the most ridiculous book as he has translated it, that I ever saw in my life. I declare that I understand not three lines together from one end of the book to the other."

In 1672 Birchensha published and wrote a preface to Salmon's *Essay to the Advancement of Musick*, and about this same time he worked on a book to be called *Syntagma Musicae* for which he was taking subscriptions. Apparently his work never saw print. Some of his manuscripts are at the British Museum, so his rather arbitrary system of composition which excited such interest in his day can still be studied. In *The Humourists* (1671), Shadwell had Brisk say, "but Berkenshaw is a rare fellow . . . for he can teach men to compose, that are deaf, dumb, and blind."

He was almost certainly the John Birchensha who was buried in the cloisters of Westminster Abbey on 14 May 1681, and though Pepys may have found him difficult, he was otherwise reported to be genteel in his person and behavior.

Bird, Mr   [*fl. 1732–1734*], *actor.*

On 27 May 1732 at the Great Booth on Windmill Hill, Mr Bird played Mopsus in *Damon and Phillida*, and on 19 June he acted the same role at Yeates's booth in Upper Moorfields. Bird was also with the troupe doing *The Gardiner's Wedding* on 30 September 1734 at Mile End Green, but his role was not billed.

Bird, Miss *(fl. 1784–1785), actress.*
During the Haymarket Theatre's off-season winter period in 1784–85 Miss Bird played two roles, Miss Walsingham in *The School for Wives* on 16 November 1784 and Aurora in *'Tis Well It's No Worse* on 25 April 1785. In the summer she was a very busy young actress with the lively troupe that played at Hammersmith. She was Mrs Trippit in *The Lying Valet* on 17 June 1785, Lucinda in *Love in a Village* on 1 July, Lady Minikin in *Bon Ton* on 6 July for her benefit with Newbold, Betty in *The Clandestine Marriage* on 8 July, Juno in *Midas* on 15 July, Belinda in *The Ghost* on 22 July, the Countess in *The Follies of the Day* on 25 July, Miss Neville in *She Stoops to Conquer* on 26 July, and Lucilla in *The Fair Penitent* on 27 July. After all this activity and what would appear to be a promising talent, her name disappeared from the London bills.

Bird, John *(fl. 1702), mountebank.*
On 8 September 1702 John and Rhymus Bird, probably relatives, along with other strollers, were advised by a notice in the *Post Man* to pay town constables the required 2s. per day for permission to perform. It is not clear whether the two Birds were performing in London, but since the notice appeared in a London paper, they were probably practicing mountebanks there.

"Bird of Paradise." *See* MAHON, MRS GILBERT.

Bird, Rhymus *(fl. 1702), mountebank. See* BIRD, JOHN.

Bird, Theophilus *1608–1663, actor.*
Theophilus Bird, alias Borne, was probably the son of the actor William Borne, alias Bird; if so, he was baptized at St Leonard, Shoreditch, on 7 December 1608. Though he may have acted as a boy with his father's company (Admiral's-Prince Henry's-Palsgrave's), his first recorded role was Paulina, sister to Vitelli in *The Renegado*, done by Queen Henrietta's men at the Cockpit in Drury Lane in 1625; he was there called Theo. Bourne. He continued playing female roles into the early 1630's, but by 1635 he acted Massanissa in *Hannibal and Scipio* with the same troupe, now styling himself Theophilus Bird. The alias Bourne is unexplained, but it appears that not very long after his father's death (probably in 1625) Theophilus chose to adopt the name of Bird permanently.

On 12 May 1637 he, along with Christopher Beeston and his son William, Ezekiel Fenn, and Michael Mohun, was called before the Privy Council for acting during a plague quarantine, and consequently performances at the Cockpit were temporarily suspended. Bird stayed at the Cockpit after Queen Henrietta's men were forced out of it, probably because of his close relationship with the Beestons. By this time he had probably married Christopher Beeston's eldest daughter Anne, and by October 1638 when Christopher died, Theophilus and Anne had a son, named after his grandfather. The son soon died, however, and was buried at St Giles in the Fields on 27 October 1638. The elder Beeston's will of 1638 left his daughter Anne and her son Christopher £300 on the condition that Beeston's two houses recently built in Covent Garden should prove worth £600; whether they did or not is unclear, but with the death of young Christopher, Anne Beeston Bird probably came into a fair sum of money.

Sometime shortly after the death of Christopher Beeston, probably between 1638 and 1641 (Hotson suggests about

1635), Bird switched to the King's Company at the Blackfriars Theatre; there he remained until the closing of the playhouses in 1642, serving, apparently, as one of the major members of the troupe. According to a Chancery suit of 1655, when Bird joined the company he deposited £200 toward clothes, books, and other theatrical necessities, entering into a £400 bond with his fellow players. When the company disbanded in 1642, Bird claimed later, the other actors ran off with his belongings; when Bird tried to reclaim his losses in 1647, his fellows threatened him with a suit because he had not paid all of his £200 deposit in the first place; how this was finally settled is not known.

On 22 January 1642 Bird's daughter Elizabeth was buried at St Giles in the Fields; birth records for the actor's other children have not been found, but in addition to Elizabeth and Christopher, both of whom died young, there were Ann (who became the actor Michael Mohun's wife), Mary, a second Elizabeth, George, and Theophilus Junior (who became an actor), all of whom survived their father.

Not all of Theophilus Bird's activities during the Interregnum are known, but he was away from London for a while, returning in 1647, so perhaps he, like several other actors, went into the military service for a while. By the early 1650's Bird was involved in theatrical real estate matters with his brother-in-law William Beeston. Serving as Beeston's agent, Bird signed for the playhouse in Salisbury Court when its purchase was completed on 25 March 1652; Beeston, in 1648, had apparently bought part of the lease himself, and now Bird signed for the rest. Bird may also have been involved in a surreptitious performance of Killigrew's *Claricilla* in early March 1653 which was raided by soldiers. *The Mercurius Democritus* of 2–9 March reported that "an ill Beest, or rather Bird (because the rest denyed him a share of their profits) be——t his own nest, causing the poor Actors to be routed by the Soul-

diery"; the "ill Beest" was probably Beeston, and the play on Bird suggests that Theophilus may also have participated.

In 1659–60 when public theatrical activity began again, there was a great deal of jockeying for position amongst the players, managers, and the imperious Master of the Revels, Sir Henry Herbert. Bird may have done some acting as early as May 1659 when Anthony Turner, Edward Shatterell, and others performed at their peril at the old Red Bull playhouse. By February or March 1660 there were probably three troupes at work: Rhodes's at the Cockpit in Drury Lane, Mohun's at the Red Bull, and Beeston's at Salisbury Court; it has been assumed that Bird joined the older players in Mohun's group, and since Mohun may by this time have become Bird's son-in-law, this assumption seems logical; yet Bird and Beeston had shared in the leasing of Salisbury Court and were also related by marriage, so Bird may have performed with him, and if so, he could have taken part in the performance of *The Rump* in early 1660. Oddly, when the single company named His Majesty's Players acted during October at the Cockpit, neither Beeston nor Bird was named a member; they may have performed without being cited in existing documents, but it would seem strange that two such important figures should remain anonymous. It may be that the pair preferred to bide their time; it was already apparent that two companies would eventually form under Davenant and Killigrew, and Bird and Beeston may have decided to remain uncommitted until that happened; or, since they were both now in their fifties, perhaps they wondered whether or not they should continue acting at all.

As it happened, Bird joined the newly formed King's Company under Killigrew on 5 November 1660 and acted with them for three days at the Red Bull before the troupe's converted tennis court in Vere Street was ready for occupancy. Records are very scanty for this period, but sometime during 1660–61 Bird may have played the Duke of Missena in *Erminia* (but the author Richard Flecknoe suggested William Cartwright as an alternate for the part), and on 7 November 1660 he may have acted Woolfort in *The Beggar's Bush*. Two other plays are connected with Bird before his death: *The Royall King*, done at Vere Street in about 1661–62, in which he played Lord Audley, and *Aglaura*, about which Pepys wrote on 24 September 1662: "Bird hath lately broke his leg, while he was fencing in 'Aglaura.'"

Bird's name figured frequently in other theatrical documents, however. On 20 December 1661 ground was obtained by the King's Company for a new playhouse in Bridges Street, and on 28 January 1662 the property was made over to the building sharers; Bird was not a sharer in the building itself, but as a member of the acting troupe he signed an agreement to perform there. He was, however, an acting sharer, and on 10 January 1662 he held one of the total of 12¾ shares in the company; only Mohun, Hart, and Lacy among the actors held larger portions. Bird's annual income on his one share could have been as high as £280, though the average yield was probably less; still, for those days, his income was very respectable. Bird was once named with Hart, Mohun, and Clun, as a representative of the company, to be paid for plays acted before royalty, and he was regularly noted as an active member of the group in livery warrants.

Even by 1660 he was referred to as "old Theoph. Bird," though he was only in his early fifties. In late March 1663, whether from old age, complications following his broken leg, or other causes, Theophilus Bird died. He made his will on 20 March, and it was proved by his widow Anne on 30 June. In it he requested burial at his parish church, St Giles in the Fields, if he should die within ten miles of there, a wish that was granted on 31 March 1663. He asked for an inexpensive funeral. To his children Ann Mohun, Mary, Elizabeth, Theophilus, and George he left 20s. each;

to the poor of his parish another 20s.; his "right and title in all the playes and play bookes that are mine by payment and survivour shipp" to his two sons; and all else to his wife.

After Bird's death his acting share in the King's Company was appropriated by manager Thomas Killigrew, creating a dispute within the troupe. It seems likely that since Bird's will made no reference to his share, he may not have paid anything on it, in which case it was available at his death to Killigrew if he wanted it.

Bird, Theophilus *d.* 1682? *actor.*

From at least 1664–65 through 1673–74 the younger Theophilus Bird served as a minor member of the King's Company to which his father Theophilus had belonged. Though he and his brother George (who was apparently not in the theatre) were bequeathed their father's rights in the plays and playbooks belonging to the elder Bird, young Theophilus seems not to have capitalized on his advantage. His name appeared periodically on livery warrants, and he was twice mentioned for roles over the years: Prospero in *Flora's Vagaries*, probably done at court on 14 February 1667 and certainly done at the Bridges Street Theatre on 5 October of that year, and Abdrahaman in Duffett's farcical *The Empress of Morocco*, performed by the King's troupe at the Lincoln's Inn Fields playhouse in December 1673. From this scanty evidence one might guess that his specialty was comedy. On 11 August 1670 he was ordered arrested for using abusive language to manager Thomas Killigrew, but otherwise his behavior appears to have been respectable. The Theophilus Bird of "cockpit Ally Dr Lane" who was buried on 10 February 1682 at St Giles in the Fields (the elder Bird's parish) was very likely the actor.

Birde. *See* **BEARD, JOHN.**

Birkenshaw. *See* **BIRCHENSHA.**

Birkett. *See* BURKITT and BIRKHEAD.

Birkhead, Mary. *See* KNIGHT, MARY.

Birkhead, Matthew *d. 1722, actor, singer, dancer.*

Hardly anything is known of Matthew Birkhead (or Burkhead, Burkett) beyond his theatrical career, which extended from 1707 to 1722. His first recorded appearance was as Worthy in *The Recruiting Officer* on 18 October 1707 at Drury Lane, a role important enough to suggest that he may already have had considerable experience. During this season he also appeared as the Dancing Master in *Love for Money* on 21 May 1708. Though most of his roles were in lighter works, he played Menelaus in *Troilus and Cressida* on 2 June 1709 and occasionally attempted other serious parts. During the next decade he played Nightingale in *Bartholomew Fair* (24 August 1711), Isander in *Timon of Athens* (17 May 1714), Abel in *The Committee* (1 December 1718), Lady Addleplot in *Love for Money* (7 July 1720), Kate Matchlock in *The Funeral* (13 April 1721), and the Doctor in *The Escapes of Harlequin* (10 January 1722).

He seems to have started his career as an actor who occasionally danced; starting about 1711–12 he also occasionally sang; by 1715–16 he was doing all three about equally; and by 1720 he was singing and dancing more than acting. In 1721 in his *Anatomical Lectures*, John Weaver named the dancing masters of that time, and among them was a Mr Birkhead, doubtless Matthew. The last theatrical notice of him was on 15 May 1722 when *Amphitryon* was done at Drury Lane for his benefit; no role was listed for him, nor had he performed in that work since 7 December 1709 when he acted Phoebus. He was probably ill, for on Sunday morning, 30 December 1722, Matthew Birkhead died, and on 5 January 1723 he was buried at St Clement Danes.

Birling. *See* BURLING.

Birnie, Mr [*fl.* 1796–1797], *house servant.*

One Birnie was listed among the house servants at Drury Lane on 3 December 1796 at a salary of £1 5s. for a six-day week; Birnie was noted again in the accounts on 10 June 1797.

Biron. *See* BYRN and BYRNE.

Birt. *See also* BURT.

Birt, [Mr?] [*fl.* 1791–1792], *house servant?*

One Birt was listed in the Covent Garden account books on 17 September 1791 at a salary of 12s. 6d. for three nights; on 2 June 1792 Birt was cited for £1 10s. covering five nights of work.

Birt, Miss S., later Mme Frederic [*fl.* 1791–1813], *dancer.*

Miss (or Mademoiselle) S. Birt was first mentioned in London playbills on 17 February 1791 when she danced the Muse of Eloquence in the ballet *Amphion et Thalie* at the Pantheon. On 22 March she was one of the Nymphs in *Telemachus in the Island of Calypso.* During the next season Miss Birt appeared briefly at Covent Garden, dancing one of the minor roles in *Blue Beard* starting on 21 December 1791. Her salary was £1 5s. weekly, but she stayed at Covent Garden only until 18 February 1792. During the summer of this year she performed at Richmond, and at some point between August 1792 and September 1797, she apparently danced at the King's Theatre in the Haymarket, and became Madame Frederic. On 1 September 1797 she danced, for that night only, at the Richmond theatre and was noted as being from the opera house. During the summer of 1798 she danced at the Birmingham theatre, but after this her activity is obscure until 1809–10 at the King's Theatre, where she was on the company list as a dancer. Madame Frederic danced again at the King's in 1812 and in 1813, being billed in the latter year as Mme Frederici. Since in her early years she was sometimes billed as Mademoiselle Bert, perhaps she was French by birth.

Birtenshaw. *See* **BIRCHENSHA.**

Bisan. *See* **BAYZAND.**

Bishop, Mr [*fl.* 1735], *singer.*
Mr Bishop, of Russell Street, sang "The Roast Beef Song" at Lincoln's Inn Fields Theatre on 22 August 1735.

Bishop, Mr [*fl.* 1738–1744], *gallery-keeper.*
Mr Bishop was gallery keeper at Drury Lane and received shared benefits from the 1737–38 season through 1743–44.

Bishop, Mr [*fl.* 1741], *actor.*
A Mr Bishop acted Quaver in *The Virgin Unmask'd* on 5 May 1741 at Goodman's Fields and on 25 May shared a benefit there with four others.

Bishop, Mr [*fl.* 1776–1777], *dancer.*
A Mr Bishop was on the roster of the Covent Garden Theatre as a dancer from November 1776 to May 1777, earning £6 per week. He was said to be making his theatrical debut on 23 November when he performed a "New Pastoral Dance," following the mainpiece. He repeated this on 30 November and on 26 and 30 December, and on 4 January 1777 he accompanied Signora Tinte in a "Rural Dance."

As far as the bills show, Bishop's *solo* or *duo* opportunities were limited, but he was frequently employed in the group dances of pastorals and pantomimes. He was living at No 15, Bateman Buildings, on 26 April 1777 when he danced with Signora Tinte a *Minuet de la cour* on his benefit night.

Bishop, Mr [*fl.* 1797–1803], *box-keeper.*
A Mr Bishop replaced Furkins as box-keeper to the theatre on Covent Garden's constant pay list, at 2s. per day, on 9 December 1797. He was employed through the 1802–3 season.

Bishop, Mrs [*fl.* 1741–1742], *dancer, actress, singer.*
Mrs Bishop was one of a small group of troupers who shared the distinction of belonging to the company in which young David Garrick made his first appearances. She danced, with Miss Medina and Master Nanfan, at Goodman's Fields Theatre on the evening of 28 April 1741. She was obscurely in the group ballets for the rest of the season, and when she returned in the fall she had added acting to her competence. In fact, on the third night of the new season, 16 September 1741, she acted the Nurse in *Love for Love*, the mainpiece, stepped into men's attire to play Sir John in *The Devil to Pay*, and danced in addition. On 18 September she was Teresa in *The Spanish Fryar*; on 25 September she was Mrs Motherly in *The Provok'd Husband*; and on 30 September she was Lady Bountiful in *The Stratagem*.

Mrs Bishop was subsequently employed in minor roles, such as one of three priestesses in a pantomime, and interesting secondary ones, like Mrs Prim in *Bold Stroke for a Wife*, Honoria in *Love Makes a Man*, Mrs Chat in *The Committee*, and the Wife in *The Anatomist*, while continuing to dance frequently. She could sing, also, for she was Lucy in *The Beggar's Opera* on 10 December and following.

Mrs Bishop disappeared from the London notices with the removal of the Giffards and their company from Goodman's Fields at the end of their season of 1741–42.

Miss Rosenfeld found a Mrs Bishop playing at Bath in 1747, Penley recorded her there at least from 1750 through 1755, and the Bath *Chronicle* of 1 July 1762 reported the death, in June, of a Mrs Bishop who had long been of the Bath theatre. It is conceivable that the decedent was our subject.

Bishop, Mrs [fl. 1776–1778?], actress.

A Mrs Bishop was in Samuel Foote's summer company at the Haymarket Theatre on 18 September 1776, playing Mrs Wisely in *The Miser*. She may have been the Mrs Bishop who was at that theatre in one of the out-of-season performances in 1778.

Bishop, Henry [fl. 1784–1790], violinist, dancing master, dancer?

Henry Bishop of No 45, Paddington Street, was identified by Doane in 1794 as a violinist, dancing master, and participant in the concerts of the New Musical Fund. He was probably the Mr Bishop listed among the first violins at the initial Handel Memorial Concerts in May and June of 1784.

The Minute Books of the Royal Society of Musicians recorded on 6 February 1785: "Mr Zeidler proposed Mr Henry Bishop as a proper person to be a member." But on 6 March 1785

Mr Bishop's recommendation was read, the members present debated thereon, a Ballot was taken, whether Mr Bishop was a proper person to be ballotted for, he being a professed Dancing Master. yeas 4 nays 20

Longman and Broderip, London, published two collections of his compositions.

Bishop, Robert [fl. 1677], trumpeter.

Robert Bishop, on 30 July 1677, was appointed to the King's Musick in place of Patrick Ray, attending "for the time being" the Lord Lieutenant of Ireland. It is not clear whether his service was restricted to Ireland, but the implication is that he

would eventually return to London and perform there.

Bithemer, Bithman, Bithmare, Bithmer. *See* BITHMERE.

Bithmere, Master [fl. 1784], dancer. *See* BITHMERE, A[UGUSTIN?].

Bithmere, A[ugustin?] [fl. 1783], dancer.

A Monsieur A. Bithmere was the father of a brood of French dancers, some members of which were in London from the fall of 1783 until the spring of 1792. (The Lord Chamberlain's accounts spell the name "Bithman.") Madame Bithmere accompanied her husband to London, as did two daughters, Marie Françoise and the younger Augustine Louis. There may also have been a son, as a British Museum manuscript pay list cites "A. Bithmer Sen" and "Bithmer Jun."

Monsieur and Madame Bithmere were not identified in the playbills until May, but they were dancing at Covent Garden on 9 October 1783 in the melodrama *The Rival Knights* and advertised as "Performers who never before appeared in this Kingdom." The piece was repeated many times during the season. The father earned £2 2s. per week, his wife £3 3s., the son (according to the manuscript cited) £2 2s., and one of the daughters 15s. 9d.

Whether Monsieur Bithmere retired to be a dancing master, died, or went back to France is not known. He was evidently not with Madame Bithmere when on 18 December 1784 she danced for the first time in the opera *corps de ballet* at the King's Theatre with luminaries like Nivelon and Mlle Dorival from the Paris Opera House.

Madame Bithmere was absent from all known London bills in the season of 1785–86. However, on 7 April 1786 of that year her younger daughter Augustine Louis danced with Ferrere in "A New Comic Dance, *The Merry Negroes*," at Astley's

Amphitheatre. On 25 April she was to be found dancing at Hughes's Royal Circus in St George's Fields, and with her there was her elder sister Marie Françoise.

Madame Bithmere reappeared at the King's Theatre in several dances on 23 December 1786 and perhaps danced there earlier in the season. She was carried in the bills for the last time on 15 March 1787, when she was for the second time a principal in an "Allegorical Ballet" by Hus, *L'heureux événement*.

One of the *filles* Bithmere was dancing at the short-lived Royalty Theatre, in Carter's pastoral *The Birthday* on 31 October 1787. The elder daughter danced at Sadler's Wells in 1788 and was "positively Siddonian," according to Dennis Arundell, when she acted there in *The Four Valiant Brothers*. Both of the girls danced at the Pantheon from 17 February through 9 July 1791 and one at the Haymarket the following summer.

Max Fuchs cites: "Bithemer, (Dlle) Danseuse, Londres 14 Avril 1792 (Bib. Opéra, la Foire de Smyrne)," but the name is not included in the bill which *The London Stage* gives for the only performance of D'Auberval's *La Foire* of that date, which was performed at the Haymarket.

Bithmere, Mme ₁*fl. 1784–1787*₁, *dancer.* See **BITHMERE, A**₁**UGUSTIN?**₁.

Bithmere, Augustine Louis ₁*fl. 1784–1787*₁, *dancer.* See **BITHMERE, A**₁**UGUSTIN?**₁.

Bithmere, Marie Françoise ₁*fl. 1784–1788*₁, *dancer, actress.* See **BITHMERE, A**₁**UGUSTIN?**₁.

Bitte. *See* **BITTI**.

Bitterton. *See* **BETTERTON**.

Bitti, Alexander ₁*fl. 1715–1730*₁, *violinist.*
Alexander Bitti (or Betti, Bitte, Bitty) was advertised as newly arrived from Italy

when he played at a concert at Hickford's music room on 6 April 1715. He may have been related to the musician Martino Bitti, one of whose compositions was played at Drury Lane and was published in January 1704. Bitti played at Drury Lane on 18 May 1716, at Hickford's on 12 April 1717, at Drury Lane on 25 May 1717, and at Stationers' Hall on 23 December 1718. It may have been about this time that he went into the service of the Duke of Chandos's academy of music at Cannons where he was one of the three first violins and received a salary of £10 per quarter, and it is probable that he played at concerts there until about 1720.

On 4 May 1722 he played a solo of his own composition at Lincoln's Inn Fields, and at some point after this he seems to have journeyed to America. In the council minutes covering November 1727 through October 1730 on the island of Jamaica, the expenses for a reception for Governor Robert Hunter included £35 "for Musick and Attendance for seven days after His Excys Arrival"; the money was to be shared by five musicians, one of whom was Alexander Bitti.

Bizan. *See* **BAYZAND**.

"Black Jack." *See* **KEMBLE, JOHN PHILIP**.

"Black Prince." *See also* **DOUGLAS, WILLIAM**.

"Black Prince, The" ₁*fl. 1700*₁, *dwarf.*
In July 1700 over against the Mews' Gate at Charing Cross was exhibited "a little *Black Man*, being but 3 foot high, and 32 years of age, straight and proportionable every way, who is distinguished by the Name of the *Black Prince*, and has been shewn before most Kings and Princes in *Christendom.*" Exhibited with him, according to the advertisement, was "his wife, the

Little Woman, NOT 3 foot high, and 30 years of Age" called the "Fairy Queen"; though "big with child," she danced, and their little *"Turkey Horse,"* a trained creature two feet high and 12 years old (who sounds very like a dog), did a "surprising Action" of some kind. The horse, stated the puff, was kept in a box.

Blackburn, Mr [*fl. 1780*], *actor.*
Mr Blackburn appeared as Saville in *Wit's Last Stake* at the Haymarket Theatre on 3 January 1780.

Blacker, Henry *b. 1724, giant.*
Henry Blacker, "The British Giant," was born near Cuckfield, Sussex, in 1724. In 1751 at the Swan in Smithfield he was

Harvard Theatre Collection
HENRY BLACKER, "the British Giant"
artist unknown

exhibited, for he had grown to a height of seven feet four inches, which, as Caulfield noted,

considerably exceeded that of a celebrated German giant, named Cajanus, who was shewn . . . some few years prior to Blacker's exhibition of himself. A great many of the first nobility and gentry honored Mr. Blacker by their frequent visits, and among others the celebrated William, Duke of Cumberland, was one of his greatest followers and admirers.

Blacker was not as tall as some giants of the time, but he was reported to have been less grotesque than the unwieldy O'Brien, who stood eight feet, two inches. An engraving of Blacker has survived, but the artist is unknown; it was first published in the *Wonderful Magazine* by C. Johnson, but the date of publication is likewise unknown. An anonymous engraving, the reverse of the *Wonderful Magazine* picture and a copy of it, was made for the *London Magazine* in 1751.

Blackey. *See* **BLAKEY.**

Blackford, Mr [*fl. 1791–1792*], *house servant?*
In the Covent Garden account books one Blackford, probably a house servant, was listed on 30 April 1791 at a salary of 2s. nightly; he was noted again on 2 June 1792 at the same salary.

Blackly, Mr [*fl. 1715*], *singer.*
The second edition of *Venus and Adonis* (1715) listed a Mr Blackly as singing Mars—probably at the 12 March 1715 performance at Drury Lane.

Blackman, T. *See* **BLACKMORE, MASTER T.**

Blackmore, Mr [*fl. 1786–1804*], *scene painter.*
Several sizeable payments to a Blackmore for painting scenes at Covent Garden

were recorded in that theatre's books between 3 January 1786 and 30 December 1788. He was not carried regularly as a resident painter until his contributions to the scenery for *Merry Sherwood* in 1795. His salary was £2 2s. per week in 1796, £2 10s. in 1797, and £3 in 1798. Other works at Covent Garden for which he helped paint or repair scenery were: *Harlequin's Treasure*, *Lad of the Hills*, *Olympus in an Uproar*, and *Harlequin Oberon* in 1796; *Raymond and Agnes*, *The Round Tower*, and *Harlequin and Quixote* in 1797; *Joan of Arc* (ballet), *Harlequin's Return*, *Ramah Droog*, and *Albert and Adelaide* in 1798, and *The Magic Oak* in 1799. On most of these projects he was, however, only an assistant to Phillips.

This was certainly also the Blackmore who had prepared scenes for Astley's Amphitheatre, including, with Lupino and Robertson, those for "the painting of Plymouth Dock" for a display called *The Royal Naval Review* and, with Whitmore and Byrne, for *The King and the Cobbler*, which opened on 6 May 1791.

Toward the end of the season of 1798–99 Blackmore went to Drury Lane to work with Marinari, Greenwood the younger, and Capon, but again as an assistant only, which is to say that he was primarily an executant, not a designer. In May of 1799 he was concerned in the lavish scenery for Sheridan's *Pizarro*. For the opening of Cross's rebuilt Royal Circus that summer he and others assisted in putting into effect Greenwood's design for the spectacular *Almoran and Hamet*. In 1800 Blackmore helped Pugh execute views for the scenic theatre at the Lyceum. For Davis at his New Royal Circus in St George's Fields he helped execute the designs of Greenwood for the scenery of *The Eclipse; or, Harlequin in China* performed on 17 August 1801. He painted, with others, Greenwood's designs for *The Golden Farmer; or, Harlequin Ploughboy*, 28 June 1802 at Cross's Royal Circus; on 11 April 1803

he did scenes for *The Rival Statues; or, Harlequin Humourist* and on 25 April for *Louisa of Lombardy*, at the same arena. In 1802 he painted Andrews's designs for *Harlequin Greenlander*. In 1803 he did all the scenes for *Number Nip*. He was intermittently employed at Covent Garden again in 1802–3 and 1803–4.

Blackmore had a wife and two sons, all of whom were rope dancers at the minor theatres and sometimes at the patent houses. In view of the fact that one of his sons appeared as "T. Blackmore," there is some chance that the painter himself was (or was related to) the Thomas Blackmore, engraver, who showed mezzotint engravings at the exhibitions of the Society of Artists of Great Britain in 1769 (at which time he was lodging "At Mr Pearson's, Duke Street, York Buildings") and at the Free Society of Artists in 1773 (when he was living at No 14, Denmark Court, the Strand).

Blackmore, Mr [*fl.* 1790], *puppeteer.*
A puppet master named Blackmore was at Bartholomew Fair in September 1790. According to the Pie Powder Court Book at London Guildhall, cited by Miss Rosenfeld, he paid 6s. for a license, 6 September.

Blackmore, Mrs [*fl.* 1791], *rope dancer.* See **BLACKMORE, MR.** [*fl.* 1786–1804].

Blackmore, Master [*fl.* 1798–1807?], *dancer, rope dancer, actor, singer, equestrian.* See **BLACKMORE, MASTER T.**

Blackmore, Master T. [*fl.* 1798–1807], *dancer, rope dancer, actor, singer, equestrian.*
Two sons of Blackmore the scene painter and his wife the rope-dancer were themselves accomplished rope-dancers. They also did specialty dances, acted, sang, and did trick riding. It is not possible, except in one instance, to say which was performing at a

given time, but their talents appear to have been identical. One Master Blackmore, doubtless very young, was on the roster of dancers at Covent Garden Theatre from 24 November until 6 June 1798, at only £5 5s. for the entire season. From 25 March through 6 June 1799 there were two Masters Blackmore in the theatre at an undisclosed salary. One was a dancer in the popular afterpiece *The Magic Oak*, for which his father painted the scenery. Through most of the period, in fact, the father was on the pay list of the theatre.

One of the boys (if not both) was finding work in the summers at the circuses. the *Monthly Mirror* for July 1798 testified that Master Blackmore's Little Lingo in the pantomime of *Harlequin Highlander* "has for the last month occasioned a complete overflow every evening" at Jones's Royal Circus. The lad played the same part on 29 May 1800, and with Miss Fisher he acted "Little Man and Wife" in *The Eclipse* on 17 May 1801, both at Davis's New Royal Circus. Again, under Cross's management at the Circus on 28 and 29 June 1802 he sang a duet with Master Standen. He was there again, as Lounger Lightfinger "(with a song)" in *Harlequin Humourist* on 11 April 1803, and on 29 April 1805 as Dubs in *Knight of the Garter*, and yet again in July 1807, when, in one bill, there was reflected "slack rope vaulting by Master T. Blackman [*sic*] who will twist round on the rope with fire works to his hands and feet, thereby forming a complete ball of fire." In the same bill a Blackmore displayed "horsemanship." By August and November 1814, a "Mr Blackmore" was performing on the slack rope at the Royal Circus, and after those dates the family appeared no more in London or locality.

Blackmore, William   ₁fl. 1754–1770₁, *tailor*.

William Blackmore identified himself in a legal deposition of 1768, testifying that he "Hath been Taylor for 13 or 14 years" at Covent Garden Theatre.

He was probably the William Blackmore who, with Ann Blackmore (his wife?) and Mary Davis, witnessed the marriage of Mary Blackmore (his daughter?) to the boxkeeper Thomas Ansell at St Paul, Covent Garden, on 2 April 1763. He also witnessed the will of John Rich, his employer at Covent Garden, on 21 May 1761.

In 1758 Blackmore was entrusted by the theatre's treasurer to make sundry payments to tradesmen. In 1769 (27 April and 2 June) and 1770 (13 June) occur three baffling payments to him in the treasurer's list: "for sending men into the gallery," £20 3s., £9 18s., and £9 16s.

Blackwell, Henry   ₁fl. 1698₁, *fencing master?*

In the *Post Boy* of 19 November 1698 the Sergeant Trumpeter Matthias Shore advertised that his servant Richard Blackwell had run off with one of the King's silver trumpets, supposedly in the company of his brother Henry Blackwell, "a pretended fencing Master." It is not certain whether or not Blackwell displayed his pretensions on stage.

"Bladderbridge, Mr"   ₁fl. 1774₁, *musician*.

Christopher Smart, alias Mrs Midnight, must have been in London in 1774, though no other activities of his are known except a performance of a Comic Ode at Dr Arne's *Temotheus* benefit on 15 March 1774 at the Haymarket. The Ode was to be performed by Bladderbridge on the hurdy-gurdy, Clatterbane on the saltbox, Shadrach Twanglyre and his assistants on the Jew's harp, and Dingdong and his assistants on the marrow bones and cleavers. These pseudonyms were typical of Smart's antic entertainments, but unfortunately we do not know who the real performers were.

Bladgen. *See* BLAGDEN.

Blaew. *See* BLOW.

Blagden, Mr [fl. 1760–1767?], dancer.

On 19 June 1760 Mr Blagden danced at Drury Lane at a benefit performance for distressed actors presented by the Richmond company. The Blagden who rented space from Drury Lane at £3 10s. per year in 1766–67 could have been this dancer, and the Master and Miss Blagden who danced at Drury Lane were very likely related to him—perhaps as his children.

Blagden, Mr [fl. 1765–1777], dresser.

Mr Blagden was one of the men's dressers at Drury Lane, receiving, according to a salary schedule dated 9 February 1765, 1s. 6d. per day or 9s. per week. He was doubtless one of the Blagdens serving as dressers during the 1776–77 season.

Blagden, [Mr?] [fl. 1776–1777], dresser.

One Blagden (or Bladgen) was a dresser at Drury Lane during the 1776–77 season earning 9s. per week; he (or she) was one of two of this name serving in the same capacity.

Blagden, Master [fl. 1755–1759], dancer.

Master Blagden participated in Noverre's *The Chinese Festival* on 8 November 1755 at Drury Lane, and it is probable that he was also in *A New Pantomime Dance* on 3 December and *The Garland* on 13 February 1756, both of which were performed by the children in the theatre's corps of dancers. His name did not appear again in the Drury Lane bills until 15 May 1759 when he danced a *New Dutch Dance* which was not repeated. On 12 December 1759 he again performed in the *Dutch Dance*, with Miss Blagden also participating. It seems likely that Master Blagden was the son of the dancer Blagden who appeared at Drury Lane in June 1760, though there is the possibility that these two are the same person and that young Blagden reached his majority at about this time.

Blagden, Miss [fl. 1759–1762], dancer.

Miss Blagden was first mentioned in the bills on 12 December 1759 when she participated at Drury Lane in *A Dutch Dance* on an occasion in which Master Blagden also appeared. Her only other notice this season was on 19 June 1760 when the Richmond company performed at Drury Lane; she was in the *Dutch Dance*, as was Mr Blagden, probably her father though possibly Master Blagden now matured. The only other mention of her in the playbills was on 21 April 1762 when she danced at Drury Lane a *Louvre and Minuet* with her teacher Settree. Since Miss Blagden's appearances were isolated, perhaps she was not a regular member of any theatrical company.

Blagden, Nicholas [fl. 1660–1668], actor.

Though Nicholas Blagden spent most of his acting career with the King's Company, he was first recorded as playing the Admiral in *The Siege of Rhodes* (both parts) on 28 and 29 June 1661 at Lincoln's Inn Fields with the Duke's Company. By December he had changed his affiliation, and on 20 December signed an agreement with Thomas Killigrew's troupe which led to the construction of the Bridges Street Theatre. Blagden was not one of the sharers in the building itself, but he was a full member of the company and agreed to perform at the new playhouse when it was completed. Only one other role is recorded for him during his career: Nibrassa in *Love's Sacrifice*, at Bridges Street in 1663–64.

Blagden's name appeared frequently in the Lord Chamberlain's accounts, however, sometimes in connection with livery payments to which he was entitled, but more often concerning suits brought against him, probably for debts. An Anthony Wood petitioned against him on 25 October 1662,

Thomas Bedford on 15 October 1663, Sir William Clarke on 26 March 1664, Thomas Letchfield on 8 July 1664 (but his permission to sue was suspended on 25 August), and Robert Toplady on 17 September 1664 (a joint suit against Blagden and his fellow actor Loveday). After the plague and fire Blagden was again with the King's Company, but no further roles or law suits are recorded for him. A livery warrant dated 8 February 1668 has his name deleted, which fact suggests that about this time he either retired or died.

Blagrave, John   [fl. 1683–1694], musician.

John Blagrave was one of the sons of Anthony Blagrave of Norwich and a student of the London musician John Hingeston. At his death in 1683 Hingeston left young Blagrave a violin. The musician also received bequests of £5 each from his uncle Thomas Blagrave in 1688 and his aunt Margaret Blagrave in 1689 and £10 from musician John Goodwin in 1694.

Blagrave, Robert   [fl. 1660–1669], instrumentalist.

Robert Blagrave, a wind player who was also proficient on the violin, may have been a brother of the more famous Thomas Blagrave and son of Richard Blagrave, wind player at the court of Charles I. Robert replaced Anthony Bassano in Charles II's wind music·in the early 1660's and was also a violinist under Nicholas Lanier and later Louis Grabu. The first specific date connected with him is 2 July 1660 when he was appointed a musician in ordinary; a warrant dated 9 November 1660 gives his salary as £58 14s. 2d. annually, one of the higher fees listed. He played a wind instrument at the coronation of Charles II in 1661, and during the ensuing years he was occasionally paid extra for musical services performed at Windsor. The last extant reference to him is a warrant of 9

January 1669 in which he is cited again as a musician for both wind instruments and violin at the same salary he had been granted in 1660. Robert Blagrave is supposed to have been mentioned in a document dated 1674 which was once in the possession of Edward Rimbault, but this may have been an error for Thomas Blagrave.

Blagrave, Thomas   d. 1688, instrumentalist, singer.

Thomas Blagrave (or Blagrove) was the eldest son of the pre-Commonwealth musician Richard Blagrave from Berkshire and his third wife Anne, née Mason, from the Isle of Wight. Thomas had an extensive musical career that included service under Charles I, Cromwell, Charles II, and James II. The first reference to him seems to be on 22 December 1637 when he was a member of the wind instrument group serving

Faculty of Music, Oxford

THOMAS BLAGRAVE

artist unknown

Charles I at table and chapel throughout the year. On 17 October 1638 he was sworn a musician for the sackbuts and oboes and an assistant to his father; his position was without fee until a vacancy occurred. This came when the elder Blagrave died in January or February 1641, and according to a warrant of 17 January 1642, Thomas was granted 1s. 8d. *per diem* in wages and a livery allowance of £16 2s. 6d. annually. On 14 October 1645 he married Margaret Clarvell (or Clarvox) of Parsons Green at St Margaret, Westminster. Blagrave served Cromwell as he had served the King, and the Protector allowed him to participate in Sir William Davenant's production of *The Siege of Rhodes* at Rutland House in 1656, sharing the role of Mustapha with Henry Purcell the elder—one of the earliest indications of Blagrave's singing ability. At Cromwell's funeral in 1658 Blagrave was one of the small group of court musicians that performed.

After 1660 he was made a member of the royal musical establishment under Charles II, serving as a violinist replacing Peter Guy (alias Pierce) and in the wind ensemble section of the King's private music. Samuel Pepys wrote on 18 March 1660 that he stopped to see Blagrave and collect on a promissory note for 40s. which Blagrave had given him two years before "as a pawn while he had my lute—so that all things are now even between him and I." On 21 June Pepys met the musician on the street and took him home to get a lesson from him on the flageolet.

Though Blagrave's chief duties were as an instrumentalist, he was also a singer in the Chapel Royal; Jeremy Noble lists him as a countertenor, but at the coronation of James II he was among the basses, and as remarkably versatile as Blagrave was, it is doubtful that he had so fantastic a vocal range. Exactly what sort of voice he had is unclear. On October 1662 he was chosen Clerk of the Cheque of the Chapel, replacing the deceased Henry Lawes, and on

10 July 1665 he was chosen by John Banister to play in the select band of violins within the King's Musick.

A document dated 1668 listed him as receiving £45 10s. 10d. yearly as one of the royal violinists; the warrant noted that Blagrave played the violin but was "for the flutes"—probably an administrative rather than a musical arrangement, though he could certainly play both. King Charles tried to retrench in 1669, and Blagrave's salary as violinist and wind instrument player dropped to £40 9s. 2d. on 9 January; this could be an error, for warrants in February and June 1669 stated that the King had exempted Blagrave and a few others from the retrenchment. Blagrave, with his multiple musical talents, was clearly one of the most valuable employees of the court.

Throughout the 1670's Blagrave served Charles II, being chosen frequently to go with the royal entourage when the King journeyed to Windsor or Dover. On one such trip, from 14 August to 26 September 1678, Blagrave was placed in charge of the musicians going to Windsor and entrusted with the money to be distributed amongst them for this extra service. By December 1679 he was earning £46 10s. 10d. yearly as a member of the wind music, in addition to which he would have received (though probably not on schedule) a livery fee and payment for duties performed out of London.

Blagrave's name does not appear in the official records during the early 1680's, though he presumably remained in the royal service. By April 1685 when James II was crowned, Blagrave had become a member of the Choir of Westminster in addition to his other positions. Records of his private life are also rare for these years, though we know he was named for a small bequest in the will of musician John Hingeston in 1683 and was appointed attorney for musician William Child in 1686. But Blagrave was well along in years by this time, and he may have curtailed his musical activities somewhat in the 1680's.

On 14 May 1686 he made his will, on 21 November 1688 he died, and on 24 November following he was buried in the North Cloister of Westminster Abbey. On 4 December 1688 his will was proved by his widow Margaret, to whom he left the bulk of his estate, including his house and land in Teddington. His will named no children, but he made bequests to a number of friends and relatives, several of them musical. Margaret Blagrave was buried on 12 October 1689 in the same grave as her husband. Her will, interestingly, left her estate to Blagrave's relatives, not her own. Dated 5 February 1789 and proved on 17 October of that year, her will listed four houses in Westminster near the Cockpit which Thomas had purchased before his death—probably at some date after he made his own will, since he did not mention them.

From the wills of Thomas and Margaret Blagrave and from that of his cousin, musician John Mason (of which Blagrave was the executor), many of Blagrave's relatives can be identified. Thomas Blagrave had at least two brothers, Anthony and Cheney; Anthony was from Norwich and had a musical son John, to whom both Thomas and Margaret left £5, and Cheney had a son Thomas, to whom his uncle left £40 and his aunt £60. There may have been a third brother, Robert, also a musician, but he was not named in the Blagrave wills and may have been dead by that time. There were also two sisters of Thomas Blagrave whose first names are not known; one married a Mr Johnson and had a son Henry, who was overseas in the late 1680's and was left £5 by Thomas and £100 (if still alive) by Margaret, and the other sister married a Mr Williams by whom she had a daughter Anne who was in Virginia in the late 1680's and was left £5 by Thomas and £60 (if still alive) by Margaret.

There were other Blagraves named in John Mason's will, but their relationships are not clear: Ann and Magdalen (possibly the wives of Anthony and Cheney), Allen, and Allen's daughter Mary. Violinist John Goodwin's relationship to Thomas Blagrave is unclear, but he was called a kinsman and given £20 and forgiveness of his debts by Thomas, and three of the houses in Westminster plus £100 by Margaret, and he was named residuary legatee of the fourth house. This fourth house was given, along with £100, to singer John Frost's wife Frances, and to her also went the house in Teddington which Blagrave had willed his wife; Margaret Blagrave called Frances Frost her niece, but whether the relationship was by blood or by marriage is not certain. The musician Ambrose Searle was also a kinsman of Thomas Blagrave and received £10 in his will; again, the exact relationship is not clear. Another probable relative of the Blagraves is named in John Mason's will: Bridgett Johnson. She may have been Thomas Blagrave's sister, though she could have beeen his niece.

Anthony Wood called Thomas Blagrave "a player for the most part on the cornet flute, and a gentile and honest man." A portrait of Blagrave is at the music school at Oxford.

Blaikes. *See* **BLAKES**.

Blair, Mr [*fl.* 1772–1791], *actor.*

Mr Blair may be unique in the annals of the London stage, for he had a career that lasted 19 years, during which he played only one role—and that one was a female. He acted Mause in *Patie and Roger* (usually called *The Gentle Shepherd*) for the first time on 21 September 1772 at the Haymarket Theatre; when the play was repeated again on 21 December, Blair was replaced by Mr Burnett. He returned to the Haymarket on 18 March 1782 and on the following 9 April to play the role again. His next stab at it was on 24 January 1785 for a single performance, and he finally gave up after acting it again on 26 September 1791 at the same theatre. It is likely Blair was from Scotland, not because of his rather odd choice of role and his persistency, but because the play, by Ramsey, was an old Scots favorite and the first performance of it in which Blair participated appears to have been done by a group of actors down from Scotland. It seems likely that Blair came to London with his colleagues periodically to put on their favorite play.

Blake. *See also* **BLAKES.**

Blake, Mr [*fl. 1753?–1798?*], *dancer, ballet master.*

A mature dancer named Blake appeared for the first time dancing at the King's Theatre in London on 6 December 1783 in D'Auberval's *The Pastimes of Terpsichore,* "an Allegorical Ballet," along with Vestris Junior and several others. He was very likely the Blake who had danced as a juvenile at Dublin's Smock Alley Theatre in the season of 1753–54. He was also probably the son of the Mr and Mrs Blake, dancers (she "from the theatre in Dublin"), who were at Covent Garden Theatre in 1760 and 1761.

Blake danced at the King's Theatre until 22 June 1784, becoming important enough to be billed as "the celebrated Blake" when he danced a hornpipe at an out-of-season performance at the Haymarket for the benefit of Delpini, on 30 April 1784. He was said to be making his first appearance at the Haymarket "by permission of the Managers of the Operahouse." In addition he danced with Delpini in "a new pantomimical dance, *The Rival Clowns.*"

Blake disappeared from all London bills until 13 May 1790, when he was named again in the opera company which in that short season sheltered sometimes at the Haymarket and sometimes at Covent Garden. He then danced "an entire new Pantomimical Dance, *The Generous Slave,*" in his own benefit performance. But he had

been with the company all season, for he was ballet master of a dance corps of 11, including Mlle Hilligsberg. His own ballet, *Les Mariages Flamands,* had been performed for the first time on 13 February. He was living that season at No 60, Haymarket.

Blake was again absent from the theatres of London until the season of 1797–98, when he danced as a featured performer at the King's Theatre from 28 November until 21 July, appearing as Silenus in *Ariadne et Bacchus,* repeated several times, and probably serving again as ballet master. In addition, he put in at least one appearance (on 9 May 1798) at Drury Lane, as Silenus in "the Grand Anacreontic Ballet, *Bacchus et Ariadne.*"

Blake, Mr [*fl. 1760–1761*], *dancer.* *See* **BLAKE, MRS** [*fl. 1761*].

Blake, Mrs [*fl. 1761*], *dancer.*

A Mrs Blake "from the theatre in Dublin" danced a hornpipe on the last night of the Covent Garden season, 23 June 1761. A Mr Blake was on the company list as a dancer for the season 1760–61. Very likely these dancers were husband and wife and stood in some relationship (probably as parents) to the Master Blake who was dancing at Smock Alley Theatre, Dublin, from 1753–54 through 1756–57. He, in turn, may have been the well-known Blake who was dancer and ballet master at the King's Theatre in the 1790's.

Blake, Benjamin 1751–1827, *violinist, violist, composer, teacher.*

Benjamin Blake was born at Kingsland, Hackney parish, near London, on 22 February 1751, according to his explicit manuscript letter to Sainsbury, and not 1761 as given in Grove and elsewhere. In 1760 he was sent by his family to a relative, a musician in Stamford, where he began to learn to play the violin. In 1768 he came to London to be instructed for two years by

Antonio Thammell, the eminent Bohemian violinist, and the celebrated William Cramer. By 1775 Blake was a member of the band of the Italian Opera, where he retained a place through 1793. In 1786 he was appointed musician in ordinary to the King's band. He was for 13 years (not 30, as in Grove) violist at the private concerts of the Prince of Wales. His pleasant personality brought him friends at the Court from his very early days in London, and the nobility pushed his enterprises forward. The powerful Duke of Cumberland was Blake's patron until the Duke's death in 1790. Blake was first violin in the Duke's band under the leadership of Blake's friend Karl Friedrich Baumgarten.

Blake was among the first violins at the initial Handel Memorial Concerts in Westminster Abbey in May and June of 1784. In 1790–91 he was among the violins in the band at the Pantheon. He played in the Professional Concerts and belonged to the Royal Society of Musicians, on the Minute Books of which he appears as a member of the Court of Assistants in 1785, 1795, 1798, and 1799. Muzio Clementi was at some point his teacher and remained his friend, and it was on Clementi's advice, strengthened by that of Baumgarten and William Dance, that he left instrumental performance in favor of private teaching in 1792. To prepare himself, he learned for the first time to play the piano, but he never played that instrument in concert. In 1793 he was engaged at Campden House boarding school, in Kensington, and he proved an efficient and sympathetic teacher. One of his pupils was the violinist and composer Luigi Borghi. His address in 1794 was No 6, Manchester Street, Manchester Square. In 1820 ill health forced him to resign his post. He was living at Hampton on 18 November 1823 and still signed himself "Musician in Ordinary to His Majesty."

Benjamin Blake was one of 13 friends left 19 guineas each in the eccentric will of John Crosdill the musician, signed in 1825. Blake died in London in 1827.

Blake stated in his letter to Sainsbury that he had published "Three Works of Six Duets each, for a Violin and Tenor," during the early part of his career, and, while he was teaching, had published "Six easy Sonatas for the Piano-forte, with an Accompaniment for the Violin," "Nine Divertissements, with a Musical Dialogue prefix'd, and separate Violin Accompaniment," "A Miscellaneous Collection of Vocal Music, with a separate Accompaniment for Harp or Piano-forte," a "Duet for the Violin and Tenor," and "Three Solos for the Tenor, with an Accompaniment for the Violoncello." Blake was a pioneer in Britain in writing works for the viola. His church music was widely collected in the last years of the eighteenth century in Busby's *Divine Harmonist* (1792), Willoughby's *Sacred Harmony* (c. 1795), and Page's *Harmonia Sacra* (1800).

Blake, James ₁*fl. 1794–1802?*₁, *singer.*

James Blake was a bass singer who sang for the Handelian Society at their concerts and perhaps elsewhere. In 1794, according to Doane, he lived on the Brixton Causeway.

Blake, Thomas ₁*fl. 1798*₁, *musician.*

In his will signed on 13 February 1798, Dr Theodore Aylward, the organist at Windsor and professor at Gresham College, provided ten guineas apiece for his "ffriends and acquaintances John Crossdall[,] Thomas Blake and Mʳ Shields Musicians."

Blakely. See **BLAKEY.**

Blakes. *See also* **BLAKE.**

Blakes, Mr ₁*fl. 1698*₁, *actor?, booth operator.*

A Mr Blakes and William Pinkethman had a booth at Bartholomew Fair on 23

August 1698 and produced *Jeptha's Rash Vow.*

Blakes, Mr *[fl. 1761]*, *fire eater.*

For 23 nights in a row, 13 October through 9 November 1761, Mr Blakes, a fire-eater, was paid 7s. 6d. for exercising his talent at Covent Garden Theatre in the afterpiece called *The Fair.*

Blakes, Charles *d. 1763, actor, singer.*

Charles Blakes was probably that young actor who played at the Haymarket on 27 May 1736 the cautionary part of Randal in *Guilt Its Own Punishment,* the less edifying one of Apollo's Bastard Son in Fielding's *Historical Register* on 21 March 1737, and the Actor in *Eurydice Hiss'd* on 13 April 1737, all at the Haymarket Theatre. From these slender beginnings he launched forth on a career as a journeyman actor of comedy which kept him on the stage every year for 27 years, almost to the day of his death in 1763.

In April 1742, people were sent for benefit tickets to his house in Cranbourn Alley, near Leicester Fields. He lived there at least through 1 April 1752, but by the same month the following year had removed to "his House in Dukes Court near Broad Court, Bow Street, Covent Garden," where he lived at least through 1756.

In December 1740 Blakes was acting with the Goodman's Fields troupe. On 15 January 1741 he signed on at Covent Garden for a short series of appearances until 14 February but returned to Goodman's Fields for the rest of the season. In the summer following he played at Turbutt's booth at Bartholomew Fair and probably toured in the provinces. When in the fall of 1742 Giffard took his company to Lincoln's Inn Fields, Blakes was with them, for we take him to be the "Blakey" playing Usher in *Lear* on 10 January 1743, according to *The London Stage.* But he also played oc-

Harvard Theatre Collection

CHARLES BLAKES, as Mons. le Médecin by Mc Ardell

casionally at Drury Lane, beginning with his Bailiff in *The Committee* on 9 October. The next season saw him act full time in that company, and from 1743–44 until the end of his career Drury Lane Theatre gave him employment in the winter seasons. His most constant summer engagment was at the Jacob's Wells Theatre, Bristol, in 1747, 1748, 1749, 1754, and every year from 1756 through 1762. In 1746 and 1752 he was in the summer company which played at Richmond and Twickenham.

The Mrs Blakes who was named in the Jacob's Wells bills for the single season of 1760 was probably Charles Blakes's wife. She was not seen in London, so far as is known.

Blakes died at his house in Castle Street, Leicester Square, on 5 or 6 May 1763. At the time that he signed his will on 14 January 1762 (witnessed by the actors Richard Smith and Thomas Mozeen) he identified himself as "of Newport Street, in the Parish of St Anne, Hatter and Hosier," and left to his wife Sarah and a son Charles all his stock in trade, unspecified. No other child was mentioned, thus it is not likely that the Miss Blakes who was playing at Kilkenny, Ireland, in 1787, was his daughter. (In 1778, 1779, and 1780 there are payments entered in the Drury Lane account books to one "Blakes, hatter.") Blakes does not seem to have been related to the fire-eater of that name.

Charles Blakes played occasionally in tragedy, but he was not very effective when he had the buskin on and was sometimes reproved by criticism for this presumption. He was, however, a more than acceptable actor of farce, pantomime, and sentimental comedy characters across a broad spectrum of lines: blunt men, eccentrics, countrymen, fops and young elegants, the bland secondary men, and foreigners, especially Frenchmen. About his performance in this last line, which finally became his specialty, there was some disagreement, represented on the one hand by *The Present State of the Stage* (1753) ("he appears in the Character of a Frenchman to vast advantage") and on the other by *An Essay upon the Present State of the Theatre . . .* (1760) ("Mr Blakes is reckoned a good mimick of a Frenchman, but we apprehend that it is by such as have not been much conversant among Frenchmen"). Blakes also sometimes amused his audiences by singing sea songs in the intervals of the play.

Here is a representative selection of the many dozens of parts of which this most energetic of actors was capable: Sharper in *The Old Bachelor*, Cassio in *Othello*, Scandal in *Love for Love*, Coachman in *The Drummer*, the Prince in *Tamerlane*, Caius in *The Merry Wives of Windsor*, the Governor in *Love Makes a Man*, Blunt in *The Committee*, Phoenix in *The Distrest Mother*, Worcester in *1 Henry IV*, Scruple in *The Recruiting Officer*, Strut in *The Double Gallant*, Elder Worthy in *Love's Last Shift*, Foigard in *The Beaux' Stratagem*, Welsh Collier in *The Recruiting Officer,* Pedro in *The Spanish Fryar*, Varole in *The Relapse*, Thessalus in *The Rival Queens*, Subtleman in *The Twin Rivals*, Marquis of Hazard in *The Gamester*, Malcolm in *Macbeth*, Quintus in *Regulus*, the Swiss in *The Amorous Goddess*, Marcus in *Cato*, Doterel in *The Astrologer*, Alcander in *Oedipus*, Seyton in *Macbeth*, Pamphlet in *Love in a Bottle*, Cleomines in *The Winter's Tale*, Sir Charles in *The Beaux' Stratagem*, Gibby in *The Wonder*, Ben Budge in *The Beggar's Opera*, Belmour in *Jane Shore*, Norfolk in *Richard III*, Randall in *Fatal Curiosity*, Young Gerald in *The Anatomist*, Transfer in *The Minor*, Dumain in *All's Well that Ends Well*, the Frenchman in *Lethe*, Clerimont in *The Miser*, Monsieur Gasconnade in *Thamas Kouli Kan*, Bedamar in *Venice Preserved*, Mordecai in *Love à la Mode*, the Scotsman in *The Apprentice*, Sancho in *Don Quixote*, Cornwall in *King Lear*, Duke Senior in *As You Like It*, and Prettyman in *The Rehearsal*.

When even he performed his memorable Monsieur le Médecin in *The Anatomist*, it was generally announced that "at the End Blakes will speak the Epilogue, Riding on an Ass, in the character of M Le Medecin." On 15 October 1742 he played both Tressel and Norfolk in *Richard III*, at a time when doubling of roles was a rare practice. At least once (13 February 1744) he sang Macheath, and he often danced. Whether playing Suffolk in *Henry VIII*, Bellamy in *The Suspicious Husband*, or Laertes in *Hamlet*, Blakes tried to sustain a reputation he had early won for submerging himself in the role and doing a workmanlike job. But his appearance and temperament destined him to wear the sock, and it is in his most famous comic part that his only likeness survives. James McArdell engraved him as Monsieur le Médecin.

Blakey, Mr (fl. 1743–1763), *actor*.

A Mr Blakely (once spelled "Blackey" in the bills) was with the Giffards in the Lincoln's Inn Fields company from at least 10 January 1743, when he was Gentleman Usher in *King Lear*. On 17 January he was Beau in *Bickerstaff's Unburied Dead* and on 3 and 4 February was Florence in *All's Well that Ends Well*. He played at that theatre occasionally during the rest of the season in such parts as Derby in *Jane Shore*, Dreary in *The Beggar's Opera*, and Young Fashion in *The Relapse*, the last on 7 April 1743 when he shared a benefit with Beckham the prompter, Edward Giffard, and Miss Storey. Lincoln's Inn Fields suspended operations after mid-April that year.

The London Stage places Blakey on both the Drury Lane and Goodman's Fields rosters for the season of 1745–46, but the name appears only once in the Drury Lane bills, as Frederick in *The Lying Lover*, on 4 April. It is probably a mistake for Charles Blakes, who played at Drury Lane all that season. Also, the "Blakes" opposite the part of Whisper in *The Busy Body*, at Goodman's Fields on 18 November 1745, is rather likely to be a mistake for Blakey, since Charles Blakes was the same evening playing in Drury Lane's mainpiece *The Way to Win Him*, as Petit.

Blakey was in the Goodman's Fields company for 1745–46 and 1746–47, acted anonymously in the minor theatres and fair booths in 1747–48, and was at the Haymarket in an irregular company on 2 May 1748 as Catesby in *Jane Shore*. He was at the Haymarket again on 26 July 1750 as Spitfire in *The Wife's Relief*, again in a company formed for the single production. (The "Blakey" cited by *The London Stage* in one performance for each of the seasons 1743–44 and 1745–46 was probably Charles Blakes.)

Blakey was a member of Theophilus Cibber's inexperienced, nearly amateur, company of young players in the summer of 1755. He must have spent the long interims between his London engagements in country companies. He is named in the part of Colonel Feignwell in *A Bold Stroke for a Wife* (and in the largest type on the bill) in a company playing in "Widow Yeates's Large Theatrical Barn Facing the Boarding-School in Croydon" on 2 October 1755. He was back with Theophilus Cibber at the Haymarket in the following July, associating again with younger players in what Cibber, in his appeals to the Duke of Grafton to grant a license, hoped would be a nursery for fledgling professionals.

Blakey was named in the company at Covent Garden in 1758–59 by *The London Stage*, but he was not in the bills. He acted a few parts there in 1759–60 and was with Foote in the summer at the Haymarket.

Blakey signed articles for the Covent Garden season of 1760–61 at 15s. per week, and though he figured in the playbills only once (26 March, as Spitfire in *The Wife's Relief*), the theatre's account book shows him to have been present through the end of the season, when he was paid £1 7s. 6d. for 11 days. There is even less information about his activities during the 1761 summer season in which, according to *The London Stage*, he was in the company of Arthur Murphy and Samuel Foote at the Haymarket. He played Transfer in *The Minor* on 21 July, but that was at Drury Lane. Foote retained him for a few performances in the winter and spring of 1761–62.

Some of Blakey's few roles, besides those named, were: Trappanti in *She Wou'd and She Wou'd Not*, Transfer in *The Minor*, Dick in *The Lying Valet*, and Catesby in *Jane Shore*.

Blame, Mr (fl. 1794), *singer*.

Doane's *Musical Directory* of 1794 lists Mr Blame, of Bell Yard, Temple Bar, as a *basso* who sang in concerts by the Handelian Society.

Blanc. *See* **BLANCK.**

Blanchard. *See also* **BLANCHET.**

Blanchard, the Misses [*fl.* 1789–1791], *dancers.*

Two Misses Blanchard, who were probably daughters of Thomas Blanchard (fl. 1766–1780) the actor, were seen in a "New Dance, *Love and Liberty*" at Astley's Amphitheatre on 20 July 1789. They were said to be "from the Opera House," but there is no other record of their employment there.

On 25 May 1791 (only), "the two young D'Egvilles, the two Miss Blanchards, Miss D'Egville, Miss De Camp," danced *La Cossaque et le pas Russe* at Drury Lane, but the Blanchards were evidently not of the permanent company.

Blanchard, Jean-Pierre *b. 1753*, *balloonist, exhibitor.*

The balloonist Jean-Pierre Blanchard arrived in England in the fall of 1784, fresh from three recent triumphs in France, to make a fourth "grand aerostatic experiment," and, not incidentally, to exhibit for money his "Globe and Vessel" at Christie's Great Room in Pall Mall. There from eight in the morning till dusk, ticket holders could be seated for one guinea or a half-guinea to watch him run through various procedures preparatory to flight. It was possible to view the apparatus more closely for another shilling. His newly completed book, *An Exact and Authentic Narrative of M. Blanchard's Third Aerial Voyage, from Rover in Normandy, on the 18th of July 1784, accompanied by M. Roby* . . . , was on sale at the exhibition. Excited people of all ranks awaited the next event. In a letter to the Shakespearean scholar Malone in Ireland, his co-editor George Steevens warned on 11 October:

"Pray tell Mr Homer that Blanchard's Balloon will ascend on Saturday next."

A print published by R. Wilkinson on 18 October 1784 of the ascent of the "Grand Aerostatic Balloon" gives full particulars:

GRAND AEROSTATIC BALLOON

in which M. Blanchard on Sat^y Octr 16th 1784 ascended from the Royal Military Academy at Little Chelsea, a fourth Time into the Atmosphere, accompanied by the ingenious Mr Sheldon—at Ten Minutes after Twelve the two gallant adventurers preceded by two small Ballons as Signals after taking leave of their generous Host & a numerous circle of Nobility & Friends arose with the most majestic grandeur & wafted by the prayers & plaudits of upwards of Four Hundred Thousand Spectators in Eighteen Minutes were lost on Æther—after a number of astonishing maneuvers & Evolutions the Travelers made a

Harvard Theatre Collection

JOHN PIERRE BLANCHARD and his "Grand Aerostatic Balloon"

artist unknown

stop at Sunbury where for the expediting the Machine the gallant Sheldon (unwillingly) descended & left his friend to pursue alone his Journey through "the tractless void" who after passing over Guildford, Farnham &c about 3 o'clock in the afternoon found the day too far spent to cross the Channel to Brest after hovering a considerable Time over Portsmouth, the Isle of Wight &c &. alighted at Rumsey near Southampton amidst universal acclamamations [sic] finished by far the most extraordinary Journey ever performed.

Evidently Blanchard's schedule of flights and exhibitions was profitable to him, for he pursued it elsewhere. A silver medal, possibly commemorative only, but more likely used for admission, is listed in Davis and Waters, *Tickets and Passes* (1922):

Obverse: A baloon with flags.
Reverse: BLANCHARDO / ARTEM / AERO-NAUTICUM / EXERCENTE / NORIMBERGAE / *mdcclxxxvii* [within a laurel wreath]

John Durang, the American actor, wrote in his *Memoir*:

In Jan'y 1793, I saw Blanchard ascend in a boat attach'd to a beautiful silk baloon out of the jail yard of Philad'a. He rose out of sight waveing a flag, cross'd the Delaware 16 miles in the Jerseys. Washington was present. Blanchard return'd on the same day; before he step'd in to his boat, Washington walk'd up to him and gave him a letter. Minute guns where [sic] fired in potter's field by our artilary.

The balloon craze was at its height, and the first flight of a manned balloon from London had occurred a month before Blanchard's ascent, on 15 September, when the pioneer Vincent Lunardi had ascended (with a dog, a cat, and a pigeon) from the Artillery Ground. Lunardi, however, did not exhibit for money. (Nearly a year earlier both Drury Lane and Covent Garden were putting balloons on their stages,

inspired by the pioneering flights of Jean François Pilâtre de Rozier in a captive fire balloon at Paris.)

The *Monthly Mirror* for July 1799 observed that "Blanchard has announced, in the Paris papers, that he shall set off for America in a balloon, by means of which he expects to cross the Atlantic in 7 or eight days." The results of this brazen publicity device are not known.

Blanchard, Thomas [*fl. 1766–1787*], *actor.*

The first Thomas Blanchard on record as an actor was performing before 1766 when he subscribed (as "T. Blanchard Comedian") for a copy of the *Poems* of John Cunningham. He was probably the Blanchard in the York Company from January 1768. The next report of him which survives came from Norwich, where he and Master [Thomas] Blanchard his son were acting in 1772. The boy, so doubtless the father, was at Stourbridge Fair, near Cambridge, in September 1772. Nothing is known of the wife of the elder Thomas.

By September 1773 father and son were both at Drury Lane. The son began to succeed at once, but the father was used that season, so far as the bills show, in a single play only: an unspecified part in *A Christmas Tale* on 27 December 1773 (but repeated as late as 11 May 1774). It is possible that he was not on the regular company list at all that season. The elder Thomas remained at Drury Lane through the season of 1776–77 playing only (but several times) Soldier in *The Committee*. He was last seen in London in an out-of-season performance at the Haymarket on 18 October 1779. But both he and his son Thomas were still flourishing at Bristol and Bath for some years afterward. The elder Blanchard (in that company denominated simply "Blanchard") played elderly characters at Bristol in 1778–79 and from 1782–83 through 1786–87. He was at Plymouth with his son in the summer of

1780 (19 July: Father Augustine in *The Duenna*). In addition to his son Thomas, the elder Thomas was the father of two girls who danced at Drury Lane and Astley's in the 1780's and 1790's.

Blanchard was an actor exclusively of characters elderly or eccentric or both—like Sir Francis Gripe in *The Busy Body* and Isaac Mendoza in *The Duenna*.

Blanchard, Thomas   1760–1797, *actor, singer, dancer.*

The second Thomas Blanchard, comic actor and tenor singer, was born in 1760, probably while his parents were on a theatrical tour in the north of England. He had sisters who danced on various London stages in the later 1780's and early 1790's. His father was first noticed at York in 1767–68. How early young Thomas was acting is not determinable, but he was certainly already performing at Norwich

Harvard Theatre Collection

THOMAS BLANCHARD, as Ralph
by De Wilde

early in 1772, and he sang at Stourbridge Fair near Cambridge that September.

Tom's first London appearance was at Drury Lane on 13 October 1773, as Cupid in *A Trip to Scotland*, in which he also sang a special song. While his father was given only one small part during the season, the lad's talents at singing, dancing, and mimicry were immediately recognized. Each of his roles was at least several times repeated during the season, as he was brought carefully along, appearing in new parts at intervals, and he tried out in a number of kinds of representations: Chief Genii ("with *song*") in *The Genii*, 25 November 1773; Messenger in *A Christmas Tale*, 27 December; Prince Arthur in *King John*, 2 February 1774; Page in *The Gamesters*, 20 April; and Beggar in *The Ladies Frolick*, 21 April.

The two Blanchards were rehired for the 1774–75 season, and young Thomas, in addition, sang once or twice in specially licensed performances at the Haymarket that winter. The younger Thomas was absent from London in 1775–76, though his father played a few times at Drury Lane.

Tom the younger was in the Bath and Bristol companies in 1778–79 and from 1783–84 through 1786–87. He may have been at Plymouth in the summer of 1780. He came back to London after 11 years, at the urging of Thomas Harris the proprietor of Covent Garden, making his first appearance ever on that stage on 3 October 1787 in a character in which he had already found fame at Bath and Bristol, the rustic Hodge in *Love in a Village*. He added that night for good measure another of his memorable portrayals, Sharp in the afterpiece *The Lying Valet*. He was advertised as from the Theatre Royal, Bath. He earned £6 that season for a variety of activity, singing and acting and probably dancing, in parts as diverse as Roderigo in *Othello* (the one tragedy part he seems to have kept for some years) and Jeffry in *Animal Magnetism*. More and more, however, the repertory which was to make him memorable emerged: bucolic bumblers, sly wits, lovable servants, and eccentrics in pastoral comedy, comic opera, and farce. But he was up against competition from others in this general line, especially from the excellent Edwin.

The season of 1788–89 opened with his playing Hodge and continued with usual portrayals. His salary was raised to £8 in 1789–90, and there it stayed throughout the rest of his career at Covent Garden until his dismissal from that theatre after 17 June 1794, because, of his heavy drinking, according to persistent rumor. Certainly his health was declining. He had also acted at Birmingham in the summer of 1790 and at Fox's Duke Street Theatre in Brighton in the summer of 1791.

Blanchard left London for Edinburgh during the theatrical seasons of 1794–95 and 1795–96, but a newspaper clipping of 14 March 1796 in the Folger Library's James Winston collection gives us the news that he was "again a candidate for a London engagement"; and by 2 April another informs us that he was "figuring away with the most wonderful success at Jones's Royal Circus, St George's Fields."

Perhaps he tired of his roles there, of singing in such pieces as *The Jew and the Gentile; or, No Bottle, No Bird* or in "An entire new Bagatelle of Music, Dancing, &c. In which will be introduced, incidental to the Piece, The Original and Celebrated Poney Races." For on 3 October 1797 a newspaper predicted that he was "engaged to perform the ensuing season at the Dublin Theatre."

His tenure at the Fishamble Street Theatre was not long. He died on 30 December 1797, according to the Bath *Journal* of the next day,

at his lodgings in Hamilton-Row, Dublin, in consequence, it is said, of the fatigue he underwent in the late storms . . . . leaving his wife and several children without any

provision. This man, who possessed very great merit in his profession, holds out a lamentable warning to the sons and daughters of Thespis, against the ruinous vice of intemperance.

The *Hibernian Journal* said that he was 37 at his death. He was buried in St Mark's churchyard, Dublin. On 16 January 1798, according to a Winston transcription from a newspaper, "The Dublin Manager gives a benefit at the Fishamble-Street Theatre, to the widow and children of the late Mr Blanchard. The eldest boy of the deceased is to speak an Address on the occasion."

Blanchard had married the singer Charlotte Wright at Bath on 19 May 1787. She had been off the London boards from her last appearance at Drury Lane in the spring of 1783 (as Miss Wright). She returned as Mrs Blanchard for her husband's benefit at Drury Lane on 5 May 1792. She was probably the daughter of Roger Wright (d. 1786) the Drury Lane harlequin. The Blanchards' daughter Charlotta was baptized at St Paul, Covent Garden, on 30 September 1788, their son Thomas John on 6 December 1789, and their daughter Elizabeth on 3 May 1791.

Mrs Blanchard continued to act long after her husband's death. Thomas John, the third Tom Blanchard (b. 1789) always identified as "Blanchard the Pantaloon," was still active at least into the late 1830's and died in 1859. He was a good pantomime player, but quarrelsome and litigious. In 1831, in addition to acting, he gave lessons in the broad and small swords at his house opposite the Cobourg Theatre. He had two daughters on the stage, Elizabeth (later Mrs Pearman) and another, whose first name is not known, but who may have been Charlotta.

During the periods of the second Thomas Blanchard's London engagements he resided at a variety of addresses: In May of 1788 he lived at No 44, corner of Broad-Court, Drury Lane. By May of 1789 he was at No 29, Bow Street, Covent Garden, where he remained until sometime in 1791. In May 1792, he was at No 11, Beaufort Buildings, Strand.

Tom Blanchard had an excellently resonant tenor voice, and "was a capital catch and glee singer." He had an open, agreeable countenance. Winston remembered that "His person was short and thick" and that he was "a good hornpipe dancer." Irresponsible and inebriate as he appears to have been, he was also a valuable performer when sober and a charming companion always. The contemporaries who noted and commented on his sudden departure from London and other companies invariably spoke of him as "poor Tom Blanchard," and on 28 March 1808, over ten years after his death, the various comic actors and the entire vocal corps of both Covent Garden and Drury Lane, including luminaries like Incledon, Braham, Kelly, Munden, Eurey, Dowton, Bellamy, Emery, and Taylor, gave a "Harmonic Meeting" at Free Masons' Hall for the benefit of his widow. A newspaper reporting the event remembered him as "remarkable for that chaste simplicity of rural character which we have never witnessed since his departure."

Blanchard's true vein is certainly accurately recalled by that last statement. As his contemporary Bellamy jingled in 1795:

> *In Rustics poor BLANCHARD long*
> *   held a first place,*
> *'Twas Nature's own work, unally'd to*
> *   Grimace,*
> *When his voice was attun'd to a pastoral*
> *   lay,*
> *He sent all his hearers in raptures away.*

As early as September 1783 a Bath contributor to a London newspaper had written:

The Gentle Shepherd . . . was, upon the whole, the compleatest theatrical exhibition I have seen for some years; the part of Patie was performed by a young fellow whose name is Blanchard, and who, I learnt, is just now emerged from obscurity in an itinerant company in the West. I have repeatedly seen the piece in London and elsewhere, but I never saw Patie half so amiable.

Though in his first seasons at Covent Garden Blanchard was up against competition from several good comic actors in some of the same sorts of characters, notably the excellent Edwin, and though later he jousted with Quick, Munden, and Harley, he gradually distanced everyone in many parts which required singing, and he held onto them. Of his Sim in *Wild Oats* (Covent Garden 16 April 1791) *The Oracle* reported:

No piece in the remembrance of this writer was ever better acted. No piece was ever better cast . . . The palm of acting, however, must be given to Blanchard. One short scene of rustic generosity, in which he gives his purse to Farmer Banks, displayed finer efforts than we ever saw before.

Among Blanchard's dozens of roles, first to last, were: Rundy in *The Farmer*, the Clown in *Dumb Cake*, Grogg in *The Positive Man*, Philippo in *The Castle of Andalusia*, Jeffry and Lafleur in *Animal Magnetism*, Gregory in *A Divertissement*, Charley in *The Highland Reel*, Robin in *Marian*, Skirmish in *The Deserter*, Jacob in *The Chapter of Accidents*, Hippy in *How to Get Rich*, William in *Rosina*, Trudge in *Inkle and Yarico*, Cymon in *The Irishman in London*, Joey in *Modern Antiques*, Taylor in *The Little Hunchback*, Filch in *The Beggar's Opera*, Tester in *The Suspicious Husband*, Daniel in *The Conscious Lovers*, Medley in *The Woodman*, Peter in *Hartford Bridge*, David in *The Rivals*, a Recruit in *The Recruiting Officer*. He had but one "tragedy" part, Roderigo in *Othello*, but he continued to make it comic.

A painting of the second Thomas Blanchard by Samuel De Wilde as Ralph in *The Maid of the Mill* is in the Garrick

Club. It was engraved by Thornthwaite for Bell's *British Library* (1791). Hall's catalogue incorrectly identifies the subject as William Blanchard. The painting belonged to the elder Charles Mathews and was No 211 in his *Catalogue raisonnée.* No 374 in the catalogue was the same subject by the same artist, a water-color drawing, but its present location is unknown.

Several songs "as sung by" Blanchard were published and survive in the British Museum's collection of published music: Sanderson's *The Merry Bells* from *Harlequin's Manner* (1796) and his *Betsy Bobbin* (1797), Shield's *The Plough Boy* from *The Farmer* (1788), and his *Patty Clover* from *Marian* (1788).

Blanchard, Mrs Thomas, Charlotte, née Wright, *b. 1761, singer, actress.*

Charlotte Wright Blanchard was the daughter of the actor Roger Wright (d. 1786). She was born about 1761 if an estimate of her age as 73 in a news story of 1834 was correct.

She is said to have attracted the favorable notice of David Garrick and at 18 appeared for the first time in public, if the announcement can be trusted, in the religious and secular oratorios at Drury Lane from 19 February through 26 March 1779. She was listed as one of the "principal singers," though her roles were not set forth, in *Judas Maccabaeus, Acis and Galatea, Samson,* and the *Messiah.* Charlotte's "first appearance [in] any character" was for Harwood's benefit on 1 May 1779, singing the part of Leonora in *The Padlock.* The bill for this performance gave her address as No 136, Drury Lane. As a consequence of this successful performance, she sang what James Winston called her "probationary character" of Polly in *The Beggar's Opera* on 5 October 1779, and the *Morning Post* reported that

Miss Wright appeared last night for the first time on the Stage, in Polly. This young Lady

is possessed of a very harmonious pipe. She was much affected by the terrors of a first nights representation, and was much embarrassed. The music of her voice, is as apparent in the common dialogue, as in her singing.

At the end of this season she lived at No 54, Drury Lane. As Miss Wright she acted and sang at Drury Lane in every successive season through that of 1782–83. In the summer of 1782 she was acting in the Liverpool company. Absent entirely from the London bills from 1783 until 5 May 1792, when Charlotte returned to the city it was to Covent Garden and as the wife of the second Thomas Blanchard, a singer and comedian of great talent and, by this time, considerable fame. They had married at Bath on 19 May 1787, when both were members of the Bath company, but evidently kept a residence in London, still regarding it as their professional home. The couple had in three of the following four years brought back children to the baptismal font of the "actors' church," St Paul, Covent Garden: Charlotta on 13 September 1788, Thomas John on 6 December 1789, and Elizabeth on 3 May 1791.

Charlotte Blanchard had begun her career with every indication of future success. Winston, who knew her, testified to her "excellent Voice, pretty face & interesting figure." She was initially approved by Garrick, given some excellent parts in oratorio, and in other ways in her first two seasons appeared well on her way to becoming a star. She "created" the small part of Eliza in William Augustus Miles's afterpiece *The Artifice* on 14 April 1779. She was seasoned in part-singing in choruses and modestly endured tertiary parts like the pastoral nymph in *Comus;* but she also came to the center of the stage on occasion, as when she was allowed to sing the traditional song "To thee, O gentle sleep!" at the end of Act IV of *Tamerlane.* She occasionally sang important roles like Semira in *Artaxerxes.* But she never built very high above this basis, especially after she left Drury Lane; and before long she found herself back in choruses, anonymous "vocal parts," assisting in mass renditions of "God Save the King" in times of national danger or of the illnesses of the third George, or singing in the "Solemn Dirge" of Juliet's funeral procession. Occasionally she was tossed parts like Emily in *The Capricious Lovers*, Miss Fleck in *A Trip to Scotland*, the First Italian in *The Critic*, Phoebe in *As You Like It*, Serina in *The Orphan*, Miss Godfrey in *The Lyar*, Victoria in *The Castle of Andalusia*, and Maria in *Just in Time*.

Mrs Blanchard never performed in London after 12 June 1793 when she acted, for the first time, Louisa in *The Duenna*. But she was playing at Edinburgh in June of 1795. In the fall of 1797 she, her husband, and their three children went to Dublin, where the father had an engagement at the Fishamble Street Theatre. By 30 December Thomas Blanchard was dead, and his widow was thrown on her own resources, which included little except her talent and the proceeds of a benefit performance organized for her by the manager at Fishamble Street. She made her first appearance at Crow Street, Dublin, on 9 February 1798 and can be traced to Limerick in October of that year. There was a "Harmonic Meeting" for her benefit at Freeman's Hall on 28 March 1808.

The last news we have of Mrs Blanchard is depressing, and it is rendered the more so by the insolent jocularity of its messenger. Among James Winston's theatrical transcriptions at the Folger Library is one from the *Morning Post* of 12 November 1834:

Nov. 11, 1834. Among the disorderlys brought up was Mrs Blanchard wife to the late & mother to the present comedian of that name: at ½ past 11 on the previous night in East Smithfield she rolled over twice on the pavement. The policeman picked her up, & put her on her legs, but in the course of half a dozen steps, she had another roll. From the respectability of her appearance, he did not wish to take her to the station House, and assisted her for some distance, but as she grew worse, & refused to give her name, felt it his duty to take her there, where she made great use of her tongue over which she had much greater controul, than over her limbs: assumed the air of a Dutchess, being decidedly drunk, she was retained for personal safety. She was in her 74th year, and rather fantastically attired, said she was overcome from fatigue, more from fatigue than any thing she had taken, having come all the way from Vauxhall, and her shoestrings pinching her, she stopped down, & the Police Man took her to the station House. She was discharged.

Blancher. *See* BLANCHARD.

Blanchet, Miss. *See* WYBROW, MRS.

Blanck, Nicholas *d. 1778, musician.* Nicholas Blanck played in the Covent Garden band, earning, as of 14 September 1767, 5s. daily. He died on 1 January 1778, and when his widow Jane appealed to the Royal Society of Musicians for financial aid on 6 February 1791, they had to refuse her on the grounds that she had been married to Blanck only 17 days when he died.

Bland, Dorothy. *See* JORDAN, DOROTHY.

Bland, George *d. 1753, actor.* George Bland, according to the bills, made his first appearance on any stage, announced as "A Gentleman," in the role of Polydore in *The Orphan* on 17 October 1751 at Covent Garden. His wife, Esther Bland, having previously acted at London, had spent several years at Smock Alley, Dublin, before returning to Covent Garden in the fall of 1751. Bland himself actually may have acted previously at Dublin, and there was a Mr Bland in the Jacob's Wells company at Bristol being paid 4s. per night in the summer of 1748.

At Covent Garden, Bland played Polydore once more on 18 October 1751 and

Harvard Theatre Collection

GEORGE BLAND
by Naish

then acted the title role of *Oroonoko* on 18 November 1751, for his own benefit, after which his name no longer appeared in the bills. On 29 October 1753 Richard Cross entered in his diary, "Mrs Bland's husband broke his leg on Friday [26 October] riding an unruly horse & dy'd yesterday." In his will, made on 6 November 1752 and proved on 13 November 1753, George Bland bequeathed all his estate to his wife and executrix, Esther Bland. Mrs Bland became Mrs John Hamilton (under which name her entry is listed) on 15 June 1754 and later became Mrs Sweeny.

Bland, George *d. 1807, actor, singer.*
George Bland was the son of Francis Bland (d. 1778) and the actress Grace Phillips (d. 1789). George's grandfather Nathaniel Bland (d. 1760) was a judge in Dublin and squire of Derriquin Castle near Sneen in County Kerry. John Bland (1721–1808), George's uncle and the judge's eldest son by his first marriage, had

been disinherited for going on the stage. Francis Bland, George's father, and the eldest son by the judge's second marriage (to Elizabeth Heaton of Mount Heaton), had also been disowned when he showed too keen an interest in the actress Grace Phillips, one of three performing daughters of a Welsh clergyman. Francis may or may not have married her (just as he may have acted with her in Dublin or may have been only a stage-hand there, and may or may not have been an officer in the army—several accounts long after the facts differ widely). But almost certainly the union was informal, inasmuch as Francis left Grace in 1774 and married a Miss Mahoney of Killarney. James Boaden in his biography of Dorothea Bland Jordan stated that the pair "lived together for several years," and had nine children. Only three besides George can now be traced: a brother Francis Bland who settled in Wales; a sister Hester Francis Bland (1759–1848), who acted at Hull and York as "Miss Hester Francis," and the Dorothea Bland (1761–1816), who as Mrs Jordan became a leading actress of the day and the mistress of the Duke of Clarence.

George Bland is said to have been given a good schooling by his father's relatives. According to the *Secret History of the Green Room* (1792), he had been placed at Oxford but had left in 1788 to join Watson's company at Cheltenham. It is possible, however, that George Bland had been acting before that time and probably never got to Oxford, for the "Master Francis" who acted at York in 1785 could very well have been George. His mother had been engaged for some years as "Mrs Francis" with Tate Wilkinson on the York circuit and was acting in that city when her daughter Dorothea Bland Jordan joined that theatre in 1782. The London press predicted on 13 October 1786 that Mrs Jordan's brother, presumably George, "who has for a great while given a fair promise of abilities in the musical line, will, it is supposed, be taken notice of by the managers, and produced to the publick eye."

The prediction was sound, for in that season (1786–87) Master Bland's name was on the pay list of Drury Lane Theatre at 12*s*. per week until it was removed on 10 March 1787. In what capacity he was engaged is uncertain since his name appeared in no bills of that season. Some four months later, on 28 July 1787, the press reported that "Young Bland, the brother of Mrs Jordan," had made his first appearance that summer at the Leeds Theatre, as Sebastian in *Twelfth Night*, with his sister as Viola, and had been received "with much applause." His second role at Leeds was as Lionel in *Lionel and Clarissa,* after which a country correspondent to a London gazette made more of "his musical than rhetorical abilities." From Leeds Bland went to Edinburgh, where the theatre was managed by his uncle John Bland (1721–1808), and then to Dundee. In the next several summers he also acted at Glasgow, York, Richmond in Yorkshire, and other places, often with his sister Dorothea.

When John Kemble took over the management of Drury Lane Theatre in September 1788, Mrs Jordan strove to have her brother engaged in the company. Kemble, however, had a low opinion of George Bland's talents, and on one occasion in January 1789, exasperated by George's presence backstage, the manager actually fined the stage doorkeeper 5*s*. for allowing him entrance. The press followed with glee the tensions between Kemble and Mrs Jordan and at one point reported a victory for the actress: "the male Jordan . . . who has been on a Northern tour with his sister . . . is, we hear, to try his skill at the old Drury this winter," but then soon after announced that "the brother of Mrs Jordan . . . is not yet to appear at Drury Lane." Perhaps to draw Mrs Jordan's attention away from her dissatisfaction with her salary, Kemble finally gave in, and on 8

February 1790 George Bland played Sebastian with his sister as Viola in *Twelfth Night*. He was announced as from the Liverpool theatre, where he had played in the summer of 1789.

Bland's figure was short, no taller than his sister's, and his strong facial resemblances to her enhanced the situations built around mistaken identities in the play. The critics reported that his voice was coarse and unpleasing but doubted not that "When Mr Bland has acquired a portion of his Sister's ease and elegance of deportment," he would become a respectable performer. But Bland was never going to be better than a mediocre actor, one more injured than helped by his relationship as brother of the exciting and news-worthy Mrs Jordan. When the liaison of the Duke of Clarence and the actress became the talk of the town in 1791, a waggish press announced: "Interest is making to have Bland the actor knighted; it is so awkward to have the brother of a Duchess a plain Mister. The title he solicits is Sir Simpleton Squeekum."

After his appearance in *Twelfth Night*, Bland played for one night at Covent Garden on 16 July 1790 as Octavio in *She Wou'd and She Wou'd Not*. He then was engaged as a regular member of the Drury Lane company from 1791–92 through 1794–95, during which period he also acted each summer at the Haymarket. His salary at Drury Lane by 1793–94 was £2 per week (not the £5 claimed by the *Secret History of the Green Room*) and at the Haymarket, £3.

Bland's roles in London were of a nondistinguished variety of tertiary supporting characters, frequently in the musical line, and included: Grey in *Henry V*, Perez in *Don Juan*, Sylvius in *As You Like It*, Campley in *Inkle and Yarico*, Charles in *The Village Lawyer*, Eugene in *The Agreeable Surprise*, William in *Taste and Feeling*, Harcourt in *The Surrender of Calais*, Belville in *The Country Girl*, the Duke of

Somerset in *The Battle of Hexham*, Hortensio in *Catherine and Petruchio*, the Italian singer in *Poor Old Drury*!!!, Tressel in *Richard III*, Beaufort in *The Citizen*, Martin in *The Haunted Tower*, and unnamed characters in *The Greek Slave*, *The Hue and Cry*, *The Mountaineers*, and *The Enchanted Wood*. Perhaps his best London review was the ironic statement of the *Thespian Magazine* concerning his performance of Arionelli in *The Son-in-Law* at the Haymarket on 11 June 1793. "It would be very remiss in us to omit the *rare* opportunity of praising Mr Bland: his performance of Arionelli is truly capital."

On 21 October 1790 Bland married the Drury Lane singer Maria Theresa Romanzini (1770–1838) at St Paul, Covent Garden. As a child she had sung at the Royal Circus and afterwards had been engaged by Daly in Dublin. Acting as Mrs Bland she was to enjoy considerably more success than her husband. She had smitten him by her "cheerfulness and vivacity," but she brought grief to the marriage by her relationship with Thomas Caulfield, the actor, by whom she had several children. In 1794 the Blands were living at No 12, St Albans Street.

By 1796, Mrs Bland was carrying on an open affair with Caulfield, and it was rumored that he was going to take her to America. They remained in London, however, living together, evidently creating such an awkward situation for Bland that he was compelled to retire from the London stage. He occasionally performed thereafter in the provincial theatres, playing at Richmond in the summer of 1797. He soon fell into heavy debt. On 25 February 1797 he wrote to the treasury of Drury Lane Theatre to request a new loan of £70 for three months, in exchange for paying "the old one of £100."

After weighing for several years upon the generosity of Mrs Jordan, George Bland went to America. Playing under the name of Wilson, he made his debut at the Park

Street Theatre in New York on 29 January 1802 as Frank Oatland in *A Cure for Heartache*. If his purposes in changing his name to Wilson were to avoid embarrassment over his recent unfortunate domestic circumstances and to come out finally from under the shadow of his sister, they were thwarted, for on 1 February 1802 the New York *Evening Post* devoted a long article to him, in which he was identified without hesitancy as Bland, the brother of Mrs Jordan. The New York press was considerably more enthusiastic about Bland's talents than any London paper had been:

His person is slim, of the middle height . . . his countenance is open and expressive his eyes large and full of meaning; his nose though not prominent, is yet . . . congenial with the rest of his face; but his greatest expression is in his mouth, which is large, but not unhandsome, and always ready to express every sensation he feels. His voice . . . is pleasing, and capable of much variety . . . His most striking peculiarity is an uncommon flexibility of muscles, which at pleasure and in an instant enables him to change his countenance from the most dull and vacant stare, to the liveliest emotions of hilarity; from the idiotic laugh of a stupid clodpate to the tear-starting expression of genuine sensibility. While his countenance is thus perfectly subservient to every emotion, his limbs seem to partake of the same rapid and expressive transitions, and his voice is in perfect unison with his whole appearance.

Becoming a useful member of the Park Theatre, Bland (as "Wilson") played Sir Benjamin Backbite in *The School for Scandal* on 28 April 1802, and for his benefit on 16 June he played Tony Lumpkin in *She Stoops to Conquer* and Jemmy Jump in *The Farmer*. According to Odell, the benefit resulted in "a great financial loss" to Bland. In the summer of 1802 he played with a group of the Park Theatre performers at Joseph Corre's Mount Vernon Gardens Theatre but was back at the Park for the season 1802–3.

According to Dunlap, "Mr Wilson" was carried off to prison on 3 December 1802 for an offense unspecified but presumably slight, for later that month he was at Boston as a member of Snelling Powell's company at the Federal Street Theatre, announced as from the Haymarket and Drury Lane. At the end of the season on 9 March 1803, after touring in the South, he appeared at the Grove Theatre in Bedlow Street, New York, as Theodore in J. C. Cross's melodrama *The Purse*, but now listed on the bill under his real name of Bland.

He was back at Boston in 1804–5, and in March of that season took $900 at his benefit. George Bland then sank into obscurity. He died at Boston in the spring of 1807, "in the utmost poverty and indigence," according to the *Gentleman's Magazine* of November 1807. When news of his death reached London in the fall, the press, in a callous cut at Maria Theresa Bland's faithlessness and her unattractive hairy face, reported, "His *disconsolate* widow, formerly Miss Romanzini, is of the Jewish persuasion, and follows their form in her mourning, which is confined to letting the beard grow!"

The question of how many children George Bland had by his wife is perplexing, complicated as it is by the reports that some of Mrs Bland's children (up to four, according to Winston) were sired by Thomas Caulfield. It is uncertain whether Caulfield's progeny include those of Mrs Bland's children who are known by name or are in addition to them. (For information on the Bland children, see the entry for BLAND, Mrs George, Maria Theresa.)

An engraving of George Bland by W. Ridley, after Naish, was published as a plate to *Parson's Minor Theatre* in 1794; a proof impression, before title, is in the Harvard Theatre Collection. The "tuppence coloured" of a Mr Bland as Pluto in *The Olympic Devils*, 1832, listed under George Bland's name in the Hall *Catalogue of Dramatic Portraits in the Harvard Theatre Collection*, is not of George, but of one of his sons, either James or Charles.

Bland, Mrs George, Esther. *See* **HAMILTON, MRS JOHN, ESTHER.**

Bland, Mrs George, Maria Theresa Catherine, née Tersi, (called Romani and Romanzini) *1770–1838, singer, actress.*

The matter of the real maiden name and heritage of Mrs George Bland, who before her marriage appeared as Maria Theresa Romanzini, is somewhat confused. During her lifetime, numerous references were made to the effect that she was a Jewess and that her parents had been Italian Jews. Several memoirs in journals at the time of her death stated her real name to have been Ida Romani and declared that she had been dubbed Romanzini ("little Roman") when she appeared as a small child-performer in London. *The Observer*, (20 January 1838) and the *Gentleman's Magazine* (March 1838) claimed that she was born on 12 September 1770. According to a manuscript in the hand of James Winston, at the Folger Library, however, she was born at Caen in Normandy, on 9 September 1770, and was baptized in the Catholic Church of Notre Dame in that city on the following day as Maria Theresa Catherine Tersi, the daughter of a strolling musician from Rome named Alexander Tersi and his wife Catherine Zeli, a Jewess from the parish of St Paul's, Florence. Standing as her godmother was one Maria Therese Le Clerck—hence her Christian name. When her mother made her will at London on 13 September 1798, she gave her name only as Catherine Romanzini, suggesting that for some reason the family had changed its name upon coming to England and that the story about the audience's settling the name of Romanzini on little Maria Theresa is a myth. The mother made no

MARIA THERESA BLAND, as Madam Belgarde

by De Wilde

mention of her husband in her will, he presumably having died by then.

Maria Theresa was brought to England by 1773, for on 10 April of that year she was announced as a "young Italian lady, about four years old," for an appearance at Bristow with her father. Upon the family's arrival soon after at London in the spring of 1773, a hairdresser named Cady helped her to obtain an engagement at Hughes's Riding School near Blackfriars Bridge. She also sang at Sadler's Wells, still so small she was perched on a table so the audience could see her. During displays of magic by the famous Philip Breslaw, she performed at Marylebone Gardens and Coachmakers' Hall, singing duets with another child,

Master Samuel Russell, who in the nineteenth century became a stage manager at Drury Lane. There is record of a benefit for her in connection with an Italian Fantoccini performance—probably by her father—in Piccadilly on 24 May 1780. By 1781 she was appearing in pantomimes at the Royal Circus under the instruction of the manager Charles Dibdin, who also conducted "a seminary to mature actors and actresses." In that season at the Royal Circus a piece called *The Boarding School Breaking Up*, in which she performed with Master J. Russell, Miss Williamson (later Mrs Mountain), and Miss DeCamp (later Mrs Charles Kemble), was interdicted by the magistrates. Songs published about this time as sung by Miss Romanzini at the Royal Circus included "Ye Jobbers, Underwriters," "I'll tell you a story," and Linley's "Ne'er ah ne'er let sorrow's sting."

By the age of 11, Miss Romanzini displayed talent enough to be given an unspecified role in *L'omaggio* at the King's Theatre on 5 June 1781 (repeated 8, 14, and 16 June). She then made her debut that fall at Drury Lane on 19 October as Cupid in *King Arthur*, announced as from the Royal Circus. The only other time her name appeared in the Drury Lane bills that season was for an unspecified role in *Don Juan* on 10 May, but her name was entered on the pay list regularly at £1 per week. She continued on the list for the following season, in which her only billed notice was for singing in the masquerade scene in Act II of *Cymbeline* on 18 February 1783 (repeated on 25 February). In 1783 she made a sensation singing in "Malbrook," in French, and in 1784 she also sang at Smock Alley, Dublin, and at Liverpool. She was engaged again at the Royal Circus between May and October 1785. On 17 April 1786 she appeared as the Savoyard Girl in *The Gates of Calais* at Sadler's Wells.

She returned to Drury Lane on 24 October 1786 when she played Antonio in an English version of Grétry's *Richard Coeur de Lion*, which had a most successful run of 38 performances. Playing Mathilda in the same production was Mrs Jordan, later to become her sister-in-law. Also in the Drury Lane company was her future husband, George Bland. That season Miss Romanzini sang again in *Cymbeline* (29 January 1787), and played Fanny in *The Maid of the Mill* (26 January), Ismene in *The Sultan* (15 February and 10 more times), Rose in *The Double Surprise* (18 April), and a character in *The Mistake of a Minute* (23 April). She remained attached to Drury Lane for most of the rest of her professional career, in the early years taking over the roles of the "singing chambermaids" after Mrs Wrighten retired. She played Sabrina in *Comus* on 4 October 1787. As Rosario in *Love in the East* on 25 February 1788, "she played her part," reported the *Morning Chronicle*, "with great innocence and naïveté, and sung her airs in a most pretty and pleasing manner." She made her first appearance as Jenny in *The Deserter* on 1 November 1788; other roles in 1788–89 included a singing witch in *Macbeth*, Annette in *Lord of the Manor*, Cherubino in *Follies of a Day*, and Ariel in *The Tempest*. In 1789–90 she played similar roles, at a salary of £5 per week. In February and March 1790 she sang Handelian selections in the oratorios at Drury Lane.

In the summer of 1789, Miss Romanzini went to Liverpool, performing on the stage and singing at concerts. According to a preposterous story in the *Secret History of the Green Room* (1795), she used all her cunning to procure a good benefit there. Knowing there were great numbers of Catholics in Liverpool, and "that they liberally patronized those of their own persuasion," Miss Romanzini "regularly displayed her devotion in their chapels." When a wag circulated the report of her being a Jewess, she sat sewing by her window on every Saturday afternoon and made her mother buy a live pig which everyone within hearing was told was meant for dinner.

On 21 October 1791, Miss Romanzini married the actor George Bland at St Paul, Covent Garden, by license. As Mrs Bland she was to achieve her greatest professional success, but the marriage would come to grief. Now billed as Mrs Bland for the first appearance of the season on 26 October 1790, she played Cicely in *The Haunted Tower* and Viletta in *Don Juan*, with her husband acting Perez in the latter piece. She then played an Italian Girl in *The Critic* (27 October), Dorothy in *No Song No Supper* (28 October), Jenny in *The Deserter* (30 November), Betsey Blossom in *The Deaf Lover* (14 December), and 47 performances of Ghita in *The Siege of Belgrade*, a role she created on 1 January 1791. She continued at Drury Lane through the decade in the same line. In 1793–94 her salary was £8 per week; it was raised to £10 in 1797–98 at which figure it remained through 1799–1800. Among her best roles at Drury Lane during this period were a Welsh peasant in *The Cherokee* (20 November 1794), in which she made popular the ballad "A Little Bird sang on a spray," and Beda in *Blue Bird* (16 January 1798), in which she and John Bannister made a great hit of their "Tink-a-tink song" and she sang "Can I my comely Turk forget."

In 1791 Colman had also engaged her for the Haymarket, and for some years she appeared in the musical dramas which he, O'Keeffe, and others wrote for that theatre, while maintaining as well her situation at Drury Lane. She made her first appearance at the Haymarket as Wowski in Colman and Arnold's *Inkle and Yarico* on 10 June 1791. On 30 July 1791 she created the role of Madelon in *The Surrender of Calais*, another piece by Colman which ran for 28 performances that summer. Other roles at the Haymarket included Araminta in *The Young Quakers* (15 June 1792), Dorcas in *The Mock Doctor* (10 December

1793), Maud in *Peeping Tom* (27 January 1794), and Jessica (with a song) in *The Merchant of Venice* on 28 August 1797. During this decade she also sang at Vauxhall.

Recognized as "perfect as an English ballad-singer," she possessed the ability to draw tears to the eyes of her listeners by singing the simple story of the loves of a street singer or beggar maid. She had a method peculiar to herself, wrote Oxberry, "of introducing in her comic ballads a word or two of speaking, and then instantly recurring to the air in a manner that was truly bewitching." In May 1794, she sang in the "Choral Nights" and the "Grand Miscellaneous Concerts" of the Oxford Musical Society in the Oxford Music Room and continued to appear at concerts there well into the early years of the nineteenth century. She also played at Richmond in August 1797. When Mme Banti was taken ill, Mrs Bland agreed on a very short notice, and with permission of Drury Lane, to sing for her in *Gli schiavi per amore* at the King's Theatre on 26 December 1798. "We congratulate her on her success," wrote the *Morning Chronicle* the next day. "Her whole performance was distinguished by the warmest approbation, particularly in her first song at the commencement of the second act, and in the favorite duet with Morelli, both of which were repeated highly to the gratification of the audience." She also sang a principal role in *La frascatana* there on 26 March 1799.

In May 1793 Mrs Bland was living at No 93, the Strand, with her husband. By May of the following year they were living at No 12, St Albans Street. By 1795, however, she was carrying on an open affair with the actor Thomas Caulfield and soon began to live with him, prompting T. Bellamy to write in *London Theatres*:

With pigmy form and ebon eyes,
Dark brown BLAND, as gipsy sly,
Trips it as she flirts along,

Yielding but to few in song:
O scandal, what an errand jade!
Would all thy sayings were unsaid,
That so our Bland might still be gay,
And green-room gossip die away.

When it was rumored that Caulfield would take her to America, John Williams, under the pseudonym of Anthony Pasquin, in *A Pin Basket to the Children of Thespis*, expressed regret that by the "base seduction of Caulfield," London would lose "one of the sweetest singers, and, as a singer one of the best comic actresses, that ever walked the boards." In America, Williams predicted, Caulfield's "boasted love will consequently be seen in its true colors." They remained in London, however, and gossip created so awkward a situation for George Bland that he was obliged to quit the London stage. (Bland subsequently went to America and acted in New York and Boston, dying at the latter city in 1807.) Mrs Bland lived with Caulfield until 1806 when he finally did leave for America, also to act at Boston. After some nine years filled with dereliction and drink, Caulfield fell down in a fit and died while acting on a Kentucky stage in 1815. (Mrs Bland's addresses while living with Caulfield were No 25, King Street, Covent Garden, in August 1797; at No 8, Cockspur Street, Charing Cross, in August 1799; at No 6, Southampton Place, Tottenham Court Road, in August 1800; at No 471, the Strand, in June 1801 and until May 1802; at No 25, Great Russell Street by May 1803; and at No 16, Charles Street by May 1804.)

On 4 March 1800 it was announced that Mrs Bland could not play that night as "one of her children was unfortunately burnt to death, by its clothes taking fire." On 17 April 1800, *The Egyptian Festival* was withdrawn "in consequence of the accouchement of Mrs Bland." But on 30 May she was back at Drury Lane introducing two songs by M. G. Lewis, "Crazy Jane" and "The Fishermen and the River Queen." She

Harvard Theatre Collection

MARIA THERESA BLAND, as Sally Shamrock

by Wageman

sang at the Haymarket in the summer of 1800, taking her benefit on 23 August as Agnes in *The Mountaineer* (in which she sang the favorite ballad of "Little Taffline, or the Silken Sash") and as Phoebe in *Rosina*. Apparently she did not perform again until almost the end of the next Drury Lane season, when on 29 May 1801, announced as her first and only appearance this season, she played Barbara in *The Iron Chest*. She did play once more, however, on 3 June 1801, when she offered Sally Shamrock in *The Shipwreck*.

Mrs Bland remained a regular member of the Drury Lane company from 1801–2 through 1821–22, including three years when the company played at the Lyceum Theatre 1809–12. Her salary in 1802–3 was at £8 6s. 8d. per week. By 1804–5 it

was £12 12s.; it was raised in 1806–7 to £15 per week, at which level it remained through 1814–15. In 1815–16, her salary was dropped to £12 per week and then in the following season to £8, where it remained through 1819–20 (in which year she was living at No 46, Gerrard Street, Soho). She was also a member of the "English Opera" at the Lyceum in the summers of 1810, 1811, and 1812. In June 1802 she sang at Vauxhall and again in June 1804. She returned to Vauxhall in the summers of 1809, 1812 (when she received a salary of £250), and 1814. In February and March of 1804 she also played at Manchester but was not well received.

Mrs Bland's last theatrical performance was on 8 June 1822 at Drury Lane in the role of Madam Belgarde in *Monsieur Tonson*, a role she created on 20 September 1821 and sang a total of 22 times that season. According to a clipping in the Enthoven Collection, she still sang a French air "as charmingly as if she were sixteen." In July 1822 she sang at Vauxhall and then took up the teaching of singing. On 17 November 1822, the press announced:

Mrs Bland, of the Theatre Royal, Drury-Lane, begs to inform her Friends and Pupils, and the Public in general, that she is Returned to Town, and continues to give Lessons in English, French, and Italian Singing. Mrs Bland being perfectly conversant with the French and Italian, is enabled to facilitate the improvement of her Pupils in the pronunciation of those languages. — Particulars to be known at Mrs Bland's Residence, No 46, Gerrard Street, Soho.

About 1824, Mrs Bland was afflicted with a serious nervous disorder, described as a "mental imbecility" which developed into a melancholy madness, probably traceable to the death of one of her children and to her other domestic troubles. It was rumored that the child who was reported as having burned to death in 1800 had really been killed by her when she shook it in anger and put it outside on a door mat. References were made in the press in July 1824 to her "lamentable condition," and it was reported that the directors of a lunatic asylum, Laverstoke House, in Salisbury, had volunteered to care for her at no charge. When the Committee of the Fund of Drury Lane Theatre proposed a benefit for her, Mrs Bland wrote to the press on 15 April 1824 claiming she was in no state of distress and had sufficient to live on with some comfort, "although not with the elegancies of life." She agreed, however, to the benefit which took place at Drury Lane on 5 July 1824. Together with a public subscription in her behalf, she received about £800. On 21 July 1824 handbills were distributed which listed the subscribers to the "Future Support of Mrs Bland." The list included the Dukes of York, Bedford, Sussex, and Devonshire, the Duchesses of Northumberland and Kent, General Phipps, Mrs Coutts, John Bell, Prince Leopold of Saxe-Coburg, Sir Francis Burdett, Alderman Birch, Lord Hamilton, Lord Carrington, and Lord Egremont. The money was handed over to Lord Egremont, who allowed her an annuity of £80 for the rest of her life.

Mrs Bland, however, still sought out a theatrical engagement, but unable to receive one, and much against the advice of her friends, she resorted to singing at White Conduit Gardens in August 1826. She took a benefit on 17 August, her last concert performance. She lived another 12 years, passing most of them at the house of a family named Western, at the Broadway, Westminster, where she died of apoplexy about eight o'clock on the evening of 15 January 1838, according to her obituary in the *Gentleman's Magazine* (March 1838). She was buried at St Margaret's Church, Westminster.

Mrs Bland had children by both George Bland and Thomas Caulfield. Mrs Catherine Romanzini, her mother, in a will dated 13 September 1798, bequeathed her estate to her daughter—"for the sole separate and peculiar use and benefit exclusive of the said George Bland, and without being subject or liable to his Debts Controul or intermeddling"—and specifically listed as residuary legatees four children of her daughter, named George, Thomas, James, and William. Probably three of these sons were by her husband. Either George or William was born on 14 September 1791, according to a clipping in the Folger Library. Michael Kelly reminisced that at the time "those who heard her masculine voice and the effeminate pipes of her husband wondered much at the circumstances of a bouncing boy." The birth date of the other son, sometime before 1798, is not known. George became a lieutenant in the Royal Navy and a Naval Knight of Windsor; he was present at his mother's funeral. Beyond the will, there is no further notice of William. Thomas Bland was born on 29 March 1796 and was christened at St Paul, Covent Garden, as the son of George and Theresa Bland, on 10 May 1796. (It is possible that Mrs Bland, who was carrying on her affair with Caulfield by now, wished to make Thomas "legitimate" by this procedure.) What became of Thomas is not known. The fourth son named in the will, James Bland, was born on 5 March 1798, according to Winston, and was no doubt sired by Caulfield. He became an opera singer, performed at the Olympic Theatre in 1838, later became known as an actor of burlesque, and died at the Strand Theatre on 17 July 1861. On 15 August 1792, the *Morning Herald* had announced that "Mrs Bland had just presented her husband with two fair daughters," neither of whom was mentioned in their grandmother's will. Winston claimed that one of these twin girls was the child who burned to death in 1800. A Miss Bland, presumably the surviving twin, is known to have sung at Sadler's Wells in 1801.

Two other sons of Mrs Bland, no doubt by Caulfield, are known. The tenor Charles Bland, born on 14 August 1802 according to Winston, made his debut as Carlos in *The Duenna* at Covent Garden in 1824. He played the title role in the original production of Weber's *Oberon* at Covent Garden on 12 April 1826 and was at the time of his mother's funeral still at that theatre. Humphrey Bland, also at the funeral and then of Leicester and probably the child born in April 1800, made his debut at the Surrey Theatre in 1834. He married first the actress Miss Somerville, and after she died at Liverpool in October 1838, he married the actress Harriet Faucit (sister to Helen Faucit), who made her debut at the Lyceum in 1843 and died in America on 5 November 1847.

In appearance Mrs Bland was unattractive. Short and thick-set, her stumpy figure was made less appealing by a gait described as "approaching to the waddle." Her face was pock-marked and dark in complexion; her hairy chin prompted unkind remarks about her Jewish background. When she and Dignum (another dark, plump figure) appeared together on the stage, Charles Lamb quipped, "And lo, two puddings smoked upon the board!" Being the "most unharmonious looking person that can be imagined," she did not please in more refined roles like that of the Widow Warren in *The Road to Ruin*. Despite these substantial liabilities she was a favorite for more than 30 years. When still young, in 1796, she was described by Waldron in *Candid and Impartial Strictures on the Performers Belonging to Drury Lane . . .* as a pleasing singer ("perhaps more than a much finer vocal performer") with action that was peculiarly appropriate to whatever she delivered. Her sweet and flexible *mezzo-soprano* voice was enhanced by a precise diction that enabled her to sing Italian music admirably and French *chansons* delightfully.

Her forte, however, was in the English ballad style. Pleyel and Haydn went to hear her at Drury Lane and confirmed Kelly's opinion that "no real judge of art could find a single blemish in her style or taste." In such pieces as the incantation in Coleridge's romantic drama *Remorse*, which was first performed at Drury Lane on 23 January 1813, she sang "with all the refreshing purity of her unsophisticated style, and with that chaste expression and tenderness of feeling," wrote Kelly, "which speak at once as it were to the heart." At the time of her death, the *Gentleman's Magazine* (March 1838) recalled that so exquisite was her ear that she could not remain in a room if anyone sang out of tune and declared her practically and theoretically "a good musician." Arch and sprightly, she was also a capable actress.

In addition to the roles mentioned above, among the many characters she played during her career were included: Nell in *The Adopted Child*, Conquetinda in *Amoroso*, Josephine in *Children in the Wood*, Claudine in *Devil's Bridge*, Emily in *False Alarms*, Jeanetta in *False and True*, Molly in *The Farmer*, Nannette in *Fontainbleau*, Dolly O'Daisy in *Hit or Miss*, Miss Notable in *Lady's Last Stake*, Jenny in *Lionel and Clarissa*, Madge in *Love in a Village*, Lisetta in *Matrimony*, Jeannet in *The Maniac*, Musca in *The Ninth Statue*, Dutch Girl in *Orange Boven*, Lucy in *Paul and Virginia*, Marinetta in *The Peasant Boy*, an unspecified part in *The Pirate*, Kathleen in *The Poor Soldier*, Nina in *The Prisoner*, Sally in *The Purse*, Lucy in *The Review*, Stella in *Robin Hood*, Mary Ann in *The School for Guardians*, Christine in *Takeli*, Taffline in *Three and the Deuce*, Lisbeth in *The Unknown Guest*, Laura in *The Woodman's Hut,* and she sang the dirge in *Romeo and Juliet*.

The following portraits and prints of Mrs Bland are known: 1. A portrait by J. Condé, engraved by the artist as a plate to the *Thespian Magazine*, 1792.   2. A portrait by W. Naish, engraved by W. Ridley as a plate to *Parson's Minor Theatre*, 1794.   3. As Sally Shamrock in *The Shipwreck*, a water color on paper by DeWilde

(1805), at the Garrick Club; engraved by R. Cooper for Cawthorn's *Minor British Theatre*, 1807. 4. As Sally Shamrock, engraved by J. Rogers, after Steeden, as a plate to Oxberry's *Dramatic Dictionary*, 1825. 5. As Sally Shamrock, by Wageman, engraved by the artist as a plate to Oxberry's *New English Drama*, 1820. 6. As Christine in *Tekeli,* a water color on paper by DeWilde, at the Garrick Club, never published. 7. As Madam Belgarde in *Monsieur Tonson,* a water color on paper, at the Garrick Club; engraved by R. Cooper and published by H. Berthoud, 1822. (In the Hall *Catalogue of Dramatic Portraits in the Harvard Theatre Collection,* Mrs Bland is incorrectly identified as playing M. Marbleu.) 8. As Beda in *Bluebeard*, by DeWilde, engraved by Bond, published 1809. 9. As Madge in *Love in a Village*, engraved by Roberts, after Brooks, as a plate to *The British Stage*, 1821. 10. As Madelon in *The Surrender of Calais*, by an unknown engraver, published as a plate to the *Carlton-House Magazine*, August 1793; another version was published in *The Attic Miscellany*, 1792. 11. As Madelon, with John Bannister as La Gloire, engraved by Barlow, published by Roach, 1791. 12. As Marinetta in *The Peasant Boy*, by an unknown engraver, published by J. West, 1811. 13. As Mary Ann in *The School for Guardians*, engraved by Audinet, after Graham, as a plate to *Bell's British Theatre*, 1797. 14. As Miss Notable in *Lady's Last Stake*, by DeWilde, engraved by Leney, as a plate to *Bell's British Theatre*, 1795. 15. As Nina in *The Prisoner*, engraved by Woolly, published 1796. 16. As Nina, with Mrs Crouch as Clara, engraved by Barlow, after Charles. 17. As Nina, engraved by Warburton, published by W. Smith, 1796. 18. A color print entitled "The Little Bland Methodist," by an unknown engraver, published by A. Beugo, 1805. 19. A satirical print entitled "A Smile to a Tear," by Cruikshank, published by Laurie and Whit-

tle, 2 March 1807, depicts Mrs Bland as Emily and John Braham as Edgar Gayland in *False Alarms*, at Drury Lane 12 January 1807. 20. A satirical print entitled "Huzza, for old Ireland, with Hubbaboo Whack!" by Cruikshank, published by Laurie and Whittle, 4 April 1810, depicts Mrs Bland as Dolly and Mr Johnstone as O'Rourke O'Daisy in the musical farce *Hit or Miss.*

Bland, James [*fl. 1784–1815*], *actor.*
James Bland was the eldest son of the Edinburgh actor-manager John Bland (1721–1808) and Nancy Bland, also an actress at Edinburgh. No doubt James acted in his father's company before 1784, when according to *The London Stage*, with other actors from Scotland, he appeared as Saville in *Wit's Last Stake* at the Haymarket, out-of-season, on 9 February. This was his only known London performance.

Bland spent the rest of his career in the provinces, with his wife, a Miss Satchell, daughter of the London instrument-maker John Satchell. She was the sister of Elizabeth Satchell, who became Mrs Stephen Kemble, of Catharine Mary Satchell, who became Mrs John Duill and later Mrs John Taylor, and of Susannah Satchell, who became Mrs Robert Benson. All the Satchell girls acted on the London stage except James Bland's wife.

The Blands were acting at Durham in 1815, according to Joseph Cowell's *Thirty Years Among the Players.* When Stephen Kemble leased the theatre at Durham to Faulkner and Anderson, he arranged that his sister-in-law, her husband, and their two children should receive a total of 25s. per week for their services in the company. The son John, aged about 12 in 1815, made the prompter's calls, and the daughter, about two years younger, played children's roles in such pieces as *Children in the Wood,* while Mrs Bland played *"short old ladies"* and Bland "delivered the messages." According to Cowell, he knew every message in any old play, but he would not or could not learn the new ones. No matter what role he played, Bland never changed any clothes but his coat. Usually frequenting one of the taverns near the theatre at curtain-time, it was Bland's habit never to appear back-stage a minute sooner than he was needed, sometimes a minute after, when his son would be in the wings "just in time to slip on a tunic or jacket, pop a little red on his face, and push him on." Well-informed, a ready and amiable wit, fond of hunting and drinking, Bland was also a careless and dissipated character. At Durham he and his wife were separated but continued to work together at the theatre, and it was droll, wrote Cowell, to hear the old actor say, "I must put on my other shirt today, for I'm invited to take a friendly cup of tea with the old lady," meaning his wife.

James Bland was related through his parents and brothers to a substantial number of theatrical people, most of whom, however, did not perform in London. His father John Bland was half-brother to the Irish actor Francis Bland who married the Irish actress Grace Phillips and became the father of the famous Dorothy Jordan and her brother the actor George Bland. James Bland himself had at least two brothers and a sister. Of one brother, Edward, little is known. The other, John Bland, an actor in his father's theatre at Edinburgh, was married to the former first wife of the actor John Mills (d. 1787). She had been born Miss Stamper, of a theatrical family. John Bland died about 1796. His wife was probably the Mrs Bland of the Swansea Theatre who died on 11 October 1808. They had four children who acted while very young on the Edinburgh stage at the beginning of the nineteenth century, including a son John who married the actress Georgianna Glover. John's children were related to the theatrical and musical families of Marsh, Connolly, Murray, and Bateman. James Bland's sister Martha was mar-

ried in July 1787 to Anthony Angelo Tremamondo (nephew of Domenico Angelo and cousin of Harry Angelo, fencing masters) and that couple had 22 children, many of whom died in infancy.

Blandford, Mr [*fl. 1789*], *actor.*

Mr Blandford acted in two performances given at the White Horse Inn, Parsons Green, Fulham. On 9 November 1789 he played Inkle in *Inkle and Yarico* and Bombardinian in *Chrononhotonthologos*; on 11 November for his benefit (shared with one other) he acted Young Belmont in *The Foundling*, Don Juan in *The Shipwreck*, and danced *The Affrighted Dwarf*.

Blandy, Mr [*fl. 1781–1787*], *constable.*

Mr Blandy was the Drury Lane constable from at least the 1780–81 season forward; the first mention of him in the bills was on 12 May 1781 when tickets delivered by Blandy and others were to be accepted at the theatre. Similar notices appeared over the years. The account books referred to him on occasion, as on 5 January 1784 when he was paid 10s. for convicting a pickpocket, or on 2 February 1787 when he was given £3 10d. to pay the "scrowrers" at the theatre. On 10 February 1787 Mr Blandy was replaced as constable by Mr Barrett.

Blaney, Miss [*fl. 1781–1782*], *actress.*

Miss Blaney played an unspecified principal role in *The Spendthrift* at the Haymarket Theatre on 12 November 1781 and Leonora in *An Adventure in St James's Park* (based on *Love in a Wood*) on 21 January 1782 at the same playhouse.

Blanfield, Mr [*fl. 1767*], *pyrotechnist.*

Sylas Neville recorded in his *Diary* on 23 January 1767 that he had seen new fireworks at Marylebone Gardens presented by Mr Blanfield.

Blanshard. *See* BLANCHARD.

Blant, Mr [*fl. 1788*], *house servant?*
The account books for Covent Garden mention a Mr Blant who was presumably a house servant, but his function in the theatre was not noted. The playbill for 27 May 1788 listed him as one whose tickets would be accepted at the theatre.

Blastock, Mr [*fl. 1735–1736*], *actor.*
Mr Blastock acted Dugard in *The Inconstant* on 17 December 1735 at the Haymarket Theatre; at the same playhouse on 19 January 1736 he played Fieri Facias in *The Rival Milliners.* At the Fielding-Hippisley booth at Bartholomew Fair from 23 to 26 August 1736 he was in the cast of *The Cheats of Scapin*, and on the following 7 September he was Doodle in *The Innocent Wife* at the old playhouse at the bottom of Mermaid Court at Southwark Fair. Blastock may have been the Mr Bostock who was active from 1742 to 1750.

Blendel, Mr [*fl. 1772*], *actor.*
Mr Blendel acted Sir William in *Patie and Roger* (better known as *The Gentle Shepherd*) at the Haymarket Theatre on 21 September 1772.

Blender. *See* BENDLER.

Blewitt, C. [*fl. 1785–1788*], *singer.*
A person named C. Blewitt was a vocalist at the Spa Gardens, Bermondsey, between 1785 and 1788.

Blewitt, Jonas *d. 1805, organist, composer.*
Considered one of the most distinguished organists of the latter half of the eighteenth century, Jonas Blewitt had been a pupil of Samuel Jarvis, and about 1795 was the organist of the united London parishes of St Margaret Pattens and St Gabriel Fenchurch and also of St Catherine Coleman, Fenchurch Street. Blewitt also wrote music for many entertainments at the Spa Gardens, Bermondsey, at the Lyceum, at Vauxhall Gardens, and at the Oxford Concerts. Some 37 such published songs are to be found at the British Museum. On 6 April 1790, his song "A Laugh and A Cry" was sung by Darley and Blanchard at Covent Garden Theatre; and on 15 May 1792, his song "Tis a mighty fine thing" was sung by Johnstone in a performance of *A Cure for a Coxcomb* at the same theatre. He composed music for a production of *The Blunt Tar* at Astley's Amphitheatre on 9 July 1791. He was the author of *A Complete Treatise on the Organ, Ten Voluntaries; or Pieces for the Organ*, and *Twelve Easy and Familiar Movements for the Organ.*

In 1794 Blewitt was living in Bermondsey Square, and according to Doane's *Musical Directory* was connected with the Apollo Gardens and the Royal Circus as well as with the Spa Gardens and Astley's. He probably played the organ at these places in addition to providing music. In the fall of 1793 he played the piano in accompaniment to G. S. Carey's readings during a revival of the *Eidophusikon* at the Great Room, late Cox's Museum, Spring Gardens. He also played the organ as the panoramic scenes of the *Eidophusikon* entertainment were displayed.

Blewitt died in 1805. His son Jonathan Blewitt (1782–1853) was a well-established organist, composer, and director of music at theatres in England and Ireland during the nineteenth century. One C. Blewitt, who was a vocalist at the Spa Gardens between 1785–88, may have been a member of the family.

"Blind Harper." *See* PARRY, JOHN.

Blinks, Miss. *See* VINCENT, MRS RICHARD.

Bliss, Mr {*fl. 1757*}, *actor.*

Mr Bliss played Harlequin in *The Restoration and Adventures of Harlequin* on 5 September 1757 at the Great Theatrical Booth in George Inn Yard at Bartholomew Fair.

Blissett, Francis *1742?–1824, actor.*

Francis Blissett's obituary in the *Bath Journal* of 23 December 1824 stated that at his death that month he was "in the 83rd year of his age." He was, then, born in 1742. (A clipping from an unidentified newspaper of 1827 declared him to have been 63 in 1800, which if accepted would mean that he had been born in 1737.)

Blissett was said to have been a native of Reading, in Berkshire, from which he ran away at 11 (or, in some accounts, at 13). His uncle, a paper stainer of London, brought him up in that business until he was 21. The story may be complicated, if

Harvard Theatre Collection

FRANCIS BLISSETT, the elder
as Baron Duberly

artist unknown

not contradicted, by an entry in the burial register of St Paul, Covent Garden, Westminster, a notation of a burial on 30 May 1745: "Francis Blissett son of Francis Blissett from St Martin in the Fields." The father in the entry could have been the actor's uncle.

Blissett came onto the stage under the management of Robert Bates in a travelling company at Shepton Mallet, but it is not known when. George Raymond placed him next at Smock Alley Theatre in Dublin early in the 1760's, then with David Fisher at Dundee, and then with David Ross at Edinburgh in 1767. He went next for an undetermined period to Birmingham, to Joseph Austin's Newcastle-on-Tyne company, and finally (after spending the summer season of 1775 at the Haymarket) to the Bath and Bristol theatres, where he acted for the rest of his long career except for summer excursions to London.

Miss Kathleen Barker finds that he was at the Bristol Theatre Royal briefly as early as 1776 but was there regularly from the spring of 1779 through at least some parts of every season through 1797–98.

Francis Blissett would have been a leading actor in London where by and large the audiences were, if more vociferously demanding, less discriminating than they were at "the Bath." But he is said to have had a superstitious dread of playing an engagement in the metropolis. He came, however, to the Haymarket at Foote's insistence in June of 1776. A popular charge of the provincial press of later years was that it was his misfortune while in London to have to "fill second-rate parts of a grave and serious cast," instead of being allowed to follow the line at which he excelled. As one of them wrote: "His forte lies in the acting of Midas, and all characters in which are painted the avarice, decrepitude, or folly of old age." This charge, however, was only partly true, for although Edwin was assigned Midas in *Midas*, while Blissett was relegated to Damaetas, and though Parsons usually shunted him out of roles like Sir Francis Wronghead in *The Provok'd Husband*, and Bannister always secured the title part in *The Quaker*, at least for a good deal of his time at the Haymarket Blissett was allowed to display the specialty which he had been developing in Bristol. Many of his London roles were in his line, though some were smaller than he might have liked: Old Gobbo in *The Merchant of Venice*, Syphax in *Cato*, Basil in *The Spanish Barber*, Justice Shallow in *The Merry Wives of Windsor*, one of the carriers in *1 Henry IV*, Dr Truby in *The Suicide*, Justice Benbow in *The Flitch of Bacon*, and Dr Julep in *The Devil Upon Two Sticks*. (For Mrs Jewell's benefit on 18 September 1778 he was even permitted to shine in Sir Francis Wronghead in *The Provok'd Husband*.) Some parts made smaller use of his talents: Lucianus (*sic*) in *Hamlet*, Flute in *The Fairy Tale* (an alteration of *A Midsummer Night's Dream*), Careful in *The Advertisement*, Peter in *The Chances*, the Taylor in *The Provok'd Wife*, Pulville in *Tony Lumpkin in Town*, the Beggar in *The Beggar's Opera*, and the Marquis in *The Gyp-*

sies. He remained at the Haymarket for the full three months of the season every summer from 1776 through 1781 and returned again in 1783. It appears that he was totally absent from London after that until 18 May 1803, when he was advertised to play Falstaff and other characters at the Haymarket. A letter of 10 December 1802 from George Colman the younger to R. W. Elliston, which is now in the Huntington Library, gives an interesting glimpse into the managerial mind and may explain what made Blissett fear London:

Thus for Blisset./ £7 per week; & a Benefit; he paying the charges. If the profits of the Benefit shd. fall short of £81, I will make good deficiencies, up to that Sum. If the profits should be more, so much the better for him, & I shall have nothing to make up to him.

Calculation

7 per week (for 17 weeks)	£119
Profits insured on Benefit	81
Total.	200

My plan is weekly Salary, *playhouse pay*:— for suppose, for instance, a calamity, a royal death, should shut up the Theatre, pro tempore:—how heavy, in that case, stipulated sums for the season wd fall upon the Property.

Blissett had married a mantua maker of Bath, Elizabeth Rudall (1749–1833), on 4 October 1779 at Walcot Church, Bath. Apparently they had no children, and she was never on the stage.

Francis Blissett's later years were spent in obscurity. In the words of one obituary "Old age and infirmity of late made him a recluse, but a small circle of ancient friends survive who regarded him living, and regret him dead." He died at Bath on 13 December 1824. By a will signed on 13 June 1823 and proved 26 March 1826 he left to Elizabeth his widow all his assets, "hoping she will lend every pecuniary assistance to my natural son Francis White

Harvard Theatre Collection

FRANCIS BLISSETT, the younger as Dr Dablancour, with Joseph Jefferson by Leslie

Blissett." (The son was the Bath, and later American, actor, who was born in 1773 and died in 1850. He did not play in London in the eighteenth century.) Blissett arranged bequests of exactly £66 13s. 4d. each to his nephew John Doll (or Dell), to his niece Mary Simmons, and to the widow of his "late relation" Thomas Blissett.

There is a large pastel drawing of Francis Blissett in the Garrick Club, incorrectly catalogued as a picture of William Blissett (1742–1824). There are in the Harvard Theatre Collection an anonymous lithograph of him as Baron Duberly in *The Heir at Law* and an engraving of a scene from the same play, with R. W. Elliston as Dr Pangloss and Blissett as Duberly, drawn and etched by A. Caldwell.

Bloe. *See* **BLOW.**

Blogg, Mr ₁*fl. 1739–1748*₁, *singer.*

Mr Blogg seems first to have been noticed in 1739 when he sang, among other pieces, "Early Horn" and "Mad Tom" at the New Wells, near London Spa. He was probably the Blogg who was a member of the company playing at Canterbury in 1741. The singer was at the New Wells again on 27 December 1742, sang at Pinchbeck and Fawkes's booth at Bartholomew Fair in the summer of 1743, and was a member of Hallam's troupe at May Fair in 1744. On 16 March 1744 at the playhouse in James Street, Blogg had entertained the audience with songs; he and Brett joined in a performance of *Solomon* at the New Wells, Lemon Street, on 1 November 1744; in the course of this year he sang at Lord Cobham's Head in Cold Bath Fields, offering selections from *Saul* and *Samson*; on 28 October 1745 at Goodman's Fields he sang and played Langoiran in *The Massacre at Paris*; and in July 1747 at the Sir John Oldcastle Tavern in Cold Bath Fields he sang such songs as "Come Rosalind" and "The Happy Pair." The singer was in the Canterbury troupe again in the summer

of 1747, playing Macheath in *The Beggar's Opera*, and in the summer of 1748 he was Sir John Loverule (with special songs) in *The Devil to Pay*.

The name Blogg does not appear again in theatrical records until 1762, again at Canterbury, but this time the performer was apparently a second generation Blogg who was primarily an actor. The elder Blogg was living at Canterbury at this time, in Lamb Lane, and his son lodged with him. The younger Blogg went on to become the Brighton theatre's co-manager in the summer of 1799, but he seems not to have been active in London.

Blond. *See* **LE BLOND.**

Blondel, Mons ₁*fl. 1742*₁, *dancer.*

Monsieur Blondel danced the *English Maggot* on 25 August 1742 at Hippisley and Chapman's booth at Bartholomew Fair.

Bloomer, Mr ₁*fl. 1784*₁, *singer.*

Mr Bloomer, a tenor, sang at the Handel Memorial Concerts at Westminster Abbey and the Pantheon on 26, 27, 29 May and 3, 5 June 1784.

Bloomfield, Mr ₁*fl. 1787–1792*₁, *actor.*

Mr Bloomfield may have made his start at the Bristol theatre in July 1787, the first mention of him in the records; he played supporting juvenile parts regularly through the 1790–91 season. During these same years he also appeared at Bath, his first notice there being on 6 October 1787; it is not clear whether he acted there as regularly as at Bristol, but he was certainly playing at Bath at the Orchard Street Theatre in January 1790 when, according to a report, bailiffs, following Bloomfield for some unspecified reason, pushed their way onto the stage and arrested him on the spot during a performance.

By the 1791–92 season he felt he was ready for London, and he made his first appearance at Covent Garden for £2 weekly on 19 September 1791 as Count Theodore in *The Count of Narbonne*. The critics were not kind. Said one, "He treads the stage like a man that has been used to it, and will make a useful performer in third, perhaps in second rate characters, but first are out of the question." Another noted that Bloomfield had "a good figure and voice, but undertook too much, when he engaged to play Theodore." And a third wrote: "He possesses a well-formed manly figure with a powerful voice, but neither musical or various, nor are his features very expressive. He has self-possession enough to call forth the talent which belongs to him. He requires much cultivation and he appears to have much to both learn and unlearn." Bloomfield fared somewhat better at his next appearance, as Paris in *Romeo and Juliet* on 26 September 1791; the critics found his action just and unembarrassed and felt he delivered the dialogue with becoming propriety of tone and manner. He was given Cornwall in *King Lear* on 4 November 1791, Lord Edmond in the afterpiece *The Prisoner at Large* on 6 March 1792, and Jack Stanmore in *Oroonoko* on 30 June—after which his name disappeared from the bills.

Bloomgarten. *See* **BAUMGARTEN, SAMUEL.**

Blore. *See* **BLOW.**

Blow, John *1649–1708, composer, organist, teacher.*

John Blow (or Blore, Blaew) was born, not in North Collingham as was once reported, but in Newark, Nottinghamshire, and was baptized there on 23 February 1649. His father was Henry Blow and his mother, before her marriage to Henry, was the widow of one Langwith. John was their second child, their first, Henry, having been baptized in 1647; their third, Katherine, was christened in 1651. The elder

Harvard Theatre Collection

JOHN BLOW
by Reader?

Blow died in 1655; Henry the younger later married and probably had a daughter named Elizabeth; and Katherine grew up to marry, apparently, a man named Cage.

Young John Blow may have received his musical education at Newark, but there is no evidence of his schooling or how he came to his interest in music. At the Restoration, when he was 12, he became a boy chorister under Henry Cooke and was considered, along with young Pelham Humphrey, "among the forwardest and brightest Children of the Chapell [Royal]." Before 1663 he had done some composing of anthems as part of his Chapel training and displayed a precocious talent. His voice broke in late 1664, whereupon Cooke was allotted the usual £40 annually for the maintenance of a boy who had "gone off" from the Chapel. Perhaps about this time Blow was tutored by musicians John Hingeston and Christopher Gibbons.

On 21 August 1667 Samuel Pepys mentioned a boy singer, "Blaew," who may have been young John Blow at 18, though one would suppose by that time the lad's voice would have become more melodious than Pepys reported:

This morning come two of Captain Cooke's boys, whose voices are broke, and are gone from the Chapel, but have extraordinary skill; and they and my boy, with his broken voice, did sing three parts; their names were Blaew and Loggings; but notwithstanding their skill, yet to hear them sing with their broken voices, which they could not command to keep in tune, would make a man mad—so bad it was.

A year later the talented Blow was appointed organist of Westminster Abbey in place of Albertus Byrne at a salary of £10 per year, and on 15 January 1669 he rejoined the Chapel Royal, replacing Giles Tompkins as "musician for the virginals." From May through June he was with Charles II at Windsor, serving as organist for a large complement of Chapel musicians, but at this time, and for several years following, he was apparently serving without a fee; not until 16 March 1674 could he be sworn a Gentleman of the Chapel Royal in ordinary, for only then did a salaried position become vacant. A few months after his appointment he was made composer for voices in the King's private music and Master of the Children of the Chapel, succeeding his recently deceased friend, Pelham Humphrey. He climaxed the year by getting married in late September of 1674.

Blow's bride was Elizabeth Braddock, daughter of Edward, a Gentleman of the Chapel Royal, Master of the Children of Westminster, and later Clerk of the Cheque of the Chapel—a father-in-law of some importance. The date of 4 September 1674 found in the St Paul, Covent Garden, register probably referred to the first publishing of the banns there, for their license was issued on 23 September. Blow declared himself a bachelor, of age about 26, from the

parish of St Margaret, Westminster; Elizabeth Braddock was from the same parish, a spinster, of age about 20. By the end of 1674, then, John Blow had achieved several important positions in the royal musical establishment, had made a most satisfactory match with another musical family, and had probably become the teacher of the talented young genius, Henry Purcell. A man of 25 could hardly have asked for more.

But Blow seems to have had boundless energy and, as Hawkins later reported, was not "totally free from the imputation of pride"; as a result, the next 25 years of his life were crammed, perhaps too fully, with accomplishments. By 1678 he had started dabbling in real estate—the results of which are evident in the eight London houses plus land at Hampton which he acquired before he died. On 10 December 1677 he was granted the degree of Doctor of Music, the earliest Lambeth degree in music on record, and by April 1679—or possibly as early as October 1676—he was made organist of the Chapel Royal. And by the end of 1683 he had sired five children and a goodly number of musical compositions.

John and Elizabeth Blow's first child was named Henry, but he died in infancy and was buried on 1 September 1676; a son John died at the age of 15 on 2 June 1693 and was buried on the eighth; a daughter Katherine (or Catherine) died on 19 May 1730 and was buried on 25 May; Elizabeth Blow Edgeworth (Mrs William) was buried on 9 September 1719; and Mary Blow was buried on 22 November 1738. The children were apparently born in the order just given, though their birth dates were not recorded, and they were all buried in the cloisters of Westminster Abbey. John Blow's wife died on 29 October 1683 in childbirth at the age of 30 and was buried two days later at the Abbey.

During this same period, from 1674 to about 1687, Blow composed much of his music, including a number of pieces for the theatre. Though he had no great penchant for theatre work, he wrote songs for *The Loyal General* in 1679, *The Princess of Cleve* in the same year, *The Royalist* in 1682, *The Lucky Chance* in 1686, and perhaps others; but his music was as forgettable as the plays for which they were written. His masque *Venus and Adonis*, on the other hand, was a work of considerable beauty, composed for the entertainment of Charles II about 1682. The role of Venus was especially designed for the King's mistress, actress Mary ("Moll") Davis, and the issue of that affair, Mary Tudor, played Cupid. From what is known of Blow's rather conservative personality, an assignment like this may have been distasteful, yet he managed to produce what was in fact a miniature opera of grace and ingenuity that has been, unfortunately but understandably, overshadowed by Purcell's more famous *Dido and Aeneas* of several years later. In addition to his theatre songs and *Venus and Adonis*, before the end of 1687 Blow had also composed, among other works, several anthems and his first—and best—Ode for St Cecilia's Day.

These years of vigorous activity also saw him appointed Almoner and Master of the Children of St Paul's, succeeding his old fellow chorister Michael Wise, and by 1685 he was the official composer in the private music of James II. The only post he seems to have relinquished during this period was his position as organist at Westminster, which he gave up to his pupil Henry Purcell. His various activities made him a prominent figure in the music world, and he was considered an authority to be turned to on matters musical, especially when organs were involved. One instance was perhaps typical. Between 1683 and 1685 he, Purcell, and Giovanni Battista Draghi were asked to judge between two organs, built respectively by Bernard Smith and Renatus Harris, which the Inner Temple was considering for purchase. Blow and Purcell played Smith's instrument and Draghi

tested Harris's; the decision was in favor of the former, but the Inner Temple, being a law group, spent two years wrangling over the award, only to decide, finally, that Blow and Purcell were right after all. All that the musicians got out of this was £4 17s. 3d. and probably an unwillingness to sell their professional opinions to amateurs again. Yet, as public servants, Blow and Purcell probably could not turn down such requests. On 30 September 1686 Purcell tested and approved another new organ by Smith for St Katherine Cree, and he, Blow, and others auditioned young organists for a position there; they voted in favor of Moses Snow, later a musician of considerable importance, and in this case the members of the vestry, though they disagreed with the judges on the second choice, gave Snow the job.

All this time Blow was busy teaching. His work as Master of the Chapel Boys, a post which he held throughout most of his active musical life, must in some ways have been an onerous one. He was paid, of course, for teaching the boys in his charge and providing for them even after their voices had broken; but he, like Henry Cooke before him, seemed to have been burdened with the task of being a parent to the children as well: going to provincial towns to fetch new boys who had been accepted (as he did in May or June of 1675 when he took a trip to Cambridge), tending to boys who were sick (as he did in October or November 1676 when he provided a nurse for one who was "sick of spotted fever" and in November or December 1677 when he paid for the "cure of a broaken legg of one of the children"), providing clothing, strings for instruments, ink, paper, heat for the classroom, thread for mending worn garments, and all the other petty necessaries for a group of youngsters which numbered anywhere from 40 to 60.

In addition, Blow taught not only organ, but lute, violin, oboe, and probably other instruments, plus singing; that he did these things well is attested by the remarkable number of illustrious students he turned out: Henry Purcell, Jeremiah Clarke, Vaughan and William Richardson, John Reading, William Holder, Francis Smith, John Robinson, William Croft, and numerous others. The job must have been time-consuming and emotionally straining, especially toward the end of Charles II's reign when his pay was often delinquent (the 1685–86 accounts indicate that some payments were over five years behind); James II, to his credit, tried to pay off Charles's debts. Since it could hardly have been greed that led Blow to stay with this burdensome job, it may have been pride or ambition, but there was also a most admirable devotion.

In the 1690's Blow's activity diminshed somewhat, yet after Purcell's death in 1695 Blow resumed the position of organist at Westminster and assumed, with Bernard Smith, Purcell's post of tuner of the royal instruments; to memorialize his famous pupil's death he and John Dryden wrote a moving *Ode*; and in 1699 he was made Composer to the Royal Chapel, a new position for which he was paid £40 annually.

After the turn of the century Blow gradually relinquished some of his duties and spent part of his time editing his musical works. In 1700 he published a collection of his music, calling it *Amphion Anglicus*; and in 1700 and again in 1704 musical anthologies were published that contained some of his pieces. By the beginning of 1708 John Blow was "sick in body," and on 3 January he made his will.

To his three surviving daughters he left the bulk of his considerable estate. To Katherine he bequeathed his two houses in the Great Sanctuary in Westminster which he had held on lease from the Dean and Chapter of Westminster. To Elizabeth he left his two houses in Orchard Street, Westminster, which he had leased from Sir Robert Pye, and a second house in the Great Sanctuary in Westminster in which

his father-in-law Edward Braddock had lived and in which, probably, Blow and his wife had also lived until her death in 1683; this house, too, he had leased from the Dean and Chapter of Westminster. To Mary, who was to get £3 annually from Elizabeth's Orchard Street holdings, he left his three houses in Duck Lane, Westminster, which he had leased from Sir Robert Pye. To all three girls he bequeathed his copyhold estate at Hampton, which he asked them to sell, sharing the profit. To his servant Elizabeth Luddington he left a generous £100 plus £10 for mourning, his rings, and his clothes. To his "sister Cage"—probably his sister Katherine—he gave £50 plus £10 for mourning clothes; to his niece Elizabeth Blow (probably his brother Henry's daughter) he gave £50 plus £6 for mourning clothes; and to Dr Ralph Battle, Sub Dean of the Chapel Royal, he gave a ring worth a guinea and asked him to serve as a trustee to assist his young daughters in the execution of the will. The rest of his estate, including any arrears in salary at the time of his death, was to be divided equally among the three girls. It was a generous will, yet oddly lacking in any remembrance of his colleagues, many of whom had been his pupils and had given him their homage while he lived.

On 1 October 1708 John Blow died. He was buried a week later near his famous pupil Henry Purcell, close to the organ loft in Westminster Abbey. The authorities could not have chosen a more appropriate spot.

Assessing John Blow's personality and his position in the history of music is not easy. On the one hand, relatively few facts have survived concerning his personal life, though there are intriguing clues here and there; on the other hand, the period in which Blow lived provided unusual opportunities for advancement which may have thrust him into higher positions than his talent actually warranted. During the Interregnum musical activity was drastically diminished, and at the Restoration many older musicians did not return to the royal service; Blow, at a very early age, was thus able to achieve positions of high importance, and he consequently exerted a profound influence on the new generation of musicians, many of whom were under his tutelage and profited greatly from the old combination of inventiveness and tradition which seemed to be part of Blow's makeup. The quality of Blow's work is also difficult to assess because he lived in an age and held a combination of positions that required him to grind out compositions at too fast a rate, the result being a musical output that was very uneven in quality—some of it remarkably fine and individual and much of it quite routine. His reputation has suffered to the point of his sometimes being ignored by lovers of his more famous and clearly more talented student, Henry Purcell, to whose greatness Blow certainly contributed; and as a man he has seemed remote and rather uninteresting.

If he was proud and ambitious, he was also generous and gave much of himself to others. He seems not to have begrudged fame for others who deserved it, and he appears to have used his influential position in the music world most charitably and to have done much to enhance his students' careers. When he relinquished his post as organist of Westminster to Purcell in 1679, he apparently did so freely, and he felt the position to be important enough to take back after Purcell's death. His colleagues loved and respected him, certainly; in 1700 when his *Amphion Anglicus* was published, his students and colleagues joined to praise Blow for being "Father of Musick and Musicians" and for "Treating Your Pupil Children as Your own." He was named in numerous wills, sometimes as witness, sometimes as executor, and most often as a beneficiary.

His contemporaries found him a convivial companion, "a very handsome man in his person, and remarkable for a gravity

and decency in his deportment. . . . He was a man of blameless morals and of a benevolent temper." That he was "not totally free from the imputation of pride" may be true, but perhaps a man who had been a faithful servant of four monarchs without (apparently) antagonizing anyone, the composer of what may really have been the first English opera, and the teacher of Henry Purcell could be permitted a little pride.

He is pictured in a Grignion engraving from life by R. White which is prefixed to his *Amphion Anglicus*. A portrait of him in the possession of Mr Algernon Ashton belonged to the family of the late Dr Detmar Blow, and an oval head and shoulders painting by Closterman in the possession of Dr W. H. Cummings belonged to the late Dr A. H. Mann. A small head of Blow by Lely is at St Michael's College, Tenbury. Blow was treated in 1937 to a full study by H. Watkins Shaw, and Grove provides an extensive list of his musical compositions and writings.

Blower, Mr [*fl.* 1777?–1791], *puppeteer, actor?*

A Mr Blower exhibited his puppets at Bartholomew Fair in 1791. Though there is not sufficient evidence to be certain, he may have been the Mr Blower who was at Covent Garden in 1787–88 and who received 12*s*. 6*d*. for three nights on 22 September 1787 and £1 9*s*. 2*d*. for seven nights on 10 June 1788. He may also have been the Blower who was paid 1*s*. on 18 August 1777 as an "Extra Man" at the Theatre Royal, Liverpool. Mr Blower may have been related to the two actresses of that name who flourished in the 1780's.

Blower, Miss A. [*fl.* 1782], *actress?*

Miss A. Blower, sister of the slightly better known Elizabeth, performed with her sister at Richmond in August 1782. One of the journals of the day reported that "The Richmond Company are going on with tolerable success. They play three nights in the week at Windsor. Miss [Elizabeth] Blower, who made her first appearance last season at Drury Lane, has joined them, as has also a younger sister to that Lady, who has made her *coup d'essai* with some *eclat*." The reporter would have been helpful if he had been less elegant and more specific, for it is not clear whether Miss A. Blower was an actress, dancer, or singer.

After her summer stint in the London area, she and her sister Elizabeth went to Dublin, where Miss A. Blower made her debut at the Crow Street Theatre on 11 November 1782. Whether or not she ever performed in London again is not certain; the 1787–88 performances by a Miss Blower at Covent Garden probably pertain to Elizabeth, but they might refer to her sister instead.

Blower, Elizabeth *b. 1763, actress, singer, author.*

Miss Elizabeth Blower was already the author of a novel, *George Bateman*, and some third-rate verse by the time she decided to try her hand at acting. On 27 April 1782, billed as "A Young Lady," she played Rosalind in *As You Like It* at Drury Lane for her first appearance on any stage. On the following 1 June she repeated the role for her benefit and made tickets available at her lodgings, No 12, Bedford Street, Covent Garden. The *Morning Post* critic was quite taken with Miss Blower's Rosalind and said on 20 May that "her stage requisites are allowed to be the most completely adapted to the character of any since Mrs Pritchard." The 30 April *Theatrical Intelligence* gave her a great deal of attention, starting out with as ambiguous a piece of journalese as one could ask: "In her stature she is sufficiently above the insipid mediocre to attract, though not tall enough to command." The review went on to laud her vivacious countenance, expressive and interesting voice, and sweet, and various, and insinuating articulation. Her

quickness of perception and intuitive rather than acquired ideas the critic felt were most praiseworthy.

Hence she gave Rosalind in a style of colouring that extorted applause from its nature and originality. We saw in her the delicacy of person, the terseness of wit, the vivacity of humour, and the sensibility of natural, not affected passion, with which Shakespeare formed the traits of his Rosalind. Her sensibility was truly nature under controul of vicissitude. She was lively without impertinence, pleasant without presumption, humorous without grimace, and distressed without [*sic*] the modesty of nature.

The review noted, however, that her costume was too slatternly "to make her appearance in before a newly-found father and an acknowledged lover"—though this may have been due to the haste with which the production was prepared.

After such praise one would expect to find Elizabeth Blower engaged by Drury Lane for the following season, but she was not. In August 1782 she and her sister were in the Richmond company, playing three nights a week at Windsor, and in the fall the two girls went to Ireland, where Elizabeth made her debut at the Crow Street Theatre in Dublin on 28 November. She apparently stayed in Ireland for the next five years.

In 1787–88 one of the Blower girls, probably Elizabeth, was back in London. At Covent Garden on 24 September 1787 she sang in the funeral procession in *Romeo and Juliet* and on 22 October she was part of the singing chorus in the triumphal entry in Act II of *Alexander the Great*. On 15 December she made her first Covent Garden appearance as an actress, playing Miss Biddy in *Miss in Her Teens* for a salary of £1 5s. weekly. She was dropped from the *Romeo and Juliet* chorus on 7 January 1788, probably because she was preparing for a similar chore in the grand chorus in Act II of *A King and No*

King. Though unnoticed in the bills, she remained in the Covent Garden troupe until the end of the season, and on 31 May 1788, the last record of her, she was one of many whose tickets were to be accepted at the theatre. The *Theatrical Intelligence* in 1782 must have seen far more talent in her than was actually there.

Bludrick, Mr [*fl. 1780*], *actor*.

Mr Bludrick (or Bludwick) was an attorney at New Inn, aged about 36, when he and the Covent Garden theatre manager determined to launch him on his stage career on 21 February 1780 playing King Lear. He was billed as "A Gentleman"— a common practice at the time—and after the critics finished with him he was probably most unhappy that the newspapers had not let him remain anonymous. One critic devoted a considerable amount of space to him and said, among other things:

His name is Bludwick [*sic*]; he has been educated, and has practised as an attorney. These circumstances have checked and regulated his passions, if he ever had any, that were disposed to eccentricity, or to swell into sublimity and greatness. They have even fixed his features, given his whole countenance that composed attention, and his eyes that cunning twinkling penetration, so observable in persons of his profession.

What induced him to think of the stage seems unaccountable. His person is diminutive; his countenance incapable of any variety of expression; and his voice feeble and unharmonious. His attempting so high and arduous an undertaking as the performance of *Lear* bespeaks his want of judgment.

The *Morning Post* was even more cutting: "so miserable was the attempt and so totally destitute did he seem of the common requisites of even a common rate actor that we caution him and the Manager against a second attempt as mutual disgrace must be the result." Bludrick apparently took the advice.

Blumb, Mr [*fl. 1792*], *imitator, pianist*.

Haydn, who visited London and recorded his impressions in 1792 in *The First London Notebook*, listed among the musical folk in the city a Mr Blumb who "imitated a parrot and accompanied himself admirably on the pianoforte."

Blume, Mr [*fl. 1783–1785*], *boxkeeper*.

Mr Blume was a boxkeeper at the King's Theatre in the Haymarket in 1783 and 1784–85. A Mrs Blume, presumably his wife, was a dresser at the King's during these same years.

Blume, Mrs [*fl. 1783–1785*], *dresser*. See BLUME, MR.

Blundell, James d. *1786, violoncellist, composer, singer*.

Though identification is uncertain, it seems likely that the Master Blundell who sang at Ranelagh in 1768 and had some of his own compositions printed and made available there was James Blundell, the violoncellist and composer of the 1770's and 1780's. Sometime prior to 22 December 1775 Blundell borrowed at least £27 from David Garrick to help finance a trip he took to the West Indies; Garrick apparently promised the cellist a place in the Drury Lane band when he returned, but when Blundell got back, no position was open. When a vacancy occurred, Garrick hired someone else, and, according to Blundell's letter to him on 22 December 1775, the musician would have starved had his friends not aided him. He studied hard at his instrument, he said, and through the help of his teacher he managed to get work.

Garrick finally found Blundell a position in the theatre band, but at a lower salary than had been paid to the musician who had left the chair vacant. Desperate and still owing Garrick £27, he took the job, and though his friends offered to pay off the debt, the cellist insisted on doing that himself. At one point in his letter Blundell told Garrick to send an account of the debt to Blundell's friend Mr Howell in Marylebone Street, but in another place he said he was relieved that the debt was now paid in full. In any case, Blundell either had paid Garrick or was now in a position to do so, and apparently he started talking to his fellow musicians about the probability of his getting a raise or leaving the band. This irritated Garrick, who thereupon hired another musician to take Blundell's place; Blundell's letter assured the manager that he had no thought of distressing him, to which Garrick responded by an endorsement on the letter: "Blundell's impudent, ungrateful ignorance."

Just what Blundell did to earn a living after leaving Drury Lane at the end of 1775 is not known, but he apparently prospered enough to permit him to marry on 2 August 1777 at St Mary Lambeth, Surrey. The bride he took was Mary Welker (or Welchor), a spinster of that parish. By 4 February 1781 Blundell was recommended to membership in the Royal Society of Musicians by William Parkinson, and on 6 May following he was accepted. James Blundell died in 1786, and though he had paid his subscription to the Royal Society to 24 June 1787, he apparently did not die well enough off to provide properly for his widow. She petitioned the Society for financial aid, noting that she and Blundell had had no children, but whether or not she was granted charity at this time is not known. On 1 September 1805 she was given three guineas for medical assistance, and on 6 April 1806 her sister, Elizabeth Welker, applied for and received £5 for funeral expenses for the late Mrs James Blundell.

Blundell seems to have spent most of his career as a performer, but he composed a few works: about 1785 his *Three Duetts for a Tenor and Violoncello* was published, and about 1790 his widow (apparently) had *A Select Collection of French, English and Scotch Airs* printed.

Blundiville, John *[fl. 1665]*, *singer.*
On 17 May 1665 Henry Cooke was granted funds for the maintenance of John Blundiville and John Blow, former members of the Children of the Chapel, whose voices had changed. Though Blow later had an illustrious musical career, Blundiville apparently did not return to singing.

Blunt, Mr *[fl. 1689]*, *actor.*
Mr Blunt played the Petitioner in *The Widow Ranter* at Drury Lane on 20 November 1689 as a member of the United Company.

Blunt, Mr *[fl. 1744]*, *actor.*
A Mr Blunt played Tyrell in *Richard III* at Richmond on 8 September 1744.

Blunt, Mrs. *See also* **HUNT, MRS.**

Blunt, Mrs *[fl. 1729–1730]*, *actress.*
A Mrs Blunt was in the Haymarket Theatre troupe during the 1729–30 season. She must have been assigned minor roles only, for her name appeared only once on the playbills: on 30 April 1730 she acted Mrs Glassring in *The Author's Farce*, which ran well into the summer.

Blunt, T. *[fl. 1794]*, *violinist.*
Doane's *Musical Directory* of 1794 listed T. Blunt, of Buckingham House, as a violinist in the King's band.

Blurton, James *b. 1756, dancer, actor, singer.*
James Blurton was stated by the Covent Garden playbill for 27 April 1767 to be 11 years old and making his first appearance on any stage when he danced *A New Tambourine* at the end of the first act of the mainpiece. He was one of three apprentices being introduced that night by Fishar, their master, ballet master of the

theatre. Master Blurton also joined another pupil, the ten-year-old Miss Besford in *A New Pantomime* ballet at the end of the second act. Though the bill stipulated "Entertainments by children for that night only," Blurton danced, alone or with Miss Besford, at least seven times more before the season ended. In 1767–68 he was making a *per diem* salary of 3*s*. 4*d*., the lowest compensation among the dancers, according to the list prepared by Arthur Murphy in 1768, where the young dancer was called "Burton."

Blurton was in Covent Garden's dance company until the end of the 1775–76 season. He appeared in the bills without the designation "Master" for the first time on 19 January 1773. He went to Drury Lane, at £2 per week, in the 1776–77 season, when he shared a benefit with Grist and Messink which netted them £136, and at which his scholar Master Staples was introduced. Blurton was at Drury Lane through 1777–78 but was absent from London then until 29 January 1779. His benefit that year, shared with Norris, Miss Simpson, and Miss Armstrong, was a disaster, grossing only £63. He was absent from London again in 1779–80.

Blurton's appearances at Drury Lane from October to April, 1780–81, were apparently separately contracted at irregular rates, and he was not on the roster. The same arrangement obtained from March through May 1782, after another absence the previous fall; but he was in the company on a regular basis from 5 October 1782 through 26 May 1783. He was absent from the city again until 18 May 1785 when, at Covent Garden, he danced an old favorite, *The Wapping Landlady*, for the benefit of the Miss Besford with whom he had made his debut.

Blurton for some reason received a cut in salary, to £1 10*s*. weekly when he returned to Covent Garden on 2 November 1785. He danced frequently until the end of the season on 5 June.

The conjecture in *The London Stage* that the "Young Gentleman" who was making his first appearance, in the part of Petit Maitre in *The Dumb Cake* at Covent Garden on 26 December 1787, was Blurton is probably correct, and what was meant was that he was then for the first time in a speaking role. From that date Blurton played small parts and also danced and sang in choruses until 1803–4. But this professional expansion did not improve his economic lot. He was still drawing a salary of £2 per week, except in 1788–89 when he was in the company only from 16 March to 18 June drawing only £1 10*s*. He may not even have been insured against old age; he had subscribed 10*s*. 6*d*. to the Drury Lane retirement fund in 1776 but had neglected his payment in 1777, and there is no record of a subscription to the Covent Garden fund.

In addition to his winter activities in London, James Blurton was in Liverpool in the summer of 1776 at £2 per week, in Bristol briefly in 1777, and at the Richmond, Surrey, Theatre in the summers of 1792, 1795, and 1797.

Blurton's line of spoken parts began with pantomime characters, like the cooper in *Harlequin Museum* and servants of no consequence, and ended only slightly more importantly with exotics and primitives like Terreeobo in *The Death of Captain Cook*, Irishmen like Fingal in *Oscar and Malvina*, Frenchmen like Picard in *Animal Magnetism*, supernaturals like Orchus in *Harlequin and Faustus*, and tiny Shakespearean parts like a traveller in *1 Henry IV*.

Blurton was married at some time before 1793, when his wife's name began to appear in the Covent Garden playbills, but neither her full maiden name nor the date of their marriage is known.

Blurton, Mrs James, Mary [*fl.* 1793–1800], *singer, actress.*

Mrs Blurton was first carried on the Covent Garden company list as a singer at

£1 5s. per week in the season of 1793–94. She probably was the "Mary Blurton . . . belong^g to Richmond" in the summer of 1793 spoken of in a manuscript commonplace book in the Folger Shakespeare Library. Presumably she was the wife of James Blurton, who had danced and acted in the company since 1785.

She was one of a number of vocalists assisting in the choruses to *Macbeth* on 30 September 1793. She also sang a "Musical Dirge," written by Shield, in Act V of *Hamlet* on 9 October and repeated it on 10 May, and she made several other choral contributions to the season. These were her musical duties the next season also, although she was not named in the bills after 9 March.

By 1795–96 Mrs Blurton had advanced nominally from "Chorus singer" to "actress" in the company lists, but her salary was the same and she was still predominantly a singer, as in her appearance with her husband and many others in yet another "Solemn Dirge," that of the "Funeral Procession of Juliet to the Monument of the Capulets" on 21 September 1795 and afterward. On 24 October 1796 she was Dolly Trull in *The Beggar's Opera*, and she repeated the part several times. She remained in London, always at Covent Garden, always in the minor employments mentioned, and invariably at the rate of £1 5s. per week, until the end of the 1803–4 season.

Boaden. *See* BOWDEN.

Boaman. *See* BOMAN.

Board. *See* BEARD.

Bocchini, Signor [fl. 1773–1774], *dancer.*

Signor Bocchini (or Bocchinini) danced at the King's Theatre in the Haymarket during the 1773–74 season, his first notice in the playbills being on 20 November 1773 when he performed in *La Bagatelle* and *A Pastoral Dance*. During the course of the season, in addition to appearing in a number of group dances, he was in a ballet entitled *The Adventures of the Harem of Ispahan* on 29 February 1774 and *Les faunes vainques* on 12 May. He appears not to have been given a benefit at the end of the season.

Bocelli. *See* BACCELLI.

Bockett. *See* BECKETT.

Boden. *See* BOWDEN.

Bodenham, Mr [fl. 1672], *musician.*

Mr Bodenham and four others were ordered arrested on 15 July 1672 for practicing the profession of music without a license.

Bodin, Mr [fl. 1742], *rope dancer, tumbler.*

In Hendrick Kerman's troupe from Holland was a rope dancer and tumbler named Bodin—not to be confused with the dancer Monsieur Baudouin, who was also in the company; they were billed as just arrived on 19 June 1742 and performed at Sadler's Wells on 3 July. Bodin did a rope dance with Mademoiselle Kerman and also tumbled.

Bodway. *See* BAUDOUIN.

Bodwin, Mr [fl. 1784], *bassoonist.*

The bassoonist Mr Bodwin played at the Handel Memorial Concerts at Westminster Abbey and the Pantheon on 26, 27, 29 May and 3, 5 June 1784.

Body, W. [fl. 1742–1745], *proprietor.*

W. Body was the proprietor of the Mulberry Garden, Clerkenwell, from 1742 to 1745. During this period, except for a rather elaborate fireworks display on 25

August 1744, Body managed to avoid charging admission and sustained the pleasure garden on money taken in from the sale of refreshments. He offered Londoners a band of wind and string instruments in which he employed only British players, for, as he said on 6 April 1743, "the manly vigour of our own native music is more suitable to the ear and heart of a Briton than the effeminate softness of the Italian." Usually the band played out-of-doors, but when the evenings were cool they performed in the long room. Fireworks displays were regular entertainments, and sometimes they were supported by music, as on 9 August 1744 when Job Baker the drummer beat out a rhythm and Bennet's music was performed. This particular pyrotechnical display was extremely popular, drawing a crowd of over 1600 people. After 1745 Body apparently relinquished the proprietorship.

Boen. *See* **BOWEN.**

Boham, Mr [fl. 1741], *actor.*
A Mr Boham played the Uncle in *The London Merchant* at the converted tennis court in James Street on 9 November 1741. It is possible that he was related to the actor Anthony Boheme.

Boheme, Anthony *d. 1731, actor.*
Anthony Boheme's birthdate is not known, but since he was by 1720 beginning to specialize in such elderly roles as Lear, the Ghost in *Hamlet*, Brabantio in *Othello*, and Caesar, it seems probable that he was then at least in his forties. Considering his high reputation, both as a comedian and a tragedian, and his relatively short but energetic stage career, it is most unfortunate that so little is known of him beyond the roles he played. Doran claimed that Boheme was a sailor before coming on the stage and had a quarter-deck walk which he was able to disguise only when he played Lear— but this story sounds strikingly like tales

Bodleian Library

ANTHONY BOHEME, as Herod
artist unknown

told of "Jubilee Dicky" Norris. If Boheme was a sailor in his younger years, there appears to be no proof of it.

The first theatrical reference to him seems to be in 1718. Davies reported that Boheme was playing with strollers at Stratford le Bow that year and was spotted by manager John Rich of the Lincoln's Inn Fields Theatre in London; Rich, said Davies, hired Boheme for a small salary and let him play Francisco in *Hamlet* for his London debut. This story cannot be substantiated either, and there is a similar version that has Boheme discovering Macklin and sponsoring him with Rich.

Boheme's first certain role was the messenger in *Cato*, done at Lincoln's Inn Fields on 16 October 1718. The following 16 January he played Lord Cobham in *Sir Walter Raleigh*, and he had gained sufficient favor in the company to share a benefit with only two others on 7 May 1719 when *Love for Love* was performed (but the cast was not published).

Starting with the 1719–20 season and continuing to the end of his life a decade later, Anthony Boheme played regularly and frequently at Lincoln's Inn Fields, chiefly in serious roles and often as the tragic heroes. He first played the Ghost in *Hamlet* on 16 November 1719, Brabantio in *Othello* on 19 March 1720, Lear on 15 October 1720, Shallow in *The Merry Wives of Windsor* on 22 October, Caesar on 1 November, Ulysses in *Troilus and Cressida* on 10 November, Angelo in *Measure for Measure* on 8 December, Titus Andronicus on 21 December, and Tamerlane on 25 April 1721. The next season he was Acasto in *The Orphan* on 5 October 1721, Shylock in *The Jew of Venice* on 17 October, Henry IV on 28 October, the Governor in *Oroonoko* on 11 November, Priuli in *Venice Preserved* on 2 December, Touchwood in *The Double Dealer* on 12 December, and Don Quixote on 31 March 1722.

This remarkable ability to prepare new roles (unless he had arrived in London with a full repertory in his head) continued in 1722–23 when he acted Cassius in *Julius Caesar* on 18 October 1722, Duncan in *Macbeth* on 20 October (instead of Seyton, which he had played before), Oedipus on 8 November, Alexander in *The Rival Queens* on 1 December, Oroonoko on 31 December (though he did not stay with this part), and Herod in *Herod and Mariamne* on 2 March 1723, opposite Anna Maria Seymour, who became his wife about 8 April. Boheme's marriage was a tragically brief one; his wife died on 10 July 1723 at Norwich where she, and presumably Boheme, were acting for the summer.

Boheme's serious acting during the regular seasons at Lincoln's Inn Fields in the early 1720's was counterbalanced by his activity at the fairs in the late summers. He performed at both Bartholomew and Southwark fairs in 1720, 1721, and 1722. On 25 August 1722 he joined with Pinkethman and Miller as a co-manager of a booth, and on 5 September he and Pinkethman alone operated a Southwark Fair booth—at least until 22 September, when Boheme was replaced by Bullock. After this year he seems to have taken well-earned summer vacations.

In 1723 it was rumored that Boheme might switch to Drury Lane. He inserted the following notice in a newspaper on 24 April 1723:

Whereas I am informed that there is a Report about the Town that the managers of the Theatre Royal in Drury Lane have lately endeavoured to seduce me from the Playhouse in Lincoln's Inn Fields: I think myself obliged (in justice to the said Managers) to declare that the said Report is entirely false; and do hereby acknowledge that I first made overtures to be receiv'd in their company, for reasons at that time to myself best known. And further that it never was proposed either by the said Managers or myself that I should quit Lincoln's Inn Fields Playhouse without six months warning given to supply my parts and a discharge in writing from the Manager of Lincoln's Inn Fields.

Anthony Boheme

It seems clear that the rumor was partly true, and since it started about the time Boheme married, perhaps his thought of changing companies had to do with hopes of better salaries for himself and his bride at Drury Lane. His income during the 1720's is not certain: manuscript house accounts at the British Museum list him as earning £1 13s. 4d. daily on 25 September 1724, but *The London Stage* gives his salary during 1724–25 as 16s. 8d. per acting day. In any case, his earnings were high by standards of the time, and to his daily pay he could add income from his yearly benefits. In view of the newspaper notice concerning Boheme's negotiations with Drury Lane, perhaps Rich raised his salary in 1724; this would account for the different fees cited.

During these years at Lincoln's Inn Fields Boheme continued to add important roles to his repertory: Banquo in *Macbeth* and Hotspur in *1 Henry IV* in 1723, Hannibal in *Sophonisba* and Wolsey in *Henry VIII* in 1726, Voltore in *Volpone* in 1727, the King in *The Maid's Tragedy* in 1729, and Cato in 1730. His activity was remarkably regular throughout the years with two exceptions: a brief period in the spring of 1727 when he was ill and an unaccountable gap between December 1728 and September 1729.

Boheme married a second time, but the date of the event is not known; it must have been before 4 June 1730, for the new Mrs Boheme made her first appearance on stage on that date, playing Selima in *Tamerlane* at her husband's benefit. But this second marriage was almost as brief as the first.

Anthony Boheme's last recorded appearance may have been as Politick in *The Coffee House Politician* on 4 December 1730 (the bill listed Chapman, but the printed edition listed Boheme). On 7 January 1731 Boheme died of consumption at his lodgings at Greenwich, Kent. He was buried there on Sunday night, 10 January, with the pall supported by Quin, Ryan, and four other fellow actors. He was highly regarded by his contemporaries, some of whom thought Boheme one of the best tragic actors in London. His manner seems to have been more vivacious than Booth's and more impressive than Wilks's. In person he was tall and dignified, and Davies said that he "gave force and authority to the various situations and passions of the character [of Lear]; the tones of his voice were equally Powerful and harmonious, and his whole action suited to the age and feelings of Lear."

The Bodleian Library has a picture of Boheme as Herod in *Herod and Mariamne* in 1726.

Boheme, Mrs Anthony the first. *See* SEYMOUR, ANNA MARIA.

Boheme, Mrs Anthony the second ⌊*fl. 1730*⌋, *actress.*

Anthony Boheme's second wife, whose maiden name is not known, made her first appearance on any stage as Selima in *Tamerlane* on 4 June 1730 at Lincoln's Inn Fields Theatre, for her husband's benefit. Her only other recorded performance was on 4 December 1730 at the same playhouse, though there is conflicting information concerning it: according to the playbill she acted Isabella in *The Coffee House Politician*, but the 1731 edition of the work gives that role to Mrs Younger and lists Mrs Boheme as Hilaret. Anthony Boheme died on 7 January 1731; how long he and his second wife had been married is not known, but they must have wed sometime after the summer of 1723, when his first wife died, and before 4 June 1730, when the new Mrs Boheme acted under her married name.

Bohen. *See* BOWEN.

Boimaison, Mr ⌊*fl. 1788–1796*⌋, *actor.*

A minor actor name Boimaison (sometimes Barmazon) played Roland in *The Four Valiant Brothers* and other roles at Sadler's Wells in 1788, when he also gave sword-fighting exhibitions with Mr Durenci on the same stage. Apparently he worked at Sadler's Wells for several years, for he is found again in an unnamed principal role in a new entertainment called *Medea's Kettle, or Harlequin Renovated* on 9 April 1792. Boimaison and his wife then engaged at Drury Lane from 1793–94 through 1795–96, each performing very minor and supernumerary roles. He regularly appeared as a tartar in *Lodoiska* (and once he played Camazin in that spectacle). Mrs Boimaison played a captive in the same piece and was a member of the general chorus in *The Pirates* and *The Mountaineers*. In 1795–96 he was on the Drury Lane pay list for £3 per week. She was on the list for £1 per week in 1793–94. Mr Boimaison also played the Earl of Douglas in *Chevy Chase* at Sadler's Wells on 4 August 1795.

Boimaison, Mrs ₁*fl. 1793–1796*₁, *actress, singer. See* BOIMAISON, MR.

Boin. *See* BOWEN.

Bois or **Boise.** *See* BOYCE, BOYES, BOYS, and DU BOIS.

Boisgérard, Mons ₁*fl. 1791–1820*₁, *dancer, choreographer.*
On 17 February 1791 when the remodelled Pantheon opened, Monsieur and Madame Boisgérard (or Boisgirard, Boisgitard) danced in *Amphion et Thalie* after the opera, apparently making their first apearance on the London stage. Monsieur Boisgérard was billed as one of the principal dancers, yet oddly his name was not included in the 1791 printed synopsis of the ballet; Madame Boisgérard danced as one of the "Habitants de la Phocide." She seems to have finished the season of 1790–91 and not to have performed again on the London stage; he, on the other hand, danced at the Pantheon for a month and was with the Pantheon troupe and then at the King's Theatre in the Haymarket in 1791–92. Not until the 1804–5 season was Boisgérard's name mentioned again in the bills, and it is probable that he had been away from London; he was at the King's Theatre almost every season from 1804–5 through 1819–20. He was both a dancer and a choreographer, at least at the beginning of his London career.

Boisgérard, Mme ₁*fl. 1791*₁, *dancer. See* BOISGÉRARD, MONS.

Boitar, Beatrice ₁*fl. 1729*₁, *actress.*
Miss Beatrice Boitar played Sukey Tawdry in *The Beggar's Opera* at Lincoln's Inn Fields on 1 January 1729 as a member of the Lilliputian Company of juvenile players.

Bolingbroke, Mrs ₁*fl. 1777*₁, *actress.*
Mrs Bolingbroke played in the summer of 1777 at the China Hall Theatre, Rotherhithe, usually in roles of some importance: Isabinda in *The Busy Body* on 20 June 1777, Jacintha in *The Suspicious Husband* on 23 June, Alicia in *Jane Shore* on 25 June, Donna Isabella in *The Wonder* and Melissa in *The Lying Valet* on 27 June, Maria in *The London Merchant* on 30 June, and Lady Loverule in *The Devil to Pay* on 2 July.

Bolla, Maria ₁*fl. 1799–1804*₁, *singer, actress.*
As a child, Signora Maria Bolla was brought from Milan to England, and after remaining six years in a school at Hampstead, she returned to Italy to take up a singing career. She performed at all the principal theatres on the Continent and came back to London in 1799, but apparently without an engagement. When on behalf of Taylor at the Opera House, Michael Kelly was seeking to engage a first woman, he was told by the singer Viganoni about Signora Bolla: "Indeed . . . you need not go so far as Italy; you have only to go over the way to Badioli's shop, and in his first floor you will find a most beautiful woman, an excellent singer and an admirable actress, who only arrived in London from the Continent last night." Kelly called upon her next morning and after making known his purpose he asked her to sing a duet with him from music found on her *pianoforte*, to which request she replied "Most willingly; I perceive you wish to hear me, before you engage me: and I think you are right."

Maria Bolla was engaged by the Opera

at £800 for the season 1799–1800. She made her first appearance in a principal role in Paisiello's *I zingari in fiera* on 11 January 1800. On 13 January the *Morning Chronicle* called her "an incomparable acquisition to the Opera." She sang in this opera 14 more times that season. She also sang Enrichetta in the comic opera *I due fratelli rivali* (on 18 February and nine more times), Coribanti in *Il capriccio drammatico* (13 May and ten times more), Gilletta in *I due svizzeri* (also 13 May and six times more), Rosina in *Il principe spazzacamino* (17 June), and the title role in *Nina* in which she took her benefit on 24 April ("tickets of Mme Bolla, No 6, Haymarket").

While engaged at the Opera, Signora Bolla acted once at Drury Lane, on 6 June 1800, as Lilla in *The Siege of Belgrade*. Kelly claimed she "gave all the points of the dialogue as if she had been for years on the English stage, and was received with just and merited applause." The *Monthly Mirror* of June 1800 reported that she spoke intelligibly but with a foreign accent, and suggested her resemblance to Nancy Storace, who had also played the role of Lilla so admirably.

Signora Bolla continued in the Opera for the next four seasons. According to the *Monthly Mirror* she was discharged in 1804.

Bologna, Signor [*fl.* 1662–1688], puppeteer.

Signor Bologna's puppets were first shown in London during the summer of 1662 when Pepys saw them in Covent Garden, probably in the Piazza. Bologna's booth was described as "within the rails," and the band included a dulcimer (the first Pepys had ever seen, so of course he was intrigued) and other strings. The Italian puppeteer performed at Whitehall on 8 October 1662, and, according to the Works accounts, a stage was also set up for him in the Queen's Guard Chamber. Bologna's

Whitehall stage measured 20' by 18' and was high enough to permit a door to be built into its side, possibly as an entry to the substage for working miniature trap doors. Bologna so pleased Charles II that the King gave him a gold chain worth £25 and a gold medal as a reward.

Pepys was also delighted with the puppets, and it is possible that the "Polichinello" who came to London to play at Moorfields in August and September 1666 and at Charing Cross in March and April 1667 was again Signor Bologna (though Speaight suggests this was another Italian puppeteer). Pepys was as enchanted in 1666–67 as he had been earlier, and on 8 April 1667 he wrote that he found the puppets "three times more sport" than the live actors in a performance of *The Surprisal* which he had just seen at the Bridges Street Theatre. In August and September at Bartholomew Fair Pepys saw puppets again; they were at Charing Cross in October; and in August 1668 they performed at the fair. Pepys usually referred to these entertainments as Polichinello, though perhaps after Bologna's initial introduction of the character of Punch to England, the nickname, under various guises and spellings, was used for all puppets, regardless of who operated them.

Signor Bologna was performing in France at the St Laurent Fair in 1678, and there he advertised the use of "changes of scenery and numerous machines." He may have returned to England in August 1688; in the poem *The Theatre of Compliment* of that year is the phrase, "And here's Punchinello, shown thrice to the King."

Bologna, Barbara [*fl.* 1786–1804], dancer.

Miss Barbara Bologna was a member of the family troupe of Italian tumblers which her father Pietro Bologna brought to England in 1786. She performed with the family in the provinces until 1792, when they went to London to play at Sadler's Wells.

In 1795 she was at the Royal Circus. She made her first billed appearance at Covent Garden as one of the principal ballet characters in *The Genoese Pirate* on 15 October 1798. She continued at that theatre in minor dancing roles at least through 1803–4. She may have been the Miss Bologna who danced at Brighton in 1808.

Bologna, John Peter *1775–1846, harlequin, dancer, tumbler, machinist.*

John ("Jack") Peter Bologna, who became one of the most celebrated harlequins in the history of pantomime, was born in 1775, probably in Italy, the son of the rope-dancer and clown Pietro Bologna. At about the age of 11 or 12, he was brought to England by his father, as a member of the family troupe of tumblers which also included his mother, a younger brother Louis, and a sister Barbara. After a successful tour in the provinces, upon the recommendation of Tate Wilkinson, the Bolognas were engaged by Wroughton at Sadler's Wells in 1792, where among other pieces John performed in a new entertainment called *Medea's Kettle, or, Harlequin Renovated.* He also appeared in "a pleasing exhibition of strength and posture work" called *Le Tableau Chinois.*

JOHN BOLOGNA as Harlequin, LUIGI BOLOGNA as Pantaloon, JOSEPH GRIMALDI as Zany, MISS SEARLE as Columbine, and MR SIMMONS as Mother Goose

in *Mother Goose*

a water-color by T. M. Grimshaw

In 1794 the family performed at Norwich, and then after leaving Sadler's Wells they joined the Royal Circus. On 11 June 1795 Jack danced on the tight rope, accompanied by his father as the aping clown. Among the earliest pieces at the Circus for which John was billed as the Harlequin was *Niobe, or, Harlequin's Ordeal* on 20 July 1797. In 1798 he played Bertrand in *The Knights of Malta*.

John also performed at Covent Garden. He made his first appearance there, billed as "Bologna Jun," on 24 November 1797, as Setric in *The Round Tower*. The *Monthly Mirror* of December 1797 judged that if he "displayed less vulgarity of trick and expression, which might better suit with the clown of an harlequinade than the hero of a serious ballet, [he] would be entitled to our approbation." He continued as a dancer and pantomimist at Covent Garden through 1804–5, earning £4 per week for the first three years and about £5 per week thereafter.

Bologna also served the theatres as a machinist and dance director. For a production of *Harlequin's Tour* at Covent Garden on 1 January 1801, in which he played Harlequin, he also assisted in devising the machinery; later in 1807 and 1808 he received extra payments for tricks and machines in such pieces as *Harlequin in his Element*. About 1803 he exhibited a mechanical device called the "Phantascopia" at the Lyceum. At the Royal Circus he provided the incidental dances to Cross's *Rinaldo Rinaldini* on 6 April 1801 and played Rinaldo in that popular spectacle. In 1802, 1803, and 1804 he was also at Sadler's Wells as a harlequin. John composed the ballet for the new burletta spectacle *Edward and Susan* at Sadler's Wells on 11 April 1803, in which his brother Louis danced a comic *pas de deux* with Banks, and Joseph Grimaldi played Clown. This production marked one of his earliest associations with the great Grimaldi.

In 1805 Bologna succeeded James Byrne as the leading house harlequin at Covent Garden, and, together with Grimaldi, he was to usher in the great age of pantomime in the English theatre. Perhaps the most famous of their productions was *Harlequin and Mother Goose, or, the Golden Egg*, by Thomas Dibdin, with Grimaldi as Clown and Bologna as Harlequin, which opened on 29 December 1806 and ran for 92 nights. On the eighty-eighth night, 9 June 1807, Bologna and Grimaldi took more than £518 in shared benefit receipts, an enormous sum. Bologna also received £73 10s. for tricks that he provided. Later on, in 1812 and 1813, Bologna took £401 14s. 6d. and £569 16s., and on 29 June 1814 he shared £426 15s. 6d. with Grimaldi.

During this period, Bologna kept busy elsewhere as well. Charles Dibdin engaged him at the Amphitheatre in Dublin from 9 November 1805 to 14 February 1806, at six guineas per week. During 1806 and 1807 he appeared in and arranged dances for a great many pantomime spectacles at the Royal Circus, including *The Cloud King*, *The False Friend*, *The Mysterious Freebooter*, *The Sorceress of Strozzi*, *Black Beard*, *Momus and Mercury*, *Buenos Ayres*, *Werter and Charlotte*, and *Edwin of the Green*. He was also granted a license in 1810 for an exhibition of mechanical and hydraulic devices, with fireworks and music, on Wednesdays and Fridays during Lent at the Sans Pareil.

On 3 June 1800, John Bologna had married Harriet Bath Barnewell at St George, Hanover Square. A Mrs Bologna who was either John's mother or wife appeared at Covent Garden in the first five years of the nineteenth century. Mrs John Bologna certainly did perform, however, as a minor dancer and vocalist at Covent Garden from about 1806 until her death about 23 April 1814. John Bologna married again on 10 April 1816 at St George, Hanover Square, to Miss Louisa Maria Bristow, the daughter of a theatrical family, the sister of the actor George Bristow and of Mary Bristow, who became the second wife of Joe Grimaldi. Louisa Maria Bristow had come on the stage at Drury Lane in *Sleeping Beauty* on 6 December 1805. In 1809–10 she was promoted to nearly 20 first-line roles, including Cordelia. According to the *Monthly Mirror*, "a prettier Cordelia was never seen," but also "a worse was never heard." It was widely hinted that her rapid advancement was owed to John Kemble's admiration for her beauty, but by the next season, 1810–11, she had been discharged from Drury Lane. She continued her career, however, as Columbine in her brother-in-law Grimaldi's harlequinades, where her association with John Bologna must have begun.

Bologna worked at Covent Garden through 1815–16 but seems not to have been there in the next two seasons. With his wife he returned to Sadler's Wells, for his first performance there in ten years, on 31 May 1819 in *The Fates, or, Harlequin's Holiday*. He spent the next fall at the Pantheon in Edinburgh whence he wrote to Elliston on 3 December 1819 to enquire if his services were desired for the Christmas pantomime at Drury Lane, as he was then making arrangements either to go to Dublin or to remain in Edinburgh. Bologna requested the salary he had formerly had at Covent Garden and an engagement until Easter. Elliston's offer was insufficient, evidently, for on 9 December Bologna wrote to Winston, the manager's assistant, that he could not go to London for less than £6 per week but that he was about to leave Edinburgh and would be in London on the way to Dublin; he would delay his Irish engagement if Drury Lane met his terms. The management eventually seems to have done so, for on 27 December 1819 Bologna appeared as Harlequin on the stage of Drury Lane.

In his later years John Bologna, according to Charles Dibdin, traveled about with "a very ingenious mechanical and philosophical Exhibition." He settled in Glasgow as a teacher of dancing; and finally in order to subsist, he was forced to take a job as "Ebony," the black-faced foil to the conjuror Anderson, "the Wizard of the North." Bologna died in extreme poverty at Glasgow in 1846 at the age of 71. According to A. E. Wilson, Bologna's son played Harlequin in the 1850's.

John Peter Bologna perhaps is best remembered for playing Harlequin to the Clown of the great Grimaldi, his close friend and brother-in-law. He had, however, a fine talent in his own right. It was reported that when John Kemble saw him play Oscar in *Oscar and Malvina*, he remarked, "If that man could speak as well as he acts pantomime, I would never appear again on the stage." There is something of an epitaph for him in *Joseph's Lament*:

> *Never shall old Bologna—old, alack!*
> *Once he was young and diamonded all*
>   *o'er—*
> *Take his particular Joseph on his back*
>   *And dance the matchless fling, so*
>   *loved of yore.*

Harvard Theatre Collection

JOHN BOLOGNA (the male dancer) and JOSEPH GRIMALDI

in *Mother Goose*

artist unknown

The London Museum has a water-color sketch drawn by the actor T. M. Grimshaw of a scene from *Harlequin and Mother Goose* which depicts John Bologna as Harlequin, his brother Louis Bologna as Old Pantaloon, Simmons as Mother Goose, and Miss Searle as Columbine. In the Harvard Theatre Collection is a large colored engraving of Bologna as a male dancer in *Mother Goose*, with Grimaldi as a female dancer. A "penny-plain" of him as Harlequin in *The Fairy of the Oak* was printed by W. West in 1812, as was a "tuppence-coloured" of him as in *Harlequin and Padmanaba, or, the Golden Fish*. In 1813, J. H. Jameson printed a penny-plain of Bologna as Kalin Azack in *Aladdin*. Bologna was also depicted in numerous other *Juvenile Prints*.

Bologna, Louis   *d. 1808, tumbler, clown, dancer, singer.*

Louis Bologna was a young member of the troupe of Italian tumblers which was brought to England by his father Pietro Bologna in 1786. Most of his career was closely tied to those of his father and of John and Barbara Bologna, his brother and sister. With his family, and usually billed as Master Bologna, Louis played in the provinces for Wilkinson, then went to Sadler's Wells in 1792, and joined the Royal Circus in 1795.

Louis Bologna made his first billed appearance at Covent Garden on 12 February 1798 as a ballet character in *Joan of Arc*, which ran for 14 performances. He performed as one of the haymakers, a vocal character, in the pantomime of *The Magic Oak* on 29 January 1799 and for 31 more times that season. He also was one of the choral boys in *Raymond and Agnes* which opened on 13 April 1799 and received 10 performances and was one of the ambassadors from Armenia in *The Princess of Georgia* on 19 April.

In the following season, 1799–1800, Louis Bologna returned to Covent Garden as a dancer and continued to appear in the pantomimes with other members of his family. In that season his wife appeared as a young dancing lass in *The Deserter of Naples*. He continued to play at Covent Garden during the early years of the nineteenth century, and in 1800–1801 was on the pay list at £1 10*s.* per week, the small salary confirming his function as a minor dancer and supernumerary. On 1 January of that season he played Harlequin's servant in a production of *Harlequin's Tour* which included his father as the lover's servant, his brother John as Harlequin, and his wife in an unnamed part in the pantomime chorus. In 1803 he was at Sadler's Wells, where on 11 April he danced a comic *pas de deux* with Banks in the ballet composed by his brother John for the burletta spectacle *Edward and Susan*.

Of all the known Bolognas, Louis is most likely to have been the Mr Bologna who performed in America in April of 1804. On 5 April 1804 a Signor Bologna, renowned pantomimist and dancer from Covent Garden, staged a pantomime called *The Vicissitudes of Harlequin* at the Grove Theatre in Bedlow Street in New York. Shortly thereafter Dunlap engaged Bologna at the Park Theatre where on 30 April, in the character of Clown, he offered *Harlequin's Statue*. Bologna remained at the Park Theatre until his second benefit on 15 June 1804 and then sailed back to England.

Louis Bologna was probably the Mr Bologna who performed Harlequin in *The Parcae, or, Harlequin in Time* at the Royal Circus in the fall of 1806. (His brother John was usually billed as Bologna, Junior.) On 29 December 1806 he opened as the Pantaloon in *Harlequin and Mother Goose, or, the Golden Egg*, with his brother John as Harlequin and his father as the landlord. This pantomime ran for 92 nights.

Louis Bologna died on 27 March 1808, according to the *Gentleman's Magazine*, "At his lodgings in Sloane-Street, where he went for the benefit of better air. . . . He had been ill for some time, having caught a violent cold from over-exertion in his professional pursuits. As a Pantaloon in Harlequinades, he excelled all his contemporaries; and as a private character he was much respected." A Miss H. Bologna, who performed at the Royal Circus in June 1806, may have been his daughter.

The London Museum has a water-color sketch drawn by the actor T. M. Grimshaw of a scene from *Harlequin and Mother Goose*, which depicts Louis Bologna as the old Pantaloon, John Bologna as Harlequin, Simmons as Mother Goose, and Miss Searle as Columbine.

Bologna, Mrs Louis *fl. 1799–1800*, *dancer.*

Although she probably made other appearances in unbilled roles when her husband performed, Mrs Louis Bologna was in the bills for only one production, as a young dancing lass in *The Deserter of Naples* at Covent Garden on 29 April 1800 and two more times that season.

Bologna, Pietro *fl. 1786–1814*, *clown, rope dancer.*

The extraordinarily versatile Pietro Bologna was born at Genoa and perhaps was descended from Simone de Bologna, a famous Arlecchino with the Gelosi company of *commedia dell'arte* players in the sixteenth century. Bologna brought to England in 1786 a troupe of tumblers, under the name of "The Italian Company," which included at least four members of his family —his wife, two sons, John and Louis, and a daughter Barbara—all of whom were performers. While touring the provinces they were engaged at Doncaster by Tate Wilkinson, who described the Bolognas as well behaved, honest people and accounted their act to be "on the whole, the best conceived and the most worthy of attention of anything of the kind I have ever beheld."

Upon Wilkinson's recommendation, the Bolognas were engaged by Wroughton for Sadler's Wells. Pietro made his debut on the slack wire there on Easter Monday, 9 April 1792. With his son John he also performed in a new entertainment called *Medea's Kettle, or Harlequin Renovated*. The Bolognas were an immediate success. One critic described Pietro as "a handsome Italian, who slung on the slack wire with amazing grace and ease, and was the most whimsical and laugh-compelling clown we ever saw. He plays on two flutes, a first and second part, through his nostrils, and on two drums, in a very *nouvelle* style." Pietro usually played the clown on the rope, the buffoon who kept the show going when the rope dancer was not in motion, and whose failure to do the tricks magnified the skill of his master. That season the family also gave "a pleasing exhibition of strength and posture work" in a new entertainment called *Le Tableau Chinois*.

In 1794 the Bolognas performed "ground and lofty tumbling, and still vaulting" in *La force de Hercule* in the Pantheon at Norwich. In that year they left Sadler's Wells to join the Royal Circus in Southwark. On 17 April 1795 Pietro played the pantaloon father in *The Prophecy* at the Royal Circus. Included in the cast as the character of Goody Blab was his wife, Mrs Bologna. On 11 June of that year he and John danced on the tight-rope. In many similar ways Pietro continued to entertain audiences at the Royal Circus regularly in summers through 1807—as the Clown in *Harlequin Highlander* and the father in *The Knights of Malta* in 1798; Tunbelly Turk in *The Golden Farmer* in 1802; as Irwin in *The Mysterious Freebooter* (21 April), Pantaloon in *The Sorceress of Strozzi* (12 May), a character in *Swiss Revels* (22 June), Governor Gouldrigg in *The Flying Island of Laputa* (4 August) in 1807, along with innumerable other performances. On 14 September 1807, one of his last appearances at the Royal Circus, Pietro played Cymbeline in a pantomime-ballet version of Shakespeare's play, entitled *Imogen, Princess of Britain.*

Pietro Bologna also engaged at Covent Garden Theatre in 1797–98 at £5 per week. Along with his son John, he made his first appearance there on 24 November 1797 in the "grand serious ballet" of *The Round Tower.* The *Monthly Mirror* of December 1797 wrote that "Mr. Bologna, Sen. certainly *embodied* the character he represented, and will give *weight* to any part he may be entrusted with in the future. In some instances, indeed, we thought him *too heavy.*" He played in *Harlequin and Quixote* on 26 December and *Joan of Arc* on 12 February. In the following season, at the same salary, he appeared in such pieces as *The Genoese Pirate, The Mouth of the Nile, Ramah Droog,* and *The Death of Captain Cook.* In 1799 the author of *Authentic Memoirs of the Green Room* complained that the Bolognas, engaged "merely for the sake of pantomime," more properly belonged to the Royal Circus, "being from their infancy in the tricks of Harlequin, and the management of the wooden sword." On 29 December 1806 Pietro played the landlord in the enormously successful *Harlequin and Mother Goose,* which ran for 92 nights, and in which his son John played Harlequin and his son Louis played Pantaloon. In 1812–13 Pietro and his son John were paid liberally for devising pantomime tricks. Pietro continued at Covent Garden at least through the season 1813–14.

Bologna, Mrs Pietro [*fl.* 1786–1798?], *tumbler, dancer, singer.*
Mrs Pietro Bologna was one of the tumblers brought to England by her husband in 1786. After touring the provinces as a member of Wilkinson's company, she performed with her husband at Sadler's Wells from 1792 to 1794 and then went with him to the Royal Circus and subsequently to Covent Garden. She made her first billed appearance at the latter theatre on 26 December 1797 as a principal vocal character in the pantomime *Harlequin and Quixote,* in which her husband played Harlequin. On 15 October 1798 she danced a principal ballet character in *The Genoese Pirate,* and on 21 October 1799 she played an island native in *The Death of Captain Cook.*

Mrs Pietro Bologna no doubt continued to perform at Covent Garden and elsewhere with her husband in the first decade of the nineteenth century, but the first wife of her son John began performing at this time as Mrs Bologna and it is difficult to discriminate in the bills. Her husband Pietro performed until about 1814. Neither of their death-dates is known.

"Bolonese." *See* GABRIELLI, TOMASO.

Bolschi. *See* BOSCHI.

Bolton. *See also* BOULTON.

Bolton, Mr [*fl.* 1730–1731], *house servant?*
On 18 June 1730 and 12 May 1731 Mr Bolton shared benefits at Goodman's Fields Theatre with two others; he was probably a house servant, but his function in the theatre was not mentioned in the bills.

Bolton, Mr [*fl.* 1773], *actor.*
A minor actor by the name of Bolton was a member of Foote's summer company at the Haymarket in 1773. He played La Fleur in *The Commissary* (2 July), one of the scholars in *The Padlock* (5 July), a Frenchman in *A Trip to Portsmouth* (11 times between 13 July–17 September), and parts in *The Orators* (3 September) and *The Macaroni* (16 September).

Bolton, Mrs [*fl.* 1789–1801], *house servant.*
Mrs Bolton was on the Drury Lane salary list as a house servant between 1789 and 1801, receiving payments in amounts of 2s. 6d. per week, usually for sweeping.

Bolton, Duchess of. *See* FENTON, LA-
VINIA.

Bolton, Mrs. *See* EYRE, MRS ED-
MUND JOHN.

Boman, Mr *b. c. 1695?, actor.*

Mr Boman was probably the son of John
and Elizabeth Boman and, if so, was born
in 1695, for Mrs John Boman was reported
as pregnant in December 1694. His first
appearance as an actor was on 11 April
1712 at the St Martin's Theatre with other
sons and daughters of patent house performers; young Boman acted the Earl of Essex in *The Unhappy Favorite* and sang, for
his benefit. During the rest of the brief season of performances by the young players,
Boman acted Aimwell in *The Stratagem*
for his second benefit on 11 June and Sir
George Airy in *The Busy Body* on 18 June.
The two benefits in quick succession indicate that the lad probably held a commanding position in the troupe.

By 1714–15 he had joined the Drury
Lane company, his first recorded role there
being Longbottom in the premiere of *The
Country Lasses* on 4 February 1715. On
8 June 1716 at a performance of *The Tempest* he shared a benefit with Weller, and
the Mrs Boman who sang in *The Death of
Dido* on 17 June was very likely his wife —
though when they married is not known.
Boman seems to have continued with the
Drury Lane players through the 1718–19
season, and though few roles are recorded
for him, we know he acted Oxford in *Richard III* and Trebonius in *Julius Caesar*. On
28 January 1719 he played this latter role
with his father acting Flavius.

During the 1722–23 season Boman and
his wife were at the Haymarket Theatre.
His first role there was Riot in *The Wife's
Relief* at a benefit he shared with Mrs Or-
feur. On 13 February 1723 he played Jaffeir in *Venice Preserved*, but after this nothing is recorded for him for several years —
unless some of the activity assigned to John

Boman at Drury Lane pertains to his son.
In 1728 at the White Swan in Norwich
Boman and his wife acted with Green's
troupe, and from 11 November of that
year they played with the United Company
in Norwich. A Boman appeared at Fielding's booth at Bartholomew Fair in August
1729, and it seems likely that this was the
younger Boman, back in London for a short
spell, and not John Boman, then in his late
seventies. By 18 January 1730 Boman was
again in Norwich, playing Iago in *Othello*,
but a year later, on 19 January 1731, he
was billed as making his first appearance at
the Goodman's Fields Theatre in London
as Vainlove in *The Old Bachelor*. By the
winter of 1733 he was at Ipswich with the
Norwich troupe, playing Edgar in *King
Lear*. On 20 January 1735, once more 'at
Norwich, Boman played Iago, and his wife
Desdemona, and this seems to be the last
record of their acting together; the couple
may well have split, for his career after this
can be traced in London and hers in Norwich.

On 29 March 1735, billed as Boman
Junior, he was Lord Foppington in *The Relapse* at Goodman's Fields, and from 1735–
36 through 1737–38 Boman was a member of the Covent Garden company. There
he acted, among other roles, Kent in *King
Lear*, Siward in *Macbeth*, Hubert in *The
Royal Merchant*, Austria in *King John*,
Glendower in *1 Henry IV*, and the Host in
The Merry Wives of Windsor. Boman also
appeared at Bartholomew Fair in August
1736, and perhaps he made other such appearances during these London years.

The records for the 1737–38 season are
baffling, for on 9 November 1737 a Boman
was billed as making his first appearance at
Covent Garden, playing Beau Mizen in *The
Fair Quaker of Deal*. The younger Boman
had been active at that playhouse for several seasons, and the elder Boman, now in
his eighties, had for years been a member
of the Drury Lane company; it seems unlikely that John Boman, who is recorded

for roles at Drury Lane this season, would also have played at the rival house, and it is probable that the "first appearance" billing was an error. At Covent Garden on 27 June 1738 "Boaman" played Brabantio in *Othello*, and on 1 August at the same house "Bowman" was Valdes in *Marina*; these surely refer to Boman the younger.

The only other records of Boman's activities come from later years, after his father died. In 1743 he played at Southwark Fair, receiving shared benefits on 18 and 25 February. On the latter date he acted Testy in *Flora*. On 16 March 1744, billed as the son of the late Boman of Drury Lane, he was Heartwell in *The Country Lasses* at the theatre in James Street, and on 1 May at Hallam's theatre at May Fair Boman played Justinian in *The Royal Hero*, a droll. His career had clearly had a falling off, and his name dropped from the bills after 1744. The last mention of him is a sad one: on 22 June 1758 at Drury Lane *The Beggar's Opera* was performed for the benefit of "some distressed actors who formerly belonged to the theatres." Boman is listed as having received £5 5s.

Boman, Mrs [*fl. 1716–1756*], *singer, dancer, actress.*

On 17 April 1716 at Drury Lane, a Mrs Boman sang Cupid in the premiere of Barton Booth's masque, *The Death of Dido*. It seems most unlikely that this was Mrs John Boman, who had not been mentioned in the bills since 1707 and by 1716 would have been about 40; it is more probable that Cupid was played by a younger, second Mrs Boman, wife of Boman Junior and daughter-in-law of the earlier performer. On the following 31 July Mrs Boman was the "Airy Spirit" in *The Tempest*, and during the following season she spent her time singing, usually at Drury Lane as *entr'acte* entertainment, but at least once (on 27 March 1717) at a Stationers' Hall concert. Through 1722 she sang at Drury Lane and at the late summer fairs, and on 25 October

1722 at Walker's booth at Southwark Fair she was billed as dancing.

The Bomans were at the Haymarket Theatre in 1722–23, but in the summer of 1723 Mrs Boman (apparently without her husband) returned to Drury Lane, where she continued singing occasionally through 1728–29; her fair appearances seem to have stopped after 1724. At Drury Lane she was once billed as dancing, and on 20 February 1726 a specific role was mentioned for her: Aurora in *Apollo and Daphne*.

In 1728 Mr and Mrs Boman were with the Greens in the Norwich Company, playing at the White Swan in that city, and from 11 November 1728 they were members of the United Company there. The Mrs Boman who turned up at Drury Lane on 28 May 1729 to sing in *The Tempest* was probably the same performer, back in London after the conclusion of the spring season in Norwich. She appears to have stayed in London for the next few years, and in June and July 1731 at Drury Lane she was Milcha in *The Tempest* and Amphitrite in *Bayes's Opera*. On 14 May 1733 she played Lucy in *The Recruiting Officer*, one of her rare London appearances in a non-singing role, after which she abandoned the big city to pursue a far more successful career in the provinces.

From the winter of 1733 through the year 1756 Mrs Boman worked with the Norwich Company, playing at Norwich, Ipswich, Colchester, and perhaps other provincial towns. Up to 1735 she acted with her husband, two of her known roles being Goneril in *King Lear* and Desdemona in *Othello*. After 1735 Boman seems to have returned to London alone, leaving his wife behind. She did remarkably well on her own, however, as some of her known roles attest: Lady Brute in *The Provoked Wife*, Rosalind in *As You Like It*, Roxana in *The Rival Queens*, Isabella in *Measure for Measure*, Millamant in *The Way of the World*, Lady Alworth in *A New Way to*

Pay Old Debts, Angelica in *Love for Love*, Lady Capulet in *Romeo and Juliet*, Katherine in *Henry V*, Lady Macduff in *Macbeth*, Berinthia in *The Relapse*, and the Countess of Rousillon in *All's Well that Ends Well*. One wonders whether the actress who managed these roles could really have been the minor singer and dancer from London, but she seems to have been.

Little else is known of Mrs Boman. In December 1737 the Norwich paper noted that "The Report of the Death of Mrs. Bowman, the fam'd Actress in the Norwich Company of Comedians, is not true, for since the Waggon went over her Body going from Bury Fair to Colchester, she is so well recover'd as to Play almost every Night." By 1750 she was afflicted with rheumatism, yet continued performing. The last mention of her seems to have been in 1756 when *All for Love* was presented for her benefit at Ipswich. It is not certain that she performed that night. Her last recorded role was in 1754 when she acted the Player Queen in *Hamlet*.

Boman, John   *c. 1651?–1739, actor, singer.*

Curll(?), in his *History of the English Stage* (1741) stated categorically that "JOHN BOMAN, Son of *John Boman*, of *Kingstreet, Westminster*, was born at *Pillerton* in *Warwickshire* (in the same House, Chamber and Bed wherein his *Mother* was Born) on the 27th of *December*, St. *John's* Day, 1664." On the other hand, he died on 23 March 1739 at the age of 88, which would place his birth about 1651, and other details of his career fit with this date; Curll, despite all his details, may have been in error, or he may have been talking about a different John Boman. Indeed, there may have been two, one a court singer and the other an actor-singer, but most of the evidence seems to suggest that there was only one, whose last name sometimes was spelled "Bowman."

For Michaelmas 1675 the Lord Chamberlain's accounts show a livery payment to a John Bowman of £16 2s. 6d. and indicate that he was a replacement for John Harding in the King's Musick. In September 1677 a John Bowman played Peter Santloe in *The Counterfeit Bridegroom* at the Dorset Garden Theatre as a member of the Duke's Company; the role required singing ability, as did the 1675 court appointment. Both instances point to a young man, which Boman would have been if he was born about 1651, and not a boy barely in his teens. That Boman may have done some performing as early as 1673, as some sources say, is quite likely, though the bills show no activity for him that early.

After his first recorded role, Boman acted such parts as Saunter in *Friendship in Fashion* (another singing role, 5 April 1678), Patroclus in Dryden's *Troilus and Cressida* (April 1679), Atticus in *Theodosius* (a singing role, September 1680), Albany in *King Lear* (March 1681), and Priuli in *Venice Preserved* (9 February 1682) – all at the Dorset Garden Theatre. Court musicians at this time were not usually allowed to hold outside positions without special permission, and Boman may have been permitted to lead a double life because of his close association with the King. One story, recorded after his death, was that he often shared a bottle with Charles II, and another concerns a party at Nell Gwynn's house in Pall Mall where Boman and others provided musical entertainment for Nell, Charles, the Duke of York, and others. It would have been quite possible for Boman, if he moved in courtly circles, to have managed two performing careers simultaneously.

By 1682 Boman had established two oddly different acting lines: the fop and the kindly friend (later to turn into the kindly father). Some of his roles, if they did not fall into one of these categories, partook of both, as Albany, for example: the hen-pecked good man. Though Boman performed in serious plays, his specialty was comedy, as Aphra Behn's joking prologue of 1682 indicates:

Bowman's *for Mischief all, and carry's on With Faun and Sneer as Gilting* Whigg *has done . . .*

In September–October 1685 Boman was appointed to the private music of James II, and at James's birthday on 14 October 1687 he lent his fine bass to a group of singers who performed Henry Purcell's "Sound the trumpet, beat the drum," which the composer wrote especially for the occasion. About this same time, Boman played Bredwel and sang John Blow's "O Love, that stronger art than Wine!" in Mrs Behn's *The Lucky Chance,* given at Drury Lane by the United Company in mid-April 1686.

In the late 1680's Boman was active as a player, though the records are too incomplete to ascertain just how frequently he appeared at the theatre. Among his known roles were Truman in *The Squire of Alsatia* and Trim in *Bury Fair,* both done at Drury Lane. During this same period the Lord Chamberlain's accounts show Boman as the recipient of £30 on 25 March 1689 for his salary and arrears in livery payments. When William III assumed the throne, Boman was retained as part of the King's Musick.

In 1690–91 Boman was especially busy at court and at the theatre; among his roles were Phoebus in *Amphitryon,* probably Derby in *Richard III,* probably Sir Fopling Flutter in *The Man of Mode,* the title role in *Alphonso,* Beau in *Greenwich Park,* and Grimbald in *King Arthur.* The calendar indicates roles for him in October, November, and December 1690, and January, April, and May 1691. In February and March he was probably at the Hague, for he was named as one of the musicians to accompany William III on his royal visit. After this, Boman's name does not appear in the Lord Chamberlain's records concerning court musicians, and it is likely that

as the actor's theatrical career developed he found it too exhausting to carry on at court as well.

On 6 August 1692 at St Mary le Bone Boman married Elizabeth Watson, the daughter of Sir Francis Watson, who had been financially ruined along with Thomas Betterton earlier that year. Mr and Mrs Betterton had taken young Elizabeth into their home after the disaster. It is probable that the Bomans' son was born about 1695.

During the 1690's John Boman's penchant for acting fops received full play, as a sample list of his character names indicates: Courtall, Brainless (a singing role), Sir Nicholas Dainty, Gayman, Sir Maggot Jingle, Lord Froth (a singing role, for which he composed "Ancient Phillis"), Tattle, Goosandelo, Airy, Treble, Spendall, Vainthroat (a singing role), and Petulant. Of these, the most famous, of course, are Tattle in *Love for Love,* which opened the Lincoln's Inn Fields Theatre on 30 April 1695 under Betterton's management, and Petulant in *The Way of the World,* performed at the same house on 5 March 1700.

As a singer Boman was much in demand during the 1690's in dramatic operas, at concerts, and on such special occasions as the Queen's birthday, and for him the greatest composer of the period, Henry Purcell, wrote "Let the dreadful engines," a song originally designed for the character of Cardenio in *1 Don Quixote* but cut from the original production in mid-May 1694 at Dorset Garden to reduce the running time; the song later became a favorite with basses and was, in 1703, sung by Boman as *entr'acte* entertainment. During the 1690's Boman also added to his repertoire the singing role of the "young, whimsical, Welsh fop" Rice ap Shinkin in *The Richmond Heiress* (April 1693).

Boman irritated playwright David Crauford in 1700 with his indolence. The dramatist had submitted his *Courtship à la Mode* to Betterton's troupe at Lincoln's Inn Fields, and Boman was assigned one of the parts;

the rehearsals were a sham, and, as Crauford later wrote in his preface, " 'tis known that Mr. *Bowman* (I mention his name to keep the reflection from other sharers) kept the first character of my play six weeks, and then cou'd hardly read six lines on't." The infuriated author took his piece to the rival Drury Lane company and saw it produced on 9 July 1700. Whether or not this was typical of Boman's behavior is not known, but the incident suggests that perhaps he played the fop both onstage and off.

During the last years of the Betterton regime at Lincoln's Inn Fields Boman appeared less frequently in foppish parts, played older roles more often, and did most of his singing as *entr'acte* entertainment. When the Queen's Theatre in the Haymarket opened in 1705 Boman continued this pattern, gradually settling into a number of fatherly roles which were to become his standard fare in years to come: Northumberland in *1 Henry IV*, Ligarius in *Julius Caesar*, Lord Suffolk in *Henry VIII*, Mentor in *Ulysses*, and Priuli in *Venice Preserved*—the role he played most frequently almost to the end of his life. In addition to his theatre work, Boman sang at concerts, as on 26 March 1707 when he performed at his own home in Brookfields (presumably the Brookfields area between St Pancras and Islington).

Boman's status was not a lofty one; in 1707 he was probably earning £70 or £80 annually and ranked in the lower half of the roster of male actors in his troupe; it may have been with hopes of bettering his opportunities that he went to Ireland for the 1707–8 season to play at Smock Alley, though the only known role for him there was the small one of Peregrine's servant in *The Spanish Wives*. By 17 June 1708 he was back in London, playing Hannibal in *Sophonisba* for his benefit at Drury Lane; then he returned to Dublin for the 1708–9 season. (The John Bowman who was appointed organist of Trinity College, Cambridge, in 1709 was presumably not the actor-singer.)

During the 1709–10 season Boman played at the Queen's Theatre, one of his new roles there being Balance in *The Recruiting Officer*. He remained at the Queen's through 18 November 1710, on which date he acted Duncan in *Macbeth*, but three days later he was Frederick in *The Rover* at Drury Lane, and there he remained for the season, adding to his repertoire the Ghost in *Hamlet* (24 March 1711) and Tiresias in *Oedipus* (18 May). He stayed at Drury Lane through the 1713–14 season, acting, among other parts, two which he continued playing with success for many years: Raymond in *The Spanish Friar* and Decius in *Cato*. In the fall of 1714 he returned to Dublin for a season, playing the small roles of the Jeweller in *Timon of Athens*, Zama in *Tamerlane*, and the third Committeeman in *The Committee*. After this Irish visit he came back to London where, apparently, he spent the rest of his long career.

Though Boman gradually reduced the number of his appearances and restricted his repertoire as the years went on, he kept playing such parts as Decius, Duncan, Priuli, and Petulant, and during the 1720's and 1730's he also acted Acasto in *The Orphan*, Petruchio in *The Chances*, Baldwin in *The Fatal Marriage*, and Atticus in *Theodosius*. He kept singing, too, though May 1729 seems to have been the date of his last recorded vocal activity. Despite his advanced age he performed with vigor. John Hoadley, apparently commenting on Boman as Priuli, later remembered him playing "with Passion & Propriety at past 80," and John Hill recalled the actor's power, too: "We remember *Bowman*, who at a time of life twenty-years beyond that at which the generality of players become disagreeable to us cou'd give such force to the character of *Raymond* in the *Spanish Fryar*, that the house never fail'd to ring with a long applause." Davies described Boman as the last of the Betterton school and noted that as the Judge in the 1731 revival of *Volpone* he "pronounced the sentence upon the several delinquents in the comedy with becoming gravity, grace, and dignity."

Boman maintained a remarkably heavy schedule for his age, as, for example, in September and October 1735, when he played Decius, Priuli, Duncan, Norfolk in *Richard III*, Suffolk in *Henry VIII*, and Northumberland in *1 Henry IV*. This last role he acted again on 19 December 1738, after which he left the stage. On 23 March 1739, after more than 60 years of performing, John Boman died. The *London Daily Post and General Advertiser* of 26 March carried an obituary:

Last week died, in the 88th Year of his Age, Mr Boman, belonging to the Drury Lane Theatre, who had the honour to perform several times before King Charles II. It is remarkable of him, that he was the oldest Player, the oldest Singer, and the oldest Ringer in England. He was a Man of good Character, a facetious, agreeable Companion, and well respected.

Chetwood testified to Boman's hardy constitution:

[I] often heard him say, he never remember'd that any Indisposition retarded his coming to the Theatre during his long Course of Life; and this Declaration was made not a Month before he died. He never met with Contempt in the latter Part of his Life; and we may end with two Lines in Jane Shore:

Age sat with decent Grace upon his Visage,
And worthily became his silver Locks.

Colley Cibber, writing just after Boman died, called him "old solemn *Boman*, the late Actor of venerable Memory" and spoke of how, when he was younger, he was "fam'd for his Voice."

Though Boman mellowed with the years, he remained something of a dandy, dapper in his dress and devious about his age. Davies noted that whenever anyone asked Boman how old he was, the actor would only answer, "Sir, I am very well." And well he was, to the end of his long career.

Boman, Mrs John, Elizabeth, née Watson 1677?–1707?, *actress, singer.*

Curll's(?) *History of the English Stage* (1741) stated that Elizabeth Watson, daughter of Sir Francis Watson, Bart, was born in the parish of St Martin-in-the-Fields in 1677; this date, if correct, would have her married at about 15 to a man a good bit older and would make her a prominent member of her acting company while still in her teens. A Sir Francis Watson is reported to have invested along with Thomas Betterton, in an East Indies adventure in 1692 which ruined both of them when their ship, returning with its profitable cargo, was captured by the French. Watson is said to have died shortly after this, and his daughter Elizabeth was taken in by the Bettertons and treated as their own child. She married the actor-singer John Boman sometime before March 1693 when, as Mrs Boman, she played Sylvia in *The Old Bachelor* at Drury Lane as a member of the United Company. If Curll was correct she would have been 16 at this time.

By December 1694, when Betterton drew up a list of complaints against managers Christopher Rich and Sir Thomas Skipwith, Mrs Boman was apparently one of the top six actresses in the rebel group, for she signed the document; she may have been so honored, however, because of her husband's established position in the company, for he, but not she, was named in the license issued to Betterton on 25 March 1695. The tangle of evidence presented by both sides in this dispute reveals that Mrs Boman was originally paid 25s. weekly but had been raised to 30s. by December 1694, a salary equal to that of the popular Mrs Corey. She was also heavy with child by this date, and the managers complained that someone else would have to learn her roles. It is possible, though not certain, that the Boman Junior who started acting in 1712 was the child she was carrying.

After the United Company split, Betterton refurbished the tennis court in Lincoln's Inn Fields, opening it as a theatre on 30 April 1695 with *Love for Love* with Mrs Boman as Mrs Foresight and her husband as Tattle. For the remaining years of the century she was very active, playing such roles as Leonora in *The Mourning Bride* and Lady Fanciful in *The Provoked Wife* and delivering a number of prologues and epilogues—an indication of her popularity with audiences. It may have been during these years that she acted Eurydice in *Oedipus*, a role which Curll singled out later when he described her as "a very pretty Player, both in her Person and Performances." Sometime between 1697 and 1701 Mrs Boman played Portia in *Julius Caesar*, and during the 1699–1700 and 1700–1701 seasons she was Regan in *King Lear*, Katherine Percy in *Henry IV*, Mrs Fainall in *The Way of the World*, and Pallas in *The Judgment of Paris*. Of the last, Congreve wrote to his friend Keally on 26 March 1701 that "Mrs Boman was not quite so well approved in Pallas" as Mrs Bracegirdle and Mrs Hodgson had been in their roles in this production at Dorset Garden. At this stage in her career she was singing occasionally, though her concentration appears to have been on heavy roles in comedies and tragedies alike; if she was born in 1677, which seems at least five years too late, she was playing remarkably mature parts in her mid-twenties.

Most of the plays she acted in up to this point also featured her husband, but during the first years of the eighteenth century she struck out on her own more frequently, and on 11 June 1703 she was given a benefit concert at Lincoln's Inn Fields. In 1704 she and her sister, Mrs Bowden, operated a shop during May Fair and Bartholomew Fair—unless a different Mrs Boman was involved.

Mr and Mrs Boman moved with the old Betterton troupe to the new Queen's Theatre in the Haymarket in 1705, and a document dating about 1707 ranks Mrs Boman fifth among the women in the company, behind Mrs Barry, Mrs Bracegirdle, Mrs Oldfield, and Mrs Rogers, at a yearly salary of £70 maximum. Curiously, though both Bomans were singers, neither was cited among the singing members of the company in this manuscript. John Boman went to Dublin in 1707 and of his wife nothing more is heard. The Mrs Boman who performed from 1716 into the 1730's may have been Elizabeth, but the evidence seems to suggest a different woman, probably the wife of Boman Junior. Interestingly, an Elizabeth Bowman was buried at St Giles in the Fields on 12 January 1707, and another was buried on 21 April 1707 at St Martin-in-the-Fields.

Bombardin, Mr ⟨*fl.* 1751⟩, *bassoonist.*

One Bombardin, a bassoonist, with the violinist Pinto, accompanied Miss Davis, age seven, at a concert at Hickford's music room on 30 April 1751.

Bombaseno. *See* BOMBAZEENO.

"Bombastini, Signor" ⟨*fl.* 1759⟩, *musician.*

"Signor and Signora Bombastini" and their daughter appeared in the burletta *Galligantus* at the Haymarket Theatre in September and October 1759. The work was probably produced by "Mrs Midnight," for the names of some of the performers and their specialties are not unlike those found in other efforts by her. On 21 September Signor Bombastini played a mock violoncello, but what he played on it was not advertised; on 25 September he joined Signora Bombastini in an "Italian Spiletta," which may have been something to watch, or hear, or both. Their daughter, on 5 October, proved that the entire family was talented by playing a solo on the French horn. It is likely that the Bombastinis were related to "Signor Bombasto," who had appeared in Mrs Midnight's offerings from 1751 through 1754 and was engaged again during the 1759–60 season. Who all these performers really were, or whether they were even people, perhaps only Christopher Smart, who was "Mrs Midnight" and created the pseudonyms for his players, could tell.

"Bombastini, Signora" [*fl.* *1759*], *dancer? See* "**BOMBASTINI, SIGNOR.**"

"Bombastini, Signorina" [*fl.* *1759*], *French-horn player. See* "**BOMBASTINI, SIGNOR.**"

"Bombasto, Signor" [*fl.* *1751–1760*], *singer, musician, dancer.*

"Signor Bombasto" was probably in *The Old Woman's Oratory* when it was first presented in late December 1751, though his name did not appear in the bills until 17 March 1752. He received a benefit on 21 March, and on 5 May he sang a *Cantata* "in the Venetian taste," accompanied by "the Vox Humaine." At *The Old Woman's Concert* on 13 March 1753 he was billed as just arrived from Padua; he was given a benefit on 7 April and accompanied "Toe" when he (or she) sang "The Dust Cart" on 10 April; what kind of an instrument Bombasto used to accompany Toe was not noted in the advertisements.

At *Mrs Midnight's New Carnival Concert* on 27 August 1754 at the Haymarket Bombasto displayed his dancing ability. Where he was, from that date until 17 September 1759, is a mystery, but when *Galligantus* was done at the Haymarket on that date, the author was identified as "Mr Bombast"—probably "Bombasto" Anglicized, or a near relative. Bombasto was certainly at the Haymarket on 14 February 1760 when *Mrs Midnight's Concert and Oratory* was presented, but what he did to entertain the audience was not mentioned in the bill. It is possible, if not probable, that Bombasto was related to "Signor Bombastini" (who

also performed at the Haymarket this season); he may, indeed, have been Bombastini. But who Bombastini was no one knows except Mrs Midnight (Christopher Smart), who concocted these pseudonyms.

"Bombazeeno, Signor" [*fl.* *1752–1754*], *dancer.*

Signor "Bombazeeno" (or Bombazeno, Bombazin) performed in *The Old Woman's Oratory* on 17 March 1752 at the Haymarket Theatre, and it is likely that he participated in this production of "Mrs Midnight's" in late December 1751 when it started. After this he went back to the Continent for a time, for when he participated in *The Old Woman's Concert* at the Haymarket on 13 March 1753, he was billed as just arrived from Italy. On 27 August 1754 at the same playhouse he danced in *Mrs Midnight's New Carnival*, after which an invention of Christopher Smart, (who was Mrs Midnight) disappeared from the bills.

Bomolle. *See* **BIMOLLE.**

Bond, Mr [*fl.* *1784*], *singer.*

Mr Bond was a tenor vocalist in the Handel concerts at Westminster Abbey and the Pantheon in May and June 1784.

Bond, John [*fl.* *1784–1807?*], *singer.*

Doane's *Musical Directory* of 1794 listed John Bond as a bass singer at Worcester and as a participant in the grand performances at Westminster Abbey.

According to an affidavit in the records of the Royal Society of Musicians made by John Bond's sister, Mrs Catherine Kerridge (wife of Henry Kerridge of No 16, London House Yard), both he and his wife, Jane Daniels Bond, were dead by 1807. Their son, George James John Bond, who had been born on 27 November 1785 and christened at St Clement Danes on 11 December of the same year, played in the bands at Drury Lane and Covent Garden in the nineteenth century and died in 1830, leaving a widow and three children.

Possibly John Bond was the J. Bond found in the Drury Lane account books as a member of the chorus between 1801 and 1807. Another J. Bond, who was listed in the same account books as a hairdresser between 1804 and 1806, could have been his wife Jane. An Edward Bond who was admitted to the Irish Musical Fund in 1809 and was still alive in 1825 may have been related.

Boneway, Mlle [fl. 1746], actress.

Mademoiselle Boneway played Colombe in *The Schemes of Harlequin* at Hussey's booth at Bartholomew Fair on 23 August 1746.

Bonfanti, Luigi [fl. 1794–1798], singer.

Luigi Bonfanti was a first *buffo* at the King's Opera from 1794 to 1798. He made his debut in London as Don Pistofolo in *L'amore contrastato* on 6 December 1794 and sang also in that season the roles of Capitan Sbaraglia in *La scola dei maritati* and Oronte in *Aci e Galatea*. In 1795–96 he sang Zaccaria in *I Traci amanti* and Don Papavero in *Il tesoro*; in 1796–97 Messala in *Evelina* and Euriso in *Merope*, the last two being serious operas. During his last season (1797–98) he sang Giorgio in *Nina* and Sandrino in *La cifra*, making his final appearance in the latter role on 13 March 1798.

Bonner. *See also* BONNOR.

Bonner, [Mrs?] [fl. 1791], actress.

A woman named Bonner sang and acted the role of Jenny in *The Gentle Shepherd* at the Haymarket out-of-season on 26 September and 12 December 1791. For the first date she was billed as *Miss* Bonner and for the second as *Mrs* Bonner. Probably she was with a group of actors from the North.

Bonnet, [Mr?] [fl. 1757–1758], house servant?

One Bonnet was named twice in the Covent Garden account books for 1757–58: on 23 September 1757 Bonnet was to receive 15s. for three days' work; on 18 May 1758 he (or she?) was cited to receive £2 5s. for nine days' work.

Bonneval, Mlle [fl. 1741–1744], dancer.

The French dancer Mlle Bonneval danced with Dubuisson at Covent Garden on 11 November 1741, that night "being the 1st time of their appearing since their arrival from Paris." She continued at that theatre for the rest of the season in specialty dances usually accompanied by Dubuisson with whom she shared a benefit on 21 April 1742. On 8 January she danced the part of Water in *The Rape of Proserpine* and was a nymph in a new grand ballet which was inserted into *The Winter's Tale* on 21 January. The next season Mlle Bonneval was at Drury Lane in similar roles, and she received a benefit there on 25 April 1743 when she performed a new serious dance at the end of Act II of *The Conscious Lovers* and a new *Hussar Dance*, with Boromeo, at the end of Act IV. She returned to Covent Garden in 1743–44. Among her roles in her final season on the London stage was Colombine in *The Rape of Proserpine* on 14 April 1744.

Bonnor. *See also* BONNER.

Bonnor, Charles [fl. 1777–1829?], actor, author.

The actor Charles Bonnor was born the son of a distiller at Bristol, and after having been apprenticed to a coachmaker he turned to the stage. Bonnor made his first appearance at the Bath theatre on 4 October 1777 as Belcour in *The West Indian*. He remained in the Bath and Bristol company through 1781–82, playing such roles as Charles Surface in *The School for Scan-*

dal, Touchstone, Granger in *Who's the Dupe?* and Ranger in *The Suspicious Husband*. He also supplied successful prologues, epilogues, and occasional addresses. In the summer of 1779 he acted at Brighton. For his benefit at Bath on 25 May 1782 he played Bob Acres in *The Rivals*, with Mrs Siddons as Julia.

On 8 May 1784 the London newspapers announced that Bonnor, of Bath, "a performer of acknowledged merit, particularly in the line of fine gentlemen, and other parts of genteel comedy, and singing," had been engaged by Colman for the coming season at Covent Garden. Bonnor was given a farewell benefit at Bath on 7 July 1783, at which he played Puff in *The Critic* and Mercutio. Before leaving for London he completed an allegorical transparent painting which was exhibited at the Bristol Theatre Royal in October of that year in commemoration of the proclamation of peace.

Engaged at £3 per week, Bonnor made his debut at Covent Garden on 19 September 1783 as Captain Brazen in *The Recruiting Officer*. Also making their first London appearances in that performance were Miss Scrace from Bath, as Sylvia, and Mrs Chalmers from York, as Rose. Before the curtain was drawn up, Bonnor delivered an "Introductory Essay" in which he compared himself to a bark venturing for the first time on the open sea, and he implored the consideration of the audience for "a fair supplicant, trembling" for their favor. One reviewer wrote that "Mr Bonnor's Captain Brazen was marked with a characteristic confidence and ease that shews his attention has been directed to the strict study of the part.—His stature is low, but he is well made, has great vivacity in his manner, free action, and a voice much resembling that of Mr Dodd."

Having met with approval from audience and critics at his debut, Bonnor played Chapeau in *Cross Purposes* on 10 October 1783 and Dupely in *The Maid of the Oaks* on 14 January 1784. He also arranged the action and John O'Keeffe supplied the words for the pantomime *Friar Bacon*, which was performed on 23 December 1783 and 15 other times; the piece was altered and brought out as *Harlequin Rambler* on 29 January 1784 and played another 18 times before the season was over.

At the middle of Bonnor's first season at Covent Garden, the management temporarily interrupted his function as an actor to send him to Paris for the purpose of exploring the possibility of establishing an English theatre in that city. No doubt he was chosen as a fitting emissary because of his versatility, tact, confidence, and an obvious facility with the French language. For a while his mission went well and the press reported on 24 March 1784 that "Letters from Mr Bonner, Plenipotentiary at Paris for the state of Covent-garden say that the negociation for establishing an English theatre has terminated most amicably, and will meet encouragement from the first personnages at the French Court." Reportedly a "superb theatre which constitutes one of the grand divisions of the Thuilleries" was taken. The plan collapsed, however, when the patronage of the French Queen was withdrawn. Something of Bonnor's efforts perhaps was salvaged, for an undated clipping in the Burney papers at the British Museum reported that Harris, the Covent Garden manager, had indeed obtained permission to perform for eight weeks at Paris in the summer of 1784 and that he intended to embark at the close of the winter season with about 14 actors, including Bonnor, John Kemble, Robson, Booth, and Mr and Mrs Chalmers.

When Bonnor returned from Paris, having been away at the usual time of his benefit, the management gave him the theatre "free of all Expense" on 14 June 1784 for a performance of the interlude afterpiece *The Manager an Actor in Spite of Himself*, which was based on Dorvigny's *La Fête de campagne*, "First Performed in Paris," and undoubtedly seen there by Bonnor. He translated the text and played all but one of the ten roles himself: Clerville, Waiter, Hair-dresser, Musician, Prompter, Machinist, Woman-dresser, Stuttering Poet, and Publican. The tenth role, that of the manager of the *fête*, was taken by Wilson of Drury Lane. The piece was never published but is found in Larpent Manuscript 37.M., and in later seasons it was sometimes acted under the title of *Transformation*.

In the late summer of 1784 (perhaps after acting at Paris) Bonnor acted at Brighthelmstone for about a fortnight and wrote an address to be spoken there at a performance of *The Beggar's Opera*. In his next and last season at Covent Garden, 1784–85, during which he lived in the Piazza, he played Petulant in *The Way of the World*, Lovelace in *Three Weeks After Marriage*, Clodio in *Love Makes a Man*, and Manuel in *Barataria*. He also played Puff in *The Critic*, a character whose spirit he did not capture with "his usual success," according to a newspaper clipping. On 14 December 1784 he replaced Thomas Holcroft in the title role of *The Marriage of Figaro*. Bonnor's last appearance at Covent Garden was on 28 May 1785 as Lord Sparkle in *Which is the Man?* and Robin in *The Contrivances*. His final connection with a London theatre was five years later when his pantomime, *The Picture of Paris, Taken in the Year 1790*, with music by William Shield and songs by Robert Merry, was played at Covent Garden on 20 December 1790 and 35 times thereafter that season. On 11 January 1791 Bonnor was paid £200 by the theatre treasury.

After retiring from the stage, Bonnor became involved with John Palmer in establishing a mail-coach service for the postal system. Palmer, who was owner of the Bath theatre and Bonnor's former manager there, had been appointed surveyor and comptroller-general of the post office. In the *Royal Kalendar* for 1788 Charles Bonnor's name appeared as the resident surveyor of the general post office at a salary of £500. Palmer also appointed him deputy-comptroller. When Palmer became involved in a power struggle with Lord Walsingham, the postmaster-general, in 1792, Bonnor turned against his benefactor for his own advantage by publishing a pamphlet, *Facts relating to the Meeting on the Fifteenth of February at the London Tavern*, in which he alleged that Palmer had called a meeting of Bath merchants for the express purpose of agitating them against the postmaster-general. Palmer suspended Bonnor and was in turn suspended by Walsingham on 7 March 1792. William Pitt suggested a court of inquiry, but Bonnor provided Walsingham with a number of compromising letters which had passed between Palmer and himself when they were still friends, whereupon Palmer was dismissed. Bonnor became comptroller of the inland department of the general post office in 1793 at a salary of £700, but two years later in April 1795 his office was abolished and he was granted a pension of £460. In 1797 Bonnor published *Mr Palmer's Case explained*, and in 1800 *A Letter to Benj. Hobhouse, Esq. M. P. on the subject of Mr. Palmer's Claim*.

Charles Bonnor's name was listed in the "Return of Persons now or formerly belonging to the Post Office Department who receive Pensions" contained in the *Parliamentary Papers* for 1829. In that same year, the *Gentleman's Magazine* for August reported the death, "lately," in Gloucestershire, of a Mr Charles Bonnor of Gloucester.

Bonomi, Giac[inta?] [*fl. 1757–1759*], *dancer.*

Signora Giac[inta?] Bonomi danced at the King's Theatre during 1757–58 and 1758–59 (and apparently did not sing there in the former season as *The London Stage* suggests). Arthur Murphy wrote in the *London Chronicle* (11–12 November) that when she danced with Gallini in the characters of a woodman and his wife on

11 November 1758, she carried the grotesque to a most entertaining extravagance —"Bonomi is allowed to excel in this way every one who has gone before her."

Bononcini, Giovanni *1670–1747, violoncellist, composer.*

Giovanni (not Giovanni Battista) Bononcini (or Buononcini) was born in Modena on 18 July 1670, the son of composer Giovanni Maria Bononcini, from whom he received part of his early musical training. He also studied at Bologna with Colonna and learned the cello under Giorgio Buoni. It was as a cellist that he entered the chapel of San Petronio in January 1687 at the age of 16; and later that year he was appointed choirmaster of San Giovanni in Monte and joined the Accademia Filarmonica. By this time the precocious Bononcini had already published some chamber music, and in 1691 when he left Bologna he had a number of chamber works, masses, and oratorios to his credit.

He was in Rome from 1691 to 1697, and it was there that he first began writing operas, his first being additions to Draghi's *Eraclea* in 1692 and his second an original work, *Xerse*. By February 1698 he was in Venice, on his way to Vienna, the city where he spent most of his next 13 years. On 1 July 1700 he was made court composer to the Emperor Leopold and also a member of the royal band. During this period he was twice invited to the court of Queen Sophia Charlotte at Berlin—in 1702 and 1704.

With his brother Antonio Maria (who was sometimes incorrectly called Marc Antonio) he returned to Italy in 1711. He was in Milan in 1713, possibly spent some time after that in Modena, and by 1719 was in Rome again. Before 1719 he had married Margherita Belletti, the sister-in-law of the actor and theatre historian Luigi Riccoboni. In 1720 Bononcini was invited to London by the newly formed Academy of Music. The singer Margherita de l'Épine had introduced songs (probably) by Bononcini as early as 15 December 1705 at Drury Lane, and on 27 May 1707 there had been an attempt to persuade authorities to invite the Italian composer to England. When he arrived in 1720, English audiences were familiar with his works and gave him a warm welcome. Just as Handel was a favorite of the Hanovers, so Bononcini was supported by such influential houses as Rutland and Marlborough, and almost as soon as he arrived Bononcini became Handel's rival. He gradually encroached on Handel's managerial prerogatives at the Academy of Music, a move which in time led to an unfortunate clash.

His first contribution to opera performances after his arrival was on 19 November 1720 at the King's Theatre in the Haymarket when his music for *Astarto* was heard; the opera was immensely successful, running for 30 performances. The next spring

Civico Museo Bibliografico Musicale, Bologna

GIOVANNI BONONCINI
artist unknown

he, Handel, and Amadei contributed an act each to the opera *Muzio scevola* which opened on 15 April 1721; the relationship between Bononcini and Handel must have been strained further when Handel carried away the honors. In the 23 June issue of the *Daily Post* Bononcini advertised his new opera *Crispo* which had been given at Rome in January but had not yet been heard in London:

Any Lady or Gentleman may have the Opera of *Crispo* rehearsed at their apartments, by all the best Performers, who will engage 20 persons or more to subscribe to Signor Bononcinis Cantatas, but it is humbly desired no one may be invited who is not already a subscriber or who does not promise to subscribe to the said Cantatas. N.B. *Crispo* is the best composition of Bononcini & is never to be performed but in this manner for his own benefit; & wherever 30 subscribers are procured Signor Bononcini will play on the Violincello [*sic*] which he never does but where he proposes a particular advantage to himself.

He was not being very honest; despite his disclaimer, *Crispo* was performed at the King's Theatre on 10 January 1722 with Senesino and Anastasia Robinson in the cast—but perhaps Bononcini never got any subscribers for his cantatas.

Though the facts are scanty, Bononcini and Mrs Robinson (later Countess of Peterborough) appear to have had some kind of liaison. With the *castrato* Senesino they were lodging at Twickenham in September 1721, and a letter from Atterbury to Pope stated that the *prima donna* "haunted" the composer. They were certainly associated in several productions of his works, including a private performance of some of the choral music he wrote for a revision of the first part of Shakespeare's *Julius Caesar* called *Marcus Brutus*. The music was apparently performed on 10 January 1723 for the young Duke of Buckingham's birthday; the Duke had revamped Shakespeare's play, and his Duchess had the choruses presented at Buckingham House by "ye best Voices Mrs A: Robinson & others & ye best Instruments of all sorts."

Bononcini's popularity grew with performances of his *Griselda* on 22 February 1722, *Erminia* on 30 March 1723, *Farnace* on 27 November 1723, *Calfurnia* on 18 April 1724, and *Astianatte* on 6 May 1727. In addition to his operas, the composer occasionally contributed cantatas (perhaps some of those he tried to peddle earlier) to potpourris at the King's Theatre and *entr'acte* entertainments at Lincoln's Inn Fields. And for the Duke of Marlborough's funeral on 15 August 1722 he composed a special anthem.

It was the young Duchess of Marlborough who, in the spring of 1723, provided Bononcini with a life income of £500 a year "provided," wrote contemporary gossip Mrs Pendarves in a letter to Anne Granville, "He will *not* compose any more for the ungrateful Academy, who do not deserve he should entertain them, since they don't know how to value his work as they ought, and likewise told him he should always be welcome to her table." A later newspaper report (1731) said Bononcini's pension was for entertaining the Duchess twice weekly with his music, and that may have been closer to the truth. The rivalry between Handel and Bononcini was warm, however, and perhaps the Duchess did want to provide the Italian with a way to dissociate himself from the Academy.

In May 1724 a satirical poem called "The Session of Musicians" was published, poking fun at a number of the musical folk in London. The poem's central character was Apollo, before whom all the musicians came so that he might judge which was the greatest.

Just then grim B[ono]nc[in]i *in the Rear,*
Most fearless of Success, came to the Bar;
Two Philharmonick Damsels *grac'd his Train,*

Whilst his strong Features redden'd with
Disdain;
Dear A[nasta]s[i]a hung upon his Arm,
Each Lisp and side-long Glance produc'd
its Charm;
Black P[e]g[g]y [Durastanti] he was
forced to hawl along,
Humming a Thorough-Base — and he a
Song:
Silent, his rolling Eyes the God survey'd.

Despite Bononcini's pair of *prima donnas* and his overweening confidence, Handel, of course, was chosen by Apollo.

Bononcini "obtained Leave of Absence for some months to go to France on private affairs"; the date of this permission has been suggested as 1731, but the summer of 1732 is more probable. What the "private affairs" were is not known for certain, but one may guess they were connected with an unfortunate controversy which virtually ruined the composer's reputation in England. Some years before, Bononcini is said to have submitted to the Academy of Ancient Music a madrigal of his which, in 1731, was found to be a transcript of one by Lotti. During the squabble over this apparent plagiarism Bononcini remained haughtily silent, and this only served to increase the growing antagonism of the public. The Churchill family eventually dropped him, and his colleagues in the music world started taking sides — some with Bononcini and some with his adversary Handel. In later years Swift wrote a joshing epigram on the two composers:

Strange! all this difference should be
'Twixt tweedle-dum and tweedle-dee!

There is some question whether Bononcini was in fact responsible for the plagiarism; he was certainly quite capable of writing a madrigal himself, and the disputed work was apparently given to the Academy not by Bononcini himself but by his friend Maurice Green (who lost his friendship with Handel during the controversy). But if Bononcini was innocent, it is odd that he made no attempt to defend himself or explain the matter; this may have been his pride, which contemporaries noted was enormous.

What had started as a plagiarism charge developed into a contest between Handel and Bononcini, and if one of them had to go, it certainly would not be Handel, despite the strong support some gave Bononcini. The preface to *The Blazing Comet* (1732), probably by Samuel Johnson of Cheshire, commented on the rivalry:

In these days, lives in *London*, without encouragement, the famous Mr. *Bononcini*, whose Musick for Celestialness of Stile, I am apt to think, will demand remembrance in the Soul after Fire has destroy'd all things in this World; and I that have translated his Sounds into our own *English* Language, cannot say enough of this great Man, who is rival'd by Mr. *Handel*, a very big Man, who writes his Musick in the *High-Dutch* Taste, with very great success: so when you peruse these two Masters you'll guess at the Men, and blush for the Taste of England.

But though he had some supporters, Bononcini's days in England were numbered. Only one more work of his was done there before he left, a fairly successful pastoral performed at the King's Theatre on 24 June 1732. Bononcini had hoped to have Signora Strada sing for him, but her husband declined the invitation for her, possibly not wanting her involved in the scandal. After this Bononcini apparently left for France where, for a while, he played cello in the chapel of Louis XV. He was in Lisbon in 1735 and Vienna in 1737, where, after several uncreative years, he once again produced an opera, *Alessandro in Sidone*. A *Te Deum* of his dated 15 February 1741 seems to have been his last work. Bononcini died in Vienna on 9 July 1747.

Despite his haughty personal manner, Bononcini put into his music a very different quality: tender, elegant, and pathetic.

There was an element of truth in Johnson's praise, and modern musicologists have found much that is fine in his work.

Bononcini's portrait is at the Civico Museo Bibliografico Musicale, Bologna; an engraving of it was made by J. Caldwall. Another portrait is in the Beard Collection. Engravings of Bononcini were made by G. van der Gucht and J. Simpson Jr.

Bonsor, Mr [*fl. 1793–1810*], *door-keeper.*

Mr Bonsor (or Bonser) was a door-keeper at Covent Garden at a salary of 12*s.* weekly in 1793–94, when his name was first mentioned in the accounts. He seems to have remained at this wage level through the years, the last mention of him being in December 1810 when he was apparently still at the theatre.

Bonville, Mr, stage name of E. N. Morgan [*fl. 1787–1789*], *actor, singer.*

"Bonville" was the stage name under which E. N. Morgan, printer of the *Cork Herald*, performed in England. As Mr Bonville he acted and sang in minor roles at Covent Garden for two seasons (1787–88 and 1788–89) at a salary of £1 5*s.* per week. His first appearance there seems to have been on 26 September 1787 when he acted in *Poor Vulcan!* On 1 October he sang one of the vocal parts in *Macbeth*. Among other minor assignments in the following season was a vocal part in the solemn dirge at Juliet's funeral procession in *Romeo and Juliet* on 22 September 1788. Bonville was also at the Plymouth theatre in the summer of 1788, where he played Captain Wilson in *The Flitch of Bacon* and the Duke in *Barataria* on 18 August, Captain Slightly in *The Romp* on 22 August, and Captain Belville in *Rosina* on 27 August, sharing a benefit on this last night with Bristow and Short. He again acted at Plymouth and at York in 1791–92. The actor G. F. Cooke wrote in his diary on 20 September 1798:

"met Mr Morgan, printer of the Cork Herald (formerly an actor in England, under the name of Bonville), with whom I had been twice in company at Dublin." A Mrs Bonville acted at Wolverhampton and Margate in 1797.

Bonwick, Miss [*fl. 1794*], *organist, singer.*

Doane's *Musical Directory* of 1794 listed Miss Bonwick, of the Old Jewry, as a soprano and an organist.

Boomar, Mr [*fl. 1719*], *singer.*

Mr Boomar made his first appearance on stage singing at Drury Lane on 2 May 1719; he is not otherwise known, so this may have been his last appearance as well.

Bootell. *See* BOUTELL and BOWTELL.

Booth, Mr [*fl. 1762–1771*], *actor.*

A male actor (or actors) by the name of Booth acted intermittently in the London theatres between 1762 and 1771. A Mr Booth was one of the orators in Foote's *Oratorical Lectures* which were given 36 times at the Haymarket in the summer of 1762. According to *The London Stage*, a Mr Booth performed at the Haymarket in 1770–71, but he is not found in the bills. An actor named Booth was performing very minor roles at Drury Lane in the three seasons 1768–71. He played Sir Harry Beagle in *The Jealous Wife* on 25 April 1769. On 6 January 1770 he performed a role in *A Trip to Scotland*, a piece often repeated in that season and in the following. He also played a Welchman in *Harlequin's Invasion* on 29 September 1770 and a character in the pantomime of *The Elopement* on 13 October 1770. On 5 May 1770 he shared a benefit with other minor actors and house servants. These allusions may have been to Joseph Cockran Booth who began to work regularly at Covent Garden in 1774–75.

Booth, Mr [*fl. 1780–1782*], *actor.*
An obscure actor named Booth performed occasionally at the Haymarket, out-
of-season, in 1780–82. He played Timothy
in *The Humours of Oxford* on 28 March
1780 and Valentine in *The Temple Beau*
on 21 September 1782.

Booth, Mr [*fl. 1784*], *singer.*
A Mr Booth was listed as a tenor vocalist
among the performers in the Handel Memorial Concerts at Westminster Abbey and
at the Pantheon in May and June 1784.

Booth, Mrs [*fl. 1740–1741*], *actress.*
A Mrs Booth, not to be confused with,
but possibly related by marriage to, Mrs
Barton Booth, played Aurora in *Cephalus*
at the Lee-Phillips booths at Bartholomew
Fair on 23 August and Southwark Fair on
9 September 1740. She appeared again as
Miss Sol-Fa in *The Devil of a Duke* on 22
August 1741 at Hippisley and Chapman's
Bartholomew Fair booth. The 1740 bills
misprinted her name as "Brooth."

Booth, Miss [*fl. 1715*], *singer.*
A Miss Booth, possibly related to actor
Barton Booth, sang at Drury Lane in the
spring and summer of 1715.

Booth, Barton *1679?–1733, actor,
manager, author.*
Born in 1679 (or possibly 1681), Barton Booth was the third and youngest son
of John Booth, a squire of Lancashire and
a member of a branch of the Warrington
family. His father's estate is said to have
become impaired, upon which the family
moved to London in 1684, but they may
not have been in very narrow straits, for
about 1688 young Barton was placed in
Westminster School under Dr Busby. There
he remained, according to his own statement, for six years. He was a schoolmate of
Nicholas Rowe and became interested in
the stage while playing Pamphilus in a
school production of Seneca's *Andria* about

Harvard Theatre Collection

BARTON BOOTH
by Vanderbank

1694 or 1695. Though some sources say
that Booth at 17 went to Cambridge, destined for a clerical career, but ran off to
join a company of strolling players to the
dismay of his parents, Booth himself stated
that after his Westminster years he went
directly into theatre work.

By the summer of 1698 he was in Dublin, acting for Joseph Ashbury at the Smock
Alley Theatre. One version of these years
has him first applying to and being refused
by Betterton and Smith at Lincoln's Inn
Fields. In any case, his first professional
role was Oroonoko at Smock Alley, probably in the summer of 1698. Chetwood
told a story of Booth's debut in black face
which may be true:

It being very warm Weather, in his last Scene
of the Play, as he waited to go on, he inadvertantly wip'd his Face, that when he
enter'd he had the Appearance of a Chimney-
Sweep (his own Words). At his Entrance, he
was surpriz'd at the Variety of Noises he

heard in the Audience (for he knew not what he had done) that a little confounded him, till he receiv'd an extraordinary Clap of Applause, which settl'd his Mind. The Play was desir'd for the next Night of Acting, when an Actress fitted a Crape to his Face with an Opening proper for the Mouth, and shap'd in form for the Nose; But in the first Scene, one Part of the Crape slip'd off. And "Zounds!" said he, (he was a little apt to swear) "I look'd like a Magpie! When I came off they Lampblack'd me for the Rest of the Night, that I was flead before it could be got off again."

Booth's Oroonoko was a success, however, and Ashbury gave the needy young actor a gift of five guineas.

During the 1698–99 season Ashbury, with a company strong in comedy, produced three Etherege works, in all of which Booth played major parts: Colonel Bruce in *The Comical Revenge*, Freeman in *She Would If She Could*, and Medley in *The Man of Mode*. Whether or not Booth stayed to play the next season in Dublin is not clear; he may have done some provincial acting in England, and he probably appeared at Mrs Mynns's Bartholomew Fair booth before reapplying to Betterton in London. He was apparently back in the big city in 1700, with a letter of introduction from Lord Fitzharding and the helping hand of actor John Boman; Betterton accepted him at Lincoln's Inn Fields, and for his London debut he played, probably in the fall of 1700, Maximus in *Valentinian*. He was impressive enough to encourage his old schoolfellow Rowe to give him the part of Artaban in *The Ambitious Stepmother* when it was performed about December 1700. About January 1701 he was Gratiano in *The Jew of Venice*. His first season in London was not spectacular, but he gained a footing, and Booth was an ambitious man.

He was also a glutton, something of a ruffian, and a heavy drinker. The first fault he clung to all his life, and it was the death of him; the second got him into some trou-

bles, but nothing serious; and the third he reformed altogether. Colley Cibber later noted that Booth about 1700 was drinking heavily, but seeing the "Contempt and Distresses [into which] *Powel* had plung'd himself by the same Vice, he was so struck with the Terror of his Example, that he fix'd a Resolution (which from that time to the End of his Days he strictly observ'd) of utterly reforming it." Cibber may have exaggerated somewhat, but apparently Booth did indeed become an abstemious man; it may have been the example of George Powell, but perhaps the death of Booth's father in 1701 also had a sobering effect on young Barton. We know from Booth's will that he helped support his brother George and sister Barbara, and this responsibility, even though he was the youngest son, may have begun soon after his father's death.

For the next few seasons Booth played important but secondary roles, but he apparently became something of a protégé of Betterton, whom he resembled in some ways and whose style he certainly studied. He was Axalla in *Tamerlane* (c. December 1701), Cassander in *The Rival Queens* (29 January 1703), Bedamar in *Venice Preserved* (15 June 1703)—these last two being noted in manuscript casts and not otherwise recorded—and Young Single in *Sir Salomon* (28 February 1704 at court). Between 25 March 1704 and the following October no roles are recorded for Booth, and it was perhaps during this time that he married.

His bride was Frances Barkham, the second daughter of Sir William Barkham, Bart., of Norfolk. Of this first marriage of Booth's virtually nothing is known; it ended with the death of his wife in 1710. It would be helpful to know if the marriage was romantic or merely convenient, for a growing pattern during Booth's early career is an establishing of important ties; by 1704 he had useful connections with Betterton, Rowe, Boman (who had a court affiliation), Dennis, Fitzharding, and now the Barkhams. They were to pay off handsomely for the actor later.

In April 1705 Betterton moved his troupe into the new Queen's Theatre in the Haymarket. Unfortunately, hardly any casts were listed for the theatre during its early months, so Booth's first role there is not known. At the end of summer, though, he joined a group at Lincoln's Inn Fields and played Florencio in *The Cares of Love* on 1 August 1705; it was one of his last appearances at the old tennis-court playhouse and one of his first as a poet: he wrote and spoke the prologue to the play.

At the Queen's Theatre he continued playing secondary but significant roles, most of them young men and many of them, even in comedies, serious. Among his parts during the next two seasons were Dick in *The Confederacy*, Telemachus in *Ulysses*, Vernon in *1 Henry IV*, Bonario in *Volpone*, Dauphine in *The Silent Woman*, the title role in *Julius Caesar*, Young Bellair in *The Man of Mode*, Cassio in *Othello*, the Duke of Buckingham in *Henry VIII*, Polydore in *The Orphan*, Alcibiades in *Timon of Athens*, and Edgworth in *Bartholomew Fair*. By this time he was in the middle rank of actors in the Queen's Theatre troupe, receiving about £100 annually or, if profits did not permit, £80. This placed him equal to Colley Cibber but below Verbruggen, Powell, Wilks, and, of course, Betterton. He had strong men ahead of him, and Wilks, especially, seems to have exerted some influence in casting and may have prevented Booth from playing top roles at this time. But Booth was a hard worker, and in time, better and better parts came his way. Before he left the Queen's, he played, in the fall of 1707, Lenox in *Macbeth* (another typically small role) but also Hotspur in *1 Henry IV* (a plum), and Laertes in *Hamlet* (another hot-blooded type, suited to the rough side of his nature).

For the last half of the 1707–8 season the players moved to Drury Lane to work under Christopher Rich. On 15 January 1708 Booth played for the first time a role which was to become one of his best and most typical: the Ghost in *Hamlet*. Though only 29 and good at volatile characters, Booth also had a solemn side to his nature, and he apparently found himself comfortable in elderly roles requiring majesty.

At Drury Lane he did not relinquish his previous roles, even small ones like Lenox or youthful ones like Laertes and Bonario, but he was able to add some new ones: Scandal in *Love for Love*, Vainlove in *The Old Bachelor*, Osmyn in *The Mourning Bride*, the Elder Worthy in *Love's Last Shift*, and Appius in *Appius and Virginia*. He had not yet played any great tragic roles, but the prompter Downes, writing in 1708, must have seen the possibilities in Booth, for he described him as "A Gentleman of liberal Education, of form Venust; of Mellifluent Pronuntiation, having proper Gesticulations, which are Graceful Attendants of true Elocution; of his time a most Compleat Tragedian."

In June 1709 Drury Lane was closed by order of the Lord Chamberlain after complaints from the actors against Christopher Rich's oppressive management. When the playhouse reopened for the 1709–10 season the new licensee, William Collier, made Aaron Hill the manager and Booth the leading tragedian. It was a season that augured well for the actor, and during it he added some important roles to his repertory: Castalio in *The Orphan*, Valentine in *Love for Love*, Brutus in *Julius Caesar*, Othello (for his 21 January 1710 benefit), and *Horatio* in Hamlet. The season was marred, however, by increasing conflicts between the actors and the new manager; Collier, the licensee, had gained control for political reasons and knew little about the theatre, and his manager Aaron Hill antagonized the players by refusing to give them sufficient say in casting. The result was a rather bloody rebellion at the end of the season.

From a letter which Hill wrote on 5 June 1710 to Vice Chamberlain Coke we can glean some of the facts. For a portion of the season Hill had apparently shared managerial duties with seven of the leading actors, Booth the foremost among them. This had not worked out, and Hill withdrew "the useless power of the seven Managers"; this "unexpected blow, was a great surprise to em, resented warmly by all." Hill then made Pack the manager of rehearsals, but Pack gave up the post within a day or two, whereupon Hill offered it to Booth. Booth refused to accept it unless all seven were restored, so Hill gave the job to his brother. Shortly after this, when Hill was out of town, some of the actors created an uproar, threw up their parts, refused to act, and threatened to run off with the theatre costumes. The nucleus of the rebels consisted of George Powell, Booth, Theophilus Keene, John Bickerstaff, and Francis Leigh. Hill rushed back to town, suspended Keene and Bickerstaff, and confronted Booth, who hurled invectives at him and tried to tell Hill who would act and when. Fearful that the rebels would make good their threat to abscond with the costumes, Hill ordered the theatre locked up.

It was apparently on the afternoon of Friday, 2 June 1710, that the riot occurred. Hill, his brother, and treasurer Zachary Baggs were in the theatre office when they heard Booth and the others "breaking open the great Doors within," the actress Lucretia Bradshaw having let the group in a private way through her lodgings next to the playhouse. The men burst into the office with swords drawn; Hill was almost stabbed by Powell, and his brother was hit on the head from behind by Leigh. Hill managed to escape, but when he came back to the theatre after an unsuccessful search for the Vice Chamberlain, he found the doors locked against him.

The result, after officials of the Lord Chamberlain's office heard Hill's story, was an order dated 14 June 1710 to Collier:

Whereas Complaint has been made to me that five of the Actors belonging to her Maj^{ts} Company of Comedians under your Managm^t vizt George Powell Barton Booth Jno Bickerstaff Thõphil^s Keen and ffranc^s Lee did not only refuse to Obey ye Orders of Mr Hill who is appointed by you to take care of the said Company, but that they did also lately in a riotous manner break open the Doors of the Play house, beating and Abusing the S^d Mr Hill and wth their Swords drawn threatning his life and have also cõmitted Sever^{ll} other other [*sic*] insolencys and disorders These are Therefore to charge and Require you imediately to dismis and remove the s^d Powell from the service of her Majesty's Company . . . and y^t you Suspend Barton Booth Theophil^s Keen Jno Bickerstaff and ffranc^s Lee from further Acting.

Since the season was at an end anyway, the punishment was rather meaningless, and by the fall, the actors were back in the good graces of the management.

During 1710, according to most sources, Booth's first wife died; when this happened and how it may have affected the actor are not known. In the fall of 1710 he was back at Drury Lane, and during the ensuing season he played Othello several times, acted Laertes in the fall and the Ghost in the spring, played Scandal again in *Love for Love*, and reverted to Polydore in *The Orphan*. Some of these changes may have come about because of his participation in the riot; Booth probably lost some ground, and the Betterton roles he had taken over in 1709–10 he now had to share with Powell. At the end of the season another shift in management was made, bringing the powerful triumvirate of Cibber, Wilks, and Doggett into the management of Drury Lane. Under them Booth retained such important roles as Othello, Hotspur, Ozmyn, the Ghost, Don Carlos, and Oroonoko, and in the last half of the 1711–12 season he was Pyrrhus in the first performance of *The Distrest Mother* and was cast again as Castalio. He was clearly a valued player, but he had not yet succeeded to some of the major roles or to the share in the management that he wanted.

The season of 1712–13, however, brought Booth triumph. On 16 December 1712 he wrote to Lord Lansdowne, recounting his history and his current grievances:

After having been six years at Westminster School, instead of going to either university to pursue my studies, my folly led me to the profession, I now must stick to while I live: as the World goes, actors are very rarely preferred to any other employment. I blush to own my Indiscretion: I was very Young; but since I have brought myself to a bad market, I must make the best of it.

I have been thirteen years an Actor—five years in Lincoln's Inn Fields under Mr. Betterton; and during that time I did not receive *Communibus annis* thirty Pounds by my salary; from thence I removed under Mr Vanbrugh and Mr Congreve, to the playhouse in the Haymarket; where for four years I far'd not much better than before: These misfortunes threw me naturally behind hand in the World and had I not married a Gentlewoman of some fortune, I must have perish'd, for the four remainding [*sic*] years I receiv'd my full pay, wch amounted to one hundred and ten pounds per ann, or thereabout—I have had success in my Benefit plays for the four years past, but never yet was able to retrieve the losses, I sustained before, I was always chearfull in my misfortunes and endeavoured, by much Industry, and application in my Business, to render myself acceptable to the town —still flattering myself with hopes, that one time, or other, actors would be encourag'd as they were at the Restoration, and many years afterwards. Volvenda dies en attulet! but Mr Wilkes, Mr Dogget & Mr Cibber only enjoy the Benefit of this alteration in our Theatrical government, Those Gentlemen have been, and are in Possession of what has already made 'em happy in their Circumstances while I must act and labour to divert the Town for a bare subsistence only. This, my Lord, is hard upon me: yet I have something to urge further, to satisfy y^r Lordship that my case is still worse, my present livelihood depends upon my Health; and even at this time I lye too much at the Mercy of my Creditors.

Thus, my Lord, if I am not redress'd, I must be a sacrifice to my Equals. Mr. Wilks, Mr. Cibber and Mr. Dogget must raise fortunes to themselves, and families, while I starve.

Booth was exaggerating his case, perhaps, but much of what he said was true; he was a hard-working actor sustaining a number of leading parts, and he deserved, at the least, a better salary.

A few months later, while Booth's letter was finding its way to the Lord Chamberlain, Booth, on 14 April 1713, "created" the title role in Addison's *Cato*; the success was so immediate and spectacular that it was now only a matter of time before the triumvirate would have to admit Booth as a fellow manager. *Cato* was a windfall for the company. It opened at a point in the season when the profits were in and the benefits were taking place, and by the end of the season the company had earned £1350. Booth was given 50 guineas by the Tories, and after some squabbling, the managers matched this with another 50 guineas so the Whigs would not think the theatre was taking sides. Cibber was convinced that this was throwing money away and that Booth would not be satisfied until he was made a manager, and Cibber was correct.

Booth, with the patronage of Bolingbroke, went to court to urge his claims, and on 11 November 1713 a new license was issued to Drury Lane with the proviso that Booth be admitted as a partner and an interest in the managers' stock sold to him. Cibber and Wilks, though reluctant, agreed to sell Booth a portion, but the stubborn Doggett refused to negotiate at all; since the stock could not be sold without the consent of all three, they were stymied. They finally settled on a plan to set the price so high that negotiations would be prolonged or they would gain enough money to satisfy Doggett. Their proposal to the Lord Chamberlain made it apparent that Booth would have to lay out £1200 to £1300 to get a fourth share; the Lord Chamberlain saw that this was ridiculously high, said that a fair value would be £600, and ordered the managers to admit Booth on those terms or lose their license. Booth was admitted (possibly having been financed by his courtly friends), and dogged Doggett walked out.

It was by this time about January 1714. For the two years that followed, Doggett had to be paid his share even though he refused to act, but after lengthy negotiations he settled for retirement, £600 for his share, and 15 percent interest since the date of the new license (presumably the one of 11 November 1713). After it was all over and tempers had cooled, it turned out that Doggett's resentment all along had been more against Wilks than against Booth. The new management was a good one, though the testy Wilks remained a problem—but Booth and Cibber agreed that it was better to live with Wilks than to act without him.

Once a sharer in the management, Booth moved into a number of roles he had longed for. On 26 April 1714 he played King Lear for the first time, and on 18 May 1715, Pinchwife in *The Country Wife* became his. He now acted Jaffeir in *Venice Preserved*, Banquo in *Macbeth* (though one would suppose he would have liked the lead), Melantius in *The Maid's Tragedy*, Bajazet in *Tamerlane*, and the title role in *Timon of Athens*—in addition to his old parts, most of which he retained. He seems not to have been interested in extending his reach but simply expanding his existing line. He was about 36 in 1715, in his prime and at the peak of his career.

The five years between 1710 and 1715 say something of Booth's bullish character. He was a hard worker, but he was also an opportunist, perfectly willing to curry favor with people in power and quite capable of fighting for what he wanted. On 19 September 1715 Dudley Ryder recorded in his *Diary* that he had heard "that Booth was the most low, vicious, debauched fellow of them all but a man of very good sense, but his conversation is full of nothing but

bawdy and profaneness." This was hearsay, but probably partly true. There was another side to Booth, however, for he was probably one of the most learned actors of the time and a poet as well. In 1716, for example, he published *The Death of Dido*, a masque for which Pepusch wrote the music; it was performed at Drury Lane on 17 April of that year.

At some point after his first wife's death in 1710, perhaps after Booth became one of the Drury Lane managers, he had an affair with Susan Mountfort, daughter of the performers William and Susanna. They must have made quite a pair. She had a £300 annuity given her on the condition that she not marry, and though Booth apparently offered marriage to her, she refused because, it is said, she loved the annuity more. Booth probably could understand that, and they settled for living together for some years. In 1714 they bought a lottery ticket, agreeing to share any winnings; according to Doran the ticket won £5000, but Susan kept the whole sum. When the relationship ended about 1718, Booth honorably returned £3200 which he had held in trust for her and which her next lover, Edward Minshull, squandered. Susan was said by George Ann Bellamy to have gone insane when Booth turned his affections to another.

The new woman in Booth's life was Hester Santlow, who had for many years been a fellow performer. She was a beautiful creature, a splendid dancer, a capable actress, and just as interested in hard work, courtly connections, money, and love affairs as Booth was. Her dancing had enraptured the young poet James Thomson, she had received gold and embraces from the Duke of Marlborough, and had been the lover of Secretary of State Craggs (by whom she had had a daughter). Booth, despite warnings from friends that she was little better than a strumpet, married her on 31 July 1719, and the couple enjoyed, surprisingly, an eminently successful marriage. Hester brought Booth a considerable fortune and made him a devoted and apparently faithful wife; for his part, Booth must have considered her wealth a reasonable compensation for her reputation, and he seems to have been sincere in his affection for her, as his poems in her praise and the conditions of his will make clear.

Meanwhile, back on the boards of Drury Lane, Booth had been his typically industrious self. He had added to his repertory in 1718 Anthony in *All for Love* and Fainall in *The Way of the World,* and though he assumed fewer and fewer new roles during the 1720's, his playing schedule, year in and year out, was a very heavy one. As he aged, however, he is said to have grown indolent. It was probably Booth that Cibber was referring to when he spoke of actors who "heavily dragg'd the Sentiment along like a dead Weight, with a long-ton'd Voice and absent Eye, as if they had fairly forgot what they were about." But a proper inspiration could bring forth Booth's energy. Doran related the story of a night when Booth was playing Othello rather languidly and then suddenly started exerting himself to the utmost. When asked what happened, Booth is supposed to have said, "I saw an Oxford man in the pit, for whose judgment I had more respect than for that of the rest of the audience." On another occasion, while playing Pyrrhus, he did the same thing when he spotted an accomplished critic, Stanyan, in the audience; offstage, after finishing the performance brilliantly, he said, "No, no! I will not have it said at Button's, that Barton Booth is losing his powers!"

Yet Booth was willing to carry a demanding load even though he did not have to. In May 1723, for example, he played, in sequence: Cato, Varanes in *Theodosius,* Brutus, Hotspur, Lear, Manly in *The Plain Dealer,* Scandal, Timon, Oroonoko, Biron in *The Fatal Marriage,* Banquo, an unspecified role in *Henry VIII,* Jaffeir, and Torresmond in *The Spanish Friar.* With

that schedule, perhaps he had good reason to perform indolently at times. He could be inspired not only by a good critic in the audience but sometimes by a good challenge from another actor. The *Lives and Characters* attributed to Theophilus Cibber contains an anecdote relating to the 7 May 1726 performance of *1 Henry IV.* Giffard had come over from Ireland to play Prince Hal to Booth's Hotspur, and Booth knew that Giffard greatly admired Thomas Elrington's playing of the fiery Percy. Consequently, Booth

exerted himself in a particular Manner, and played the whole Part with such Fire, and Energy of Spirit, as rouzed his Auditors to an Extravagance of Applause, and made Mr Giffard confess (as he has often done in my Hearing) that, notwithstanding his Prepossession in favour of Mr Elrington,—Mr Booth, in Power, Spirit, and Judgment, went far beyond him in this Part; as he afterwards, with Admiration confessed,—he did in every other.

During the 1720's, as one of the trio of Drury Lane managers, Booth was also burdened with administrative affairs. After the departure of Doggett, Sir Richard Steele had become involved in the running of the troupe. At first, with his helpful connections, Steele was a useful silent partner, but over the years he and the managers were entangled in a complicated series of financial maneuvers, suits, and counter suits. Booth was probably on the fringes of much of this, yet any actions taken by the sharers involved him to some degree, willy-nilly. From 18 June 1723 onward, the triumvirate recompensed themselves for the extra work they were obliged to assume because of Steele's continual absence.

The relationship of the three managers themselves was not always smooth. Cibber was traditionally the mediator, as he had been when Doggett was a manager; though Booth was far easier to work with than his predecessor had been, he was frequently at odds with Wilks. In his *Apology* Cibber told of a typical squabble that apparently took place during the winter of 1725–26. Wilks had been complaining of overwork (he, like Booth, carried a fantastically heavy acting load), so Booth proposed doing a play without him. The company gathered for the distribution of roles in Vanbrugh's revised version of *The Provoked Wife*. Wilks had chosen the role of Constant for himself, but Cibber urged him, since it was a small one, to give it to Booth. Wilks was annoyed by this treatment and accused his partners of trying to ease him out of the company, but Cibber explained they were only trying to ease Wilk's burden, since he had complained of being "over-labour'd." Wilks threw his part down and sulked. Booth said he thought acting daily was good exercise; it "kept the Spirits in motion, and always gave him a good Stomach." Anne Oldfield tittered behind her fan. Wilks said he would leave it up to her who should play Constant, since she was to play Lady Brute, his mistress. With her usual frankness, Mrs Oldfield said, "Pooh! you are all a Parcel of Fools, to make a rout about nothing." This kind of petty wrangling apparently went on much of the time, adding to the strain under which the managers must have been working.

Though Booth may have thought daily acting was good for the stomach, his stomach did not agree. The *Daily Journal* of 30 September 1726 reported that "Mr Booth, the excellent Tragedian, continues so much indisposed, that he keeps his Chamber." He had been ill before on occasion; this indisposition, however, was more serious, and a little over a year later he was forced to leave the stage. Between 15 September 1726 and 16 January 1727, apparently, he was plagued by a 46-day fever and suspended acting, but then he worked at his usual compulsive pace until 8 May, took his summer vacation, and began again in the fall of 1727. Theobald's *The Double Falsehood* was in preparation, and Booth, know-

ing his own condition, took the precaution of having Charles Williams understudy his role of Julio. When opening night came on 13 December 1727, Booth had a relapse, and Williams stepped into the part. At the entreaty of the author Booth managed to perform from the fifth to the twelfth nights, but after acting Julio on 9 January 1728, he left the stage for good.

According to Victor, in his *Life of Booth*, Doctors Broxham and Colehatch examined the actor and diagnosed his affliction as "inveterate Jaundice." Dr Mead was called in and recommended a trip to Bath, which the Booths took on 11 April, but to no avail. After 11 weeks they were back in London, stayed three weeks, and then went to Ostend and thence to Antwerp to consult Dr Boerhaave. The Dutch physician was of little help, and they returned to England. By 2 June 1730 (or more likely 1731) Booth so despaired that he made his will, and sometime in 1731 the couple took Lady Mansell's house at Hampstead. Under the advice of his surgeon Mr Small, Booth chewed rhubarb and began a slow but only temporary recovery. The years of culinary indulgence had taken their toll.

On 13 July 1732 the *Daily Courant* reported that Booth "hath sold his share [*recte*, half of it] & interest in the Stock & Management of [Drury Lane] to John Highmore" for £2500; after Booth's death his widow sold the other half to Henry Giffard. By 22 December 1732 Aaron Hill thought Booth was well enough that he wrote him a letter urging him to return to the stage, if only to speak a prologue; but shortly afterwards the actor had another relapse, and for the remaining six months of his life he had violent monthly recurrences of colic; before he quite recovered from one attack, another was upon him. In March 1733 the colic was accompanied by intermittent fevers which continued until 22 April, after which, with the use of cortex, he seemed to be improving. On 3 May, having read a book on the use of mercury, he consulted the author, a doctor unidentified in the sources, who assured Booth that a mercurial course would prevent the return of the fever and cure him of his complaints. On the fourth Booth began to take mercury as directed by the doctor, and he had, by the eighth, consumed nearly two pounds. On this day the actor complained of a great ache in his forehead, much restlessness, and a severe pain in his bowels. He continued dosages of mercury for another day, but on 9 May Mrs Booth sent for Dr Hans Sloane.

Sloane ordered plasters on the feet and nine ounces of blood to be drawn from the jugular for the easing of the head pain; this did not help Booth pass the mercury, however, and a purging draught was administered, followed by a cordial mixture as a cathartic. This, proving ineffectual, was followed by a glyster. On 10 May plasters were applied to Booth's scalp and new cathartics tried, but nothing helped. After all this torture, climaxing over six years of illness, Barton Booth died. His death was placed by *Read's Journal* on Thursday, 10 May 1733, between four and five in the afternoon (a manuscript genealogy at the Folger Shakespeare Library says 8 May at 8 p m). In the presence of Dr Sloane, the surgeon Alexander Small performed an autopsy and found one large and five small gallstones and the intestines nearly rotted. Most of the crude mercury was still in the intestinal tract. The whole wretched business was a most ignominious end for a player who had so loved the dignity of majesty.

According to Booth's wish, he was taken from his house at No 4, Charles Street, Covent Garden (to which he had returned for his last days) and buried privately at Cowley Church, near Uxbridge, on the morning of 17 May 1733. His corpse was attended by Colonel John Mercer and his son Captain John Mercer as relations, and John Cook, James Wallace, John High-

more, Richard Glover, Alexander Small, and Samuel Wrexham. Oddly, Colley Cibber, who was a neighbor at No 3, Charles Street, and a long-time colleague, was not among the pallbearers.

Booth had made his will on 2 June 1730 (or, according to Victor, 1731, with whom details of the will would agree). To his father's old servant Christian Hannah he left £5, and to his wife Hester he bequeathed everything else. Booth felt it necessary to explain to his relatives why he had excluded them:

I have considered my Circumstances, and finding, upon a strict Examination, that all I am now possessed of, does not amount to two Thirds of the Fortune my said Wife brought me on the Day of our Marriage, together with the yearly Additions and Advantages, since arising from her laborious Employment on the Stage, during twelve Years past; I thought myself bound by Honesty, Honour, and Gratitude due to her constant Affection, not to give away any Part of the Remainder of her Fortune at my Death, having already bestow'd in free Gifts upon my Sister, BARBARA ROGERS, upwards of 1300 *l. out of my Wife's Substance*, and full 400 *l.* of her mony upon my undeserving Brother, GEORGE BOOTH, (besides the Gifts they received before my Marriage) and all these Benefits were conferred on my said Brother and Sister, from time to time, at the earnest Solicitation of my Wife, who was perpetually intreating me to continue the Allowances I gave my Relations before my Marriage. The inhuman Return that has been made my Wife for these Obligations by my Sister, I forbear to mention.

Victor emphasized the actor's support of his family. His father had been a spendthrift and left little to his survivors; Barton undertook the support of his mother, provided handsomely for his ungrateful sister, lent his brothers large sums and put them in "genteel ways of Business," and made a dresser at the theatre of one of his brother's two daughters. Booth had thirsted for fame and fortune, but he had nevertheless been generous with what he had gained.

Hester Booth proved her husband's will on 11 May 1733, retired from the stage, and disappeared from public notice. After providing him with a monument in Westminster Abbey in 1772, she died, about 15 January 1773.

Victor described Booth as being "of middle Stature, five Feet eight, his Form inclined to the athletic, though nothing clumsey or heavy." He is said to have had large muscles and a ruddy, round face. "His Air and Deportment [were] naturally graceful; he had a marking Eye, and a manly Sweetness in his Countenance. . . . His Voice was compleatly harmonious, from the Softness of the Flute to the Extent of the Trumpet" and his "Attitudes were all picturesque; he was noble in his Designs, and happy in his Execution."

Cibber felt that Booth had not "that Conscious Aspect of Intelligence nor requisite Variation of Voice" that gave Betterton's performances their natural air. This led to an excess of gravity, and, despite his occasional bursts of fire, Booth lacked the kind of excitement that exemplified Wilk's acting. Cibber thought Booth "seem'd too much to heave up his Words" and had "too solemn a Regard to Harmony," yet Cibber liked his full, strong voice and, paradoxically, thought Booth excelled in "the more Turbulent Transports of the Heart."

Though Cibber seems contradictory, apparently Booth was an odd combination of fire and ice. "Patrick Fitz-Crambo," in *Tyranny Triumphant* (1743), praised Booth's combination of fine voice, noble and graceful action, and great judgment, yet cited his fire as Hotspur, his dignity as Brutus, and his gravity as Cato. The airy quality that marked Wilk's comedy was not in Booth, so he was best at the more sober roles like Pinchwife, and his classical scholarship well served dignified parts like Cato; but his roughness and his solid physique were suited to the more volatile roles like Hotspur, Othello, and Lear.

Aaron Hill wrote a perceptive analysis of Booth in one of his letters:

Two advantages distinguish'd him, in the strongest light, from the rest of his fraternity. He had *learning*, to understand perfectly whatever it was his part to speak; and judgment to know, how far it agreed, or disagreed, with the character. Hence, arose a peculiar *grace*, which was visible to every spectator, tho' few were at the pains of examining into the *cause* of their pleasure: he could soften, and slide over, with a kind of elegant negligence, the *improprieties*, in a part he acted, while on the contrary, he would dwell, with energy, upon the *beauties*, as if he exerted a latent spirit, which had been kept back for such an occasion, that he might alarm, awaken, and transport, in those places only, where the *dignity* of his own *good-sense* could be *supported*, by that of his *author*.

A LITTLE reflection, upon this remarkable quality, will help us to account for that manifest *languor*, which has sometimes, been observ'd in his *action*, and which was generally, tho' I think, *falsely*, imputed to the natural indolence of his temper.

Hill commented that Booth's personality was not excited by comedy:

Like a deep loaden *ship*, he was too heavy for a common breeze, which, therefore, serv'd but to make him *roll* and *heave*: —But, in a *gale*, that threatn'd shipwreck to the cock-boats of the Theatre, he was sure to display his streamers; and sail'd steady and majestic, as if the force of a tempest had just breath enough to move him. . . .

HE had a talent at discovering the passions, where they lay *hid*, in some celebrated parts; having been buried under a prescription of *rantings* and *monotony*, by the practice of other actors: When he had *discover'd*, he soon grew able to *express* 'em. And his secret, by which he attain'd this great lesson of the Theatre, was an association, or adaptation of his *look* to his *voice*; by which artful imitation of *nature*, the variations, in the sound of his words, gave propriety to every change in his countenance. So that, among *Players*, in whom it is common to hear *pity* pronounc'd with a *frown* upon the forehead, sorrow express'd, by a *grin* upon the Eye, and *anger* thunder'd out, with a look of unnatural *serenity*, it was Mr. *Booth's* peculiar felicity, to be *heard*, and *seen* the same; whether as the *pleas'd*, the *griev'd*, the *pitying*, the *reproachful* or the *angry*: one would almost be tempted to borrow the aid of a very bold figure, and to express this excellence the more significantly, beg permission to affirm, that the *blind* might have seen him, in his *voice*, and the *deaf* have *heard* him, in his *visage*.

Almost, Hill said, but not quite. Booth must have had a splendid talent, but something was missing that prevented him from being another Betterton.

Between the lines of many comments is the hint that Booth never quite reconciled the poet and peasant within him. In an adulatory poem on his wife's dancing he himself wrote,

> *Order and Grace together join'd,*
> *Sweetness and Majesty combin'd,*
> *To make the beauteous Form compleat.*

This, perhaps, was what he tried for himself, and sometimes achieved, but even when he succeeded, it was not enough. Cibber tried to put his finger on the problem in discussing Booth's Morat in *Aureng-Zebe*.

There are in this fierce Character so many Sentiments of avow'd Barbarity, Insolence, and Vain-glory, that they blaze even to a ludicrous Lustre, and doubtless the Poet intended those to make his Spectators laugh while they admir'd them; but *Booth* thought it depreciated the Dignity of Tragedy to raise a Smile in any part of it, and therefore cover'd these kind of Sentiments with a scrupulous Coldness and unmov'd Delivery, as if he had fear'd the Audience might take too familiar a notice of them.

Colley noted that "*Booth* seem'd to think nothing valuable that was not tragically

Great or Marvellous" but "having no Taste of Humour himself, he might be too much inclin'd to depreciate the Acting of it in others." Theophilus Cibber also felt Booth went too far in "his Reverence for the Buskin" and wished he had followed "the bold Flights of the Author." The actor's learning may have been a dangerous thing; in his efforts to achieve "the beauteous Form" he may have exercized too much control, rather than not enough.

Cibber had high praise for Booth's voice:

The tones of his voice were all musical, and he had so excellent an ear, no one ever heard a dissonant note come from him. He was not only harmonious, but properly so; while he filled the ear he spoke to the heart; avoiding a monotone, which has been too frequently perceived in some other actors of merit. . . . And his articulation was so excellent, he was heard to the farthest part of the theatre when he almost whispered.

Further,

He had the deportment of a nobleman, and so well became a Star and Garter, he seemed born to it; and would have made as good a figure in the drawing-room as on the stage. His countenance had a manly sweetness, so happily formed for expression, that he could mark every passion with a strength to reach the eye of the most distant spectator, without losing that comeliness which charmed those who sat near him.

Despite the occasional references to his fiery spirit when acting a role like Hotspur, most of the commentary on Booth runs in this vein, emphasizing his ability to create majesty on stage.

Victor, describing Booth as Pyrrhus, noted:

His entrance—his walking and mounting to the throne—his sitting down—his manner of giving his answer to the ambassador—his rising from the throne—his descending and leaving the stage—though circumstances of a very common nature in theatrical performances, yet were executed by him with a grandeur not to be described.

Macklin, according to Cooke, was similarly struck by this same scene; at one performance, just as Macklin was going into the pit,

Booth was making his approach to the throne; which struck [Macklin] so powerfully, from the grandeur and dignity of his manner, that he thought himself in the royal presence: but where he came to that line,

Am I, am I the last of all the scepter'd heroes, he repeated it so awfully impressive, and accompanied it with such an air of majesty, that [Macklin] stood fixt with amazement; nor could he take his seat till Pyrrhus left the audience chamber.

Booth's style left its imprint on actors who followed him—especially James Quin. But majesty was not enough; Betterton had gone beyond that, and so would David Garrick. What Booth seemed to be afraid of putting into his acting was humanity; but this was perhaps typical of the transitional period between Betterton and Garrick, which Barton Booth, as the leading tragic actor of his time, exemplified.

In addition to his masque, *The Death of Dido,* Booth wrote an afterpiece, *The Burgomaster Tricked,* which was performed at the Haymarket Theatre on 12 January 1734 with music by Arne. He also wrote some good imitations of Horace, a few songs, and a handful of poems, two of which concerned Hester Booth and are quoted in her entry.

A caricature of Booth, Wilks, and Cibber, showing them in Newgate and titled "A Just View of the British Stage," was drawn by William Hogarth in 1724. Engravings of Booth as Brutus were made by T. Wageman and J. Rogers and by W. Evans. Other engravings of the actor were done by J. Vanderbank and G. van der Gucht, G. White (mezzotint), G. Clint and E. Smith, and W. Evans, J. Storer drew and engraved a view of the monument erected in Booth's memory by his widow in 1772 at Westminster Abbey. The Garrick Club has John Vanderbank's painting of Booth, as well as a full-length portrait by an unknown hand, titled "Booth," which was probably done after the actor's death.

Booth, Mrs Barton the second, Hester, née Santlow   *c. 1690–1773, dancer, actress.*

Hester Santlow's origins are not known, the approximate time of her birth (c. 1690) is conjectural, and one cannot even be certain how her name was spelled: St Lo, St Loe, St Low, Saintlow, Sandlow, Santlow, or Shantlow. It was probably around 1704 that she became a student of the dancing master Cherrier; and apparently about 1706 the two drew up a contract splitting equally between them her income from dancing. On 28 February 1706 at Drury Lane she made her first stage appearance, dancing with her master-agent some new pieces composed by him. She danced for the rest of the season and received a solo benefit on 16 April. She continued to be billed as Miss Santlow until about 1711, after which the billing changed to "Mrs"—suggesting that she had just reached her majority and thus had been born about 1690. Winston noted that she was "upwards of 90" in 1772, but this would place her birthdate in the early 1680's and would not fit with the other facts.

Though she was infrequently named in the bills for the next several seasons, she seems to have appeared regularly in dances after the plays. In January 1708 she switched her engagement to the new Queen's Theatre in the Haymarket and began dancing there on 21 February at a salary of £1 3s. 4d. weekly (the accounts, surely in error, list this fee as *per diem*). She stayed at the Queen's through the end of the 1708–9 season, receiving a benefit

HESTER BOOTH
engraved by R. B. Parkes, after Kneller?

on 12 April 1709, after which she returned to Drury Lane.

Though she continued her dancing career for many more years, in the fall of 1709 she also began acting. For her debut on 3 December she chose Prue in *Love for Love*; on the seventeenth she played Corinna in *The Confederacy*; and on 14 February 1710 she acted Ophelia in *Hamlet*. It was not her Ophelia that attracted attention, however, but her Dorcas, the leading role in *The Fair Quaker of Deal*, which she filled at the premier performance on 25 February. Colley Cibber did not think much of the play, but he later wrote that Miss Santlow's person

was then in the full Bloom of what Beauty she might pretend to: Before this she had only been admired as the most excellent Dancer, which might not a little contribute to the favourable Reception she now met

with as an Actress, in this Character which so happily suited her Figure and Capacity: The gentle Softness of her Voice, the composed Innocence of her Aspect, the Modesty of her Dress, the reserv'd Decency of her Gesture, and the Simplicity of the Sentiments that naturally fell from her, made her seem the amiable Maid she represented.

The same role brought praise from von Uffenbach (*London in 1710*), who saw her on 13 June 1710 (an otherwise unrecorded performance); he called her "a person well known throughout England . . . She is universally admired for her beauty, matchless figure and the unusual elegance of her dancing and acting, and she is visited by those of the highest fashion in England." For a young woman of about 20, Hester Santlow had made astounding progress.

During the next two seasons she danced occasionally but concentrated on her acting career. Some of her new roles were Lady Percy in *1 Henry IV* (2 December 1710), Gatty in *She Would If She Could* (21 December), Meriel in *The Jovial Crew* (19 January 1711), Harriet in *The Man of Mode* (22 February), and Flora in *Hob* (6 October 1711). She played Flora again on 23 September 1712 just as the new season was beginning at Drury Lane, and then her name suddenly disappeared from the bills for a year. It is very likely that during this interim she gave birth to a child by her lover James Craggs.

Craggs was perhaps one of "those of the highest fashion in England" who visited Hester when she blossomed into an actress. In 1712 he was 26, and within the next six years he was to become a member of the House of Commons, Secretary of War, and finally Secretary of State. Gay called him "Bold, generous Craggs" and Pope said he had "A Soul as full of Worth, as void of Pride, / Which nothing seeks to show, or needs to hide." He was personable, gallant, handsome, and a favorite with the ladies, yet he never married. Cibber later told a story (without naming names) of an incident that took place about this time and involved Hester Santlow, a Captain Montague, and Craggs.

Hester was sitting in an upper box at the King's Theatre watching a performance when Captain Montague tried to strike up a conversation with her. She was indifferent; he was abusive. When she next appeared on stage at Drury Lane, Montague was in the audience, mocking her and finally throwing trash at her. Craggs was watching the performance from backstage, came to her rescue, called Montague a bully, and accepted the Captain's demand for satisfaction. A duel was fought at Hyde Park the next morning, and Montague had to beg for his life.

(The issue of the affair between Craggs and Hester Santlow was undoubtedly Harriet, Cragg's natural daughter, who was born in 1712. Harriet married Richard Eliot at an early age and had by him nine children, one of whom, Edward, was created Baron Eliot of St German's in 1784; and another, their fifth, was named Hester. After Richard Eliot's death Harriet married the Honourable John Hamilton and had a son by him who became the second viscount and first marquis of Abercorn. Harriet died in 1769, a few years before her mother.)

Hester Santlow, either before or after (or possibly even during) her affair with Craggs, seems also to have had a liaison with the Duke of Marlborough. Contemporary gossip about 1712 had it that Craggs was Marlborough's procurer of both money and women, and there is the possibility that at some point Craggs supplied the Duke with Hester Santlow; after Craggs became Secretary of State in 1718 the Duchess of Marlborough accused him of some unspecified impertinence back in 1712, and this may have been it. In any case, when John Galt, in 1831, described Hester as "celebrated for her beauty, her money, her jewels and her incontinency," he may not have been far from the mark.

When Hester Santlow reappeared at Drury Lane for the 1713–14 season, she reassumed her old roles and dancing chores. Over the next few seasons she expanded her repertory to include Cordelia in *King Lear*, Alithea in *The Country Wife*, Desdemona in *Othello*, Celia in *Volpone*, and a number of less familiar roles of the same type: whether in comedy or tragedy, her line was innocent young women. She began to dance more frequently now that her acting career was solidified, and she apparently worked out an arrangement with the managers of Drury Lane to permit her to perform on occasion at the King's (formerly the Queen's) Theatre in the Haymarket where operas were given. On 4 and 11 December 1714, for example, she danced at the King's, and, in between, on the ninth, she played Cordelia at Drury Lane. It may have been her requests to be allowed to do this that led the Drury Lane managers to provide more dancing opportunities for her, and on 2 March 1717 they produced *The Loves of Mars and Venus*, probably choreographed by John Weaver, with Hester as Venus. By the 1718–19 season she was dividing her time equally between acting and dancing at Drury Lane, and in April and May 1719 she danced almost exclusively.

By this time her affair with Craggs (and /or the Duke of Marlborough) seems to have ended, and she turned her attention to an actor with whom she had worked for 10 years, Barton Booth. Coincidentally, Booth had shed his mistress, the actress Susan Mountfort, in 1718 and had become so enamoured of Hester Santlow that he proposed marriage. The story goes that when Susan heard of this, furious with jealousy she barged onstage when Hester was playing Ophelia and had to be forcibly taken home. She died, insane, two years later.

Booth was ridiculed for considering marriage with Hester Santlow. She was called a strumpet by some, and his friends assured him that such a match could never work. The *Theatrick Squabble* in 1733 contained a poem on Hester, reflecting on her earlier years:

My little Lady's *Choler does so rise*
That, could she reach, she'd tear out all
*   their Eyes:*
Continual Scandal does her Mind so
*   rack,*
She'll Empty all the Venom—on her
*   Back.*

But by 1719 Booth was about 38 and Hester about 29; they had both sewn their wild oats and were perhaps ready to settle down. On 31 July 1719 they were married, and to everyone's surprise, the match turned out to be a remarkably happy one. Later Booth wrote a tender poem on their marriage:

Happy the hour when first our Souls
*   were joined!*
The social virtues and the cheerful
*   mind*
Have ever crowned our days, beguiled
*   our pain;*
Strangers to discord and her clamorous
*   train*
Connubial friendship, hail!

The Booths could easily have retired from the frantic life of the theatre, for as the leading tragedian and one of the managers of Drury Lane Booth was certainly well off, and Hester, for her part, was wealthy and brought Booth a small fortune as her dowry. But they had both been and continued to be extremely hard workers who took their careers seriously. After the summer of 1719 they returned to the theatre and continued their arduous schedules. During the 1720's Mrs Booth took on some new roles, such as Aspatia in *The Maid's Tragedy* and Lucinda in *The Conscious Lovers*, and kept a number of old parts that must have been her favorites: Ophelia, Cordelia, Harriet, Celia, Dorcas, and Lady

Percy. About a third of her time was now spent as a dancer, sometimes in specialty dances such as *Hussar, Country Lads and Lasses*, and *Harlequins* which she did with Shaw, and sometimes in pantomimes such as *The Escapes of Harlequin* in which she danced the Harlequin Woman. Frequently she would act a role and present a specialty dance as well, especially at her benefits. The only respite seems to have been in the summers when neither she nor Booth usually performed and when, perhaps, they relaxed at Booth's country home in Cowley.

In the fall of 1726 Booth's health started failing, and though he continued acting when he could, he reduced his work schedule drastically, and on 9 January 1728 gave his last performance. During these years Mrs Booth kept performing with remarkable regularity, but she, too, by 1728 was beginning to lose ground. *Mist's Weekly Journal* on 2 March wrote that "To the soft Flute B—th trips in vain, / Nor longer draws the applauding Throng."

The Booths went to Bath on 11 April 1728 for 11 weeks, hoping that the waters might help the ailing actor; the next month Mrs Booth must have returned to London —or perhaps she commuted—for she performed at Drury Lane on 1, 10, and 20 May. It was probably in the summer of 1728 that the pair went to Holland to consult the specialist Dr Boerhaave, but this trip proved no more helpful to Booth than had the one to Bath. Back in London, Mrs Booth was able to continue performing fairly regularly from 1728–29 through 1732–33. In 1731 the couple took Lady Mansell's house in Hampstead, but at some point before Booth's death they returned to No 4, Charles Street, Covent Garden. Booth spent the last half of 1732 in almost constant pain, and all his wife could do was stand by and watch a series of doctors attempt various cruel cures which proved useless.

The *Daily Post* for 25 January 1733 reported that "Mrs Booth has been very ill but is recovered"—possibly an error for Barton Booth, though Hester may well have collapsed momentarily under the strain. On 6 February 1733 she played Helen in *The Judgment of Paris*, her last recorded role at Drury Lane. A course of mercury recommended by a quack doctor made Booth even more miserable, and Mrs Booth called in Dr Hans Sloane in a last effort to save her husband's life, but it was too late. On 10 May 1733 Booth died, and a week later he was buried at Cowley.

Booth's will, proved on 11 May, left virtually everything to his wife. In it he noted honestly that most of what he possessed had been brought to him by Hester when they married and that he did not want to give any of what remained to his ungrateful brother and sister. He stated that he had given them considerable amounts over the years at Hester's urging, yet Booth's sister Barbara Rogers had been "inhuman" in her treatment of Mrs Booth.

Booth had sold half of his share in Drury Lane in July 1732, and after his death Mrs Booth sold the other half to Henry Giffard of the Goodman's Fields Theatre, apparently with the odd stipulation that it not be resold to the actors. On 22 September 1733 the *Universal Spectator* reported that she had resolved to leave the stage. The Mrs Booth who did a comic dance on 4 September 1733 at the Cibber-Griffin-Bullock-Hallam booth at Bartholomew Fair may have been Hester (or possibly the Mrs Booth who flourished 1740–41); if she was Mrs Barton Booth, this was a sad conclusion to her stage career.

Just as Mrs Booth's early life is a virtual blank, so are her years after her husband's death. In William "Gentleman" Smith's letters is his recollection of her about 1755 coming backstage at the theatre to see the "Young *Gentleman*." And on 24 September 1772 she had a memorial to her husband erected in Westminster Abbey. Granger reported that "Soon after it was put up, attended by some friends, Mrs. Booth went

to look at it; and after considering it for some time, with attention and considerable emotion, she returned back to her house, from which she never went out any more, but died shortly after at a very advanced age." On 15 January 1773 (other sources say 21 or 31 January) Hester Santlow Booth died at her house in Great Russell Street at about 83; she was buried beside her husband at Cowley on 21 January—a date which, if correct, would make the 15th her proper death date.

Mrs Booth had made her will on 2 February 1769, and it was proved on 3 March 1773. She described herself as of Great Russell Street in the parish of St George, Bloomsbury, and asked to be buried beside the remains of her mother and her husband. Her mother, therefore, may have been from Cowley, as were the Booths, or she may simply have moved there after Barton and Hester married. To Elizabeth Lally, widow of the dancer Michael, she left a diamond ring, and to Mrs Frances Perrin she bequeathed another. To Benjamin Victor, who wrote the most detailed early biography of her husband, she bequeathed 50 guineas, describing him as of Maiden Lane, Covent Garden. Two Mrs Blakes, sisters, of Great Russell Street were to receive £5 each, and £20 was to go to Mrs Booth's agent, Mr Beruda(?) of Southampton Row. To her servant Ann Evans she left £50; to Annabella, wife of Thomas Plukenet, £100; to her former servant Margaret Dobson £10; and to her current servants £5 each, plus a £20 annuity for Thomas Child.

Mrs Booth's other bequests concerned her deceased daughter Harriet's offspring. The Honourable Harriet Hamilton had died in 1769, probably shortly before Mrs Booth made her will; by her two husbands, Richard Eliot and John Hamilton, she had apparently had eleven children. Harriet outlived both husbands and was described in Mrs Booth's will as late of Wigmore Street, Cavendish Square, widow, deceased.

The will does not always distinguish between the Eliots and the Hamiltons, but it would appear that in 1769 five children of Richard and Harriet Eliot were still living: Elizabeth (then Mrs Charles Cooke), Edward, Harriet (then Mrs Pendock Neale), John, and Catherine. The two children of Harriet's marriage with John Hamilton were still alive: John and Ann, then apparently Mrs Bonfoy and the mother of a daughter named Ann—Mrs Booth's only great-grandchild.

To Edward Eliot, of Port Eliot, Cornwall, Mrs Booth left most of her pictures, but one of herself and one of Barton Booth she bequeathed to Charles Cooke. To Elizabeth Cooke she left £200, and to Edward Eliot's wife she bequeathed 20 guineas. She asked that her executors, Edward Eliot and Samuel Salt of the Inner Temple, call in and sell all her property and invest the income in government securities in trust for four of her grandchildren: one fourth for Harriet Neale and the other three-fourths for John Eliot, Governor of West Florida, Ann Bonfoy of Wimpole Street, and Catherine Eliot. Mrs Booth stated that she hoped Edward Eliot and Elizabeth Cooke would not impute any disparity in the will to any inequality in her affection for the five Eliot offspring, for she loved all of them equally, she said, but felt the fortunes of Edward and Elizabeth were already better advanced than those of the other children.

To John Hamilton she left 20 guineas; to Ann Bonfoy she left her tea service (plus the share in the trust noted above); and to Ann's daughter Miss Ann Bonfoy she left 20 guineas.

Though Hester Santlow Booth played some very important roles during her career, and kept them over many years, she seems not to have been a very extraordinary actress. Davies felt that "Mrs Booth's figure, voice, and deportment, for [Ophelia], raised in the minds of the spectators, an amiable picture of an innocent, unhappy maid: but she went no farther." In a letter to Dr Cranston dated 3 April 1725 the young poet James Thomson wrote that "Mrs. Booth acts some things very well, and particularly Ophelia's madness in Hamlet inimitably; but then she dances so deliciously, has such melting lascivious motions, airs and postures, as, indeed according to what you suspect, almost throws the material part of me into action too." It was her dancing, not her acting, that excited her contemporaries.

Theophilus Cibber found "the celebrated Mrs. *Hester Santlow* . . . a beautiful Woman, lovely in her Countenance, delicate in her Form, a pleasing *Actress*, and a most admirable *Dancer*; generally allowed, in the last-mentioned part of her Profession, to have been superior to all who had been seen before her, and perhaps she has not been since excelled."

The dancer John Essex, in the preface to his translation of Rameau's *The Dancing Master*, was even more enthusiastic:

WE HAVE had a great many Women attempt to be theatrical dancers, but no one ever arrived to that Height and Pitch of Applause as the incomparable Mrs. Booth, in whom Art and Nature are so beautifully wove together, that the Whole Web is of a Piece so exquisitely formed to Length and Breadth, that the Produce of the many different Characters she represents is the Wonder and Admiration of the present Age, and will scarce be credited by the Succeeding. I shall beg leave to mention the Chaconne, Saraband, Menuet, in all of which she appears with the Grace, Softness, and Address none can look on but with Attention, Pleasure, and Surprise. She far excells all that went before her and must be the just Subject of Imitation to all that dare attempt to copy her.

Gay called her "Santlow famed for dance," and in 1732 the *Comedian* felt that she "has not an equal in England, nor perhaps in the World; the easy and genteel Air which appears in the Variety of her Steps, and her every other Motion, is easyer conceived than described."

The father of English pantomime, John Weaver, said "Art and Nature have combin'd to produce a beautiful Figure, allow'd by all Judges in our Art to be the most graceful, most agreeable, the most correct Performer in the World." And though she may have had a fairly narrow line in acting, she was apparently excellent in all the categories of dancing described by Weaver: the serious, the grotesque and the "scenical."

But the last praise should properly come from Barton Booth, who wrote "On Mira Dancing," a tribute to his beloved Hester:

*She comes! The God of Love asserts his
   Reign,
Resistless o'er the gazing Throng!
Alone she fills the spacious Scene!
The Charm of ev'ry Eye! The Praise of
   ev'ry Tongue!*

*Order and Grace together join'd,
Sweetness and Majesty combin'd,
To make the beauteous Form compleat.
On ev'ry Step and Motion wait.*

*Now to a slow and melting air she
   moves!
Her eyes their Softness steal from
   Venus' Doves!
So like in Shape, in Air, and Mien,
She passes for the Paphian Queen!
The Graces all around her play; the
   wondering Gazers die away.*

*But now the flying Fingers strike the
   Lyre!
The sprightlier Notes the Nymph in-
   spire!
She whirls around! She bounds! She
   springs!
As if Jove's messenger had lent her
   Wings!*

*Such Daphne was, when near old
   Peneus' Stream
She fled to shun a loath'd Embrace!
(Of antient Bards the frequent theme)
Such were her lovely limbs, so flush'd
   her Charming face!*

*So round her Neck, her Eyes so fair!
So rose her swelling Chest, so flow'd her
   Amber Hair!
While her swift Feet outstripp'd the
   Wind,
And left th'enamour'd God of Day
   behind.*

*While the light footed Fairy flies,
Our mounting Spirits nimbly rise!
The Pulse still answers to the strains,
And the Blood dances in our Veins.*

In the Penicuik House collection is a painting by Kneller of a Mrs Booth, probably Hester, and an engraving of her was made by R. B. Parkes.

Booth, Charles *[fl. 1660?–1682?], prompter.*

John Downes, who served as prompter for the Duke's Company during the Restoration period, identified the rival King's Company prompter as Charles Booth. How early Booth began working with Thomas Killigrew's players and when his tenure ended is not known; it is possible he was with the King's troupe when it organized in 1660, and since Downes was prompter for the United Company that formed when the rival groups merged in 1682, perhaps Booth ended his service at that time. The Lord Chamberlain's accounts, which frequently name theatre personnel, contain no reference to Booth.

Booth, Cockran Joseph *d. 1789, actor, singer.*

Cockran Joseph Booth may have been acting as early as 1762 in *The Orators* for Foote at the Haymarket. He may also have been the Booth who performed very minor roles at Drury Lane between 1768 and 1771 and the Booth who played Hamlet on 2 March 1771 at the new theatre at Stratford and appeared in 11 more plays there that summer. Cockran Joseph Booth was certainly the Booth who, with J. Kennedy, leased the new Barton Street Theatre at Gloucester for the summer of 1772.

Harvard Theatre Collection

COCKRAN JOSEPH BOOTH as Lord Froth
by Roberts

Again with Kennedy, Booth brought a strolling company to play at Cooper's Hall, next to the Bristol Theatre on King Street, in November 1772. They advertised "A Concert of Music with Specimens of Rhetorick," but they were informed against and fined a total of £200 on four charges of illegal playing. Almost immediately, nevertheless, they resumed playing at Bristol and continued until April 1773. Booth and Kennedy then took the company to act at the Richmond theatre, which was under their management in the summer of 1773, and returned it to Bristol about October, remaining there until the company dissolved about February 1774. Booth, however, returned alone to Bristol in the next summer, where on 20 June 1774 he played Stukely in *The Gamester*.

C. J. Booth made his first appearance at Covent Garden on 4 October 1774 as Po-

lyperchon in *Alexander the Great*. Before the season was over he had played at least ten additional roles, no doubt supported in this task by his provincial experience. These included Stockwell in *The West Indian*, Paris in *Romeo and Juliet*, Buckingham in *Richard III*, Salisbury in *King Henry II, or, The Fall of Rosamond*, the officer in *The Grecian Daughter*, Patrico in *The Jovial Crew*, Don Luis in *She Wou'd and She Wou'd Not*, Don John in *Much Ado About Nothing*, Teramenes in *Cleonice*, Blunt in *1 Henry IV* and Cloten in *Cymbeline*. On 27 May 1775 he shared tickets with some house servants and minor actors. In *Miscellanies in Prose and Verse*, written during this season, William Hawkins referred to Booth as an "inferior" actor.

Booth was re-engaged at Covent Garden for 1775–76 and his wife was now a member of the company. Among other roles this season he played Harry Bevil in *Cross Purposes*, Barberino in *A Duke and No Duke*, and Bull in *The Man of Quality*. He was then to remain at that theatre for the next 13 years. Through 1786–87, he received £3 per week; in 1787–88 he was advanced to £4, and in 1788–89, his last season, to £5.

In the summer of 1777 Booth played at Liverpool for £2 per week. He was also announced as one of the group of actors from Covent Garden which was to be taken by Harris to perform for eight weeks at Paris in the summer of 1784, but we do not know if they went. When Wild broke his leg in 1784–85, Booth also took his place as prompter at Covent Garden, and upon Wild's return to service Booth continued as his assistant. He played at the Haymarket in the summer of 1785 and 1786. Booth also appeared twice at Drury Lane: on 5 April 1780 he performed Joseph Surface in *The School for Scandal* for Miss Farren's benefit, and in the following week, on 11 April, he performed Granger in *Who's the Dupe?* for Mrs Wrighten's benefit.

Booth's line was mainly that of older character men in comedy. In addition to the roles already mentioned, he frequently played Le Beau and Duke Senior in *As You Like It*, Fluellen in *Henry V*, the Irishman in *Rosina,* O'Cutter in *The Jealous Wife*, Captain Bygrove in *Know Your Own Mind*, Boniface in *The Beaux' Stratagem*, Sir John Bull in *Fontainbleau*, and Father Luke in *The Poor Soldier*. His last performance on the London stage was as Colonel Heavyside in *The Pharo Table* on 13 April 1789 at Covent Garden.

At the beginning of his career at Covent Garden, Booth lived at No 35, Brownlow Street, Long Acre, where he remained at least until May 1781. By April 1785 he was living at No 22, Great Queen Street, in Lincoln's Inn Fields. In the next year he moved to No 18, Broad Court, Bow Street, Long Acre. From that address on 3 June

Courtesy of the Garrick Club

COCKRAN JOSEPH BOOTH as Father Luke

by R. Dighton

1789 he expressed his regrets to the public that he could not play at his own benefit on that night because of his "long, severe, and still-continuing illness." On 6 July 1789 it was reported in the press that Booth was now dangerously ill, without hopes of recovery. The unfeeling writer for one journal added unkindly, "Whatever may be his loss to society as a man, the Stage would not suffer by his death as an actor."

Cockran Joseph Booth died on 7 July 1789. His obituary notices pronounced him to have been an actor of various talents, and if not an excellent player, "there were but few parts both in tragedy and comedy in which he could not make at least a very respectable figure." He left to his wife and a minor son his one-fourth share in the new Theatre Royal, Margate, which he had purchased in 1787 from Thomas Robson.

A drawing by J. Roberts of Booth as Lord Froth in *The Double Dealer* was engraved by D. Reading for a plate to *Bell's British Theatre*, 1777. A water-color drawing of him as Father Luke in *The Poor Soldier* was done by Robert Dighton and is in the Garrick Club.

Booth, Mrs Cockran Joseph [*fl. 1774–1791*], *actress.*

Mrs Cockran Joseph Booth seems to have begun her career under her husband's provincial management. She was a member of his company of strollers when it played at Cooper's Hall in King Street, Bristol, next to the Bristol Theatre, from November 1772 to April 1773. The company then went to play at the theatre in Richmond, which Booth and Kennedy managed in the summer season of 1773, but returned to Bristol about October to resume playing in King Street until February 1774. Mrs Booth played again at Bristol in 1775.

Mrs Booth made her first appearance in London at Covent Garden on 4 November 1776 in the role of Isabella in *The Conscious Lovers*. No doubt she had been in

London the year before, for her husband became a member of the Covent Garden company in 1775–76 but apparently she was not acting. Mrs Booth next essayed the role of Mrs Fulmer in *The West Indian* on 5 February 1777, and that of Mrs Olive in *The Device* on 5 May 1777. After this single season, apparently, she never again played at London, despite the fact that her husband continued in his career there until his death on 7 July 1789. About a year after his death, Mrs Booth shared tickets with some minor functionaries at Covent Garden on 8 June 1790, but there is no evidence that she was then serving the theatre in any capacity.

By her husband's will, Mrs Booth received a 25% share in the Theater Royal, Margate. As the executrix of his will, she also became responsible for his debts which she managed to liquidate, except for about £100. According to Winston in *The Theatric Tourist*, in order to make up for this deficiency she secured her share in the Margate Theatre to Wilmot Wells, until "her son should become of age, and capable of claiming his father's legacy," in exchange for the £100 and a promise of marriage from him. Wells forgot the promise, which was apparently verbal and not part of the written bond, and then dismissed Mrs Booth, who was then a performer in the company, from her engagement at Margate. She never performed again.

She and her husband were not the Mrs and Mr Booth who acted in Belfast in the 1770's, for they were engaged at London on some of the same dates. She seems also not to have been the Mrs Booth, the Irish actress, who in 1790 began to act in Dublin as Mrs Mason.

According to Mrs Inchbald's *Memoirs*, Mrs Cockran Joseph Booth died before 1797.

Booth, John *d. 1779, performer?*

A John Booth subscribed 10*s.* 6*d.* to the Drury Lane Theatrical Fund in 1776.

According to James Winston's notation on the Fund Book, Booth died in August 1779. Possibly he was the John Booth, the Drury Lane tailor, to whom Mrs Ursula Agnes Booth, the actress, was married, but more likely he was her father-in-law. Also he may have been one (or all) of the Booths carried on the bills of various London theatres in the 1760's.

Booth, John [*fl.* 1780–1796], *tailor.*

John Booth was a tailor at Drury Lane Theatre from at least 1780 through 1796. During most of this period his salary was £1 16*s.* per week, but in 1791–92 it was raised to £2 per week. Most likely it was this John Booth who was married to the actress Mrs Ursula Agnes Booth, who died in 1803. He would, then, have been the father of Elizabeth Field and the grandfather of her children by both Dr Granger and William Wallack. No doubt he was the son of the John Booth of Drury Lane, who died in 1779.

Booth, Mrs John, Ursula Agnes *1740–1803, actress, singer.*

Ursula Anne Booth was born in 1740, according to a notation in the Drury Lane Fund Book, which in 1797 put her age at 57. She first was noticed in the Covent Garden bills on 1 November 1775 when she played the servant Lucy in *The Rivals*. On 3 November she played Laura in *The Man's the Master* and on 4 November Miss Mechlin in *The Commissary*. On 15 May 1776 she played Lady Constant in *The Way to Keep Him*. After this season at Covent Garden she moved over to Drury Lane in 1776–77 where she would remain for 20 years. Mrs Booth made her first billed appearance there singing in *Macbeth* on 25 November 1776. She filled a vocal part in *Harlequin's Invasion* on 1 January 1777 and was one of the chorus of spirits in *The Tempest* on 4 January 1777. Throughout the rest of her career she continued to play third-line and very minor characters and to sing unnamed vocal parts in the entertainments and pantomimes. Such roles included the Duchess of York in *Richard III*, Madge in *The Gentle Shepherd*, Mrs Sagely in *The Heiress*, Audrey in *As You Like It*, Miss Bridget in *All the World's a Stage*, Maud in *The Haunted Tower*, the Lady in the Balcony in *The Manager in Distress*, and characters in *The Hurly-Burly* and *The Caldron*.

During the last decade of her career, although she continued to appear occasionally in the choruses and crowds, she limited herself almost wholly to the line of older inferior women such as the nurses in *The Chances* and *Love for Love*, the landladies in *Harlequin Captive* and *The Prisoner at Large*, Old Colombine in *Harlequin Junior*, Mrs Maggs in *The London Hermit*, Curtis in *Catherine and Petruchio*, and Mrs Caddy in *The Prize*. On 8 May 1794 she played the character of Jabal in the first performance of Cumberland's *The Jew*. In the *Druriad* of 1798, the author alluded to Mrs Booth as "the ancient crone" who was always there to "Lead in the queen, or stand behind the throne." The author of *Candid and Impartial Strictures* in 1795 referred to her as "A very useful piece of theatrical antiquity."

Mrs Booth's salary at Drury Lane was £1 per week until 1789–90 when it was raised to £2, and it remained at that figure for the rest of her time there. In May 1780 she was living at No 10, corner of Martlett Court, in Bow Street, Covent Garden. By May 1781 she was at No 8, Broad Court, Longacre, and in 1794 at Duke's Court, in Bow Street. She also acted regularly in summers at the Haymarket in the same line of roles in 1791 and from 1793 to 1797. She perhaps was the Mrs Booth who acted at Birmingham in 1791 and 1792, and she acted at Richmond in 1793.

At the end of the season 1796–97, Mrs Booth was dismissed from Drury Lane and claimed assistance from the Theatrical Fund to which she had first subscribed in 1776. Her last performance at Drury Lane was as Mrs Sagely in *The Heiress* on 16 June 1797. She played that summer at the Haymarket, where she made her final appearance on the London stage as Gradisca in *The Italian Monk* on 14 September 1797.

Her husband, we believe, was not the John Booth who died in 1779 but the John Booth who was a tailor at Drury Lane between 1780 and 1796.

Mrs Booth was the mother of the actress Elizabeth Field who married William Wallack. The Wallacks had at least four children who married people in the profession. Before her marriage to Wallack, however, Elizabeth Field had been married to a Dr Granger. Her daughter by him, Miss Julia Granger, was raised by her grandmother, Mrs Booth. In her enthusiasm for forwarding the interests of her granddaughter, Mrs Booth encouraged her in an affair with the dancing master J. E. Burghall, whose wife was the niece of Mrs Booth's husband. An account of Mrs Booth's duplicity and of Burghall's ultimate separation from his wife, without gaining Miss Granger, was given by the dancing master in a sixteen-page pamphlet entitled *A Statement of Facts* which he published in February 1797. Julia Granger married an actor named Jones in 1800, with whom she went to act at Boston, Massachusetts. By the end of the nineteenth century the two branches of the family tree issuing from Mr and Mrs John Booth through the Wallacks and the Joneses yielded a large number of theatrical people, including the American Wallacks and Simpsons.

According to Winston's notation in the Theatrical Fund Book, Mrs Booth died in August 1803.

Booth, Joseph stage name of Mr Martin *d. 1797, actor, exhibitor.*

"Joseph Booth" was the stage name of a Mr Martin who earlier in life was a hosier at Marsfield, Nottinghamshire. Having neglected his business, he went on the stage, deserted his family, and moved to London, where under the name of Joseph Booth he opened an exhibition of "Polygraphic Paintings." According to his obituary in the *Gentleman's Magazine* for February 1797, he was an "ingenious inventor of the polygraphic art, and of the more important art of manufacturing cloth by a perfectly original process." He died in Cumberland Gardens, Vauxhall, on 25 February 1797.

Joseph Booth's wife, Mrs Martin (née Mallatratt) also acted. She ended her provincial theatrical career of more than 26 years in 1797. Their son, William Martin (1769–1810) became a well-known naturalist, author, and provincial actor. He married a widowed actress, a Mrs Adams, and by her had six children, among them the well-known writer on natural history, William Charles Linnaeus Martin (1798–1864).

Boothby, Mr *[fl. 1735–1736]*, actor.

Though *The London Stage* mistakenly placed Mr Boothby in the New Haymarket company during the summer of 1735, he played at Lincoln's Inn Fields during this period. His first recorded role was Modern Wit in *Squire Basinghall* on 23 July 1735. During August he was Doodle in *The Tragedy of Tragedies*, Granius in *Caius Marius*, Rover in *Bartholomew Fair*, and Crambo in *The Stage Mutineers*.

During the 1735–36 season Boothby acted principally at the Haymarket Theatre, though he began the season doing Belmour in *Jane Shore* on 29 September 1735 at York Buildings. On 13 December at the Haymarket he played Brazen in *The Recruiting Officer*, and among his other roles there in 1735–36 were Petit in *The Inconstant*, Filch in *The Beggar's Opera*, and the Doctor in *The Mock Doctor*.

Latreille recorded that Boothby was in Fielding's *Pasquin* in 1736 at the Haymarket, but *The London Stage*, citing the cast list in the 1736 edition, makes no mention of him.

Bopins. *See* BEAUPINS.

Boquet, Louis-René   *1717–1814, scenery and costume designer, decorator.*

Monsieur Louis-René Boquet, born at Paris in 1717, was by 1748 a costume designer at the Paris Opéra and eventually became one of the leading scenery and costume designers of the century, working for the French court at Versailles, at the Opéra Comique, as well as in many other theatres in Europe. He was especially noted for the costume designs he created for the ballets of Noverre, and it was in this connection that he probably went to London in 1755 with the great choreographer. In preparation for his engagement at Drury Lane in 1755–56, Noverre wrote to Garrick on 7 May 1755 that

The Sieur Boquet wishes to undertake to go to London, to have executed his four décours and have made before his eyes all the costumes necessary to my ballets, have your theatre arranged without a chandelier and, finally, make it the most agreeable in London. He asks for this, for the journey and for his efforts and the supply of his drawings, one hundred and fifty louis, on the condition that you supply him with workmen because his time is precious and he could only remain in London for six weeks.

Since Garrick replied on 24 May with great enthusiasm, it is assumed that Boquet did indeed go to London as planned, to carry out his designs for the scenery and costumes for the tumultuous production of *Les Fêtes Chinoises* in November 1755. *Les Fêtes Chinoises* opened on 8 November; anti-French feeling created such a continuing uproar in the theatre that Garrick was obliged to withdraw the piece after the performance on 18 November, but not before the audience had rioted and had done extensive damage to the theatre. According to a *Lettre écrite de Londre* by someone who was a member of the *corps de ballet* in 1755, Boquet's scenery and costumes for the London production of *Les Fêtes Chinoises* were more superb and magnificent than those created for the brilliant success at Paris. Curiously enough Boquet's scenery seems to have been spared the wrath of the Drury Lane patriots, and Garrick's "fertile judgement and economy" probably brought the settings.to good use four years later in a production of *The Orphan of China*.

After a long and varied theatrical career in Europe, Boquet died at Paris on 7 December 1814. (For an account of his activities on the Continent see the *Enciclopedia dello spettacolo* and Bert States, "Servandoni's Successors at the French Opera," *Theatre Survey*, III [1962].) A son, Pierre-Louis Boquet (1741–c. 1815), also became a chief painter at the Paris Opéra.

Borde. *See* LABORDE.

Bordoni. *See* FAUSTINA.

Borghi, Luigi ₁*fl. 1772–1794₁, violinist, composer, manager.*

A pupil of Pugnani, Luigi Borghi was an esteemed musician, who, according to Grove and van der Straeten, appeared in London as a violinist in 1774 and as a violist in 1777. Borghi seems, however, to have been there even earlier, for it was he who recommended to Giardini, the manager of the Opera, the employment of William Shield in 1772. Also in that year at London, William Napier published *Six Solos for a Violin and Bass* by Borghi.

With others in 1783, Borghi composed *The Celebrated Opera Dances, as perform'd at the King's Theatre . . . 1783 for the Harpsichord, Violin, &c*, which were published in four parts by W. Forster. He also played in the King's Theatre band in 1783–84 and 1784–85. Borghi was among the second violins at the Handel Memorial Concerts in Westminster Abbey and the

Pantheon in May and June of 1784, and he was also second violinist in the quartet which played at Wilhelm Cramer's Professional Concerts. On 1 May 1785, he was recommended for admission to the Royal Society of Musicians. Unfortunately, the papers relating to his recommendation have been lost. He was admitted on 2 July 1785, and the next day a Mr Blake signed the book for him and paid his subscription.

Van der Straeten places Borghi in Berlin in 1788, since a violin concerto bearing the date 24 October 1788 is in the Royal house-library there. But under the leadership of Cramer, in 1790 Borghi played the violin in the orchestra for the London Opera company (which, because of the great fire at the King's Theatre in the previous year, performed at the Haymarket from 7 January to 12 June and from 15 June to 17 July). Borghi was appointed acting manager of the Opera company for the season of 1791 at the Pantheon, and under his care were performed 55 nights of operas and ballets between 17 February and 19 July. Singing in the Pantheon company that season was the soprano Signora Anna Casentini, whom he soon married. In 1794 they lived at No 14, Hanover Street, Hanover Square.

Luigi Borghi's works published at London included: *Sixty-Four Cadences or Solos for the Violin*, about 1790; *Six Duetts for a Violin and Violoncello*, about 1785; *Six Overtures . . . with Hautboys and French Horns*, with a title page engraved by F. Bartolozzi, 1785. *Six sonates à deux violins* were published at Berlin and Amsterdam about 1780. He also wrote a number of canzonets, divertissements and other incidental pieces of instrumental music, and a song, *The Lovely Spring*, which was published at Dublin about 1780.

Borghi, Signora Luigi, Anna, née Casentini ₁*fl. 1790–1797₁, singer.*

As Anna Casentini Signora Borghi was engaged by the King's Theatre as *prima buffa* soprano in the comic operas for 1790–91. She made her first appearance at the Pantheon (where the King's company played that season) on 1 March 1791 as Dorinda in Guglielmi's *La bella pescatrice*. On the next day the *Morning Post* reported that "the new *Buffa* is an elegant and graceful woman. Her voice has uncommon Sweetness, and from the well-managed swell which distinguishes her modulations, we think she is of the School of Pachierotti. She was well received and loudly applauded." *La bella pescatrice* was repeated 21 more times, and during the rest of the season Signora Casentini sang Rachelina in *La molinarella* (10 times) and Guerina in *La locandra* (eight times), the latter opera by Bertati having been "written expressly for this Theatre and the only Opera ever composed by the great Master for an English audience." In the following season at the Pantheon she sang Eurilla in *La pastorella nobile* on 17 December 1791. After the Pantheon burned down on 14 January 1792, the opera company finished its season at the Haymarket, where she sang Ortensia in *Le trame deluse* (seven times), Donna Aurora in *La discordia conjugale* (five times), and again in *La bella pescatrice* (10 times) and *La locandra* (22 times).

Sometime soon after the season of 1791–92 Signora Casentini married the violinist Luigi Borghi, under whose management she had recently worked at the Pantheon. She seems not to have performed in 1792–93, but in 1793–94 she was at the King's Theatre as Signora Borghi, when she sang Carolina in *Il matrimonio segreto* (six times), Giannina in *I contadini bizzarri* (14 times), and again in *La bella pescatrice* (four times). In 1794 she lived with her husband at No 14, Hanover Street, Hanover Square.

Signora Borghi, whom Lord Mount-Edgcumbe described as "a pretty woman and a genteel actress," left the Opera after 1793–94 because her voice was too weak for the very large King's Theatre to which the company had returned. In 1797 she sang in Giovanni Battista Borghi's (not her husband) *Semiramide* at Vienna. She may have been the "Signora Castini" who sang in Sacchini's *L'avaro* at Dublin about 1779.

Bornal, Mr [*fl.* 1796], *puppeteer.*
Speaight lists a Mr Bornal as a puppeteer active at Bartholomew Fair in 1796.

Borne, Constantine [*fl.* 1768], *freak.*
The *Gentleman's Magazine* for May 1768, under its "List of Deaths for 1768," carried the notation: "Constantine Borne, aged 70, formerly shewn as an hermaphrodite."

Borne, Theophilus. *See* BIRD, THEOPHILUS 1608–c. 1663.

Boromeo, Signor [*fl.* 1742–1743], *dancer.*
Signor Boromeo and Signora Costanza danced a *Tyrolean Dance* at Drury Lane on 21 September 1742, billed as making their first appearance on that stage. Where Boromeo had been dancing prior to this is unclear. The performances of Boromeo and the other dancers in the troupe certainly did not appeal to an anonymous actor at Drury Lane that season who found them "long and tedious." He thought the dancers were "great performers but in bad taste and without grace." Boromeo seems not to have risen to stardom during the season; his benefit on 16 May 1743 was shared with two others, and after the 1742–43 season his name disappeared from the London playbills.

Borosini, Francesco *b. c. 1690, singer.*
Francesco Borosini (or Borseni) was the son and student of singer Antonio Borosini. Francesco was born in Modena about 1690. A tenor, he sang at Venice in 1708, was part of the Viennese imperial court music

in 1712, sang at Modena in June 1720, and was a great success at Prague in 1723 when he sang in the coronation opera, *Costanza e fortezza.* In 1724–25 he was in London, but even before the season opened he received unfavorable notices; the *London Journal* of 17 October 1724 said, "We hear there is a new Opera now in Practice . . . called, Tamerlane, the Musick by Mynheer Hendel, and that Signior Borseni, newly arriv'd from Italy, is to sing the Part of the Tyrant Bajazet. N.B. It is commonly reported this Gentleman was never *cut out for a Singer.*"

Tamerlane opened on 31 October 1724 at the King's Theatre in the Haymarket and was followed on 1 December by *Artaserse,* in which Borosini sang the title role. His other parts during the season included Sesto Pompeo in *Giulio Cesare* on 2 January 1725, Grimoaldo in *Rodelinda* on 13 February, Siderme in *Dario* on 10 April, and Vitige in *Elpidia* on 11 May. The Signora "Sorosini" who sang in the last two operas this season was probably not, as some sources have reported, Borosini's wife, but rather Benedetta Sorosina. It was probably after his return to Vienna that Borosini married Rosa (not, as in some sources, Leonora) d'Ambreville, a singer who appeared in several continental cities but not in London.

On 4 November 1746 at the King's Theatre *Annibale in Capua* was performed, and Dr Burney listed a Borosini—presumably the same singer—in the cast. For the rest of the 1746–47 opera season no casts were listed, but Borosini probably remained in London and participated in *Mitridate, Phaeton, Roxana,* and *Bellerophonte.* A Signor Borosini collected *One Hundred Cantici in Italian after the Manner of English Canons and Catches,* published in London about 1747, and this, too, may have been Francesco.

Boroughs. *See* **BURROUGHS** and **BURROWS.**

Borowlaski. *See* **BORUWLASKI.**

Borromeo. *See* **BOROMEO.**

Borroughs or **Borrows.** *See* **BURROUGHS** and **BURROWS.**

Borselli, Fausto [*fl.* 1789–1790], *singer.*

Fausto and Elisabetta Borselli came from Palermo to London to sing at the King's Theatre in the Haymarket from 10 January to 11 July 1789. Their contract was for £190 each and a free shared benefit, but the burning of the playhouse before the end of the season seems to have lost them this opportunity to augment their income. During their initial season Borselli was the first *buffo* and his wife sang serious women's roles. Both singers made their London debuts in *La cosa rara* on 10 January 1789, Fausto singing Lubino and Elisabetta taking the role of Ghita. On 24 March he was Marcone and she Rinuccia in *La villana riconosciuta;* on 9 May he played Cardone and she Lauretta in *La vendemmia;* and on 28 May both had principal roles, unnamed in the bill, in *La buona figliuola.* She sang Erissena in *La generosità d'Alessandro* on 2 June and he was Figaro in *Il barbiere di Siviglia* on 11 June. When the King's Theatre burned to the ground on 17 June, the company moved to Covent Garden to complete the season, but the Borsellis sang no more new roles.

The couple was re-engaged for the next season, this time with Fausto serving as second *buffo.* They were both in *Ninetta* on 7 January 1790, he singing Gianfabrizo and she Mirandolina; in *Li due castellani burlati* on 2 February he was Gradasso and she Carlotta; and in *La villanella rapita* on 27 February he played Pippo and she Giannina. Elisabetta sang Creusa in *L'usurpator innocente* on 6 April; both had major parts in *Gli schiavi per amore* on 27 May; and she sang Ermione in *Andromaca* on 29 May. During this season the opera company played at the Haymarket Theatre until the middle of June 1790 and then moved to Covent Garden for their last few performances.

The critics paid little attention to Signora Borselli, but of her husband the January 1789 issue of the *Biographical and Imperial Magazine* wrote: "Borselli, the new bass, has good qualities in his voice, and appears to be a tolerable musician: as an actor he has also merit; but the excellence of Morelli is not fully supplied in any respect by his substitute."

Borselli, Signora Fausto, Elisabetta [*fl.* 1789–1790], *singer. See* **BORSELLI, FAUSTO.**

Borseni. *See* **BOROSINI.**

Boruwlaski, Joseph *1739–1837, dwarf, guitarist, fiddler.*

The dwarf Joseph Boruwlaski was born, according to his own account, near Halicz, Polish Galicia, in 1739. He had no legal right to the title of Count, by which he styled himself, but he was an untitled member of the Polish nobility. Boruwlaski was one of six children, three of whom were dwarfs. His eldest brother was only 41 inches high; but the second brother, who died in battle at the age of 26, was six feet, four inches tall. One of his sisters, Anastasia, who died aged 20, measured two feet, four inches in stature. Joseph, himself, did not reach quite 39 inches at maturity.

Having been cared for first by the Starostin de Caorlix and then transferred to the patronage of Countess Humiecka, Boruwlaski grew up in a court atmosphere. Both as a member of the nobility and as a curiosity, he was welcomed by royalty throughout Europe, and in his *Memoirs* he relates many of his travels and court visits. In Poland, he married Isabella Barboutan, a lady of normal height, despite the efforts of his patroness to break off the relationship. When the King of Poland gave him a small

pension, Boruwlaski embarked on a career of wandering, made easier by the novelty of his size, which his hosts found entertaining and intriguing. Between 1761 and 1781, he grew about ten inches.

Upon the encouragement of Sir Robert Murray Keith, he traveled to England by way of Presburg, Belgrade, Adrianople, Damascus (where a dangerous illness was cured by a Jewish physician), Astrakan, Lapland, Finland, and through Croatia, Dalmatia, and Germany. He lived mainly upon the proceeds of concerts and the gifts of his acquaintances.

In England, armed with letters of introduction to the Dukes of Gloucester and Cumberland, he was granted an audience with George III. At Blenheim he left a pair of his little shoes for the Duke of Marlborough's cabinet of curiosities. After an at-

Harvard Theatre Collection
JOSEPH BORUWLASKI
by W. Hincks

tempt to provide for his support by a sub-scription failed, Boruwlaski's only means of income were occasional concerts. One such concert was given by him at Gallini's Rooms in London on 13 June 1783 and was attended by Sylas Neville:

This little gentleman, who is not taller than a child of 5 years old & tollerably well-shaped, is a very great natural curiosity. . . . The count is clever & extremely polite & well-bred. During the first act he was in the dress of his own country Polish Russia & then changed to that of a modern fine gentleman. He performed several airs on the guitar with good taste, elevated on a table in front of the orchestra. He was lifted on & off the orchestra & table like a child. Notwithstanding what is said about the regularity of his features &c, his countenance has much of the *Nain* [Fr: dwarf] in it.

In February 1789 Boruwlaski exhibited himself and gave concerts in Edinburgh. He announced his entertainment in the *Edinburgh Advertiser*, 17 February 1789, to be given at No 4, St Andrew's Street, New Town, admission, half-a-crown: "he speaks several languages, plays on various musical instruments, and is no less astonishing for the regularity of his proportions than the liveliness of his conversation."

After a trip to France just before the Revolution, Boruwlaski returned to England and then traveled "through the whole of Ireland, beginning with Cork." It was reported that his appearance at Ballinasloe caused such commotion that the militia had to be turned out. After a plan to go to America was abandoned, in 1800 he received a residence, the Bank's Cottage, near Durham, from the prebendaries of the Cathedral. The charity of his friends enabled him to live out the rest of his life in peace and comfort.

In his *Memoirs*, which he published in both French and English in 1788 (and which he sold for 5s. at his appearances), Boruwlaski spoke little of his family af-

fairs. He had four sons of ordinary size. It is not known when his wife died. Boruwlaski did not occupy the house provided by the Cathedral but lived for nearly the last 30 years of his life in a small cottage on ground that now forms No 12, South Bailey, with the Misses Ebdon, daughters of a violinist. He continued to earn a shilling or two from passing strangers who wanted to see the curiosity, although his pride did not allow him to admit that people paid to see him and he continued in the fiction that visitors merely gave his valet a gratuity for opening the door.

Joseph Boruwlaski died on 5 September 1837 at the age of 98. He was buried near the remains of one of his friends, John Leybourne, deputy-receiver of the Dean and Chapter, in the west end of Durham Cathedral near the doorway leading into the northern tower, and not, as has been usually reported, by the side of his friend Stephen Kemble in the Nine Altars. His grave was marked by his initials J. B., and there is also a monument to his memory in the Church of St Mary in the South Bailey.

A copper plate engraving by W. Hincks which was published as the frontispiece to the first edition of Boruwlaski's *Memoirs* shows the dwarf in regimentals standing before a full-sized woman who holds a child on her lap. The caption reads, "Mysterious Nature! who thy Works shall scan? / Behold a Child in Size, in Sense a Man." In 1924, Mr Charles Drury owned the original water-color sketch by Hincks. The engraving was copied by R. Cooper and published by J. Robbins in 1822. A full-figure portrait of him was done by R. Hancock for the second edition of the *Memoirs* published at Birmingham in 1792. A third edition was published at Durham in 1820 with a frontispiece from a drawing by John Dowman.

In Kay's *Edinburgh Portraits,* there is a picture of Boruwlaski, "taken from life," with Neil Fergusson, an Edinburgh advocate. An oil painting of him by Hastings belongs to the Corporation of the City of Durham. An engraving shows him standing with P. O'Brien, the Irish Giant. Several caricatures of him in the British Museum include: "The Dwarf taking an Airing," which pictures him playing a fiddle and singing, published January 1787 by S. W. Fores; a scene of an "Exhibition at Bullock's Museum of Bonepartes Carriage," in which the Polish Dwarf is shown in a print on the wall of the museum; and T. Rowlandson's drawing in 1786 of "The Polish Dwarf Performing Before the Grand Seignior." In 1862 some scarce portraits of him, autograph letters, and some effects were sold at the auction of the Fillingham Collection. One of Boruwlaski's shoes, five and seven-eighths inches long, and a glove are in the Bristol Philosophical Institution. A full cast of him taken by Joseph Bonomi just before the dwarf's death is in the Museum of Durham University with a suit of clothes, hat, stick, knife and fork, undergarments, shoes, and the violin that belonged to him.

Bosbery. *See* BUSBY, THOMAS.

Boscawen, Mr (fl. 1735), *actor.*
For his benefit at York Buildings on 3 March 1735 a Mr Boscawen acted Macheath in *The Beggar's Opera* and Friendly in *Flora*; the latter role he repeated on 7 April at Southwark at the Great Booth on the Bowling Green. Perhaps Boscawen was the "Boskotin" of 1732.

Bosch, Frederick (fl. 1739–1743), *musician.*
Frederick Bosch was one of the original subscribers to the Royal Society of Musicians on 28 August 1739. He is doubtless the Bosch who shared a benefit with Richter at Hickford's music room on 5 March, and it is probable that he was the Mr Bush who played a violin solo at the Goodman's Fields Theatre on 2 April 1741. On 15 March 1743 Bosch and three others shared a benefit at Lincoln's Inn Fields. The Min-ute Books of the Royal Society of Musicians contain a notation of 6 February 1785 to the effect that Mrs Bosch had recently died; this was presumably Frederick Bosch's wife, though the "Mrs" could be a scribal error for "Mr."

Boschetti, Signora Mengis (fl. 1770–1772), *singer.*
Signora Mengis Boschetti sang Tonina in *Il disertore* on 19 May 1770 at the King's Theatre in the Haymarket, and she was mentioned in the bills again at that theatre on 21 February 1772 when she sang in a concert of vocal and instrumental music. *The London Stage* errs in listing a Boschetti on the 1769–70 season roster for the King's Theatre as a male.

Boschi, Giuseppe Maria (fl. 1710–1728), *singer.*
Giuseppe Boschi (or sometimes, in error, Girolamo Bolschi) was born in Viterbo, and though he became a bass singer of considerable fame, the dates of his birth and death have remained obscure. He sang in the choir at St Mark's in Venice early in his career and may have taken the role of Polifemo in Handel's cantata, *Aci, Galatea e Polifemo* in 1709 at Naples. He and his wife Francesca Vanini-Boschi came to London to sing in 1710 when he was in his prime, though by then her voice was "on the Decay." Boschi's first London appearance was as Artaserse in *Idaspe fedele* at the Queen's Theatre on 22 November 1710. On 10 January 1711 he sang the title role in *Etearco*; on 24 February he was Argante in Handel's first London opera, *Rinaldo*; and on 5 May he and his wife shared a benefit when Handel's work was performed again. Galliard's notes to Tosi's *Observations* (1743) indicate that Signora Vanini-Boschi returned to Venice after this season, leaving her husband behind "for several Years."
If Boschi was in England during the next few years, however, he certainly was not on

the London stage, and his activity remains a mystery. Handel found him in Dresden in 1719 and engaged him for the 1720–21 season, which he opened by singing Phoenicius in *Astarto* at the King's Theatre on 19 November 1720. He remained busy throughout the 1720–21 season, singing bass roles in *Radamisto*, *Arsace*, *Muzio Scevola*, and *Ciro*, as well as participating in concerts at the King's Theatre. During the 1721–22 season he added to his repertory roles in *Floridante*, *Crispo*, and *Griselda*; in 1722–23 he sang in *Ottone*, *Coriolano*, *Erminia*, and *Flavio*; in 1723–24 he was in *Farnace*, *Vespasiano*, *Giulio Cesare*, *Calfurnia*, and *Aquilio consolo*; and in 1724–25 he appeared in *Tamerlano*, *Artaserse*, *Rodelinda*, *Dario*, and *Elpidia*. Boschi sang in *Elisa*, *Scipione*, and *Alessandro* in 1725–26; in *Lucio vero*, *Admeto*, and *Astianatte* in 1726–27; and in *Teuzzone*, *Riccardo primo*, *Siroe*, and *Tolomeo* in his last London season, 1727–28.

In June 1728 the Academy of Music, deep in financial difficulties, ended its final season, and the Italian singers, including Boschi, Senesino, Cuzzoni, and Faustina, all of whom had excited London audiences, returned to Italy.

Boschi was apparently possessed of a splendid bass voice, though one contemporary report indicates that he was prone to bellowing:

A useful performer for several years in the Italian operas, for if any of the audience chanced unhappily to be lulled to sleep by these soothing entertainments, he never failed of rousing them up again, and by the extraordinary fury both of his voice and action, made it manifest that, though only a tailor by profession, he was *nine* times more a *man* than any of his fellow-warblers.

Boschi, Signora Giuseppe Maria, [née?] **Francesca Vanini** [fl. 1710–1711], *singer*.

Signora Francesca Vanini-Boschi, wife of the famed *basso* Giuseppe Maria Boschi,

was past her prime by the time she and her husband arrived in London in the fall of 1710. A contralto, she had been a singer of some importance. Tosi, in his *Observations* (1743), noted that she had proved that women might well instruct men in singing, and Galliard's footnote to this said "She was a Mistress of Musick, but her Voice was on the Decay when she came here." During her one English season at the Queen's Theatre in the Haymarket she sang in *Pirro e Demetrio* on 9 December 1710, *Etearco* on 10 January 1711, and *Rinaldo* on 24 February. At a performance of *Rinaldo* on 5 May she shared a benefit with her husband. Galliard said that after 1710–11 she returned to Venice and left "her Husband behind for several Years."

Boskotin, Mr [fl. 1732], *actor*.

A Mr Boskotin (or Baskotin) played Damon in Cibber's ballad opera *Damon and Phillida* at the Haymarket Theatre on 29 November 1732. He may have been the Mr Boscawen of 1735.

Bossi, Cesare *d. 1802, composer, instrumentalist*.

Cesare Bossi was in London by 1795 and became associated with the King's Theatre in the Haymarket from 1795–96 through 1799–1800; he served as leader of the band and wrote the music for a number of ballets. Shortly after he joined the staff he married Mademoiselle del Caro, one of two dancing sisters in the company; her name began to appear in the bills as Madame Bossi or Signora Bossi del Caro as early as 6 February 1796. By 2 June 1800 she and her husband were living at No 1, Great Suffolk Street.

Apparently all of Bossi's ballet composing was confined to the 1796–1800 period, during which he turned out music for *Acis and Galatea*, *L'amant statue*, *L'amour vangé* (or at least some airs for it), *Bacchus and Ariadne*, *Barader*, *Les délassements mili-*

taires (or at least part of it), *Les deux jumelles*, *Flore et Zephire*, *L'heureux retour*, *Hylas et Témire*, *Les jeux d'Eglé*, *Laura et Lenza*, *Le marchand de Smyrne*, *L'offrande a Terpsichore*, *Le triomphe de Thémis*, and (with d'Egville) *Télémaque*. He also composed "Little Peggy's Love," a Scotch ballad.

The *Monthly Mirror* in September 1802 reported that Bossi had died "In the King's Bench Prison, of a deep decline." The paper called him "a Musical Professor of eminent talents."

Bossi Del Caro. *See* DEL CARO.

Bossy, Frederick ₁*fl. 1794*₁, *violinist.*
Doane's *Musical Directory* of 1794 listed Frederick Bossy, of No 9, Bunhill Row, Moorfields, as a violinist who played at the Apollo Gardens.

Bostock, Mr ₁*fl. 1742–1750*₁, *actor.*
Mr Bostock, who may have been the same as the Mr Blastock who was active in 1735–36, played Telemachus in *Ulysses* at the converted tennis court in James Street on 31 May 1742 for his benefit with Mr Evans. When Hill's *The Actor* was published in 1750, it contained a description of Bostock; *Tamerlane* had been performed "at the new theatre" with Bostock as Bajazet. Though Hill did not identify the date and place more precisely, it was probably the New Wells, Shepherd's Market, for the play was done there on 10 May 1750, but no cast was announced. At the new theatre, wrote Hill, there was

a heroe, who makes a figure there under the name of *Bostock*. This gentleman is humble enough in his private vocation to walk before the chair of a lady at that end of the town; but when he assumes the buskin he grows unmeasurably great swells to twice his ordinary size, and like the priestess of the Delphic God, becomes another creature: But such is the joy of this sudden change of for-

tune, such his satisfaction in his own performance, that we have seen a settled smile upon his face thro' the whole part of Bajazet.

There is a possibility that the actor was the Christopher Bostock of St Paul, Covent Garden, a bachelor, who married Mary Leazer (or Leaser), spinster, on 25 April 1760.

Boswell, Mr ₁*fl. 1788–1795*₁, *house servant?*
One Boswell was named on a half-value ticket list in the Covent Garden Theatre accounts for 1788–89; he may have been one of the theatre's employees whose tickets were accepted at a performance, but he received only half the value of each ticket. On 29 November 1794 Boswell was noted in the books as receiving £1 16s. 8d. for six nights, and on 7 February 1795 he was being paid a constant salary of £1 for six nights.

Botarelli, Mrs ₁*fl. 1778–1784*₁, *singer.*
Mrs Botarelli was probably the wife of the librettist Giovanni Gualberto Botarelli, though she may have been married to his son, the translator, F. Botarelli. She sang at Edinburgh at the Theatre Royal in December 1778 and again in 1779, and she was a singer at Brighton under Buckle's management on 21 July and 18 October 1783. She appeared at Ranelagh in 1784 and probably in a few subsequent years, two of her songs there being "To the Greenwood gang wi me" and "The Nightingale."

Boteler. *See* BUTLER.

Botelli, Signor ₁*fl. 1717*₁, *singer.*
Signor Botelli, billed as lately arrived from Italy, sang a concert at Hickford's music room on 20 March 1717 for his benefit.

Botham, William [*fl. 1663*], *actor?*
William Botham was listed as a member of the Duke's Company on a warrant dated 31 March 1663, but his function in the troupe was not mentioned.

Bothmar, Mr [Baron?] [*fl. 1734*], *oboist.*
The Earl of Egmont's diary for 1734 mentions a Mr Bothmar—possibly Baron Bothmar—who played the oboe on 15 February and 8 March; these may have been private performances.

Bott, [Richard?] [*fl. 1785–1787*], *house servant?*
A Mr Bott was named frequently in the Covent Garden account books from 24 September 1785 through 8 December 1787; his salary was 7s. 6d. for three nights, and it is probable that he was one of the house servants.

There is a fair possibility that Bott's first name was Richard. A Richard Bott was named in three wills that have theatrical connections: he witnessed the will of Anna Giffard on 18 November 1776, received a bequest in Theodosius Forrest's will dated 21 November 1783, and was named for another bequest in the will of Edward Wilford dated 9 February 1788. In the last will cited, Richard Bott was described as living in Chancery Lane. It is probable, though not certain, that all three references to Richard Bott are to the same person, and since the Giffards, Forrests, and Wilfords were all theatrical families, Richard Bott may well be the Mr Bott named in the Covent Garden accounts described above.

Bottarelli. *See* BOTARELLI.

"Bottle Conjurer." *See* NICHOLAS, WILLIAM.

Boubert, Marie E. A. *See* MILLARD, MISS.

Boucher. *See also* BOUCHIER, BOWCHER, *and* BUTCHER.

Boucher, Anthony [*fl. 1689–1696*], *actor.*
Anthony Boucher was ordered arrested on 9 September 1689 for acting drolls illegally—presumably in London. He was probably the same performer who was cited in the *Flying Post* of 15–18 August 1696: "Mr Boucher, a Player, having formerly won 36,000 Pistols from the Elector of Bavaria, who promis'd to pay him at a convenient time, his Highness hath now sent for him to come and take his Money; And we hear he goes accordingly with this Convoy."

Boucher, Thomas *d. 1755, dancer, prompter, boxkeeper, sub-treasurer.*
Though there may have been two or more people named Boucher active at the theatres from 1729 through 1754, it is possible that there was only one, Thomas Boucher. He first appeared in the records in the 1729–30 season at Goodman's Fields as a prompter; a shared benefit was billed for him there on 4 June 1730. On 27 April and 2 June 1731 at the same theatre he received benefits, the second perhaps granted because the returns at the first may have been small. At the second benefit he participated in the "Waterman's Dance" in *The Tempest*, his only recorded stage appearance. On 17 May 1732 he had his last benefit as a prompter, for the next year, on 22 May 1733 he shared a benefit but was designated boxkeeper.

The records do not name him again until 28 April 1736, again at Goodman's Fields; on this date benefit tickets he had sold were accepted at the theatre. He joined Giffard's company at Lincoln's Inn Fields for the 1736–37 season, still serving as boxkeeper, and shared a benefit on 18 May 1737. The following season he moved to Covent Garden, and the accounts and bills there mention him regularly through 9

May 1743; his duty may still have been boxkeeper, for the benefit bills usually name him with other front-of-the-house servants. The accounts show that in 1740–41 he was earning 1s. 9d. daily.

Boucher's name was next cited in the bills on 4 May 1753 at Drury Lane, where his position was sub-treasurer; the date of his move to this theatre is not certain, but it must have been after 8 February 1750 when the Covent Garden accounts show a payment to him of 8s. He had a partial benefit on 9 May 1754 at Drury Lane, his last. On 19 February 1755 he died, and on 24 February he was buried at St Paul, Covent Garden, described as from St Giles in the Fields. His widow was granted benefit tickets at Drury Lane on 30 April 1755.

Bouchier. *See also* **BOUCHER** and **BUTCHER.**

Bouchier, Josias *d. 1695, singer.*

Josias (or Jonas, Joseph) Bouchier was probably the son of Josias and Sara Woodbourne Boucher who were married at St Alphage, London Wall, on 7 June 1652. The younger Josias was very likely born sometime in the 1650's and was married by the early 1680's. His wife Margaret bore him a son Nicholas who died a child and was buried in the Westminster Abbey cloisters on 21 April 1685; a daughter Margaret was baptized at the Abbey on 20 January 1687. A Josiah Boucher, possibly their son, was admitted vicar choral of Armagh on 11 September 1747 and may also have been a vicar choral of St Patrick's, Dublin.

Josias Bouchier was sworn a Gentleman of the Chapel Royal on 6 August 1682 at Windsor, replacing the deceased Thomas Purcell. A countertenor, he sang at the coronation of James II on 23 April 1685 and again when William and Mary were crowned on 11 April 1689. The "Jonas Bourchier" who was appointed to the King's private music on 18 July 1689 was doubtless Josias, and references in the early 1690's to a Joseph Boucher or Bouchier who sang at St Cecilia Day festivities and on birthdays for the Queen probably also concerned Josias of the Chapel Royal. In January 1691 he was one of the singers chosen to accompany William III on his trip to Holland.

Bouchier died on 6 December 1695 and was buried in the East Cloister of Westminster Abbey on the eleventh. His wife died on 29 October 1724 at the age of 75 and was interred in the South Cloister of the Abbey on 2 November.

Boudet, Mons [fl. 1726], *dancer.*

Monsieur Boudet had been the *maître des ballets* at the Opéra Comique in Paris until he was replaced by Sallé. On 24 March 1726 a French troupe in which he was a featured dancer opened at the Haymarket Theatre for a two-month engagement. Boudet and Mademoiselle Boudet, probably his daughter, were specifically mentioned in the bills as dancing on 13 April when they did *Pierrot and Pierrottess.* A Madame Boudet was also named in the bills as dancing in the company; this would presumably have been Boudet's wife unless the "Mme" was an error for "Mlle."

Boudet, Mme [fl. 1726], *dancer. See* BOUDET, MONS.

Boudet, Mlle [fl. 1726], *dancer. See* BOUDET, MONS.

Boudin, Boudoin, Boudon, Boudouin. *See* BAUDOUIN.

Bougier, Mlle [fl. 1791], *dancer.*

Mademoiselle Bougier was one of the nymphs in the ballet *Telemachus in the Island of Calypso* at the Pantheon on 22 March 1791 and at subsequent performances; she was probably in other ballets during the season, but her participation was apparently not notable enough to deserve mention in the playbills.

Boule, Philip [Jean Philippe?]
1697?–1744? scene painter.

The identity of the scene painter Philip Boule who worked in London in 1710 is uncertain, but he was probably the Frenchman Jean Philippe Boulle who was born perhaps in 1679 and died in 1744. Boulle has sometimes been described as of Flemish origin. He spent some years in Italy before coming to England. For the premiere of *Marplot* at Drury Lane on 30 December 1710 he painted "an intire sett of a pleasant Wood . . . after the Italian Manner." The artist was probably the Philip Boul who did a series of sketches of Derbyshire.

Bouloinge, Mr [fl. 1799], *house servant?*

One Bouloinge, possibly a house servant, was listed in the Drury Lane account books on 1 January 1799 at a salary of 16s. (probably weekly).

Boultby, Mrs [fl. 1740–1741], *actress.*

Mrs Boultby made her first appearance on any stage at Drury Lane on 4 May 1740 when she played Amanda in *Love's Last Shift,* for her benefit. She was living at this time at the "corner of Moor's Street in Compton Street." The following season she acted briefly at Covent Garden, appearing on 22 October 1740 in the same role, but starting on 27 November she performed at Goodman's Fields, acting Lady Easy in *The Careless Husband.* She played Amanda in *The Relapse* on 8 December, and for her benefit on 9 February 1741 she acted Alicia in *Jane Shore.* After this rather striking period of activity, Mrs Boultby seems to have left the London stage.

Boulton. *See also* BOLTON.

Boulton, Mr [fl. 1794], *house servant.*

On 26 April 1794 Mr Boulton's name was entered in the Drury Lane accounts for 2s. 6d. daily wages as "Box Book office Sweeper."

Boultry. *See* BOULTBY.

Bounty, William *d. 1687?, trumpeter.*
William Bounty was playing in the King's Musick by 22 September 1661, if not earlier, but the warrant appointing him a trumpeter in ordinary was dated 19 December 1661. During the 1660's he was on the move frequently; he went to Tunbridge with the King from 10 June to 7 July 1663 and to Bath from 20 August to 1 October of the same year, and on 19 September 1664 he was assigned service with Prince Rupert, along with two fellow trumpeters. By 10 December, however, all three had deserted the Prince, and a warrant was issued for their apprehension.

On 9 April 1667 Bounty and three other trumpeters were paid £15 each and assigned to attend Lord Hollis and Henry Coventry, ambassadors to the United Netherlands; he journeyed to Breda from 15 April to 25 September 1667, after which he apparently returned to London to stay. On 17 December 1669 he was granted a new silver trumpet in place of his old one, and on 15 February 1675 he played in the masque *Calisto* at court. Bounty was reappointed under James II on 16 May 1685, but sometime before 30 March 1688 he died, for on that date a warrant was issued appointing John Shore as his successor. The William Bounty who was buried on 31 July 1687 at St James, Westminster, was probably the trumpeter.

Bouquet, James [fl. 1794], *violinist.*
Doane's *Musical Directory* of 1794 listed James Bouquet, of Montague Street, Spitalfields, as playing the violin in performances given by the Cecilian Society.

Bouqueton, Mons [fl. 1775–1776], *ballet master.*
Monsieur Bouqueton was engaged as ballet master at the King's Theatre in the

Haymarket for the 1775–76 season; except for an announcement at the beginning of the season, on 30 October 1775, that he was in the company, his name did not appear in the theatre's bills.

Bourchier. *See* BOUCHIER.

Bourdon. *See also* BURDEN and BURDON.

Bourdon, Mr [Gabriel?] [fl. 1700–1737?], *singer.*

Mr Bourdon (or Burdon) sang Daniel Purcell's "Sabina has a thousand Charms" in *The Reformed Wife* at Drury Lane, probably in March 1700; the song was published in 1700, and though the playbill cited Mrs Erwin as the singer, the printed song listed Bourdon. It is likely that they both sang it, but at different times. Bourdon and Mrs Lucas sang a duet in *The Bath*, probably at the Drury Lane premier performance on 31 May 1701. Bourdon seems not to have been a regular member of the company but rather a free-lance singer.

Bourdon was paid £2 3s. for singing Weldon's music for Congreve's *The Judgment of Paris* at Lincoln's Inn Fields and possibly at Southampton House for the Duke of Bedford. When this happened is not certain; the work had been performed in March 1701 at Dorset Garden and Weldon gave entertainments in May 1702 at Stationers' Hall and Somerset House Garden. Performances at Lincoln's Inn Fields and Southampton House may have taken place about this same time.

There is a possibility that Bourdon was the Gabriel Bourdon of St Ann, Westminster, who bought a share in the Lincoln's Inn Fields Theatre on 1 February 1722 and sold it to John Rich on 31 October 1737.

Bourg, du. *See* DUBOURG.

Bourgeois, Mlle [fl. 1793], *dancer.*

Mademoiselle Bourgeois was engaged to dance at the King's Theatre in the Haymarket from 26 February to 16 April 1793, her only specific mention in the bills that season being on 26 February when she was one of the Graces in a new Noverre ballet, *Venus and Adonis.*

Bourk. *See also* BURK.

Bourk, Miss. *See* BOURK, MRS WILLIAM.

Bourk, William [fl. 1780–1797], *dancer.*

William Bourk was a minor dancer at Drury Lane from 1780 to 1795. His name first appeared in the bills, however, when he danced a hornpipe on 20 May 1785, an evening when he shared tickets with other minor personnel. On 6 June 1786 he shared a benefit, at which time he lived at No 13, Little Russell Street.

Bourk married Miss Elizabeth Bradshaw, also a dancer, on 27 January 1788 at St George's in the East. A few months later they danced a double hornpipe at Drury Lane on 29 April 1788. Bourke also performed at the Royalty in 1787–88. He remained at Drury Lane as chorus dancer in such pieces as *Robinson Cruso, Harlequin's Frolicks, The Pirates,* and *Lodoiska* at least through 1794–95. In 1789–90 he was being paid £1 per week.

In the *Morning Herald* of 16 October 1797 he advertised as a dancing master.

Bourk, Mrs William, Elizabeth, née Bradshaw [fl. 1779–1793], *dancer.*

According to a letter written by the actress Mrs Mary Bradshaw to Garrick on 11 October 1779, she had "the expense of supporting an orphan relation," who was known as Miss Elizabeth Bradshaw. The *Gentleman's Magazine* for October 1780 suggested, however, that the girl was probably in actuality Mrs Bradshaw's daughter.

Miss Bradshaw, in any event, was well cared for, despite her guardian's meager means, and upon her return from schooling in France she danced at the Plymouth Theatre in July 1780. Her appearance is said to have resulted in the tragic demise of Mrs Bradshaw. Upon hearing the girl being hissed, she fell into a fit of madness from which she never recovered.

The assessment of Miss Bradshaw's talents by the Plymouth audience was doubtless accurate, for she had a slight stage career. Although she was not specified in the bills for 1786–87, she shared in tickets at Drury Lane on 1 June 1787. She also worked at the Royalty Theatre in 1787–88. On 27 January 1788 at St George's in the East she married William Bourk, also a dancer at the Royalty. Several months later, on 29 April 1788 at the Haymarket, William Bourk danced a double hornpipe with a "Miss" Bourk, who was probably his new wife, and not a daughter by a previous marriage. The designations "Mrs Bourk" and "Miss Bourk" are found in the Drury Lane bills also from 1790–91 through 1796–97, usually for dancing, sometimes for singing, but we believe them to be the same person. Mrs Bourk remained an obscure chorus dancer in such pieces as *The Pirates* and *The Cherokee*. Her last performance of record was in *A Country Dance and Scotch Reel* at the end of the mainpiece on 10 June 1797.

Bourlier. *See* BOURRELIER.

Bourne, [Barnard?] [*fl. 1733–1760*], actor.

On 5 February 1733 a Mr Bourne played Foresight in *Love for Love* at the Rainsford Street playhouse in Dublin; the same actor was Don Charino in *Love Makes a Man* at Smock Alley, probably on 11 December 1735; and on 17 January 1745 he acted Tubal in *The Merchant of Venice* at the Capel Street Theatre. This last venture brought Bourne under the managership of the famous harlequin Phillips, and perhaps through Phillips he made contact with Hallam at the Goodman's Fields playhouse in London.

On 19 December 1745 at Goodman's Fields the role of Skelton in *Perkin Warbeck* was performed by Barnard Bourn "for his Diversion." This terminology certainly suggests an amateur, but we believe that he was Mr Bourne from Dublin. He made no other appearances during the season, but on 22 March 1746 he was granted tickets to sell for his profit—possibly a way Hallam devised for reimbursing him for playing Skelton *gratis*. Chetwood reported in 1749 that at that time Bourne was still in England, but Clark shows him back in Ireland, acting at Cork, in 1760.

A Miss Bourne who performed in Ireland in the late 1740's may well have been a relative, possibly Bourne's daughter. The musician Barnard Bourne of London, who became a freeman in 1766 and would thus have been born about 1745, may have been the actors' son.

Bourne, Barnard   *b. c. 1745, musician.*

Barnard Bourne became a freeman and was admitted to livery in the Worshipful Company of Musicians on 25 November 1766; he was then living in White Chapel. He would, presumably, have been born about 1745 and was probably the son of the Irish actor of the same name.

Bourne, Theophilus. *See* BIRD, THEOPHILUS   *1608–c. 1663.*

Bournonville, Antoine   *1760–1843, dancer.*

Antoine Bournonville was the son of Amable Louis Bournonville and his wife Jeanne, *née* Evrard; he and his twin brother Wilhem were born at Lyon in 1760, but Wilhem died at Vienna at the age of 10. At Vienna Antoine studied under Noverre, after which he went to Cassel where in 1778 he made his debut as a dancer. He stayed at Cassel until 1780 but without an engagement, and in the fall of 1781 he came to London for a season at the King's Theatre in the Haymarket. On 17 November 1781 he was noticed in the bills as participating in a pastoral dance and in two Noverre works, *A Divertissement Dance* and *Les amans réunis*. On 21 February 1782 he was added to the ballet *Les petits riens*, and on 19 March he danced in another Noverre work, *La rosière de Salency*.

After his stay in London Bournonville went to Stockholm from which city, though he was engaged to 1795, he left in 1792 for Copenhagen; he died at Fredensborg, Denmark, on 11 January 1843. Bournonville was twice married, first to Marianne Jensen, an actress and dancer who bore him two children, and then to Louise Sundberg, who bore him three children. Of his offspring, only Antoine Auguste (1805–1879) pursued a successful career as a dancer.

Bourrelier, Mr ₁*fl. 1785–1790*₁, *house servant.*

Mr Bourrelier (or Bruillier) was apparently a house servant at Covent Garden Theatre; the account books and bills there first noted him on 29 October 1785, and he worked regularly through the 1789–90 season at a steady salary of 15s. per week.

Boutcher. *See* **BOUCHER.**

Boutell. *See also* **BOUTET** and **BOW-TELL.**

Boutell, Henry ₁*fl. 1687–1689*₁, *actor.*

Henry Boutell was listed in a warrant dated 12 January 1688 as an actor in the United Company, and he may also have been in the troupe the following season. His name appeared at about the same time that Elizabeth Bowtell returned to the stage after a ten-year absence, but there is no evidence to establish a clear relationship be-

tween the two. Her name was frequently spelled "Boutell"; her husband's name was Barnaby, and Henry Boutell may have been one of Barnaby's relatives.

Boutet, ₁**Mons?**₁ ₁*fl. 1675*₁, *instrumentalist.*

One Boutet (or Boutell), probably of French origin, played the recorder—and perhaps other instruments—in the masque *Calisto* at court on 15 February 1675. A warrant dated 27 May 1675 listed him under the French violins and oboes, and at that date he and other performers had not yet been paid for their services.

Boutflower, Mr ₁*fl. 1784*₁, *violinist.*

Mr Boutflower was a first violinist at the Handel Memorial Concerts at Westminster Abbey and the Pantheon on 26, 27, 29 May and 3, 5 June 1784.

Bouton, Miss ₁*fl. 1784*₁, *actress.*

Miss Bouton acted Myra in *Wit's Last Stake* at the Haymarket Theatre on 9 February 1784.

Bouzilarico. *See* **BUZILARICO.**

Boval, ₁**Mons?**₁ ₁*fl. 1714–1760?*₁, *dancer.*

One Boval (or Bovil), probably a Frenchman, was a dancer, and dancing master at Lincoln's Inn Fields Theatre during the 1714–15 season, at Drury Lane in 1716–17, at Lincoln's Inn Fields again in the spring of 1719, and then at Drury Lane once more from 1719–20 through 1729–30. He reappeared at Drury Lane in 1733–34 but signed articles at Covent Garden for the 1734–35 season—his last one. His first appearance on record was on 22 December 1714 and his last on 2 June 1735; during the numerous periods when he is not known to have been active in London, he may nevertheless have been there. But, again, he may have been on the Continent. The full story of his career is not known.

He appeared regularly in *entr'acte* dances and pantomimes, one of his favorite characters being Punch. One of his students was Miss Brett, who first appeared during the 1727–28 season and later married the prompter W. R. Chetwood. A Mr Boval sold benefit tickets at Covent Garden on 9 December 1760 and received his half value of £15 15s. 6d., but there is no certainty that this was Boval the dancer of earlier years.

Boval, William (*fl. 1739*), *musician*.
William Boval, possibly related to the dancer Boval, was one of the original subscribers to the Royal Society of Musicians when it formed on 28 August 1739.

Bowan, Mr (*fl. 1780*), *actor*.
Mr Bowan, probably a Scotsman who came down with others of his country to perform in London, played a principal role in *The Double Amour* at the Haymarket Theatre on 25 September 1780 as an afterpiece to *The Gentle Shepherd*.

Bowcher. *See* BOUCHER.

Bowden, Mrs (*fl. 1699–1704*), *actress*.
Mrs Bowden played Doris in *Achilles* at Drury Lane in December 1699 as a member of Christopher Rich's company; she was probably the Mrs Bowden who operated a booth at May Fair on 4 May 1704 with her sister, Mrs John Boman the actress.

Bowden, Wright *1752–1823, singer, actor*.
Wright Bowden was born in 1752 at Manchester. His father kept a theatrical public house in that city. (When John Edwin applied to James Whitely for a job at Manchester, Whitely gave him an excellent lecture on the profession of actor at Bowden's tap-room in November 1766.)

After an apprenticeship to a cotton manufactory and an unsuccessful attempt at mercantile life, Wright Bowden, at the urging of his friends, decided to go upon the stage. He made his first appearance on any stage in the title role in *Robin Hood* at Covent Garden on 18 October 1787. The debut was a success and Bowden's "deep tenor" voice, which he used with "good taste," was greatly applauded. Two of the songs which he sang that night—*When gen'rous wine* and Shield's *Charming Corinda*—were published in that year. *Robin Hood* was performed as a mainpiece 29 times that season. Bowden, who was being paid £10 per week, a substantial salary for a novice, also performed Ferdinand in *The Duenna* nine times and Don Caesar in *The Castle of Andalusia* four times. At his benefit on 5 February 1788, in which he cleared about £180 (tickets to be had of him at No 5, John Street, Great Portland Street) he sang the title role in *Comus* and in Act II also gave the celebrated "Laughing Song" from *L'Allegro ed il Penseroso*.

After this initial season in London, Bowden went to Ireland to play at Limerick during race week in July 1788. He also played at Crow Street, Dublin, and at Cork. Despite his apparent success in his first London engagement, he did not return to the capitol in 1788–89 but toured principal towns in the Three Kingdoms. He was at Cork and Limerick again in the summer of 1790; he made his first appearance at Edinburgh in the role of Macheath in *The Beggar's Opera* on 19 January 1792, when the *Courier* wrote, "to speak of this gentleman as a singer, no encomium can be too high."

In the following season Bowden was reengaged at Edinburgh to support the appearances of Mrs Billington. The season was intended to open with her, with Bowden's engagement made accordingly, but she decided to visit Ireland first, and it was not until 25 February 1793 that she appeared in Edinburgh, as Rosetta in *Love in*

WRIGHT BOWDEN at the age of 71
by Minasi

a Village. Bowden, meanwhile contracted at £10 per night and a benefit, had been used for operatic roles on three occasions only (including Hawthorn in *Love in a Village* on 14 January). While awaiting Mrs Billington's arrival, and aggrieved, he began a process against the theatre. When Mrs Billington did arrive, Bowden was out of favor, and the singer Meadows supported her in performance. On 27 February 1793, Bowden published a handbill which set forth his case.

TO THE PUBLIC.

When Mrs Billington's engagement was first announced, Mr Bowden was announced at the same time. Hence the public were certainly led to expect that she was to be supported by that capital singer. Instead of which an attempt has been made to support her by Mr Meadows, who may be a very worthy man, but certainly is in a very unhappy predicament as a performer, it being perfectly obvious on Monday last that he could neither sing nor say. In this situation, it is highly proper the Pit should exercise their undoubted right of interfering; and, this night they should call for Mr Williamson the manager, and demand the reasons why the Public is so shamefully insulted, and why Mr Bowden is not suffered to appear, who is still in Edinburgh, and ready to renew his engagements on the same terms that were originally offered.

The public did not respond as Bowden hoped, for Meadows continued to sing with Mrs Billington. Bowden's case came before the sheriff on 11 December 1793 and he was awarded his full salary of £180 plus £5 expenses.

In his first London appearance in seven years, Bowden returned to Covent Garden to perform at Incledon's benefit on 2 May 1794. He played Robin Hood in the mainpiece and Captain Cable in *Naples Bay* in the afterpiece, and he also sang Carter's "Stand to your Guns, my Hearts of Oak" and, with Incledon, Shield's "May our Navy old England forever protect." On 8 May he repeated Robin Hood.

Bowden then engaged at Covent Garden for the next three years, 1794–97, at a salary of £8 per week. On 22 September 1794 he sang one of the vocal parts in *Macbeth.* That season he also sang Ferdinand in *The Duenna,* Silcno in *Midas,* and Fairlop in *The Woodman.* He made a number of appearances to sing patriotic songs in such pieces as *The Naval Volunteers* and *The Death of Captain Faulknor.* For his benefit on 16 May 1795 (tickets of him at No 9, Lower Brook Street, Grosvenor Square) he played Inkle in *Inkle and Yarico,* for the first time, (with additional songs from Handel) and sang "O bring me wine" and "How shall we mortals spend our hours" in *England's Glory.* The *Secret History of the Green Room* (1795) found him much improved by his practice in the country: "Mr Bowden is a firm and manly singer, possessing a bass voice of considerable compass and melody. His figure is well enough, but his face incapacitates him for a Lover, and Opera has little better to offer him in its present state."

Bowden sang similar parts and songs during his next two seasons at Covent Garden. Some such songs which were published included Reeve's "The Bugle Horn" and "The Friar" from *Merry Sherwood* and Reeve's "The Land we live in" from *Harlequin and Oberon*. On 30 November 1795 and 26 September 1796 he played Hecate in *Macbeth*. Each year he took his benefit in the role of Fairlop in *The Woodman*, and for his last benefit on 20 May 1797, he cleared about £131. He was still living at No 6, Lower Brook Street. In the summer of 1796, Bowden acted again at Limerick and Cork.

In August 1797 the *Monthly Mirror* announced that Bowden had "given in his resignation" at Covent Garden. His engagement at Richmond that summer seems to have been his last connection with the stage. According to notations on a manuscript in the Garrick Club, after leaving the theatre Bowden was employed as a broker on the stock exchange. He died on 16 April 1823, at the age of 71, and was buried in St Mary's churchyard, Manchester.

Waldron wrote that "this gentleman's musical powers will always entitle him to a respectable rank in the theatre," but of his acting exclaimed—"No more of that Hal if thou lov'st me!"

A painting of Bowden as Robin Hood by Gainsborough Dupont is in the Garrick Club. The Folger Library has a small watercolor of him as Robin Hood, "Taken from Life," by W. Loftis. An engraving by J. R. Smith of Bowden in this character was published in 1787. A portrait of Bowden as an older man, just before his death, was drawn by J. A. Minasi in October 1822 and published in an engraving by the artist at Manchester in April 1823.

Bowen, Mr *fl. 1734–1735*, *actor*.

Mr Bowen, possibly a relative of either Jemmy or William Bowen of earlier in the eighteenth century, played Juba in *Cato* on 23 May 1734 at the "Lilliputians' Theatre" (the converted tennis court in James Street). On 13 December 1735 his name again appeared on the bills, this time as Worthy in *The Recruiting Officer* at the Haymarket Theatre.

Bowen, Mr *fl. 1784*, *singer*.

Mr Bowen was a countertenor who sang at the Handel Memorial Concerts at Westminster Abbey and the Pantheon on 26, 27, 29 May and 3, 5 June 1784.

Bowen, Jemmy *b. c. 1685, singer*.

Young Jemmy Bowen (or Bowin, Boyn) may have been related to the actor-singer William Bowen, who is said to have had several children, including one illegitimate one. Among them may have been James, or as he was affectionately called for several years, Jemmy, the remarkable boy singer of the 1690's. No proof of a relationship has been found, however, and the name Bowen was a very common one.

When and where Jemmy began his stage career is uncertain, but it may have been about 1691–92 when *The Libertine* was revived at Drury Lane; one of Henry Purcell's songs, "To arms, heroic Prince," was sung by "the boy," identified in *Orpheus Britannicus* (1702) as Bowen. Jemmy must have been very young in 1691–92— perhaps about six; he was still referred to as a youth in the late 1690's, and his disappearance from the records after 1701 suggests that his voice may have broken in that year.

During the 1690's the theatrical records contain frequent references to an unidentified boy singing, but which ones refer to Jemmy cannot be ascertained. He was probably the boy who sang for Queen Mary's birthday on 30 April 1693, in *Abdelazer* at Drury Lane on 1 April 1695, and possibly the role of the God of Dreams in the April 1695 revival of *The Indian Queen* at Dorset Garden. By the 1695–96 season he had become popular enough to be named more specifically in the bills, on one occasion (at Richmond Wells in 1696) even being formally called Mr James Bowen. In November 1698 he appeared in *The Island Princess* at Drury Lane; other singing engagements in 1698 for a Mr Bowen, such as concerts on 28 May and 7 June at York Buildings, may have been Jemmy's but could have been William Bowen's. The last record of his activity is at the music room at Hampstead Wells on 15 September 1701 where he "sang and two men performed on the violin."

Jemmy Bowen, before Henry Purcell's death in 1695, had worked with the great composer, and Anthony Aston later told a story of a rehearsal during which members of the band tried to advise the lad; Purcell stopped them and said, "O let him alone . . . he will grace it more naturally than you, or I, can teach him."

Bowen, William *1666–1718, actor.*

The early history of William Bowen is not clear. Chetwood said he was born in Ireland in 1666, but Bowen is such a common name in both Irish and British records that it is difficult to determine who William's relatives might have been. One, however, we know about for certain: a nephew John Bowen who was a tidesman and eventually Surveyor of Customs at Leigh, Essex. The boy singer Jemmy Bowen may also have been related, and some scholars have suggested that he may have been William's son, but there is not evidence sufficient to be sure. There were at least eight Bowens who served under the Duke of Ormonde between 1644 and 1686, and one, Captain Griffith Bowen, may well have been related to the actor and may have given his name to that one of William's sons so christened. At the Restoration Captain Bowen obtained property in Milton

County, Pembroke, from Phillip Bowen; and during his life the captain was connected with the Customs service (as was William) and came to the attention of the Ormondes (as did William). Captain Bowen died insolvent sometime before 7 December 1709.

But though the actor may have been related to Griffith Bowen, and perhaps to Phillip Bowen as well, there were Bowens in London in Caroline times from whom he may have descended. The actor John Shank, for example, had a daughter Elizabeth Bowen and a grandchild Winifred Bowen to whom he left bequests in his will dated 31 December 1635. And Alice Bowen, widow of Thomas Bowen, married the actor-manager William Beeston in 1642. These Bowens may have been related to one another and related as well to our William Bowen of later in the century.

Aline Taylor has suggested that Bowen may have begun his acting career at the Smock Alley Theatre in Dublin about 1683 for by the time he joined the United Company at Drury Lane in London he was given a salary of 40s. weekly—more than a neophyte would have been paid. His first recorded role was the Valet in *Bury Fair* when it was first done in April 1689 at Drury Lane. From this time until the breakup of the company in 1694–95, Bowen played mostly comic parts and gradually worked up to major roles. For example, he acted the Shoemaker in *The Man of Mode* about 1690–91, Sir Gentle Golding in *Sir Anthony Love* in late September 1690, Monsieur Le Prate in *Love for Money* in January 1691, Sir William Thoughtless in mid-April 1691, Callow in *The Marriage-Hater Matched* in January 1692, and Sir Symphony in *The Maid's Last Prayer* at the end of February 1693. His friend Congreve tailored Sir Joseph in *The Old Bachelor* to Bowen's strong voice in March 1693, the first of three such roles. By this time Bowen had established himself sufficiently with the public to be referred to as "a notable Joker" in D'Urfey's *The Richmond Heiress* in mid-April 1693 (in which Bowen played Cummington). And in 1693 his salary was raised by 10s. weekly, a sure sign of his popularity. Just before the United Company split, in May 1694, Bowen was assigned the title role in both parts of *Don Quixote*.

Betterton, the leading actor in the United Company, had reservations about Bowen, however. Sometime prior to December 1694 Bowen and Thomas Doggett had rebelled, been discharged, and, at Betterton's suggestion, had not been readmitted until they had negotiated separately with the troupe. Betterton (in the legal documents concerning the splitting of the company) testified that he thought Bowen was not worth the 50s. per week he was being paid, and he noted that Bowen was easily drawn to mutiny—yet Betterton admitted that the actor was a quick study and performed with commendable vigor. When Betterton seceded from the United Company and formed a new group, he took on Bowen but did not make him one of the sharers. This is the earliest record of Bowen's intractable personality, a quality that would finally bring about his death.

His first role with Betterton's troupe was Jeremy in *Love for Love* on 30 April 1695 at the reconverted tennis court in Lincoln's Inn Fields—the second role tailored for him by Congreve. He was called upon frequently to deliver prologues and epilogues —another sign of his popularity with audiences—and he continued in his comic line, playing such roles as Rasor in *The Provoked Wife*, Cheatall in *The Innocent Mistress,* and Nickycracky in *The Pretenders*. Rarely did he appear in tragedies, though he is recorded as Cinna the Poet in a manuscript cast for *Julius Caesar*, probably in 1697–98 before he left for Ireland. Once during these few seasons with Betterton's company Bowen was in trouble with the law, though the details are not known, and Bowen, apparently, was not at fault: a warrant dated 4 June 1696 called for the arrest of several men who had falsely apprehended the actor.

In May 1698 Bowen spoke the prologue to *The Fatal Friendship* and shortly afterwards sailed for Ireland. During the 1698–99 season he acted in Joseph Ashbury's company at Smock Alley, but no details have been found about his roles there. He may have arrived in Dublin soon enough to go with the players to Kilkenny Castle to entertain the recently arrived second Duke of Ormonde; if so, perhaps he was able to curry favor with the Duke and play upon any connections earlier Bowens had had with Ormonde's father. In any case, after the theatrical season in Dublin ended, Bowen was appointed one of the 17 land-carriagemen of the Port of London on 8 June 1699 at a salary of £35. This was less than the salary he was making as an actor, but the two salaries combined must have made him fairly well off. What the duties of the office were is not known, and it was probably a sinecure. He contrived to keep both careers going simultaneously in London, whence he returned for the 1699–1700 season with Betterton's company. His first role upon his arrival was probably Francis in Betterton's version of *Henry IV*, on 9 January 1700, and on 5 March he was Witwoud in *The Way of the World*—the third part created especially for him by Congreve.

By this time Bowen had probably married, and perhaps by now his two sons that we know of, William and Griffin (or Griffith), had been born. It was apparently about this time that the actor Robert Wilks, who had acted with Bowen in Dublin in 1698–99, left his infant son Robert under Bowen's care. Little else is known of this arrangement except that the child soon died.

Bowen started the fall season in 1700 on 25 September sharing a benefit with Hodgson, and then, in November, he abruptly left the stage. The *Post Boy* for

14–16 November contained a report on him:

We hear that this day Mr. William Bowen, the late famous Comedian of the New Playhouse, being convinc'd by Mr. Collier's Book against the Stage, and satisfied that a Shopkeeper's life was the readier way to Heaven of the two, opens a Cane Shop, next door to the King's-head Tavern in Middle-Row, Holborn, where it is not question'd but all manner of Canes, Toys, and other Curiosities, will be Sold at reasonable Rates. This sudden Change is much admir'd at, as well as the Reason which induced him to leave such a profitable Employ; but the most Judicious conclude, it is the Effect of a certain Person's good Nature, who has more Compassion for his Soul than for his own.

The "certain person" remains unidentified, but whoever it was could not have been very persuasive after all, for Bowen was acting again in four months. The *Post Boy* of 1–4 March explained the matter:

We are informed that the famous Comedian Mr. William Bowen, who has for some months discontinued acting on account of some Difference between him and the rest of the Sharers of the New Theatre, is to have the Committee, Sir Robert Howard's Celebrated Comedy play'd at the said theatre for his benefit on Thursday next the 6th instant; the part of Teague is that which he has made choice of for himself in it, and it's the opinion of the best Judges in Town that no person in either of the Theatres can come so Near the Performance of the famous Original Mr. [John] Lacy as he can; It is reported that after this performance which is to be his last on the English Stage, he designs for Ireland, which will be a great advantage to that state, and in all Probability no small loss to this.

The difference may well have been over salary, for Betterton's group had earlier excluded Bowen from the select group of sharers. He hardly needed to worry, however; he was a popular actor, had useful connections at court through the Ormondes, still held his landcarriageman sinecure, and probably maintained his interest in the cane shop he had opened.

Having announced his intention to leave England, he probably surprised no one when he turned up at Drury Lane on 11 June 1701 playing Jacomo in *The Libertine*. Somehow he contrived to have this play given for his benefit, his third of the season. He stayed at Drury Lane for the next two seasons, playing such parts as Puzzle in *The Funeral*, Teague in *The Twin Rivals*, and de Pistole in *The Old Mode and the New*. The two latter roles he played during the 1702–3 season—the only ones recorded for him; perhaps he acted other parts, for the records for this period are far from complete, but he may well have curtailed his stage work because of his extra-theatrical activities.

Sometime between March and August of 1702 Bowen got himself into what turned out to be very lucrative trouble. A Mr Forde spoke some "insolent and disrespectful words . . . against her Majesty's royal title" and the fiery Bowen took umbrage, fought Forde, and was wounded. In recompence the Queen granted Bowen a £100 bounty on 12 August 1702. Perhaps encouraged by this royal favor, Bowen applied on 10 November 1702 for a position in the Customs; it is not clear whether the post was granted or not, but it seems likely that it was. His earlier appointment as landcarriageman may now have expired—if, indeed, it had continued this long.

After the 1702–3 season at Drury Lane Bowen belatedly made good his promise to return to Ireland, and his trip was coincidental with the arrival there, once again, of the Duke of Ormonde. Ormonde was present in Ireland from 21 September 1703 to June 1705 for his first vice-regal term. In 1703–4, then, Bowen probably acted at the Smock Alley Theatre, but at some point he "left off Playing on account of some Disgust" (or so it was reported in Dublin the following 23 January 1705). What caused the disgust this time is not certain, though later events would suggest that Bowen had been trying to get a share in the Smock Alley company.

By the winter of 1704 he was back in London, apparently in the Drury Lane company, though no roles are recorded for him. On 27 November 1704 Christopher Rich, the troupe's manager, complained that Bowen was being wooed away by the management of the new Queen's Theatre in the Haymarket in preparation for their opening. The wooing was successful, for on 26 April 1705 Bowen acted the title role in *The Humorous Lieutenant* there, and on the thirtieth he played Don Quixote.

On 6 June 1705 he was granted permission to carry on his duties as one of the messengers of the Revenue in Ireland *in absentia*; this new duty he seems to have acquired during his 1703–4 stay in Dublin. The records are far from clear, so it is not known whether his Customs appointment (assuming he was granted it back in 1702 or 1703) now ended or whether he was allowed to hold both positions simultaneously. In any case, his new revenue post was ideal, for his place was supplied by a deputy whenever he was in England, and he collected the salary.

Bowen began the 1705–6 season by playing Teague in *The Committee* at Lincoln's Inn Fields, billed as newly arrived from Ireland, where he may have spent the summer. On 20 October he acted Raggou in *The Old Troop*, and when Betterton's company moved back to the Queen's he followed the venerable leader and played out the rest of the season there. His roles were mostly those he had done before, and almost all of them were leading parts. During the two following seasons he added a number of new roles to his line: Crack in *Sir Courtly Nice*, Gripe in *The Confederacy*, Osric in *Hamlet*, Foigard in *The Beaux' Stratagem* (now called *The Stratagem*), Ascanio Sforza in *Caesar Borgia*, Captain

Strut in *The Double Gallant*, and one of the witches in *Macbeth*. On 14 May 1708 his permission to serve as a messenger of the Revenue by deputy was extended, and he seems to have decided to settle for a while in London.

In 1708–9 Bowen found himself in trouble far more serious than anything he had encountered before: he killed a man, or it certainly seems he did. The details of his case are so closely parallel to another one, involving his nephew, that one cannot be sure which was which or what, exactly, happened; and during the period in question the actor William Bowen carried on a performance schedule as though nothing untoward had occurred.

On 9 September 1708, according to Luttrell, Bowen "the custom house officer" was "convicted at the Old Bailey of murther, having sworn he would kill the next man he mett, and accordingly stabb'd a pattin maker [actually, a patten-maker's assistant, on Tower Hill] in 3 several places, of which he died." On 7 October, however, Bowen was busy at Drury Lane playing Jeremy in *Love for Love*, and he appears to have acted fairly regularly through the end of December, playing, among other parts, Roderigo in *Othello* (9 October) and La Roch in *Bury Fair* (31 December). In January 1709 he acted Fourbin in *The Soldier's Fortune* on the seventeenth, the Shoemaker in *The Man of Mode* on the twenty-ninth; on 1 February he played Jaqueline in *The Fatal Marriage*; and on 3 March he acted Foigard in *The Stratagem*. On 10 March he was at the Old Bailey, where he entered an appeal. On 15 March he played Jaques in *The Pilgrim* at Drury Lane. He completed the season there, and on 20 June signed a contract with manager Owen Swiney of the Queen's Theatre to act there for five years starting 1 July 1709 at a salary of £75 annually and a benefit every April with £50 house charges, plus a vacation from 10 June to 10 September each year. Given this schedule, he certainly could not have spent much time in prison, and his treatment, even before his official trial, suggests remarkable lenience and possibly the influence of well-placed friends.

All the reports of the murder and of Bowen's court case cite him as "Bowen of the custom house," which would seem to be a clear enough identification, but his theatrical affiliation was not mentioned, and this might raise a doubt as to whether a different Bowen was the murderer. In fact, another Bowen, the actor's nephew John, was involved in a startlingly similar (if not the same) murder.

John Bowen had been appointed to a tidesman's post on 9 July 1706, was discharged in connection with alleged fraud charges on 5 January 1709, and at some point prior to mid-January 1709 was charged with killing one William Smith. The *Post Boy* of 15–18 January reported that "Mr. Bowen, who lies condemn'd in Newgate, for the Murder of a young Man, made his Escape from thence, last Saturday in the evening, disguis'd like a Barber, as if he came from shaving one in the said Prison, but was retaken that Night, at the Swan-Ale-house in Thames-street." In the same paper on 10–12 May it was reported that John Bowen (so named, this time) appeared "upon an Appeal for the Murder of William Smith" and "was remanded to Prison till Saturday next." John Bowen was finally released and, apparently on the grounds that he had been illegally charged, was rewarded £30 for his services. On 9 February 1710 he petitioned for an increase in his reward, and on 15 November 1712 he asked for a "farther reward, and to be restored to his place, being deprived of it by being convicted illegally for killing a man." After the death of Queen Anne in 1714 he was rewarded indeed by being made Surveyor of Customs at Leigh, Essex, at £40 a year. Later, on 1 April 1718, he seized a smuggling boat near Gravesend and took a prize of about £3000 from it.

There seem to have been two different Bowen cases, but at times they sound almost identical, and it is quite possible that the details of one case were confused with the other in contemporary reports: the barber disguise certainly sounds like a clever actor's trick, for instance.

Whether this was the second or third show of violence on the part of William Bowen is not certain. There was another incident, reported in 1718 but referring to a much earlier period, which involved Bowen and the actor Francis Leigh, son of the famed Restoration comedian Anthony. Francis testified that Bowen had thrice attempted to take his life,

and once particularly as he [Leigh] was sitting at his Father's Door, *Mr. Bowen* passed by him and asked him how he did . . . and coming back in about half-an-hour, while he was still sitting there, without any Provocation called him ill Names, drew his Sword, cut him over the Head, and he rising and retreating backward into the House he happened to fall, whereupon he made two Passes at him with his Sword, but happened to miss him, he putting it by with his hand, and somebody coming by, and taking hold of him, he was shortening his Sword to have stabb'd him as he lay on the ground, but was prevented by Persons [Thomas Alpress, for one] running to his Assistance. That thereupon he advised *Sir Peter King* in order to prosecute him, but by the Mediation of some Great Men on Mr. Bowen's Account, did make it up with him.

The date of this incident is not clear. The phrasing suggests that Francis's father Anthony was still alive, which would place the event before December 1692, but the reference to Sir Peter King, who was knighted on 12 September 1708, could place it shortly before, or perhaps after, the murder trial of 1708–9. In any case, William Bowen was a good man to stay away from; he was prone to violence, and he had friends in high places.

Bowen acted at the Queen's Theatre under his new contract in the 1709–10 season, playing several of his old roles as well as such new ones as the King of Brentford in *The Rehearsal*, Littlewit in *Bartholomew Fair*, and the title role in *The Cheats of Scapin*. Meanwhile, his trial came up (on 9 November 1709, the day after he blithely played Foigard), and though the charge was murder, the verdict was manslaughter, and Bowen was acting again by 18 November.

He began the 1710–11 season at the Queen's Theatre, but by mid-season the playhouses had altered their managerial arrangements again and he moved with the actors to Drury Lane. He retained many of his old roles, but he had to share some of them with others, and his annual salary dropped to £60 annually. He faced considerable competition in his comic line from such players as Cibber, Estcourt, Johnson, and Pinkethman, and as a result he was less frequently billed during the ensuing seasons. In 1713–14, for example, after appearing once in November, his name dropped from the notices until the following May, and perhaps it was during these years that Bowen made another try for a Dublin theatre patent.

It is likely that he had tried to gain a footing at Smock Alley before and had failed; this time his chances were somewhat better. His petition (undated, but probably about this time) noted that he had been 30 years an actor, and that the current patentee Joseph Ashbury was now ancient and that his heir Charles had died. Bowen asked the Queen for a patent for himself and his son William. Ashbury, understandably alarmed, went to England to plead with Queen Anne sometime before 13 October 1713, and it is noteworthy that the Duke of Ormonde's term as viceroy in Ireland was ending at just this time. The appropriate point for Bowen to have pressed his case would have been in 1712–13, but the fact that his plea was denied suggests that his timing was off or that he misjudged the influence he had with

Ormonde. If he used the blank months on his theatrical calendar between December 1713 and April 1714 to follow up his petition, he certainly would have been too late.

Bowen finished his stage career at Drury Lane, still clinging to some of his favorite roles: Captain Strut, Jeremy, Foigard, Osric, Roderigo, and a few others. But he was past his prime and no longer as useful to the players as he once had been. In 1715–16, for instance, he is recorded for only four roles, and inactivity probably did not set well with him. He was 50 now, but still, according to Chetwood, "fiery to a Fault and passionate to his Prejudice." On 8 May 1717 he played Jacomo in *The Libertine* (retitled *Don John*) for his benefit, and on 9 August, his last recorded appearance, he acted Dashwell in *The Unlucky Lover*. Perhaps he was still at Drury Lane the following season, though no roles are recorded for him, and the company may have dropped him. He still held his customs post (for he was named when it was applied for after his death), but it is not known whether his position in the Revenue had been extended this long.

In April 1718 Bowen let his Irish temper fly for the last time. On the afternoon of the seventeenth, James Quin, the promising new actor at Lincoln's Inn Fields, met Bowen by accident at the Fleece Tavern in Cornhill. According to the evidence given at Quin's trial later, *"Mr. Bowen* reflected on *Mr. Quinn,* that he had acted Tamerlane in a loose sort of manner," in response to which *"Mr. Quinn* replied that *Mr. Bowen* had no great occasion to value himself for his Performance in that *Mr. Johnson* who had acted it but seldom, acted the part of *Jacomo* in *The Libertine* as well as he, who had acted it often." (This was not precisely true, for Johnson, since he started playing the role in 1708, had probably acted it more often than Bowen, but Jacomo was indeed one of Bowen's favorite roles.) This exchange of unpleasantries was bound to set two Irishmen at physical odds, and so it did. They

fell into a Discourse about their Honesty, and *Mr. Bowen* giving himself the Character of *as honest a man as any was in the World* . . . *Mr. Quinn* replied by asking *Mr. Bowen* if he should tell the Story of the Court, *Mr. Bowen* said no, it was no matter; but at last said he might tell it if he would, which *Mr. Quinn* did, and *Mr. Bowen* still persisting to abide by the assertion of his Honesty, they proceeded so far as to lay Wagers about it, and Money was laid down. *Mr. Quinn* charged *Mr. Bowen* with sometimes drinking Healths to the Duke of Ormond and at other times refusing it. Asking *Mr. Martin*, to whom the Decision of the Wager was left; how could he be as honest a man as any was in the World who acted upon two different Principles? That thereupon *Mr. Martin* told *Mr. Bowen*, that if he insisted upon it, as to his being as Honest a Man as any was in the World, he must needs give it against him. That this discourse was all the while carry'd on with a joucular air, but upon this *Mr. Bowen* rose up, flung down some Money for the Reckoning, saying he could not bear it, and must be gone.

The "Story of the Court" was probably a reference to Bowen's manslaughter case, and Quin's talk of Bowen's varying fidelity to the Duke of Ormonde could well have referred to his not getting the Smock Alley patent.

Bowen, though he stormed out of the tavern, would not let the matter drop. He sent a porter for Quin, and the two walked to a room in the Pope's Head Tavern where they ordered wine. After he downed a glass, Bowen suddenly "rose, and barricaded the door with two chairs, and told [Quin] that he had injured him past verbal reparation, and nothing but fighting should make him amends." Bowen threatened to pin Quin to the wainscot if he failed to draw at once. Quin drew to defend himself, and in the ensuing scuffle Bowen was fatally wounded. After the bloodletting of the duel had

quieted Bowen's temper, he said before witnesses that "*the Gentleman has done it fairly. If I die I forgive him.*" But then, in a more Bowenesque spirit: "but if I live I will be revenged of him." Three days later he died. Quin was later charged with manslaughter, the punishment for which was being burned in the hand, and was convicted, but there is no record to indicate that any such sentence was actually carried out; a cold iron may have been used, since Quin was a favored performer.

William Bowen died on 20 April 1718, leaving a wife, a son William and, reputedly, an illegitimate son who was a street urchin calling himself "Rugged and Tough." Bowen was buried with strange pomp arranged by Mr Arne, the fashionable undertaker of King's Street, Covent Garden. His corpse, on 25 April, was "put on board the Prince Frederick Yacht, lately built by his Nephew [John], an Officer in the Customs, in order to be carried to Leigh in Essex to be Interr'd; while they are going thither a Gun is to be fired every Minute, and they are to Salute all Ports with the falling of a Sail." After this pompous passage to his burying ground, Bowen's name was kept alive at the theatre by a series of annual benefits for his widow which lasted through 1726, an extraordinary show of charity.

Bower, Mrs *[fl. 1721]*, *singer.*

Mrs Bower appeared for the first time on stage at Lincoln's Inn Fields on 18 December 1721, singing in Italian and English. The *Daily Journal* announced that she would sing on the next day as well, but other newspapers listed "the little Boy" as singing on that date.

Bower, Henry *[fl. 1664–1667]*, *wardrobe keeper.*

Henry Bower was wardrobe keeper for the Duke's Company, probably from 1664–65 through 1666–67, though he may have been with the troupe both before and after these dates.

Bowers, Mr [*fl. 1757–1773*], *box-keeper.*

Mr Bowers was a boxkeeper at Drury Lane from at least 1757–58 through 1772–73, sharing benefits each season with several other house servants. In 1764–65 he was on the pay list at 12*s.* per week. He received his last benefit on 1 June 1773 and died sometime before 24 May 1774, on which date his widow was given a shared benefit.

Bowes, James. *See* **WINSTON, JAMES.**

Bowford, Mr [*fl. 1733*], *dancer.*

Mr Bowford (or Bewford) danced at the Haymarket Theatre on 28 May 1733.

Bowin. *See* **BOWEN.**

Bowington, Mr [*fl. 1737*], *actor.*

Mr Bowington played Appletree in *The Recruiting Officer* on 15 June 1737 at the Lincoln's Inn Fields Theatre.

Bowles, Miss [*fl. 1779*], *actress.*

A Miss Bowles played an unnamed principal part in *The Touchstone of Invention* at the Haymarket, out-of-season, on 18 October 1779. A Miss Bowles acted at the Crow Street Theatre, Dublin, in 1794 and at Belfast in 1796.

Bowles, Mrs Henry Robert. *See* **AICKIN, MRS GRAVES.**

Bowles, Robert *1748–1806, actor, singer.*

The actor Robert Bowles was born in 1748. He spent most of his professional life as a provincial actor. As a young man, according to John Bernard, Robert Bowles had accompanied an old manager, Mr Fisher, to St Petersburg to establish an English theatre under the patronage of the Empress Catherine. Perhaps he was the Mr Bowles mentioned by James Winston as manager of a strolling company which visited Andover every two years or so before about 1770. He was engaged by R. Griffith at Norwich in 1772. On 13 August 1774 the proprietors of that theatre denied his request for "an advance of Salary" but they must have complied soon after, for on 8 February 1775, they ordered the treasurer to bring to his account the sums advanced to several performers including £3 12*s.* from Mr Bowles, who then had 5*s.* per week deducted from his salary for repayment. On 15 June of that year Bowles was with the Norwich company at Bungay. He continued at Norwich through the summer season of 1777 at £1 11*s.* 6*d.* per week, but then, either discharged or leaving Norwich on his own, Bowles went to London. (On 31 October 1777 the proprietors at Norwich directed Griffith "to engage a Singer to perform in the Room of Mr Bowles on the best terms he can.")

Engaged at £3 per week, Bowles made his first billed appearance at Covent Garden as Harman in *Lionel and Clarissa* on 3 October 1777, but he may have played Leander in *The Padlock* earlier, on 22 September. While at Covent Garden he also appeared at the Haymarket, out-of-season, as Tradelove in *A Bold Stroke for a Wife* on 31 March 1778 and as the Chaplain in *The Orphan* and Bates in *The Irish Widow* on 9 April. In May and June 1778 at China Hall, in the Lower Road, Rotherhithe, Bowles acted a series of featured roles (an opportunity never his at Covent Garden) such as Don Lopez in *The Wonder*, Old Norval in *Douglas,* Sir Charles Marlow in *She Stoops to Conquer*, and Dumont in *Jane Shore*. That summer he was also at Richmond. Bowles was not at Covent Garden for 1778–79 but returned to Norwich. He also acted at York and Plymouth in 1780.

On 29 August 1780 Bowles made one more excursion onto the London stage when he played Harman in *Lionel and Clarissa* at the Haymarket, for the benefit of Miss Harper. He then passed the remainder of his career in the provinces. At Norwich in 1783, his financial problems continued. On 30 May the proprietors took his note for £7 9s. 6d. for the balance he owed them from his benefit charges, the note to be paid at his next summer benefit. But soon he was at odds with the proprietors, who apparently discharged him and then ordered on 19 December 1783 "if Mr Bowles's Note be not already discharged that his Security at Lynn be immediately applied to the Payment." His request for re-admission to the company was turned down on 24 February 1784, but on 29 April he was engaged at one guinea per week, a salary somewhat lower than he had received from that theatre in 1777. He also played at the Crow Street Theatre in Dublin in 1780 and at Limerick in 1782.

Although there are no notices of him at the Norwich theatre after 1785, Bowles seems to have lived out his life in that city and at Lynn. He seems to have been a worthy man, with a reputation for telling strange stories and playing practical jokes. Bernard thought that "Bowles was a great romancer, but the most humourous in his nonsense I ever listened to." Bowles died on 15 October 1806, probably at Norwich. His widow, Mrs Sarah Bowles, died at Lynn in April 1811.

Robert Bowles was the father of the provincial actor Henry Robert Bowles (1774–1830), who managed the Norwich theatre in 1806. The son had married the widow of Graves Aickin in 1806. After a handsome benefit on 10 February 1810 the couple ended their theatrical careers to open a day school for boys at Yarmouth. He was also a co-pastor of the Yarmouth Unitarian Chapel. The first Mrs Henry Robert Bowles died in 1814, and Bowles married Elizabeth Marshall, who died in 1823.

Henry Robert Bowles died in 1830. His daughter Jane by his first wife married a Mr Swan, and their daughter Elinor (Mrs Hely), as Elinor Aickin, acted late in the nineteenth century as a member of the Compton Comedy Company.

Bowley, Mr [fl. 1792–1820], *boxkeeper, officekeeper.*

Mr Bowley was first noted in the Drury Lane accounts in 1792–93 when he was listed simply as a member of the company. A benefit he shared with others on 30 May 1795 identified him as one of the theatre's boxkeepers, and the accounts regularly listed him in that capacity after the turn of the century. In 1797 he apparently served also as an officekeeper. He was still a boxkeeper in the 1819–20 season, earning the same 12s. weekly that had been paid him during most of his years of service (only in two seasons did he earn more: 1800–1801 when he was paid 15s. and 1812–13 when he received 18s.).

The St Paul, Covent Garden, parish registers contain several mentions of a John Bowley, and perhaps this was the boxkeeper. Mary Ann, daughter of John and Mary Bowley, was baptized on 30 November 1790; another daughter, Maria, was born on 8 August 1794; and Mary Bowley —probably John's wife—was buried 22 October 1822. The last entry describes Mary Bowley, aged 68, as of Bridges Street, which would place her very close to the playhouse, but no mention is made of John. The only other reference to John Bowley is on 7 June 1818 when Bowley witnessed the wedding of widower Benjamin Handy the equestrian star, and widow Mary Grant.

Bowley, Mrs [fl. 1746–1747], *house servant?*

A Mrs Bowley, possibly related to Bowley the boxkeeper, worked in some capacity for 10s. weekly at Covent Garden in the 1746–47 season.

Bowman. *See also* **BOMAN.**

Bowman, Mr [fl. 1792–1794], *actor*.

Mr Bowman, possibly a descendant of the acting family of Bomans earlier in the eighteenth century, played Campley in *Inkle and Yarico* and Captain Loveit in *Miss In Her Teens* on 16 January 1792 at the Crown Inn, Islington. He was probably the Bowman who was Pantaloon in *The Life and Death of Harlequin* at Mrs Sturmer's booth at Bartholomew Fair in 1794.

Bownty. *See* BOUNTY.

Bowtell, Mrs Barnaby, Elizabeth née Ridley [fl. 1662?–1697], *actress*.

About 1669 Elizabeth Ridley married Barnaby Bowtell (or Boutell, Bootell), and as Mrs Bowtell she joined the King's Company at the Bridges Street Theatre where her first certain stage appearance was made in August 1670 as Aurelia, a breeches part, in *The Roman Empress*. In his *Roscius Anglicanus* the prompter John Downes implied that Mrs Bowtell acted much earlier than this, presumably as Elizabeth Ridley; *The London Stage* records her as possibly playing Estifania in *Rule a Wife and Have a Wife* at the Vere Street Theatre on 28 January 1662, Aspatia in *The Maid's Tragedy* at Bridges Street on 7 December 1666, Donna Theodosia in *An Evening's Love* on 12 June 1668, and St Catherine in *Tyrannic Love* on 24 June 1669—but *The London Stage* says that though she doubtless played these parts later, it is unlikely that she came on the stage before 1670. Indeed, when Mrs Bowtell left the stage in 1696 she was lauded for having retired before growing old, and her marriage about 1669 would suggest a birth date in the early 1650's; hence she would have been too young in the 1660's for the major roles listed above.

Her husband was the son of Barnaby Bowtell, Esquire, of Parham Hall, Suffolk; he was commissioned a lieutenant in the Holland Regiment of William III's on 2 December 1681, and some of his wife's absences from the stage late in her career may have some connection with his military assignments.

Mrs Bowtell's breeches role in *The Roman Empress* was one of many such parts that she sustained throughout her career; others included some of the most important roles in Restoration drama: Benzayda in *The Conquest of Granada* (December 1670 and January 1671), Melantha in *Marriage à la Mode* (c. April 1672), Margery Pinchwife in *The Country Wife* (12 January 1675), probably Rosalinda in *Sophonisba* (3 April 1675), and Fidelia in *The Plain Dealer* (11 December 1676). But her most famous role was in skirts: the loving and trustful Queen Statira in *The Rival Queens*, which she "created" at Drury Lane on 17 March 1677. Opposite her in later years was Elizabeth Barry as the vengeful Roxana, and at one of the performances, according to Curll, a dispute between the two actresses led to Mrs Bowtell's being wounded:

It happened these Two Persons before they appeared to the Audience, unfortunately had some Dispute about a *Veil* which Mrs. *Boutel* by the Partiality of the Property-Man obtained; this offending the haughty *Roxana*, they had warm Disputes behind the Scenes, which spirited the Rivals with such a natural Resentment to each other, they were so violent in performing their Parts, and acted with such Vivacity, that *Statira* on hearing the King was nigh, *begs the Gods to help her for that Moment*; on which *Roxana* hastening the designed Blow, struck with such Force, that tho' the Point of the Dagger was blunted, it made way through Mrs. *Boutel's* Stayes, and entered about a Quarter of an Inch in the Flesh.

This Accident made a great Bustle in the House, and alarmed the Town; many different Stories were told; some affirmed, Mrs. *Barry* was jealous of Mrs. *Boutel* and Lord *Rochester*, which made them suppose she did it with Design to destroy her; but by all that could be discovered on the strictest Examination of both Parties, it was only the *Veil* these two Ladies contended for.

There was apparently good reason for some to suspect that jealousy might have caused the argument, (though Curll was wrong in citing Rochester, who died before this encounter) for Elizabeth Bowtell was apparently a very talented, popular, beautiful, and promiscuous young woman.

Curll described her as "a very considerable Actress; she was low of Stature, had very agreeable Features, a good Complexion, but a Childish Look. Her Voice was weak, tho' very mellow . . . [and] she was a Favourite of the Town; and besides what she saved by Playing, the Generosity of some happy Lovers enabled her to quit the Stage before she grew old." A lampoon written about 1678 said

> *Betty Bowtall is true to whom shee*
> *pᵉtend*
> *Then happy is hee whom shee Chuses*
> *for freind*
> *Shee faine would hang out widdows*
> *peak for a signe*
> *But ther's noe need of Bush where there*
> *is so good wine*

And in the 1688 *Session of Ladyes* she was called "Chestnut-man'd Boutel, whom all the Town F——ks."

Mrs Bowtell's stage career during the 1670's had been busy and successful, but in the two decades that followed, her appearances were infrequent and her whereabouts difficult to trace. About the time Barnaby Bowtell received his commission in 1681, the King's Company to which his wife belonged was crumbling, and a union with the Duke's troupe was imminent. Prompter John Downes said that Mrs Bowtell joined the United Company in 1682, but from March 1678 to April 1688 no roles are recorded for her, and she may well have gone to the Continent with her husband. She acted again from the spring of 1688 through the end of the 1689–90 season

—or perhaps a season or two longer; but her appearances were not frequent, and the most significant new roles she played were probably Mrs Termagant in *The Squire of Alsatia* on 3 May 1688 and Desdemona in *Othello* about 1688–89. By September 1692 she was living in an English Benedictine covent in Paris and had just received a sizeable sum of money—source unknown. Shortly after this she returned to England for a year, accompanied by actress Elizabeth Price; for some mysterious reason both women travelled under Mrs Bowtell's maiden name of Ridley. She probably did not return to the stage during this stay, and on 26 December 1693 she was granted a pass to go to Holland with her maid.

By 1694 Mrs Bowtell was again in London and performing. She may have joined the United Company just before it split, or she may have engaged in some unrecorded acting at the summer fairs; Mrs Lee, a booth operator at Southwark Fair, stated (c. 1735) that she and her mother's troupes had been nurseries of such great performers as Mrs Bowtell, but any fair-acting Mrs Bowtell might have done for the Lees probably would have been late, rather than early in her career, since they operated late in the seventeenth century. In the fall of 1695 she began acting regularly with Thomas Betterton's company at Lincoln's Inn Fields, one of her new parts being Constantia in *The She-Gallants* which she acted in late December. Her last recorded role was Estifania ("the prettiest rogue that e'er you looked upon") in *Rule a Wife and Have a Wife* in October 1696. On 1 November 1697 she was granted a pass to return to Holland and join her husband. Barnaby Bowtell left his regiment on 24 January 1705, but whether or not his wife was still with him or, indeed, still alive, is not known. The lively actress of the 1670's who so excelled as "the young, innocent Lady whom all the Heroes are mad in Love with" became a woman of mystery during the following two decades.

Bowyer, Mrs [fl. 1798–1799], singer.

Mrs Bowyer was in the singing chorus at Drury Lane from 14 November 1798, when she was one of the peasants in *The Captive of Spilburg*, to 24 May 1799, when she sang in *Pizarro*; between these dates she also swelled the choruses of such works as *Aurelio and Miranda* (29 December 1798) and *Feudal Times* (19 January 1799).

Boxley, Edward [fl. 1773], musician.

On 16 January 1773 young John Hindmarsh was bound apprentice to Edward Boxley, citizen and musician, who turned Hindmarsh over to George Buckland—citizen, "plaisterer," and a musician by profession—for a term's training. Boxley's address was given as the Town Clerk's Office, Guildhall. All this information was duly recorded in the books of the Worshipful Company of Musicians.

Boyack, Mr [fl. 1766–1776], actor, singer.

Mr Boyack, apparently a Scotsman, played in *The Gentle Shepherd* (sometimes billed as *Patie and Roger*) at the Haymarket Theatre several times over a period of ten years. He was first mentioned in the bills on 19 May 1766, but the advertisement stated that this was the last time the work was to be performed that season, so presumably he had appeared earlier than this date. He acted Glaud and introduced the *Cries of Edinburgh* into the performance. Boyack was back in London again on 19 December 1768, this time playing Sir William, but on 21 September 1772 he reverted to the role of Glaud and again sang the *Cries*. He stayed with this part for performances of the pastoral on 20 February 1775, 20 November 1775, and 7 October 1776; on this last date he made his exit from the London theatre world in style by also playing Carbuncle in the afterpiece, *The Prejudice of Fashion*.

Boyce. *See also* BOYES *and* BOYS.

Boyce, John [fl. 1701–1710], actor.

The first recorded appearance of John Boyce (or Boise) was about March 1701 at Lincoln's Inn Fields when he acted Bassilius in *The Czar of Muscovy*. A warrant in the Lord Chamberlain's accounts names him as one of 22 comedians sworn on 23 February 1702—presumably a renewal of his contract. Among the few roles recorded for Boyce in this early period were Castruccio in the premiere of *The Patriot* at Drury Lane about December 1702, after he switched companies, and Crimp in *The Old Mode and the New*, which he played at the same house on 11 March 1703. After a break of seven years his name reappeared on the bills: he had a benefit at *The Fair Quaker of Deal* at Drury Lane on 25 March 1710, and at Pinkethman's theatre at Greenwich he played Hubert in *The Fond Husband* on 12 August and the French Pirate in *The Sea Voyage* on 24 August 1710.

Boyce, Thomas d. 1794, dancer, actor.

Thomas, "Son of Samuel Boyce by Anne his Wife," was christened at St Paul, Covent Garden, on 23 June 1755, and may be the Thomas of the following essay. It is at least conceivable that the engraver-dramatist Samuel Boyce, who died on 21 March 1775, was the father of the subject of the parish-register entry.

Thomas Boyce was a dancer employed by Sadler's Wells from about 1786 until his death in 1794. He was also at Covent Garden Theatre from the beginning of the 1788–89 season, when he appeared in an account entry of 20 September, having been paid 15s. for three nights. He was first named as Harlequin in John O'Keeffe's new pantomime *Aladin; or, the Wonderful Lamp*, on 26 December, and repeated many times afterward. The *Biographical and Imperial Magazine* for January 1789 called him the joint producer, with Carlo Delpini, of this harlequinade; it is not certain what was "produced" beyond, perhaps, the choreography.

For such an auspicious start, Boyce seems to have been strangely obscure for the rest of the season. He was apparently in no other named parts. Chorus dancing was still his lot for most of the 1789–90 season, though his salary was raised to £2 per week. On 19 September he was paid an extra fee of £15 for "attention to the pantomime." He was a principal dancer in "A Grand Ballet of Action" called *The Deserter*, Don Pedro Commandant in *Don Juan*, and Harlequin again in *Harlequin Chaplet*, a farrago of scenes from 11 favorite pantomimes by James Wild, repeated many times after its first appearance on 21 December. He danced, with Byrn, Miss DeCamp, and others, in "a new dance," *The Generous Sportsman*, for his last named appearance of this season, on 25 June.

In 1790–91 Boyce was excluded from even the smaller parts except for dancing as Harlequin among the "pantomimical characters" in Charles Bonner and Robert Merry's *The Picture of Paris*, 20 December 1790, repeated many times through 25 February. Mrs Boyce was a "dancing nymph" in this production. Boyce did not appear in the bills thereafter but was probably dancing at the theatre until the end of the season.

In 1791–92 Boyce shifted his services to Drury Lane, where he was on the rolls as an "actor," but apparently this change did not improve his rank. He was seen in the bills only as one of many priests in *The Cave of Trophonius*. Back at Covent Garden the next season, he was again Harlequin, this time in *Harlequin Museum*, which was repeated 47 times from 20 December through 23 February. In his final season, 1793–94, he took Simpson's place as Harlequin in *Harlequin Chaplet* on 28 October, and from 19 December to 8 May he appeared many times in *Harlequin Dr Faustus* as a chorus dancer.

He was also appearing regularly at Sadler's Wells that season, and it was as a Wells performer that he was spoken of in the *Gentleman's Magazine* for October 1794, which reported his death on 30 October:

After a short illness, brought on by one of those overheats to which those of his pantomimic industry are so liable, Mr Boyce, the Sadler's Wells Harlequin. No man, in theatrical recollection, ever united so much active ability with such a constant and steady attention to the business of the stage. The managers of the Wells, as a proper tribute to his public and private worth, have since kindly given a benefit to his widow and children.

A clipping from some newspaper of 10 October 1794 conveys Mrs Boyce's "Heartfelt Acknowledgments for the very liberal Patronage which attended her Benefit Night on Wednesday last." Mrs Boyce had been a dancer at Sadler's Wells also, and she returned there for some period of time after her husband's death. On 31 August 1795 she was a "lass" in *Englands Glory* at the Wells; and a copy of a benefit ticket for her night, 10 October 1796, survives.

The Boyces had three children. The

Harvard Theatre Collection

BENEFIT TICKET FOR MRS BOYCE

Susannah Boyce, dancer, who signed a petition to the King for establishment of a third
patent theatre in 1810 is on surviving pay
lists at Drury Lane as an actress from
1805 through 1819, and she must have
been the Miss Boyce whom Charles Dibdin
remembered as being in the Sadler's Wells
company of 1802–3. Dibdin testified that
she was still at Drury Lane about 1830.
She also acted at Brighton in the summers.
It is probable that she was a daughter of
Mr and Mrs Thomas Boyce. James Winston
recorded data in his notebooks concerning
a Miss Boyce: "Many years an actress at D
Lane—daughter of Boyce a celebrated Harlequin—married a son of Mrs Klanert, of
the Richmond Theatre, not half her age."

Boyce, Mrs Thomas *[fl. 1790–1796],
dancer. See* **BOYCE, THOMAS.**

Boyce, William *1710–1779, composer, organist, teacher, conductor.*
William Boyce was by many estimates
the greatest English-born composer of the
eighteenth century, rivalled in eminence
only by his contemporary, Thomas Augustine Arne. He was the son of John Boyce
(d. 1753), who was beadle of the Joiners'
Company from 1722 until 1752. Burney
declared that Boyce had been born about
1710 "at Joyner's Hall in the City" of
London and had lived with his father
"during his celibacy," but perhaps neither
statement should be taken literally. William
had one brother, John (d. 1755), who
succeeded his father briefly in the office of
beadle, and a sister, Elizabeth, who married
Francis Wyndham, a tailor of Salisbury
Court, Fleet Street. Neither displayed the
slightest musical talent.

As a young chorister of St Paul's Cathedral, Boyce studied under Charles King and
was later apprenticed to the excellent
teacher Dr Maurice Greene, organist of the
Cathedral, with whom he remained in
cordial friendship until Greene's death in

Harvard Theatre Collection

WILLIAM BOYCE
by J. K. Sherwin

1755. From about 1737 he also studied
theory with Johann Christoph Pepusch,
who seems to have been responsible for
Boyce's intense interest in the history of
music.

When Boyce was about 23 he received
his first appointment as a church organist,
to Oxford Chapel in Vere Street, Cavendish
Square. He supplemented his income by
teaching harpsichord at Mr Cavaller's seminary for girls in Queen Street, Bloomsbury. On 21 June 1736 he was sworn as
composer to the Chapel Royal, on the
strength of his remarkable early compositions, replacing John Weldon, who had
died on 7 May. At the same time Jonathan
Martin was given Weldon's place as principal organist, and the two young men
signed a rather amusing agreement:

Whereas the place of Organist has much more duty and attendance belonging to it than the place of Composer (both which were enjoyed by Mr. Weldon lately deceased, during whose long indisposition the two places were joyntly supply'd by the two persons aforesaid), I the said William Boyce do promise and agree that so long as I shall continue in the place of Composer I will perform one third part of the duty and attendance belonging to the Organist, provided that I am allow'd one third part of the travelling charges belonging to the place. And I Jonathan Martin promise to compose Anthems or services for the use of his Majesty's Chapel whenever required by the Subdean for the time being.

In 1737, and for many years thereafter, Boyce conducted the meeting of the Three Choirs of Gloucester, Worcester, and Hereford. In 1739 he became one of the organizers and charter members of the Royal Society of Musicians.

During the terminal illness of his old friend and teacher Dr Greene, Master of the King's Music, Boyce performed Greene's duties, succeeding to the office at his death in 1755, by the nomination of the Duke of Grafton. Boyce was formally sworn in 1757 and continued in this important place until his death. He also followed Greene as conductor of the annual Festivals of the Sons of the Clergy.

From 1747 through 1768 Boyce was organist at St Michael's, Cornhill, and (from 1749 through 1768) simultaneously at All Hallows, Thames Street. He resigned the latter post in 1769, because of his increasing deafness. He retained for life his post as principal organist of the Chapel Royal, which he gained in 1758 in addition to his composership. During all his other endeavors, Boyce continued teaching privately. Marmaduke Overend, the composer, organist, and theorist, and John Stafford Smith, the organist, tenor singer, and composer, were among his notable pupils. He was also much in demand to

grace solemn occasions, such, for instance, as the funeral of Thomas Coram the celebrated philanthropist who was buried on 3 April 1751, aged 84, under the chapel of the Foundling Hospital, for which he had obtained a royal charter. According to *The Student; or, The Oxford and Cambridge Monthly Miscellany*

the burial service was sung by the gentlemen belonging to the choir of St. Paul's, which was composed by doctor Boyce, who played the same on a small organ set on one side of the chapel; and when the minister had read all the service but the last collect, an anthem composed by Dr. Boyce, was sung by Mr. Beard, Mr. Mence, and Mr. Savage, and the chorus parts by the other Gentlemen of Westminster and St. Paul's.

Boyce seldom refused any such demand imposed on his time, talents, or spirit. His physique and physiognomy were comfortably rotund; his approach to life easy. He dispensed a calm and cheerful benevolence from his lofty position as Master of the King's Band and foremost composer in England after the death of Handel in 1759. Burney said that "there was no professor [of music] who I was ever acquainted with that I loved, honoured, and respected more." Boyce was to Jonathan Battishill "the only man in the musical profession whose friendship I . . . laboured years to gain" (he lamented that an act of discourtesy on his part had forfeited Boyce's good opinion of him). The Reverend Charles Wesley wrote that "A more modest man than Dr Boyce I have never known. I never heard him speak a vain or ill-natured word, either to exalt himself or depreciate another." Sir John Hawkins, a strict judge, thought Boyce a moral paragon:

He was endowed with the qualities of truth, justice and integrity, was mild and gentle in deportment, above all resentment against such as envied his reputation, communicative of his knowledge, sedulous and punctual in the discharge of the duties of his several employments.

William Boyce was in most musical matters a conservative who did not chafe under the dominance of Handel as did his rival Arne. He managed, nevertheless, to express his own charming originality from his solid base on the Italian tradition. His music was of a considerable variety. Production of his theatrical contributions was concentrated almost entirely within the thirteen years between 1747 and 1760, during which time he wrote for masques and pantomimes and did incidental music for farces, and choruses and dirges for tragedy. During the famous *Romeo and Juliet* contention of 1750 between the rival patent houses (with Romeo played by Barry at Covent Garden and by Garrick at Drury Lane) T. A. Arne composed a solemn dirge for the procession of Juliet's *cortège* toward her Covent Garden tomb. Garrick immediately commissioned Boyce to provide a dirge for Drury Lane's procession, and competition between these famous productions was much intensified by the rivalry between the two eminent composers.

Boyce wrote some of the finest and best-known songs of his century, including the rousing "Hearts of Oak" in *Harlequin's Invasion* and the favorite "With Horns and Hounds," in his setting of Dryden's *Secular Masque*. He is probably best remembered today for his symphonies, his anthems, and his gorgeous organ voluntaries, but he also wrote much music for other single instruments.

Boyce was a conscientious dependent of the Crown, and as Master of the King's Music he composed large numbers of excellent musical odes on the occasions of royal birthdays, weddings, and deaths, and for New Year's Day and other Feast Days. These duties dovetailed nicely with the special performances required of his charges in the King's Band. For instance, on 4 June 1762 Boyce led a band of "upwards of fifty performers" stationed inside a "temple" which was "illuminated with upwards of 4,000 lamps," which had been caused by the Queen to be erected in secrecy outside St James's palace, contrived as "an amusement for His Majesty on his birthnight."

In 1749 Boyce was called to Cambridge to set to music an ode composed by William Mason for the installation of the Duke of Newcastle as Chancellor of the University on 1 July. At the commencement convocation on the day after the installation, Boyce's anthem "O be joyful" was performed as his exercise for the degrees of Bachelor of Music and Doctor of Music, which were conferred on him simultaneously on 3 July. (For an excellent brief assessment of Boyce's work and a nearly complete catalogue of his productions see the entry by Harold Watkins Shaw in *Grove's Dictionary of Music and Musicians*, fifth edition, edited by Eric Blom. Of particular interest to students of the theatre is the list included there of Boyce's scores for the stage, prepared by Alfred Loewenberg. An interesting critique of Boyce, measuring him against his greatest native contemporary, is the article by Charles Cudworth, "Boyce and Arne: 'The Generation of 1710,'" *Music and Letters*, XLI [1960], 137–45.)

In addition to his achievement in composition, which is only in this century beginning to be evaluated truly, Boyce had a scholarly and antiquary side to which musicians remain deeply indebted. He greatly augmented the collections of English music which had been made from 1735 onwards by John Alcock and Maurice Greene, publishing the whole in three volumes, from 1760 through 1778, under the title *Cathedral Music*. The collection preserved some works from each of 26 Tudor and Stuart composers and standardized the readings for them. In 1755 Maurice Greene had willed to his friend "William Boyce Doctor in Music," his large collection of "Music MS or printed and all Books relating to that Science," Boyce having promised not to publish any of Greene's own works.

William Boyce had at some date before 1749 married a girl whose first name was Hannah but whose last name is not now known. Their daughter Elizabeth was born on 29 April 1749. She later became Mrs Fenn, and then, according to one account, Mrs John Stafford Smith. Fifteen years after her birth, on 25 March 1764, Boyce's son William was born. He became a theatrical singer and a double-bass player of some distinction.

The elder William Boyce died at his house in Kensington, probably on 9 February 1779, and was buried beneath a brass grating under the center of the dome of St Paul's Cathedral. A service was sung by the combined choirs of Westminster Abbey and the Cathedral. His epitaph reads: "Happy in his compositions, much happier in a constant flow of harmony, through every Scene of Life, Relative or Domestic, the Husband, Father, Friend."

Boyce had been plagued by gout frequently through his later career, and in 1763 the concert bills had carried the information that he had been "prevented by a severe Fit of Illness from executing" with Avison and Giardini, a projected oratorio called *Ruth* for the benefit of the Lock Hospital on 25 April. But his will was made while he was "in perfect health" on 24 June 1775. It was proved on 20 February 1779. His widow Hannah and his daughter Elizabeth were designated executrices of his estate, which was to be disposed of in equal thirds to them and to his minor son William. The property, not itemized, and unvalued in the will, consisted of:

Government stock and security plate Jewels Rings China Pictures Household Goods Wearing Apparel Laces Linen of every Denomination for Personal Wear as well as for the Bed Table and other Uses my Music Printed and of the various other Authors my Musical Instruments Engraved Music Plates

with my Printed Books of every sort and whatever else may be omitted in the above enumeration.

A very exact idea of most of what was included under "the above enumeration" can be gained from a perusal of the catalogue of the sale at auction, on 14–16 April 1779, of Boyce's library and musical instruments. (Some items were evidently bid in on behalf of his son, William, but around 1802 the composer John Wall Callcott acquired the manuscript collections of Boyce and his pupil, Marmaduke Overend, from Overend's widow.) Among the 267 lots of the Boyce sale, principally of sheet music in manuscript and printed, are: "An elegant large Morocco Case, with Asses Skins prepared, with Lines for Musical Characters, particularly serviceable to Composers," "An exceeding fine Original Picture of Corelli," "A very curious Original Picture of Hen. Purcel," "A most excellent antient Picture of Orlando de Lassus, an undoubted Original," "A fine toned Cremona Violin," "A Stainer Violin in fine Preservation," and "A Most capital Violoncello, finely preserved, by Antonious Straduarius of Cremona, the Signature of the Maker in his own Hand-writing on the Inside, with the Year 1700."

William Boyce seems to have had only three addresses during the whole of his life: his father's residence in or near Joiners' Hall, Upper Thames Street; after his marriage, about 1748, an apartment in Quality Court, Chancery Lane; and, until 1762, his house in Kensington.

Sir Joshua Reynolds painted a fine portrait of Boyce. Another, by Hudson, belongs now to the Music School in Oxford. F. K. Sherwin drew and engraved a portrait for frontispiece to the first volume of the second edition of the composer's *Cathedral Music*, edited by Sir John Hawkins in 1788, and prefixed also to the *Collection of Anthems* published by Mrs Boyce in 1790.

Boyce, William *1764–1823? singer, double-bass player.*

William Boyce was born to the great English composer of the same name and his wife Hannah on 25 March 1764. He was baptized on 25 April at Hammersmith. He was 15 years younger than his sister Elizabeth, Dr Boyce's only other child.

William matriculated at Magdalen College, Oxford, 11 months after his father's death and shortly before he was 16, on 27 January 1780, but the *Alumni Oxonienses* does not show that he took a degree. No record of his early musical education survives, but it is reasonable to surmise that at least some of it had been furnished by his distinguished parent.

A Boyce, probably William, was listed among the bass singers at the Handel Memorial Concerts at Westminster Abbey and the Pantheon on 26, 27, and 29 May and 3 and 5 June 1784. "Wm Boyce," a "Bass Voice," was paid £4 14s. 6d. by the Academy of Ancient Music for singing in its concerts in the 1787–88 season. He was employed as a double-bass player in the spring oratorios of the Ashleys from 1789 until far into the nineteenth century. He was probably the Boyce who, according to J. P. Kemble's notes, was being engaged as "extra bass, chorus" at Drury Lane Theatre from before 1790 through 1795–96, but was first named in the playbills there, "Boyce" only, singing among some 40 others in "The Chorus of Youths and Maidens" accompanying the "Triumphal Entry of Publius into Rome," in the fifth act of a performance of William Whitehead's *The Roman Father* on 15 November 1794. The music of the Chorus, according to the bill, was by "Boyce," i.e., Dr William Boyce the celebrated composer. This year Doane's *Musical Directory* cited the younger William as living at Hungerford Market and said he had been concerned in the Concerts of Ancient Music and had played at Ranelagh. .(The *Directory* listed him both as "Do[uble] Bass" and "Bass," and the latter usually means bass voice.)

Boyce was listed as singing again, one among many, in the choruses accompanying *The Cherokee* on 20 December 1794 and *The Pirates* on 8 January 1796. Both these pieces were repeated many times. He was employed by the Haymarket in the summers of 1795 and 1796, again for the anonymous background of massed voices. After 1796 he does not seem to have been mentioned again as a vocalist.

Boyce had been proposed as a member of the Royal Society of Musicians on 7 February 1792. He was said then to be "employed at the Haymarket Theatre, at Covent Garden Theatre, and Ranelagh and private concerts, has a wife but no children. Is in good health and aged twentyeight years." He was elected by 11 yeas and one nay at the meeting of 6 May and paid his subscription and signed the membership book on 3 June 1792. Boyce was assigned by the Governors to play the double bass every year from 1792 through 1803 at the annual May benefit concerts sponsored by the Society at St Paul's Cathedral. He was himself elected a Governor in 1796.

Boyce was in the Covent Garden band until at least 1816–17 when his pay was £2 per week. He was also, in 1817, in the band for the opera at the King's Theatre, and Sainsbury cited him as playing at the Birmingham Music Festival in 1820. He died about 1823.

William Boyce the younger had inherited one-third of the value of the property of his father, who had died when the boy was 15. Dr Boyce's music library, embracing that of his teacher Dr Maurice Greene, and also some valuable musical instruments, had been sold at auction in 1779. But evidently some of this property had been bid in for the son, for when his own library was sold (on 29 March 1824) it included "the choicest portion of the Property which formerly belonged to the celebrated Doctor Boyce." He had been even more fortunate in 1808, when the eccentric and miserly organist John Rice the younger, who died possessed of over

£40,000, made Boyce the beneficiary of £7000.

Boyd, Miss. *See* COLLES, MRS.

Boyer, Mr [*fl. 1789–1794?*], *singer.*
A Mr Boyer was in the cast of the ballad opera *The Island of St Marguerite* at Drury Lane on 13 November 1789, and though he was named as playing one of the principal characters, his role was not cited. This may have been Boyer's only performance on stage, but if, as seems likely, he was a singer in 1789 at Drury Lane, perhaps he was the Mr Boyer reported in Doane's *Musical Directory* of 1794 who was a *basso* living in Pall Mall. This Mr Boyer sang at concerts sponsored by the Longacre Society and participated in the Handelian performances at Westminster Abbey.

Boyes. *See also* BOYCE and BOYS.

Boyes, Mr *d. 1791, actor.*
A Mr Boyes, who had previously acted at Worcester and Shrewsbury, played the part of Doiley in *Who's the Dupe* at Drury Lane Theatre on 22 April 1790. John Philip Kemble left a memorandum on this attempt: "Mr Boyes, formerly Partner with Mr Hatchett the Coach-maker, made his first Appearance in Old Doiley. He is very like Mr. Parsons in his Face; but not in his acting."
Boyes went discreetly back to provincial acting after this single performance in London. He died in Worcester on 4 March 1791.

Boyn. *See* BOWEN.

Boys. *See also* BOYCE and BOYES.

Bozoni. *See* BUZZONI.

Brabant, Francis [*fl. 1669–1690*], *kettledrummer.*
Francis Brabant was kettledrummer to Sir Philip Howard, at least in the early part

of his career; a warrant dated 1 July 1669 so described him and ordered a payment of £7 from the royal coffers for the gilding and painting of his two kettledrum banners. On 9 March 1690—after two decades in which his name did not appear in the Lord Chamberlain's accounts—he was granted livery as a kettledrummer in the Troop of Guards.

Bracegirdle, Anne *c. 1663–1748, actress, singer.*
Anne Bracegirdle was the daughter of Justinian and Martha Bracegirdle of Northamptonshire (and the wealthy clergyman Justinian Bracegirdle who died on 25 October 1625 may have been a near relation). Anthony Aston noted that the common opinion was that her father was a coachman, coachmaker, or coach renter of Northampton, and a poem about Anne's admirer the Earl of Scarsdale, written about 1700, spoke of her father as the keeper of an inn for carriers in Northampton. The murder trial following William Mountfort's death in 1692 confirmed that Anne's mother was, indeed, named Martha, and that she had a brother Hamlet. Various wills, including Anne's, show that she also had a brother John (who apparently had a son Justinian and a daughter Martha) and a sister Frances. Anne may have been related in some way to the Staffordshire Bracegirdles, in which case she would have been distantly related to the Astons and the Congreves. The Funeral Book at Westminster Abbey shows Anne's death to have been on 12 September 1748 at the age of 85, which would place her birth about 1663; references to her throughout her career fit nicely with this date, arguments in favor of her having been born about a decade later notwithstanding.
We have very little information about Anne Bracegirdle from before 1688. Curll said that her father fell on hard times and was forced to place Anne in her infancy with Thomas and Mary Betterton, and through them, one may guess, she became

interested in, and trained for, the stage. A number of references to little girls in play-bills before 1688 suggest that Anne may have appeared on stage at least once or per-haps several times before she was officially recognized. The epilogue to *Don Carlos* on 8 June 1676 at Dorset Garden was spoken by a "Girle" in the Duke's Company, and the epilogue to *Abdelazer* on 3 July was given by "Little Mis. Ariell." The latter opens, "With late Success being blest, I'm

come agen" and closes with "Since then I'm grown at least an Inch in height, / And shall e'er long be full-blown for Delight." Perhaps these were delivered by Anne at about 13, exaggerating her growth a bit. When *The Orphan* was performed in late February 1680, "The Little Girl" played the page Cordelio; Curll cited this as Anne's first role, though he said she was less than six when she played it—possibly a scribal error for 16, which would have been almost

Harvard Theatre Collection

ANNE BRACEGIRDLE as Semernia
engraved by W. Vincent

right for Anne at this date. When *The Duke of Guise* was performed by the United Company in 1683, the epilogue asked, "Wou'd any of you Sparks, if Nan or Mally / Tipts you th'inviting Wink, stand shall I, shall I?" "Nan" may have been a reference to Anne, then about 20. However, there must have been other young girls during these years who occasionally spoke epilogues, and without further evidence it is difficult to assign any to Anne with certainty.

On 12 January 1688, when she was about 25, Anne's name first appeared in the Lord Chamberlain's accounts as a member of the United Company, and on 6 February, billed as Mrs Bracegirdle, she acted Atelina in Mountfort's *The Injured Lovers*. Though theatrical records are woefully incomplete for this period, we know of a few roles that Anne played, among which were Semernia on 20 November 1689 in *The Widow Ranter* (her first breeches part—a type she henceforth played frequently), Biancha in Mountfort's *The Successful Strangers*, and Marcelia in *The Treacherous Brothers*—both in January 1690. As early as 16 March 1690 she may have inherited Mrs Bowtell's part of Statira in *The Rival Queens*, opposite the Alexander of William Mountfort; it was to become in time one of Anne's most famous roles. Other characters from the early years of her career were Julia in *The English Friar*, Rosania in *The Amorous Bigot*, Cleomira in *Distressed Innocence*, Maria in *Edward III* (another work in which Mountfort may have had a hand), and Emmeline in *King Arthur*. Most significant among her roles about this time were Lady Anne in *Richard III* and Desdemona in *Othello*, both of which she may have played about 1690–91, according to manuscript casts that have survived. Even at this early date she found pathetic roles in tragedies and sophisticated heroines in comedies most suited to her talent.

In addition to her acting assignments, Anne regularly spoke prologues and epi-

logues—an indication of her popularity with audiences; during the 1690's alone she was called upon for such tasks for at least 20 plays. She had, in a very few years, become one of the important members of the United Company and a favorite with the town.

Colley Cibber, remembering Anne in 1690 when he joined the troupe, said she was just then

blooming to her Maturity; her Reputation as an actress gradually rising with that of her Person; never any Woman was in such general Favour of her Spectators, which, to the last Scene of her Dramatick Life, she maintain'd by not being unguarded in her private Character. This Discretion contributed not a little to make her the *Cara*, the Darling of the Theatre: For it will be no extravagant thing to say, Scarce an Audience saw her that were less than half of them Lovers, without a suspected Favourite among them: And tho' she might be said to have been the Universal Passion, and under the highest Temptations, her Constancy in resisting them served but to increase the number of her Admirers . . . [Yet] she had no greater Claim to Beauty than what the most desirable *Brunette* might pretend to. But her Youth and lively Aspect threw out such a Glow of Health and Chearfulness, that on the Stage few Spectators that were not past it could behold her without Desire. It was even a Fashion among the Gay and Young to have a Taste or *Tendre* for Mrs. *Bracegirdle*.

One of the young blades who developed a *tendre* for her was Captain Richard Hill, and another, very likely, was the actor-playwright William Mountfort, with whom she had worked closely for several years.

On 10 December 1692 Narcissus Luttrell recorded the bare outline of the celebrated tragedy which occurred as a result of their conflicting interests:

Last night Lord Mohun, captain Hill of collonel Earles regiment, and others pursued Mountfort the actor from the playhouse to his lodgings in Norfolk Street, where one kist him while Hill run him thro' the belly: they ran away, but his lordship was this morning seized and committed to prison. Mountfort died of his wounds this afternoon. The quarrell was about Bracegirdle the actress, whom they would have trapan'd away, but Mountfort prevented it, wherefore they murthered him thus.

Not all of these facts were correct, but the conclusions to which Luttrell jumped were probably similar to those arrived at by other Londoners who heard of the murder. The trial of Lord Mohun brought out many more details and corrected a number of errors.

According to the testimony, Hill was infatuated with Mrs Bracegirdle, and she had firmly refused his proposal of marriage. He believed that Mountfort was Anne's successful lover and that it was the actor who stood in his way. Hill had openly spoken of doing away with Mountfort, but he seems to have had the abduction of Mrs Bracegirdle as his first concern. On 9 December 1692 Hill and Lord Mohun planned to abduct Mrs Bracegirdle after her morning rehearsal at Drury Lane and whisk her off to Totteridge. They appeared at the theatre and eyed the actress, who then tried to hide; Lord Mohun found her, but she made her escape. The men met at the playhouse again at six, failed to find Anne, and then went to her house in Howard Street only to discover she was having supper at Gawen Page's house in Princess Street. They then went to the Horseshoe Tavern in Drury Lane where, according to one witness, they were joined by Anne's brother Hamlet, who agreed to let them know when Anne would leave Page's house and what route she would take to her home. Whether Hamlet informed on his sister or provided the information quite innocently is not known, but when Anne, her mother Martha, Hamlet, and Mr Page walked down Drury Lane toward Anne's house, Hill, Lord Mohun, and about six soldiers they had hired were waiting with a coach.

The soldiers parted Anne and Mr Page and almost knocked Anne's mother down, but they were prevented from getting the actress into the coach, partly by Martha's clinging to her daughter and partly by the alarm Mr Page raised as he warded off with his cane the attack of Hill, who had drawn his sword. Hill, realizing that his plan had misfired, took the nearly-swooning actress by the hand and led her and her mother to their house in Howard Street about a quarter of a mile away. He apparently gave excuses, said his design was honorable, and begged Anne's pardon, but Martha Bracegirdle accused Hill of trying to steal her daughter, and Anne refused to accept an apology or see Hill again. With Lord Mohun, Hill remained in the street outside Anne's house for over an hour, threatening vengeance on Mountfort, the actress's presumed lover. The actor then appeared, apparently going toward the Bracegirdle house. Lord Mohun greeted him and asked if he had come because of the thwarted abduction; Mountfort said he had no knowledge of it but had come up Howard Street by chance, and that Mrs Bracegirdle was no concern of his. Then Mountfort said it was a dishonor for Lord Mohun to "keep Company with Captain *Hill*," whereupon Hill struck Mountfort on the head and ran him through with his sword, apparently before the actor had a chance to draw and defend himself. By the next day, Mountfort was dead. Hill escaped, but Lord Mohun gave himself up, stood trial, and was acquitted; five years later Hill was killed in a tavern brawl, and in 1712 Lord Mohun died in a duel.

That Anne Bracegirdle was shaken by the dreadful affair is evident from the theatrical records: she had played (or was supposed to have played) the Countess of Essex in *The Unhappy Favorite* on 9 December 1692, the day of the murder, and her next recorded performance was as Lady Trickitt in *The Maid's Last Prayer* at the end of February 1693, about a month after

Lord Mohun's trial. In March 1693 she acted Araminta in Congreve's first play, *The Old Bachelor*, but the Drury Lane box office and Mrs Bracegirdle's reputation had suffered from the Mountfort affair. It was probably *The Richmond Heiress*, performed in mid-April, with music by John Eccles, that redeemed Anne's popularity. She played Fulvia, a heroine who emerges victorious after a series of abduction attempts—an obvious parallel to the events of the previous December. Eccles, who became Anne's singing teacher, provided her with songs, including a particularly pointed one, "I am a maid, I'm still of Vestas train." She thus became perhaps the first singing actress of the period, for previously the songs in plays had been handled by professional singers who were not assigned acting roles. Dryden, in a letter to Walsh on 9 or 10 May 1693, was enthusiastic about her and about his friend Thomas Doggett (called "Solon"): D'Urfey's "Second Act, was wonderfully diverting; where the scene was in Bedlam: & Mrs Bracegirdle and Solon were both mad: the Singing was wonderfully good, And the two whom I nam'd, sung better than Redding and Mrs Ayloff, whose trade it was: at least our partiality carried it for them. The rest was woefull stuff, & concluded with Catcalls."

D'Urfey, too, had praise for Anne's singing in another production, his second part of *Don Quixote*, performed in late May 1694, in which she played Marcella and sang Eccles's "I burn, I burn." In the preface to the printed edition D'Urfey apparently referred to this song when he said it was "so incomparably well sung, and acted by Mrs Bracegirdle, that the most envious do allow, as well as the most ingenious affirm, that 'tis the best of that kind ever done before."

By 1694 Mrs Bracegirdle was one of the leading members of the United Company and reaching her full development as an actress; Congreve and other dramatists were writing roles especially for her, and her

skill as a high comedienne was being fully recognized. But the United Company, which had existed since 1682, was in trouble. Christopher Rich had gained control of the group in the 1690's, and his tyrannical ways had antagonized many of the more mature members of the company. Typical of his practices was one which involved Anne Bracegirdle: Rich gave some of Betterton's roles to young George Powell and tried to give some of Mrs Barry's roles to Anne—but Anne sensibly refused them. His financial manipulations and attempts to economize at the actors' expense also antagonized the older members of the troupe. To be fair, however, Mrs Bracegirdle was apparently capable of being quite demanding, as when she insisted upon a benefit each year and all the profits from it, a demand which in the early 1690's was most unusual.

In December 1694 Thomas Betterton, as leader of the older players, placed a long letter of grievances before the Lord Chamberlain, and when the company suspended acting on 22 December because of the illness of Queen Mary, Betterton and his cohorts took the opportunity to press their charges. Sir Robert Howard, the Lord Chamberlain, was won over by their pleas, and he in turn persuaded the King to grant the rebels a license. By March 1695 Betterton's faction had seceded from the company, hired the old tennis court in Lincoln's Inn Fields, and started reconverting it for stage use. The group was given a license on 25 March 1695 after the King gave a private hearing to the leaders, Betterton, Elizabeth Barry, and Anne Bracegirdle. At about 32, and in her prime, Anne had arrived at the top of her profession.

Waiting in the wings to write for her a succession of brilliant roles was William Congreve. His *Love for Love* opened the new theatre in Lincoln's Inn Fields, the second on that site. Anne played Angelica, a role tailored to her talents, and spoke the epilogue. A prologue by an unknown hand was also written, intended for her delivery; in breeches she was to say "You see I'm Young, and to that Air of Youth, / Some will add Beauty, and a little Truth." The *Love for Love* cast was a brilliant one, the production a triumph, and the new troupe was off to a splendid start. Within the next five years Anne Bracegirdle played, among other roles in less familiar plays, Almeria in Congreve's *The Mourning Bride*, Bellinda in *The Provoked Wife*, Isabella in Gildon's version of *Measure for Measure*, and—the finest role ever written for her—Millamant in Congreve's *The Way of the World*, first performed on 5 March 1700.

But Betterton's company was apparently not well managed by the veteran actor and his two leading ladies. In 1698 or perhaps a little later, the actor John Verbruggen lodged a complaint against the trio, noting that Betterton, Barry, and Bracegirdle kept the company's books secret and made huge profits for themselves. He had been told when he joined the troupe in 1696 that the company debts were not over £200, but he found them later to be about £800. Further, he complained, the managers stopped his weekly 20s. payment and yet ordered benefits for themselves. Whether or not conditions were as bad as Verbruggen claimed, it would appear that the managers were being as high-handed in their way as Christopher Rich had been in his.

After the turn of the century and until her sudden retirement in 1707, Mrs Bracegirdle continued to attract writers, among whom was Nicholas Rowe, who fashioned roles for her talents. According to Davies, Rowe courted Anne through his plays, designing Selima in *Tamerlane*, Lavinia in *The Fair Penitent*, and Semanthe in *Ulysses* especially for her. Congreve, too, continued to create parts for her; she was his Venus in *The Judgment of Paris*, brought out at Dorset Garden. On 26 March 1701, a few days after the performance, Congreve wrote to his friend Keally, "Our friend Venus performed to a miracle." Manuscript casts

ANNE BRACEGIRDLE

engraved by J. Stow, after *Harding's Biographical Mirrour*

for this period also show her playing Victoria in Southerne's *The Fatal Marriage* on 24 April 1701, Cordelia in Tate's version of *King Lear* on 19 May (or possibly 27 January, or both), and Evandra in Shadwell's *Timon of Athens* on 3 February 1702. It may also have been about this time that she played Ophelia in *Hamlet* (Shakespeare's version, for a change), but though she is recorded as having played this role, the date on which she first acted it is not known.

By about 1705 Mrs Bracegirdle was earning an assured £3 per week; when profits were good, her weekly salary may have run as high as £5—a very handsome income for the time. By 1707 she was probably receiving even more: a minimum of £120 annually or, when profits climbed, £150. Her salary was equal to that of Mrs Barry among the women and of Betterton, Verbruggen, Powell, and Wilks among the men.

Her last season on the stage was 1706-7 at the new Queen's Theatre in the Haymarket. Among other roles she played were a few new ones (though she may have acted some of these before; the records are too incomplete to tell): Aspasia in *The Maid's Tragedy* on 2 November 1706, Harriet in *The Man of Mode* on 9 November, Estifania in *Rule a Wife and Have a Wife* on 20 November, Ophelia in *Hamlet* on 10 December, and Portia in *Julius Caesar* on 14 January 1707.

It is probable that during this season Anne also played the title role in *The Amorous Widow*, though no performance date is known. In the Queen's Theatre company in 1706-7 was Anne Oldfield, a rising young star who was beginning to challenge Mrs Bracegirdle in comedy roles. The story told by Mrs Oldfield's biographer ("Egerton," probably a pseudonym for Curll) was that a contest was arranged between the two actresses to determine which was the best comedienne. *The Amorous Widow* was to be played twice, with the leading role taken by Mrs Bracegirdle one night and Mrs Oldfield the next. The older actress performed the role to "Admiration" as expected, but the next night Anne Oldfield

had spoke but ten Lines, [and] such was the gracefulness and beauty of her Person, so enchanting the harmony of her Voice and justness of her Delivery, and so inimitable her Action, that she charm'd the whole Audience to that Degree, they almost forgot they had ever seen Mrs. *Bracegirdle*, and universally adjudged her the Preheminence; which so much disgusted her celebrated Antagonist, that in a short time after she quitted the Stage.

The story is a good one, and despite Curll's recounting it, probably true. During this one season the two actresses were indeed in the same company, and Anne Bracegirdle "quitted" the stage before the 1706-7 season was over. Evidence to support the story also comes from the *Memorial of*

Jane Rogers (1711), a pamphlet which contains a postscript saying that Mrs Bracegirdle "left her Employment upon Mr. *Swiney's* ill Treatment of her to oblige Mrs. Oldfield." Swiney was managing the company at the Queen's Theatre during Mrs Bracegirdle's last season there.

On 18 February 1707 Anne played Lavinia in *Caius Marius* and then retired. The retirement was temporary, for she returned for a sentimental benefit on 7 April 1709 to honor Betterton, so her last role was Angelica in *Love for Love*. But in February 1707 she really completed her career at about 44 years of age when, despite the conjectural duel with Anne Oldfield, she was still at the height of her powers and one of London's most wanted women.

The bewitching effect Anne Bracegirdle had on her male admirers caused a great deal of ink to be spilt. But that was better than blood, and after the Mountfort affair no one was seriously wounded—if one excepts hearts and reputations. Much that was rumored or written about the actress could be dismissed as gossip, yet out of the mass of stories, letters, poems, reports, toasts, and arguments, one can gain an impression of Anne's character and an understanding of the quality she must have brought to the characters she played. If Millamant was the greatest character ever written for her, it was because Anne was the perfect woman to play her.

Whether Captain Hill was justified in his suspicions about William Mountfort or not, the scandal-mongers from that time forth were certainly inclined to believe he was, so that the actor was the first of a long line of admirers about whom the gossips speculated. Even the sworn evidence in the trial suggested the possibility of something more than a platonic working relationship between the two performers.

The Player's Tragedy (1693), a novel inspired by the Mountfort murder, thinly disguised Anne as Bracilla, Hill as Montano, and Mountfort as Monfredo. In the

novel Bracilla probably gave herself to
Monfredo, inciting the jealousy of Montano. Montano was advised that "Bracilla,
from a Child has been train'd up in the
Playhouse, and Interest was instill'd with
all the little Arts of Design into her before
she cou'd take any more generous Sentiments. In short: 'tis Money that must buy
your satisfaction . . ." Whereupon Montano tried to get Bracilla through a pro-
curess, who duped him with another girl;
after this, he attempted the abduction.

When Tom Brown wrote his *Letters
from the Dead to the Living* in 1703 he
created a scurrilous letter purportedly written by the ghost of Aphra Behn to "the
Famous Virgin Actress"; she was blunt
about Mountfort's conquest:

[P]eeping by chance into the Breast of your
old Acquaintance, where his Sins were as
plainly scor'd as Tavern Reckonings upon a
Bar-board, there did I behold, amongst his
numberless Transgressions, your Name registered so often in the Black-List, that Forni-
cation with Madam *B——* came so often into
the score, that it seem'd to me like a Chorus
at the end of every Stanza in an old Ballad.

In another letter from the shades Brown
described Mountfort suffering from an ach-
ing back, which he "got in the other world,
with overheaving [himself]"; a girdle was
suggested to him, but he replied, "[H]ow
can a single *girdle* do me good, when a
Brace was my destruction?"

But Mountfort, being dead, was a less interesting target than the numerous train of
Bracegirdle admirers among the living,
foremost among whom, for a long while,
was Congreve. Probably from his first association with the theatre in 1693 Congreve
had been attracted to Anne, and it was supposed later by Cibber that in the words of
his heroes the playwright was pleading his
own love for the actress. It was certainly no
secret at the time. In the preface to an
anonymous pamphlet published on 8 Sep-

tember 1698 entitled *Animadversions on
Mr. Congreve's Late Answer to Mr. [Jer-
emy] Collier*, the author chided Congreve
about Mrs Bracegirdle: he "need not covet
to go to Heaven at all, but to stay and Ogle
his dear Bracilla, with sneaking looks under his Hat, in the little side Box" at the
playhouse.

As with others, so with Congreve: Anne
was coolly aloof, a perfect Millamant—at
least in public. The tongues wagged again,
and foremost, Tom Brown's; he noted in
Amusements Serious and Comical (1700)
that Mrs Bracegirdle

looks to a miracle, when she is acting a part
in one of [Congreve's] own plays. Would
not any one think it pity she should not have
an humble servant, when Mrs. Abigail, who
is one of her attendants, can be brought to
bed of a living child without any manner of
notice taken of her? Look upon him once
more, I say; if she goes to her shift, 'tis ten to
one but he follows her, not that I would say,
for never so much, to take up her smock! He
dines with her almost every day, yet she's a
maid; he rides out with her, and visits her
almost every day, yet she's a maid; if I had
not a particular respect for her, I should go
near to say he lies with her, yet she's a maid.
Now I leave the world to judge whether it
be his or her fault that she has so long kept
her maidenhead, since gentlemen of his profession have generally a greater respect for
the ladies than that comes to.

It was probably in 1703 that Congreve
wrote a poem which many have assumed
was addressed to the actress:

> False tho' you've been to me, and Love,
>   I nere can take revenge,
> (So   much   your   wondrous   beautys
>   move)
>   Tho' I resent your change.

> In hours of bliss we oft have met,
>   They could not allways last;
> And tho' the present I regret
>   I still am Gratefull for the past.

Other poems of the time went further, especially *The Tryal of Skill* (1704):

> *When C——ve brimfull of his Mistresses Charms,*
> *Who had likewise made bold with Molier,*
> *Came in piping hot from his B——s Arms,*
> *And would have it his Title was clear.*

And Apollo, in this satire, told Congreve, "you are said to make a Wife of a Play'r." Indeed, in 1707 a poem "On the Marriage of Mr Congreve to Mrs Bracegirdle" was published in *Martial Redevivus*.

In the *Poems on Affairs of State* of 1707 the implication that Congreve had married Anne was put even more boldly:

> *Shall a Place be put down when we see it affords*
> *Fit Wives for great Poets, and W——s for great Lords?*
> *Since Angellica blest with a singular Grace*
> *Had by her fine Acting preserv'd all his Plays,*
> *In an amorous Rapture young Valentine said,*
> *One so fit for his Plays, might be fit for his Bed;*
> *He warmly pursu'd her, she yielded her Charms,*
> *And blest the Kind Youngster in her Kinder Arms:*
> *But at length the poor Nymph did for Justice implore,*
> *H'as married her now, tho he'd —— her before.*

There is no actual evidence that Anne Bracegirdle ever married anyone, nor any to prove the scandalous allegations of the satires of the time, but bewitching Bracegirdle continued to inspire gossip about her private life.

In addition to Congreve, and at about the same time, the Earl of Scarsdale (Robert Leke) was infatuated with Anne. Dryden hinted at it in a letter to Mrs Steward on 23 February 1700: "my Lord Scarsdale is the patron of Betterton's house, being in love with somebody there." At about this time a poem was written entitled "The 4th Ode of the 2nd Booke of Horace / imitated / Ld Granville to the Earle of Scarsdale," a manuscript of which is in the Essex Record Office. The work has been attributed by Fyvie and Hodges to Nicholas Rowe and was published in Rowe's works as "Lord Griffin to the Earl of Scarsdale." The opening stanza chides Scarsdale:

> *Doe not most fragrant Earle disclaime*
> *Thy bright, thy reputable Flame*
> *ffor Bracegirdle the Browne*
> *But publickly espouse the Dame*
> *And say G——d——ne the Towne.*

After noting that Anne's father was a humble innkeeper, the poem goes on:

> 5.
> *Of Proffers large the choice had shee*
> *Of Jewells Plate & Land in Fee*
> *Which she with scorne rejected*
> *And can a nymph so virtuous bee*
> *Of base-borne Blood suspected.*

> 6.
> *Her slender wast & Roguish Eye*
> *Her twining armes & taper Thigh*
> *I alwaies thought provoking*
> *But faith tho I talke waggishly*
> *I meane no more but Joking.*

The Earl of Scarsdale may not have done much about his love for Anne while he lived, but when he died, his will (proved 2 January 1708) left her £1000 and specified that she should be the first to be paid. It may not be a coincidence that Anne had chosen to retire less than a year before.

Another nobleman entranced by Mrs Bracegirdle was Lord Lovelace, of whom Anthony Aston reported that Anne was very shy. He used to send his servant daily to Mrs Bracegirdle's lodgings to inquire for her, but she never gave him any encouragement. Lord Burlington, too, courted her. One day, according to Horace Walpole, he sent her a gift of fine china, but she told his servant that it must have been a mistake and that the china was probably intended for Lady Burlington; whereupon the servant delivered the gift to the countess, who astounded her Lord with her gratitude when he came home to supper.

Then there was Nicholas Rowe, who was apparently as infatuated with Anne as Congreve was but did less about it. And, to balance the picture, there were Lord Halifax, the Dukes of Devonshire and Dorset, and others, who extolled Mrs Bracegirdle's virtuous behavior. Aston reported that over a bottle Lord Halifax proposed to the group that they present "this incomparable Woman with something worthy her acceptance," upon which he deposited 200 guineas and the others made it up to 800 to send her with "Encomiums on her Virtue."

Much that was written about Anne Bracegirdle was not connected with any specific admirers. She was called by Gildon in 1702 "the *Celebrated Virgin*," a nicely ambiguous phrase which may or may not have been ironic. In this year *A Comparison Between the Two Stages*, probably by Gildon, roasted practically everyone connected with the theatre of the time. When the character Ramble asks about Mrs Bracegirdle, his friend Critick replies that she is "a haughty conceited Woman, that has got more Money by dissembling her Lewdness, than others by professing it."

SULL[EN]. But does that *Romantick Virgin* still keep up her great Reputation?

CRIT. D'ye mean her Reputation for Acting?

SULL. I mean her Reputation for not Acting; you understand me ——.

CRIT. I do; but if I were to be sav'd for believing that single Article, I cou'd not do't: 'Tis all, all a Juggle, 'tis Legerdemain; the best on't is, she falls into good Hands, and the secrecy of the Intrigue secures her; but as to her Innocence, I believe no more on't than I believe of *John Mandevil*.

The Tom Brown *Letters from the Dead* of 1703 contain the most complete (and scurrilous) examination of Mrs Bracegirdle's character. Tom has Aphra Behn write to Anne:

Madam,

I Vow to Gad Lady, of all the Fair Sex that ever occupied their Faculties upon the publick Stage, I think your pretty self the only Miracle! For a Woman to cloak the frailties of Nature with such admirable cunning as you have done hitherto, merits, in my Opinion, the Wonder and Applause of the whole Kingdom! How many chast *Diana's* in your station have lost their Reputation before they have done any thing to deserve it? But for a Woman of your Quality to first surrender her Honour, and afterwards preserve her Character, shows a discreet management beyond the Policy of a Statesman: Your appearance upon the Stage puts the Court Ladies to the Blush, when they reflect that a mercenary Player should be more renown'd for her Vertue than all the Glorious Train of fair Spectators, who, like true Women, hear your praises whisper'd with regret, and behold your Person with insupportable Envy. The *Roman* Empress *Messalina* was never half so famous for her Lust, as you are for your Chastity; nor the Most Christian King's Favourite, Madam *Maintenon*, more Eminent for her parts, than you are for your cunning; for nothing is a greater manifestation of a Womans Conduct, than for her to be Vicious without mistrust, and to gratifie her looser inclinations without discovery; at which sort of managements you are an absolute Artist . . . [T]hat which makes me admire your good Huswifery above all your Sex is, that notwithstanding your Powdering-Tub has been so often polluted, yet you have kept your Flesh in such Credit and good Order, that the nicest Appetite in the Town would be glad to make a meal on't. . . . I commend you for the Liberty you take to oblige your chosen Friends, and the Prudence you use to conceal it from the envious Number you think unworthy of your smiles.

Yours
A. Behn

One cannot know now where the grains of truth may lie, not only in Brown's writings, but in all the scribbling that Anne provoked. Most of what was written was irresponsible gossip, backbiting, envy, or sport. But a woman who could inspire all this must have been a dazzling creature indeed. Nearly all that has been quoted here was written during the ten years before Mrs Bracegirdle's retirement when she was at the peak of her powers and the town's favorite. She apparently ignored it all, which must have made the scandal-mongers even more furious. It probably matters little what the truth was; what is important is that Anne Bracegirdle was apparently charged with a very special combination of qualities, which bewitched and bewildered London playgoers.

Though some critical comments on Anne's acting were made, none, unfortunately, are as extensive as the numerous examinations into her virtue or lack of it. Her style in tragedy was pathetic, and when the anonymous comedy *The Female Wits* was performed in October 1696 a parody of Mrs Bracegirdle's tragic style was introduced. In the play Marsilia (a satire on Mrs Manley) instructs the actress Miss Cross how to speak a tragic line: "Give me leave to instruct you in a moving Cry. Oh! there's a great deal of Art in crying; Hold your Handkerchief thus; let it meet your Eyes, thus; your Head declin'd, thus; now, in a perfect whine, crying out these words, 'By these Tears, which never cease to Flow.'"

Cibber wrote more seriously: "If any thing could excuse that desperate Extravagance of Love, that almost frantick Passion of *Lee's Alexander the Great*, it must have been when Mrs. *Bracegirdle* was his *Statira*."

Some of this quality apparently spilled over into her comic creations, for though she seems to have had the necessary *hauteur*, it was tempered by charm. Cibber wrote that "when she acted *Millamant* all

the Faults, Follies, and Affectations of that aggreeable Tyrant were venielly melted down into so many Charms and Attractions of a conscious Beauty. In other Characters, where Singing was a necessary part of them, her Voice and Action gave a Pleasure which good Sense, in those Days, was not asham'd to give Praise to." It is a pity that Cibber was so frequently at a loss for words and lapsed so often into meaningless praise, for he might have told us more if he had tried.

Anthony Aston called Anne "that *Diana* of the Stage" and was proud to think he might be related to her. Typically, he was very candid and helpful in his description of her. He said she was "of a lovely Height, with dark-brown Hair and Eye-brows, black sparkling Eyes, and a fresh blushy Complexion; and, whenever she exerted herself, had an involuntary Flushing in her Breast, Neck and Face, having continually a chearful Aspect, and a fine Set of even white Teeth." Tony liked her best in genteel comedy, though she was fine in breeches, and he remarked that her only noticeable defect was her right shoulder, which was a little "protended." When in man's clothes she wore a long or campaign peruke to cover it. Yet, he said, she was "finely shap'd, and had very handsome Legs and Feet; and her Gait, or Walk, was free, manlike, and modest, when in Breeches." Any woman who could be free, manlike, and modest simultaneously must have been quite an actress.

Very little seems to have been written by her contemporaries concerning her charitable nature, though Aston mentioned it, saying that Anne was often "going into *Clare-Market*, and giving Money to the poor unemploy'd Basket-women, insomuch that she could not pass that Neighbourhood without the thankful Acclamations of People of all Degrees; so that if any Person had affronted her, they would have been in Danger of being killed directly." She was also generous to fellow performers, such as

Mary Porter; Anne and Mrs Barry are said to have discovered Mrs Porter acting at Bartholomew Fair and to have given her an introduction to the patent house, where she became, in her day, a splendid tragic actress.

Some of the many qualities that made up Anne Bracegirdle's character were captured in portraits, though no one picture could hope to catch them all. The Kneller painting at Hampton Court shows a very handsome and tantalizing woman indeed; there is a faraway look in her eyes that gives her face a gentle, soft, shy quality. The sparkle, the "chearfulness" that Cibber and Aston noted, was captured in other portraits; typically, artists showed her wide-eyed, with an astonished look bordering on defiance.

In words, it was probably Congreve who came closest to hitting the mark:

> PIOUS Celinda goes to Pray'rs,
>   Whene'er I ask the favour;
> Yet, the tender Fool's in Tears,
>   When she believes I'll leave her.
> Wou'd I were free from this Restraint,
>   Or else had Power to win her!
> Wou'd she cou'd make of me a Saint,
>   Or I of her a Sinner!

Anne Bracegirdle may have retired in 1707 simply because she could then afford to, and she was probably wise not to work past her prime. Except for her momentary return to the stage for Betterton's benefit in 1709, she withdrew from the public eye and spent the next 39 years in a quiet retirement which, significantly, the public appears to have respected. She was certainly well off, if not wealthy, for she had done well financially as an actress, had been given many gifts, and, upon the death of the Earl of Scarsdale had received a handsome bequest in January 1708. Curiously, when Mrs Barry died she left Anne £20, plus £200 to save her "harmless from any debt of the Playhouse." That will was signed on 4 November 1713, by which time one supposes Anne's connections with

the theatre had been severed, but perhaps she still had a financial interest and, at that date, stood in danger of debt.

Anne's friendship with Congreve continued long after he turned his affections toward the Duchess of Marlborough, and they were good neighbors in Howard Street. On 26 February 1726 Congreve drafted his will, and one of the few items he did not cancel by a codicil on 29 January 1728 was a legacy of £200 to Anne. Another friend who made a bequest to Anne was Edward Porter, her brother-in-law and a friend of Congreve; he left bequests to "our Sister" Anne, "our Brother" Hamlet Bracegirdle, and to Justinian, apparently John Bracegirdle's son.

Mrs Bracegirdle lived on quietly in Howard Street among paintings of herself, Mrs Barry, Betterton, and Congreve and with the frequent company of her living friends, among whom were Horace Walpole, Colley Cibber, Tom Davies, and many other wits of the town. She occasionally went to the theatre (on 17 February 1728, for instance, she had two free tickets to that new sensation *The Beggar's Opera*) and often talked of the old days. On 26 May 1742 she visited Walpole for breakfast and, wanting her clogs to leave, joshed about how at the theatre years before they used to call for "Mrs Oldfield's chair! Mrs Barry's clogs! and Mrs Bracegirdle's pattens!" And with Colley Cibber at her own house in 1742 she chatted of current theatrical events. Cibber spoke disparagingly of the rising young star, David Garrick; Mrs Bracegirdle "tapped Colley with her fan," according to Walpole, and said, " 'Come, come, Cibber, tell me if there is not something like envy in your character of this young gentleman. The actor who pleases everybody must be a man of merit.' Colley smiled, tapped his box, took a pinch, and, catching the generosity of the lady, replied: 'Faith, Bracey, I believe you are right; the young fellow *is* clever.' "

Indeed, in 1742, when Anne Bracegirdle

was almost 80, a brilliant new generation of actors, of whom Garrick was the chief, had started their careers; the age of Cibber, Booth, and Wilks was past; and the era of Betterton, Barry, and Bracegirdle was only a memory.

Sometime in the early 1740's Mrs Bracegirdle moved from the lodgings in Howard Street, where she had spent most of her life, to the home of Mr Chute (perhaps Francis Chute, brother of John Chute of The Vyne). It was apparently there, on Monday, 12 September 1748 at the age of 85, that Anne Bracegirdle died. She was buried at Westminster Abbey six days later.

She had written her will on 28 November 1747, describing herself as of St Clement Danes, spinster. Unless there was a scribal error in the records, the will was proved on the day of her death by her niece and executrix Martha. To the poor of her parish Anne left £10; to her nephew Justinian (her brother John's son, presumably) she bequeathed £400; and to Mrs Ann Hodge, spinster, she gave £100. The rest of her estate she left to her niece Martha (John's daughter). She asked that she be buried "in a leaden Coffin in Westminster Abbey" if she died in London. Anne's servant, Elizabeth Parker, testified to the validity of the handwriting when the will was proved.

The finest portrait of Anne Bracegirdle is a portion of a large painting of the equestrian William III at Hampton Court, executed by Sir Godfrey Kneller in 1697. (The two emblematic figures were identified as Mrs Bracegirdle [standing] and Mrs Barry [kneeling] by Lucyle Hook in *Theatre Notebook*, XV, where many of the other Bracegirdle portraits are discussed.) A preliminary sketch for this work had been done by Kneller, and Horace Walpole claimed it was much finer; it was once in the Common Parlour at Houghton Hall, Norfolk, Sir Robert Walpole's home, but has been lost.

At the Garrick Club are two portraits called Anne Bracegirdle. One is a painting probably done by Thomas Bradwell about 1755, showing Anne with a small dog. The second is a plumbago drawing of 1737 by J. Smith.

There are two mezzotints of Anne as Semernia, the Indian Queen, in Behn's *The Widow Ranter*. One is a small unsigned oval in the Enthoven Collection at the Victoria and Albert Museum; the other is signed J. Smith and was engraved by W. Vincent, showing Anne with two black boys, one carrying her train and the other holding a parasol over her head. This, with variations, was also engraved by E. Cooper, B. Lens, and two anonymous engravers.

Another mezzotint, attributed to William Vincent, is in the Kenneth W. Sanderson Collection. It shows Anne in armor and with shield, possibly as Placentia in Motteux's *Beauty in Distress* (1698).

She was pictured on the title page of the musical anthology *Deliciae Musicae* (1695–96), sitting, probably singing. This engraving was by Frederik Henrik Van den Hoven. The British Museum has an unpublished engraving by J. Stow that was made for Harding's *Biographical Mirrour*.

The Harding-Stow engraving in the third volume of the *Biographical Mirrour* bears no resemblance to Anne Bracegirdle as she is shown in the other pictures.

Bracht, Walter van. *See* VAN BRIGHT, WALTER.

Bracker. *See* BRUCKER.

Bracy, Mr [fl. 1677], *gallerykeeper*.
Among the few financial records that have survived from the Restoration period are receipts for performances at Drury Lane on 12 and 26 December 1677; a Mr Bracy (or Bray) was listed on them as one of the theatre's gallerykeepers.

Bradcourt, Captain. *See* PRENCOURT, CAPTAIN.

Braddeley. *See* BADDELEY.

Braddock, Edward *d. 1708, singer.*

Tenor Edward Braddock became a member of the Chapel Royal in August 1660, apparently replacing the deceased George Cooke. On 16 February 1661 he was officially installed as a singing man, along with the elder Henry Purcell, and on 23 April of that year he participated in the coronation of Charles II. By 1670 he had become a lay-clerk of Westminster Abbey, and in that year he was made Master of the Choristers there. During the next decade, in addition to his London duties, he occasionally attended the King on trips to Windsor.

Braddock sang at the coronation of James II on 23 April 1685; he was made Clerk of the Cheque of the Chapel Royal on 21 November 1688 replacing the deceased Thomas Blagrave; and on 11 April 1689 he participated in the coronation of William and Mary. His active career in the Chapel Royal extended at least until the spring of 1704, but details of his work are scarce despite the high positions he held.

He died on 12 June 1708 and was buried in the North Cloister of Westminster Abbey on the seventeenth. Describing himself as of St Margaret, Westminster, he had made his will on 21 May, and it was proved by his son Edward on 28 June. The legatees were Edward and the elder Braddock's four granddaughters—Katherine, Elizabeth, and Mary Blow, and Arabella Braddock (probably the younger Edward's daughter). Of Braddock's wife, nothing seems to be known, and since she was not named in his will, she probably died before he did. His only daughter, Elizabeth, (c. 1654–1683) married the famous musician John Blow in September 1674. Edward Braddock the younger was apparently Braddock's only son, though the boy singer Hugh Braddock may have been related. References to a William Braddock, musician of the 1660's, seem to be errors for Edward. At the time of his death, Edward Braddock was probably living in a house in the Great Sanctuary in Westminster which John Blow had leased from the Dean and Chapter of Westminster; judging from his daughter's birthyear of about 1654 (she was "about 20" when she married in 1674), Braddock was probably born in the 1630's and thus lived to a ripe old age, one of the last of the older generation of Restoration musicians.

Braddock, Hugh [*fl. 1679*], *singer.*

Hugh Braddock, possibly a relative of Edward Braddock of the Chapel Royal, was a boy singer in 1679; warrants for payments to him as a former Chapel boy have been found dated as late as 7 January 1696, but whether this indicates delinquent payments or his continued service in the royal musical establishment is unclear.

Bradfield, Axford [*fl. 1794*], *singer.*

Doane's *Musical Directory* of 1794 listed Axford Bradfield of No 5, Dean Street, Holborn, as a tenor who participated in concerts presented by the Choral Fund and the Handelian Society.

Bradford, Mrs [*fl. 1775*], *singer?*

Mrs Bradford, possibly related to the violoncellist Bradford, was one of Thomas Augustine Arne's pupils and apparently a singer. Arne seems to have persuaded David Garrick to give Mrs Bradford a chance to perform at Drury Lane, but she did not do well. In a letter to Arne dated 21 August 1775 Garrick said, "I try'd Mrs Bradford, Miss Weller and I now have Mr Faucet; the two first (As I in a most friendly manner foretold) did no credit to you or myself by appearing in a Piece which you obstinately insisted upon bringing out, tho you knew it would be the means of making a coolness between us." Mrs Bradford's Drury Lane appearance was apparently too insignificant to be noticed in the bills.

Bradford, [Thomas?] [*fl. 1778–1784?*], *violoncellist.*

A Mr Bradford, along with Lolli and Danby, was paid on 24 January 1778 by the Drury Lane Theatre for music copying; the trio submitted three bills totalling £5 18s. Bradford was very likely a member of the theatre band. It may have been this same Bradford who played violoncello at the Handel Memorial Concerts at Westminster Abbey and the Pantheon on 26, 27, 29 May and 3, 5 June 1784. It is also possible that this musician was Thomas Bradford, the composer and music publisher who appeared in concerts in New York as early as 1788 and may have gone to Charleston, South Carolina, in 1791 to set up a music store there.

Bradley, John [fl. 1673], tailor.

On 10 April 1673 John Bradley was sworn as a tailor in the King's Company, then performing temporarily at the Lincoln's Inn Fields playhouse.

Bradley, Mrs M. [fl. 1772–1777], singer.

On 22 September 1772 Mrs M. Bradley, one of Dr Arne's students, made her first appearance on any stage playing Lucy in *The Beggar's Opera* at Drury Lane. Hopkins wrote in his *Diary* that she was "Tall & a good figure for Lucy and acquitted herself very well in that character" but a variant reading of the *Diary* by MacMillan runs: "Mrs Bradley,—very tall, and appears to have blackguard requisites enough for Lucy, but will not do for anything else." Kemble noted that she later became the husband of a Mr Prior "the Builder." The *Town and Country Magazine* called Mrs Bradley's figure "genteel" and had high praise for her "great spirit, vivacity and Propriety, and her singing being so well suited to the character, she so much eclipsed Polly [played by Mrs Bradley's fellow student Miss Weller], that the audience formed a more indifferent opinion of her abilities than she deserved." Mrs Bradley appeared on stage once again, on 6 October 1777 at the Haymarket, and tried playing Lucy once more. This time there were no reports of her efforts.

Bradley, Richard [fl. 1694–1700], musician.

Richard Bradley was appointed to the King's Musick on 22 June 1694, replacing the deceased violinist and wind player Robert Strong; whether or not Bradley also specialized in both strings and wind instruments is not known, but it is likely that he did. He was mentioned regularly in the livery accounts through Michaelmas 1700 and presumably continued in the royal service after the turn of the century.

Bradney, Mr [fl. 1775], actor.

Mr Bradney played Young Meadows in *Love in a Village* on 2 February 1775 at the Haymarket Theatre. On the following 23 March he was Lorenzo in *The Merchant of Venice* and in the cast of *The Snuff Box* at the same playhouse.

Bradock. *See* BRADDOCK.

Brads, Charles [fl. 1794], violinist.

Doane's *Musical Directory* of 1794 listed Charles Brads, of No 45, Poland Street, as a violinist.

Bradshaw, Mr [fl. 1680's?], boxkeeper.

Mr Bradshaw, the father of Lucretia Bradshaw, is said to have been a Drury Lane boxkeeper, probably in the 1680's.

Bradshaw, Mrs [fl. 1785], performer.

A Mrs Bradshaw appeared as one of the vocal and rhetorical characters in *A Musical Interlude* at the Haymarket, out-of-season, on 10 February 1785.

Bradshaw, Elizabeth. *See* BOURK, MRS WILLIAM.

Bradshaw, Lucretia, later Mrs Martin Folkes d. c. 1755, actress, singer.

Lucretia Bradshaw's early history is obscure, though she was reportedly the daughter of a Drury Lane boxkeeper. She came on stage quite young; her first recorded appearance was in April 1696, when she spoke the epilogue to *The Royal Mischief* at Betterton's Lincoln's Inn Fields Theatre. In June 1697 she played the Child of Hercules in *Hercules*, and in late November 1697 she spoke the epilogue to *The Deceiver Deceived*. A year later, on 15 December 1698, she was given a benefit at a vocal and instrumental concert at York Buildings, and on 8 May 1700 at the same place she shared a benefit at another concert. Though at this time she was still referred to as "Miss," she must have been close to 20, for in November 1703 when she acted Mariana in *The Different Widows* at Lincoln's Inn Fields she was styled Mrs Bradshaw. This would suggest that she was born sometime between 1680 and 1685.

She appears to have performed only sporadically between 1703 and 1706, but the records for these years are very incomplete, and she may have been acting regularly. During these years she was mentioned as playing Celinda in *Love at First Sight* (25 March 1704), possibly Ann Page in *The Merry Wives of Windsor* (24 April 1704 at court), Lisena in *The Cares of Love* (1 August 1705), Corinna in *The Confederacy* (30 October 1705), and Constantia in *The Faithful General* (3 January 1706) — the last two at the new Queen's Theatre in the Haymarket. She was engaged in at least one subscription concert during these years — in May 1704 — and she may have displayed her singing talent at other times as well.

The records of Lucretia Bradshaw's activity become much fuller starting with the 1706–7 season at the Queen's Theatre; through 1714 she performed regularly and frequently in both tragedies and comedies; she often played nice young women, but her range included sophisticated ladies and pathetic heroines as well, and some of her roles gave her an opportunity to sing. She seems to have been a protégée of Elizabeth Barry, and after Mrs Barry retired, Lucretia succeeded to some of her major parts. The list of only her more significant roles in familiar plays is impressive: Corinna in *The Confederacy* on 11 December 1706, Anna Bullen in *Henry VIII* on 15 February 1707, Dorinda in *The Stratagem* on 8 March 1707, Calphurnia in *Julius Caesar* on 1 April 1707, Ophelia in *Hamlet* on 28 April 1707 (her benefit), Melissa in *Timon of Athens* on 4 July 1707, Hillaria in *Love's Last Shift* on 18 October 1707, Mrs Wellborn in *Bartholomew Fair* on 22 October 1707, Sylvia in *The Double Gallant* on 1 November 1707, 1st Constantia in *The Chances* on 24 February 1708, Araminta in *The Old Bachelor* on 15 March 1708, Almeria in *The Mourning Bride* on 25 March 1708, Charlotte in *Oroonoko* on 19 April 1708, Mrs Mavis in *The Silent Woman* on 21 April 1708, Harriet in *The Man of Mode* on 29 April 1708 (her benefit), Desdemona in *Othello* on 9 October 1708, Cordelia in *King Lear* on 21 October 1708, Eurydice in *Oedipus* on 23 October 1708, Alithea in *The Country Wife* on 14 April 1709, Cressida in *Troilus and Cressida* on 2 June 1709, Indamora in *Aureng Zebe* on 23 November 1709, Monimia in *The Orphan* on 30 November 1709, Angelica in *Love for Love* on 3 December 1709, Lucina in *Valentinian* on 28 January 1710 (her benefit), Lavinia in *Caius Marius* on 18 February 1710, Imoinda in *Oroonoko* on 21 April 1710, Portia in *Julius Caesar* on 22 April 1710, Elvira in *The Spanish Friar* on 7 November 1710, Portia in *The Jew of Venice* on 3 February 1711, Kate in *1 Henry IV* on 8 May 1711, Madam Fickle in *Madam Fickle* on 29 September 1711, Belvidera in *Venice Preserved* on 13 May 1713 (her benefit).

These roles were played at the Queen's Theatre (through November 1707), then at Drury Lane (through April 1710), at the Queen's again (November 1710), and back at Drury Lane (through May 1713). On 20 July 1714 Lucretia Bradshaw played her last recorded role, Angelica in *The Gamester* at Drury Lane.

During these busy years she was involved in occasional theatrical conflicts, though probably no more than other leading players. In December 1707, for example, she and other players had to apologize for removing themselves from the Queen's Theatre to Drury Lane without proper authorization. A second instance was far more serious, though Mrs Bradshaw may have been an innocent party. In the spring of 1710 Aaron Hill was managing the Drury Lane troupe and having constant difficulties with a nucleus of actors led by George Powell who wanted to handle the management their way. At this time Mrs Bradshaw was living next door to the theatre and had direct access to it from her house. When Powell and his colleagues rioted, they gained entrance to the playhouse because, as Hill put it, "Mrs Bradshaw had let 'em in through a private way, from her lodgings." Once within the theatre, the players attacked Hill, his brother, and treasurer Zachary Baggs; fortunately, no one was seriously wounded, but the rioters were suspended. Whether or not Mrs Bradshaw was in on the plot is not clear; she may have let the men into the theatre quite unaware of their desperate intentions.

Of Lucretia Bradshaw's acting there are frustratingly few descriptions. Gildon, writing in 1710, spoke of her as "that Conduct of the other Hopes of the English Stage"—an obscure phrase but apparently intended to place her as the logical successor to Mrs Barry, since he went on to say that if Mrs Bradshaw "be not the best Actress the Stage has known, she has hindered Mrs. *Barry* from being the only Actress." This was high praise indeed, though it does not define her excellence. Another description is more useful, but it has variants: either Mrs Bradshaw or Mrs Barry said "she endeavour'd first to make herself Mistress of her Part, and left the Figure and Action to

Nature." Since the two actresses were sometimes compared, perhaps the quote is applicable to both. Another comment on her acting appeared in *The Spectator* of May 1712; in an anonymous letter a playgoer said that Mrs Bradshaw's Lavinia in *Caius Marius* was her greatest role. Curll (or Oldys), writing in 1741 called her behavior exemplary and prudent; Cibber strangely made no mention of her at all; and Anthony Aston referred to her, but only obliquely: he noted Mrs Barry's way of drawing out her words which, he felt, was effective with her but not becoming to Mrs Bradshaw and Mrs Porter, her successors. From all this one can gain little, and it is unfortunate that criticism was so niggardly with an actress who was obviously considered first-rate by her public.

Mrs Bradshaw left the stage after the 1713–14 season to marry. On 18 October 1714 at St Helen's, Bishopsgate, she wed Martin Folkes, Esq. He was the son (probably not, as one source says, the grandson) of Martin Folkes, a bencher of Gray's Inn, and his wife Dorothy, née Hovell, co-heiress of Sir William Hovell of Hillington Hall, Norfolk. Young Martin was born between 1685 and 1690 and studied at Westminster School, Clare Hall, Cambridge, and Saumur. His intimate and enemy Stukely said that before Martin "was at age" he married Lucretia Bradshaw of Drury Lane Theatre, a beautiful, discreet, and even exemplary woman. Martin's mother, on hearing of the marriage, threw herself out of a window, fortunately sustaining no injury but a broken arm; apparently she felt that she wanted no actress, exemplary or not, marrying her young son. Folkes went on to a brilliant though controversial career. He was named vice-president of the Royal Society by Newton in 1722–23 and unsuccessfully contested the presidency with Sir Hans Sloane when Newton died in 1727. Folkes finally succeeded Sloane as president, became a foreign member of the Académie des Sciences, and president of the Society of Antiquaries. Oxford granted him his D.C.L. before his own university did. He wrote papers on a variety of subjects but was charged by some with being "an errant infidel and loud scoffer."

Lucretia and Martin Folkes had a son Martin and a daughter Dorothy before 1723, and in that year their third child, Lucretia, was born. About 1728–30 Folkes and his wife were in Rome with their son, and it was there that the ex-actress went "mad upon religion" and was brought home to a house for lunatics in Chelsea. Martin the younger was killed in a fall from his horse while studying in France, apparently sometime after his mother's seizure. In 1751 Dr Folkes resigned the presidency of the Royal Society after he suffered a paralytic attack, but he lived until 1754. He was buried at his mother's ancestral home at Hillington, near Lynn. In his will he directed that his daughters Lucretia and Dorothy should receive £12,000 each, and Lucretia, in addition, was to have Folkes's library and his fine collection of coins and other curious objects. Dorothy ran away with an indigent bookkeeper named Rishton who "used her very ill," and Lucretia, in 1756 at the age of 34, married Richard Bettenson (also described as an "indigent person" by Stukely) and sold her father's library and collection. Two years later the younger Lucretia died. What year Lucretia Bradshaw Folkes died is not certain; most sources say 1755. She was still at Chelsea when her husband died in 1754. It is not known whether or not she ever regained her reason.

Bradshaw, [William?] [fl. 1735–1745], boxkeeper, box bookkeeper.

Mr Bradshaw, possibly William, husband of Mary, was first mentioned as a boxkeeper at Drury Lane in 1735–36, though he may have been working at the theatre for some time before this. He was noticed again on 25 May 1739 when he shared a benefit and sold tickets for it at the Black Boy and Sugar Loaf, on the corner of Stanhope Street. By 26 May 1741 when he was granted a solo benefit, he was described as boxkeeper and box bookkeeper, and by the following 5 September he was selling tickets at the King's Arms in Russell Street, near the Drury Lane playhouse. In addition to vending tickets for his own benefits, Bradshaw seems to have served as an agent for others, at least in the spring of 1742.

In 1742–43 Bradshaw apparently relinquished his box bookkeeper position to Hobson, though he retained his old boxkeeper post. For his 17 May 1744 benefit he advertised himself as living in a house near the Bull and Gate in Holborn. His last recorded benefit was on 1 May 1745, shared with three others.

Bradshaw, Mrs [William?], Mary d. 1780, actress.

The actress Mrs Mary Bradshaw was probably the wife of the boxkeeper Bradshaw who was at Drury Lane in the 1740's. (Kahrl gives her husband's name as William.) Although she was frequently billed early in her career as Miss Bradshaw, she was married to Bradshaw by the time she made her first attempt on any stage as Nell in *The Devil to Pay* at Lincoln's Inn Fields on 7 January 1743. On 14 February 1743 she played Lucy in *The Beggar's Opera* at the same theatre. Several days later, on 18 February, she appeared as Miss Prue in a production of *Love for Love* which was given in a theatrical booth on the Bowling Green at Southwark, and on 14 April she played Lappit in *The Miser* and Lucy in *The Virgin Unmasked*, for her own benefit, at the Haymarket.

At the beginning of the season 1743–44, Mrs Bradshaw joined the company at Drury Lane, where she was to remain, with the exception of several seasons, for 37 years. During this long career she seldom played a role of the first line and never was paid more than £2 per week. In her earlier years

Enthoven Collection, Victoria and Albert Museum

MARY BRADSHAW and DAVID GARRICK
in *The Farmer's Return*
by Zoffany

most of her roles were those of young comic ladies and hoydens in the farce afterpieces and in her later years those of old character women. Her first role at Drury Lane was as Kitty Pry in *The Lying Valet* on 17 September 1743. That season she also played Amice in *The Jovial Crew* on 9 April and Lappit in *The Miser* on 8 May, when she shared a benefit with Collins and Gray. On 17 May 1744 she acted Phillis in *The Conscious Lovers* and Nell in *The Devil to Pay* for the benefit of Mr Bradshaw the boxkeeper. In the following season she also appeared for Bradshaw's

benefit (his last) on 1 May 1745, as Miss Prue in *Love for Love*. In that season and in the following, 1745–46, Mrs Bradshaw played also Mrs Chat in *The Committee*, Mrs Topknot in *The Gamester*, Angelica in *The Anatomist*, Phillis in *The Picture*, Doris in *The Quacks*, Venus in *Chronon-hotonthologos*, and Molly Brazen in *The Beggar's Opera*.

After 1745–46, Mrs Bradshaw's name disappeared from the London bills, and her activities are unknown to us, until she performed Emilia in *Othello* at the New Wells, Lemon Street, on 16 November 1752. Several weeks later, on 28 November at the same place, she played Nell in *The Devil to Pay*. Her next part was Melinda in *The Recruiting Officer*, on 30 November. She returned to Drury Lane in 1753–54 to stay for the rest of her career. In addition to the roles already cited, during the next seven years her parts in the repertory included unnamed characters in *Harlequin's Invasion* (many times) and *Queen Mab*, Setup in *The Double Gallant,* an orange woman in *The Man of Mode*, Mrs Day in *The Committee*, Mignionet in *The Way to Keep Him* (in which Garrick played Lovemore), Inis in *The Wonder*, the nurse in *Polly Honeycombe*, Mrs Amlet in *The Confederacy*, Mrs Prim in *A Bold Stroke for a Wife*, Bromia in *Amphitryon*, and Necessary in *Woman is a Riddle*. In 1759 she played Phillis in *The Conscious Lovers* in John Arthur's company at his new theatre in Plymouth.

Probably Mrs Bradshaw's finest opportunity and her greatest success came when she was chosen by Garrick to play the farmer's wife to his farmer in the two-character interlude, *The Farmer's Return from London,* which opened on 20 March 1762 and ran for 14 nights. In the next season, however, she continued to play her customary roles. In 1756–57 and 1759–60 she shared in benefit tickets with minor performers and house servants. Her salary in 1764–65 was 6s. 8d. per day or £2 per week. In May of 1766, when she shared a benefit with Ackman, tickets could be had of her "at Mr Ash's, Grocer, the Corner of Craven-building, Drury-lane." By May 1778, benefit tickets could be had of her at Mrs Norfolk's, glazier, Little Russell Street, and in 1779 and 1780 at Nichol's, baker, in Bridges Street, Covent Garden.

On 18 November 1766, Mrs Bradshaw played the role of Mrs Stockwell in the first performance of Garrick's farce *Neck or Nothing*. She also played Dorcas in the first performance of Garrick's extravagant *Cymon* on 2 January 1767. Among the many other roles which she played regularly in her last years at Drury Lane were Audrey in *As You Like It* (Gentleman, *The Theatres*: "a store of Comic humour makes us wish for more"), the nurse in *Love for Love*, Margaret in *Much Ado About Nothing*, Scentwell in *The Busy Body*, Mrs Dripping in *New Brooms!*, Tib in *Every Man in his Humour*, Mrs Quickly in *The Merry Wives of Windsor*, and Mrs Overdone in *Measure for Measure*. She occasionally performed such specialty acts as *Linco's Travels*, with Thomas King, and *Three Old Women Weatherwise*, with Hartry and Mrs Dorman. Also she appeared at least twice at Covent Garden: on 9 October 1775 she acted the nurse in *Romeo and Juliet*, and on 22 May 1777 she acted Lady Sycamore in *The Maid of the Mill* for the benefit of the boxkeepers Ansell and Green.

After some 36 years at Drury Lane, and still being paid £2 per week, Mrs Bradshaw wrote to Garrick on 11 October 1778 about her financial distress. She had spent the previous summer at Plymouth, but the "publick alarm that prevailed there" kept houses very thin, and she was now very deep in debt. She thanked Garrick for £50 he had sent her, but she had to repay Hull £20 which he had loaned her while she was on a sick bed, and the rest had gone to release her "goods" which she had pawned. If Mr King ("God bless him") had not given her £20, she would never have been able to get out of London at the end of the last season. She asked Garrick for another £50.

In this sad letter, written when she was no doubt well over 60 years of age, Mrs Bradshaw also mentioned the expense of supporting an "orphan relation," who was more likely really her daughter. The girl, who had just returned from schooling in France, made her dancing debut, as Miss Elizabeth Bradshaw, on 19 July 1780 at Plymouth on the same evening when Mrs Bradshaw, who was engaged there again for the summer, was billed to play Mrs Drugget in *Three Weeks After Marriage*.

Courtesy of the Garrick Club

MARY BRADSHAW, as Dorcas
by Parkinson

According to the *Gentleman's Magazine* (October 1780), "whether from the length of the dance, the timidity of the performer, or the ill-nature or ignorance of the audience," the young Miss Bradshaw was hissed. So distressed was the old actress that "she fell into fits instantly, was conveyed home raging mad, and died in a short time after," in early August. A confused account of the incident gave rise to the false report that Miss Jarrat, who was also acting at Plymouth, had died while playing a comic character. Miss Elizabeth Bradshaw danced at Drury Lane in 1786–87. In 1788 she married William Bourk, a dancer, and performed at Drury Lane and the Royalty as Mrs Bourk.

A painting by T. Parkinson of Mrs Mary Bradshaw as Dorcas in *Cymon* is in the Garrick Club. She was also painted by Zoffany with Garrick in a scene from *The Farmer's Return*. The farmer's wife in this painting was incorrectly identified by Lady Manners in *John Zoffany* as Mrs Cibber, who never played the role, and by Mander and Mitchenson as Lucretia Bradshaw, who had died c. 1755. This picture was bought at the Garrick auction in 1823 by a Mr Sequer for £33 12s. In 1920 the painting was in the collection of the Earl of Durham.

Brady, Mr *[fl. 1774–1775?]*, *actor.*
A Mr Brady was a supernumerary at Drury Lane, apparently during the 1774–75 season.

Brady, Mr *[fl. 1795]*, *actor.*
Mr Brady was one of the Satraps in the lavish production of *Alexander the Great* at Drury Lane on 12 February 1795. His services were needed until 28 February for this work, and perhaps he was employed for the full season as an extra.

Brady, Master *[fl. 1785]*, *dancer.*
Master Brady, apparently a student of Delpini, appeared as the Dancing Master in *The Peasant Metamorphosis* on 14 February 1785 at the Haymarket Theatre. Delpini was the director of the production and danced the title role.

Brady, Charles *[fl. 1783–1785]*, *stage doorkeeper.*
Charles Brady was stage doorkeeper at the King's Theatre in the Haymarket from at least 1783 through the end of the 1784–85 season.

Brady, Patrick *[fl. 1779–1816]*, *barber, hair dresser.*
Patrick Brady was the Drury Lane barber, apparently on the staff of the theatre, from at least 2 October 1779 when the accounts first identified him, through 1816 when he was last noted as a hair dresser.

During the early years he seems to have submitted bills to the theatre for barbering he had done, and the accounts frequently show lump sums of as much as £40 7s. 6d. (covering May, June, and July 1806). But some account entries indicate that Brady had a regular salary of £1 4s. weekly; most of these citations are after the turn of the century. The accounts also mention payments to Brady for wigs, but it is not clear whether he made them or procured them for the theatre; the large payments to him may well have been for wigs rather than barbering. On 17 September 1807 an A. Brady is mentioned as wig maker; he may have been a relative of Patrick's, and possibly he was Brady's source of supply. Patrick's wife was also a dresser and barber at Drury Lane, though she seems to have worked only in the early nineteenth century.

Brady, Thomas *[fl. 1686]*, *kettle-drummer.*

On 6 May 1686 kettledrummer Thomas Brady was directed to attend the Lord Lieutenant of Ireland, but whether he served only there or in London as well is not known.

Braggin. *See* **Brangin.**

Braghetti, Prospero *[fl. 1793–1810]*, *singer.*

Prospero Braghetti (or Barghetti), a *buffo*, sang at the King's Theatre in the Haymarket for 17 years, but except for a single comment by Haydn in 1795, the critics paid little attention to him, and the roles he was given were chiefly secondary. But he seems to have been a dependable and useful member of the company, as a list of his roles over the years may suggest: Filosseno in *I giuochi d'agrigento* on 5 February 1793, Conte di Belfiore in *Le nozze di Dorina* on 26 February 1793, Eleuterio in *I zingari in fiera* on 14 May 1793, Paolino in *Il matrimonio segreto* on 11 Jan-

uary 1794, Il Marchese in *I contadini bizzari* on 1 February 1794, Gelindo Scagliozzi in *Il capriccio drammatico* on 1 March 1794, Don Ottavio in *Don Giovanni* (Gazzaniga's) on 1 March 1794, Celidoro in *La bella pescatrice* on 18 March 1794, A major part in *La prova dell'opera* on 1 April 1794, Oroe in *Semiramide* on 26 April 1794, Giocondo in *Il burbero di buon cuore* on 17 May 1794, Il Cavaliere Giocondo in *La frascatana* on 5 June 1794, Don Calloandro in *L'amore contrasto* on 6 December 1794, Licinio in *Zenobia in Palmira* on 20 December 1794, Barbadoro in *I zingari in fiera* on 10 January 1795, Lisia in *Aci e Galatea* on 21 March 1795, Gran Sacerdote in *Alceste* (Gluck's) on 30 April 1795, Osmano in *I Traci amanti* on 16 February 1795, Prete in *Ifigenia in Tauride* on 7 April 1796, Adrasto in *Antigona* on 24 May 1796, Verigola in *Il tesoro* on 14 June 1796, Modred in *Evelina* on 10 January 1797, Adrasto in *Merope* on 10 June 1797, Plistene in *Ipermestra* on 28 November 1797, Valerio in *La scuola dei maritati* on 23 January 1798, Agrippa in *Cinna* on 20 February 1798, Leandro in *La cifra* on 10 March 1798, Siveno in *Elfrida* on 26 April 1798, possibly Araspe in *Didone* on 30 May 1799, Zopiro in *Zenobia of Armenia* on 22 May 1800.

When Haydn heard the singer on 28 March 1795 in *Aci e Galatea* he called him "good old Braghetti" but noted that the singers at that performance "all deserved, and received, not the least applause."

After the turn of the century Braghetti remained faithful to the King's Theatre, repeating some of his old roles and creating many new ones, though he remained to the end of his career in London in 1810 only a supporting player. A sampling of his work during the first decade of the new century might include Arbate in *La morte di Mitridate*, Tamete in *La vergine del sole*, Podesta in *La cosa rara*, Annio in *La clemenza di Tito*, Giovinetto in *Il barbiere di*

Siviglia (by Paisiello), and, during his final season in 1809–10, roles in *La Scommessa, Romeo e Giuletta, Il matrimonio per susurro,* and *La buona figliuola.* His final appearance was on 21 June 1810 in the last-mentioned work, after which he may have retired or left England.

Braham, John   *1777–1856, singer, composer, manager.*

John Braham, by virtue of his long career and renowned talents, ranks as one of the greatest singers in the history of the English musical stage. He was born in London on 20 March 1777, according to a memoir in the *Illustrated London News* which appeared on 20 March 1852 (his seventy-fifth birthday), and not in 1774 as understood by several biographers. John Levien, in *The Singing of John Braham* (1945), stated that Braham's father was a Portuguese Jew who lived at Rotherhithe, but the evidence weighs in favor of the statement by Boase, in *Modern English Biography* (1892), that the singer was the son of John Abraham, a German Jew who at about the time of John's birth lived in Goodman's Fields.

None of John Braham's biographers connected him with brothers or sisters, but it seems certain that he was the youngest of John Abraham's talented children who had musical careers at London including the singers Miss G. Abrams, Eliza Abrams, Harriet Abrams (1760–1825?), Flora Abrams, Jane Abrams (fl. 1794), Theodosia Abrams (c. 1761–1849), and the instrumentalists David Bramah Abrahams (1775–1837), and William Abrams (fl. 1794). Their father, John Abraham, who himself may have been employed at Drury Lane between 1775 and 1779, received directly until 1779 the salaries of Miss Harriet and Miss G. Abrams. David Bramah Abrahams, the violinist, was born two years before John Braham in Duke's Place, where the Great Synagogue was located. All the family were associated with addresses at

Charlotte Street, Rathbone Place, and at Wellclose Square. (Possibly also related to the family were Anne Philadelphia Braham, who as a minor married Eccles Nixon at St Mary le Bone, by consent of her guardian Edward Burman, on 6 April 1773, and Susannah Braham, who married William James at St George, Hanover Square, on 28 August 1803.)

The story that John Braham was orphaned when young is only half true. While notices of his father cease after 1779, his mother Esther Abrams (Abraham) was still living at Wellclose Square in 1798, according to her sworn deposition to the Royal Society of Musicians. Braham and his family experienced the poverty and other abuses of ghetto immigrants, at least until the children began their professional careers; and reportedly during his childhood

Harvard Theatre Collection

JOHN BRAHAM
by T. C. Wageman

John sold pencils in the streets. His father may have been a musician by profession, for his children all turned to music when young, probably receiving their educations in the Great Synagogue in Duke's Place, Aldgate, where it is known that John Braham first grew to love music. After his father's death, Braham came under the protection of his uncle, Michael Leoni (d. 1797), who was a chorister of the Great Synagogue. Leoni, a celebrated Jewish singer, was not Italian; his real name was Myer Lyon and he was probably the brother of Esther Abrams.

At the age of 10 on 21 April 1787, billed as Master Braham and a pupil of Leoni, John Braham made his debut on the Covent Garden stage by delivering two songs: "The Soldier tir'd of War's Alarms" and "Ma chère amie." The evening was for the benefit of Leoni, whose address was given as No 1, Wellclose Square. When John Palmer opened his Royalty Theatre in Wellclose Square on 20 June 1787 with *As You Like It*, Master Braham, billed as "a little boy" sang "The Soldier tir'd of War's Alarms" as an *entr'acte*. Again at the Royalty on 31 October 1787, he sang a principal character in the musical pastoral *The Birthday*. In the same performance, which was for the young boy's benefit, he also performed Willy in *A Scotch Pastoral Entertainment*, and introduced some favorite songs usually sung by Mrs Billington and Madame Mara. Leoni was present to sing Handel's "Water Parted from the Sea."

A Master Abrahams appeared at Sadler's Wells in 1788 in *Saint Monday; or, a Cure for a Scold*. Since John had already established the stage name of Braham, perhaps this person was really his brother David Bramah Abrahams. That year at Covent Garden, on 2 July 1788, Master Braham made his first appearance in a speaking part, as Joe in *Poor Vulcan!* for the benefit of Leoni, and on the next night he sang again "The Soldier tir'd of War's Alarms." Near the end of that summer, he made his first appearance at the Haymarket, when from 22 to 29 August 1788 he sang a part in *The Catch Club*, a series of concerts given by the Sons of Anacreon.

Soon after, when his master, Leoni, fell on bad times, went bankrupt, and was compelled to flee to Jamaica, Braham was thrown upon his own resources. His boyish voice broke (even in these early days it was remarkable, with a compass of two octaves), and his future seemed doubtful until he was taken up by a generous patron, Abraham Goldsmid (1756?–1810). A prominent leader of the Jewish community in the East End, Goldsmid rendered great service to the British government during the Napoleonic Wars by floating loans at very favorable terms. Frequent visitors to his home were such notable people as Pitt, Lord Nelson, and the musicians Thomas Attwood, J. P. Salomon, and Haydn. Enjoying advantages of Goldsmid's protection, Braham supposedly continued to sing under a feigned name at Norwich and at Ranelagh Gardens, but mainly he occupied himself with the teaching of piano—even at this age he was a sound musician.

Once he had recovered his vocal powers, Braham went to Bath, upon the advice of the flutist Ashe, for instruction from Rauzzini, who taught him for three years and introduced him in some concerts there in 1794. In 1796, upon the recommendation of J. P. Salomon, Braham was engaged at Drury Lane for an opera which Stephen Storace was preparing. The composer died while the work, *Mahoud*, was in progress, but it was completed by his sister Nancy Storace, with a text by Prince Hoare, and presented on 30 April 1796 with a cast which included Braham, Charles Kemble, Mrs Bland, and Miss Storace. Encored three times in the role of Noureddin, Braham was an immediate success. The *Morning Herald* (2 May) enthusiastically reported that he possessed "all the science of Harrison, the melody of Incledon, and the pleasing articulation of the late Mrs Kennedy," and did not hesitate to pronounce him "the first public singer of the present day." It was noted, however, that Braham's "action is indifferent, and his dialogue scarcely audible," faults he never overcame but which were overlooked in deference to his extraordinary vocal talents. For the 15 performances of *Mahoud* that season Braham reportedly received £200, the beginning of the fortune his voice would bring to him. On 9 May 1796 he also played Woodly in *My Grandmother*, for the benefit of Nancy Storace.

In the following season, 1796–97, Braham joined the opera at the King's Theatre, to become one of the first English-born singers to achieve acclaim in that calling. He made his debut as Azor in *Zémire et Azor* on 26 November 1796. The *Morning Chronicle* (28 November) took heart from the performance in which Braham had been so brilliant that "we trust he will give us an example that shall induce us to chace from an English stage the degrading and disgusting form of a *Castrato*." The critic assured that, "When he has learnt to moderate his decorations, and to suffer the exquisite melody of his voice to be felt unencumbered by the weight of ornament he will gratify the most scientific as well as the natural ear." Braham evidently never really mastered the "scientific" precision of singing, but, as Crabb Robinson—who knew and cared "nothing about the Science of Singing"—exclaimed later, Braham's pure melody and expressiveness delighted him "in a sensual way." *Zémire et Azor* was given four times that season. Braham also sang Vellino in *Evelina* (10 January 1797 and 12 more times) and Silvio in *L'arbore di Diana* (18 April and six more times).

In the spring of 1797, Braham performed in the oratorios at Covent Garden, and on 21 June, made his first appearance in a theatrical piece at that theatre since the days of his childhood, as Carlos in *The Duenna*, with the permission of the King's Theatre. He also sang in the Three Choirs Festival at Gloucester. In the summer of 1797 he sang on 31 July at the Birmingham Theatre, and according to Richard Suett, whenever in that town in later years he would attend the meetings of the Birmingham Anacreontic Society which Suett had instituted there in 1793.

The fact that Braham was born a Jew seldom escaped the notice of early bigots, and his short bow-legged figure and swarthy face gave them opportunity for abuse. Yet, even the scurrilous John Williams in *A Pin Basket to the Children of Thespis* (1797) grudgingly had to acknowledge Braham's substantial talents at this early stage of his adult career. After some introductory anti-Semitism, Williams wrote:

> *His voice and his judgment completely atone*
> *For that heap of repulsion he cannot disown;*
> *When he pours forth his note, how he cleaves to our will!*
> *'Tis a test of most exquisite order and skill*

Contrary to other testimonies of Braham's humanity of voice, which seems always to have been one of his greatest attributes, Williams concluded:

> *Yet though thus is the cadence, though thus is the feat,*
> *There's no soul to his ditty—no sauce to his meat.*

Despite the opportunities now available to him in the London theatres, Braham took the advice of the fencer Monsieur St George and decided to study singing in Italy. In the fall of 1797 he left for the Continent in the company of Nancy Storace, with whom he lived for some time, arriving first at Paris where they remained for eight months, the two of them giving concerts under the patronage of Joséphine Beauharnais. According to Oxberry, whose *Dra-*

matic Biography must always be approached cautiously, at Paris the public thronged to their concerts at the price of a louis per ticket although the general admission was usually only six francs, and had their purpose been emoluments, Braham and Storace could have engaged permanently in that city at an annual salary of 1400 louis. In October 1797 the *Monthly Mirror* reported intelligence of their debut at the Théâtre de la Rue Federace: "these singers, besides two solo pieces, performed a duet, in which they displayed that unison, harmony, and happy execution which belongs, we repeat, only to Italians." The *Monthly Mirror* took umbrage at the failure of the French reporter to discern that both singers were born in London.

Going on to Italy in 1798, Braham made his debut at La Pergola in Florence in Basili's *Il ritorno di Ulisse* and Monesta's *Oreste*. In Italy he met the celebrated Italian vocalist, the elder David, who is reported to have proclaimed, "There are only two singers in the world, I and the Englishman." Braham sang with brilliant success in Nasolini's *Il trionfo di Clelia* with Nancy Storace at La Scala in Milan, where he remained for two years. At Milan he also sang with Mrs Billington, and their first encounter forced him into an unfortunate rivalry with her, owing to the machinations of that singer's husband Felissant. Apprehensive of any challenge to his wife's applause, Felissant used his influence to have one of Braham's best arias in *Il trionfo di Clelia* cut at the first performance. The aria was restored on the second night, however, in consequence of the public's displeasure, and Braham retaliated. Having a quick ear, he had mastered the florid embellishments of Mrs Billington's first aria, which although supposedly "improvised," had been carefully rehearsed by the *prima donna*— who was really not capable of any sort of improvisation. In his own first aria, which preceded hers, Braham appropriated all of Mrs Billington's embellishments, leaving

her in a state of embarrassment. She refused to sing again with him, but soon the quarrel was reconciled and they became good friends.

Braham also sang at Venice—where Cimarosa wrote the opera *Artemisa* for him but did not live to complete it—and at Leghorn, Trieste, and Genoa. While in Italy he was a frequent visitor to the Leghorn residence of Admiral Nelson, whose wife he had tutored in music in 1795. Here he also met General Abercrombie. In later years Braham composed "The Death of Abercrombie," and "The Death of Nelson," singing both pieces regularly to thousands of people.

Receiving offers at Vienna from the London managers, Braham and Storace returned to England through Hamburg, without stopping to sing in Germany, arriving home early in the winter of 1801. Engaged at Covent Garden for 1801–2 at a salary of £500, Braham performed again in London after an absence of four years on 9 December. *The Chains of the Heart*, a slight and commonplace piece by Prince Hoare with music by Mazzinghi and Reeve which lasted only a few nights, was his vehicle. He next sang with Storace in Dibdin's *The Cabinet* on 9 February 1802, for which Braham wrote the music of his own part of Orlando, including the well-known "Bird Song." Upon hearing Braham in *The Cabinet* Jane Porter in her diary compared him to Orpheus's lyre, calling him "without any exception, the most glorious singer that ever appeared in the world." From this point Braham became a figure of public adulation, and his appearance in a piece virtually assured its success. Jane Porter wrote of the "ecstasy" and the "delerium" to which Braham transported her whenever she heard him sing, so enraptured that she wondered she might "well nigh run mad with pleasure." The musical pieces, all unworthy of his great powers, in which he sang over the next several years at Covent Garden included *The Siege of Belgrade*

(15 March 1802), Dibdin's *Family Quarrels* (18 December 1802) with music by Braham, Moorehead, and Reeve, and *The English Fleet in 1342* (13 December 1803). The music of the latter opera was composed entirely by Braham, including one of his best-known compositions, the duet "All's Well." By 1803–4, Braham's salary was £1000 a year.

In 1803–4 he also had a falling out with the management of Covent Garden over a selection of songs for Signora Storace's benefit. Signora Storace advertised in March 1804 that she would perform *The Siege of Belgrade* at her benefit, with songs to be introduced from other operas, "according to the usual practice." John Philip Kemble, on the other hand, gave strict orders forbidding any pieces from other operas to be used, whereupon Braham protested to the proprietor, Thomas Harris, of discrimination against Signora Storace and himself, "who bring as much money to the house as any performers, tragic, comic, or operatic." In a letter dated 26 March 1804, Braham resigned from Covent Garden, stating that he had already received £600 of his salary, and would forfeit the remaining £400 and his benefit. The matter was resolved, however, and Braham indeed took his benefit on 24 April 1804, receiving £359 11s. 6d. (in the previous season he had taken £278 5s. 6d.).

In the next season Braham continued at Covent Garden. With Reeve, he wrote music to *The Paragraph, Thirty Thousand,* and *Out of Place.* He also appeared at the King's Theatre in 1805 and 1806: his operatic performances there included a role in *Gli Orazi e I Curiazi* ("the duet by Braham and Grassini . . . was raptuously encored" 2 May 1805 and 7 January 1806), the Prince in *La cosa rara* (13 July and 14 December 1805), roles in *Argenide e Serse* (25 January 1806), *La morte di Cleopatra* (4 March 1806), and *Camilla* (1 May 1806). On 27 March 1806 he sang Sesto in *La clemenza di Tito,* the first per-

formance of this Mozart opera in England, in which he sang "admirably." Also at the King's Theatre, on 7 December 1805, he performed in the melodrama-ballet, *The Naval Victory and the Triumph of Lord Nelson on the Memorable 21st October, 1805,* which was presented only this once, "this work being considered," according to the *Morning Chronicle* (9 December 1805), "to be lacking in taste and decorum so soon after Nelson's death."

In the summer of 1805 he and Signora Storace sang for six nights at Brighton. On one of these nights, when an imperfect drummer behind the scenes threatened a great *scena* of Braham's in *The Haunted Tower,* Signora Storace took over the tympany accompaniment with distinction. That fall both singers returned to London to take up engagements, not at Covent Garden

Harvard Theatre Collection

JOHN BRAHAM, as Prince Orlando
by R. Dighton

as previously, but at Drury Lane, in which company Braham continued through 1814–15. Among the operas in which he sang and for which he also composed the music were *False Alarms* (3 January 1807) in collaboration with King, *Kais* (11 February 1808) with Reeve, *The Devil's Bridge* (10 October 1812), *Narensky* (11 January 1814) with Reeve, and *Zuma* (1 February 1818) with Bishop. His salary for his first season at Drury Lane was £30 per week with a clear benefit of £387 8s. 6d. By 1807–8 he was receiving £48 per week, with the privilege of writing an unlimited number of orders for house tickets. His benefit that season brought him another £365 8s. 6d. By 1809–10, the season in which Drury Lane burned down, Braham's salary was £1300, plus a benefit. In 1809 he engaged for 15 nights at the Royal Theatre, Dublin, at a salary of 2000 guineas, when his performance created so great an excitement that the engagement was extended to 36 nights at appropriate terms.

In April 1810, Braham was living at No 16, Caroline Street, Bedford Square. After two seasons with the Drury Lane company at the Lyceum, where his opera *The Americans* (composed with M. P. King) was performed on 27 April 1811, Braham entered into negotiations with Samuel J. Arnold about his engagement at the new Drury Lane Theatre. In letters written on 10 and 12 November 1812, from his new address at No 22, Great Marlborough Street, he called Arnold "the most abusive man alive" (Arnold had previously called him "the most impudent man alive") for being so noncommittal about terms for dresses, composing, and the precise period of the contract, complaining that had he realized Arnold was going to be so difficult, "I should at this moment be in Ireland—where they offered me £2000 for 24 Nights." Arnold offered him £750 for 20 nights of singing and a benefit, an arrangement much inferior to the one Braham had enjoyed at the previous and smaller Drury Lane The-

atre. Braham now requested either one clear benefit or two paid ones. The problem seems to have been resolved by the latter arrangement and in 1812–13 Braham took £729 9s. 6d. in benefit receipts. The following season he received benefits totaling £635 18s. During these years with the Drury Lane company Braham also performed in innumerable provincial festival concerts and oratorios including the sixth Chester Music Festival in September 1814. He was a constant favorite at the Oxford Music Room during this time, and made regular visits to perform in the Bath concerts given by Rauzzini, his old master. When Rauzzini died in 1810, Braham and Signora Storace reverently erected a monument to his memory at Bath Abbey. Braham also performed at the new Bath Theatre Royal in Beaufort Square at the end of the 1809–10 season, and again in January 1812, when he played for nine nights in opera at the playhouse and gave concerts in the morning at the music rooms.

After a ten-year absence, Braham returned in 1816 to the King's Theatre in the Haymarket to take up his old roles of Sesto in Mozart's *Clemenza di Tito* and Guglielmo in *Cosi fan tutte*. His vocal powers, reported the *Morning Chronicle* on 4 March, were "in their fullest vigor." By now those defects in his acting abilities noticed earlier in his career had been somewhat alleviated by his years of experience, and his new skills as an actor "immediately struck the whole audience with surprise." In this same year, Braham's domestic circumstances altered considerably and rapidly. Despite Byron's designation of the Braham-Storace *amour* as the "Only thing of this kind known to last," for reasons now unclear Braham deserted the soprano who had lived with him as his wife for many years. He ran off to France, it seems, with a Mrs Wright, whose husband sued Braham for criminal conversation. On 16 March 1816 Braham was hissed during the oratorio of *Israel in Egypt* at Drury Lane on account of the pending suit. At the conclusion of his song, Braham stepped forward to address the audience: "I am now before you as a public character. If, in that situation, I have given offence, you have an undoubted right to call for an apology or defence; but if I have erred as a private individual, the nature of that error cannot with discretion come under your notice. It will be probably investigated before a court, constituted to hear both the accuser and the accused, and where justice only can be done." The litigation was settled on 23 July 1816 by an award of £1000 in damages to Wright. In the same year, Braham married a Miss Bolton of Ardwick, near Manchester. The marriage, it was said, hastened the death of the deserted Nancy Storace. She died about a year later on 24 August 1817.

Braham returned to Drury Lane on 5 October 1819, for his first appearance there in four years, at a salary of 25 guineas per night, for 20 nights guaranteed, with a clear benefit. Living at No 3, Tavistock Square in January 1820, he also became associated with Attwood and Beale in the unfortunate speculation of rebuilding the Argyle Rooms and presenting concerts, a scheme which included an association of 21 principal professors of music for the purpose of printing the best music at a moderate profit. Known as the Royal Harmonic Institution, the speculators gave some concerts in the Argyle Rooms from 1820 until 1829, when the great expense of the operation caused the principals to withdraw. During the decade Braham performed Max in the first production in England of Weber's *Der Freischütz* at the Lyceum on 20 July 1824, receiving the immense salary of £150 per week during its run. He also played Sir Huon in the same composer's *Oberon* at Covent Garden on 12 April 1826; the grand *scena* "O 'tis a glorious sight to see" was written especially to provide Braham with an extraordinary opportunity to exhibit his declamatory powers, although Weber was not pleased with having to write such florid ornamentation. The composer wrote to his wife, "What can I do? Braham knows his public and is idolized by them." For the Lyceum he also wrote portions of *Isidore de Merida* (1827) and *The Taming of a Shrew* (1828). Between 1824 and 1828, Braham was living at No 69, Baker Street.

By now Braham was at the zenith of his fame and talent, averaging some £14,000 *per annum*. He lived in magnificent style, with nobility sometimes at his table. As an outstanding personality in English life, he was a great hero to London Jews. He turned now to the extremely hazardous business of theatrical management, a decision which was to drain his large fortune and energies. In 1831, jointly with Yates, he purchased the Colosseum in Regent's Park for £30,000 (and not the £40,000 stated by the *Dictionary of National Biography*); by 1837 he had poured over £100,000 into the buildings and its enterprises which included a public house, shops, and rooms for music and dancing. Expanding his speculations in 1835, he built the St James's Theatre, an "elegant little theatre," at the cost of £30,000, plus £3000 for the freehold of the land. The project was protested against by local property owners who petitioned the King not to grant a license for a theatre "in the immediate neighbourhood of Your Majesty's Court causing in this quiet and orderly situation a daily and nightly assemblage of the abandoned and dangerous characters who are accustomed to resort to the approaches of Theatres." But the license was granted.

The St James's Theatre opened on 14 December 1835 with three new pieces, *Agnes Sorel*, an operatic burletta by A'Beckett, an interlude entitled *A Clear Case*, and a farce, *A French Company*. In the role of Count Dunois in *Agnes Sorel*, Braham was "received with the most enthusiastic cordiality," singing "with an expression of skill and taste which would justify us in saying that he is still our first English tenor." Both ventures, at the Colosseum and St James's Theatre, proved to be disastrous. On 22 November 1837 Braham wrote to his bankers about his financial condition, proposing to borrow £20,000, out of which he would retire a judgment-bond of £14,400 due to Horner's Trustees, lest he should lose the Colosseum. He offered to pay back the new mortgage at £1000 per year, at five percent interest and assured the bankers that "The profits of the Colosseum, on the old buildings alone, have always exceeded £4000 a year, & including the new have averaged from £7000 to £8000." It is not known whether or not the mortgage was granted, but Braham's association with the Colosseum soon ceased. By the end of 1838, he was also forced to abandon the St James's Theatre to Bunn who reopened it with a troupe of wild animals and "highly trained monkeys, dogs, and goats."

In his attempts to keep the St James's Theatre, Braham, whose "stout heart and spirit remained unquenched," had performed in two pieces per night "with the fire and vigor of five-and-twenty." Even as late as 1834, when Lord Mount-Edgcumbe heard him sing at the Handel Festival in Westminster Abbey, Braham's splendid voice seemed to this critic to be still in its prime: "it had become neither weak nor husky nor tremulous, but filled with its volume all the vast space with the finest effect." When it was put forward by some that Braham should retire, Thomas Williams asked in *A Treatise on Singing* (1834): "Why should he retire? Is there anyone to fill the chasm? Why should people take only silver when gold is to be had?" But time soon depleted his energy and weakened his voice, and when he returned to the Drury Lane stage in 1838–39, his range was diminished, he was no longer able to support his old tenor parts, and he sang the baritone title-roles in Rossini's *William Tell* and Mozart's *Don Giovanni*.

Following the example of other English stars who sought fortunes across the Atlantic, Braham undertook an American tour with his son Charles in 1840–42. He made his first appearance at the National Theatre, Philadelphia, as Henry Bertram in *Guy Mannering*. According to the *Stage Reminiscences* of an anonymous machinist who was working back-stage that evening, when Braham, with his short legs which "shuffled in his gait, worse . . . than any other man that ever trod the boards," came upon the stage not a hand of applause welcomed him. Indeed the audience tittered at the diminutive size of Braham, who was about five feet and one inch in height, contrasted to the striking five feet ten inches of his leading lady of the night, a Miss J. Inverarity, "a handsome, strapping Scotch lassie then about twenty years of age." So disappointed was Braham by this initial reception that tears rolled down his cheeks at his first exit. But when he returned to sing the stirring "Twas in Trafalgar's bay," the house became "electrified" and gave him a tumultuous ovation which demanded two encores of the air. In November 1840 he gave a concert at the Tabernacle in New York, and then with star billing sang again in *Guy Mannering* at the Park Theatre. Concert audiences in America were moved by his vaunted dramatic power and brilliant technique, but in opera he was less successful.

Upon Braham's return to England in 1842 he continued to sing in London concerts and at provincial festivals. His spirit continued dauntless. On a tour to the Channel Islands in 1843, with his son Charles and friend Torre, he made a crossing in a small open boat from Guernsey to Jersey, taking 15 hours in a rough sea, without food or sleep, a most perilous journey for a man in his sixty-sixth year. He gave his final public performance at one of the Wednesday concerts in March 1852, and after 65 years on the stage he retired to the Grange, Brompton, where he had resided from time to time since, probably, 1834. (When he made his will on 22 May 1854, however, he gave his address as No 44, Great Ormond Street, Queen Square, but lately at Conduit Street, Hanover Square.) Braham died on 17 February 1856, and was buried in Kensal Green Cemetery, under the wall to the right of the main entrance. According to the *Gentleman's Magazine* of May 1856 Braham had converted to the Anglican Church.

By his wife Miss Bolton, Braham had two daughters and four sons. Three of his sons followed musical careers at some time: Charles Braham, born 20 December 1823, who made his debut as Adelman in *Leonine* at the Princess's Theatre on 26 October 1848; Augustus Braham, who made his singing debut at the Metropolitan Hall in New York and in 1852 performed at Philadelphia, according to Wemyss, and who made his London debut at the Lyceum on 30 August 1853 as Edgard in *Lucia di Lammermoor*; and Hamilton Braham, a *basso* who was very popular in Germany. The fourth son, Ward Soane Braham, not a performer, was the only son mentioned in John Braham's will, administration of which was granted to him on 30 May 1856. As Mrs Braham was not mentioned in the will, presumably she was dead by 1854, when it was drawn. One of the daughters, Frances Elizabeth Anne (1821–1879) married four times. In 1839 she married John Henry Waldegrave (1802–1840) of Navestock, Essex, eldest and illegitimate son of the sixth Earl of Waldegrave; upon his death she was married on 28 September 1840 to his half-brother, the seventh Earl of Waldegrave (1816–1846). By these first two marriages she acquired the vast Waldegrave estates in Essex, Somerset, and elsewhere. On 30 September 1847 she married George Granville Vernon Harcourt (1785–1861); and on 20 January 1863, Chichester Samuel Parkinson-Fortescue (1823–1898), who was created Baron Carlingford in 1874 and became the Irish Baron of Clermont in 1877.

John Braham also sired a son of Nancy Storace, named William Spencer Harris Braham, who was born at Leicester Square on 3 May 1802. His grandmother, Elizabeth Storace, of Herne Hill, sent him to Winchester College, and by her will dated 12 September 1817, left him her estate in trust, provided that at the age of 23 he would take the final surname of Storace instead of or in addition to Braham. On 21 May 1824, administration of his grandmother's will was granted to Braham's natural son under the conditions specified. Eventually he took orders in the Anglican Church and changed his name to Meadows in 1851. The possibility that Braham actually had a total of three children by Nancy Storace should be noted. In a satirical print published at the time of Braham's elopement with Mrs Wright in 1816, Signora Storace is pictured as a deserted woman in England, reclining on the ground in a theatrical pose, singing "Far from me my lover flies / a faithless lover he / In vain my Tears in vain my Sighs / No longer true to me / He seeks another." Standing behind her are three children, of equal height, singing vigorously. Braham, himself, across the Channel in France, is pictured carrying a plump vocalist and two infants on his back.

In addition to the roles already mentioned, other parts which John Braham played over his long career included: Lord Winlove in *Fontainbleau*, Alphonso in *The Castle of Andalusia*, the Indian Prince in *Polly*, Foreski in *Lodoiska*, Edwin in *Robin Hood*, Julian in *The Peasant Boy*, Rodolf in *The Unknown Guest*, and Apollo in *Midas*. He also composed music with Moorhead and Davy, for T. J. Dibdin's pantomime *Harlequin Habeas* (1802), and with Cooke for the drama *Isidore and Merida; or, The Devil's Creek* (1827).

Many of his contemporaries pronounced John Braham the greatest English vocalist of his day. Weber, whose music Braham sang in 1824 and 1826, declared him "the greatest singer in Europe!" Clearly his career was exceptional by reason of its length as well as because of its brilliance. He made his debut in the year Edmund Kean was born, and was still performing when Charles Kean was in his hey-day at the Princess's Theatre. He sang before Napoleon's Josephine and gave lessons to Nelson's wife, and when he retired the Victorian age was already fifteen years old. Charles Lamb wrote to a friend: "Braham's singing, when it is impassioned, is finer than Mrs Siddons's or Mr Kemble's acting; and when it is not impassioned, it is as good as hearing a person of fine sense talking." For Lamb, Braham sang with the same consummate understanding with which Kemble delivered dialogue. "He could sing the Commandments," Lamb wrote in *Essays of Elia*, "and give an appropriate character to each prohibition." A technical analysis of Braham's singing appeared in *The Musical Quarterly* for 1818:

Gifted with the most extraordinary genius and aptitude for the exercise of his profession that was ever implanted in a human being . . . The whole compass of Mr Braham's voice is 19 notes, and if not all of equal strength, they yet differ so little in power perceptibly to the auditor, that is seems as if the singer could at pleasure produce any given quality of tone from pianissimo to fortissimo upon any one of them. Mr Braham can take his falsetto upon any note from D to A at pleasure and the juncture is so nice managed that in an experiment to which this gentleman had the kindness to submit, of ascending and descending by semitones, it was impossible to distinguish at what point he substituted the falsetto for the natural note.

Possessed of an "astonishing flexibility" and a "pure and unvaried tone," as well as a magnificent declamation, Braham could sing to perfection when he chose. Many accused him of vulgar, sensational effects by which he appealed to the groundlings. Some claimed even that he was "corrupting

the taste of the age," as he frittered away his talents. He was never invited to sing at the concerts of the gentlemen's Catch Club at the Thatched House Tavern in St James Street, a matter which, according to Henry Phillips in *Musical and Personal Recollections* (1864), "was at all times a sad thorn in his path." For Leigh Hunt, one of the few dissenters as to his greatness, Braham typified a "popular and not very refined style of bravura singing. . . . It was what might be called the loud and soft style," which consisted of being very soft on such words as "love" and "peace," and then rising to roars of triumph on such words as "war" and "glory."

On one occasion, so the story is told, when he entertained the Duke of Sussex (who was godfather to his son Augustus) at dinner with a selection of songs delivered to perfection, the Duke asked, "Why, Braham, don't you always sing like that?" "If I did," replied the singer, "I should not have the honour of entertaining your royal highness tonight." Julian Young, author of the life of his father, the actor Charles Mayne Young, described hearing Braham render the best sacred music at the house of friends whom he knew to be refined musicians in a "glorious and worthy" manner, and then hearing him in an oratorio at the theatre the very next night give the same air with florid interpolations. Braham was never an impressive actor, although improvement in this regard was indicated in his mature years. Walter Scott, in whose *Guy Mannering* Braham often sang, spoke of him as "a beast of an actor, though an angel of a singer." He was, however, clearly a singer of extraordinary dramatic force, who threw his soul into his voice, and, as Crabb Robinson wrote, when he sang "his whole frame is awakened—his gestures and looks are equally impassioned." His immense popularity with women was no doubt enhanced by his ability to give pleasure "in a sensual way," and by his unrivalled expression of strong pathos. Jane Porter, for example, found him to have pensive eyes and a pathos in his voice, with amiable but grave manners, "even to melancholy," which she attributed to "an unfortunate connection with Signora Storace [which] seems to have clouded his happiness."

Most of his career was passed on the popular stage, yet Braham was celebrated for his *bel canto* on the operatic stage; his early visit to Italy prompted the Italians to declare there was no tenor in their country like him. Many people believed, indeed, his singing in Italian far transcended his English performances. Braham's voice and style seemed especially suited, moreover, to concerts and Handelian oratorios. According to Leigh Hunt:

When he stood in the concert room or oratorio, and opened his mouth with plain, heroic utterance in the mighty strains of "Deeper and Deeper Still," or "Sound an Alarm" . . . you felt indeed you had a great singer before you. His voice . . . now became a veritable trumpet of grandeur and exaltation; the tabernacle of his creed seemed to open before him in its most victorious days; and you might have fancied yourself in the presence of one of the sons of Aaron, calling out to the host of the people from some platform occupied by their prophets.

Joseph Heywood, of Manchester, in the *Cornhill Magazine* (December 1865), reminisced of a deeply religious experience he had shared with the audience at a performance of Handel's *Israel in Egypt*. Braham rose to sing:

"But the Children of Israel went on dry land," and then paused and every sound was hushed throughout the great space. And then, as if carved out upon the solid stillness, came these three words: "through the sea"; our breath failed us, our pulses ceased to beat, and we bent our heads, as all the wonder of the miracle seemed to pass over us with these accents. Awful, resonant, radiant, triumphant, he sat down, while the whole house thundered its applause.

Obviously Braham's talents waned with the years. For Crabb Robinson, who declared upon hearing him in *The Siege of Belgrade* in 1820, that "he had lost none of his fascination in singing," the charm had passed away by the time Braham sang in *Fra Diavolo* at Covent Garden on 24 January 1832: "Braham's voice seems gone. . . . The rich middle tones are lost entirely." Yet when he sang in London upon his return from America in 1842 it was said that he exhibited "a wonderful increase of power and energy," at least compared to the impairment and decline apparent just previous to his departure from England. Writing in 1839, John Adolphus spoke of Braham almost with an air of apology and with the careful courtesies one extends to faded greatness; he reminded his readers that Braham had been a professional performer for over fifty years by then, "and by his taste and industry" still contributed to their gratification.

The many songs which Braham composed achieved vast popularity. He had a gift for flattering the average Briton's pride in his country and for inflaming his patriotism. Most of Braham's compositions, however, were undistinguished. They relied heavily on the embellishments with which Braham himself sang them.

About 40 different portraits and engravings of Braham were executed, most of them in character. Among the better portraits are an oil painting by Opie and an anonymous water color of John as a boy singing "The soldier tir'd of War's alarms" at Covent Garden; in 1945 both were in the collection of Lord Strachie at Sutton Court, Pensford, Somerset (Lord Strachie's mother was the daughter of John Braham's son Charles.) A small painting by an unknown artist of Braham as a young man, dated about 1800, is in the Garrick Club.

Other portraits include vignettes by Ridley, after Allingham (1803); by Cardon after J. S. Wood (1806); an engraving by Adlard, "Mr Braham in 1800," published in Busby's *Concert Room Anecdotes*; and an engraving published in *The Beauties of Melody* (1827), a collection of airs, duets, and glees compiled by W. H. Plumstead. A miniature attributed to Sir William C. Ross and an oil by Robert Dighton are at the National Portrait Gallery. Dighton also did a colored full-length of Braham as Prince Orlando, in fantastically elaborate dress, which was published as an engraving by the artist in 1802. Other engravings of him as Prince Orlando were done by J. Rogers, after Kennerly, as a plate to Oxberry's *Dramatic Biography* (1825), and by T. Woolnoth, after Wageman, as plates to Cumberland's *British Theatre* (1828), and *Ladies Monthly Museum* (1827). An engraving by G. A. Glover of Braham as Sir Huon in *Oberon* was published in 1826; another in the same character was published by William West in the same year.

An engraving by Cruikshank of Braham as Don Alfonso in *The Castle of Andalusia* was published as a plate to *British Stage* (1817). An anonymous engraving of Braham as Henry Bertram in *Guy Mannering*, at the Haymarket on 22 September 1820, was published by T. Williams. Among the latest pictures executed was that of Braham as Count Julian de Beauvais in *Wanted, a Brigand*, a lithograph drawn and engraved by W. Newman in 1837. A satirical print by Cruikshank entitled "A Smile to a Tear," showing Braham as Edgar Gayland, with Mrs Bland as Emily, in *False Alarms*, was published in 1807. A pen and ink drawing by Richard Doyle of Braham in *Masaniello*, at the St James's Theatre, 29 November 1839, is at the British Museum.

An anonymous engraving shows Braham in a high collar and stock; another is an oval small bust; and Roberts engraved a bust that was published by T. Kelly. R. Woodman, Jr engraved a profile portrait of Braham for Bysh's *New Musical and Vocal Cabinet;* W. M. Thackeray drew a caricature of the singer, and an anonymous engraving of it was published by Thomas Hurst as a plate to the *National Standard*. George B. Ellis engraved a plate to Key and Biddle's *American Singer's Own Book* which shows Braham and seven others making a toast. George Cruikshank drew the singer in five different characters as a plate to the *Universal Songster* (1826). An anonymous engraving shows a bust of Braham; the plate also contains a scene and six other portraits. A. Ashley drew and J. Bingley engraved Braham's likeness for Bingley's *Select Vocalist*. A penny-plain picture of Braham shows him as Abo Cassen. Kennerley engraved him as Count Amaranth in *Philandering*. An anonymous engraver showed him as Count Belino in *Devil's Bridge*.

Kennerley engraved Braham as Fenton in *The Merry Wives of Windsor*. An anonymous engraving shows him in *Gli Orazzi;* this served as a plate to the *Theatrical Recorder*. He was pictured in an anonymous color etching as Kais, and R. Page drew him as Koyan in *The Travellers* for the *Drama* (1823). Foster drew Braham as Lord Aimworth in *The Maid of the Mill;* this drawing was engraved by Thomson and served as a plate to Oxberry's *New English Drama* in 1818.

Two anonymous artists drew the singer as Prince Orlando. An engraving by D. Barber shows him with Mr Nickinson in *Der Freischutz*. J. Fairburn published a twopence colored and W. S. Johnson a pennyplain of Braham as Tom Tug singing "The Bay of Biscay." An anonymous picture shows him in character in a uniform with a high ruff collar; another, published by Sherwood in 1824 shows him posing in character. An anonymous artist drew Braham and Miss Stephens singing "I love thee Night and Day, Love." Laurie and Whittle published a picture in 1805 of Braham singing "Love and Glory."

A street between Leman Street and Mansell Street in Aldgate, where Braham had close associations, bears his name.

Braithwaite, Mr *d. 1773, master tailor.*

Mr Braithwaite was the master tailor at Drury Lane at least during the 1771–72 season and possibly earlier. Francis Gentleman (under the pseudonym Sir Nicholas Nipclose) in *The Theatres* in 1772 wrote of

> The valiant Brathwaite, arm'd with steel
> and goose,
> Lets all a taylor's mighty genius loose.

A 27 April 1772 letter from David to George Garrick mentions Braithwaite in passing, and the Drury Lane Theatre accounts contain a payment of £3 3s. to him for men's costumes. He died on 16 December 1773, and the playhouse accounts note that on 5 December 1774 a payment of £1 7d. was made to cover the late Mr Braithwaite's bill for Mr Barry (a costume for Barry, presumably). Other Braithwaites were active at about this same time and may well have been relatives of the tailor. A Booth Brathwaite, bachelor, married Ann Mitford, spinster, at St George, Hanover Square, on 26 March 1761; he could have been the tailor, but there is no proof.

Braithwaite, Mr *fl. 1776–1777,* *dresser.*

One Braithwaite (or Brathwit) was being paid 9s. per week as a dresser at Drury Lane during the 1776–77 season. He was doubtless related to the tailor Braithwaite who died in 1773.

Braithwaite, Ann *fl. 1775–1790,* *actress, dancer.*

There are several references in theatrical documents to a Mrs (sometimes Miss)

Braithwaite, and it is probable that all of these refer to Ann Braithwaite. In 1775 Ann subscribed 10s. 6d. to the Drury Lane pension fund; on 23 September 1776 a Mrs Braithwaite danced in Roger Johnstone's company at Bristol; and during the 1776–77 Drury Lane season a Mrs Braithwaite was twice noted in the account books as an actress at a salary of £1 per week. She is said to have played Molly Brazen in *The Beggar's Opera*, and since the work was done in 1781–82 and 1782–83 at Drury Lane with that role unassigned in the bills, perhaps she acted Molly during those seasons. Her name did not appear on any bills, however, and in March 1783 she seems to have submitted a claim to the theatre fund for financial help. She may have remained in the Drury Lane troupe until 1790.

An Ann Mitford, spinster, married Booth Brathwaite at St George, Hanover Square, on 26 March 1761; this may have been the performer, and her husband may have been Braithwaite the Drury Lane tailor. Ann Braithwaite may also have been related to the other theatre folk of this name who were active during the 1770's and 1780's.

Bramah, D. *See* ABRAHAMS, DAVID BRAMAH.

Bramsbottom, Abraham *fl. 1794,* *musician.*

Abraham Bramsbottom was admitted to livery in the Worshipful Company of Musicians on 3 October 1794, at which time he was living in Great Bell Alley.

Bramstone, Mr *fl. 1752, actor?*

Drury Lane prompter Cross noted that on 15 December 1752 when *The Beggar's Opera* and *Harlequin Ranger* were performed, Mr Bramstone (who is otherwise unrecorded) ran across the stage drunk, fell, and was carried off like a tragic hero.

Bramwell, Mr *[fl. 1794–1804], singer.*

The Drury Lane account books indicate that a Mr Bramwell was in the company in 1794 and left it on 29 October 1796. In the latter year he was earning 6s. 8d. daily. Bramwell then went to Edinburgh and performed for a season, and in 1803–4 his name appeared briefly in the Covent Garden accounts. At Covent Garden he seems to have been working at a salary of £2 weekly as a member of the singing chorus. His dates and type of activity are parallel to Mrs Georgiana Bramwell's, and it is very likely that they were husband and wife.

Bramwell, Georgiana *[fl. 1791–1804], singer, actress.*

At £1 weekly on 15 October 1791, Mrs Georgiana Bramwell began acting for the Drury Lane company at the King's Theatre in the Haymarket, playing one of the priestesses in *The Cave of Trophonius*. During the course of the 1791–92 season she was in the choruses of *Macbeth* (18 February 1792), *The Surrender of Calais* (29 March), and *Dido Queen of Carthage* (23 May). She worked in the summer at the Haymarket Theatre, singing again in the chorus of *The Surrender of Calais*. In 1792–93 she made some slight progress; in addition to chorus work in *The Pirates*, *The Mountaineers*, and *Caernarvon Castle*, she was cast as Honoria in *Love Makes a Man* (4 October 1792) at the King's and a Pastoral Nymph in *Comus* (2 September 1793) at the Haymarket.

She continued the same pattern in 1793–94, serving as a Bridesmaid in *Royal Clemency* and in the chorus of *Thomas and Sally*—among other chores—at the Haymarket Theatre where many of the Drury Lane players acted while the new playhouse was being completed. When the grand new Drury Lane opened its dramatic season on 21 April 1794 with a lavish production of *Macbeth*, there was Mrs Bramwell, swelling the chorus—but her contribution was not significant enough to warrant keeping her in the cast from 28 April on. On 26 April 1794 she played Nelly in *No Song No Supper*, a role she kept in ensuing seasons. She also played Cicely in *The Quaker* on 8 May 1794 and was one of the captives in *Lodoiska* on 9 June.

Mrs Bramwell's 1794–95 season was her most successful and active one. Her pay was raised to £1 16s. 8d., she was now able to start contributing 10s. 6d. to the retirement fund at the theatre, and she was frequently named in the bills, occasionally in name roles. She played Nelly again, was in the chorus of *The Glorious First of June* on 14 October 1794, sang and also played Partheca in *The Cherokee* on 20 December, was Jenny Diver in *The Beggar's Opera* on 6 February 1795, acted an Amazon in *Alexander the Great* on 12 February, and sang in the chorus of *The Triumph of Hymen* on 6 May. During 1795–96 she was engaged in the same routine, but her schedule was somewhat lighter; on 18 January she sang in *Harlequin Captive*, on 7 June was Katharine in *Don Juan*, and shared a benefit with three others on 8 June. After this benefit the profit to be split four ways was a bit over £135.

Mrs Bramwell began the 1796–97 season at Drury Lane, playing Nelly again and serving as a peasant in *Richard Coeur de Lion*, but after singing in a performance of the latter on 8 November 1796 she left the London stage. In 1797–98 she was acting at the Theatre Royal, Edinburgh, and in 1803–4 she was at Covent Garden. On 19 April 1803, however, George Colman had written to Elliston in connection with the coming season at the Haymarket: "I wd. not give twopence for Mrs Bramwell." She seems, in short, to have had a rather undistinguished career which gradually faded into obscurity.

Mrs Bramwell was reported by Doane in 1794 as living in Prospect Row, Lambeth, and participating that year in oratorios as well as theatrical performances. The Mr Bramwell, whose dates seem to match hers, was very likely her husband.

Brancourt, Captain. *See* PRENCOURT, CAPTAIN.

Brand, Miss *[fl. 1780]*, *actress.*

A Miss Brand acted a principal role in *The Double Amour* at the Haymarket, out-of-season on 25 September 1780.

Brand, Hannah *d. 1821, actress, dramatist.*

Hannah Brand was born the daughter of a tanner at Norwich and the sister of John Brand (d. 1808), the clergyman and political writer. She had two sisters, Mary and Sarah, who, unlike Hannah, lived out their lives as spinster school mistresses. After keeping a school at Norwich for a while with her elder sister Mary, Hannah Brand turned to the stage, a profession for which she proved to be temperamentally unsuited. Announced as a young lady who was making her first appearance on any stage, she acted the role of Agmunda in her own tragedy of *Huniades* with the Drury Lane company at the King's Theatre on 18 January 1792. The play was bad and Miss Brand's performance did not contribute usefully. The work was withdrawn after this first performance but was again produced on 2 February 1792 under the new title of *Agmunda*, with Miss Brand in that character but with the former title role of Huniades, which had been played by John Kemble, now omitted. This curious alteration, which was ridiculed by the Earl of Guilford in the House of Lords, was no more successful than the original, and "piece and author vanished from London."

Two years later, Miss Brand acted with Wilkinson's company at York. On 20 March 1794 in that city she played Lady Townley in *The Provok'd Husband*, but, according to Wilkinson, her performance was "too formal for the school of gaiety in 1794," and her "dialect was as provincial, as if her education had been entirely neglected." Refusing to acquiesce to the low-cut bodices of contemporary fashion and demonstrating a starched manner which was interpreted as haughty disdain, she stirred against herself an antagonism from the feminine portion of the audience, so that her first appearance at York "so far from being well received, met with rude marks of disgustful behaviour, and that from ladies who did not add by such demeanour addition to their politeness or good understanding." Miss Brand stayed at York, however, until the last night of the season on 21 May 1794, when she again acted in *Agmunda*, "in which she was derided." At Liverpool that summer she met with a similar reception.

Hannah Brand soon retired from the stage to become a governess to a married woman, and even in this profession her eccentric conduct caused friction, now between that lady and her husband. According to Wilkinson, who has drawn an amusing picture of her in his *Wandering Patentee,* Hannah Brand was "very sensible, but too learned." Wilkinson's curious stories of her reveal how highly she had overestimated her histrionic talents. But her failure on the stage she attributed to the jealousy of the Kembles and Mrs Siddons. When her tragedy *Agmunda* was performed, in fear of having it stolen she copied out the entire manuscript for the prompter except her own part which she reserved. Wilkinson found her to be, however, a person of estimable private character with good and generous understanding—"Now take this lady from her tragedy and her acting," he wrote, "and she possesses many good, ay shining qualities."

In 1798 Miss Brand published at Norwich a volume of *Plays and Poems*, which included: *Adelinda*, an alteration of Destouches's *La Force du naturel*; *The Conflict, or, Love, Honour, and Pride*, an adaptation of Corneille's *Don Sanche d'Arragon*; and *Huniades*, along with miscellaneous poems.

Hannah Brand died in March 1821, probably at Norwich. When she drew up her will on 13 October 1811, she was residing with Ann Livie, widow, in the Liberty of the Tower of London. In this will, which was very long and complex for the disposition of a very modest estate and which was proved at London on 19 October 1821, she left her books, book cases, and writing desk to her sister Mary Brand, of Woodbridge, spinster; £50 each to her cousins Elizabeth Brand and John Brand, of Woodbridge and of Trinity College, Cambridge; and small bequests to her sister Sarah Brand and to her nieces Hannah and Elizabeth Brand, daughters of her late brother, Reverend John Brand. The residue of her estate, including about £200 in 5 percent annuities, she left to Mary Ware, widow, of Norfolk. Mrs Ware was named as a co-trustee with Ann Beever, of Norfolk, the wife of Thomas Beever, Hannah's cousin John Brand, and Ann Livie.

Brandi, Gaetano [*fl. 1784–1818?*], oboist, flutist?

Gaetano Brandi played oboe at the Handel Memorial Concerts at Westminster Abbey and the Pantheon on 26, 27, and 29 May and 3 and 5 June 1784. He was a member of the band at the Pantheon for the opera season that ran from 17 February to 19 July 1791, and he played at the Haymarket on 15 January 1798 when the *Messiah* was performed. A flutist named Brandi was on the company list at the King's Theatre in the Haymarket in 1818, and it is possible that he was Gaetano.

Brandon, James William 1754–1825, box bookkeeper, housekeeper.

James William Brandon was christened at St Paul, Covent Garden, on 17 June 1754, the son of Josiah John Brandon by Martha his wife. His mother Martha Brandon was probably the Mrs Brandon who for so many years supervised the fruit concession at Covent Garden Theatre; and the John Brandon who served in the treasury office there was probably his brother. About 1770 James William Brandon became a house servant at Covent Garden. He was to remain in the employ of that theatre for some 55 years. In 1774–75 and 1775–76 he shared tickets with other minor house servants. In 1777 he seems to have been promoted to the fairly important position of housekeeper, overseeing cleaning and maintenance personnel, and serving as their pay master. By 1782 he had also taken on the very influential position of box bookkeeper, a situation which kept him in close contact with the more affluent and important frequenters of the theatre. He continued to share benefit tickets with others through 1791–92, but in the following season he began to receive his benefit by himself.

Brandon continued in his positions as housekeeper and box bookkeeper up to his death in 1825. The Covent Garden account books over the years record numerous sums given to him for paying the charwomen and other minor personnel. Brandon him-

JAMES BRANDON

self seems to have been on a constant salary of 12*s.* per week, at least from 1776 through 1803, but by virtue of his position, which gave him some considerable persuasion over the box keepers and ticket takers, and also evidently because he was very popular with the public, Brandon always took in especially high benefit receipts for himself. On 1 June 1797 he sold tickets in the amount of £348 2*s.* 6*d.* On 3 June 1799 his benefit receipts were £505 9*s.* 6*d.*, less house charges. Thomas Dutton in *The Dramatic Censor* described a benefit on 29 May 1800, when *The Chapter of Accidents* "was this evening revived for the benefit of Mr Brandon, whose assiduities and attention to the functions of his office, attracted a very numerous, a very splendid and fashionable audience. The side and dress boxes boasted some of the loveliest and most elegant ladies, that ever graced a public assembly with their presence." Brandon's receipts that night were £410 4*s.*, presumably less the house charges. Benefit receipts entered in the account books for Brandon in the nineteenth century are even higher and average almost £600 per year—for example: 8 June 1807, £591 3*s.*; 14 June 1810, £615 7*s.*; and 28 June 1814, £555 1*s.*

Despite his popularity, Brandon's responsibilities in the house sometimes put him in danger of audiences which could be terrifying in their violent rowdiness. On 26 December 1802 a riot ensued when the farce was suddenly changed from the announced *The Review* to *The Jew and the Doctor.* Before the farce, a bottle thrown from the slips by a drunken sailor narrowly missed Mr Betterton on the stage, and then at the commencement of the farce the riot became serious, despite the apologies of the management:

the actors successively appeared, amid showers of apples, oranges, penny-pieces, &c. and skipped about, to the great amusement of the galleries, tho' at the expence of their own

limbs. The ladies were in the utmost terror, and at the end of the farce, which was converted into a pantomime, and that a very short one, the one and two shilling deities, for some time, kept possession of their regions, but were at length compelled to resign their *thunder* to the *staff* of the constables, headed by Mr Brandon, the housekeeper.

At the end of that season, nevertheless, the *Monthly Mirror* reported that on 7 June 1802, "Mr Brandon had one of the most profitable houses of the season; a recompense to which his assiduity and services are justly entitled."

Brandon also played a key role in the famous "Old Price Riots" which occurred at the opening of the new Covent Garden Theatre in the fall of 1809. As an important Covent Garden official he became a notorious figure to the "O. P." faction and almost ended as a professional casualty. He brought charges against one of the riot leaders, Clifford, but the case, *Brandon v. Clifford*, brought to trial on 5 December 1809, was settled against Brandon by a jury which evaded the central question of whether or not Clifford was guilty of riot. A number of caricature prints were published about the event. One, entitled "English Discipline For Meddling Servants," which was printed in December 1809 by S. W. Fores of No 50, Piccadilly, depicts John Bull, with the letters O. P. on his hat, kicking and thrashing Brandon; a caption reads, "Now Mr *Brandon* I'll Kick you Out of your Place! for dareing to meddle with the *O Ps* and makeing Yourself so Buiey [sic], in Spoiling Our *Dances*." In another part of the design a weeping Brandon kneels abjectly before John Bull, imploring forgiveness. In an engraved colored impression by Cruikshank, Brandon, depicted as burly and brandy-faced, is hooted out of Westminster Hall, with Kemble, after his trial. Brandon has his hands to his ears and exclaims *"Oh D—— n the OPs."* Another satirical print shows Brandon at his desk with a large pen behind his ear; the caption reads, "This is the Box-Book Keeper, who pockets the Pelf, . . . and prays for the Tool that ruin'd the Man."

In September 1799 James Brandon married Miss Lucinda Mallinson, who perhaps was the daughter of Mr and Mrs Joseph Mallinson, performers at Bath. By her, Brandon had at least four children, all baptized at St Paul, Covent Garden: James William Brandon, born 21 October 1800 and christened 16 November 1800; Charlotte Harris Brandon, born 7 April 1802 and christened 21 August 1802; Mary Ann Brandon, born 27 November 1809 and christened 7 April 1814 (at which time the Brandons lived in Hart Street, Covent Garden); and another child, name unknown. On 7 January 1825, then living at No 100, Longacre, Brandon wrote a letter to W. Dawes in interest of one of his daughters who wished to make her appearance at the Concert for the Choral Fund.

James William Brandon died at his house at Upper Marylebone Street on 13 May 1825, aged 71. According to the *Monthly Mirror* of May 1825, he left a widow and four children "unprovided for." Brandon's namesake son died in Upper Marylebone Street on 3 September 1828.

Brandon, John   *fl. 1789–1813*, *treasurer.*

John Brandon was probably the son of Josiah John and Martha Brandon of the parish of St Paul, Covent Garden, and the brother of James William Brandon, the boxkeeper at Covent Garden Theatre. By 1789, John Brandon seems to have been serving some function in the treasury office of the same theatre. On 26 August 1795 he was paid a total of £13 17s. 6d. for travel expenses for 1789, 1793, and 1794, a delay in reimbursement which seems extraordinary. On 6 August 1796 the treasury received from John Brandon half the value of tickets which he apparently had out. And in July 1802 he was paid £11 6s.

3d. for his travel expenses to Newington. In July 1813 he was paid £210 by Covent Garden, an amount which also included the residue of his salary for 1810–11.

He was no doubt the John Brandon who subscribed to John Cross's *Parnassian Trifles* in 1792. "John Brandon of the Theatre Royal Covent Garden" appeared before a notary public to testify to the validity of the handwriting of James Wild, the prompter, in his will of 14 August 1801, and John Brandon of White Horse Yard witnessed the will of Jane Banks, the actress, in 1810. This person was probably also the J. Brandon who witnessed the will of John Ledge of Covent Garden Theatre in 1806.

A John Brandon, bachelor, married Sarah Ward, spinster, both of the parish, at St Paul, Covent Garden, on 10 June 1794. On 14 December 1811, at the same church, Sir Thomas Lighton of the parish, bachelor, married Sylvia Brandon of the parish of St Giles in the Fields; she was a spinster and minor, and the marriage took place "by & with Consent of John Brandon Esq. her natural and lawful father," and was witnessed by him and by a "J. H. Brandon," probably a scribal error for J[ames] W[illiam] Brandon, the boxkeeper.

One James William Brandon, who died on 3 September 1828, at the age of 36, in Upper Marylebone Street, according to the *Gentleman's Magazine*, was the "eldest son of the late John Brandon, treasurer of Covent Garden Theatre." While it is possible that John Brandon had a son by this name, we believe that the *Gentleman's Magazine* may have confused him with the James William Brandon who was namesake and son of the boxkeeper.

Notices of John Brandon seem not to have continued after 1813, but some of those we have associated with James William Brandon may be instead about him. A John Brandon, of 13 Rose Street, who was buried at St Paul, Covent Garden, on 30 September 1845, at age 51, probably was a son.

Brandon, [Martha?] 1727?–1798, concessionaire.

For many years Mrs Brandon supervised the fruit concession at Covent Garden Theatre, at which were also sold the playbooks and copies of songs. She paid the theatre £80 for "fruit rent" on 17 July 1781 and another £80 on 21 June 1783. Payments of £20 each for "fruit rent" were made by her on 30 November 1785, 18 June 1787, 17 December 1787, and 27 November 1788. On 10 January 1791 it seems that she received a gratuity of £30 from the management for one year and another annual gratuity on 6 January 1792 (suggesting that she had by then retired?). In October of 1798 the *Monthly Mirror* reported the death of Mrs Brandon of Covent Garden Theatre, "in her 71st year." We believe Mrs Brandon to have been the Martha Brandon who was the wife of Josiah John Brandon and the mother of James William Brandon, the Covent Garden boxkeeper. She was probably also the mother of John Brandon who was in the treasury office of that theatre for many years.

Brangin, Mr [fl. 1781–1791], house servant?

A Mr Brangin (or Braggin) was on the Covent Garden staff, probably as a minor house functionary, at a steady salary of £1 per week from 22 September 1781 through 15 June 1791; the only period during which he appears to have been inactive in the 1784–85 season, during which the account book makes no mention of him. He was probably related to the actress Miss Rhoda Brangin.

Brangin, Rhoda, later Mrs James Spriggs [fl. 1779–1791], actress.

Rhoda Brangin (or Braggin) was probably related to the Covent Garden employee Mr Brangin of the 1780's, for their years of service at that playhouse are parallel. Miss Brangin made her first appearance on the stage as Miranda in *The Busy Body* at the Haymarket Theatre on 13 October 1779. On 27 December she delivered the epilogue to *Falstaff's Wedding*; on 28 March 1780 she was Kitty in *The Humours of Oxford*; and on 5 April she had a principal but unnamed role in *A School for Ladies* and acted Mrs Brittle in *No Wit Like a Woman's*. After this season at the Haymarket she was engaged at £1 weekly to play Harry Paddington in *The Lady's Opera* (an adaptation of *The Beggar's Opera*) at Covent Garden on 16 and 18 October 1781, after which her name disappeared from the bills for two years.

On 14 October 1783 she played Betty Doxey in *The Beggar's Opera* at Covent Garden, beginning an engagement at that house that lasted until 1791. Her roles throughout her seasons of service were small ones, almost all comic, and usually in afterpieces; during the summer months she regularly moved with many patent house players to the Haymarket, and there she sometimes had opportunities for slightly more significant roles. But most of her seasons were not unlike her first full one of 1783–84: after Betty Doxey she played Trusty in *Epicoene* (starting on 26 April 1784), and at the Haymarket in the summer she was Corinna in *The Citizen* (8 July), the Chambermaid in *The Genius of Nonsense* (19 July), one of the actresses in *The Manager in Distress* (28 July), the Ghost of Goody Black and Blue in *The What D'Ye Call It* (10 August), and Lady Godiva in *Peeping Tom* (6 September).

Some roles, like Lady Godiva, she continued playing over the years; among these were Zapphira in *A Mogul Tale*, Bianca in *Catherine and Petruchio*, Agnes in *The Follies of a Day*, Miss La Blond in *The Romp*, Pink in *The Young Quaker*, Betty in *The Hypocrite*, Jenny in *The Tender Husband*, and Miss Bronze in *The Sword of Peace*. Miss Brangin occasionally appeared in plays of some significance, too; in addition to *Epicoene* she was in *The Way of the World* (but played an unnamed maid), *The Rehearsal*, *The Beggar's Opera* (as Mrs Coaxer), *The Conscious Lovers* (as Lucinda), *The Provoked Husband* (as Myrtilla), *A Duke and No Duke* (as Prudentia), *A Bold Stroke for a Wife* (as the Masked Lady), and *King Lear* (but as an added character named Arante).

Throughout the years she remained at a steady salary of £1 per week, making little progress but working steadily and serving faithfully. Her best season was 1785–86 when she was frequently named in the bills both in the winter at Covent Garden and in the summer at the Haymarket, but her brisker activity this season did not lead to better roles or higher pay. Suddenly, in April 1790, her name dropped from the bills; she acted Bianca in *Catherine and Petruchio* on 6 April and, instead of finishing out the season and spending the summer at the Haymarket, she left the theatre until the following November. In 1790–91 she played less frequently than usual at Covent Garden and on 5 April 1791 made her last appearance as Miss Brangin, playing the maid servant in *Two Strings to Your Bow*. She was gone for a month, and on 19 May 1791 reappeared as Mrs James Spriggs, thus explaining her rather erratic schedule of the previous year. On 13 June she played in *Two Strings to Your Bow* again and then left the stage for good.

Branman, Mr *[fl. 1795], watchman.*

Mr Branman, along with his colleagues Gell and Vaughan, was paid £18 on 17 October 1795 for serving as a watchman at Drury Lane during the summer when the theatre was dark. His weekly salary was 12s.

Bransby, Astley *d. 1789, actor.*

Astley Bransby acted on the London stage for some 33 years, yet almost nothing is known of his personal life nor was he ever the subject of a contemporary memoir or biographical notice. His first appearance of record was as Plume in *The Recruiting Office* at the Haymarket on 23 April 1744, at which time he was apparently one of a group of young actors, including Samuel Foote, being trained by Charles Macklin. In the following season Bransby played once, at Drury Lane for the benefit of Morgan on 5 June 1745, in the role of Friendly in *The School Boy*. At the beginning of the next season he became a regular member of the Drury Lane company, in which he remained through his career, except for four seasons (1749–53) when he was at Covent Garden.

Almost without reputation, Bransby worked nightly in numerous supporting roles in the repertory. He seems never to have played a leading role in London, and only on occasion, as with Kent in *King Lear*, was a featured part his. In his earlier years he frequently doubled in several small roles within a production, such as Capucius and Brandon in *Henry VIII* and Oxford and Tyrrel in *Richard III*. He made his first appearance as a regular member of the company at Drury Lane as Doodle in *The Tragedy of Tragedies* on 8 October 1745, and in that season he also played Thomas in *The Virgin Unmask'd*, Phormio in *The Comical Lovers*, Montano in *Othello*, a bravo in *The Lady's Last Stake*, Curio in *Twelfth Night*, the Constable in *The Sea Voyage*, the clerk in *The Humours of the Army*, and Francisco in *The Tempest*. In the following season, 1746–47, he added: the player in *The Beggar's Opera*, Slap in *The Intriguing Chambermaid*, Buckram in *Love for Love*, Stratton in *The Comical Lovers*, the second murderer in *Macbeth*, the lawyer in *Love's Last Shift*, Robin in *The Artful Lover*, Chatillion in *King John*, Sparkle in *The Miser*, and Harrow in *Marry or Do Worse*.

After four seasons at Drury Lane, Bransby went over to Covent Garden in 1749–50, where he remained through 1752–53, playing in a similar line of small

Enthoven Collection, Victoria and Albert
Museum

ASTLEY BRANSBY, as Aesop

by Zoffany

secondary and tertiary roles, many of them
Shakespearean: Guildenstern, Norfolk in
Richard III, Montano in *Othello*, Siward in
Macbeth, Shallow in *Measure for Measure*,
Metellus in *Julius Caesar*, and Worcester in
I Henry IV. His salary at Covent Garden in
1749–50 was 5*s*. per day.

In 1753–54 Bransby returned to Drury
Lane. Over the next 24 years he regularly
played dozens of roles, of great variety,
but with an emphasis it seems on serious
older men or somewhat extravagant comic
characters. In addition to the above-mentioned, an incomplete list includes: Clerimont in *The Miser*, Stanmore and Captain
Driver in *Oroonoko*, Stanley in *Richard III*,
Gibbet in *The Stratagem*, Escalus in *Romeo
and Juliet*, Phoenix in *The Distrest Mother*,
Downright in *Every Man in his Humour*,
Dervise in *Tamerlane*, Acasto in *The Orphan*, Waitwell in *The Way of the World*,
the Duke in *The Merchant of Venice*, Raleigh in *The Earl of Essex*, the Duke in
Venice Preserv'd, and Don John in *Much
Ado About Nothing*. On 21 April 1759
Bransby played the role of Octar in the

first performance of Murphy's *The Orphan
of China*.

In his last season on the stage, 1776–77,
Bransby was still playing many of the roles
which had been his for years, including Old
Bevil in *The Conscious Lovers*, Lucius in
Cymbeline, and Duncan in *Macbeth*. His
last performance at Drury Lane was as
Sackbut in *A Bold Stroke for a Wife* on
2 June 1777. In that final season he was
being paid £3 10*s*. per week, the salary at
which he had been on the pay list since at
least 1764–65. Bransby seems not to have
taken regular benefits, perhaps having a
salary adjustment in lieu of them, but in
the few years when he did, they were
shared with other supporting players such
as Burton and Packer. On 23 April 1777,
his last benefit, when he played Russet in
The Jealous Wife, he shared a net of £132
with Burton. Between 1765 and 1777,
Bransby lived at No 10, New Pye Street,
Westminster.

Bransby was involved for awhile with
provincial management. In 1762 he and
Burton were managers of the theatre at
Richmond, but not being very successful,
they soon sold out to James Love. Bransby
acted for Love at Richmond in 1765,
1766, and 1767. He was also a member of
Foote's summer company at the Haymarket in the summer of 1772. In November of that year he sold his interest in the
Bristol theatre to Parsons and Buckley.

Bransby retired from the stage at the end
of the season 1776–77 apparently because
of ill health. He claimed against the Drury
Lane Fund in the middle of 1777. On 25
April 1778 Bransby wrote a peremptory
note to an unidentified addressee inquiring
when he would receive a draft of 20 guineas "that you told me Mr Garrick was so
kind to let me have; as I am in the greatest distress at this time." According to Winston's notation on the Fundbook, Bransby
died in August 1780, but unless there was
another Bransby of Drury Lane Winston
was mistaken. The *European Magazine* for
March 1789 announced in its obituary col-

umn that "Mr Bransby, formerly of Drury-Lane Theatre" had died "at his lodgings, Rochester-row, Tothill fields" on 24 February 1789.

Astley Bransby was a very tall man, or as Churchill put it, "a mighty Gulliver in Lilliput." Churchill thought Bransby excelled as Kent in *King Lear* and Downright in *Every Man in his Humour*, finding in these portrayals "a justness of conception not often to be met with." In *A General View of the Stage*, Samuel Derrick (under the pseudonym of Thomas Wilkes) considered it odd that Bransby was "like to have been overlooked in the crowd, . . . as he is no very trifling object: indeed, neither his person, nor his talents are diminutive." Other critics confirmed Bransby's physical stature, but not his talents. The author of *The Rational Rosciad* wrote of him in 1767:

> Bransby, the great Goliah of the stage,
> Beneath a diadem can fiercely rage,
> His majesterial taste so meanly poor,
> Is an unchanged monotony of roar,
> And constitutionally fond of nokes,
> All his long periods, are so many jokes.

Earlier, in 1761, the author of *The Anti-Rosciad* had proclaimed, "Nor can his size gigantic *Bransby* save, / Though voice and stature both denote him brave." Francis Gentleman (1772) referred to him and Burton as "gentle opiates," who when playing together were as "Dull, heavy, cold as dark November weather." As the ghost in *Hamlet*, Bransby was judged by the *Theatrical Review* (1772) to be "the shadow of a shade," and the *Smithfield Rosciad* (1763) asked, "Don't Bransby tread too heavy for a ghost?" Perhaps Kelly's description in *Thespis* (1766) of Bransby as a humble and careful actor, who "Avoids all censure, if he meets no praise," was the most succinct and reliable assessment of the actor's abilities.

Bransby appears in the character of Aesop in *Lethe* in two fine paintings by Zof-

fany which are in the Birmingham Museum and Art Gallery. In one painting he is shown with William Parsons as the Old Man and Watkins as the servant, and in the other with Ellis Ackman as Bowman and Garrick as Lord Chalkstone. The scenes are from the revival of *Lethe* at Drury Lane in 1765–66. Bransby is also probably represented as Kent in the painting by Benjamin Wilson of Garrick as Lear in the storm. This painting was engraved by MacArdell in 1762.

Branscomb, J. *d. c. 1815, machinist, proprietor.*

Mr J. Branscomb was for many years the chief machinist at the Royal Circus; the first notice of him seems to be on 23 April 1798 when he did the machinery for a production of *Blackbeard* at the Circus. The next season he provided machines for *Cora; or the Virgin of the Sun*, and on 23 June 1800 he handled the machinery for *The Magic Flute; Or, Harlequin Champion*. Over the next 12 years he was regularly billed as machinist for such productions as *Rinaldo Rinaldini* on 6 April 1801, *The Fire King* on 20 June 1801, *The Golden Farmer* on 28 June 1802, the *Mogul Tale* on 3 June 1805 (and for this summer he had done "the whole Architectural Alterations in the Theatre"), *The Rival Clowns* on 17 July 1809, and the *Seven Wonders of the World* on 13 July 1812. The bills occasionally noted that tickets could be had of Branscomb at the Circus Coffee House, but it is not certain that his lodgings were connected with this establishment. Once during this period, on 6 November 1809, Branscomb apparently came on stage; when *The Jubilee* was staged, into it was introduced "a Match of Single Stick, by Mr. S. Slader and Mr. Branscomb."

Branscomb normally took full credit for machinery in Royal Circus productions, though once, on 7 June 1813, he shared the billing with Mr Sutton when *Llewelyn, Prince of Wales* was performed; rarely were other machinists cited in the bills, however, though the advertisements made it clear that Branscomb had a team of assistants working under him.

The Royal Circus became the Surrey Theatre, and in 1814 Branscomb and Dunn became the new proprietors. Despite this new position, Branscomb continued to create machines for the productions, one of his last being devised in July 1814 for the equestrian spectacle called *The Tiger Horde*. On 13 November 1815 at the Surrey Theatre a benefit was held for Mr Honeyman, "Executor to Mr J. Branscomb, Late proprietor of this Theatre," but Branscomb's date of death is not known.

Branson, Mr [*fl. 1767–1784*], *house servant?*

The Covent Garden account books contain numerous entries concerning a Mr Branson (not to be confused with Brandon the boxkeeper), but there is no clue as to his function in the house. The first reference to him is dated 19 June, apparently 1769 but covering 1767–69; the payment noted is £23 17*s*. 6*d*. Over the years his daily salary seems to have been £1 weekly but an entry dated 29 May 1770 for £24 is called extra salary for the season, so Branson must sometimes have worked overtime or in a second theatrical position. The last reference to him is dated 3 June 1784—a payment of £1 10*s*. for nine nights—and its existence precludes our assigning him as husband to the Mrs Branson who acted at Covent Garden in walk-ons in 1767 and 1768, for she was widowed by May 1783. Mr Branson may have been related to the Miss Branston (or Branson?) who married actor William Powell in 1759 and later acted at Bristol.

Branson, Mrs [*fl. 1767–1784*], *actress.*

Mrs Branson walked on in *The Coronation* at Covent Garden when it was performed on 22, 23, 24 September 1767, receiving 5*s*. nightly for her efforts. She repeated this silent part on 22 September 1768 at the same fee and then disappeared from the records until 16 and 18 October 1781. At that time she played Molly Brazen in *The Beggar's Opera* at Covent Garden, her fee for the two performances being £1. She was married, but her husband's first name is not known; he could not have been the Mr Branson who worked at Covent Garden from 1767 to 1784, however, for on 21 May 1783 Mrs Branson shared a benefit and was styled Widow Branson. She was cited at benefit time the following season, on 15 May 1784, but after that her name dropped from the records for good. Mrs Branson may have been related to the Miss Branston (or Branson?) who married actor William Powell in 1759.

Brasgirdle. *See* **BRACEGIRDLE.**

Brassey, Mr [*fl. 1728–1748*], *actor.*
Mr Brassey played Thimble in the opera *Penelope* on 8 May 1728 at the Haymarket Theatre. He was possibly the Brassey who was at Norwich in 1743 and played at the Lee and Yeates booth at Bartholomew Fair in August 1748.

Brathwaite, Brathwayt, or **Brathwit.** *See* **BRAITHWAITE.**

Braville, Mr [*fl. 1776–1777*], *puppeteer.*
With Meniucci as his partner, Mr Braville displayed his Chinese shadow puppets in St Alban's Street in 1776–77.

Brawford. *See* **CRAWFORD.**

Brawn. *See* **BROWN, MISS** [*fl. 1767–1778*].

Bray. *See also* **BRACY** and **DUPRÉ.**

Bray, Mr [*fl. 1689–1695*], *dancer, dancing master.*
From 1689 to 1694 Mr Bray was a dancer and the dancing master in the

United Company; he is known to have performed in *The Rape of Europa* at Dorset Garden during the winter of 1693–94. When the company split, Bray joined Betterton's troupe at Lincoln's Inn Fields, but whether or not he stayed there beyond 1695 is not certain. His name could be an error for another, such as Dupré.

Bray, Mrs *d. 1752, proprietress, actress.*

Mrs Bray played Lady Wealthy in *The Unnatural Parents* on 22 August 1727 at the Lee and Harper booth at Bartholomew Fair, and it is probable that she was the same Mrs Bray who was the proprietress of Mulberry Gardens, Clerkenwell, from 1745 to 1752. She was described as "one of the fattest women in London" and had "an excellent good character." Mrs Bray died on 1 March 1752. (Mrs Henrietta Maria Bray [1676–1737] was active at Norwich from 1728 to her death and may have been related to the London woman; Henrietta Maria was buried in 1737 at St Peter Mancroft, Norwich.)

Brayzant. *See* BAYZAND.

Brazong, Mr [*fl. 1691*], *musician.*

One Brazong was apparently among those members of the King's Musick who accompanied William III to Holland in the spring of 1691.

Breame. *See* DE BREAME.

Brearley, Mr [*fl. 1783–1785*], *box-keeper, lobby keeper.*

Mr Brearley was a box and lobby keeper at the King's Theatre in the Haymarket during the period 1783–85.

Brécourt. *See* DE BRÉCOURT.

Breil. *See* DU BREIL.

Breillat, George [*fl. 1794*], *singer.*

Doane's *Musical Directory* of 1794 listed George Breillat, of No 60, Aldermanbury, as a participant in concerts presented by the Longacre Society, Cecilian Society, Surrey Chapel Society, and the Handelian Society. He was a composer and a tenor (presumably tenor singer, not tenor horn player).

Brent, Mr [*fl. 1797*], *actor. See* BRENT, MRS [*fl. 1787–1797*].

Brent, Mrs [*fl. 1787–1797*], *actress.*

Mrs Brent appeared as Woodcock in *Love in a Village* at the Haymarket Theatre for a single performance on 8 January 1787. Ten years later she and Mr Brent were at the same playhouse on 23 and 26 January 1797. On the twenty-third Mr Brent had a principal role in *The Battle of Eddington* and played Old Random in *Ways and Means*; in the afterpiece Mrs Brent acted Harriet. On the twenty-sixth both Brents were in *Barnaby Brittle*, she playing Damaris and he Clodpole.

Brent, Charles *1693–1770, singer, fencing master.*

Charles Brent, a countertenor, created the role of Hamor in the first performance of Handel's *Jeptha* at Covent Garden on 26 February 1752. The piece was repeated on 28 February and 4 March. Brent also may have sung Micah in *Samson* on 6 March 1752. At Ranelagh in 1758 he accompanied Beard in the "Salt Box Song," playing on that instrument, in the first performance of Bonnell Thornton's burlesque *Ode on St Caecilia's Day.*

Brent was also a fencing master and the father of the singer Charlotte Brent, who became the second wife of the violinist Thomas Pinto. Charles Brent died on 8 August 1770 at age 77, according to Burney.

Brent, Charlotte. *See* PINTO, MRS THOMAS THE SECOND.

Brerecloth. *See* BERECLOTH.

Brerely, Mr [*fl.* 1777], *actor.*

Mr Brerely played Sir George Hastings in *A Word to the Wise* at the Haymarket Theatre on 1 May 1777.

Brereton, Mr [*fl.* 1771–1788], *house servant.*

A Mr Brereton was a minor house servant at Covent Garden from as early as 1771–72 through at least 1787–88. In most of these seasons he shared benefits with other minor house personnel. In 1771–72 his wages were 9*s.* per week; in 1779–80 they were raised to 15*s.*, and in 1780–81 to £1, at which figure they remained through 10 June 1788.

Brereton, William *1751–1787, actor.*

William Brereton was born in 1751, probably at Bath, the son of Major William Brereton, Master of Ceremonies of the Lower Rooms at Bath, and descended from an old Cheshire family. As a young man of 17, endowed with good looks and a fine voice, Brereton went upon the stage. He had the additional advantage of an acquaintance with David Garrick, through his father, whom Garrick was soon to support in a dispute relating to the position of Master of Ceremonies at Bath. Brereton made his first appearance on any stage at Drury Lane on 10 November 1768, announced as "A Young Gentleman," in the title role in *Douglas.* "He is a pretty figure," wrote Sylas Neville in his diary after seeing Brereton's third appearance in the role on 15 November 1768, "but wants lemon in his voice, as Mr Garrick calls it." Brereton acted Douglas six times that season, apparently his only billed role.

Under Garrick's tutelage Brereton was brought on in the following season in the roles of Trueman in *The London Merchant* on 26 December 1769, Laertes in *Hamlet* on 2 May 1770, and Romeo, for his benefit, on 8 May 1770, when tickets could be

had of him in Maiden Lane, Covent Garden. He remained at Drury Lane for the rest of his career, playing a line of similar young attractive men in both comedy and tragedy, usually in a mediocre fashion, for, despite Garrick's help, Brereton acquired a reputation of being no greater than a walking gentleman.

In 1770–71 he played the title roles of *Theodosius* on 23 April, *Tancred* on 1 May, for his benefit, and Orlando in *As You Like It* on 8 May. Earlier that season, on 17 October 1770, and again on 7 March he had acted Chamont in *The Orphan* (with Mrs Barry as Monimia) almost without notice, but when he played the role again in the following season on 15 October 1771 the *Theatrical Review,* no longer able to restrain itself, declared never to have seen it "so miserably executed before." Castigating Garrick for foisting upon the public this "insult to Common Sense," the critic described Brereton's conception, action, voice, and expression as "too contemptible for Criticism . . . His Action and Utterance, with numberless other Defects," rendered his performance "the highest Burlesque on the Character," causing the audience to laugh in places they were accustomed to weep. (Perhaps heeding the attack, Garrick replaced Brereton with Crofts when the play was next done on 21 February 1772, but on 22 December 1772 Brereton was back in the role.)

After the blast upon him as Chamont, the *Theatrical Review* gave Brereton a *coup de grace* when it wrote of his performance of Altamont in *The Fair Penitent* on 12 November 1771 that he was a "blubbering, bloody-murderer of Blank verse, who should never attempt any Character of more importance than that of *Jemmy Twinkle* in the *Trip to Scotland.*" Francis Gentleman, more cryptic, called Brereton a "cypher." The twenty-one-year-old actor managed to survive this onslaught and on 13 May 1772 played Hardy in *The Funeral, or, Grief a la Mode* for his own bene-

Harvard Theatre Collection

WILLIAM BRERETON, as Douglas
by Hone

fit, at which he took a modest profit of £49 3s. At this time he lived at Mr Pritchard's, shoemaker, in York Street, Covent Garden.

In 1772–73, when he lodged at Mr Gravock's, at the corner of St Martin's Street in Leicester Fields, Brereton acted, among other roles, Orsino in *Twelfth Night*, Don Frederick in *The Chances*, and the title role in *Philaster*. He went to play leading roles at Bristol in the summer of 1773, and in the next season at Drury Lane, engaged at a salary of £3 per week, he added Mercury in *Amphitryon* to his repertory on 20 May 1774. On 17 February 1775 he created the role of Mendoza in Jephson's *Braganza*, a performance which, according to Davies, gave evidence of improvement in Brereton's acting. "When he has thrown off that diffidence which hangs about him,

and has acquired a greater confidence in his powers to please," wrote Davies, "I venture to prophesy he will be an excellent performer." Brereton played six other roles for the first time in 1774–75: Belville in *The School for Wives*, Tyrrel in *The Fashionable Lover*, Young Bevil in *The Conscious Lovers*, Dolabella in *All for Love*, Posthumus in *Cymbeline*, and Jaffeir in *Venice Preserv'd*, the last-mentioned for his benefit on 3 May 1775. Also played on that night was Charles Dibdin's musical afterpiece, *The Quaker*, which Dibdin sold to Brereton for £70. Brereton's net benefit receipts for that night were only £36 1s. 6d., but Brereton had reserved a right to sell *The Quaker* to the theatre, according to Dibdin, "if he could prevail on the managers to buy it at a better price." A few months later, although first refusing to pay the requested amount of £100, Garrick did buy the piece for that sum.

Brereton went to Ireland in the summer of 1775 to act in Spranger Barry's company at Cork and at Crow Street, Dublin. On 24 June 1775 he wrote Garrick that Barry intended to open the Crow Street Theatre in the next winter and had offered him "a first situation" in the company with articles for two years, at seven guineas per week the first year and eight the next. Since his present salary at Drury Lane of £3 per week is "much below what I can live upon in London," he knows Garrick will not blame him for accepting Barry's offer, yet if Garrick will raise him to £6 per week he prefers to return as "my heart is and ever will be at Drury Lane while you are concern'd in it."

About 29 June 1775 Garrick replied that he considered Brereton "ungenteel" for not letting him know of 'his "inclination to quit Drury Lane at the time of yʳ going for Ireland," since the manager had only just stopped his office from writing him about debts Brereton owed to the company. (On 8 November 1774 the treasurer had given Brereton £20 on note.) In a maneuver not untypical, Garrick claimed that he had already decided to raise his salary, even retroactively for the past season, but he could not meet Brereton's proposal of £6 per week—"I will make y^r Salary four pounds for last Season—five & five for ye two next & Six for the third." In a generous way he closed the letter by assuring Brereton of a place in the Drury Lane company as long as he was manager, but "If you prefer ye Situation in Ireland . . . I wish you Joy of it." Brereton in the meantime, however, had signed articles with Barry. When he advised Garrick so, the manager responded in a hurt but firm manner, accusing him of chicanery, having heard from a friend that Brereton had announced his engagement to Barry in the papers, to which Brereton replied on 30 July: "I never cou'd be guilty of such low chicane as to send any thing relative to myself to the newspapers and am very much concern'd that you cou'd entertain such an opinion of me." Brereton's was a lame defense considering he had indeed signed with Barry. On 9 August, Garrick cut him down:

It must first be known what advantages You *will* gain, & what lose—I will venture to fore tell, that You have lost the very Critical time of your Theatrical Life, and that you will sorely repent Your unkind, I had very nearly said, Ungrateful Behaviour to me: What! does Mr Brereton (To whom, & to whose Family I have Shewn the most immoveable Attachment) offer me his Services after having Engag'd them to another?—This Sir, I did not expect from *You* of all Men—& I will even continue my open Behaviour to You, and Assure You that it is impossible that You can ever be engag'd with *me* again —I wish you no harm, but hope when you meet with a better Friend of a Manager that you will treat him more kindly

No doubt shaken by this reply, Brereton offered to break his contract with Barry, a proposition which Garrick told him on 9 September was "adding worse to bad" and one he would never consent to had Brereton "all the talents of the great Actors put together. . . . I once more assure you that it will not be in my power to give you the Situation you might have had. . . . You may depend upon it that this is the resolution of your once very Sincere friend and not your Ill wisher even now."

Despite his "resolution," Garrick relented on his principle, and Brereton returned to Drury Lane in 1775–76, at £5 per week, making his appearance on 25 October 1775 as Nerestan in *Zara.* On 31 October he played Constant in *The Provok'd Wife* for the first time. On 26 December his acting of Barnwell in *The London Merchant,* for the first time, prompted William Hopkins to write in his diary "very well." He played Seyward in *The Hypocrite* for the first time on 3 January and Dauphine in *Epicoene* on 13 January. In this latter production the title role was played by Mrs Siddons, in an incongruous piece of casting since the denouement depends on the character being a male. As Dauphine, according to the *Westminster Magazine,* Brereton displayed "a bloated vulgarity."

His patron Garrick having retired from the stage in June 1776, Brereton continued at Drury Lane under Sheridan's management, at £5 per week. Among the characters he played over the next ten years were (with date of first appearance) Richmond in *Richard III* (6 December 1776), Colonel Briton in *The Wonder* (18 December 1776), Colonel Standard in *The Constant Couple* (16 April 1779), the Prince of Wales in *1 Henry IV* (20 December 1779), Faulkland in *The Rivals* (22 February 1780), Hastings in *Jane Shore* (17 October 1780) and Alonzo in *The Revenge* (24 April 1783). According to his benefit bills, in 1779 and 1780 he lived at No 11, Tavistock Street, in 1782 at No 14, Catherine Street, Strand, and from 1784 through May 1786 at No 10, Charles Street. In lieu of benefits he was paid £100 in 1776–77, £50 in 1777–78. When he did take a regular benefit the net receipts to him were small, £31 15s. 6d. in 1782–83, £38 17s. 2d. in 1783–84, and £41 18s. 8d. in 1784–85.

On 26 September 1777 at Bath, Brereton married the young actress Miss Priscilla Hopkins (1756–1845), the daughter of the Drury Lane prompter William Hopkins. She continued, however, to be billed as Miss P. Hopkins in 1777–78, and not until 6 October 1778 did she perform as Mrs Brereton. After her husband's death in 1787 she soon married the great actor John Philip Kemble and performed as Mrs Kemble until her retirement in 1796. She no doubt had been a good wife to Brereton, but the story circulated that Brereton had an unrequited infatuation for Mrs Siddons, whose reputed heartlessness contributed to the madness which finally afflicted Brereton. He had played Jaffeir to Mrs Siddons's Belvidera in *Venice Preserv'd* at Drury Lane in December 1782. Stimulated by her power of genius, Brereton evidently rose to the occasion and performed a fourth act fully worthy of her and perhaps gave the best of his otherwise uninspired career. In the scene of their embrace, however, according to the author of *A Review of Mrs Crawford and Mrs Siddons in the Character of Belvidera* (1782), Mrs Siddons gave him only a "comfortable hug." "Lost in dulness 'till the Siddons came, / Who fir'd his soul, and push'd him on to fame," wrote the *New Rosciad* (1785). They acted together at Dublin in the summer of 1784, when, contrary to rumors that she had refused to appear for his benefit, she played *Jane Shore* on his night, 19 August 1784. The rumor persisted, however, and when she came onstage at Drury Lane again as Mrs Beverley in *The Gamester* on 5 October 1784, she was hissed. "A considerable period of time was lost; it might be forty minutes before the play began," reported the *Town and Country Magazine* for October 1784. "We

could perceive that the lady supported herself with a great degree of firmness under this very awful trial—a trial which, in great measure, determined her future fame—perhaps her residence in this metropolis."

Brereton played in the summer of 1785 at Portsmouth, where hints of his mental illness emerged, perhaps brought on by excessive drinking. One day in front of a public house run by Coombs, later a property man at Covent Garden, Brereton, with Williams and Staunton, in a fit of inebriety, pelted the carriage of the magistrate Sir John Carr and were required to make a public apology. On the Portsmouth stage, as Lovel in *The Clandestine Marriage*, he obliged Mrs Brereton, as Fanny, to dance a minuet which had no relationship to the text. As Posthumus "he came dancing on the stage, and altered a number of speeches," reported Winston in *The Theatric Tourist*, and in *Alexander the Great*, "In the scene where Statira says—'Hold off, and let me rush into his arms,' he turned short round, went off the stage, and left her to make the best of it. When she lay dead, he walked up to her, and exclaimed 'O my poor dear little ——, who could have used you so?' "

Although engaged for the entire season of 1785–86 at Drury Lane, Brereton played on until 3 November 1785, when he made his last appearance on the stage as Frederick in *The Chances*. In 1786 he claimed against the Drury Lane Theatrical Fund. It was said that he tried at least once to commit suicide and that when he also tried to kill his wife, he was put under restraint at a Hoxton asylum, where he died on 17 February 1787. He was buried in Shoreditch Churchyard, in a grave marked by a tombstone with the inscription, "William Brereton / Died 17th February 1787 / Aged 36 Years."

In his 18 years at Drury Lane William Brereton had been a performer of not very great merit. William Hawkins called him an "inferior" actor. Even Davies, who had hopes for him, wished that he "would avoid tones in speaking which approach something like singing." Brereton was not void of grace in person, but evidently he was lacking in energy and was laconic on stage. In a kind of epitaph for Brereton, John Williams (under the pseudonym of A. Pasquin) in 1786 wrote of him in *The Children of Thespis*:

> Lo, Brereton *comes—to his feelings a prey,*
> To damp our enjoyments, and darken our day;
> The hand of disease has laid waste his meek mind,
> To shew her great triumph o'er worth and mankind.
> When lofty ambition his pray'r had denied,
> His senses were madden'd, his reason it died.

An anonymous engraving of Brereton as Barnwell, wearing a close-fitting full-face black mask, was published by I. Wenman in 1777. Another picture of him as Barnwell by R. Dighton was engraved by Walker as a plate to the *New English Theatre*, published by T. Lowndes in 1776. J. Roberts did a line drawing of him as Don Alonzo in *The Revenge* which was engraved anonymously for a plate to *Bell's British Theatre*, 1777. Another picture of him, as Douglas, was done by N. Hone and engraved by S. Harding who published it in 1795; the same engraving appeared as a plate in the *European Magazine*, June 1796. Dighton did a line drawing of him as Troilus which he engraved for a plate to *Bell's British Theatre*, 1776.

Brereton's father, Major William Brereton, was involved in a contention over the successor to the position of Master of Ceremonies at Bath left vacant by the death of Samuel Derrick on 28 March 1769. A fierce competition, supported by pamphlets, epigrams, and broadsheets, ensued among Major Brereton, Plomer, and

Wade, which culminated in a riot at the Assembly Rooms. According to a document among the Garrick papers in the Forster Collection, Garrick supported Brereton. A committee especially appointed for the problem resolved on 17 April 1769 to declare Wade the Master of Ceremonies and to award Brereton "the Sum of Five Hundred Pounds part of the Surplus Money Subscribed to the Balls during this Season." Brereton was furthermore to have an annual ball in November as long as he continued to reside at Bath, at a guaranteed benefit of £200. Major Brereton died at Holt on 18 January 1813, in his ninetieth year. A line drawing of him, done by T. Hickey and engraved by J. Collyer, was published in 1778. His brother, George Brereton, uncle of the actor, a bombardier in the Royal Horse Artillary, died in 1805, and the administration of his estate was granted to Major Brereton on 10 May 1805.

Brereton, Mrs William, Priscilla. *See* KEMBLE, MRS JOHN PHILIP.

Breslaw, Philip *1726–1803, conjurer.*
Philip Breslaw (or, infrequently, but probably more correctly, Breslau) was born in Berlin in 1726 but spent much of his life in England and Ireland. The first mention of him appears to be an affidavit in *Faulkner's Dublin Journal* on 14 March 1767 when he identified himself as an equilibrist. Though he may have begun by balancing things, his chief fame was as a magician. One of his first recorded appearances was at the old music hall in Fishamble Street, Dublin, in 1768, but the particulars of his performance have not survived.

By 21 May 1771 he was in London, holding forth at what was to become a favorite address, a "commodious" house near Pinchbeck's in Cockspur Street. He claimed he would exhibit his "grand Performances, particularly on Watches," but he failed to go into any detail until a later bill that year advertising his fourth night in Cock-spur Street. This time he described his quarters as "Mr BRESLAW's new Long Room, prepared with Pit and Boxes in the most elegant and grand Manner," and he promised to exhibit "his new amazing Performances with Pocket-pieces, Rings, Sleeve buttons, Purses, Snuff-boxes, Swords, Cards, Hours, Dice, Letters, Thoughts, Numbers, Watches, and particularly with a Leg of Mutton; and to conclude with several live Pigeons, in an amazing Manner." The leg

Harvard Theatre Collection
PHILIP BRESLAW
artist unknown

of mutton trick was apparently one of his favorites: he carved a pack of cards out of a leg of mutton brought smoking hot from the spit.

Breslaw's exact whereabouts during the next three years are not clear, but he was at the Capel Street Theatre in Dublin some time after it was remodelled in 1773; the Duchess of Northumberland reported him in Cockspur Street again in 1773, offering his "deceptions"; and at about this same time he was associated with the equestrian Hughes at his British Horse Academy on the Surrey side of Blackfriars Bridge.

In the summer of 1774 he was touring the provinces with an Italian troupe, and it may have been this year that he gulled the churchwardens of Canterbury into furnishing the cost of the house on the promise that he would feed the poor of the parish; he fed the poor, not of the parish—but of his own troupe. A July 1774 advertisement gave the conjurer's itinerary:

BRESLAW and his ITALIANS, on their way for Worcester Races, will perform at the Town-Hall, in the City of Litchfield, this present Thursday, and To-morrow, being Friday, the 28th and 29th instant; at the Green Dragon in Walfall on Monday and Tuesday, the 1st and 2d of August; at the Red Lion in Wolverhampton on Wednesday and Thursday, the 3d and 4th of August; at the Talbot in Stourbridge on Friday the 5th of August: in each Place the Exhibition will begin precisely at Seven o'Clock. The Particulars of the Performances will be expressed in the Bills—Admittance Two Shillings each person.

Note, BRESLAW and his ITALIANS will likewise perform at the Town-Hall in the City of Worcester on Tuesday the 9th of August, in the Forenoon, precisely at Eleven o'Clock, being the first Day of the Races.—Admittance Half a Crown each Person.

Those were probably the Italians who were the singers who performed with Breslaw on 3 June 1776 when he exhibited his sleight of hand at Marylebone Gardens.

In 1776–77 Breslaw was still working

with his Italian friends, and the pattern of their performances was to intersperse songs, instrumental music, whistling, bird imitations, and the like by the Italian performers with five appearances by Breslaw and his bag of tricks. This season they toured their medley again in the west of England, playing at Worcester, Wolverhampton, Bridgnorth, Kidderminster, Stourbridge, Bromsgrove, Stafford, Litchfield, and Warwick in December 1776 and January 1777. They were at their home base in Cockspur Street, London, by 29 January and played through June. From 19 June to 15 July Breslaw's group moved to the Great Room in Panton Street where, in addition to their presentations, Chinese shadow puppets were exhibited by Brunn, Ambrose, and one of Breslaw's Italians, Gelmeena.

The conjurer was entertaining fans on 4 June 1781 at the Great Room in Cornhill, previously the King's Arms Tavern, and living at No 23, Haymarket. In Cornhill he offered other entertainments, as before, but this time not the Italian troupe. During this year he also advertised performances at Greenwood's Room where he exhibited card deception and "thought communication" and advertised that he would teach deception privately "on reasonable terms." He had on his program the whistler Sieur Andrea.

At Astley's Amphitheatre on 28 March 1783 *Natural Magic Revealed* was performed, and though Breslaw apparently had no part in it, the show promised to discover every "experiment by Mr. Pizetti, Mr. Breslaw, Mr. Astley's Little Learned Horse, as well as other performers of the like sagacity."

By 1792 Breslaw was back in Dublin, performing at the Capel Street Theatre. The *Dublin Post* of 30 August that year announced:

Mr. Breslaw, by permission of the Right Honourable Lord Mayor, will display a Variety of his new invented magical Card Deception, Letters, Numbers, Silver Medals, Gold Boxes, Oranges . . . He will command a fresh Egg to Dance a Hornpipe upon a Stick on the middle of the Stage by itself, Dressing several real Pancakes in any Gentleman's Hat, a Philosophical Bottle and hovel, Rings and Seals Answering Questions, Cutting the bodies of Aprons and Cloaks, An Experiment on Six or Eight Watches, Firing Two Mechanical Pistols, etc, etc: Music will attend. To commence at eight. Boxes and Lattices 3s.3d. Pit and Gallery 2s. 2d.

The *Post* lamented that with the Theatre Royal closed "the public amusements of this great capital have been confined solely to Breslaw's Exhibitions, which however entertaining, and they certainly are much so, can hardly be deemed sufficient for the town."

Philip Breslaw died at the Bull and Punch-Bowl in Liverpool on 16 May 1803 at the age of 77 after 44 years in England and Ireland. A woodcut of him has survived, showing him performing a "decapitation," but the artist is not known.

Bresmes. *See* DE BREAME.

Brett, Mr [*fl.* 1740–1750], *singer, actor.*

Mr Brett was first noticed in the bills on 10 October 1740 at Covent Garden when he was a Villager in *Orpheus and Eurydice*; he played the role again on 5 January 1741 and then moved to Goodman's Fields where, on 3 March, he was Mercury in *Harlequin Student*. On 5 April and 3 July 1742 he appeared at Sadler's Wells, singing with Hendrick Kerman's troupe, and on 1 November 1743 he was at the New Wells, Lemon Street, singing in *Solomon* with Blogg. At this last performance he was repeating an earlier one, for the bill noted that *Solomon* would be presented "as it was performed at Ruckholt House by Lowe and Brett"; the November 1743 performance was the first "on any stage." At the Haymarket Theatre on 1 November 1744 Brett sang in a concert connected with Theophilus Cibber's Academy.

In the spring of 1745 Brett performed at Lemon Street, Goodman's Fields, playing Pluto in *The Tempest* (and Neptune in the masque) on 1 February, Sir John in *The Devil to Pay* on 26 March, and a Sportsman (with the song, "The Early Horn") in *The Jealous Farmer* on 28 March. He sang frequently at Goodman's Fields in 1745–46, and on 10 March 1746 at Hickford's Room in Panton Street was advertised "Brett, the surprising voice of the famous African who sings several songs, with Mock Voices, particularly in Imitation of a Young Child." The puff is ambiguous, but one supposes that Brett did an imitation of some African singer who had recently performed in London. Brett sang regularly again at Goodman's Fields in 1746–47 and acted occasionally, as on 9 January 1747 when he played Pistol in *The Merry Wives of Windsor* or on 26 January when he was Friendly in *Flora*. In the summer of 1750 he was with the Richmond company, in which also was a Master Brett who may have been his son; possibly Master Brett was the William Brett who sang later in the century.

Brett, Master [*fl. 1750*], *actor?*

Master Brett, probably the son of the Mr Brett of the same period, was in the summer company at Richmond in 1750; whether he was an actor or not is unclear —he may have been a dancer or singer. There is a possibility that Master Brett was William, who had a successful career as a singer in the 1770's and 1780's.

Brett, Anne. *See* CHETWOOD, MRS WILLIAM RUFUS THE SECOND.

Brett, Mrs Dawson, Elizabeth, née Cibber *b. 1701, actress, dancer.*

Elizabeth Cibber, the daughter of Colley and Katherine, was baptized at St Paul, Covent Garden, on 16 March 1701. She married Dawson Brett, Junior and by him

had at least two children: Catherine, baptized on 4 April and buried on 8 April 1719, and Anne, baptized on 8 May 1720 —both at St Paul, Covent Garden. Her daughter Anne made her first stage appearance in 1727–28 and ten years later married William Rufus Chetwood.

The first recorded role for Elizabeth Brett was Mirabel in *The Rival Fools* at Drury Lane on 4 January 1722; the only other part mentioned for her in the bills this season was Rose in *The Recruiting Officer* on 3 May 1722 for her benefit shared with Harper. In 1722 she was likewise rarely cited, though on 24 May 1723 she shared a benefit with Mrs Campbell and played Lucia in *The Squire of Alsatia*. During the summer of 1723, on the other hand, she was very busy acting and dancing at Drury Lane, and perhaps her exposure there caused John Rich to engage her for the 1723–24 season at Lincoln's Inn Fields. There she was given a number of important dancing and acting assignments, including Alinda in *The Pilgrim* on 16 November 1723, Panthea in *A King and No King* on 26 February 1724, and Cordelia in *King Lear* on 28 February. For her benefit on 29 April with Mrs Sterling she both danced and spoke the epilogue to *Don Sebastian*.

Though he was paying her only 10s. daily, Rich discharged Mrs Brett on 10 September 1724; for some reason she continued appearing at Lincoln's Inn Fields in October and November, but by February 1725 she was back at Drury Lane where she spent the rest of her career. She played occasional dramatic roles, such as Mademoiselle D'Epingle in *The Funeral* and Mademoiselle in *The Provoked Wife*, but the bulk of her assignments were dancing parts in pantomimes or specialty dances. She was fairly active in 1727–28, the season during which her daughter Anne made her first appearance, but in April and May of 1728 she performed only on occasion, and the following season the bills did not notice her. Drury Lane kept her on the roster for 1729–30, though she was unmentioned in the bills, and after this season she apparently retired. It is possible that during her last few years in the theatre she may have devoted her time to helping Anne Brett with her budding career.

The two Bretts can usually be distinguished in the 1720's, but occasional references to a Mrs Brett in the 1730's are confusing; they probably refer to young Anne, who would have (supposedly) reached her majority in 1741, but perhaps some point to Elizabeth Brett's having made occasional appearances. One citation was on 11 April 1735 when a Mrs Brett was billed as dancing at Drury Lane; a cluster of "Mrs Brett" billings from September through November 1737 are probably errors for Anne: Florella in *The Orphan*, Sylvia in *The Old Bachelor*, Sukey in *The Beggar's Opera*, and Doll Mavis in *The Silent Woman*.

Elizabeth Brett was in London during her brother Theophilus Cibber's court case in 1738, but she seems not to have been much involved in it. On 23 November of this year the parish registers of St Paul, Covent Garden, recorded the burial of Dawson Brett; this was probably her husband. At some later time, but before 1753, she married Joseph Marples.

On 28 April 1742 Elizabeth Brett was mentioned in a Drury Lane bill; a benefit was given this date for the two daughters of Theophilus Cibber and his late wife Jane, and tickets for it were available at their aunt's (Mrs Brett) in Berwick Street, near Soho. She was mentioned again in 1753, this time in her father Colley Cibber's will, and it was a slighting mention indeed: he bequeathed her £5. About 1756, when Elizabeth was 55, she opened an eating house in Fullwood's Rent, near Gray's Inn, according to her wayward sister Charlotte Clarke. After this, there seems to be no further record of her.

Brett, Frances. *See* HODGKINSON, MRS JOHN THE SECOND.

Brett, Frances R. *See* CHAPMAN, MRS GEORGE.

Brett, William *d. 1789, singer, actor.*
William Brett probably acted at the Crow Street Theatre in Dublin in 1769, though this is not certain; there may have been a second Mr Brett, doubtless related to William, who performed in Ireland at least through 1792 and sired the actress Frances R. Brett who eventually married George Chapman. William Brett was probably acting in the 1760's, however, and by 1771 he had married and had a daughter Frances, who eventually became the second Mrs John Hodgkinson. During the winter of 1772–73 William and his wife Hannah were members of Roger Kemble's troupe at Worcester, after which they moved to Bath. There, on 17 December 1773, their son William was baptized.

Brett's first appearance in London was on 27 June 1774 with Foote's company at the Haymarket Theatre, playing Leander in *The Padlock*. He followed this with Sir John in *The Devil to Pay* (6 July) and the Squire in *Thomas and Sally* (11 July). Mrs Brett was with William this summer, but the following year he acted in Foote's summer group while she stayed home (possibly at Bath) to prepare for their next child. During this summer of 1775 Brett acted Sir John and the Squire again, had roles in *The Rehearsal* and *A Trip to Portsmouth*, and played Sir William in *The Dutchman*. On 16 July 1775 the Bretts had a daughter, Elizabeth, and on 18 October 1775 she was baptized, as had been their son William, at Bath Abbey. Brett joined the Haymarket company again in the summer of 1776, repeated his Sir John and Leander, and was assigned singing chores: a hunting song after the play on 2 September 1776 and Mat in *The Beggar's Opera* on 16 September. Brett presumably spent his winters with the company at Bath.

The London *Morning Chronicle* finally

gave Brett some attention when he came back to the Haymarket in the summer of 1778, accompanied by his wife. On 3 June he began his season as Young Meadows in *Love in a Village*, and on 11 June the paper reported that Brett had "a fine clear voice, but he wants sensibility; in other words, he did not feel the character." By 26 June the same paper had apparently seen and heard enough more of Brett (as Apollo in *The Spanish Barber* and Ben in *Buxom Joan*) that they begged the patent houses to engage him: "The winter managers are out of their senses if they suffer Mr. Edwin & Mr. Brett to return to the Bath playhouse. We have not so good a burletta singer as Edwin, nor a better singer in general than Brett." This opinion may have encouraged the Haymarket to make more use of Brett that summer, for he went on to be Lord Aimworth in *The Maid of the Mill*, Lelio in *The Gipsies*, Count Folatre in *April-Day*, Captain Greville in *The Flitch of Bacon*, and Lubin in *The Quaker*. He also sang in the production of *Macbeth*.

The winter managers apparently paid no attention to the *Morning Chronicle*, for Brett's next several years were spent with the Bath and Bristol company with at least one side trip, in October 1778, to Brighton. By 1782 the Bretts' precocious son William was making a name for himself as a singer at Bristol, and so was one of the Brett girls, probably Frances. Mrs Siddons was playing at Bath in the spring of 1782, and about the time she was ready to end her season William Brett did something unseemly—perhaps connected with her, perhaps not—which caused the Bath management to announce on 21 June that Brett had been discharged for "exceeding ill behaviour on Wednesday night." This finished Brett as far as Bath was concerned, and for the next several seasons he pursued his career in London.

He introduced his son to London audiences at the Haymarket in the summer of 1782 and performed frequently himself. By now he had become a specialist in Captain

Greville, Young Meadows, and Sir John, roles which he continued performing in the years to come. This summer he added a few others which also became standards in his repertory: the Soldier in *The Tobacco Box* (songs from which he frequently sang apart from the work), the Genius of Ireland in *Harlequin Teague*, and Colin in *Rose and Colin*. He also received two plums which may have helped him gain his patent house engagement in the fall: Compton in *The Agreeable Surprise* (replacing Bannister) and Macheath in *The Beggar's Opera*.

Covent Garden hired him for 1782–83, and he opened with Farmer Giles in *The Maid of the Mill* on 25 September 1782; he pleased the critics, especially with the bigness of his voice: "In a small house he must crack the ears of an auditory, and it fills the spacious Theatre of Covent Garden completely." They were also pleased with the purity with which he went through difficult vocal passages. Brett followed Farmer Giles with Young Meadows; then, on 9 October, he was Carlos in *The Duenna*, on 16 October Cable in *The Positive Man*, and on 22 October Macheath. Of this part one paper noted that

he sung the songs with his usual strength and spirit, and received warm and just commendation; but his acting was not equal to his vocal performance. He was deficient in the ease and gallantry of manners which are the characteristics of Macheath.—Mr. Brett is better formed for the blunt and rough countryman, than the fine gentleman.

After this Brett offered Covent Garden audiences his Captain Greville and played, on 2 November, Philippo in *The Castle of Andalusia*. It must have been right after this that his talented little son William died, for he was buried at St Paul, Covent Garden, on 8 November, and Brett did not play another new part at Covent Garden until 3 March 1783 when he was Joe in *Poor Vulcan!* Just before this, in February, his wife Hannah had another girl, and she was christened Arabella Hannah on 16 February at St Paul, Covent Garden. Brett completed the season at Covent Garden, receiving a weekly salary of £6, appeared again at the Haymarket in the summer, as was his wont, and returned in the fall at £7 a week to Covent Garden.

Through the season of 1786–87 Brett worked regularly at Covent Garden, sometimes being joined by his wife or daughter, playing most of his old roles as regularly as clockwork, and taking yearly benefits that normally brought him a handsome profit (£143 13s. in 1784, for instance, or £166 2s. in 1786), but adding over the years only a few parts of significance (Scarlet in *Robin Hood,* Lionel in *Lionel and Clarissa,* Captain Belville in *Rosina,* and Hawthorne in *Love in a Village*). In the spring of 1784 the Bretts lived at No 7, Catherine Street, Strand; by summer Brett advertised that benefit tickets from him would be available at Warburton's, Haymarket (possibly the Bretts' lodgings); and by April 1785 they were at No 73, Longacre, where they remained for several years. Brett seems to have been a competent performer but certainly not an exceptional one, and he did little during his career to expand his talent. On 18 September 1786, apparently just as the fall season at Covent Garden was about to begin, Brett, for reasons unknown, was discharged. He played in October at Brighton and then went to Ireland where, by 1 April 1787, he had started contributing to the Irish Musical Fund. William Brett died in Dublin on 2 April 1789. He was survived by his wife and at least three of his daughters: Frances (Mrs John Hodgkinson), Arabella, and "W." (Mrs William King), all of whom performed in America with their mother.

Brett, Mrs William, Hannah *d. c. 1804, actress, singer.*

The first theatrical notice of Hannah Brett seems to be for November 1772 when she and her husband William were members of Roger Kemble's company at Worcester. By this time the couple had a daughter Frances, born in 1771, who in time would become the wife of John Hodgkinson, and another daughter whose initial was W., who grew up to marry William King.

Kemble's group played at Worcester through May 1773, after which the Bretts went to Bath, where William apparently performed and Hannah gave birth to a son, William, who was baptized at Bath Abbey on 17 December 1773. In the summer of 1774 both Bretts were in Foote's company at the Haymarket Theatre in London, Mrs Brett making her first appearance there as Nell in *The Devil to Pay* on 20 July. This seems to have been the only billed role she was given, and she played it last on 29 August. In the fall, on 17 September, she was the Niece in *The Fair Orphan* at the Haymarket, but for that night only.

The Bretts probably returned to Bath for the winter, and though William came back to London for the summer of 1775, Hannah stayed at Bath, where she gave birth to a daughter, Elizabeth, on 16 July; the child was baptized at Bath Abbey on 18 October. While her children were young Mrs Brett may have given up the stage, for she was not mentioned in the bills again until the summer of 1778. Back at the Haymarket, Mrs Brett appeared as Mrs Bundle in *The Waterman* (11 June), the Mother in *Buxom Joan* (25 June), Floretta in *The Quaker* (21 August), and a member of the chorus in *Macbeth* (7 September). William performed with her, and after the summer season ended, they went to Brighton, where Mr Brett acted until the end of October. For the next few years the Bretts were affiliated with the Bristol company, and in the winter and spring of 1782 they were acting and singing at Bath. For some indiscretion, William was discharged from the company there, and the Bretts came again to London. Their precocious son William, who had pleased audiences at Bristol and London with his singing, died on 30 October 1782. Another Brett daughter, Arabella Hannah, was baptized at St Paul, Covent Garden, on 16 February 1783.

By the summer of 1783 Mrs Brett was acting again, playing a role in *The Separate Maintenance* and Audrey in *As You Like It* at the Haymarket Theatre. At the same playhouse on 27 July 1784 Mrs Brett played Lady Rounceval in *The Young Quaker* for William Brett's benefit, replacing, for that performance only, Mrs Webb. During this summer a Miss Brett, presumably one of their girls (but not the Elizabeth who was born in 1775), was acting with the Haymarket troupe. By 1784 the Bretts were living at No 7, Catherine Street, the Strand, though William's 27 July benefit notice said that tickets would be available from him at Warburton's, Haymarket. The family had moved by 15 April 1785 to No 73, Longacre.

In the summer of 1786 Mrs Brett performed again at the Haymarket, acting Mrs Fustian in *The Separate Maintenance*, Fidget in *Summer Amusement*, and Lucy in *The Beggar's Opera*. After this, she may have retired temporarily from the stage. She probably followed her husband to Brighton in October 1786 and then to Ireland, where he died on 2 April 1789. Mrs Brett acted again on 19 October 1791 at Bristol, playing Nelly in *No Song No Supper,* and presumably she stayed with the company for the full season.

By 2 or 5 November 1795 Mrs Brett was in America, making her debut at the Federal Street Theatre in Boston as Mrs Bromly in *Know Your Own Mind*. She acted at the John Street Theatre in New York in February 1796 when the American Company moved there, playing Lady Wronghead in *The Provoked Husband*. She was probably in New York when her daughter Arabella made her debut in 1796. Mrs Brett performed at Hartford in 1796 and 1797 and with her two daughters in

Boston in 1797 at the Haymarket Theatre as members of John Hodgkinson's troupe. Mrs Brett's weekly salary in November 1798 in Boston was $28, but this included her daughter Arabella as well. Still a member of her son-in-law's company in the spring of 1799, Mrs Brett was popular enough at her benefit to draw $240. In the summer of 1799 she acted at Portland (at the assembly hall in King Street), and she appears to have continued as a member of the American Company until 1803. Her retirement that year was probably brought about by the death of her daughter Frances (Mrs Hodgkinson) in September. Shortly after this, perhaps in 1804, Mrs William Brett died.

Brett, William *1773–1782, singer.*
Master William Brett, son of performers William and Hannah, was baptized at Bath Abbey on 17 December 1773. Before coming to London he played occasional children's roles in 1780–81 and 1781–82 at Bristol; on 19 June 1782 with his sister he sang a pastoral dialogue called "Arcas and Rosetta" as *entr'acte* entertainment at his mother's benefit. With his father he appeared at the Haymarket Theatre in London on 17 August 1782 as the Giant of the Causeway in *Harlequin Teague*; in it he sang "Fee-Faw-Fum" "with astonishing strength and harmony of voice." One other song is recorded for him: "I've rifled Flora's painted Bower," but when and where he warbled this inappropriate ditty is not known. The precocious boy died on 30 October 1782 and was buried at St Paul, Covent Garden, on 8 November.

Brewman, Mr [*fl.* 1789], *actor.*
Mr Brewman played Medium in *Inkle and Yarico* at the King's Head, Southwark, on 16 September 1789.

Brewster, Henry *c. 1747–1788, organist, harpsichordist, singer, composer.*
Henry Brewster was born about 1747, served a musical apprenticeship, and on 6

August 1780 at the age of 32 was recommended to the Royal Society of Musicians by Casper Flack. By that date he had become the organist of St Benet Fink and had a job playing harpsichord at the Haymarket Theatre. He was admitted to the Royal Society on 7 January 1781.

It is probable, though not certain, that the Mr Brewster who was a *basso* at the Handel Memorial Concerts at Westminster Abbey and the Pantheon on 26, 27, 29 May and 3, 5 June 1784 was Henry, for he was a song writer as well as an instrumentalist, and it is likely that he was a singer too. On 2 March 1785 Henry Brewster married; he described himself as of the parish of St Marylebone and a bachelor, and his bride was Elizabeth Glandfield, spinster, of the same parish. Their witnesses were Elizabeth Sell and John Glandfield, possibly the bride's father.

On 5 October 1788 Brewster suffered a "very dangerous fit of illness" and his doctor recommended that he move to the country. In a plea to the Royal Society of Musicians for financial help, Brewster stated that such a move would prevent him from earning a living; this suggests that, though ill, Brewster may still have been active in the music world and could "profit by his business" only in London. His chief income, then, was probably as a performer, not a composer. Apparently the Royal Society did not act in time to save Brewster's life; on 4 January 1789 Elizabeth Brewster told the Society that her husband had died insolvent and she had no means of subsistence. Brewster must have died shortly before this plea, perhaps in December 1788. The Royal Society granted Widow Brewster £8 toward the funeral expenses and a pension of 2½ guineas per month for her support. Brewster left no children.

How long Mrs Brewster's pension lasted is not clear. She did not appeal to the Society for aid again until 5 November 1815, when she was almost 70. They gave her £3 1s. 6d. to cover an apothecary's bill, and this amount apparently provided for her sufficiently until 2 March 1817 when she was granted three guineas for medical aid. From that time forward she received regular grants for medical expenses. In March 1819 she was living in Sadler's Wells Row, Islington. On 4 February 1821 she was reported as very ill, and before 3 June of that year she died.

Henry Brewster was a minor composer, but in the 1770's some of his songs, popular at Vauxhall and Finch's Gardens, were published; one of his serious pieces was *A Set of Lessons for the Harpsichord or Piano Forte with the Grand Chorus in the Messiah*, published about 1785.

Brian. *See* BRYAN.

Brice, Mr [*fl.* 1793–1801], *house servant.*

Mr Brice was a house servant at the Covent Garden Theatre at a constant salary of 12s. per week from 1793 through the 1800–1801 season except for two seasons unaccounted for: 1798–99 and 1799–1800; this gap may simply be due to incomplete records, though Brice may have been away from the theatre for two seasons.

Brice, Miss [*fl.* 1782], *actress.*

Miss Brice played in two premieres at the Haymarket Theatre in the spring of 1782: *Love at a Venture* on 21 March and *The Fashionable Wit* on 6 May. Unfortunately, the bills did not assign characters to the players.

Bricklayer, Miss [*fl.* 1756–1757], *singer.*

Billed as a "Young Gentlewoman," Miss Bricklayer made her first appearance on any stage as a nymph in *Comus* at Drury Lane on 24 November 1756. That night the prompter Cross entered in his diary, "Miss Bricklayer sung Indiff[erently]." On 20 December, she sang the role of the Second Shepherdess in the premier London performance of Thomas A. Arne's *Eliza*, which was repeated on 17, 21, and 28 January 1757. (But see Miss BRICKLER.)

Brickler, Miss [*fl.* 1758–1767], *singer.*

Miss Brickler made her first appearance on any stage, announced as a "Young Gentlewoman who never acted before," in the role of Polly in *The Beggar's Opera* at Covent Garden on 30 March 1758. In the following fall she again sang Polly at that theatre on 9 October 1758, advertised as her "2nd time on any stage." She seems then to have been absent from the London stage for some ten years, until she (or another person by that name) sang again at Covent Garden on 21 February 1767, when she was announced as a "Young Gentlewoman" in the role of Penelope in *Love in the City*. On 16 May of that year she sang a favorite song from *Judith*, accompanied by Dibdin "on a new instrument, call'd Piano Forte." That season she was on the Covent Garden pay list at 6s. 8d. per day. Miss Brickler may have been identical with the Miss Bricklayer who was singing at Drury Lane in 1756–57.

Brida, Luigi [*fl.* 1794–1795], *singer.*

Luigi Brida was billed as making his first appearance in England when he sang Aureliano in *Zenobia in Palmira* at the King's Theatre in the Haymarket on 20 December 1794. The *Morning Chronicle* two days later made a guarded comment on the new tenor: "Signor Brida has a very fine voice and as he is young, we think it more than probable that he may become a very valuable acquisition to the Theatre." The opera company found Brida valuable enough to keep him remarkably busy the rest of the season. He sang Conte Lelio in *La scola dei maritati* on 27 January 1795, a part in the oratorio *Debora and Sisara* on 20 February, an air in the Handel concert on 13 March, Aci in Bianchi's version of *Aci e Galatea* on 21 March, Sandrino in *Il conte*

ridicolo on 14 April, Evandro in *Alceste* on 30 April, Micheletto in *L'isola del piacere* on 26 May, a role in the *intermezzo Le nozzi de' contadini spagnuoli* on 28 May, and Masotto in *Le nozze di Dorina* probably on 16 and certainly on 23 June. Haydn heard Brida sing in *Aci e Galatea* in March and noted that "Brida is a good youngster with a beautiful voice, but with very little musical feeling."

Bride, Mr [*fl.* 1741?–1761], *scene-shifter.*

The London Stage lists a Mr Bride, dancer, as a member of the Drury Lane company in 1741–42, but the calendar of performances seems to contain no reference to him, and the only other Bride in the troupe was the scene-shifter who was named regularly in the bills at benefit time from 24 May 1743 through 21 May 1761. The "Mr Bride" of 1741–42, then, may well be an error for the stagehand. The *Town and Country Magazine* of October 1769 identified Mr Bride as a scene-shifter and father of Miss Bride the dancer. It is likely that the Mrs Bride who was a Drury Lane dresser in 1765 was the scene-shifter's wife.

Bride, Mrs [*fl.* 1765], *dresser.*

A salary schedule for Drury Lane dated 9 February 1765 listed Mrs Bride as a dresser being paid 1s. 6d. daily or 9s. weekly. She may have been the wife of Mr Bride the Drury Lane scene-shifter, and, if so, she was the mother of Elizabeth Bride the dancer.

Bride, Elizabeth, later Mrs Lefevre, [later Mrs Samworth?] *d. 1826, actress, dancer.*

Elizabeth Bride (or, in error, Pride) was very possibly the daughter of the Drury Lane scene-shifter (fl. 1741–1761) and, probably, the same theatre's dresser (fl. 1765). Elizabeth performed several times before her official debut, the first occasion being on 8 November 1755 when she was one of the children who danced in *The Chinese Festival* at Drury Lane; it is likely that the pantomime dance by the children, performed on 3 December, was salvaged from *The Chinese Festival* and included little Miss Bride. She was referred to later as having been a figure dancer, and it may have been during these early years that she did most of her dancing. Her next appearance, also as a child, was as Loveit in *Miss In Her Teens* on 5 April 1759; the entire cast was made up of children, and they performed the work again on 20 April and 23 and 24 May. On the last date Mr Bride was granted his benefit. During the run of this novelty Miss Bride was also an extra in *The Heiress* on 21 May. Her last appearances before her formal debut were as Prince John in *1 Henry IV* on 28 April 1760, Maria in *The London Merchant* on 13 May (for her benefit, shared with three others), and Mariana in *The Miser* on 29 July.

On 18 October 1760 she made her official debut as Lucia in *Cato,* billed as "A Gentlewoman," and Hopkins noted in his *Diary* that he had great expectations for her. Her acting career from this point forward was most peculiar, for she played some significant roles yet was not frequently mentioned in the bills; this suggests that she may have contracted to act only on occasion, for her parts were not those a utility actress would have played. Her name did not appear again on the bills during 1760–61, despite Hopkins's enthusiasm at her debut. In 1761–62 she was Imogen in *Cymbeline* on 28 November 1761, Polyxena in *Hecuba* on 11 December, Mariana in *The Miser* again on 20 January 1762, Juliet in *Romeo and Juliet* on 25 January (but she gave the role up on 13 May), Lady Harriet in *The Funeral* on 15 March, and Angelica in *The Constant Couple* on 1 April. For her 28 April benefit (shared with Noverre) she played Imogen.

The following season she acted Angelica and Mariana again and added Sylvia in *The Two Gentlemen of Verona* on 22 December 1762, Almayda in *Elvira* on 19 January 1763, Louisa Medway in *The Discovery* on 3 February, Clarinda in *The Double Gallant* on 14 March, and, for her 19 April benefit with Mrs Davies, Jacintha in *The Suspicious Husband*. During her final season, 1763–64, she again played Angelica, Imogen, and Lady Harriet, adding only one new role: Arethusa in *Philaster* (8 October 1763). On 19 November Hopkins noted that "it was currently reported in the Green Room that Miss Bride was taken into keeping by Mr Calcraft." This was apparently not news to Garrick, for he had written Colman from Paris on 8 October, "Mr Calcraft's behaviour astonishes me, but I hope Lacy will be firm." Lacy apparently was not. On 27 April 1764, according to Hopkins, "Miss Bride, being with child, could not go into breeches, Mrs Palmer played Imogen." The naughty girl played Arethusa on 2 May and then left the stage.

The Calcraft who had lured Miss Bride was John the elder (1726–72) who led a lively life as a politician, business man, and debauchee. He had according to a clipping in the Burney collection, three sons and a daughter by Miss Bride. Some reports have it that John Calcraft the younger, born on 16 October 1765, was Miss Bride's son. When the elder Calcraft died in 1772 he made Elizabeth Bride the guardian of his children Katherine, John, Grandby, and Richard Calcraft; if these are in chronological order, one may guess that Katherine was the child Miss Bride was carrying when her stage career ended. Calcraft left Miss Bride £3000, a clear annuity for life of £1000, another of £500 to expire should she remarry, and £10,000 for each of his children by her, according to the anonymous newspaper source.

Miss Bride married a Mr Lefevre at some point after Calcraft's death and on 4 September 1795 was reported by the *Telegraph* as "still living in a beautiful Gothic Villa, near Northfleet, on the River." *The Age* of 10 September 1826 recorded the death of Mrs Lefevre, formerly Miss Bride, but the wording of the obituary is somewhat ambiguous and seems to imply that Mrs Lefevre may have remarried shortly before her death. If so, then the will of Elizabeth Samworth, "formerly Lefebvre [*sic*]," probably refers to the ex-actress. Elizabeth Samworth made her will on 30 November 1824 and identified herself as the wife of John Samworth of Greenwich, Kent; she described herself as late Elizabeth Lefebvre, widow, sick and weak in body. To her sister Mary Wright, widow, she left her clothes; to her niece Anna Maria Shed (Mrs Charles) of Greenwich she left candlesticks and other silverware, and to her cousin Mary Phillips she bequeathed a £30 annuity for life out of East India Company stock which John Samworth had settled on Elizabeth when they married. The will was proved by John Samworth on 7 May 1827, a date which fits well with the reported death of Elizabeth Bride Lefevre in September 1826.

The Mrs Lefevre who acted from 1778 to 1791 was probably a different person, though this is not certain.

Brider, Miss [*fl.* 1765], *dancer.*

A Drury Lane salary schedule dated 9 February 1765 listed a Miss Brider, dancer, at 2s. 6d. daily or 15s. weekly. This seems to be the only reference to her, and it could be an error for dancer Elizabeth Bride — though Miss Bride is said to have left the stage in May 1764.

Bridgeman. *See also* BRIDGMAN.

Bridgeman, Mr [*fl.* 1794], *house servant?*

One Bridgeman, possibly a relative of the actress Mrs Bridgman, was on the staff at the Haymarket Theatre during the summer season of 1794; the accounts note his discharge on 20 October of that year from the "Summer Theatre."

Bridges, Mr [*fl.* 1690–1692], *actor.*

Mr Bridges was a minor actor in the United Company at Drury Lane; he is recorded as having played Turrington in *Edward III* in November 1690, Vincentio in *Alphonso* in December 1690, and Aumerle in *Henry II* on 8 November 1692.

Bridges, Mr [*fl.* 1728?–1751], *actor.*

Mr Bridges the actor may have been the William Bridges who subscribed to Henry Ward's *Works* in 1746, but there is no certainty of this. He may also have been the Bridges who was in *The Beggar's Opera* at Bristol about 1728–29, though his later roles would suggest that he was not. He was certainly the Mr Bridges active in Dublin from at least 1737 to 1740, for it was from Ireland that he came to London, already an accomplished performer. The records show a benefit for him on 9 May 1737 at Aungier Street, Dublin, another there in February 1739, and a third on 7 June 1740.

On 7 April 1743 Bridges appeared at Drury Lane playing Pinchwife in *The Country Wife*, replacing Garrick, who refused to act; Bridges was billed as "a Gentleman from the Theatre Royal in Dublin," and when he repeated the role on 28 April his name was cited in the bill. This engagement appears to have been for this role only but it led to Bridges's permanent engagement at Drury Lane the following season. On 15 September 1743 he acted Balance in *The Recruiting Officer*, after which followed a remarkably heavy schedule which probably presented Bridges in most of the roles he had established as his during his Dublin days. They included Sir Sampson in *Love for Love*, Sir Jealous in *The Busy Body*, the Governor in *Love Makes a Man*, Syphax in *Cato*, the Governor in *Oroonoko*, the Uncle in *The London Merchant*, Acasto in *The Orphan*, Boniface in *The Stratagem*, Blister in *The Virgin Unmasked*, Gonzales in *The Mourning Bride*, the title roles in *Aesop*, *The Spanish Friar*, and *Tamerlane*, Pierre in *Venice Pre-*

served, Gloster in *Jane Shore*, Heartwell in *The Old Bachelor*, Sealand in *The Conscious Lovers*, Sciolto in *The Fair Penitent*, Ross in *Macbeth*, Creon in *Oedipus*, and Bellguard in *Sir Courtly Nice*.

In the 1744–45 season Bridges was joined by his wife, who played minor roles through 1748–49. On 15 September 1744, when she made her first appearance as the Nurse in *Love for Love*, Bridges was Sir Sampson. Through the 1746–47 season Bridges and his wife remained at Drury Lane, using their summers of 1746 and 1747 to act at Richmond and Twickenham. During this period Bridges added a number of other roles to his line; among the more significant ones were Claudius in *Hamlet*, Gloucester in *King Lear*, Buckingham in *Richard III*, Subtle in *The Alchemist*, Sir Tunbelly in *The Relapse*, Medley in *The Man of Mode*, and Decius in *Julius Caesar*.

In 1747–48 Mr and Mrs Bridges changed to Covent Garden, his roles there being essentially the same ones he had played at Drury Lane; he was able, however, to add Falstaff in *The Merry Wives of Windsor*, Volpone, and the King in *1 Henry IV* to his repertory. After beginning the new season playing Kite in *The Recruiting Officer* on 23 September 1748, Bridges and his wife went back to Drury Lane where he remained through 1750–51. His roles remained virtually unchanged through the years, but he added to his summer activity by joining with Cross, Burton, and Vaughan to operate a booth at Bartholomew Fair in August 1748; the following two summers he and Cross alone were the proprietors. By 1749 Bridges and his wife were advertising that tickets for their joint benefit would be available at Mr Courteen's in Bow Street, Covent Garden—possibly their lodgings—but by April 1751 Bridges had moved to York Street, Covent Garden. His last benefit was on 20 April 1751, shared with Blakes (since Mrs Bridges was no longer acting), and his last recorded appearance was on 8 May when he played his old role of Balance in *The Recruiting Officer*. The young actor Bridges who appeared a year later may have been the son of this Mr and Mrs Bridges.

Bridges, Mr (*fl.* 1752–1761), *actor.*

Mr Bridges made his first appearance on any stage on 13 May 1752 at Covent Garden when he played Lothario in *The Fair Penitent*. After this one performance Bridges may have gone to the provinces, for the next record of him is in 1760–61 when he was acting at Norwich. On 17 October 1761 he made his first Drury Lane appearance as Othello, billed as a "Young Gentleman," an on 4 November he played Moneses in *Tamerlane*. He seems not to have played any other roles named in the bills this season, and, again, perhaps he left for the provinces.

Mr Bridges may have been the same person who acted at Cork in October 1761, Dublin in 1762, and Edinburgh in 1764. If so, he probably had a wife named Fredericka, who played in Ireland from 1760 to 1793, and possibly a daughter who acted in the 1790's in Ireland.

Bridges, Mrs (*fl.* 1744–1749), *actress, singer.*

Mrs Bridges joined her husband (*fl.* 1728?–1751) at Drury Lane in the 1744–45 season, playing for her first role there the Nurse in *Love for Love* on 15 September 1744. On 18 September she was Lady Darling in *The Constant Couple* and the Wife in *The Anatomist*; on the twentieth she played Lady Bountiful in *The Stratagem*; on 1 November she was Mrs Motherly in *The Provoked Husband*; and on 11 February 1745 she acted the China Woman in *The Double Gallant*. Her parts the next season were similarly small and motherly. In the summers of 1746, 1747, and 1748 she and Mr Bridges acted at Richmond and Twickenham, and in 1748–49 they played a season at Covent Garden. There she was Diana Trapes in *The Beg-*

gar's Opera (an indication of her singing ability), Mrs Fruitful in Aesop, and Mrs Goodfellow in Tunbridge Walks—among other minor roles.

She acted at the booth operated by her husband and others at Bartholomew Fair in August 1784, returned to Covent Garden briefly in the fall of the year, and then transferred back to Drury Lane, where she played her last season. After a benefit shared with her husband on 13 April 1749, when they advertised that tickets would be available at Mr Courteen's in Bow Street, Covent Garden, she appears to have left the stage.

Bridges, Paul Francis [fl. 1660–1673], viola da gamba and bass viol player.

Before coming (or perhaps returning) to England, Paul Francis Bridges held a position as musician to the King of Spain at Brussels. In 1660 he accepted an appointment in the private music of Charles II as a viola da gamba player; a warrant dated 4 September 1662 confirmed the position and listed Bridges as receiving a yearly salary of £40 plus £16 2s. 6d. for livery. He played the bass viol as well, for on 18 November 1662 he was to be paid £10 for an instrument. In June 1664 he was living at Mr Perkins's house in Hatton Grounds for a rent of 5s. weekly, paid out of the exchequer. As was the case with many of the King's musicians, Bridges's pay was often in arrears, and it may have been due to this that Sarah Glascock, widow, sued him on 29 March 1671 for a £10 debt. A warrant was issued on 23 May 1673 appointing John Young as Bridges's replacement in the King's private music, Bridges having surrendered his post.

Bridgetower, George Augustus Polgreen 1778–1860, violinist.

George Augustus Polgreen Bridgetower was born on 11 October 1778, possibly at Biala, Galicia (Poland), but more likely in the British West Indies. He was the son of an African (known in London as the "Abyssinian Prince" because of the elegant social circles in which he moved) and of a European mother. George had a brother who was a cellist, but the brother seems not to have appeared in England, nor did he gain anything like George's fame as a virtuoso. At the age of nine young George made his debut as a violinist at the Concert Spirituel in Paris on 13 April 1789, and a year later he was in London to play at the Drury Lane oratorio concerts that ran that season from 19 February to 26 March 1790. On the first day he played a concerto after the second part of the Messiah, and it was probably to this appearance that a critic on 20 March referred when he called the performance "equal to any of his former wonderful exhibitions."

After his debut he was much patronized, and on 2 June 1790 he and the youthful Viennese violinist Franz Clement gave a concert sponsored by the Prince of Wales. He then became a student of Barthélemon and Giornovichi for the violin and Attwood for composition, played first violin in the Prince of Wales's private music, performed in the Haydn-Salomon concerts in 1791, appeared at the King's Theatre during the February and March oratorio season in 1792, and played in Barthélemon's concerts in 1792 and 1794. In 1794 Doane listed Bridgetower as living at No 20, Eaton Street, Pimlico, and as participating in the Handelian concerts at Westminster Abbey. Bridgetower also performed at the oratorios produced at Covent Garden from 1795 through 1799 during Lent.

In 1802 the violinist visited his mother and brother at Dresden and gave concerts there on 24 July 1802 and 18 March 1803. After this visit he made an even more important one to Vienna, where on 17 and 24 May 1803 he performed the "Kreutzer" Sonata of Beethoven with the composer at the piano. According to Bridgetower, who may have been exaggerating, when the violinist altered one passage as he was going along, Beethoven was so delighted that he leapt from the piano, embraced "Brischdower" and begged him to play it again. Apparently the master liked the violinist's temperamental playing, but Czerny reported that his gestures when performing were so extravagant that they were laughable.

Bridgetower returned to England, and on 5 July 1807 he was recommended by W. Dance to membership in the Royal Society of Musicians. Dance described the violinist as single, born on 11 October 1778, currently in the service (again) of the Prince of Wales, a teacher, and proficient not only on the violin but on the viola, violoncello, and piano. Bridgetower signed his name to the recommendation without the middle "e," though on his will in 1859 he used it. He was elected to membership with seven yeas and two nays on 4 October 1807, and he paid as his initial subscription to the musical fund £5 6s. He was supposed to play in the Society's annual May concert at St Paul's in 1808 but sent a deputy without permission and in June was ordered to attend the general meeting and explain himself. The upshot of this was simply that in several later years when he was scheduled to play in the May concert, he remembered to ask permission to send a substitute. This permission was granted in 1809, 1811, and 1813—the only years in which the Minute Books indicate that he was supposed to play.

In June 1811 he took his Bachelor of Music degree from Cambridge, and when the Philharmonic Society was formed in 1813, Bridgetower was one of the associates who, presumably, assisted at the first performance of the orchestra on 8 March. On 9 March 1816 at St George, Hanover Square, Bridgetower married spinster Mary Leach Leake; of his wife little is known except that she predeceased him. Grove notes that Bridgetower lived abroad for some time in Paris, Rome, and elsewhere; this

was after 7 December 1828 when he asked the Royal Society of Musicians to drop his membership because he was going abroad. He was back in England in 1843.

On 4 September 1859 Bridgetower made his will, describing himself as of Peckham, Surrey, and noting that he was about to leave for Paris. He left all his possessions to his late wife's sister, Clara Leach Leake Stuart of Scotland; he asked his friend Samuel Appleby of Harpur Street to be his executor. The violinist died on 28 February 1860 at Peckham and the will was proved on 3 July. Appleby found the estate to be worth under £1000.

Bridgewater. *See* **BRIDGWATER.**

Bridgman. *See also* **BRIDGEMAN.**

Bridgman, Mr ₍*fl.* 1742₎, *actor.*
Mr Bridgman acted the role of Eurymachus in *Ulysses* at the converted tennis court in James Street on 31 May 1742.

Bridgman, Mrs ₍*fl.* 1794₎, *actress.*
Billed as "A Young Lady," Mrs Bridgman made her first and last appearance on the stage as Euphrasia in *The Grecian Daughter* at Covent Garden on 1 October 1794. The work was given only once again at Covent Garden, on 27 December, shortly after Mrs Siddons had played Euphrasia at Drury Lane; when it was revived, Mrs Bridgman was replaced by Miss Wallis. She may have been related to the Bridgman who was on the summer staff at the Haymarket in 1794.

Bridgman, William ₍*fl.* 1684₎, *musician?*
Henry Purcell named William Bridgman in his dedication to *A Musical Entertainment* (1684) as one of the four Stewards of the Musical Society. Since the other Stewards cited were professional musicians, it seems likely that Bridgman may have been

too, though there is no record of his activity.

Bridgtower. *See* BRIDGETOWER.

Bridgwater, Roger *d. 1754, actor, dancer.*

Roger Bridgwater may have made his first appearance on stage as the Earl of Northampton in *Sir Thomas Overbury* on 12 June 1723 at Drury Lane, but not until the following October did his name appear on the playbills; he was noticed in printed casts of 1723 and later, and some were for plays done earlier than October. The first bill carrying his name was on 15 October 1723 when he was listed as playing Garcia in *The Mourning Bride* at Drury Lane—a younger man's part, which suggests that perhaps Bridgwater was born around the turn of the century. In addition to being an actor, he was also a dancer in his early career, but the bulk of his time was spent playing dramatic roles, usually heavy ones. From the start he seems to have held a strong position in the company, and for his benefit, on 12 May 1724, he played the Duke in *The Chances* and shared receipts with only one other performer.

During the summer of 1724 Bridgwater played at Richmond, Lincoln's Inn Fields, and Pinkethman's booths at Bartholomew and Southwark Fairs. Several of his summer parts were of first importance: Archer in *The Stratagem*, Marplot in *The Busy Body,* and the title role in *A Duke and No Duke.* Back at Drury Lane from 1724–25 through 1729–30 he played such youthful roles as Duart in *Love Makes a Man*, Belfond Junior in *The Squire of Alsatia*, Aimwell in *The Stratagem*, Kastril in *The Alchemist*, and Hippolitus in *Phaedra and Hippolitus*—but he also attempted more mature parts like Theodosius, Alcibiades in *Timon of Athens*, the Ghost in *Hamlet*, and Banquo in *Macbeth.*

Before the rebellion of Theophilus Cibber and his followers in the fall of 1733,

Bridgwater added a number of other significant roles to his growing repertory: Shore in *Jane Shore*, the Governor in *Oroonoko*, Thorowgood in *The London Merchant* (at the premiere on 22 June 1731), Tamerlane, Cassio in *Othello*, Hotspur in *1 Henry IV*, Valentine in *Love for Love*, Mirabel in *The Way of the World*, Polydore in *The Orphan*, Horner in *The Country Wife*, and Buckingham in *Henry VIII.* Though he may have been well suited to some of these parts, others he probably succeeded to because of the loss of such performers as Wilks, Watson, and Williams who had played many of them previously. In 1732 he was considered an asset to the house in tragedy, but *The Theatrick Squabble* in 1733 described him as a bombastic actor:

> *Hark! a loud Noise a palls the list'-*
> *   ning Ears!*
> *All think it Thunder, —— Br—dg—wa*
> *——r appears:*
> *His Brazen Front he thinks will do far*
> *   more*
> *Than B[oo]th, W[il]ks, M[il]ls, or*
> *   C[i]bber did before . . .*

When Theophilus Cibber revolted against Highmore's control of Drury Lane in September 1733, he took with him to the Haymarket Theatre most of the best actors; Bridgwater, perhaps recognizing an opportunity to succeed to some good new roles, stayed at Drury Lane. For the brief period when the dissenting actors were gone, Bridgwater did not get many windfalls, but he was given the Copper Captain in *Rule a Wife and Have a Wife*, Kite in *The Recruiting Officer*, Trincalo in *The Tempest*, and Aboan in *Oroonoko*; he continued in some of his old parts, but the Drury Lane troupe, bereft of its best performers, turned to light entertainments during this period, and Bridgwater made few gains. After the seceders returned, Bridgwater may have felt his opportunities at Drury Lane were limited, for on 26 April and 9 May 1734 he played at Lincoln's Inn Fields, and after doing Frederick in *The Miser* at Drury Lane on 16 May, he left the company and became affiliated with John Rich at Covent Garden.

In 1734–35 with his new colleagues he moved into some important parts, almost exclusively weightier roles such as Manly in *The Plain Dealer*, Sullen in *The Stratagem*, the King (and sometimes Falstaff) in *1 Henry IV*, Balance in *The Recruiting Officer*, Buckingham in *Richard III*, Sir John Brute in *The Provoked Wife*, the title role in *The Old Bachelor*, and Gloucester in *King Lear*. On 22 March 1735 he was given a solo benefit at Covent Garden and advertised that tickets were available from him at No 16, Craven Buildings. His first season with Rich had certainly been encouraging, and he had wisely dropped lighter roles for which he seems to have been unsuited.

In the seasons through 1736–37 he continued in many of his old parts, but there were some interesting changes: he played the first Gravedigger in *Hamlet* instead of the Ghost; he shifted to the lesser part of Leontine in *Theodosius* (he had previously played the lead or, more often, Varanes); he lost Tamerlane and moved down to Dervise; he added *Julius Caesar* to his repertory; he changed from the major part of Aboan in *Oroonoko* back to the smaller one of the Governor; and he gave up Banquo to play Duncan in *Macbeth*. Among his other new roles during these seasons were Creon in *Oedipus*, Voltore in *Volpone*, Priuli in *Venice Preserved*, and Teague in *The Committee*.

In May 1737 Bridgwater and a few other London actors were lured by Lewis Duval to Dublin to play at Smock Alley during June. There he acted a principal role (unnamed in the bill) in *The Orphan* on 24 June, Cassius in *Julius Caesar* on 27 June, and Corbaccio in *Volpone* on 30 June; the leading roles were taken by his fellow travelers Denis Delane and Adam Hallam.

Back in London in the fall of 1737, Bridgwater rejoined the Covent Garden company, and there he remained for the rest of his career. He kept most of his old roles, though again he made some significant changes: on 17 January 1738 he switched to Claudius in *Hamlet*; on 13 and 16 February he played Falstaff in both parts of *Henry IV* (and this became his regular role henceforth); and on 15 September 1738 he changed from his small part in *Theodosius* to the melodramatic character of Marcian. By the time of his benefit on 7 April 1739 he was living beside the Red Lion in Bow Street, Drury Lane.

On 15 September 1739 he was playing Sohemus in *Marianne* and, apparently inadvertantly, wounded his fellow actor Rosco in the Act V fight; Rosco, fortunately, recovered fairly quickly. By the 1740–41 season Bridgwater was earning a daily salary of 16s. 8d.; at this time in his career he was seldom adding any new roles to his list, and the bulk of his parts were now mature or elderly. Occasionally and unaccountably he still acted younger men, as on 10 December 1740 when he played Kastril in *The Alchemist*. But his health was none too good now, and when he advertised his benefit on 9 April 1741, he offered an apology:

I humbly hope my Friends will excuse my personal application, it being publickly known how unfortunate I have been in my health for some months past, & though I have ventured abroad I find myself so weak & so incapable [because] of fatigue that I hope my friends will accept of this publick notice— that my Benefit is on Thursday the 9*th* of April . . .

He had been missing from the bills from 13 February to 1 April 1741, and though he pleaded poor health, he played a role in which Quin much admired him, Hubert in *King Arthur*, at his benefit and finished out the season with frequent appearances.

By 27 March 1742 he was living at the

lower end of Water Lane in Fleet Street and for his benefit that day he chose, oddly, Ben in *Love for Love*, a part for which one would suppose he was not suited. As the years passed, he continued acting regularly, and only infrequently did he attempt new roles. Three interesting new ones, however, were Pinchwife in *The Country Wife*, Morose in *The Silent Woman*, and Adam in *As You Like It*. Such strenuous parts as Falstaff he now dropped, but he continued acting Gloucester, Balance, Priuli, and Caesar.

During the 1740's or perhaps earlier, Bridgwater set up business as a coal dealer at a wharf near Whitefriars, perhaps not far from where the old Dorset Garden Theatre had stood in Restoration times. He may have had to augment his theatre income during these declining years of his life; on 29 May 1747 he was getting £2 per week at Covent Garden, and since he was now less useful to the troupe and had another activity, he began, as Davies reported, to neglect his duties at the playhouse. The spring of 1754 was his last one in the theatre. He played Sir John in *The Conscious Lovers*—one of his favorite parts—on 26 March, Priuli in *Venice Preserved* on 30 March, King Henry in *Richard III* on 2 April, the Constable in *Henry V* on 17 April, Sir John Brute in *The Provoked Wife* on 18 April, and Trusty in *The Funeral* on 23 April. During May several plays in which he normally would have acted were performed, but other actors took his roles. Bridgwater died at Bath on 20 August 1754, and the prompter Cross, taking note of it, described him as "an Old Actor & an honest Man."

Writing 25 years later, Davies had mixed views of Bridgwater's abilities:

Bridgewater was esteemed a general player; and it was with some a doubt whether he acted best or worst in tragedy or comedy; and, though it may seem paradoxical, yet he certainly was equally well and ill in both.

For example, in the Ventidius of Dryden in his All for Love, he was a true portrait of the rough, brave, old soldier; in Tamerlane he was solemnly drowsy in speaking, and struttingly insignificant in action. He was a very judicious player in the character of the Suspicious Husband, and disagreeable in the Lover of the Miser. His Hubert in King John was as characteristically just as his King Henry in Richard the Third was truly offensive. In short, Bridgewater made it doubtful, whether he pleased or displeased most.

A will for a Roger Bridgewater written on 17 and proved on 31 August 1754 was very likely the actor's. To a William Bridgewater and his wife of Ripley, Surrey, he left £20 each, with the admonition that they

not go into mourning for me but employ the money for the benefit of themselves and family and I desire them to take care of their graceless son William who has disobliged me in the highest degree but notwithstanding that as I took him to do something for him at the instigation of Mr. Villett apothecary I do hereby give unto the said Mr. Villett the sum of twenty pounds in trust to place out the said William Bridgewater the son an apprentice . . .

Despite his rancor at young William's behavior, Bridgwater also left £30 to be given the lad when he reached 21. To each of four sisters he gave £10. He also made bequests to two servants and to the son of a friend, Thomas Smith "who lodges in my house." The bulk of his estate he left to George Villett, his clerk.

Brief, [Mr?] [*fl. 1734*], *actor.*
One Brief played "Galloon" (Gallono) in *The Covent Garden Tragedy* at the Haymarket Theatre on 17 April 1734.

Brigg. *See also* BRIGGS.

Brigg, Mr [*fl. 1781–1803*], *dancer.*
Mr Brigg (or Briggs) danced at Drury Lane off and on for over 20 years; he was

also a dancing master, but he apparently restricted his teaching to private instruction. The accounts first mention him in 1781–82, and on 21 November 1782 he was paid £11 3s. 4d. for dancing the previous season—but how many days of work this covered was not stated. His first playbill notice was at the end of that first season, on 6 May 1782 when he danced a minuet with one of his scholars, an unidentified young lady. On that day tickets he had delivered were accepted at the door. In the spring of 1783 and 1784 he was again granted tickets to sell, though no appearances were noted for him in the bills, nor did his name appear in the accounts. On 18 December 1784 he returned to the treasurer £4, which represented four weeks in which he had not worked at the playhouse, but the dates of his absence were not specified. On the following 1 January 1785 he was back on the salary list, and on 20 May 1785 he danced a *Minuet de la cour* with Miss Stageldoir.

On 6 June 1786 Brigg was given his first real benefit, shared with three others, and he advertised that tickets from him were available at (presumably) his lodgings, No 6, Little Russell Street, Covent Garden. At the performance he danced, with others, a *Minuet and Quadrille*. He received a benefit again on 31 May 1787, dancing the *Minuet de la cour* with Miss J. Stageldoir once more and sharing his profits with three other performers. His 3 June 1788 benefit was likewise shared with three others, but there was no indication on the bill that Brigg performed. During these seasons of 1784–85 through 1787–88 the account books show no salary for Brigg, though he was apparently receiving something and working regularly.

On 29 November 1788 he was dropped from the roster and returned an unspecified amount that had been paid him for days he had not worked. The books do not indicate his return as a salaried member of the company until 1795, though on 2 June

1790 his tickets were accepted and he danced the *Minuet de la cour* with his wife at what was probably her first appearance. After this he made no further appearances at Drury Lane or anywhere else in London for five years, though he may have been teaching; his wife, on the other hand, worked at Drury Lane throughout the 1790's.

On 25 April 1795 Brigg was put back on the salary list at Drury Lane at £1 5s. weekly, and at that fee he stayed for the rest of his career. The playbills make no mention of his performing, though he probably did, and the accounts cite him in 1796 and again in 1800–1801 through 1802–3.

Brigg, Mrs [*fl.* 1790–1802], *dancer, actress, singer.*

Mrs Brigg (or Briggs) made her first appearance on the stage dancing a *Minuet de la cour* with her husband at Drury Lane on 2 June 1790. In the fall she was engaged again from 26 October to 1 December 1790, dancing in the afterpiece *Don Juan* at a weekly salary of £1 5s. This short contract was repeated at the same salary in the fall of 1791 when she appeared in *Don Juan* again, but on 27 September 1791 she also had a vocal part in *Poor Old Drury!!* at the King's Theatre, to which the Drury Lane troupe removed while their new playhouse was being built. She was hired for the full season in 1792–93, again at £1 5s. weekly, and was noted in the bills as acting a vintager in *The Pirates*, starting 21 November 1792, and dancing in *Harlequin's Invasion*, starting 27 December —again at the King's Theatre.

Her activity during the rest of the 1790's was remarkably similar: she served sometimes as a singer or actress but mostly as a dancer, performed full seasons most of the time but occasionally (as in May 1794) joined the Drury Lane company only for a limited engagement, and was seldom billed as anything grander than a member of the chorus or part of a group. She was, for instance, in the chorus of *The Cherokee* and one of the female slaves in *Blue Beard* for several seasons. Occasionally she was billed as participating in a specialty dance or ballet, as on 10 June 1797 when she was in a country dance and a Scotch reel, or on 16 May 1798 when she danced in the ballet *Kitty and Jemmy.*

Her salary stayed at £1 5s. until after the turn of the century, though on 23 October 1802, the last notice of her in the accounts, she was paid only £1 10d. per week. After this she seems to have given up the stage.

A listing of Mrs Briggs on 4 June 1787 in *The London Stage* may be an error for her husband, yet seems correct: he had received a shared benefit on 31 May, and on 4 June "Mrs Briggs" was listed as one of many whose tickets would be accepted at Drury Lane that date. She is not otherwise known to have been in the troupe this early.

Briggs. *See also* **BRIGG.**

Briggs, Mr [*fl.* 1776–1777], *doorkeeper.*

Mr Briggs was a doorkeeper at Drury Lane in 1776–77, but his salary was not noted in the account books.

Briggs, Mr [*fl.* 1781], *actor.*

Mr Briggs played Lovewell in *Love and a Bottle* on 26 March 1781 at the Haymarket Theatre; the play received only this one performance. He may have been the same Briggs who had a leading role in *Columbus* and was in *Indians* at the Theatre Royal, Bath, in 1795.

Briggs, Mr [*fl.* 1784], *singer.*

Mr Briggs, a *basso*, sang in the Handel Memorial Concerts at Westminster Abbey and the Pantheon on 26, 27, 29 May and 3, 5 June 1784.

Bright, Mr [*fl.* 1711], *musician?*

A document at Harvard ascribed to the manager Owen Swiney of the Queen's Theatre in the Haymarket lists payments to various employees, including one Bright who was paid £520 for "Mus." This was probably a payment for all the members of the band, since the amount is far greater than any others on the list for individual performers; Bright may have been one of the musicians at the theatre or perhaps the manager of the band. The payment covered the months of March, April, and May 1711.

Bright, Mr [*fl.* 1733], *actor, singer.*

Mr Bright played the Constable in *The Harlot's Progress*, a ballad opera, on 28 September 1733 at "a large commodious Room in Artichoke Yard at Mile-End during the time of the [Southwark?] Fair." He may have been related to the Mr Bright of the Queen's Theatre in 1711; he is probably not to be identified with George Bright of the Restoration period, though he may have been a relative.

Bright, Mrs [*fl.* 1750], *actress.*

Mrs Bright appeared in the spring of 1750 with the "English Anti-Gallic Company" which produced several English and French works in French. Her first appearance was as Mariane in *L'Avare* on 26 February, after which she played Madelon in *Les Précieuses ridicules* on 8 March, and the title role in *Arlequin fourbe Anglois* on 13 March. The company apparently disbanded after this last date.

Bright, George [*fl. c.* 1677–1707], *actor.*

George Bright apparently began his theatrical career in Dublin in the 1670's at the Smock Alley Theatre. The first recorded role for him was the fairly important part of Marone, the bank officer, in *Belphagor*, performed about 1677. He may well have been at Smock Alley for some years before this, of course, and it is likely that he stayed in Dublin until shortly before his first known role in London, Ajax in *Troilus and Cressida* at Dorset Garden in April 1679 with the Duke's Company.

For the United Company in the early 1680's he acted minor characters (such as a plebeian in *Julius Caesar* in 1683–84 at Drury Lane), but beginning in the fall of 1690 he moved into larger roles, and his activity was more completely recorded. Among his parts were Waitwell in *Sir Anthony Love* (late September 1690), Polidas in *Amphitryon* (21 October 1690), Old Zachary Baggs in *Love for Money* (January 1691), Dulhead in *Win Her and Take Her* (1691–92), Sir Formal Trifle in *The Virtuoso* (after 1692), Sir Quibble Quere in *The Richmond Heiress* (mid-April 1693), Sir Timothy Witless in *The Female Vertuosos* (May 1693), and Vincent in *1 Don Quixote* (mid-May 1694). His specialties, as even his character names suggest, were comic dullards, fops, and bouncy servants.

When the United Company split in late 1694 Bright signed with Betterton and subsequently acted at the Lincoln's Inn Fields playhouse. In mid-April 1697 he was the Justice of the Peace in *The Provoked Wife*; in March 1698 he acted Captain Bownceby in *The Pretenders*; about 1698–99 he was Old Bellair in *The Man of Mode*; on 9 January 1700 he played Bardolph in Betterton's version of *Henry IV*; and at the premier performance of *The Way of the World* on 5 March 1700 he acted the inventive servant Waitwell.

When the surge of complaints against the immorality of the stage came at the end of the seventeenth century, Bright was one of the actors accused by the authorities: as Old Bellair in *The Man of Mode* he had delivered the lines, "Please you Sir to Commission a young couple to go to bed together a' Gods name," which struck the purifiers as bawdy beyond words

and blasphemous to boot. The actor testified that since the words had been printed,

ye said Bright did humbly conceive y^t there was neither imorality or prophainess therein, ye said Bright as well as sev:^{11} others, haveing often Exprest y^e said words publickly on y^e stage, & no notice ever before taken threof. But some Maliciously buissy person or psons informing ag.st y^e said Bright, have taken hold of y^e Law, prosecuted him unknowingly, & have surroptitiously obtain'd a verdict against him for 10.$^£$ besides Cost & Charges, wch amounts to as much more, so y^t the s^d Bright is in a Continuall Danger of being taken up for y^e s^d: 10$^£$: & Cost & Committed to Goal. The said Bright therefore humbly Begs yor Honor to consider the hardness of this his Case, & hopes y^t since the whole Company are Equally concernd in this matter, That you will be Please to Order it so, that y^e sd Company may be Equall Sharers in y^e payment of y^e sd 10$^£$ wth Cost of suit, since by Law it is ordered to be paid, or y^t you would be please to protect him, otherwise the s^d. Bright & family must suffer.

Poor George seems to have been one of the players harder hit by the purge, and there is an intimation in his plea that his colleagues were letting him be a scapegoat; but other performers were cited too, and the acting companies probably had their hands full. Whether or not Bright was out of danger by 19 May 1701, at least he was acting again, for on that date he played the Gentleman Usher in *King Lear*. The charges against the players dragged through the courts for some time, and the final disposition of Bright's case is obscure.

Bright's activity in the early years of the new century is only partly documented; he stayed with Betterton's troupe until the new Queen's Theatre in the Haymarket was built, played there in 1705 (Don Felix in *The Mistake* on 27 December 1705 was one of his roles), and moved to Drury Lane shortly thereafter. In 1707 when the troupes were reorganizing, Bright was listed as one of the players to receive a guinea per performance whenever he acted, plus a base salary of £40 yearly, indicating that he was playing only sporadically. Grouped with him on an organizational list about this time were other actors who appeared only on occasion—Doggett, Johnson, Pinkethman, and Underhill; all were considerably above Bright in salary, Doggett, for instance, receiving £1000 *per annum*.

This limited service was apparently not of Bright's choosing, for he was in dire financial straits. An undated document that probably belongs to 1707–8 is a petition by Bright to the Chancellor of the Exchequer in which the actor reviewed his 25 years on the stage and noted that though he was supposed to be paid 40s. per week now, insufficient company income often reduced this figure to 8s., and that Bright had gone into debt to support his family. He was arrested for debt, he said, and imprisoned in Marshalsea for eight weeks; his playhouse pay had been stopped—something not previously done to actors, he claimed. While in prison he had been visited by Mills, one of the members of the company (either Drury Lane or the Queen's, depending on the petition's date); Mills had brought with him a lawyer and an agreement for Bright to sign which would have approved of the company's selling costumes to Sir John Vanbrugh for £500. Mills had also brought Bright some money but would not have given it to him unless he had signed the agreement. Desperate, Bright had signed and was released from prison, but he found himself shut out of the playhouse and deprived of his salary. In his petition Bright pleaded for reinstatement and his arrears in pay. Whether his complaint was heeded is unknown, but the likelihood is that it was not. There seems to be no further record of his theatrical activity, and his colleagues were obviously trying to squeeze him out of his position in the company. His useful days were over.

Bright, Molly [*fl. 1783–1785*], *wardrobe keeper.*
Molly Bright was mentioned in the King's Theatre accounts as being the keeper of the wardrobe in 1783 and 1784–85, and it is possible that she worked there before and after these dates.

Bright, Walter van. *See* VAN BRIGHT, WALTER.

Bright, William [*fl. 1794*], *singer?*
Doane's *Musical Directory* of 1794 listed William Bright, of Holborn, as a bass (singer, probably, but possibly a bass viol player) who participated in concerts given by the New Musical Fund. He may have been the William Bright of Hart Street who was buried on 20 January 1814 at St Paul, Covent Garden, having died at the age of 42.

Brightwell, Peter [*fl. 1689*], *actor.*
Peter Brightwell was ordered arrested for acting drolls illegally, presumably in London, by a warrant dated 9 September 1689.

Brila, Mons [*fl. 1742*], *acrobat.*
Monsieur and Madame Brila, with their little son of three years, came from Paris to perform "several curiosities of Balancing" at the New Wells, near the London Spa, Clerkenwell, on 3 July 1742.

Brila, Mme [*fl. 1742*], *acrobat. See* BRILA, MONS.

Brila fils *b. c. 1739, acrobat. See* BRILA, MONS.

Brill. *See* DU BRIEL.

Brinley, Matthew [*fl. 1671–1677*], *scenekeeper.*
On 20 March 1671 Matthew Brumley was listed as a member of the King's Company, and on 22 March 1677 a similar list named Matthew Brinley as a member of

the troupe; the two names doubtless represent the same man, a scenekeeper, but which spelling is correct is a pretty question.

Brinsley, Mr [*fl.* *1781–1782*], *actor.*
Mr Brinsley appeared as Sir John Freeman in *The Artifice* on 16 October 1781 and as Colonel Standard in *The Constant Couple* on 14 January 1782 at the Haymarket Theatre; the plays were given once each.

"Brischdower." *See* BRIDGETOWER.

Bristow, Mrs, later Mrs Robert Skinner [*fl.* *1797–1804*], *singer.*
Mrs Bristow appeared on the London stage in an unnamed vocal part in the mainpiece *De Montfort* at Drury Lane on 29 April 1800. She repeated her performance on 30 April and 2 May, but on 3 May her name was omitted from the bills of this production.

She was the wife of Mr Bristow the provincial actor, who played at Plymouth in 1788, at Bristol in 1787–90, at York in 1791 and 1792, and at Tunbridge Wells in 1797. Probably Mrs Bristow accompanied him on these tours. Mr Bristow was also at Drury Lane from 1800–1801 through 1802–3 at £1 per week.

Mrs Bristow was the mother of George Bristow (at first billed as Master Bristow), who acted at Covent Garden and Edinburgh in the first two decades of the nineteenth century; of Mary Bristow, who made her debut at Drury Lane as a singer in the fall of 1800 and became the second wife of Joe Grimaldi shortly thereafter; and of Louisa Maria Bristow, who acted at Covent Garden, 1805–10, and married the harlequin John Bologna in June 1818. A Maria Bristow, who seems also to have been acting at Covent Garden in the early part of the nineteenth century and who received £75 from the will of Joe Grimaldi in 1837, was probably another daughter.

By December 1803, Mrs Bristow's husband had died, and in that month she married the Edinburgh actor Robert Skinner at Sterling. As Mrs Skinner she was in the Edinburgh company in 1804.

Bristow, George [*fl.* *1671*], *actor.*
George Bristow was ordered on 27 December 1671 to be apprehended for acting without a license, presumably in London.

Britain, Mr [*fl.* *1675–1678*], *pitkeeper.*
Mr Britain was one of the King's Company pitkeepers at the Drury Lane Theatre. On 9 December 1675 new rules for the government of the troupe were drawn up, and Britain was assigned to guard the tiring house door; this may have been only at certain times, or he may have served in this backstage position before moving to a post in the pit. For productions done on 12 and 26 December 1677 the receipts have survived, and Britain at that time was named pitkeeper. He may well have served before the earliest mention of him, and possibly he continued at the theatre beyond the 1677–78 season. The actor "Briten" of the early 1660's may have been Britain himself, or a relative.

Briten, Mr [*fl.* *1661–1664*], *actor.*
In a manuscript cast for the King's Company production c. 1661–1664 at Vere Street or Bridges Street of *Love's Sacrifice*, a Mr Briten is listed for the role of Nebrassa; a second manuscript cast shows Nicholas Blagden in this part. "Briten" could be an error for Blagden, but it is possible this was a different person, perhaps to be identified as or related to Mr Britain the scenekeeper of the 1670's.

Brithmere. *See* BITHMERE.

"British Giant." *See* BLACKER, HENRY.

Britt. *See* BRETT.

Britton, Mrs [*fl. 1729–1731*], *actress, dancer.*

The London Stage lists Mrs Britton among the dancers at the Haymarket Theatre in 1729–30, and she may have danced minor roles before her first billed appearance as an actress. On 7 July 1730 she attempted the sizeable role of Lavinia in *The Fair Penitent*, and on the seventeenth she was one of the peasant women in *The Amorous Adventure*. At Reynolds's booth at Tottenham Court on 1 August she served as a member of the troupe, but her specific participation is not known. Her last billed appearance was as ambitious as her first: at the Haymarket on 4 May 1731 she played Monimia in *The Orphan*.

Britton, Thomas 1644–1714, *instrumentalist, impresario.*

Thomas Britton was one of the most charmingly fascinating men of his time; skilled in music, chemistry, and bibliography, intimate with some of the most fashionable people of his day, he remained throughout his life a humble and industrious hawker of small coal in the streets of London. He was born at Rushden, near Higham Ferrers, Northamptonshire, on 14 January 1644, and was apprenticed when young to a small coal vendor in St John Street, Clerkenwell. After serving his apprenticeship he established his own business in an old stable at the northeast corner of Jerusalem Passage in Aylesbury Street where the Bull's Head Inn later stood. On the lower floor Britton had his coal shop, and on the upper he constructed a long, low room accessible only from the outside by a ladder-like stair. His jolly neighbor Ned Ward described it:

His Hut wherein he dwells looks without side as if some of his Ancestors had happened to be executors to old Snorling Diogenes and that they had carefully transplanted the Athenian Tub into Clerkenwell; for his House is not much higher than a Canary-pipe, and the Windows of his State Room, but very little bigger than the Bunghole of a Cask.

For this humble place Britton, in 1677, paid a rental of £4 annually.

With his coal sack over his shoulder and measuring cup in his hand, Britton spent his days selling small coal in the streets, but at some time in his early days he had developed a love for music and an intellectual curiosity that led him to spend his leisure hours at more elevated work. Beginning in 1678 Britton sponsored, in the long room over his shop, concerts of music not unlike those which John Banister had instituted a few years before, and over the years he attracted not only the most elegant audiences imaginable (despite the awkward stairs and uncomfortable surroundings) but the foremost musicians of his time. He was an accomplished *viola da gamba* player

Harvard Theatre Collection

THOMAS BRITTON
after Woollaston

himself, and, to judge by the charming portrait of him tuning a harpsichord, he must have been a keyboard expert as well. With him over the years performed John Banister the younger, Matthew Dubourg, Pepusch, Needler, Symonds, Wichello, Shuttleworth, and the poet John Hughes, the painter Woollaston, and, on Britton's little five-stop organ, Handel.

Britton developed an interest in rare books and manuscripts, too, and in addition to building a valuable collection of his own, he helped other bibliophiles find scarce items, so that in time he counted among his friends Sir Roger L'Estrange (who, it is said, helped Britton start his concerts), Ralph Thoresby and Thomas Hearne the antiquaries, the Earls of Oxford (Robert Harley), Pembroke, Sunderland, and Winchelsea, the Duke of Devonshire, and John Bagford—all fellow book collectors—and such fashionable lady lovers of the arts as the Duchess of Queensberry.

Walpole reported in later years that Britton's concerts were by an annual 10*s*. subscription and that coffee was served for a penny a dish, but though this may have been true when, temporarily, Britton moved to a more spacious room next door, or toward the end of his life, the early concerts were given by him free of charge. Either from the beginning or shortly after the concerts started, the meetings became a kind of club for musicians, or, as Ned Ward described it, a "Harmonious society of tickle-fiddle gentlemen" that met Thursdays for nearly 40 years. Britton's fellow music lovers and performers did not seem to mind the little loft where they met, and when Britton moved the concerts next door to larger quarters "that the company might not stew in the Summer-Time like sweaty dancers at a Buttock Ball," as Ward said, the change was not successful, and the group returned to Britton's attic. When Ralph Thoresby visited a meeting he noted in his diary on 5 June 1712 that he had heard "a noble concert of music, vocal and instrumental, the best in town, which for many years [Britton] has had weekly for his own entertainment, and of the gentry, &c., gratis, to which most foreigners of distinction, for the fancy of it, occasionally went."

In addition to his musical and bibliographical interests, Britton was an amateur chemist and student of the occult. He seems to have picked up his interest in chemistry from his neighbor Dr Garencier, physician to the French Embassy, and to the astonishment of the antiquarian Hearne he built at small expense "an amazing elaboratory" which so fascinated a Welshman who saw it that he commissioned Britton to build him a duplicate. What experiments the coal dealer may have carried on are not known, nor is it clear how deeply he went into the study of the occult, but his library relating to physics, chemistry, theology, history, and Rosicrucian philosophy was impressive and suggests his serious interest. Some people thought him very odd indeed, and many who saw (or heard) his activities only from a distance accused him of being an atheist, a Jesuit, a sectary, and a conjurer.

How Britton managed financially is a mystery, for his income could hardly have been large. His book collecting brought him money occasionally; it is said that for £500 he sold a portion of his collection to Lord Somers. But as often as not he contributed to the libraries of his friends, as when he helped the Earl of Oxford form the famous Harleian collection. At his death his own library of 1400 books and his musical instruments, including a Ruckers virginal, fetched only £180 (some sources say £100) for his widow.

The story of Britton's death is as curious as that of his life. Legend has it that a prankster friend of his, the magistrate Robe, brought the amateur ventriloquist Honeyman, a blacksmith, to visit the unwitting small coal man. As a joke, knowing Britton's superstitiousness, Robe had the ventriloquist throw his voice and call out to

THOMAS BRITTON

artist unknown

*Tho' mean thy rank yet in thy humble
    cell*
*Did gentle peace and arts unpurchased
    dwell;*
*Well pleased Apollo thither led his
    train,*
*And music warbled in her sweetest
    strain.*

Prior wrote in the same vein:

*Tho' doomed to Small Coal, yet to arts
    ally'd,*
*Rich without wealth, and famous with-
    out pride;*
*Music's best patron, judge of books and
    men,*
Belov'd and honour'd by Apollo's train;
*In Greece or Rome, sure never did ap-
    pear,*
So bright a genius in so dark a sphere;
More of the man had artfully been sav'd,
Had KNELLER *painted, and had* VERTUE
grav'd.

Woollaston painted Britton twice, once in
his smock with his coal measure in his
hand, and a second time tuning a harpsichord. The first picture is in the National
Portrait Gallery, and an engraving in mezzotint was made of it by J. Simon, under
which Hughes's lines were printed. Mad-
docks also made an engraving from this
first portrait. The second Woollaston painting has been lost, unfortunately, but a mezzotint engraving of it was made by Thomas
Johnson, accompanied by the Prior verses
(which end with a rather uncomplimentary
note on the painter and engraver). Another
engraving by C. Grignion shows Britton's
head, and still another pictures him full
length hawking his coal; the latter was
printed in the *London Magazine* in February 1777. Of the various pictures, the
Woollaston portrait of Britton and his harpsichord is the most ingratiating, despite
Prior's complaints; it shows a short, friendly
man on whom it would seem most cruel to
play a joke of any kind.

Britton that his death was near unless he
fell to his knees and repeated the Lord's
Prayer. Trembling with fear, Britton did
as he was bid, but the fright so shook him
that he died a few days later. Whether or
not the story is true, it seems probable
enough that so quaint a little man should
die so oddly. He quit this world on 27 September 1714 at the age of 70 and was
buried the following 1 October at St
James, Clerkenwell.

His contemporaries found Britton a personable and ingenuous man; he was praised
for his probity, ingenuity, diligence, and
humility. John Hughes, violinist and poet,
sang of him:

Broad, Mr 〔*fl. 1754–1769*〕, *box-keeper.*

Mr Broad, a boxkeeper at Drury Lane, was regularly listed in the bills at benefit time from 20 May 1754 through 20 May 1769. His salary on 9 February 1765 was 2s. daily or 12s. weekly, a standard wage paid all five boxkeepers.

Broad, Mr 〔*fl. 1760–1761*〕, *door-keeper.*

The Covent Garden accounts for 1760–61 list a Mr Broad as doorkeeper.

Broad, Mrs 〔*fl. 1735–1736*〕, *house servant.*

Mrs Broad was a "chairwoman" at Covent Garden Theatre in 1735–36 (and possibly before and after), a menial job for which she received a mean salary: 1s. per night. For 179 days of work she was paid £8 19s.

Broad, George *b. 1777, double-bass player, pianist, composer.*

George Broad was born at Wychinford on 8 November 1777, the son of Sarah Broad, and he was baptized at Worcester on 3 January 1778. His mother attested to these facts on 3 June 1805 when her son was being considered for membership in the Royal Society of Musicians; by that time she was living in Chapel Street, Tottenham Court Road. Though her testimony did not mention her husband—for he was probably dead by 1805, his name was George.

Dibdin, writing in 1828, stated that Broad was Astley's composer and pianist in 1797–98 at the "Royal Amphitheatre of Arts." This is the only evidence of Broad's professional activity in London before the turn of the century.

On 1 September 1805 he was recommended to the Royal Society and was then described as 28, married, and with two children: George Frederick, nearing six years of age, and Sarah Ann, age nine months. The recommendation noted that Broad had served an apprenticeship with the late John Danby and was, in 1805, engaged as a double bass player at the Drury Lane Theatre and Vauxhall. In addition, he had "scholars and a Chapel." The Drury Lane accounts show that Broad was still working at the theatre on 16 September 1807 and was paid £1 15s. weekly as a member of the band.

At the very time Broad was being considered for Royal Society membership, his wife, according to Dibdin, was engaged by that manager to perform at the Amphitheatre in Peter Street, Dublin, from 9 November 1805 to 14 February 1806. What her specialty was is unknown, and it seems odd that with a child less than a year old she would go off to Ireland, apparently leaving her husband behind. In any case, George Broad was admitted to the Royal Society on 5 January 1806, participated in the annual St Paul's concert in May of that year, played there again in 1811, 1812, and 1813, and then, at some time after that, went to Ireland.

On 7 December 1823, though in Ireland, Broad was granted £10 for medical aid by the Society back in London, and medical aid continued coming to him for the next 15 years. Dibdin noted in 1828 that Broad, "a good-natured, worthy man," was "comfortably settled in a farm in the County of Mayo, Ireland, and teaches Music the country round." A later notice of him in the Royal Society books is dated 6 March 1836: it was reported that he was in better health and had been told by Mr Kelly, a professor of music in Dublin, that he could find work in the city if he returned there. By this time, however, George Broad was an old man (as the Society books on 7 October 1838 indicated), and he may not have chosen to leave his country home. Since no records exist for him after this date, perhaps he died shortly thereafter.

Broadhurst, Miss *b. c. 1775, singer, actress.*

Miss Broadhurst was born about 1775 if the report was true that she was 16 at her 1791 debut; she was the daughter of a miniature-painter of Hatton Garden who apprenticed her to a composer and singing teacher named Percy. It was during her training period that her father died. By 10 January 1791, or perhaps a month earlier, she was reported as "well known in the Musical World" and ready to make her first appearance at some theatre in a new afterpiece called *Will o th' Wisp*. Whether this actually occurred or not is uncertain, but her singing master did contrive to have her engaged at Covent Garden for a debut as Polly in *The Beggar's Opera* on 15 January 1791, billed as "A Young Lady."

After her first appearance the *European Magazine* reported that Miss Broadhurst had a good figure and pleasing face, a clear, sweet voice of great compass, meticulous execution, and polished taste. By 10 February she was billed by name and played Leonora in *The Padlock*, this being her sixth appearance on the stage. After this brief duty at Covent Garden she went to Drury Lane for the oratorio season from 11 March through 15 April, singing a number of selections from Handel's works, including "Oh had I Jubal's Lyre" from *Saul*, "Abraham enough" from *Susanna*, and "Gentle Airs, melodious Strains" from *Athalia*. She returned to Covent Garden after the oratorio season and was given the singing role of Nancy in *The Union* on 18 May and a Pastoral Nymph in *Comus* on 27 May. For her 3 June benefit she played Lydia in *The Cottage Maid* and made tickets available at Mr Percy's, No 13, Tavistock Street, Bedford Square. The receipts for the evening were £202 9s.

She was engaged again by Covent Garden in 1791–92, at a weekly salary of £4. Her work during the season was not particularly distinguished: she sang Polly again and played bit parts in such productions as *Oscar and Malvina*, *The Woodman*, and *Zelma*. She also sang in the choruses that were included during this era in *Romeo and Juliet*, *Macbeth*, and *Alexander the Great*. In the summer of 1792 she played at the Richmond theatre, and when she returned to Covent Garden in the fall she embarked on a remarkably busy schedule. In addition to her old roles and her participation in choruses, she was Clara in *The Duenna*, Norah in *The Poor Soldier*, Eliza in *The Flitch of Bacon,* Celia in *Fontainbleau*, Ismene in *The Sultan*, Jenny in *The Highland Reel*, Bercilla in *The Midnight Wanderers*, and Emily in *The Invasion*.

Miss Broadhurst travelled with her mother to America, making her first appearance there at Annapolis in 1793. During her stay of several years she played at the Chestnut Street Theatre in Philadelphia (Catalina in *The Castle of Andalusia*), the John Street Theatre in New York (Yarico in *Inkle and Yarico*), the Vauxhall Gardens in New York, and the Haymarket Theatre in Boston. Dunlap was not as impressed with her as London had been; he found her "a genteel and amiable young lady" but found that she "had science, but not personal beauty, or skill as an actress, to recommend her." She was, however, quite popular with American audiences,

Harvard Theatre Collection

MISS BROADHURST
by Barlow

played frequently in Philadelphia and New York, and after the turn of the century was with Placide's company at Charleston.

As early as 28 March 1796, shortly after she had made her New York debut, she was reported in the *Morning Herald* as married and retired from the stage; though she apparently did marry in America, she certainly did not retire for several years after this date. Dibdin said that she was engaged for the 1803 season at Sadler's Wells, and perhaps she did return to London briefly, but the *Thespian Dictionary* of 1805 was probably correct in saying that she had married and settled in America.

Barlow made an engraving from a painting of Miss Broadhurst (artist unknown) which W. Lock published in 1792.

Broaks. *See* **BROOKS.**

Broc. *See* **DE BROC.**

Brocas, Mr *fl. 1755*, *actor.*

Mr Brocas played Perriwinkle in *A Bold Stroke for a Wife* on 2 October 1755 at Widow Yeates's "Large Theatrical Barn Facing the Boarding-School in Croydon." He may have been the William Brocas who was buried at St Paul, Covent Garden, on 14 July 1762.

Brock, James *b. 1727, pyrotechnist.* *See* **BROCK, JOHN** *b. 1700.*

Brock, John *d. 1720, pyrotechnist.*

The first of a long line of fireworks specialists that stretches into the twentieth century, John Brock the elder was probably responsible for a cruel pyrotechnic display at the Bear Garden, Hockley-in-the-Hole, where bears, dogs, bulls, and other animals were baited with fireworks. He lived in Islington Road, and by his wife Eleanor he had three children: John (born 25 November 1700), Mary (died 27 November 1720), and Paul (dates unknown). His son John followed in Brock's footsteps. The

elder Brock died on 5 November 1720 and was buried at St James, Clerkenwell.

Brock, John *b. 1700, pyrotechnist.*

John Brock the younger, son of the founder of the Brock family of pyrotechnists, was born on 25 November 1700. He married a woman named Martha and by her had two sons, John (born 1728) and James (born 1727). It was Brock's son John who continued the family line, though it was his son James who followed his father's trade. Little is known of the work of either John or his son, but it was probably John who worked with Morel Torré at Marylebone Gardens in the 1750's. Perhaps James worked with him, but all that is known of James is that he was a pyrotechnist like his father and grandfather and that he married a woman named Mary, by whom he had a daughter Martha (born 1750), a daughter Sarah (born 1752), and a son Abraham who was born in 1753 and died in 1754.

John Brock's wife Martha died in 1750 and was buried at the family church, St James, Clerkenwell; John's death date is not known.

Brock, Thomas *1756–1819, pyrotechnist.*

The fireworks expert Thomas Brock, one of the numerous Brocks in that trade, was born in 1756, the third son of John and the grandson of the John Brock who founded the line. He had two brothers, John and William, but the former chose not to follow in the family specialty. Thomas was married in 1788 at the Charlotte Chapel, St Pancras, to a woman named Mary, and by her had six sons and six daughters. Of this sizeable brood two became pyrotechnists: William, born in 1779, and Thomas, born in 1797. William married a woman named Elizabeth, and by her he had four sons and four daughters, all born in the nineteenth century; it was through William's son William that the

Brock line continued into the present century, and most of the offspring were pyrotechnists. William died in 1849.

Of all the Brocks, only Thomas, William's father, was spoken of in any detail in his time. He worked at Ranelagh in 1792, apparently with the same Morel Torré with whom his grandfather John had worked in the 1750's. The *Morning Chronicle* of 1 June 1812 announced "the greatest feast for the eye ever exhibited is a superb firework by that unparalleled artist, Mr Brock, Engineer." A few years later, on 5 August 1816, were advertised "superb Fire-Works, at the Ben Johnson Tea-Gardens, Stepney, by Mr Brock, Engineer to Vauxhall, the Original Ranelagh, and Spa Gardens, Bermondsey." Thomas, identified as of Red Lion Street, Spitalfields, died in 1819. The Mr Brock who worked at the Swan Bowling Green, Stratford, in 1820 and at Highbury House on 8 September 1823 was probably his son William.

Brock, William *b. 1752, pyrotechnist.*
William Brock, born in 1752, was one of the three sons of John Brock, grandson of the John Brock who was the grand progenitor of the huge family of fireworks experts. William had a brother John (the fourth of that name) who did not choose to follow the family trade, but he also had a brother Thomas who shared with him his interest in pyrotechnics. William married widow Elizabeth Powell of St Pancras at St George's, Queen Square, in 1774. They had a daughter Mary who was baptized at Islington in 1780, six years before her mother died at Mile End Old Town. Of William's work as a pyrotechnist, unfortunately, nothing seems to be known.

Brock, William *1779–1849, pyrotechnist. See* **BROCK, THOMAS** *1756–1819.*

Brockin, Mr ₁*fl. 1776–1790*₁, *dresser.*
One Brockin (or Brochin) was a Drury Lane dresser earning 9s. weekly in 1776–

77, and it is likely that the Brockin cited in the theatre account book on 19 September 1789 at that salary was the same person. He probably worked during the intervening years, but there seems to be no certain evidence.

Brockin, Mrs ₁*fl. 1765*₁, *dresser.*
Mrs Brockin, doubtless a relative of Mr Brockin (or Brochin) the dresser, was listed at a daily salary of 1s. 6d. or weekly pay of 9s. on a Drury Lane salary schedule dated 9 February 1765; Mrs Brockin was one of the women's dressers, all of whom received the same fee.

Brockwell, Benjamin ₁*fl. 1665*₁, *musician.*
The only reference to Benjamin Brockwell may be an error for the more important musician Henry Brockwell. In 1665 Benjamin Brockwell and John Atkinson (*recte* Atkins) were advised not to take positions outside the King's household; it was about this time that Henry Brockwell performed at the Bridges Street Theatre, but his work there seems to have been authorized.

Brockwell, Henry ₁*fl. 1661–1688*₁, *violinist.*
As early as 24 January 1661 Henry Brockwell (or Brocknell, Brookwell) was a member of the private music of Charles II, for on that date he and others at court were given New Year's gifts; it is likely that he had been in the royal employ since the Restoration. On 2 December 1661 he and five other musicians complained that Nicholas Lanier, Master of the King's Musick, had not been allowing them into the practice room to rehearse with the other players, and Lanier was issued a warning to cease this preferential treatment. Throughout the reign of Charles II Brockwell was chosen to join the small group of select musicians who attended the King on his trips to Windsor, Hampton Court, Dover, and

Newmarket, and when Thomas Killigrew at the Bridges Street Theatre needed the services of royal musicians on 20 December 1664, Brockwell was among the nine chosen. On 10 July 1665 he was appointed to John Banister's elite band of violins serving the King.

Like many musicians in the royal service during this period, Brockwell was sometimes late in receiving his salary and occasionally had to borrow money; one such occasion appears to have been on 13 August 1667 when £5 15s. of his pay was stopped and paid instead to a Mr Morris. On or about 20 February 1668, however, Brockwell received a promotion, replacing Richard Hudson as keeper of the lutes and viols, a position he kept for the following two decades. By this time he was receiving a yearly salary of £45 10s. 10d. as one of the band of violins, plus £18 5s. as keeper of the instruments, plus £46 10s. 10d. as a member of the King's private music. His post as keeper was an important one, and at times, as on 13 August 1669, for instance, he had warrants issued to remind all the King's musicians to turn in their instruments to him after using them and not to keep them for their private use. In 1670 he received payment on behalf of the band, which suggests again that he was one of its highest ranking members. His keeper's post had its drawbacks, however; by 27 February 1672 a creditor of Richard Hudson, previous keeper of the instruments, had contrived to have one of Hudson's old debts to him transferred to Brockwell, so that Brockwell's pay was stopped and given to the creditor, Alphonso Maley. Hudson's debt was probably an official one, and Brockwell inherited not only the prestige but also the delinquencies of his predecessor.

On 15 February 1675, as one of the regular band of 24 violins, Brockwell played at the performance of the last great court masque, *Calisto*. Two years later, on 8 May 1677, he and four other violinists

petitioned against Master of the Revels Charles Killigrew (Thomas's son) for dismissing them from attendance at the playhouse—very likely Drury Lane—where they had been playing, probably officially. By 13 December 1679 Brockwell's salary as a member of the violins had risen to £46 10s. 10d., to which was supposedly added the fees for his other posts, and since he was paid extra for royal trips out of London and for other special service, his total income was probably very handsome—if he received it on schedule.

A warrant dated 26 January 1681 indicates that Brockwell surrendered his keeper's position to Richard Robinson, but he was apparently reappointed to it under James II and was so serving as of 31 August 1685. On 27 October 1687, however, he relinquished it permanently to Richard Lewis. The last discovered reference to Brockwell was dated 7 March 1688, when he was paid for attending the King at Windsor the previous summer and fall. He may well have been fairly old by this time, and the absence of his name from later records could indicate that he retired from the royal service at the accession of William and Mary.

Brodas, Mr [*fl.* 1750], *tailor*.

Mr Brodas, a tailor, was paid £13 8s. for two dancing costumes made for Mr Jossett and Miss Hilyard, performers at Covent Garden, on 8 January 1750. Brodas may have been on the theatre staff, though he could have been a private tailor.

Broderick, Mr [*fl.* 1771–1776], *actor, singer*.

On 28 January 1771 at the Haymarket Theatre, Mr Broderick (or Brodrick) played Patrick O'Carrol, a singing role, in *The Register Office*. In the entertainment, *Teague's Rambles to London*, he played the Knife Grinder and Captain O'Brallaghan, in which character he sang a song from *Love à la Mode*. He reappeared at the Haymarket on 7 October 1776 as O'Cargo in *The Prejudice of Fashion*, another role with a song in it; and on 18 October he delivered a monologue, re-using the title *Teague's Rambles to London*, and now taking the role of Captain O'Blunder, at the China Hall, Rotherhithe.

Brogden, Mr [fl. 1730], *actor*.

At the Oates-Fielding booth at Bartholomew Fair starting 20 August 1730, Mr Brogden acted the Captain in *The Generous Free Mason*; he was not listed in the company when the group performed that same play at Southwark Fair on 9 September.

"Broileau, the Mlles" [fl. 1753], *performers*.

What the pair of Mademoiselles Broileau did when they appeared in "Mrs Midnight's" production of *The Old Woman's Concert* on 13 March 1753 was not mentioned in the bills. Their name was a pseudonym concocted by Christopher Smart, who was Mrs Midnight; who the actual performers were is not known.

Broke. *See* DE BROC.

Bromley, Master [fl. 1763–1782], *harpist*.

Master Bromley played the harp at Covent Garden on 11 April 1763, billed as "a Blind Youth" making his first appearance on any stage. He was probably the Bromley who played harp solos at the Oxford Music Room on 28 March 1778 and 1 December 1782.

Bromley, John [fl. 1778–1802], *scene painter*.

John Bromley was the son of the scene painter William Bromley and probably learned the trade from his father. The first record of him may have been as early as 14 May 1773 when a J. Bromley sent a letter and an account to Richard Brinsley Sheridan; he was certainly the painter who

irritated Sheridan in late 1777, causing the manager to reply with a curt note on 4 January 1778. Bromley had apparently written Sheridan of the unfortunate circumstances of Mrs French, widow of the Drury Lane scene painter who had worked under Garrick; Sheridan, in reply, told Bromley that keeping the playhouse accounts was not his business and that he should apply to Mr Evans of the theatre treasury and have Mrs French do her own complaining. At this time Bromley was living in Little Queen Street.

Starting at least as early as the 1792–93 season, John Bromley was a scene painter at Covent Garden, working with his father. The accounts indicate that he was probably paid 10s. 6d. daily, the same wage his father was granted. After the turn of the century William Bromley moved to Drury Lane, and John may have gone with him, though the earliest mention of John in the Drury Lane accounts was on 4 March 1802, after his father had been there for about two years. Since the accounts seldom discriminated between the two Bromleys, it is impossible to be certain how long after March 1802 John Bromley continued working.

He may have been the John Bromley of Tavistock Row who was buried at St Paul, Covent Garden, on 31 March 1815 at the age of 74. A John S. Bromley was a scene painter in Boston, Massachusetts and died at Charleston, South Carolina, on 25 November 1801; he may have been related to the London Bromleys.

Bromley, William [fl. 1780–1803], *scene painter*.

William Bromley served as Greenwood's assistant scene painter at Drury Lane from at least as early as 2 November 1780 when the accounts mention a payment to Bromley and Benson of £22 9s. Thereafter he was cited regularly in the accounts through 9 December 1788. This last payment was apparently for work done at Drury Lane earlier, for on 7 February 1788 Bromley (presumably William and not his son John) was paid £6 6s. for painting at Covent Garden. At Covent Garden he appears to have been paid a regular salary rather than in lump sums for work done; his weekly income was 10s. 6d. daily. Bromley worked at Covent Garden through the 1799–1800 season, during part of which time he was associated with his son John, also a scene painter. The accounts do not usually indicate which Bromley is being referred to, so it is difficult to separate the work of the two.

By 15 November 1800 William Bromley had returned to Drury Lane, perhaps accompanied by John (who was certainly there by March 1802); there he worked at least through the 1802–3 season.

William Bromley may have been related to the family of Bromley, engravers, of the eighteenth and nineteenth centuries, though he seems not to have been the William Bromley, engraver, who died in 1842.

Brook. *See also* BROOKE, BROOKES, BROOKS.

Brook, J. ₁fl. 1722–1723₁, *house servant?*

On 19 October 1722 Thomas Wood, the Lincoln's Inn Fields treasurer, and a J. Brook witnessed a notice by John Rich concerning two performers he had just hired; it is likely that Brook was one of Rich's office workers. On 28 May 1723 a benefit was held for Coe, the pit office-keeper, and for Brook—doubtless the same J. Brook.

Brookam, Mrs ₁fl. 1779₁, *dresser.*

In correspondence with Jane Pope, Kitty Clive declared on 22 June 1779 that

I cryd for that poor good creature Mrs Brookam till I was quite ill. I cannot find out what they can mean by dischar[g]ing Old Servants with such trifling salaries who are able to do their business, they must have such

people unless the[y] propose the Actresses' dressing themselves.

Brooke. *See also* BROOK, BROOKES, BROOKS.

Brooke, Mr ₁fl. 1788–1789₁, *actor.*

A Mr Brooke played Sanford in *Who's the Dupe?* on 22 December 1788 at the Haymarket, out of season. On 16 September 1789 he played Trudge in *Inkle and Yarico* at the King's Head Inn in Southwark. On 9 November of the same year he acted the same role at the White Horse Inn, Fulham, and on 11 November at the same place he played Major Belford in *The Deuce is in Him* and Don Ferdindo (with a song) in the pantomimical interlude *The Shipwreck.* The Miss Brooke who appeared on the same bills at the King's Head and the White Horse was probably related to him.

Brooke, Miss ₁fl. 1781–1789₁, *actress.*

A Miss Brooke acted Christiana in *Adventure in St James's Park* on 21 January 1782 at the Haymarket, out of season. A Miss Brooke played Patty in *Inkle and Yarico* at the King's Head Inn, Southwark, on 16 September 1789, and she also acted three roles in a bill of plays given at the White Horse Inn on 11 November of the same year: Rosette in *The Foundling,* Bell in *The Deuce is in Him,* and Cleone in *The Shipwreck.* Doubtless she was related to the Mr Brooke who also appeared in the latter two places in the same company.

Brooke, James ₁fl. 1773–1784₁, *proprietor.*

In 1773 James Brooke was granted a license for Italian opera at the King's Theatre from Michaelmas 1773 to Michaelmas 1774. Co-grantees were Richard and Mary Ann Yates. Brooke's actual role in the affairs of the Opera is elusive. He was a proprietor in the seasons 1776–77 and 1777–

78 and still seems to have been involved in 1784 when he was named as a co-defendant with a number of other King's people in a case in Chancery brought by Thomas Harris and John Gallini. He should not be confused with John Brooke or his wife Frances who were also proprietors of the Opera at the same time.

Brooke, Mrs John, Frances, née Moore *1724–1789, author, proprietor, actress.*

Frances Moore was born in 1724, one of the children of the Rev William Moore by his second wife Miss Secker. She married the Rev John Brooke D. D., rector of Colony, Norfolk, about 1765, and as Frances Brooke she became best known as an author and journalist. Soon after her marriage she and her husband left for Quebec, where he had an appointment as chaplain to the garrison. A story current at the time related that at a farewell party Dr Johnson took her into a separate room to kiss her goodbye, which he "did not chuse to do before so much company."

Mrs Brooke's role in the proprietorship of the King's Theatre is unclear. She met the actress Mrs Mary Ann Yates by chance and they immediately became intimate friends. According to *The London Stage*, Mrs Brooke joined the Yateses in the joint management of the Opera in 1773. She and her husband still had some share in the opera license in 1784 when they were named as co-defendants in a case in Chancery brought by Thomas Harris and John Gallini.

The year of her marriage she published her first play, *Virginia*, along with some poems and an account of its rejection by Garrick. Her other writings for the theatre include a tragedy, *The Siege of Sinope*, in which Mrs Yates acted for 10 nights in 1780–81, the very popular entertainment *Rosina* in 1782–83 with music by William Shield, and *Marian* in 1788–89, again with music by Shield, all at Covent Garden. She

translated Madame Riccoboni's *Lady Juliet Catesby*, the *Memoirs of the Marquis de St Forlaix*, and Millot's *History of England*. Her original non-dramatic works include three novels, *The History of Lady Julia Mandeville*, *Emily Montague*, and *The Excursion* (in which Garrick is attacked).

Under the pseudonym of Miss Mary Singleton, Mrs Brooke also published, from 15 November 1755 to 24 July 1756, *The Old Maid*, a weekly periodical which was devoted primarily to general topics of morals and manners but also contained essays on Shakespeare and criticisms of contemporary theatrical productions. Among these essays is a detailed account (13 March 1756) of Spranger Barry's acting of King Lear and her denunciation of Nahum Tate's "wretched alteration" of Shakespeare's play.

Frances Brooke died at Sleaford, Lincolnshire, on either 23 or 26 January 1789, predeceased by only a few days by her husband on 21 January 1789. The Brookes were survived by a son, the Rev John Moore Brooke, M.A., fellow of Trinity College, Cambridge.

A painting by T. Worlidge, engraved by R. Houston, which is listed in the *British Museum Catalogue of Engraved British Portraits* as a portrait of Mrs John Brooks, the wife of the well-known engraver, may possibly be of Frances Brooke. A version of this portrait engraved by C. Spooner is mistakenly listed in the Hall *Catalogue of Dramatic Portraits in the Harvard Theatre Collection* as item two under Mrs Brooks, *née* Watson.

Brooke, Richard [*fl. 1672–1673*], actor.

Richard Brooke (or Brooks) was an actor in the King's Company at least during the 1672–73 season and was named in a Lord Chamberlain's warrant dated 11 December 1672.

Brooker, Rebecca. *See* GRIMALDI, MRS GIUSEPPE, REBECCA.

Brookes. *See also* **BROOK, BROOKE, BROOKS.**

Brookes, Mr ₁*fl. 1778*₁, *actor.*

A Mr Brookes acted in *The Quaker* at the Richmond Theatre on 27 June 1778.

Brookes, Miss ₁*fl. 1774–1775?*₁, *dancer.*

According to a manuscript in the Forster Collection at the Victoria and Albert Museum ("Garrick Correspondence" add. XVIII), a Miss Brookes was a dancer at Drury Lane about 1774–75. She is not found in any other lists or bills.

Brookes, Robert ₁*fl. 1702*₁, *actor.*

The *Post Man* of 3 October 1702 named Robert Brookes as one of the strolling players required to pay town constables 2*s.* per day when he performed; he probably acted in London, since the newspaper was published there.

Brooks. *See also* **BROOK, BROOKE, BROOKES.**

Brooks, Mr *d. 1750, house servant, actor?*

A Mr Brooks shared benefits with house servants and minor actors at Drury Lane regularly each year from 1741–42 through 1746–47. He must have continued in that theatre until 3 March 1750 when the prompter William Cross wrote in his manuscript diary "Brooks dead and remov'd from Salary list."

Brooks, Mr ₁*fl. 1774*₁, *animal trainer?*

A Mr Brooks was paid £7 3*s.* at Covent Garden on 18 June 1774 for "attending with the Camels &c in the Fair." The production of *The Fair* on 28 October 1773

included real animals, and Mr Brooks probably was their keeper or trainer.

Brooks, Mr ₁*fl. 1783–1785*₁ *constable.*

A Mr Brooks was house constable at the King's Theatre at least from 1783 to 1785.

Brooks, ₁Mr?₁ ₁*fl. 1794*₁, *actor?*

According to a Folger manuscript, a person named Brooks was discharged on 20 October 1794 from the "Summer Theatre" (i.e. Haymarket).

Brooks, Mrs ₁*fl. 1760–1767*₁, *charwoman.*

A Mrs Brooks was paid 1*s.* 2*d.* per day as charwoman at Covent Garden in 1760–61 and 1766–67.

Brooks, Mrs, née Watson ₁*fl. 1786–1794*₁, *actress.*

According to a biographical notice in the *Thespian Magazine*, Mrs Brooks was the daughter of a man named Watson who originally lived in Scotland. After he lost his property in 1745—by his "adherence to the Stuart family"—he settled in London and went into the "mercantile line." He died about 1763 while on a business trip in Jamaica, leaving behind his widow and six children, of whom the future actress was the youngest. Apparently well provided for, the mother gave her a genteel education at a fine boarding school and sent her to France to complete it. Upon her return she served for a while as tutoress in a noble family and then at the age of 18 married Mr Brooks, a successful wall-paper manufacturer. But his business failed, and he went bankrupt; she turned to the stage— "for the most laudable of all motives"—to help support her family.

Announced as a gentlewoman who was making her first appearance on any stage,

Harvard Theatre Collection

MRS BROOKS (Watson)
by J. Condé

Mrs Brooks played Lady Townley in *The Provok'd Husband* at the Haymarket on 19 July 1786. After playing that role three more times that summer at the Haymarket (and perhaps once at the Windsor Castle Inn at Hammersmith on 24 July 1786), she took up a successful engagement at Dublin by invitation of Daly. She returned for another summer at the Haymarket in 1787 in which she played Elvira in *The Spanish Fryar*, Florinda in *Tit for Tat*, and Mrs Oakly in *The Jealous Wife*; she then went to Edinburgh in the next winter to play Yarico in the first performance of *Inkle and Yarico* in that city. From 1788 through 1794 she played regular summer engagements at the Haymarket but seems never to have engaged at a London winter house, perhaps by her own choice, she being

"an affectionate wife and tender mother." Her roles at the Haymarket included, in addition to those mentioned: Fanny in *A Mogul Tale*, Elvira in *A Key to the Lock*, Miss Richland in *The Good-Natured Man*, Mrs Love in *A Quarter of an Hour Before Dinner*, Mariana in *The Miser*, Cecilia in *The Chapter of Accidents*, Emily in *The Married Man*, Primrose in *The Young Quaker*, and Lady Euston in *I'll Tell You What*.

Tall, with an elegant figure, and a beautiful face, and moving with a natural ease and grace, she was most successful in the line of young ladies endowed with artless innocence and rural simplicity. At first her voice proved weak but it strengthened with experience. Mrs Brooke seems to have taken Elizabeth Farren as her model, and according to the *Secret History of the Green Room* (1795), she copied every attitude and gesture, even taking the Farren style of enunciation.

While professionally active in London she lived at Mr Woodmason's, Nos 66–68, Pall Mall. Of her family and her life after 1794 nothing is known. Possibly she was the Mrs Brooks who acted Lady Randolph in *Douglas* for a shared benefit at Wheatley's Riding School in Greenwich on 8 July 1798.

A drawing of her by Condé, engraved by him for the *Thespian Magazine* (October 1793) shows her to be the delicate and pretty woman of report. A portrait of her by Samuel De Wilde as Leonora in *The Revenge* — a role she did not play — was engraved by J. Chapman for a plate to *Bell's British Library*, 1793. Items two and four in Hall's *Catalogue of Dramatic Portraits in the Harvard Theatre Collection* under her name are not pictures of her.

Brooks, Mrs [*fl.* 1798], *actress.*

A Mrs Brooks acted Lady Randolph in *Douglas* at Wheatley's Riding School, Greenwich, on 8 June 1798 for a benefit which she shared with other actors, some of whom, like Twaits, Ives, and a Hallam, were professionals.

Brooks, the Masters *fl. 1737–1739*, *dancers.*

Two boys by the name of Master Brooks, one called Senior and the other Junior and doubtless brothers, danced at Drury Lane in 1737–38 and 1738–39. They appeared in such pieces as *The Burgomaster Trick'd* and *The Harlot's Progress* billed as the "Lilliputian" dancing scholars of Leviez. In September 1738 one of them, perhaps both, performed in *The Dragon of Wantley* at Hallam's booth in the George Inn Yard.

Brooks, Ann. *See* HATTON, MRS WILLIAM T., ANN.

Brooks, James *fl. 1749*, *house servant?*

In a manuscript in the British Museum is a notation pertaining to Covent Garden for 8 September 1749, informing that James Brooks, "husband to the late Jane Savidge Lee died £2–2," which could mean the weekly paylist was now reduced by that amount or that the theatre paid some funeral expenses.

Brooks, James *1760–1809, violinist, band leader.*

In a recommendation for admission to the Royal Society of Musicians on 2 March 1783, the musician Parke described James Brooks, 23, as a violinist who had practiced music professionally for seven years, as a married man with a child one year old, and as "engaged at the opera &c." He was no doubt the Brooks listed by Burney as a first violinist at the Handel Memorial Concerts given at Westminster Abbey and the Pantheon in May and June 1784. He also played at the annual spring concerts at St Paul's for benefit of the clergy in 1792 and 1794.

It is possible that James Brooks was the "Mr Brooks Jun" who played a concerto on the violin at Bath on 23 April 1782 and was the son of Mr Brooks, also a violinist and a teacher of music in that city. If so, his mother was doubtless Mrs Sarah Brooks who died at Bath on 8 August 1787 and was noticed in the *Bath Chronicle* of 16 August 1787 as the widow of Mr Brooks of the Theatre Royal in that city. The younger Brooks also played at Bristol in 1791, 1792, and 1798. Most likely it was he who was announced in the *Monthly Mirror* in February 1800 as "Brooks of Bath" to be the leader of the Vauxhall band for the next season in place of Mr Mountain. He may also have played in the Drury Lane band in 1807–8 (two persons named Brooke and Brooks are on the pay list that season as members of the band at £1 10s. and £2 5s. per week respectively).

James Brooks published *A Concerto for the Violin in Nine Parts . . . No 1* in 1795, *Two Duets for One Performer on the Violin*, and *Twelve English Ballads, adapted for the Piano Forte & Harp* about 1800. Eight published songs which he composed for Vauxhall Gardens are in the British Museum collection of printed music.

On 1 October 1809 James Brooks was granted five guineas by the Governors of the Fund of the Royal Society of Musicians on account of his illness, which prevented him from attending the meeting. Apparently the illness was serious, for he died, probably in late December. On 7 January 1810 his widow Mrs Ann Barnard Brooks was granted £8 for funeral costs and £2 12s. 6d. per month allowance. Three years later, on 7 November 1813, the Governors gave the widow £5 for her own medical relief, and on 6 February 1814 they gave her another £5, at which time it was noted in the Minute Book that she was suffering from "severe paralytic affliction." She survived, however, for another seven years. Her daughter Caroline announced to the Governors on 4 March 1821 that her mother had died recently; Caroline was granted £8 for funeral costs.

Brooksbank, Miss _[fl. 1785]_, _actress._
Miss Brooksbank played Princess Elizabeth in _King Charles I_ at the Haymarket Theatre on 31 January 1785.

Brookwell. _See_ BROCKWELL.

"Broomstickado, Mynheer Von Poop-Poop" _[fl. 1757–1760]_, _bassoonist._
"Mynheer Von Poop-Poop Broomstickado" made his first appearance on the London stage, not, as has sometimes been reported, on 2 September 1757, but on the previous 28 June at the Haymarket Theatre as an accompanist for "Signora Mimicotti" in "Mrs Midnight's" _A Medley Concert_. The reason for the erroneous dating of his debut is doubtless confusion over the variant spelling of his name, which on 28 June was given as "Myn Heer Van-Poop Broomsticato"; the two performers are clearly identical, for on 2 September his assignment was again as an accompanist for Signora Mimicotti. He played, appropriately, the bassoon, or some instrument resembling it. He was also a participant in _The Old Woman's Oratory_ on 18 May 1758, another Midnight production.

He may have left London to tour after this season, for his name did not reappear in the bills until 14 February 1760, again at the Haymarket and again in one of Mrs Midnight's presentations, her _Concert and Oratory_. He was billed as "Mynheer Broomsticado," another variant spelling, and labelled part of Mrs Midnight's band of originals. His last appearance was on 8 September 1760 at the Haymarket when he joined once again with Signora Mimicotti, playing his bassoon while she offered a _Mock Italian Air_. After this, his name disappeared from the bills. "Broomstickado" was a pseudonym created by Christopher Smart (Mrs Midnight) for some performer, but who he actually was and what he really did remains a mystery.

Brooth. _See_ BOOTH.

Broschi. _See_ FARINELLI.

Brouden or **Broudin.** _See_ BRUODIN.

Brous, Mr _[fl. 1708]_, _tailor._
Mr Brous was on the payroll of the Queen's Theatre in the Haymarket as a tailor for the operas; his daily salary was 7s. 6d., and on 13 January 1708 he was paid £110 11s. 6d. for costumes.

Brown. _See also_ BROWNE.

Brown, Mr, stage name of J. B. Williamson. _See_ WILLIAMSON, J. B.

Brown, Mr _[fl. 1708]_, _boxkeeper._
The Mr Brown who was paid £7 3s. on 13 January 1708 by the Queen's Theatre in the Haymarket was probably Brown the boxkeeper who was listed on 8 March 1708 at a salary of 4s. per day. He was very possibly related to the Mrs Brown who was a dresser at the opera at this time, and he could have been the Brown who served at Lincoln's Inn Fields from 1719 to 1729.

Brown, Mr _[fl. 1719–1729]_, _boxkeeper or officekeeper._
A Mr Brown (or Browne) shared benefits at Lincoln's Inn Fields Theatre on 3 June 1719 and 23 May 1720, and a Mr Brown appears in the theatre's accounts starting 13 September 1728 as an officekeeper or boxkeeper. The two may be the same, and, indeed, this Brown could be the Brown who was boxkeeper at the Queen's Theatre in 1708.

Brown, Mr _[fl. 1724]_, _actor._
A Mr Brown (or Browne) was listed as a member of the Haymarket Theatre troupe in 1723–24. He acted Farewell in _Sir Courtly Nice_ on 5 February 1724 and shared a benefit on 20 February. This actor may have been the "Browme" who played

Tiresias in *Oedipus* at the Bullock-Spiller booth at Southwark Fair on 24 September 1724.

Brown, Mr [fl. 1748–1751], actor, dancer, singer.

Though the following references may have involved two different Browns, the dates suggest that perhaps one person was concerned. A Mr Brown played Scrawl in *The Consequences of Industry and Idleness* at Yates's booth at Bartholomew Fair on 24 August 1748, and on 7 September at Phillips's booth at Southwark Fair he was Antonio in *The Tempest*. It was probably this same Mr Brown who was billed as singing and dancing at the New Wells, Clerkenwell, on 27 November 1749, with Mrs Smith. At the Haymarket Theatre on 16 February a Mr Brown played Jacques in the French version of *The Beggar's Opera* called *L'opéra de gueux*, and on 7 September 1750 at Phillips's Southwark Fair Booth a Brown acted Porter in *The Imprisonment of Harlequin*.

There was a Mr Brown performing with the summer company at Richmond in 1751, and on 18 September of this year at Southwark Fair a Brown played Sharp in *The Lying Valet*. The last reference to a Mr Brown who might fit into the above sequence is on 9 September 1751 at Phillips's Southwark Fair booth; a Mr Brown played Colonel Sorenzo in *No Fool Like the Old One*. The Mrs Brown in the troupe at this time may have been his wife; she had been playing since 1736, but her activity, like Mr Brown's, seems to have stopped after 1751. If they were husband and wife, perhaps the Master John Brown who flourished 1732–36 was their son.

Brown, Mr [fl. 1763–1764], actor.

Mr Brown played Sullen in *The Beaux' Stratagem* and a role in *The Contented Cuckold* on 5 September 1763 as one of the members of Foote's company at the Haymarket Theatre. In the summer of 1764 he

was busy again with Foote's group, acting Staytape in *The Patron* on 13 June, a role in *The Orators* on 6 July, Dapper in *The Citizen* on the thirteenth, Gargle in *The Apprentice* on the twenty-third, Drawcansir in *The Rehearsal* on 20 August, and Cobb in *Every Man In His Humour* on 1 September. The Mrs Brown who also acted in *The Apprentice* and *The Rehearsal* was probably his wife.

Brown, Mr [fl. 1768?–1817?], singer.

Though proof is lacking, it is quite possible that the Master Brown, pupil of Dr Arne, who sang at the theatres and pleasure gardens in London from 1768 to 1773 was the Mr Brown who served in singing choruses at Drury Lane and the Haymarket from 1776 to possibly as late as 1817.

The first notice of Master Brown was on 25 May 1768 when he sang in a performance of *Ruth* at the Lock Hospital. During the summer of this year he was engaged at four guineas per week at Marylebone Gardens, and on 16 March 1769 at Drury Lane he made his first stage appearance as Ariel in *The Tempest*, billed as Dr Arne's pupil and substituting for Mrs Arne who was ill at Bristol and could not take the normally female role. It is not likely that he was a regular member of the Drury Lane troupe, but he made enough of an impression as Ariel to be invited to sing on 5 April in *Ruth*, this time at the King's Theatre in the Haymarket. In August 1769 he was back at Marylebone Gardens, entertaining patrons in a pastoral *serenata* called *Love and Innocence*. Some of the songs he sang were published with his name attached, namely "Jemmy and Nanny" and "When Innocent Pastime our Pleasure did Crown." In September 1769 he participated in *Judith* at the Stratford Jubilee.

On 27 March 1770 he sang in the fourth act of *The Tender Husband* at Drury Lane, and on 7 June he warbled some catches and glees there with Mrs Scott and Mrs Wrighten. Drury Lane engaged him for the

1771–72 season at £2 5s., one of his assignments being in *Harlequin's Invasion* in October and December 1771. Master Brown sang again in the summer of 1773 at Marylebone Gardens, and then his name disappeared from the bills.

It is possible that the Mr Brown who sang in the *Macbeth* chorus on 25 November 1776 at Drury Lane, at a salary of £2 10s., was the same person; the lapse of three years would suggest that Master Brown's voice broke and that he now returned as an adult singer. He is recorded as singing in the *Romeo and Juliet* chorus from 10 December onward. He was a tenor, if the account book references for this season point to him, and though he subscribed to the pension fund at 10s. 6d., the books show him discharged at the end of the season.

What happened to Mr Brown during the following years is not known, but it was probably he who joined the Drury Lane company in 1790–91, now as a bass; the bills do not cite him until the 1792–93 season, however. On 11 October he was a Priest in *The Cave of Trophonius*; on 18 October he was one of the soldiers in *The Prisoner*; on 21 November he was in the chorus of *The Pirates*; and on 7 March he was in the chorus of *Ozmyn and Daraxa*. During the summer of 1793 he sang in the choruses in *The Surrender of Calais* and *The Mountaineers* at the Haymarket Theatre, two works in which he was to participate frequently for the rest of the century.

In 1793–94 he was not with Drury Lane but appeared on 10 October 1793 at the Haymarket as a Brideman in *Royal Clemency*, and he sang in the chorus again at the Haymarket in the summer of 1794. This year he was living in Duke Street, Lincoln's Inn Fields, and Doane the same year reported that Brown had sung in the Handelian concerts at Westminster Abbey and still participated in the oratorio performances at Drury Lane. In the fall of 1794 he rejoined the Drury Lane chorus, lending his bass to performances of *The Pirates*, *The Mountaineers*, *The Roman Father*, and *The Cherokee*. Again, he spent the summer singing in the Haymarket chorus, and this same pattern he repeated in 1795–96.

He seems not to have sung at Drury Lane in 1796–97, but he was at the Haymarket in the summer of 1797, and perhaps the Mrs Brown (fl. 1790–1797) who sang as a fellow member of the chorus in *The Italian Monk* on 15 August was his wife. Brown returned to Drury Lane in the fall and thereafter sang regularly there in the winters and at the Haymarket in the summers until the end of the century. His salary during the 1790's seems to have remained a steady £1 5s. weekly. A Mr Brown was noted in the Drury Lane accounts as late as 1816–17 at this salary, and perhaps he was the singer; there was, however, a dancer named Brown in the company at the same time, and perhaps the singer did not continue his career this late.

Brown, Mr *(fl. 1770?–1808?)*, *actor*.

A Mr Brown acted with a company of players at Glasgow in January, February, and March 1770, probably appearing in *The Provoked Wife*, *The Citizen*, and *Jane Shore*. It is likely that he was the same Mr Brown who played Dapper in *The Citizen* at the Haymarket Theatre in London on 16 November 1770 and then became a member of the Theatre Royal, Edinburgh. He was acting at Edinburgh on 8 April 1775, at any rate, and it was probably he who popped up again at the Haymarket in London for a single performance as Gibbet in *The Beaux' Stratagem* on 23 September 1776. He remained in London this trip to play Eumenes in *Alexander the Great* on 7 October at the China Hall, Rotherhithe, after which he returned to Edinburgh to stay until 1779.

The next record of Brown, assuming the same person was concerned, is for 15 March 1779 at the Haymarket, when he spoke the prologue to *The Wrangling Lovers*; almost a year later, on 27 December 1779, he was Huncks in *The Rival Milliners*, and on 3 January 1780 he played Crambo in *The Modish Wife* at the same playhouse. On 19 July 1780 he was at Plymouth, playing Father Paul in *The Duenna*, and on 13 November of that year he came to London again to act Dunk Donald in *The City Association* and M'Intosh in *The Detection* at the Haymarket, billed as from the Theatre Royal, Edinburgh. A Mr Browne, possibly the same actor, was in the cast of *The Taylors* on 25 November 1782, and certainly the Edinburgh man was Richmond in *Richard III* on 15 December 1783.

With other Edinburgh actors Brown, as Item, was in *Wit's Last Stake* at the Haymarket on 9 February 1784 and was Manage in *The Man's Bewitched* on 8 March; a year later at the same house he spoke an address before the mainpiece on 25 April 1785 and played Simon in *The Suspicious Husband* on the next night. A Mr Browne acted at Plymouth in August and September 1788, playing Justice Benbow in *The Flitch of Bacon*, the Clown in *The Recruiting Serjeant*, and an Irishman in *Rosina*—and this, too, may have been the Edinburgh actor. The last notices of a Mr Brown who falls into the above pattern are in 1805–6 and 1806–7, when he was acting again at the Theatre Royal, Edinburgh.

Brown, Mr *[fl. 1771]*, *equestrian*.
A Mr Brown, equestrian, performed at The Three Hats, Islington, under Sampson's management in 1771.

Brown, Mr *[fl. 1776–1777]*, *dresser*.
One Brown was a dresser at Drury Lane at 9s. weekly in 1776–77.

Brown, [Mr?] *[fl. 1776–1777]*, *performer*.
A Brown was an actor or actress at £1 weekly at Drury Lane during the 1776–77 season.

Brown, Mr *[fl. 1791]*, *exhibitor*.
A Mr Brown presented some sort of exhibit at Bartholomew Fair in 1791.

Brown, Mr *[fl. 1794]*, *singer?*
Doane in 1794 listed a Mr Brown of Packington who was a tenor (singer, probably) who participated in Handelian Society concerts at Westminster Abbey.

Brown, Mr *[fl. 1798–1799]*, *actor*.
A Mr Brown played the title roles in *Douglas* and *Sylvester Daggerwood* at Wheatley's Riding School, Greenwich, on 8 June 1798; the plays were given only once. In the spring of 1799 he appeared as Chicane in *The Agreeable Surprise* at the same playhouse on 17 May and may have participated in other performances there, but the bills have been lost.

Brown, Mrs *[fl. 1662]*, *actress*.
A Mrs Brown played Dorothea in *Ignoramus* on 1 November 1662 as a member of the Duke's Company at court.

Brown, Mrs *[fl. 1707]*, *actress*.
Situp in *The Double Gallant* at the Queen's Theatre in the Haymarket was played by a Mrs Brown on 1 November 1707.

Brown, Mrs *[fl. 1708]*, *dresser*.
Mrs Brown, probably related to Brown the boxkeeper of 1708, served as a dresser at the Queen's Theatre in the Haymarket at a salary of 5s. per day, according to a company list dated 8 March 1708.

Brown, Mrs *[fl. 1736–1751]*, *actress*.
On 24 March 1736 at Lincoln's Inn Fields a "Mrs Browne" (afterwards always "Brown") played Araminta in *The Confederacy* for her first appearance on any stage. Three days later at Covent Garden she was a Woman in *The City Ramble*, and on the following 23 August at the Hallam-Chapman booth at Bartholomew Fair a

Mrs Brown, probably the same woman, played Cleora in *Fair Rosamond*. The Master John Brown who acted Cupid in this work may have been her son.

On 29 December 1746 at the New Wells, Goodman's Fields, Mrs Brown was Trapes in *The Beggar's Opera*, but the bills made no other mention of her during the season. On 23 August 1749 she played Bromia in *The Descent of the Heathen Gods* at Yates's booth at Bartholomew Fair, and on 9 September 1751 she was Colombine in *Harlequin Statue* at Phillips's Southwark Fair booth. The Mr Brown who was in Phillips's company this summer and had been active since 1748, may have been her husband.

Brown, Mrs [*fl. 1764*], *actress.*

A Mrs Brown was a member of Foote's summer company at the Haymarket in 1764, her roles being Lucy in *The Minor* on 16 July, Charlotte in *The Apprentice* on the twenty-third, a role in *The Lyar* on the thirtieth, and Amaryllis in *The Rehearsal* on 20 August. The Mr Brown (fl. 1763–1764) in the company this summer was probably her husband.

Brown, Mrs [*fl. 1776–1778*], *dresser.*

A Mrs Brown served as a dresser at Drury Lane in the fall of 1776, and though the accounts contain too many Browns to be certain, she is probably the one who received a weekly wage of £1 and worked at least from 23 November 1776 to 14 November 1778.

Brown, Mrs [*fl. 1786*], *performer?*

A Mrs Brown had £5, representing two weeks' pay, omitted from her pay on 27 June 1786. A salary that high would suggest a performer, not a house servant, but just what Mrs Brown did is not clear.

Brown, Mrs [*fl. c. 1786–1787*], *singer.*

A clipping at the British Museum dated 24 December 1787 speaks of "a Mrs. Brown, formerly a singer at Sadler's Wells, a publick toast, and afterwards in keeping by a nobleman, who being reduced by age and misfortunes to pick up bones about the Streets, was turned out by Lydia Hall [an infamous landlady] when incapable by illness to walk, and after lying three days in a shed was removed to the parish workhouse."

Brown, Mrs [*fl. 1790–1797*], *actress, singer.*

Mrs Brown, billed only as "A Gentlewoman," made her first appearance on any stage on 16 June 1790 at the Haymarket Theatre playing Amelia in *The English Merchant*. A Mrs Brown, perhaps the same person, sang in the general chorus of nuns in *The Italian Monk* on 15 August 1797 at the Haymarket; singing in the chorus of assassins was a Mr Brown (fl. 1776–1799) who may have been her husband.

Brown, Mrs, née Biggs [*fl. 1798–1801*], *actress.*

Mrs Brown was the daughter of James and Sarah Biggs who had a theatrical company at Barnstaple, where she acted frequently with her sisters Anne and Binney and her brother James. On 28 August 1798 at the Haymarket Theatre, billed as "A Young Gentlewoman," she played Yarico in *Inkle and Yarico*; the *Monthly Mirror* for September 1798 identified her as Mrs Brown and reported that her "figure is good, and she delivered the dialogue with ease and propriety: but she wanted feeling and spirit in the impassioned scenes, and neither her action nor deportment were entirely free from embarassment."

This may have frightened Mrs Brown out of London, for she tried Birmingham next, on 15 September 1800, and sometime in 1800–1801 she acted Euphrasia in *The Grecian Daughter* at Hull. The *Monthly Mirror* tracked her down there and reported that "she rather failed to portray with effect the soft and affectionate tenderness of Euphrasia: neither does she appear to have sufficient dignity for the higher department of tragedy." After that, apparently, Mrs Brown gave up.

Brown, Miss, stage name of Miss Hester Sowdon. *See* JACKSON, MRS JOHN.

Brown, Miss *[fl. 1767–1778]*, dancer, actress.

A Drury Lane pay list dated 24 January 1767 has a dancer named "Brawn" down for 2s. 6d. daily or 15s. weekly. The name is otherwise unknown, and it is likely that this was the Miss Brown, also a dancer (and the only Brown of many at this time who was) on the Covent Garden pay list of 14 September 1767. There she was earning 4s. 2d. daily. The same Miss Brown may have been the girl who played Isabinda in *The Busy Body* at the China Hall, Rotherhithe, on 3 June 1778.

Brown, Miss *[fl. 1782]*, actress.

On 26 October 1782 at Drury Lane, Miss Brown made her first appearance on any stage, billed as "A Young Lady," playing Fanny in *The Maid of the Mill*. She seems not to have made any billed performances after this.

Brown, Miss *[fl. 1791]*, actress.

A Miss Brown had a role in *The Advertisement* at the Haymarket Theatre on 7 March 1791.

Brown, Abraham *[fl. 1739–1768]*, violinist, composer.

On 28 August 1739 violinist Abraham Brown became one of the original subscribers to the newly formed Royal Society of Musicians and by that time was an accomplished performer. He was given a benefit concert at Hickford's Music Room on 3 March 1740; he played first violin at a Stationers' Hall concert on 9 February 1744, at the Castle Tavern on 14 January 1745, at the Devil Tavern on 14 March, at Hickford's on 10 March 1746, and at the Haymarket Theatre on 14 March 1751. In the mid-1740's he was living in Margaret Street, near Cavendish Square. He had a benefit concert in James Street on 5 March 1752, and during this year succeeded Michael Festing at Ranelagh Gardens. Burney noted that Brown had "a clear, sprightly and loud tone, with a strong hand" but his playing consisted of *"des notes, rien que des notes"* with no real expression.

In addition to his playing at Ranelagh at this time, Brown also participated in concerts at the Swan Tavern and was a member of the King's Musick (a 22 April 1754 warrant in the Lord Chamberlain's accounts granted him £32 for livery). In May 1754 he played violin at a performance of the *Messiah* at the Foundling Hospital for a fee of £1 1s., and in 1755 he led the orchestra at the meeting of the Three Choirs in Worcester, supporting singers Bear, Wass, and Miss Turner. He was first violin at the performance of *Acis and Galatea* on 1 April 1758 in Dean Street, Soho, and in May 1758 he played in the *Messiah* again at the Foundling Hospital.

By 1763 when *Mortimer's London Directory* came out, Brown was living in Meard's Court, Dean Street, Soho, and was still serving as first violin at Ranelagh and playing in the King's band. The last mention of Brown seems to be on 19 September 1768 when musician James Nicholson empowered Brown as his attorney; both were described as musicians to the King. In Haydn's *London Notebook* under 3 August 1794 is a comment that probably concerned Abraham Brown, but one cannot be certain; Haydn met a Miss Brown at Bath, "a charming person of the best *conduit*; a good pianoforte player, her mother a most beautiful woman." These may have been Abraham's daughter and wife, but the lack of a specific mention of Brown himself leaves the matter in doubt; if Miss and Mrs Brown were in fact his family, perhaps Brown by this time was dead.

Brown, Ann. *See* CARGILL, MRS R.

Brown, Anne. *See* BARRY, MRS SPRANGER.

Brown, Miss E. [fl. 1797–1798], actress.

On 1 and 15 September 1797 Miss E. Brown was in the bills at Richmond, and in October she played at Birmingham. On 25 September the Birmingham papers had prepared the public for Miss Brown's arrival by noting that her father, the manager of the theatre at Litchfield, "has in the most cheerful manner subscribed his own and daughter's aid, whose infantile abilities have been the admiration of every audience she has appeared before."

Despite this, when she appeared as Lydia Languish in *The Rivals* at Drury Lane on 10 November 1798 (for that night only), she did not appeal to the *Monthly Mirror* critic:

A child, of the name of Brown, was injudiciously suffered to excite the commiseration of the public in the part of Lydia Languish. We have seen such little girls, and such performances, occasionally, at boarding schools, where the mistresses, more vain than wise, have authorised the representation of plays before *breaking up*. By the way, the deplorable mischief is becoming more and more prevalent in the *academies for young ladies and gentlemen* about town, and daily engendering swarms of *spouting clubs*, and *private theatres*, which every obscure alley in London is now ambitious of emulating. But, notwithstanding the youth of Miss Brown, and notwithstanding the bills, which declared it to be her *first appearance on any stage*, our pretty Miss amused herself for *a whole season*, the summer before last, on the boards of the Richmond theatre.

After this blast, Miss E. Brown seems to have faded into obscurity where she perhaps belonged.

Brown, Henry *d. 1770, actor.*

In 1751–52 Henry Brown managed Simpson's "playroom" at Bath, and the house became known as "Mr Brown's theatre." Either before or after this he was in Ireland, for when he made his first appearance in London on 23 February 1753 at Drury Lane playing Richard III, he was noted as being "from Ireland and Bath." He was not successful in London, and Cross jotted down in his diary that the actor was "very bad, but no hissing." Brown seems to have given only this single performance in London, after which he had a theatre at Chester. By 27 November 1756 he was at Bath again, to which he may have returned as early as 1754.

By this time he had achieved the nickname of the Copper Captain, having acted that role in *Rule a Wife and Have a Wife* at Bath with some success. On 1 December 1757 he made his Edinburgh debut, after which he went to Ireland to play at the Smock Alley Theatre. The *Thespian Dictionary* (1805) reported that Brown was much esteemed as a comedian and succeeded Sheridan as the Smock Alley manager. With Dublin as his home base, he journeyed to Edinburgh again to play Abel Drugger in *The Alchemist* on 3 January 1758, was a frequent performer at Cork, and appeared briefly at Belfast, Newry, and Kilkenny. About 1770 or perhaps earlier, Brown married the actress Miss E. Slack, and probably the daughter of this union was the "Miss Browne" who married John Jackson. According to *Faulkner's Dublin Journal* of 27 February 1770, Henry Brown died shortly before at Glasgow.

The *Thespian Dictionary* stated that Brown had a treacherous memory, but he had "a peculiar *laugh* which always put the audience into good humour, and gave himself sufficient time for recollection."

Brown, Mrs Henry. *See* SLACK, MISS E.

Brown, J. *d. 1818, actor, acrobat, singer.*

Mr J. Brown made his Irish debut at the Crow Street Theatre on 18 January 1776 in *Cymon*, billed as "A Gentleman." From Dublin he seems to have gone to Norwich, where he acted from 1778 to 1782 (with trips to Cork in October 1779 and Plymouth in July 1780, apparently). At Norwich he was earning a guinea and a half weekly. In 1781 he married the widow of William Ross, who brought him two daughters, Frances Mary and Anna, and who in time bore him a son, John Mills Brown, who was to have a performing career in America in the following century. In 1782–83 and 1783–84 the Browns acted with the Bath-Bristol company, but they left that group before 26 May 1784 and joined the troupe at York. On 2 April there the Browns shared a benefit, and to dazzle his audience Brown, as Harlequin, flew from the stage to the upper gallery and returned "head foremost" to the back of the stage; to prove there was no deception, he took off his hat and threw it to the spectators in the pit as he ascended. He was a specialist at leaps, too, and in another sequence in *Neck or Nothing, or Harlequin's Flight to the Gods* in which the drawbridge at Hull was scenically depicted, Brown leaped over the bridge when it was drawn up. Later in the performance he jumped into a stage window seven feet off the floor.

The Browns played at Hull in 1784, at Norwich in 1785–86, and in January 1786 they came to London for an engagement at Covent Garden. Brown's salary was £2 10s. weekly, and his first London appearance was as Coupée in *The Virgin Unmasked* on 31 January, replacing the ill Edwin. Brown completed the season playing Lord Sparkle in *Which Is the Man?* on 16 February, Young Meadows in *Love in a Village* on

16 March, Ballad in *The Country Madcap* on 9 May, a role in *Small Talk* on 11 May, and the Squire in *Poor Vulcan!* on 30 May.

He returned to Covent Garden for the 1786–87 season, playing such roles as Captain Belville in *Rosina*, Dick in *Hob in the Well*, Harlequin in *The Enchanted Castle*, Sparkish (with a song) in *The Country Girl*, and Lovel in *High Life Below Stairs*. When he and Mrs Brown had their benefit on 18 May 1787, they advertised that tickets would be available from them at No 147, Drury Lane, and that Brown would play Vane in *The Chapter of Accidents*, deliver Goldsmith's epilogue in the character of Harlequin, and "conclude with a Leap eight feet high." In 1787–88 Brown acted, among other parts, Simon Pure in *A Bold Stroke for a Wife*, Sly in *The Cheats of Scapin*, a footman in *She Stoops to Conquer*, Fag in *The Rivals*, and the title role (for his benefit on 16 May 1788 only) in *Cymon*. At this performance he also played Jupiter in *The Royal Chace* and spoke an occasional epilogue written by his stepdaughter Miss Ross. Miss Ross also contributed to the evening by playing Sylvia in *Cymon*.

In late summer the Browns, with Miss Ross, went to Plymouth for an engagement; he played Captain Greville in *The Flitch of Bacon*, Careless (with a song) in *The School for Scandal*, and Gibbet in *The Beaux' Stratagem*, among other parts, in August and September 1788. In November he was playing at the Crow Street Theatre in Dublin, and he reappeared briefly at Covent Garden on 5 June 1789 to be a footman again in *She Stoops to Conquer*—apparently as a replacement for an ailing actor. In 1790 he was back in Ireland, playing at Limerick and Ennis. He also acted at Norwich this year; and beginning in August 1791 he was with the Theatre Royal at York again, where he remained through the fall of 1794. The last record of him appears to be on 18 March 1795 when he was acting at Belfast. The following year the Browns' son Henry, billed as "The Child of Promise," age eight, excited the interest of Belfast playgoers, and perhaps with the beginning of his son's career, Mr J. Brown withdrew from the scene. He died in 1818.

Brown, Mrs J., née Mills, formerly Mrs William Ross   *d. 1823, actress, singer.*

Mrs J. Brown was born Miss Mills, the sister of the Covent Garden actor John, of Mrs Chalmers who also acted at Covent Garden, and of Mrs Sparks of Edinburgh. She married William Ross and by him had two daughters; one of the daughters, Frances Mary (1765–1855), later became Mrs Thomas Shaftoe Robertson, and the other, Anna (born 1773), became the wife of the younger John Brunton. As Mrs Ross, our subject acted at Norwich from 1774 to 1780, but she made a trip to Ireland in

Harvard Theatre Collection
MRS J. BROWN, as Grace
by Prattent

1779 to play at the Crow Street theatre and at Cork. William Ross died shortly before 7 February 1781, when the Norwich Committee Books show a payment to his widow of £5 to cover Ross's funeral expenses.

She remarried sometime in 1781, to J. Brown, an actor and singer who had performed with her in the Norwich company. One of her earliest mentions as Mrs Brown seems to be a bill for *The Miniature Picture* on 12 August 1782 when the Norwich troupe was playing at Colchester. The Browns went to Bath from 1782 to 1784 and then to York, Hull, and back to Norwich by 1785–86. On 28 January 1786 she played Prue in *Love for Love* as her first appearance in London at Covent Garden. The *London Gazette* wrote that

The lady has a good figure with a face highly expressive, and a voice full of musical sweetness. She is an experienced actress, and comes before the London audience enriched by study as well as nature, with the requisite endowments for her profession. . . . In person she is short and plump; in countenance and features lively and pleasing; in voice clear, interesting and effective; and in manner, action, and deportment, perfectly easy and unembarrassed.

The reviewer went on to note that the Mills family from which Mrs Brown stemmed virtually had formed a full acting company in themselves in earlier years and had played in most of the towns in the north of England.

Mrs Brown imitated Mrs Jordan in her style of acting, but, as Genest noted, she was no competition for the younger and well-established comedienne. During the spring of 1786 after her London debut, Mrs Brown acted Miss Lucy in *The Virgin Unmasked*, Audrey in *As You Like It*, the title role in *The Country Wife*, Miss Biddy in *Miss in her Teens*, Miss Pendragon in *Which Is the Man?*, Miss Notable in *The Lady's Last Stake*, Mary the Buxom in

Barataria, Catalina in *The Castle of Anda-lusia*, and Miss Dolly in *Fontainbleau*.

The Browns were re-engaged in 1786–87 at Covent Garden, Mrs Brown receiving a salary of £2 10s. weekly. During the season she repeated most of her old roles, and her new offerings were in a similar line: Margery in *Love in a Village*, Grace in *Poor Vulcan!*, Miss Jenny in *The Provoked Husband*, Nell in *The Devil to Pay*, and Bridget in *The Chapter of Accidents*. During the summer she (without her husband) acted at the Haymarket Theatre as Fanny in *A Mogul Tale*, Maud in *Peeping Tom*, Comfit in *The Dead Alive*, and other roles.

Mrs Brown's last London season was 1787–88 at Covent Garden; and for her benefit with her husband on 16 May 1788 her daughter, Anna Ross, joined Mr Brown in *Cymon* and also wrote a special epilogue for him to speak; oddly, Mrs Brown seems not to have participated in the performance. Her last London role was on 2 June when she again played Grace in *Poor Vulcan!*

Harvard Theatre Collection
MRS J. BROWN, as Biddy Bellair
artist unknown

In the late summer of 1788 the Browns were at Plymouth, Mrs Brown acting Letty in *Tit for Tat*, Mary Buxom, Charlotte in her daughter Anna's play *The Cottagers*, the title role in *The Romp*, and Cherry in *The Beaux' Stratagem*. The Browns then went to York to play in Tate Wilkinson's company from 1790–91 through the summer of 1793. During this last year she was not well, and her benefit on 2 May with her husband was a late one due to her indisposition "since the commencement of the season." During 1794–95 she was at Belfast, where for her benefit on 27 February 1795 she delivered an address and sang a comic song and during the season entertained patrons with a number of roles usually reserved for men. That year saw her little son Henry's debut. In 1796 Mrs Brown played at Belfast and Derry, after which she may have retired from the stage.

Four engravings of Mrs J. Brown are known. One, by an anonymous engraver, is a formal portrait; a second, by Prattent, depicts her as Grace in *Poor Vulcan!* and was published on 1 March 1786 in the *Lady's Magazine*; a third by Stothard and Scott, shows her as Lucy in *The Virgin Unmasked* and was published on 30 June 1786 in *New English Theatre*; and the fourth, by an anonymous engraver, pictures her as Miss Biddy in *Miss in Her Teens*.

Brown, James [*fl. 1794*], *trumpeter.*
Doane listed James Brown, of No 44, George Street, Portman Square, as a trumpeter who participated in concerts presented by the New Musical Fund in 1794.

Brown, John [*fl. 1732–1736*], *singer, actor.*
Though the John Brown and Master Brown of the 1730's may have been two people, it would appear that they are one and the same. John Brown was billed as singing Mordecai and the Israelite Boy in *Esther* at the Crown and Anchor Tavern in the Strand on 23 February 1732. On

20 March 1733 at the Haymarket Theatre a Brown, apparently Master Brown, played James in *The Mock Doctor*, and on 21 and 26 March he was the Pedlar in *Love Runs All Dangers*. On 28 September of this year a Master Brown played Julio in *The Harlot's Progress* at the Room in Artichoke Yard at Mile End Green; and on 23 August 1736 Master Brown was Cupid in *Fair Rosamond* and the Page in *The Modern Pimp* at the Hallam-Chapman Bartholomew Fair booth. When Master Brown played Cupid a Mrs Brown was Cleora; this may have been his mother, and, if so, his father may have been the Mr Brown who flourished 1748–51.

Brown, [Owen?] [*fl.* 1794], *actor.*

Billed as "A Young Gentleman," a Mr Brown made his first appearance on any stage at Covent Garden, playing Jack Conner in *The Prisoner at Large*. The *Thespian Magazine* identified him as Brown and commented that the young actor "seemed to think an acquaintance with the performers, and chattering with them, were sufficient to recommend him to the public notice." After this, Brown apparently did not act again, unless he could be identified as Owen Brown, who signed a receipt for performances at Covent Garden in 1808.

Brown, Sarah 1757–1806, *dancer.*

Mrs Sarah Brown apparently joined the Drury Lane company as a dancer in 1774–75, and in 1775 she subscribed 10s. 6d. to the pension fund. She worked during the 1776–77 season for £1 weekly, and in 1785 she started claiming her pension, having, presumably, retired. She died on 5 December 1806 at the age of 49.

Brown, Thomas [*fl.* 1715–1740], *violinist, composer.*

Thomas Brown, "fidler," was noted in the parish registers of St Giles, Cripplegate, as having a daughter Elizabeth by his wife Anne, born on 29 February and baptized

on 8 March 1721. Their son Thomas was born on 21 July and baptized on 12 August 1722; a daughter Ann was born on 11 December 1722 and baptized on 5 January 1723 (though this is possibly another Thomas Brown's child); and a son James was born on 31 January and baptized on 28 February 1725. This Thomas Brown was possibly the composer who had several songs published between 1715 and 1740, including *Love is Lost* (c. 1715), *Bacchus's Feast* (c. 1720, sung by Mr Platt at Sadler's Wells), and *Return, my lovely Nymph* (c. 1740).

Brown, Thomas [*fl.* 1794], *singer.*

In 1794 Doane listed Thomas Brown, of Bear Street, Leicester Square, as a participant in oratorios at Drury Lane and concerts presented by the Choral Fund and the Handelian Society.

Brown, William [*fl.* 1789–1794], *violoncellist.*

The parish records of Christ Church, Spitalfields, for 1789 show that William and Susannah Brown had a child baptized that year; Brown was described as a musician. Doane, in 1794, listed him as a violoncellist who played at Cecilian Society concerts.

Browne. *See also* BROWN.

Browne, Mr [*fl.* 1749–1756], *house servant?*

A Mr Browne (once spelled Browse) was noted in the Covent Garden accounts and bills from 29 September 1749, when he was paid 3s. 4d. for two days work, through 24 May 1756, when he had a shared benefit. The various references to him over the years do not specify his duties, but he was probably a minor house servant.

Browne, Charles [*ff.* 1739], *musician.*

Charles Browne, a professional musician, was one of the original subscribers to the

Royal Society of Musicians when it formed on 28 August 1739.

Browne, Matthew Campbell [fl. 1778–1806], actor.

It is probable that the Mr Browne who appeared at Richmond, Surrey, in mid-June 1778, billed as from Bath, was Matthew Campbell Browne. Clark places him at the Crow Street Theatre, Dublin, in 1779, billed as from Edinburgh, after which, in the fall of 1779, he acted at Cork. By 1780 he had returned to Bath, where he played until 1784, except for a Capel Street, Dublin, appearance in 1782. By 22 January 1785 he was again in Ireland, making his Smock Alley debut, billed as from Bath; then he went to Norwich, where, on 6 August 1785, he was hailed as from Dublin. On 11 January 1786 he appeared for the first time at Hull and was referred to as from Bath and previously of Dublin and Edinburgh. By July 1786 he had returned to Richmond, and it was from there that he was described as coming when he finally made his London debut on 18 May 1787 at the Haymarket Theatre as Hamlet.

The *Thespian Dictionary* (1805), in noting his London appearance, observed that he was said to have come originally from America. Browne spent the summer at the Haymarket, playing Benedict in *Much Ado About Nothing*, Major Cyprus in *I'll Tell You What!*, Count Almaviva in *The Spanish Barber*, Beril in *The Two Connoisseurs*, Frederick Wayward in *The County Attorney*, Jaffeir in *Venice Preserved*, and the title role in *Comus*. He acted Jaffeir for his benefit, advertising that tickets would be available from him at No 13, King Street, Covent Garden. On 25 July 1787 he refused to play Clifford in *Henry II*, whereupon Williamson took the role and Browne finished his London visit.

In 1789 he played at Cork and Waterford in Ireland, and perhaps after this he left the stage to follow other interests. On 22 September 1795 a report appeared in the London papers that "*Matthew Brown* the Actor who was suppos'd to have some Connection with the Scotch Convention is now in the Metropolis." His business in London was not reported.

Browne returned to the London stage for one appearance only, on 27 November 1801. He was much heralded: the *Monthly Mirror* in October 1799 announced that "A Mr. Brown, who formerly played at Bath with great applause, and at the Haymarket when Palmer commenced the Royalty undertaking [1787], is shortly to appear at this theatre." Which theatre was meant is unclear, but on 27 November 1801 it was on the Covent Garden stage that Brown finally did appear. The December *Monthly Mirror* reported the event:

Besides the novelty of Mr. Cooke in the part of Stukely, a gentleman of the name of BROWNE, who, at the time Mr. Palmer embarked on the Royalty scheme, filled that actor's situation at the Haymarket with great respectability, made his first appearance on the Covent-Garden stage, in Mr. Beverly [in *The Gamester*], and was received with the most flattering applause. Mr. Browne delivered the text with the most critical propriety, and, throughout the whole character, displayed very superior judgment, and strong sensibility. . . . Mr. Browne, in countenance and person, reminded us a good deal of the late Mr. Farren, and the tones of his voice occasionally resembled Mr. Wroughton's. He trod the stage with freedom, his action was unrestrained and judicious, and his manner and appearance were very much those of a gentleman. Mr. Browne's time of life is, perhaps, a little too advanced for the representative of Mr. Beverly, whose addiction to gaming is only entitled to compassion as the vice of a young man; but there are many characters in which the circumstance would prove rather serviceable, than otherwise, to Mr. B's reputation as an actor.

After this encouragement, one might expect to find Browne's name popping up regularly in the bills thereafter, but the only other notice of him seems to be for 7 August 1806 at Windsor when he played an unspecified role in either *The Stranger* or *The Agreeable Surprise*.

Matthew Campbell Browne's wife Tabitha, born Donner, was buried on 28 June 1801 at St Mary, Lambeth; she seems not to have been a performer (it appears that the Mrs Brown who acted during Matthew's London summer season was a different woman).

Browne, Rachell [*fl.* 1666–1670], tirewoman.

During the 1666–67 season Rachell Browne was a tirewoman for the King's Company at the Bridges Street playhouse; on 29 January 1670 she was cited in the same capacity but designated a widow. She is the earliest of several Browns (or Brownes) who were house servants at theatres, and though the name is a very common one, perhaps some of these folk were related.

Browne, Richard [*fl.* 1670–1675], violinist.

The Richard Browne, violinist, who was admitted to the King's Musick on 5 December 1670 may have been the same as the organist and composer of later decades. The violinist was admitted without fee to serve in the absence of Henry Comer, but he was still serving on 21 February 1672, and Comer's salary was finally stopped and given to him. This apparently amounted to giving him a permanent position, for later mentions of him do not suggest he was thought of as a replacement. On 4 July 1674 he and other musicians were directed to practice under Monsieur Cambert at the Whitehall theatre and to perform shortly after that at Windsor for the King's pleasure. The last notice of Browne was a payment for a group of musicians who had played at Windsor from 18 May to 3 September 1674 in the chapel. It would appear

that Browne had split his time this summer between London and Windsor.

Browne, Thomas [*fl.* 1675–1683], violinist.

On 15 February 1675 Thomas Browne played violin in the court masque *Calisto* as one of the regular band of 24; he was probably the Thomas Browne who was sworn a Gentleman of the Chapel Royal extraordinary (without fee until a permanent position became available) in 1683.

Brownhill, Thomas Robson. *See* ROBSON, THOMAS.

Browning, Mr [1784], bassoonist.

Mr Browning played bassoon at the Handel Memorial Concerts at Westminster Abbey and the Pantheon on 26, 27, 29 May and 3, 5, June 1784. He may have been the Browning who worked at Covent Garden in 1785–86.

Browning, Mr [*fl.* 1785–86], house servant? bassoonist?

One Browning was paid £1 5s. per week at Covent Garden during the 1785–86 season; his name was noted for payments in the account books on 24 September and again the following 8 April. Judging from the salary, Browning may have been a house servant, but if he is to be identified with Browning the bassoonist of 1784, he doubtless played in the theatre band.

Browning, Miss [*fl.* 1785–1786], singer, dancer.

On 23 September 1785 Miss Browning was a bacchante in *Comus* at Covent Garden; four days later she was a figure dancer in a pantomime dance at Astley's; on 5 October she performed in a burletta there; and on 17 October she was part of the singing chorus in Act V of *The Roman Father* at Covent Garden. Her last stage appearance seems to have been at a performance of this last piece on 9 January 1786.

Brownsmith, John [fl. 1751–1779], prompter, actor, author.

John Brownsmith worked at Norwich in 1751 and the Jacob's Wells summer theatre at Bristol in 1754 before joining the Drury Lane company for the 1757–58 season. At Drury Lane he was an assistant to Cross the prompter and also played occasional small roles, his first recorded one being a servant in *The Gamesters* on 22 December 1757. On 9 May 1758 he shared a benefit with at least five others, so his standing in the company was not high. In 1758–59 he acted such parts as Tribulation in *The Alchemist*, the Captain in *Chrononhotonthologos*, a servant in *The Heiress*, and Goodwill in *The Virgin Unmask'd*.

Brownsmith's whereabouts for the next several years are not certain, though it is probable that he stayed at Drury Lane during the winters as under-prompter, taking over from Cross in January 1760 and continuing until Hopkins was made prompter in 1762. After this he may again have worked as an assistant prompter for several more years. It is odd, however, that no further roles are recorded for him at Drury Lane, for if he was on the staff there one would expect to find that he acted occasionally. During the summers he went out of London for employment, his name being connected with the theatre at Bath in 1759 and at Salisbury in 1776.

He began turning some of his experiences into books in 1759, his first effort being *The Dangers of a Lee Shore* in which he identified himself as late prompter at the Bath theatre. In this work he detailed his difficulties with the manager John Lee; he also mentioned a Mrs "B********h" whom one takes to be the prompter's wife. Brownsmith complained bitterly about the slave wages Lee paid, how Mrs Brownsmith was treated like a neophyte despite her 12

years of acting experience, and how she was ultimately discharged. Judging by a reference in the work to a 24 November that fell on a Saturday, the Brownsmiths were working at Bath in the winter of either 1759 or 1753, the latter being more probable in view of the publication date of the work. Mrs Brownsmith, though she may have acted in the provinces for some time, apparently never appeared in London.

In 1767 three more works by Brownsmith were published. *The Theatrical Alphabet* contained a list of several hundred parts in popular plays of the time with an indication of the type of play and the number of "lengths" or sides to the role—a device which Brownsmith hoped would assist theatre managers and performers in determining how long it might take for an actor to prepare a part. The second 1767 publication by Brownsmith was *The Rescue, or Thespian Scourge*, written in Hudibrastic verse and commenting on the poem *Thespis*. The last work was *The Dramatic Time-Piece: or Perpetual Monitor*. This handy volume provided theatre folk with the running-times of the acts of most of the popular plays done at the London theatres.

During the summer of 1767 Brownsmith joined Foote's company at the Haymarket Theatre, serving as prompter and playing such parts as Thrifty in *The Cheats of Scapin*, Charon in *Lethe*, Poundage in *The Provoked Husband*, and Sir Gregory Gazette in *The Knights*. He joined Foote again in the summer of 1768 but played only one role that was mentioned in the bills: La Fleur in *The Commissary*. On 19 September 1768 he was Tom Thimble in *The Rehearsal*. He apparently did not work with Foote in the summer of 1769, but he was with him in 1770 and acted Dr Catgut in *The Commissary* on 18 May. His last work in London for a while was during the winter season of 1770–71 at the Haymarket Theatre; he prompted and acted Mixum in *The Vintner Tricked*, Sir Francis Gripe in *The Busy Body*, and Priuli in *Venice Preserved* (one of his rare appearances in a serious work).

It is likely that he left London after this, for when he was there he certainly made his presence noticed. The next record of him occurred in 1776 when his pamphlet *The Contrast* was published. This was "a Peep behind the curtain of the Salisbury Theatre, in 1776" by the "Late *Nominal* Prompter to the said Theatre." He returned to the Haymarket in London to prompt in the 1776–77 season, and though no roles were noted for him, he played Poundage in *The Provoked Husband* the next season, on 18 September 1778. He worked through the summer of 1779 and on 18 October 1779, when the new theatrical season began, Brownsmith's first play was produced at the Haymarket: *The Touchstone of Invention; or, The Soldier's Fortune*, an alteration of Otway. Brownsmith probably continued working at the Haymarket as prompter during the rest of the 1779–80 season, though the records contain no further mention of him after the premiere of his play.

Browse. *See* **BROWNE, MR** [*fl.* 1749–1756].

Bruce, Mr [*fl.* 1794–1795], *doorkeeper.*
One Bruce was doorkeeper at Covent Garden in 1794–95 at a salary of 12*s.* weekly.

Bruce, Mrs [*fl.* 1705–1706], *dancer.*
Advertised as a student of Mrs Elford, Mrs Bruce made her first appearance at Lincoln's Inn Fields Theatre on 28 September 1705. Starting on 2 January 1706 she danced at the Queen's Theatre in the Haymarket, sharing a benefit with Young and l'Abbé there on 29 May; on that date she spoke the epilogue to *The Unhappy Favorite*—her first and apparently last vocal appearance in public. She danced again on 29 June 1706 at the Queen's and then faded into obscurity.

Bruce, William [*fl.* 1730–1751], *musician.*
The baptismal records of St George in the East, Stepney, identify William Bruce as a musician and list his addresses over the years. In 1730 and 1732 he was noted as living at Mayfields Buildings, in 1738 in Church Lane, in 1749 off Ratcliff Highway, and in 1751 in Denmark Street.

Brucker, Mr [*fl.* 1795], *house servant?*
One Brucker (or Bracker?) was noted in the Drury Lane accounts on 25 April 1795 as receiving a wage of 1*s.* 5*d.*—presumably for one day's work.

Brudnal, Mr [*fl.* 1753], *actor.*
Mr Brudnal was a member of the summer company playing at Richmond in 1753, but what roles he may have acted are not known.

Brugier. *See* **BRUGUIER.**

Brugner, Mr [*fl.* 1766–1767], *lobby doorkeeper.*
One Brugner was paid 2*s.* per day as lobby doorkeeper at Covent Garden in the 1766–67 season; the accounts are somewhat unclear, and it may be that there were two people of this name, both lobby doorkeepers.

Bruguier, Anthony [*fl.* 1786–1798], *dancing master.*
Anthony Bruguier became the Sadler's Wells dancing master in 1786, a position which he retained for at least the following 12 years. He had two or perhaps three dancing daughters: Sophia and Susan, who appeared in London and Birmingham, and (though her relationship is conjectural) a Miss E. Bruguier who is known to have performed only at Birmingham. Anthony presumably trained his daughters.

A Miss "Bruquier"—probably Sophia or Susan—played a principal character in *Maedea's Kettle, or Harlequin Renovated* at Sadler's Wells on 9 April 1792, the earliest notice of one of the girls performing in public. At Birmingham in 1797 Miss E. Bruguier danced, and she was joined by either Sophia or Susan or perhaps both. Sophia and Susan danced at Sadler's Wells in the summer of 1798, and one of the girls was Columbine on 19 September in an unnamed piece. Due to an economy move by the Wells manager Richard Hughes, Anthony, Sophia, and Susan received, jointly, only £4 4s. weekly for their work.

On 23 April 1799 at Covent Garden a Miss "Brugier"—again probably Sophia or Susan—danced in *The Highland Lovers*; and on 14 May she did *Del Caro's Hornpipe* as a solo. One of the Bruguier girls was at the Birmingham theatre on 4 June 1799 dancing *The Drunken Swiss* with Mr West.

Bruguier, Sophia ₍*fl.* 1798–1799₎, *dancer. See* BRUGUIER, ANTHONY.

Bruguier, Susan ₍*fl.* 1798–1799₎, *dancer. See* BRUGUIER, ANTHONY.

Bruillier. *See* BOURRELIER.

Bruley. *See* BEWLEY.

Brumen, Miss ₍*fl.* 1794₎, *singer.*
Miss Brumen sang in the Handel oratorio performances at Covent Garden from 7 March to 11 April 1794, but the bills did not mention any specific songs for her; one can assume she was in the chorus. Doane's *Musical Directory* of 1794 listed her as living in Pimlico Terrace and noted that she also participated in concerts at Westminster Abbey.

Brumley. *See* BRINLEY.

Brummell, William ₍*fl.* 1785?₎, *performer?*
William Brummell, probably a performer at the King's Theatre in the Haymarket about 1784–85, was a defendant in a Chancery trial connected with the finances of the theatre. This was probably, though not certainly, the trial described in *The London Stage* (the 1784–85 season introduction) in which the opera manager Gallini was involved.

Brumoro. *See* BRUNORO.

Brun or Brunn. *See* LE BRUN.

Brunatti, Antonio ₍*fl.* 1663–1667₎, *scenekeeper.*
Antonio Brunatti was probably active with the King's Company from 1663–64 through 1666–67, but he was mentioned in the records only at the beginning and end of this period. A warrant dated 12 July 1664 designated him a scenekeeper, and it is possible he was related to the painter Brunetti of the eighteenth century.

"Brunette." *See* CARGILL, MRS.

Brunette, Miss ₍*fl.* 1734–1742₎, *actress, dancer.*
Miss Brunette made her first appearance on any stage at Lincoln's Inn Fields on 12 October 1734 as Rose in *The Recruiting Officer*. For a newcomer and a girl who was probably still in her minority, Miss Brunette was kept very busy indeed during her first year. She was a country lass in *The Rape of Proserpine* on 30 December 1734 (evidence that she had some dancing ability), Lettice in *The School Boy* on 9 May 1735, Maria in *The London Merchant* on 15 July, Jenny in *The Provoked Husband* on 18 July, the maid in *The Anatomist* on 1 August, Jenny in *The Beggar's Opera* on 12 August, Combrush in *The Honest Yorkshireman* on 14 August, the Nut Woman in *Bartholomew Fair* on 25 August, Cherry

in *The Stratagem* on 26 August, Tom Thumb in *The Tragedy of Tragedies* on 2 September (suggesting that she was petite), and Corinna in *The Carnival* on 5 September. Her winter season performances were at Covent Garden or Lincoln's Inn Fields (the company used both playhouses); during July and August she was at the Haymarket Theatre; and the September appearances were at Lincoln's Inn Fields.

The London Stage erroneously places Miss Brunette at the Haymarket Theatre in 1735–36, but she was with the Covent Garden troupe, earning a flat salary; British Museum clippings show Miss Brunette was allowed 172 nights at only 20*d.* per night or £14 6*s.* 8*d.*; she received no benefit. During the season she was mentioned as being in *The Rape of Proserpine* again, and she also played a peasant in *Apollo and Daphne*, a nymph in *The Royal Chace*, Arabella in *The Committee*, and Betty in *The Happy Lovers*; this season she did not continue acting into the summer, but her roles remained as before—pretty young girls and small parts in pantomimes. In the 1736–37 season she added a few new roles: Lesbia in *Achilles*, Lucy in *Wit Without Money*, Caelia in *The Woman Captain*, Mrs Vixen in *The Beggar's Opera*, Prue in *Three Hours after Marriage*, and Charlotte in *The Mock Doctor*. By the end of the season she was living at Mr Heath's, the auctioneer, at the Golden Head in Hart Street, Covent Garden.

Miss Brunette is not recorded for any parts in the fall of 1737, and she played infrequently in the spring of 1738. Her 1738–39 season at Covent Garden, on the other hand, was a busy one, and she added a number of roles to her repertory, though few of any size: Lucy in *Oroonoko,* Advocate in *The Fair Quaker of Deal*, Mincing in *The Way of the World*, Lucia in *The Cheats of Scapin*, Lucia in *The Squire of Alsatia*, Flora in *Don Quixote*, Honoria in *Love Makes a Man*, Ursula in *Much Ado*

about Nothing, and Teresa in *The Spanish Friar* were among her new parts. She continued in the same pattern in 1739–40, staying with many of her earlier roles, especially Rose in *The Recruiting Officer*, and adding such others as Myrtilla in *The Provoked Husband*, Delia in *Theodosius*, Pert in *The Man of Mode*, Prue in *Love for Love*, Loveit in *The Provoked Wife*, and Isabinda in *The Busy Body*.

By the 1740–41 season she was earning 4*s.* 2*d.* daily and each spring was given benefit tickets to sell but she had obviously fallen into a rather rigid pattern. The thought of spending the rest of her career playing such tiny roles as Mincing may have led her, near the end of the 1740–41 season, to take her slender talents to Drury Lane. She first appeared at the elder house on 28 May 1741 playing Trusty in *The Provoked Husband*. During 1741–42, however, she played few billed roles at Drury Lane, and only two were new ones: Peggy in *The King and the Miller of Mansfield* and Lucinda in *The Conscious Lovers*. She started the next season at Drury Lane, playing Charlotte in *The Mock Doctor* on 11 September 1742, but within two months she had joined Giffard's troupe at Lincoln's Inn Fields. With this company she acted Edging in *The Careless Husband* on 24 November, Scentwell in *The Busy Body* on 29 November, Mrs Chat in *The Committee* on 1 December, and Parthenope in *The Rehearsal* on 6 December. After this, no new parts are mentioned for her in the bills, and when Giffard's project floundered before the end of the 1742–43 season, Miss Brunette seems to have given up her stage career.

Brunetti, Gaetano *d. 1758, scene painter.*

Gaetano Brunetti collaborated with Amiconi on decorative paintings and is said to have painted scenery for the King's Theatre in the Haymarket in the first half of the eighteenth century. He died in 1758.

Brunetti may have been related to the Restoration scenekeeper Brunatti.

Brunetts, Mons [fl. 1675], *manager?*

Monsieur Brunetts—if that is his correct name, for it looks neither French nor Italian and may be misspelled—was named to receive the goods shipped to England by Fiorelli's troupe of comedians. The warrant, dated 20 June 1675, permitted the goods, probably costumes and properties, to pass custom free and be delivered into Brunetts's hands: the goods were allowed a similar free export on 4 October. Brunetts may have been the company manager or possibly one of the actors assigned to look after the troupe's belongings.

Bruni, Domenico [fl. 1793], *singer.*

Domenico (not Gaetano) Bruni was engaged by the King's Theatre in the Haymarket for the period 5 February to 15 June 1793 at £1800. He made his first appearance in England as Clearco in *I giuochi d'Agrigento* on 5 February, and the *Morning Chronicle* reported the next day that the new male soprano "justified every expectation that was formed of him. His voice has exquisite sweetness and considerable volume . . . One admirable recommendation is that he sings perfectly in tune; which we hope he will continue to do." Perhaps Bruni did not so continue, for Mount-Edgcumbe, who had heard him before at Florence, said "He certainly was improved since that time, but still he was very weak and poor in comparison with his predecessors." Bruni sang only two more roles during the season, Agilulfo in *Teodolinda*, which opened on 19 March, and Odenato in *Odenato and Zenobia* on 11 June. Parke found Bruni's singing "chaste and expressive. If he did not surprise like Mara, he gratified by his plaintive melody." Doane's *Musical Directory* of 1794 noted that Bruni lived in London at No 2, Union Street, Lambeth, and in addition to his ap-

pearances at the King's Theatre participated in the Concert of Ancient Music, Salomon's Concert, the Professional Concert, and, in Oxford, the Oxford Meeting. After his season in London, perhaps Bruni returned to the opera house in Milan, whence he had come.

Brunn, Mr [fl. 1775–1778], *puppeteer, dancer.*

On 5 November 1775 Antonio Ambroise and a Mr Brunn (possibly an error for Le Brun) announced the opening of an *Ombres Chinoises* repertory at the Great Room in Panton Street, saying that their show had been played the previous February before Louis XVI. Their season in London lasted through April and consisted of sketches and episodes with musical accompaniment; among the pieces in the Ambroise-Brunn repertory were *The Metamorphosis of a Magician, African Lion Hunt, Storm at Sea, and Escape of a Highwayman from Prison.*

The partners returned in the winter of 1776–77 to Panton Street, now billed as the *Original Ombres Chinoises* so that patrons could distinguish them from the rival Braville-Meniucci company. They performed through July 1777. After this the pair apparently separated and Brunn went to Ireland; he returned in March 1778 with at least some of the numbers he had presented in Dublin: *The Broken Bridge, The Carpenter's Shop,* and *The Spanish Bull Fight.* As a diversion, Brunn also appeared on the slack wire, but his *pièce de résistance* was a Spanish castanet dance which he performed, blindfolded, through a pattern of eggs laid on the stage—without breaking any.

Brunoro, Signor [fl. 1742], *dancer.*

On 9 October 1742 Signor Brunoro (or Brumoro)—not to be confused with his fellow dancer Boromeo—made his first appearance at Drury Lane dancing in two new comic pieces, *La Mascarade* and *Les*

Matelotes. He was billed as making his first appearance at that playhouse, but there seems to be no record of his previous activity. On 25 October he and others did *The Turkish Seraglio*. His engagement at the theatre may have been a limited one, for he was not named in any of the new dances introduced later in the season, and perhaps he left Drury Lane about November 1742.

Brunsdon, John ₁*fl. 1774–1781*₁, actor.

When John Brunsdon made his first appearance in London as Marplot "(with an address to the Town)" in *The Busy Body* at the Haymarket Theatre on 24 January 1774, he was billed as being from the Edinburgh theatre. How long he may have performed at Edinburgh before this date is not certain. On his London debut night he also played Young Philpot in *The Citizen*, after which he apparently left the big city for a few years. In the summer of 1774 he was at Bristol, playing Sir Brilliant Fashion in *The Way to Keep Him* at the King Street Theatre on 20 July, and sometime in 1775 he was apparently performing at Bath.

In 1778–79 he was back in London and joined the Covent Garden company at £1 5s. weekly for two seasons. His first role was Razor in *The Provoked Wife* on 25 September 1778, after which he played frequently in comic parts, especially in afterpieces. He was, to cite a few examples, the Gentleman Usher in *King Lear*, Tattoo in *The Invasion*, Sancho in *Love Makes a Man*, the Music Master in *Catherine and Petruchio*, Dromio of Syracuse in *The Comedy of Errors*, Bronze in *The Liverpool Prize*, Quillet in *Illumination*, and Thicket in *The Chelsea-Pensioner*. He continued in many of these parts in 1779–80 and added such roles as Lord Heartless in *Plymouth in an Uproar*, La Pierre in *The Shepherdess of the Alps*, the French Valet in *The Belle's Stratagem*, Captain Strutt in *The Double Gallant*, and (his last Covent

Harvard Theatre Collection

JOHN BRUNSDON, as Dromio

artist unknown

Garden appearance) Brush in *All in the Wrong* on 17 May 1780.

On 23 January 1781, billed as from Covent Garden, Brunsdon made his Irish debut at the Smock Alley Theatre, and a year later he was at Bath. There he was Perez in *The Mourning Bride* on 9 February and Gradus in *Who's the Dupe?* on 21 March 1782. During this season he also performed at Bristol again, playing his usual line of sparks.

An anonymous artist pictured Brunsdon as *Dromio of Syracuse*; the picture was published by Harrison on 1 March 1779.

Brunton, Anne. See WIGNELL, MRS THOMAS, ANNE.

Brunton, Elizabeth, later Mrs Peter Columbine *c. 1772–1799, actress.*
Elizabeth Brunton was the second of the five known daughters of the actor-manager,

John Brunton (1741–1822), under whose entry her brothers and sisters are listed. According to clippings in the Folger Library she was reported as making "her first appearance on any stage" at Norwich in February 1789, but unless there was another Miss E. Brunton, who died early, Elizabeth was playing children's roles at Bristol as early as 1782.

For her debut at Norwich Elizabeth played Amanthis in *The Child of Nature*. The press described her as appearing to be about 16 years of age, of about medium stature, "her whole figure in the finest proportion, which receives additional effect from easy, graceful, and unembarrassed action." She had a fine, open and expressive face, a refined nature, and a clear, powerful and harmonious voice. Displaying a bewitching simplicity and elegant *naïveté* in the performance, "as could only be equalled by her sister [Anne]," she so pleased the overflow audience that it shouted its approval. Her father was an inveterate supplier of newspaper puffs, so perhaps the reporter's enthusiasm deserves some scepticism, but when she appeared in the same role on 8 March, now described as "a girl of seventeen," her audience was the most brilliant assemblage ever seen in Norwich. By April she had played five nights "to over-flowing houses," and for her benefit on 11 April 1789, in which she played Polly Honeycombe and Sylvia in *The Desert Island,* all places were taken a week ahead of time. Her sister Anne came back to Norwich for the event but could not act because of restrictions in her contract with Covent Garden.

On 24 May 1790 the press announced that the "Norwich people are in raptures" because Elizabeth Brunton was going to join her sister at Covent Garden. For over five months periodic puffs in the London papers had reported her Norwich triumphs, culminating on 4 May 1790 with praise of her beauty and comic powers which promised "to rank her with a Goodall or a Jor-dan." She finally appeared, at her sister's benefit on 5 May 1790, as Miss Hoyden in the afterpiece *The Man of Quality.* Her sister Anne introduced her in an elegant poetical address, which she gave with "affecting sensibility," at one point becoming so overwhelmed "by her sororal feelings" that tears momentarily prevented her from continuing. When the time came for Elizabeth's entrance as Miss Hoyden, she was so overcome, perhaps by emotion but more likely by fear, that she could not speak for some time. The *Biographical Magazine* (May 1790) described the event:

We know not what cynics may say upon the subject, but we will venture to affirm, that the theatre, on this evening, presented so striking and amiable an instance of relative tenderness, that every feeling and generous character must have retired with improved sensibility, and a heart more calculated to expand to social virtue and affection. Nor was the interest thus inspired in behalf of Miss E. Brunton disappointed by the performance of that lovely little actress: her figure is eminently interesting; her features are regular, soft, flexible, and capable of the most vivacious expressions, and her eyes exceedingly bright and attractive; while her voice is perhaps one of the most harmonious ever heard; and conspired with that extreme agitation which she discovered at her entrance to give us the most favourable idea of her sensibility, a quality by no means unimportant in a player. Her excessive timidity and embarrassment, which for some time robbed her of the power of speech, naturally obscured some portion of her vivacity: but still she discovered so much of comic inspiration, as left us only to lament that her part was so short, and that we had not the satisfaction of hearing when we should witness her next performance.

But the next performance so eagerly awaited by the reporter never occurred. For reasons unknown, Elizabeth Brunton, despite the influence of her sister, never again acted in London. She returned to play at Norwich, and on 15 January 1798 the press announced she had retired from the stage in consequence of her impending marriage to Peter Columbine, Junior, of that city, which took place on 4 February 1798. The *Gentleman's Magazine* reported in November 1799 that she had died (perhaps in childbirth?) on 10 November 1799.

Brunton, John   *1741–1822, actor, manager.*

John Brunton was born in 1741 at Norwich, the son of a soapmaker. After serving an apprenticeship for seven years to a wholesale grocer in Norwich, he left that city with his wife, a Miss Friend—who was, according to William Dunlap, from Bristol—and went to London to "carry on business as a grocer and tea-dealer in Drury Lane." Brunton's interest in the theatre began when his friend J. Younger, the prompter at Covent Garden, persuaded him to appear for Younger's benefit in the title role of *Cyrus* on 11 April 1774, for which Brunton was announced only as "A Gentleman" making his first appearance on the stage. Several weeks later, on 3 May, he played Hamlet at the same theatre, announced as "the Young Gentleman who played Cyrus," for the benefit of Mr and Mrs Kniveton. The fact that Brunton could present himself at a patent theatre in two leading roles of such consequence, especially Hamlet, would seem to suggest that he had had some prior theatrical experience in the provinces, yet the records of the eighteenth-century theatre contain many instances of novices assuming major roles for their London debuts. Although there seems to be no assessment in the press of these first performances, Brunton no doubt was successful enough to decide on abandoning his business and entering the theatrical profession.

He soon returned to Norwich, and became "esteemed the best actor that had appeared on that stage," or anywhere on the circuit traveled by the Norwich company. Few bills for this circuit survive, but there is a record of his playing Villars in *A Word to the Wise* at Bungay on 15 June 1775.

On 1 July 1780 Brunton returned to London for a single performance at the Haymarket, when he acted Richard III. The *Gazetteer* (3 July) was "completely disappointed" with this actor who it understood had earned at Norwich the appellation of "the Northern Roscius," stating that he performed without "the least ray of dignity or grace" and displayed "that air of slovenly negligence which is frequently mistaken for ease, and which, where merit is wanting, is most disgusting." The *Morning Chronicle* (3 July) was more impressed and acknowledged surprise at Brunton's showing "more merit than we expected." Although the audience did not care for him at first, he soon grew in their esteem. "At present," continued that paper's critic, "we presume he plays the part as well as any one actor who treads not on a London stage, but he would play it much better if he did not seem to be so intimately acquainted with the character," by hurrying through the dialogue "without sufficiently discriminating between the ordinary declamatory passages, & those which peculiarly discover the deep designs & artful views of the all inspiring Gloster." Although his performance lacked a degree of dignity and weight, the *Morning Chronicle*, in another article on 8 July, assured its readers that, contrary to some press reports that Brunton had received a cold reception, he met with the "unanimous plaudits of a large audience."

Despite the *Chronicle*'s opinion that he was deserving of a London engagement, evidently no offer was forthcoming, and Brunton passed the rest of that summer playing leading roles at Bristol. In the fall he made his debut at Bath on 19 September 1780 as Dumont, with the young Mrs Siddons, in *Jane Shore*. Brunton remained at Bath for five years, largely in secondary roles such as Grey in *The Chapter of Accidents*, Sciolto in *The Fair Penitent*, Adam in *As You Like It* and Austin in *The Count of Narbonne*. He also played the more important roles of Richard III and King John; for his benefit on 5 June 1782 he acted Lusignan in *Zara* ("tickets . . . of Mr Brunton, at Mr Staines's, in Bridge-street"). For his benefit in his first season he took £39 17s., small in comparison to receipts taken by others in the company and indicative of his modest position and popularity. He took somewhat more, £104, at his second benefit, in 1781. While at Bath he also acted at Bristol every season. According to Dunlap, during these five years Brunton had settled his family in an "elegant cottage."

Brunton made another single appearance at London on 28 October 1785 when he played Evander in *The Grecian Daughter* at Covent Garden. Playing the title role was his daughter Anne Brunton, who had made her London debut only 11 days earlier on 17 October, at the age of 15, in the same theatre as Horatia in *The Roman Father*. Her father had introduced her to audiences at Bristol and Bath in the previous season, and her debut at Bath on 17 February 1785, for which Brunton had delivered a proud prologue, was in Haslewood's words "a phenomenon in the theatrical hemisphere." Harris had brought her up to Covent Garden in hopes of making a stand against Mrs Siddons at the other house. To prepare for his London appearance, Brunton carried on one of the most indefatigable campaigns of puffing on record in the London papers. Anne Brunton's debut was a great success, although "the public curiosity was raised to such a pitch it was scarcely possible for her to equal expectation" (see her entry as WIGNELL, Mrs Thomas). When her father joined her on the Covent Garden stage for the performance of *The Grecian Daughter*, they drew a numerous crowd of the curious. The *Morning Herald* (29 October 1785) judged Brunton not much good in his role and lacking regality, the same fault found

in his earlier London appearances. His voice was reported to be resonant, but he could not manage it properly, it was felt.

This performance with his daughter proved to be John Brunton's last in London, where he had appeared a total of only four times. He devoted the rest of his theatrical life to the theatres at Norwich and its circuit, the lease of which he acquired by permission of the proprietors from Giles L. Barrett on 15 May 1788. On 20 May 1788 he posted a bond in the amount of £2000 with William Elwin of Gerard Street, Soho, a merchant, as his surety "for the payment of the Rent & Performance of the Covenants in the Lease." The lease was renewed for seven years on 3 August 1790 at the yearly rent of £300 and then again in 1796. At the time Norwich was one of the most important provincial theatres in England and was the center of a prosperous touring circuit in East Anglia, which included playhouses at Colchester, Ipswich, King's Lynn, Cambridge, Yarmouth, Barnwell, Beccles, Bury, and "Stirbitch." They seem to have prospered under Brunton's care. For example, his company in 1789 began to visit King's Lynn regularly each year from mid-February to mid-March, and according to the *Norfolk Chronicle* (14 March 1789), their first season was an unprecedented success: "the very high estimation in which the company was held, and the novelty produced by them drew crouded audiences every evening. . . . The profits of this trip will, we doubt not, prove the most fortunate circumstance, that has happened in Mr Brunton's management." In the same year the company had the most successful season ever known at Cambridge, taking £60 to £70 a night.

The minute books of the Norwich theatre record the preparations for Brunton's retirement on 28 May 1800. In December 1798 advertisements for receiving proposals from interested lessees were placed by the proprietors in the newspapers, and on 10 January 1799 they agreed to grant to William Wilkins, an architect, the lease for 14 years "from the Expiration of Mr Brunton's Lease." The proprietors also negotiated with Brunton in respect to compensation for the depreciation of the circuit theatres.

The manner in which John Brunton passed the remaining years of his life is unknown, but no doubt his responsibilities for his large family kept him busy, and their various theatrical careers offered him the usual mixed shares of satisfaction and concern. His wife, who seems not to have acted, had her fourteenth child on 26 June 1789. Some of them evidently died young. (A William Brunton was buried at St Paul, Covent Garden, on 17 November 1778.) Six survivors had stage careers of varying success and lengths, and by their marriages they connected themselves to an enormous network of theatrical people on both sides of the Atlantic.

John Brunton (1775–1849), the eldest son, made his debut at Bristol in 1782, at the age of seven, acted at Norwich from 1795 to 1800, and made his first appearance in London on 22 September 1800 at Covent Garden as Frederick in *Lover's Vows*. In 1804 he became manager of the theatre at Brighton, and later he managed the theatres at Norwich, Birmingham, and Lynn. In 1823 he was manager of the West London Theatre. On 6 September 1792, he married Miss Anna Ross (b. 1773), daughter of William Ross (d. 1781), and Mrs Ross (later Mrs J. Brown, d. 1823), sister of Frances Mary Ross (1765–1855) and half-sister of the American John Mills Brown. All were actors. The Ross family had connections to the large theatrical families named Ashmore, Brown, and Sparks. Through Frances Mary Ross's marriage to Thomas Shaftoe Robertson they were related to the numerous acting family Robertson, culminating in Forbes Robertson. John and Anna Brunton had at least four children: Elizabeth Brunton (1799–1860), who made her debut at Covent Garden in 1817 and married Frederick Yates (1797–1842) the actor-manager, leading to Yateses and Morrisons; Maria (Fanny?) Brunton (1804–1883), who made her debut at Covent Garden in 1822 and married William Daly (1796–1857), leading to more theatrical Dalys; a son, name unknown; and "his second son," John Brunton, a lieutenant in the Royal Navy, who died on 17 July 1749, leaving a widow and ten children.

Anne Brunton (1769–1808), mentioned above as making her debut at Covent Garden on 17 October 1785, later married the poet Robert Merry (1755–1798), then Thomas Wignell (d. 1802), and finally became the second wife of William Warren (1767–1832). She died at Alexandria, Virginia, in 1808 (see her as WIGNELL, Mrs Thomas).

Elizabeth Brunton (d. 1799), who made her debut at Covent Garden on 5 May 1790 and married Peter Columbine, of Norwich, in 1798.

Louisa Brunton (1785–1860), who made her debut at Covent Garden on 5 October 1803 and after marrying William, the second Earl of Craven, in 1807 retired from the stage as the Countess of Craven.

Harriet Brunton (1778–1859), who acted as a child at Bristol and married Francis Noverre (1773–1840), the son of Augustin Noverre (1729–1805) and the nephew of the great Jean Georges Noverre.

Kitty Brunton, who acted at Brighton in 1805.

Thomas Brunton, who also acted at Brighton in 1805.

John Brunton died on 19 December 1822, aged 82, at Hampstead Park, the seat of the Earl of Craven, husband of his daughter Louisa. Mrs John Brunton died in July 1826.

Brunton, Mrs John, Anna, née Ross
b. 1773, actress, dramatist.

Mrs John Brunton, the wife of the younger John Brunton (1775–1849, actor at Covent Garden in the nineteenth century and son of the Norwich manager of the same name), was born Anna Ross in 1773. She was the daughter of the performers William Ross (d. 1781) and his wife, who later became Mrs J. Brown (d. 1823). Anna was sister to Frances Mary Ross (1765–1855) and half-sister to the American actor John Mills Brown.

At the age of 15, Anna Ross wrote the comic opera *The Cottagers* which was published in 1788 and was first played at the Crow Street Theatre, Dublin, on 19 May 1789. She made her first and apparently only appearance in London when at Covent Garden on 16 May 1788 she played Sylvia in *Cymon* for the benefit of her step-father and mother, Mr and Mrs J. Brown. At the end of the afterpiece *The Royal Chace*, Mrs Brown, in the character of Harlequin, gave an "Occasional Epilogue" written by Anna.

Miss Ross played at Norwich between 1789 and 1792, then went to play at Edinburgh where on 25 February 1792 she acted Lady Amaranth in O'Keeffe's *Wild Oats*, "being her second appearance in Scotland." Soon after, on 6 September 1792, she married the younger John Brunton. As Mrs Brunton she acted at Norwich from 1794 to at least 1800, and she also was a member of her husband's company at Brighton in 1809.

By John Brunton she had at least four children, who are noticed in the entry of the elder John Brunton (1741–1822).

Brunton, W. *See* BURTON, W.

Bruodin, Mr [fl. 1749], actor.

Mr Bruodin (or Broudin) and his wife acted at the Capel Street playhouse in Dublin under William Phillips; and in August and September 1749 Bruodin, but apparently not his wife, played for Phillips at his booths at the London fairs. Starting 23 August at Bartholomew Fair he acted Prospero in *The Tempest*, and from 7

September at Southwark Fair he was Slango in *The Industrious Lovers*. Bruodin remained in London in the fall, playing Othello for his benefit (shared with Mrs Hutton) at the Haymarket Theatre on 17 October 1749. After this performance he may have returned to Ireland. Chetwood reported that at Dublin Bruodin played Morochius in *The Merchant of Venice* and his wife acted Nerissa, but he did not date the performance.

Bruquier or Bruquire. *See* BRUGUIER.

"Brush." *See* COLLINS, JOHN.

Bryan. *See also* BRYARS.

Bryan, Mr [fl. 1713?–1726], musician.

Mr Bryan was one of the musicians playing at the Queen's Theatre in the Haymarket about 1713, when he was earning a salary of 11s. 6d. (per week, presumably). On 2 March 1726 he shared a benefit with musician Betty Smith at the Haymarket Theatre. He may have played at theatres during the intervening years, but there seems to be no clear evidence.

Bryan, Mr [fl. 1750], actor?

A Mr Bryan was in the company that played at Richmond and Twickenham in the summer of 1750; he was probably an actor.

Bryan, Mr [fl. 1784], singer.

A tenor, Mr Bryan sang at the Handel Memorial Concerts at Westminster Abbey and the Pantheon on 26, 27, 29 May and 3, 5 June 1784.

Bryan, Daniel [fl. 1670], scenekeeper.

On a warrant dated 11 November 1670, Daniel Bryan was listed as a scenekeeper in the King's Company at the Bridges Street playhouse; a duplicate warrant of the same date has his name marked "discharged," but the discharge is cancelled.

Bryan, [Frederick?] d. 1770?, prompter.

Mr Bryan, the Covent Garden prompter, was first mentioned in the theatre's account books on 24 January 1767, though he may have been employed earlier than this. On 7 March his salary was noted as £2 weekly, but this was raised to £3 on 25 April; he received a clear benefit on 14 May. In addition to prompting, Bryan was also paid for writing out parts, and occasionally the accounts indicate payments for this added duty, as on 9 January 1768 when he was paid £1 9s. After the 1768–69 season his name disappeared from the Covent Garden books, but in 1769–70 a Mr Bryan, prompter, turned up at York. The registers of St Michael le Belfry at York record the burial of Frederick Bryan, "comedian," on 6 March 1770; whether or not this was Bryan the prompter is not clear, though the fact that the York theatrical records contain no further mention of Bryan suggests that this may have been he.

Back at Covent Garden on 18 February 1773, however, Mr Bryan's name reappeared in the account book; the entry simply gives his last name and the date, with no indication of service so the reference may have been to a different Bryan.

Bryan, John d. 1769, musician.

Musgrave's *Obituary* notes the death of John (or Jonathan) Bryan, formerly of the King's band of music, on 22 April 1769.

Bryars, Mrs [fl. 1723–1724], boxkeeper.

Mrs Bryars (or Bryan; Bryers?) was possibly related to Mr Bryers, boxkeeper at the King's Theatre in the Haymarket in 1716. She worked at the Haymarket Theatre and is recorded for shared benefits as a boxkeeper on 22 April 1723 and 9 March 1724.

Bryers, Mr [fl. 1716], boxkeeper.

Mr Bryers was one of the keepers of the front boxes at the King's Theatre in the Haymarket on 15 December 1716. How long he may have served at the opera is not known, for records for this period are far from complete. It is likely that he was related to the Mrs Bryars who was active 1723–24.

Bryne. See BRYAN and BYRNE.

Brynham. See BYNAM.

Bubb, [Elizabeth?] [fl. 1723–1727], dresser.

Mrs Bubb was given a benefit at the Lincoln's Inn Fields Theatre on 31 May 1723 "on account of arrears." She was apparently a dresser at the playhouse at this time, or had been. She was cited in the theatre accounts in 1724, and when she was paid £10 on account on 4 March 1726 she was identified as Mrs Bubb, "late dresser," the implication being that she was now in business as a costume supplier on her own. On 25 March 1727 she was paid for 50 black feather "falls."

One might be tempted to interpret the phrase "late dresser" as indicating that Mrs Bubb had died, especially in view of a burial at St Paul, Covent Garden, on 27 December 1725 of an Elizabeth Bubb. This, however, would leave the 1726 payment "on account" and the 1727 payment unexplained, unless Mrs Bubb's business was carried on after her death by another Mrs Bubb.

Buber. See BUHER.

Buchan, Mr d. 1800, watchman, sweeper.

On 19 September 1789 Mr Buchan's name first appeared in the Drury Lane account books; what his position was is not known, but he was receiving 9s. per week. On 17 May 1794 he was paid 2s. 6d. per day, and this must have been for his summer work as theatre watchman, for the accounts show a sequence of payments to Buchan and Mr Potts of £2 10s. 6d. weekly for the two. One may suppose that he continued working winters in some capacity, though the accounts make no mention of him again until 8 November 1800 when he was reported dead and his small salary of 6s. daily as a sweeper was taken off the books. He was probably the husband of the Mrs Buchan who served Drury Lane as a dresser from 1789 to 1794.

Buchan, Mrs [fl. 1789–1794], dresser.

On 19 September 1789 Mrs Buchan was first noticed in the Drury Lane account books; she was described then simply as a house servant earning 4s. weekly. Her name was entered again in February 1794 for 5s. per week as a dresser, and she was last mentioned on 22 April 1794. It is probable that she was the wife of the watchman and sweeper at Drury Lane about this same time.

Buchanan, Mr [fl. 1724], actor.

On 20 February 1724 Mr Buchanan shared a benefit at the Haymarket Theatre with three others, and on 24 September of the same year he played Diocles in Oedipus at the Bullock-Spiller booth at Southwark Fair. He may have been related to the actress Elizabeth Buchanan of a few years later, but there is no evidence to connect them.

Buchanan, Mrs Charles, Elizabeth d. 1736, actress.

Elizabeth Buchanan made a brief appearance at Lincoln's Inn Fields a year before she became a permanent member of the company there: on 21 October 1727 she played Gertrude in Hamlet for one performance only. The following summer she played the Queen in The Spanish Friar at the Haymarket Theatre on 9 August 1728 and Anne in Bateman at the Hall-Miller booth at Bartholomew Fair on 24 August. Of her husband nothing is known except that his name was Charles Buchanan (the actor Buchanan of 1724?) and that he married Elizabeth sometime before she first appeared in London.

On 20 November 1728 she played Calphurnia in Julius Caesar as a regular member of the Lincoln's Inn Fields troupe. During the 1728–29 season she also played Gertrude again (19 December), Araminta in The Old Bachelor (31 December), Isabella in Measure for Measure (13 January 1729), Dorinda in The Stratagem (28 January), Lady Macduff (31 January) and Lady Macbeth (28 April) in Macbeth, Desdemona in Othello (3 February), Belvidera in Venice Preserved (7 February), and Hillaria in Love's Last Shift (10 April). When she played Lady Macbeth it was for her benefit shared with Mrs Benson, which brought in £36 16s. 6d. in money and the sizeable sum of £121 8s. in tickets. To have been given these roles during her first season she surely must have arrived with a considerable reputation in both tragedy and comedy; her specialty seems to have been tragic heroines, of both the tender and tough varieties. In the next two seasons she appeared in similar parts: Goneril in King Lear (12 September 1729), Aspatia in The Maid's Tragedy (8 November 1729), the title role in Marianne (6 May 1730), Indiana in The Conscious Lovers (23 November 1730), and Angelica in The Constant Couple (22 March 1731).

During the ensuing four seasons before her tragic death she continued in most of the roles she had acted previously and added such parts as Arabella in The Committee, Lady Grace in The Provoked Husband, Almeyda in Don Sebastian, Milwood in The London Merchant, Melinda in The Recruiting *Officer*, Mrs Fainall in *The Way of the World* (at the opening of Covent Garden on 7 December 1732), Fidelia in *The Plain Dealer*, the title role in *The Fair Penitent*, the Duchess of York in *Richard III*, Andromache in *Troilus and Cressida*, Melissa in *Timon of Athens*, Lady Graveairs in *The Careless Husband*, Zara in *The Mourning Bride*, Selima in *Tamerlane*, and Octavia in *All for Love*.

On 1 October 1736, though pregnant, she played Mrs Fainall; after her performance she was watching the afterpiece, *The Necromancer*, and during it one of the flying machines carrying four performers crashed to the stage floor when its supporting cables snapped. One actor was killed and several others were seriously injured. Mrs Buchanan, according to Thomas Gray who witnessed the scene, was "put into a chair in such a fright that as she is big with child, I question whether it may not kill her." Though shaken by the experience, Mrs Buchanan performed on 13 and 22 October and played Euridice in *Oedipus*—her last appearance—on 1 November 1736. On 19 November she gave birth to twins, but they were either stillborn or died within a few days. By the evening of 27 November she was reported at the point of death, and on the morning of 28 November she died.

Elizabeth Buchanan's lodgings have been reported in some sources as being in Great Russell Street, Covent Garden, and in others as in Bow Street in the same parish. On 21 January 1737 at the Covent Garden Theatre *The Confederacy* was performed for the benefit of her surviving children, but how many there were, or whether or not her husband survived her, is not known. Only Davies seems to have mentioned her acting, and he wrote precious little: "a very fine woman and a pleasing actress"—but the roles she was given would suggest that she was, for a brief period, the leading tragedienne in her company.

Buchinger. *See also* **BUCKINGER.**

Buchinger, Mr [fl. 1735], *flutist*.

In September and October 1735 a Mr Buchinger performed on the German flute at Goodman's Fields Theatre. Though Matthew Buckinger is not otherwise recorded this late, this may have been he. On 4 November 1746 at St George's Chapel, Hyde Park Corner, a Matthias Buckinger married Mrs Frances Kninington of Kensington; he may have been the flutist of 1735 or, again, Matthew Buckinger. Since the famous Matthew had numerous offspring, however, it is more likely that Mr Buchinger the flutist was one of his sons.

Buck, [Mr?] [fl. 1760–1761], *doorkeeper*.

The 1760–61 accounts at Covent Garden list a Buck as doorkeeper.

Buck, [Mr?] [fl. 1761], *property man*.

On 16 November 1761 one Buck was paid £4 4s. for 14 "Tamberines" for the production of *The Fair* at Covent Garden the month before. He was doubtless related to the other Bucks working at Covent Garden at this time.

Buck, Timothy *d. 1741, swordsman, actor*.

There may have been, in the early eighteenth century, two Bucks named Timothy, one who was a swordsman and one who acted, and a third Buck called Tom, also a swordsman; but their careers dovetail so neatly that it seems highly probable that all were the same person.

Sir Richard Steele, in the 21 July 1712 issue of *The Spectator*, wrote a delightful account of his trip on 16 July to the bear garden at Hockley-in-the-Hole where a trial of skill was held between Serjeant James Miller, lately come from Portugal, and Timothy Buck of London. Miller had challenged Buck at several weapons: back sword, sword and dagger, sword and buckler, single falchion, case of falchions, and quarterstaff. Steele said he hoped they might, as did knights of old, do battle because of a difference of opinion over a maiden's beauty, but, alas, they were only fighting for money. After both gladiators had entered the arena, Steele noted that

Miller had an audacious look, that took the eye; Buck a perfect composure, that engaged the judgment. Buck came on in a plain coat, and kept all his air till the instant of engaging; at which time he undressed to his shirt, his arm adorned with a bandage of red riband. No one can describe the sudden concern in the whole assembly; the most tumultuous crowd in Nature was as still and as much engaged, as if all their lives depended on the first blow. The combatants met in the middle of the stage, and shaking hands as removing all malice, they retired with much grace to the extremities of it; from whence they immediately faced about and approached each other, Miller with an heart full of resolution, Buck with a watchful untroubled countenance; Buck regarded principally his own defence, Miller chiefly thoughtful of annoying his opponent. It is not easy to describe the many escapes and imperceptible defences between two men of quick eyes and ready limbs; but Miller's heat laid him open to the rebuke of the calm Buck by a large cut on the forehead. Much effusion of blood covered his eyes in a moment, and the huzzas of the crowd undoubtedly quickened the anguish. The assembly was divided into parties upon their different ways of fighting; while a poor nymph in one of the galleries apparently suffered for Miller, and burst into a flood of tears. As soon as his wound was wrapped up, he came on again with a little rage, which still disabled him further. But what brave man can be wounded into more patience and caution? The next was a warm eager onset, which ended in a decisive stroke on the left leg of Miller. The lady in the gallery, during this second strife, covered her face; and for my part I could not keep my thoughts from being mostly employed on the consideration of her unhappy circumstance that moment, hearing the clash of swords and apprehending life or victory concerned her lover in every blow, but not daring to satisfy herself on

whom they fell. The wound was exposed to the view of all who could delight in it, and sewed up on the stage. The surly second of Miller declared at this time, that he would that day fortnight fight Mr Buck at the same weapons, declaring himself the master of the renowned Gorman; but Buck denied the honour of that courageous disciple, and asserting that he himself had taught that champion, accepted the challenge.

Steele's account, unfortunately, seems to be all we have concerning Timothy Buck's early career as a swordsman. He presumably went on to fight Miller's second, and perhaps he continued in his precarious occupation for a few more years.

By 1715 Buck had theatrical connections. Genest (but not *The London Stage*) lists a benefit for "Tim" Buck on 31 July 1715 to "release him out of prison." On 12 June 1717 a Mr Buck, presumably the same Timothy, shared a Lincoln's Inn Fields Theatre benefit, but the records reveal nothing of his function, if any, at the playhouse. Fitzgerald in his *New History of the English Stage* quoted a 12 April 1722 inventory of players at this theatre, and a Timothy Buck was named on the list. It was he, then, who played Countryman in *Hanging and Marriage* on 15 March 1722 and shared a benefit on 16 May. On 24 September 1724 at Bullock and Spiller's Southwark Fair booth Buck acted Haemon in *Oedipus*. He may well have been active as a player in London from 1715 through 1724 but in small parts that the bills ignored.

In 1725 a Tom Buck (an error for Tim, perhaps) was bested at swordplay by the noted James Figg, who made a habit of defeating practically all his opponents. Since Timothy Buck's career as an actor is blank this year, perhaps this was he, taking a last fling at swordsmanship to see if he liked it better than acting on the legitimate stage.

From 1725 to 1741 a Timothy Buck acted at Norwich and other provincial towns, and this, again, was our man. Sybil Rosenfeld, in *Strolling Players*, found that

Buck used to "supplement his income by teaching small sword and quarter-staff to the gentlemen of the cities which he visited." We know that Buck was in Dymer's Company at Canterbury in early 1732 and that he played Bassanio in *The Jew of Venice* at Ipswich in June 1736, but most of his provincial career remains obscure. Buck died at Colchester (or, according to one report, Bury St Edmunds) a few days before 27 October 1741. In January 1742 a benefit was given at Norwich for his orphan child. Buck's wife Ann (1705–1737) acted at Norwich from 1727 until her death, the beginning of her stage career there almost coinciding with Timothy's; her epitaph stated that she had been on the stage for 14 years, so she had performed elsewhere for four years before appearing at Norwich. She is not known to have acted in London. Ann Buck, too, was buried at Colchester. A Miss Buck, who was probably related to Timothy and Ann and may have been their child, acted at Norwich from about 1735 to 1738.

Buck, Tom. *See* BUCK, TIMOTHY.

Buck, William *d. 1777, actor.*

William Buck, the minor but industrious Covent Garden actor of the 1750's and 1760's, may have been the Mr Buck who was lessee of the theatre at Ipswich up to 1749 and/or the Mr Buck who was active at Norwich in 1753. His first London appearance was on 3 December 1755 at Covent Garden when he played Westmoreland in *Henry V*. He was also noticed in the bills as Charles in *As You Like It* on 17 May 1756, and on 21 May he shared a benefit with two others. During his second season he repeated Charles and added the Herald in *The Humorous Lieutenant*, Sebastian in *The Rover*, a servant in *The Twin Rivals*, Tatter in *The Funeral*, and Charon in *Lethe*. At the beginning of his Covent Garden career Buck was earning £1 per week. Over the years his salary

gradually increased to a little over £2 15s. weekly, though he remained among the fourth rank of actors in the troupe. His benefits were usually shared with two or three others, sometimes bringing him a small profit, but on at least one occasion (14 May 1767) a small loss.

His roles were usually small, but Buck was apparently a dependable utility actor, capable of handling both serious and comic parts. Among the characters he played were Nym in *The Merry Wives of Windsor*, Gadshill in *1 Henry IV*, Austria in *King John*, Norfolk in *Richard III*, Cob in *Every Man In His Humour*, Hack'em in *The Squire of Alsatia*, an Officer in *Venice Preserved*, the first Murderer in *Macbeth*, Mouldy in *2 Henry IV*, a recruit in *The Recruiting Officer*, the second Gravedigger in *Hamlet*, and Lepidus in *Julius Caesar*. His last appearance was as Austria in *King John* on 28 May 1767.

During the summers William Buck may have augmented his income by playing at Bristol. A Mr Buck was there in 1754, 1755, and 1761 through 1764. A Mrs Buck was also at Bristol in 1761 and died on 22 November 1763. Though there is a possibility that this woman was William Buck's wife, his acting schedule at the time of her death would seem to deny it, for he performed at Covent Garden on 23, 24, 26, and 28 November as though nothing unusual had happened in his private life.

Buck is said to have kept an inn at Kendal after his Covent Garden days, and he may have managed a provincial circuit covering Carlisle, Kendal, Durham, and Berwick. On 4 April 1776 he and other players were reported to be shipping off to Lisbon to act, and it was at Antigua in the Canaries, in February 1777, that William Buck died.

Buckholtz, Mr [*fl. 1791–1801*], *music copyist.*

The Drury Lane accounts first cite Mr Buckholtz on 22 October 1791 as a music copyist, though on this date no amount was noted as paid to him. In later years the books show varying payments from which one can judge that as copyist he averaged about £3 per week when he had such work to do. It is likely that he also earned an income as an instrumentalist—perhaps he was in the theatre band—but the accounts indicate no such activity. The last mention of Buckholtz in the accounts is on 11 November 1801 when he was paid £2 2s.

Buckinger. *See also* BUCHINGER.

Buckinger, Miss ⌊fl. 1761–1769⌋, *dancer.*

Miss Buckinger (or Buchinger) was first noticed in the bills on 23 June 1761 when she danced in a ballet titled *Les Chasseurs and les Bergères* at the Haymarket Theatre. She reappeared at the same playhouse two summers later, on 20 July 1763, performing a new dance with Rogier, and on 1 July 1769 she was named in the Richmond bills as participating in productions of *Comus* and *The Recruiting Officer.*

Buckinger, Joseph ⌊fl. 1784–1805⌋, *viola and bass viol player, lutenist.*

Joseph Buckinger, the grandson of Matthew Buckinger, played viola in the Handel Memorial Concerts at Westminster Abbey and the Pantheon on 26, 27, 29 May and 3, 5 June 1784. In 1794, when Doane's *Musical Directory* was published, Buckinger was living at No 443, the Strand, and was listed as a performer on the viola and bass, a music seller, and a participant in concerts presented by the New Musical Fund as well as Handelian performances at the Abbey. The Drury Lane account books show a Mr Buckinger on 7 January 1798 being paid £3 15s. 6d. for music copying, though this may have been an error for the copyist Buckholtz. At the Haymarket Theatre on 15 January of that year Buckinger played viola when the *Messiah* was performed, and on 7 January 1805—the last notice of him—he was paid £8 16s.

for "attending" Mrs Jordan in her songs at Drury Lane. Caulfield reported that Buckinger was also a skilled lutenist.

Buckinger, Matthew *b. 1674, musician, painter, inventor, freak.*

Born, according to his own testimony, on 2 June 1674 "in Germany in the Marquisate of Brandenburgh, near to Nurenburgh . . . without Hands, Feet, or Thighs," Matthew (or Matthias) Buckinger (or Buchinger) was the last of nine children—eight sons and a daughter. His parents encouraged the boy to study as though he were normal. As a result of their compassion and good sense, Buckinger became amazingly adept at several musical instruments, "not in the manner of general amateurs," said Caulfield, "but in the style of a finished master." Similarly, he learned to draw and write with astounding minuteness and was an inventor of no mean ability. Though his parents did not exhibit him when he was young, after he grew to his full height of two feet (or, according to some sources, 29 inches) he willingly performed before company and, in fact, supported himself and his family very handsomely on the income he made by showing himself and his works.

In painting he specialized in coats of arms, portraits, and landscapes, mostly done with pen and India ink. Edward Godfrey observed Buckinger at work and described a piece he was finishing for Sir Robert Walpole:

It is about the bigness of a sheet of paper; the body of it is drawn in perspective with statues, and on one side is the little man's own picture, in the compass of six inches by four, very like him. Instead of shades for the curls of his peruke are psalms written in different characters which at some distance look like shades done with a hair pencil. On the other side at the top is Sir Robert's arms.

This may have been the drawing described by Caulfield which Mr Herbert of Chest-

MATTHEW BUCKINGER
by himself

nut, Hertfordshire, had in his collection; the Herbert picture, done on vellum, had Psalms 27, 121, 128, 140, 149, and 150 plus the Lord's Prayer worked into the curls of the wig. This fantastic decorative work Buckinger did by holding a pen or pencil between his handless wrists, as can be seen in Tillemans's sketch of him.

The little man was no less marvelous in music. He learned to play with great skill the oboe, bagpipe, trumpet, dulcimer, and "Strange Flute" (probably the German transverse flute). It was probably to enable him to play musical instruments that he developed an interest in mechanical devices and invented—or at least worked on—a rig designed to play the violin and German flute. Just what this machine was is obscure, but it was apparently not like an automatic band, but rather something which would help him play various instruments—singly, not simultaneously. Allied to his talent in music was Buckinger's ability, despite his

stumps, to dance a hornpipe; painter John Devoto pictured him thus, in highland garb.

As if all this were not enough, Buckinger was skilled at games and tricks as well. He could perform with cups and balls, corn, and live birds, and he played skittles and nine pins. As one might expect, he could shave himself with ease.

When he was in England in 1723—one of several visits—he billed himself as having performed "before three Emperors, and most of the Kings and Princes in Europe, and in particular, several times before his Majesty King GEORGE." During this particular stay he exhibited himself next door to the Two Blackamoors' Heads in Holborn at the hours of ten, twelve, two, four, six, and eight; his stamina, too, was astounding. At these exhibitions he would demonstrate his skills and sell his drawings, which together brought him a comfortable income.

Buckinger would have needed such an income to support his very sizeable family. He married four times and had one child by his first wife, three by his second, six by his third, and one by his last (though another report of his skill at procreation says he had 14 offspring: one by his first wife, three by his second, six by his third, and four by his fourth). One of his wives, probably the fourth, was said to have been a handsome, tall woman who traveled from country to country with him. It was perhaps one of the other wives who made a practice of beating the little man, but, as Caulfield reported, one day Buckinger had enough, somehow got her down on the floor, and buffeted *her*.

Matthew Buckinger's death was once reported as 1722, but he was in England, alive and well, in 1723, did a sketch of himself in London on 29 April 1724 (stating on it that he was 24 inches tall and a "wonderful little man"), and he was still alive about 1730. Caulfield stated that one of Buckinger's grandsons once kept a music shop in the Strand and was an excellent lutenist; this would have been Joseph

Buckinger (fl. 1784–1805). Other Buckingers who may have been related to Matthew are more difficult to identify with certainty. The Mr Buchinger who was a flutist in 1735 may have been a relative or, indeed, Matthew himself. The parish registers of St George's Chapel, Hyde Park Corner, show a marriage on 4 November 1746 between a Mr Matthias Buckinger and Mrs Frances Kninington of Kensington; this man may have been the flutist of 1735, but at the time the famous Matthew would have been 72 if he was still alive, and if he was, perhaps he was again in the marrying mood. It is more likely that this was one of his children.

Of the various pictures of Buckinger mentioned above, the Devoto sketch, an incomplete work, is in the collection of Sir Edward Croft-Murray. The Tillemans drawing still exists, apparently, but its location now is not known; the work was commissioned by Dr Macro. Macro also asked Edward Godfrey to draw Buckinger, but it is not known whether or not the work was ever finished. Buckinger's self-portrait with the psalms and the Lord's Prayer worked into the wig was copied by an anonymous engraver and is reproduced here. G. Scott engraved a copy for Kirby's *Wonderful Museum* in 1804, and a similar engraving was made anonymously about the same time. E. Beck engraved a picture of Buckinger that featured 13 representations of the little man's performances, along with his autograph, in the margin. For Caulfield's *Remarkable Persons* in 1819 R. Grave engraved a portrait, and at an unknown date G. Smeaton published an engraving of Buckinger by J. Gleadah. The engravings all show Buckinger seated on a cushion.

Buckingham, James (fl. 1784–1794), singer.

At the Handel Memorial Concerts at Westminster Abbey and the Pantheon on 26, 27, 29 May and 3, 5 June 1784, James Buckingham was one of the *bassos*. He was still participating in Handelian concerts at the Abbey in 1794 when Doane's *Musical Directory* was printed, as well as in oratorios at Drury Lane and concerts by the New Musical Fund. Doane gave Buckingham's address as Great Bandy Legg Walk, Gravel Lane, Southwark.

Buckland, George (fl. 1773), musician.

On 16 January 1773 John Hindmarsh, who was in time to become an important violinist and violist, was bound apprentice to musician Edward Boxley, who turned him over for the term to George Buckland, citizen and "plaisterer," who was a musician by profession. There seems to be no other indication of Buckland's musical activity.

Buckler, Mrs (fl. 1789–1797), actress.

A Mrs Buckler who acted at the Crow Street Theatre in Dublin in 1789 and, with her husband, at Kilkenny and Waterford in 1792 was probably the Mrs Buckler who was performing at the Richmond Theatre on 1 September 1797 when *The Way to Get Married* and *The Maid of the Mill* were acted.

Buckler, Augustin (fl. 1682), trumpeter.

As a member of the King's Musick, Augustin Buckler was appointed trumpeter in Captain Legg's troop, replacing Thomas Barwell, on 8 March 1682.

Buckler, Edward (fl. c. 1677?), singer.

At some period before 15 April 1678 Edward Buckler (or Butler) was one of the boys in the Chapel Royal under the tutelage of James Hart; on that date the first of a series of warrants was written providing payment for clothes for Buckler—a standard pension for Chapel boys whose voices had changed.

Buckley. *See also* **BULKELY** and **BULK-LEY.**

Buckley, Mr ₁*fl. 1742*₁, *doorkeeper.*
A Mr Buckley shared a benefit on 15 May 1742 with three other doorkeepers at Drury Lane.

Buckley, ₁**Thomas?**₁ ₁*fl. 1784?–1794*₁, *violoncellist.*
A Mr Buckley, living in Manchester in 1794, was said by Doane to have played in the Handelian observances at Westminster Abbey in 1784 or following and at the Manchester Music Meeting.

(A Thomas Buckley married Arabella Wall Callcott on 25 August 1803 at St George, Hanover Square. She was probably the sister of John Wall Callcott, organist and composer, and the daughter of Thomas Callcott, bricklayer and builder, by his wife Charlotte Wall.)

Buckley, John *d. 1805, flutist, harpsichordist, organist.*
When John Buckley was proposed by Benjamin Blake for membership in the Royal Society of Musicians in June 1780, it was said of him that he had "practiced Music for a livelihood for seven years, is an organist of St. James's Church Teaches the Harpsichord, and flute, is a single Man." He was admitted to the Society on 4 June.

He must be identified with the Mr Buckley who was listed among the flutes at the Handel Memorial Concerts at Westminster Abbey and the Pantheon on 26, 27, and 29 May and 3 and 5 June 1784.

In each of the first five months of 1785, a Buckley, doubtless John, was listed as one of the Governors of the Royal Society. On 6 January 1793 he was set down in the minutes as a member of the Society's Court of Assistants, an office to which he was also named in 1794, 1797, 1799, 1801, and from 1803 through 1805.

In 1794 Doane noted that John Buckley was still organist at St James's Church and played in the Professional Concerts. He resided then in "Glass-house-street, Swallow-st."

John Buckley died sometime between the Society's January 1805 meeting and that of 5 January 1806, when Mr Potter, his executor, rose to inform the Society that it had been the beneficiary of £40 in the will of Mr Buckley. On 2 March the Society received the £36 residue, after deduction of "the duty of £4."

Buckley, Richard ₁*fl. 1694–1716*₁, *actor.*
In 1694 the Smock Alley manager Joseph Ashbury came to London from Dublin to recruit players for his company, and among the younger actors he took back with him were a married pair, Richard and Elizabeth Buckley. Ashbury may have found them in a provincial troupe, for there is no record of the Buckleys acting in London, but the theatrical records for the London playhouses in the 1690's are too incomplete to rule out the possibility of their playing there. Shortly after their arrival in Dublin the Buckleys had a daughter, Elizabeth, who was baptized at St John's on 4 July 1695. After this, Mrs Buckley apparently acted for Ashbury until after the turn of the century. Richard was talented enough to be noted by John Dunton in 1698 as being in no way inferior to players in London, and he continued his career in Dublin until 1716.

Buckley, Mrs Richard, Elizabeth ₁*fl. 1694–1700*₁, *actress. See* **BUCKLEY, RICHARD.**

Bucknall, Thomas ₁*fl. 1739–1746?*₁, *musician.*
When the Royal Society of Musicians was established on 28 August 1739, Thomas Bucknall was one of the original subscribers. It is possible that the Mr Bucknall who shared a benefit at the Goodman's Fields Theatre on 18 March 1746 was

Thomas, but the playbill contains too little information to be certain.

Bud, Mrs (fl. 1697–1701), *actress.*

Mrs Bud (or Budd) played with Betterton's company at Lincoln's Inn Fields, her first notice being in June 1697 when she was Clara in *All Without Money.* She was also billed as playing Flora in *The Ladies' Visiting Day* about January 1701 and Betty in *The Gentleman Cully* about August of the same year.

"Budd, Mr." See BERNARD, JOHN.

Budd, Master (fl. c. 1745–1750), *singer.*

Master Budd sang "Hail to the Myrtle Shade" at the New Wells—probably Clerkenwell—about 1745. He was surely the same Master Budd who sang the role of the First Priest in T. A. Arne's *The Sacrifice of Iphigenia* there on 16 April 1750. It is difficult to determine whether or not Master Budd grew up to be one of the musical Budds of Richmond, Surrey, for his dates do not seem to fit with theirs, but he may well have been related.

Budd, Benjamin Richard (fl. 1794), *violinist, composer.*

Doane listed Benjamin Richard Budd of Richmond, Surrey, as a composer and violinist who participated in the Handelian concerts at Westminster Abbey and performances given by the New Musical Fund in 1794. Budd's Richmond address suggests that he was related to the other musical Budds of that town.

Budd, Thomas b. c. 1751, *musician.*

Thomas Budd of Richmond, Surrey, was admitted to livery in the Worshipful Company of Musicians on 29 April 1772, having just completed his apprenticeship. He was probably apprenticed at 14, so one may guess that he was born about 1751.

Budd, Thomas c. 1761–1789, *violinist, violoncellist, harpist.*

Thomas Budd was born about 1761, the son of musician Thomas Budd of Richmond, Surrey. On 10 November 1774 he was bound apprentice to his father for seven years, and on 4 January 1782, giving his address as No 20, Heming's Row, St Martin's Lane, he was granted livery as a freeman in the Worshipful Company of Musicians. On 2 March 1783 he was recommended to the Royal Society of Musicians, described as a single man, age 22, with seven years of performing on the violin, violoncello, and harp, having "a great deal of Business." He was admitted, and perhaps at about this same time he married. His wife, named Sarah, bore him four children before his premature death: Elizabeth Walters, born 15 February 1784; Thomas, born 10 October 1785; Isabella, born 1 September 1787; and an unnamed female child, born 5 April 1789. Of Thomas Budd's professional career little is known beyond the fact that he played violin at the St Paul's concerts on 10 and 12 May 1785. Sometime shortly before 3 May 1789 he died.

Thomas's widow, Sarah, applied to the Royal Society of Musicians for a funeral allowance on 4 October 1789 and received £8; she had already been granted a monthly allowance of two and a half guineas for herself and 15s. for her children. By 1792 Mrs Budd had set up a school of some sort which at first prospered but by 6 April 1805 was not earning a profit; the Royal Society looked into the matter and continued Mrs Budd on a reduced allowance of £2 4s. 2d. The last notice of her in the Society's Minute Books is on 7 June 1812 when she was refused further aid.

Budd, Thomas (fl. 1774–1794?), *musician.*

Thomas Budd the elder, of Richmond, Surrey, was one of at least three Thomas Budds, all musicians, active in the late eighteenth century. On 10 November 1774 Thomas Budd the younger was bound apprentice to his father, a citizen and musician of London, for a period of seven years; the younger Thomas, then, was born about 1760–61, and Thomas the elder was probably born some two decades before that. It is likely that the elder Budd was the one who shared a benefit at Covent Garden on 21 May 1776, and we may guess he was a member of the theatre band. He may also have been the Thomas Bud who lived at No 5, Valentine Place, Blackfriars Road, Surrey, in 1794; the will of Jonathan Oldfield refers to this property on 20 May 1794 and cites Bud as the tenant.

Budgell, Anne Eustace *c. 1726–c. 1755, actress, singer.*

Anne Eustace Budgell, the natural daughter of author Eustace Budgell, was born about 1726. When Budgell, his mind deranged, committed suicide in May 1737, he left a scrap of a will leaving his estate to Anne, then about 11 years old. On 31 October 1741 Miss Budgell made her first stage appearance as a Lady of Pleasure in *The Harlot's Progess* at Drury Lane, and on 11 November she was a Gipsey Woman in *The Fortune Tellers.* At the end of the season on 25 May 1742 she was one of many whose tickets were to be accepted at the theatre.

Her name disappeared from the bills for the next season, but she was back at Drury Lane in 1743–44 playing small parts too insignificant to be mentioned in the bills until 13 February 1744, when she appeared as Polly in *The Beggar's Opera.* The *Daily Advertiser* reported that she "met with such unusual applause that several persons of quality have requested the same performance tomorrow [16 February]." Writing later, Davies noted that Miss Budgell was a very short girl with good understanding, a critical ear, a musical voice, and much propriety and sensibility in her delivery. Her success as Polly led to more frequent billings, though her parts were not always large. During the rest of the spring of 1744 she played such roles as Manto in *Oedipus,* Meriel in *The Jovial Crew,* Nell in *The Devil to Pay,* Foible in *The Way of the World,* and the title role in *Flora.*

She remained at Drury Lane for two more seasons, adding such roles as Lavinia and Calista in *The Fair Penitent,* Rose in *The Recruiting Officer,* Octavia in *All for Love,* and, her most important attempt, Monimia in *The Orphan* (on 17 April 1746). Her last role at Drury Lane was Prince Edward in *Richard III* on 22 April 1746. For the 1746–47 season she joined Hallam's troupe at Goodman's Fields and there played a number of leading roles, including Polly, Calista, and Nell, which she had done previously. Among her new parts were Lady Macbeth, Belvidera in *Venice Preserved,* Sigismunda in *Tancred and Sigismunda,* Indiana in *The Conscious Lovers,* Cordelia in *King Lear,* Ophelia in *Hamlet,* and Isabella in *The Fatal Marriage.* Her last appearance was probably on the day the Hallam venture at Goodman's Fields ended, 11 April 1747; on that day *The Fair Penitent* and *Miss in Her Teens* were performed but the casts were not listed. After so auspicious a season it is odd that theatrical records contain no further mention of Anne Eustace Budgell's acting. She died at Bath about 1755.

Buett, Hugh [fl. 1651–1662], musician.

The Middlesex County Sessions Books identify Hugh Buett as a musician in the parish of St Giles in the Fields from about 1651 to 1662; according to these records one of his pupils was John Pike.

Buffon, [Mons?] [fl. 1734–1735], actor.

The London Stage lists one Buffon as performing during the 1734–35 winter season at the Haymarket Theatre, presumably with the troupe of French players who arrived shortly before 26 October 1734 and remained most of the season, but no roles are recorded for him.

Bugani or **Buggiani**. *See* **BUGIANI**.

"Bug-Nose" [*fl. 1754*], *dancer.*

A dancer at Sadler's Wells about 1754 was called "Bug-Nose" because of the warts on his nose; his name, unfortunately, has been lost, as has a painting by Hayman which the Sadler's Wells manager Thomas Rosoman commissioned. The painting was a group picture of Rosoman and his friends which once hung in the Sir Hugh Myddleton's Tavern, near Sadler's Wells; Hayman depicted "Bug-Nose" pointing at his unfortunate affliction.

Bugiani, Signor [*fl. 1753–1754*], *dancer.*

At Covent Garden on 30 April 1753 Signor Bugiani (or Bugani) danced a minuet with his daughter, Signora Elizabetta Bugiani; at her benefit the next year, on 30 March 1754, he joined her in a "Mock Minuet." He was apparently not a regular member of the company, and these two appearances may have been his only ones in London.

Bugiani, Elizabetta [*fl. 1752–1757*], *dancer.*

On 9 October 1752 Signora Elizabetta Bugiani arrived from the Paris Opéra with Signor Cassimo (or Cosimo) Maranesi to appear at Covent Garden. Though styled as adults, the pair were youngsters, and it is probable that they came over with Elizabetta's father who was also a dancer. For their introduction to English audiences the pair offered two dances which proved popular throughout the season: *Les charbonniers* and *Les sabotiers Tyrolese*. Their second appearance was on 1 November, and James Winston saved a clipping describing them: "They were just[ly] admired by the whole House for great Execution

and amazing Variety of Comic Gestures . . . [They] are both very young. The Lady, as we are informed, not being above 15, and Signior Maranesi about 16 years old." The *duo* danced throughout the season, and on 30 April 1753 Elizabetta's father joined her in a minuet.

After spending the summer in Paris the couple returned to Covent Garden for the 1753–54 season. On 7 March 1754 Elizabetta was a Shepherdess in the afterpiece *The Sheep Shearing* and did a new dance with Maranesi called *Les jardiniers*; for her benefit on 30 March her father again joined her in a minuet, and with Maranesi she danced another new piece, *Le matelot*.

For the 1754–55 season the young couple joined the King's Theatre in the Haymarket, first appearing there on 9 November 1754. At their benefit on 18 March 1755 Elizabetta performed a new pantomime dance in men's clothes and did a minuet with Maranesi. They continued pleasing the opera audiences through the 1755–56 season, their last benefit being on 6 April 1756. A note in the Burney Collection at the British Museum indicates that Signora Bugiani and Signor Maranesi were at this time living in Dean Street, Soho; if the 1752 report of their ages was correct, they would now have been about 20 and 21 respectively. For the 1756–57 season Signora Bugiani danced at the Smock Alley Theatre, Dublin, after which she may have returned to the Continent.

Buher, Mr [*fl. 1683*], *actor.*

A Mr Buher (or Buber) player Master Sentwell in *The Jovial Crew* at Drury Lane in December 1683. This is the only occurrence of this name in the theatrical records, and it could be a scribal error.

Bulbrick. *See* **BULLBRICK**.

Buling, Hans [*fl. 1670*], *mountebank, actor.*

Granger's *Biographical History of England* states that "Hans Buling, a Dutchman,

Harvard Theatre Collection

HANS BULING
by Laroon

was well known in London as a mountebank. He was an odd figure of a man, and
was extremely fantastical in his dress. He
was attended by a monkey, which he had
trained up to act the part of Jack Pudding;
a part which he had formerly acted himself." A picture of him with his ape and
chest of medicine and his harlequin coming
from behind a curtain was embellished with
the following verses:

> *See Sirs, see here!*
> *a Doctor rare,*
> *who Travels much at Home,*
> *Here take my Bills,*
> *I cure all Ills*
> *past, present and to come:*
> *The Cramp, the Itch,*
> *The gout, the [tw]itch*
> *The Squirt, the stone, the P—x:*
> *The Mulligrubs,*

> *The Bonny Scrubbs,*
> *and all Pandora's Box:*
> *Thousands I've Dissected,*
> *Thousands new erected,*
> *and such cures effected,*
> *as none e're can tell.*
> *Let the Palsie shake ye,*
> *Let the Chollick rack ye,*
> *Let the Crinckum break ye,*
> *Let the Murrain take ye,*
> *take this and you are well,*
> *Come wits so keen*
> *Devour'd with Spleen,*
> *come Beaus who sprain'd your backs,*
> *Great Belly'd Maids*
> *Old Founder'd Jades,*
> *and pepper'd Vizard Cracks.*
> *I soon remove,*
> *The pains of Love,*
> *and cure the Love-sick Maid;*
> *The Hot, the Cold*
> *The Young, the Old,*
> *the Living, and the Dead*
> *I clear the Lass,*
> *With Wainscot Face,*
> *and from Pimpinets free,*
> *Plump Ladys red,*
> *Like Saracen's Head,*
> *with toaping Rattafia*
> *This with a Jirk,*
> *Will do your Work*
> *and Scour you o're and o're*
> *Read, Judge and Try*
> *And if you Die*
> *never believe me more.*

The engraving, dated 1670 in George's
Catalogue of Political and Personal Satires,
was titled "The Infallible Mountebank or
Quack Doctor." The figure of Buling alone
was published in Marcellus Laroon's *Cries
of London*, engraved by G. Walker.

Buling was also pictured on a Delft
plate as "a Mountebank of great Notoriety
who frequently exhibited in Covent Garden," a copy of which was engraved by
I. R. Cruikshank.

Bulkeley, Mrs [*fl. 1769*], *equestri-
enne.*

In the middle of June 1769 a Mrs Bulkeley began to give equestrian performances
with the well-known trick rider Hyam at

"Mr Kearney's Manage in Channel Row, near Smithfield," Dublin. An advertisement of 8 July 1769 proclaimed that for "one British shilling" admission might be gained to view these performers who have "exhibited before their Majesties at Kew." She was perhaps Mrs George Bulkley.

Bulkely, Mr *fl. 1742–1743?, actor.*

The name "Buckley" appeared in the Lincoln's Inn Fields playhouse bill of 3 December 1742 opposite the character of Bull in *The Relapse.* There is hardly any doubt that he was the representer of Beau and Virtuoso in *Bickerstaff's Unburied Dead* at the same theatre on 14 January 1743, though his name was then spelled "Bulkely." On 14 February (as "Buckley"), he was Paddington in *The Beggar's Opera,* and on 24 March the bill announced that "Tickets deliver'd out for . . . Bulkely . . . will be taken." Neither name appeared again in London bills for many years afterward.

It is possible that he was the "Mr Bulkley" who was at Edinburgh and had a benefit on 1 February 1734. A "Mrs Bulkeley" was with him and was still there in 1735–36.

Bulkley, Mr *fl. 1709?, musician.*

On 21 November 1709 a benefit concert was given for Mr Bulkley at Godwin's Dancing School, and on 30 November he performed at a concert at Stationers' Hall. The instrument of his specialty is not known. He was, one would suppose, the father of the Bulkley Junior of 1713.

Bulkley, Mr *fl. 1713?, musician?*

A "Bulkley Junior," probably the son of the 1709 musician, shared a benefit with Pitchford at a Hampstead Wells concert on 27 June 1713; the advertisement did not indicate whether he performed or, if he did, what instrument he played.

Bulkley, George *d. 1784, violinist.*

The first known public mention of George Bulkley was in a list of payments to Covent Garden Theatre performers as of 14 September 1767, drawn up by Arthur Murphy, in which Bulkley was placed among the musicians in the pit band at a *per diem* salary of 6s. 8d. He had been married at Chelsea on 9 August to Mary Wilford, the dancer, daughter of Edward Wilford, brother-in-law of the Covent Garden patentee John Rich. (Burney calls him "G. Bulkley, builder," and this may have been his secondary occupation.) The Bulkleys' daughter Mary Elizabeth was baptized at St Paul, Covent Garden, on 9 November 1768. The William Fisher Bulkley who was left £400 by Edward Wilford and who was about 20 years old in 1780 must have been the George Bulkleys' son.

The marriage proved uncongenial, and by 1773 at the latest Mrs Bulkley had begun her long love affair with James Dodd. In 1774 she and her lover eloped to Dublin.

Bulkley was at some date before 1768 violinist and leader in the band of the Bristol Theatre, in which he acquired a quarter share from Robert Bensley in December 1772. He remained for some years in the bands of Covent Garden in the winter and of the Haymarket in the summer. Reed's "Notitia Dramatica" under date of 21 August 1784 notes: "From the opening of the Haymarket to this time 6 Persons belonging to that Theatre have died," and "Bulkeley," a musician, is among them. Mary Wilford Bulkley, his widow, married Ebenezer Barrisford in 1788.

George Bulkley may have been related to the other Bulkleys we have noticed or to the Mr and Mrs Bulkley who were acting at Edinburgh in 1728 through 1735, but no connection has been established.

Bulkley, Mrs George, Mary, née Wilford, later Mrs Ebenezer Barrisford, *1748–1792, actress, dancer.*

Mary Wilford was the daughter of Edward Wilford (d. 1789), a minor official of Covent Garden Theatre and of the Auditor's Office. He was the brother of Priscilla

Wilford, who had married John Rich, the Covent Garden patentee.

John Jackson the Edinburgh manager remembered seeing Mary at Rich's country house at Cowley, near Uxbridge, "where I used to be upon a visit for weeks together. . . . She was then about fourteen or fifteen years of age, possessed of an elegant figure, and had every advantage of education to render her accomplishments complete."

She had also, of course, the advantage of being related to the management. Yet her beauty and talents would have sufficed without that good fortune. At perhaps eight or nine years of age she was given into the care and tutelage of the competent dancer Michael Poitier. She made her first appearance on any stage dancing with Master Banti on 11 April 1758 for Poitier's benefit, and she danced publicly once or twice again during her apprentice years.

Mary was signed on at Covent Garden at a salary of £1 3s. 4d. per week in 1761–62 as a dancer; and even after her first appearance as an actress, in the role of Miranda in *The Busy Body* for her own benefit on 23 April 1765, she was known chiefly for her dancing. Her second appearance in a leading role was as Estifania in *Rule a Wife and Have a Wife* on 16 October, which made the owner of that part, the erstwhile favorite of Rich's family, George Ann Bellamy, bitterly resentful. Mary remained at Covent Garden as Miss Wilford until her marriage with George Bulkley, a violinist in the Covent Garden band, at Chelsea on 9 August 1767; and she continued, under her married name, until the end of the season of 1779–80 (though on 4 May 1770 she was borrowed by Drury Lane to play Harriet in *The Funeral*). She was somewhere out of London in 1780–81 and was at Edinburgh in 1781–82, though she played at the Haymarket from 6 June through 11 September 1782. John Jackson had engaged her as a lead, with lavish promises, to decorate his first season as manager of the Edinburgh house. Unfortunately her

best roles stood in the exact line of Mrs Jackson, and a paper war with her manager's wife ensued in the Edinburgh *Courant*. Mrs Bulkley evidently won, for Jackson later became her enthusiastic partisan.

Mrs Bulkley played her first role as a regular member of the Drury Lane company, performing Viola in *Twelfth Night*, on 21 September 1782, and followed a full season there with a busy summer at the Haymarket again. She remained in the Drury Lane Company in the winter of 1783–84, summering again at the Haymarket. A sudden dip in her popularity in 1783–84, attributable probably to an unusually brazen love affair, left her after her benefit night with a deficiency of £28 17s. 2d. From 1785–86 through 1787–88, she was playing again at Edinburgh in the win-

Harvard Theatre Collection

MARY BULKLEY, as Mrs Wilding

by J. Roberts

ters but she signed on at the Haymarket regularly in the summers. She was on the Haymarket bills as Mrs Bulkley from 12 June through 14 July 1788. On 22 July she married Captain Ebenezer Barrisford of the East India trade at St George, Hanover Square, and continued through 13 September acting under her new name. She was not employed at either Covent Garden or Drury Lane the following winter; but she was at the Haymarket from 18 May 1789 until her last London appearance, on 15 September, when she substituted for Mrs Kemble, as Margaret in *The Battle of Hexham*.

The Bulkleys' daughter Mary Elizabeth had been baptized at St Paul, Covent Garden, on 9 November 1768, but nothing is known about her. Edward Wilford, in a codicil to his will dated 15 March 1788, left £400 in stock to a William Fisher Bulkley who apparently was then 20 years old. The Bulkleys' marriage seems to have been very quickly in trouble. Mary's great beauty and small powers of resistance attracted many admirers. She may have been the Mrs Bulkley who was with Hyam the equestrian in Dublin in June 1769, and her name was vaguely linked in *amour* with other performers.

George Bulkley had been at some time leader of the Bristol theatre's band. In December 1772, he had bought one half of Robert Bensley's half share of the Bristol theatrical enterprise. The other half share seems to have been owned by James Dodd, an actor of fops and beaux, and himself a foppish little man. Mrs Bulkley had played leading parts at Bristol during breaks in her London schedule in 1768, 1769, and 1771, and after her husband entered the management, she acted there again. There was gossip about a "celebrated actress at Bristol" being "detected in bed with the sing-song insignificant Mr D" in the *Bath Chronicle* of 20 August 1772. In the summer of 1774 Mary Bulkley and Dodd ran off from London to Ireland together. William Smith the actor (who had himself left his wife in London and eloped to Dublin with Mrs Hartley that summer) wrote to Garrick on 12 July that Mrs Bulkley would not earn much in the Irish capital. Indeed, it seems that neither she nor her *innamorato* earned much, owing to the somewhat unfairly discriminatory disapprobation of the Dublin public because of their flaunting of convention (the Smith-Hartley liaison seems to have provoked no comparable reaction in Dublin). On 8 September, Garrick wrote to the actor John Moody, "Dodd has been much worse for his voyage (as I suppose he is not ye better for his intrigue) he is money bound in Dublin and I shall release him . . . Mrs Bakley [*sic*] is returned safe to her husband." She was not "safe" for very long, for Tate Wilkinson engaged her and Dodd at York in 1777.

The chronology of her other notorious affairs is conjectural. She seems, however, to have had a protracted connection with John ("Big") Banks, the harlequin and provincial manager, who was succeeded as her lover by John (or James) Brown Williamson (really Williams), while the three votaries of Venus were acting together at Edinburgh in 1781. According to the somewhat indignant account in the *Secret History of the Green Room*, Williamson had "two or three fine children," as well as a wife. But Mrs Bulkley conceived a ruthless passion for him and made him send his family to live with relations in London. "Mr BANKS, who had hitherto been Mrs BULKELEY's gallant, could not submit passively to this change. He challenged Mr. WILLIAMSON, and even struck him in the Dressingroom; but without affecting any alteration in the Lady's mind." Williamson went to Liverpool in the summer of 1782

at the same time Mrs Bulkeley first appeared at the Haymarket; and so strong was the passion of that Lady, that she sent several sums of money to him; and miserable when out of his society, she exerted every nerve to have him engaged at the same Theatre in London, and at last she accomplished it.

But Williamson's debut as Hamlet at the Haymarket in 1783 failed to gain him much attention. He played secondary roles at the Haymarket through the summer of 1792 and was never on the stage of a London patent theatre but once (as a substitute for Wroughton at Drury Lane on 11 February 1784). He later went to the Continent, failing in a theatrical venture at Hamburg in 1794, and in 1796 he turned up in America. He died in Charleston, South Carolina, on 26 March 1802. How long his affair with Mrs Bulkley lasted is not known. Perhaps it did not overlap her marriage with Captain Barrisford in 1788, but the contrary is much to be feared. She and Williamson were together in the Edinburgh company, where the *Thespian Dictionary* says he was named deputy-manager by Mrs Esten in the season of 1791–92, not long before Mary Bulkley died.

On 6 January 1785, at Edinburgh, Mrs Bulkley, who had been advertised to open the season as Clarinda in *The Suspicious Husband,* had been injured when her carriage overturned on the North Bridge on the way to the theatre from her lodgings at the house of the painter Stevenson. Possibly there were lasting effects from the accident. She evidently drank heavily in her final years.

According to the *Newcastle Courant* of 29 December 1792, Mrs Barrisford died at Dumfries on 19 December 1792, aged 44. In the Folger Library's copy of James Dibdin's *The Annals of the Edinburgh Stage* (1888) there is affixed a much earlier manuscript note by Charles Kirkpatrick Sharpe:

Mrs Bulkeley, the celebrated comic actress, whose portrait frequently occurs in the first Edition of Bell's British Theatre, . . . belonged to Williamson's company of players . . . she was buried in the Church yard of Dumfries, not far from where Burns lies—or lay—she was in wretched pecuniary circumstances—I know that my father frequently gave her money, and, I believe, contributed to her funeral expences—I saw her play Clarinda in the Suspicious Husband—excellently well—far better than the vulgar trulls, not excepting Mrs Jordan, whom I have since seen—tho' she was then old—sickly—and with a very red face; which was attributed to too much tenderness for cordial waters.

Mrs Bulkley seems to have been a woman of spirit as well as talent. On 20 November 1779, while playing Portia, she was received with hissing and catcalls. Advancing to the footlights she announced "that as an actress she had always done her best to oblige the public, and as to her private character she begged to be excused." She had another such crisis of audience disapproval in 1783–84. But for most of her career her unusual beauty and undeniable abilities carried her easily over the objections put forward by the growing number of public moralists in the London audiences, and the grumbling about her conduct in the public prints was easily balanced by poems of praise.

The year 1767, when she was still principally a young dancer but had begun speaking parts in comedy, was particularly fruitful in compliments, some of it no doubt inspired by the managers. An anonymous verse, surviving in a newspaper clipping, is a good sample of these vacuities:

How various are the shapes she wears
How lovely she's in all!
Applauding multitudes she chears,
Admirers hopeless fall.

The last stanza sounds, knowing what we now know, somewhat ironic, until we remember that she was then only 19:

Yet (blessings on the pious care
That rear'd the tender frame)
One here hath claim to all that share,
And Wilford is her name.

Perhaps *The Rational Rosciad* of the same year was a little more prescient:

Wilford, all flame, vivacity and life,
Shines in a young coquet, or modish
    wife,
But often overdoes her part too much,
And causes strict propriety to blush.

Francis Gentleman in *The Dramatic Censor* (1770) complained "Why is she so neglected by the managers?" and gave her good marks as Imogen in *Cymbeline*, Angelina in *Love Makes a Man*, and Lady Grace in *The Provok'd Husband*, for her "very amiable appearance, easy deportment, and unaffected delivery." Though in Miranda in *The Busy Body* he placed her second only to Miss Macklin, he finally summed her up as essentially just a "pretty woman," and "agreeable" actress, "where nothing great is wanted." Over the twenty years after this judgment her repertoire increased and she learned the lessons that only experience can add to talent, but there is no reason to modify Gentleman's early assessment by very much, though in some certain parts she was above everyone. John Jackson said that her Lady Racket would be remembered as long as one who had heard it was alive. She was more than competent, but less than uniformly brilliant, and though in the earlier years assiduous study refined her technique, in the later ones dissipation began to coarsen it. As Sharpe's testimony shows, however, her native ability to the last pushed her ahead of the common ruck of comediennes toward the end of the century.

Mary Wilford Bulkley Barrisford in her day played many parts and "created" not a few—among them Miss Richland in Goldsmith's *The Good-Natured Man*, Miss Hardcastle in *She Stoops to Conquer*, and Julia in Sheridan's *The Rivals*. Sheridan, writing (as "Aristarchus") to the *Morning Chronicle* of 2 February 1775, was doubtless puffing his new production but perhaps telling truth too. He thought that "Mrs Bulkeley never appeared to more advantage than in the amiable and elegant Julia."

From among her numerous other characters one might select as illustrative of her range and quality the following: Portia in *The Merchant of Venice*, Sylvia in *The Recruiting Officer*, Mrs Sullen in *The Stratagem*, Dame Kitely in *Every Man in His Humour*, Phillis in *The Conscious Lovers*, Flora in *The Country Lasses*, Mrs Harlow in *The Old Maid*, Violante in *The Wonder*, Maria in *The Citizen*, Lady Louisa in *The Double Mistake*, Jessica in *The Merchant of Venice*, Rosalind in *As You Like It*, Beatrice in *Much Ado About Nothing*, Angelina in *Love Makes a Man*, Mariana in *The Miser*, Valeria in *The Roman Father*, Molly in *The English Merchant*, Mrs Oakly in *The Jealous Wife*, Isabella in *The Wonder*, Lavinia in *The Fair Penitent*, Statira in *The Rival Queens*, Mrs Lovemore in *The Way to Keep Him*, Caelia in *The Fox*, Anne Bullen in *King Henry VIII*, Mrs Frail in *Love for Love*, Queen Mary in *The Albion Queen*, Oriana in *The Inconstant*, Elvira in *The Spanish Fryar*, Viola in *Twelfth Night*, Lady Alton in *The English Merchant*, and Bridget in *The Chapter of Accidents*.

For all that she acted Cordelia well in her youth, the overwhelming preponderance of her effort, as the list shows, was in comedy.

Roberts sketched in India ink, and Thornthwaite engraved, a portrait of Mrs Bulkley as Lady Dainty in *The Double Gallant* for *Bell's British Theatre* in 1777, and the sketch is in the British Museum. The same artists drew and engraved her portrait in costume as Angelina in Cibber's *Love Makes a Man* in 1776 and as Mrs Wilding in Garrick's *Gamesters* in 1778; and an anonymous engraver produced her likeness from J. Roberts's portrait of her as Mrs Ford in *The Merry Wives of Windsor* as a plate to Bell's edition of Shakespeare, 1776. In 1785 J. H. Ramberg drew and Thornthwaite engraved her as the Princess of France in *Love's Labour's Lost* for *Bell's British Theatre*. The original is in the British Museum; it was re-engraved by B. Reading in 1785. E. Roffe re-engraved the Roberts portrait of Mrs Bulkley as Mrs Wilding in 1878.

"Bull Speaker." *See* AMNER, RALPH.

Bull, Mr [*fl.* 1797], *actor.*

At the Haymarket Theatre on 4 December 1797 a Mr Bull made his only London appearance on record, playing the title role in *Cato.*

Bull, Thomas [*fl.* 1794], *bassoonist, bass player?*

Doane's *Musical Directory* of 1794 listed Thomas Bull, of Lower Grosvenor Street, as a bassoonist and a bass (viol player, presumably, but he may have been a bass singer). He participated in concerts put on by the Portland Chapel Society.

Bull, William [*fl.* 1666–1700], *trumpeter, instrument maker.*

William Bull was made a trumpeter extraordinary—that is, without pay until a position became vacant—in the King's Musick on 2 July 1666. By the time he was granted a position in ordinary in 1677, replacing the deceased John Christmas, Bull had already started an instrument making and repair business. He worked not only on trumpets, but also on French horns, speaking trumpets, hearing horns, powder flasks, and "wind guns" (early air rifles). Some of his work, especially toward the end of the century, was of exceptional quality.

Bull's service with the court continued into the reigns of James II and William III, and the accounts show that from about 1685 onward the royal musicians brought their broken instruments to Bull for repairs, and he became the official trumpet-maker to the King. In the early part of 1691 Bull was one of the musicians chosen to accompany William III on his trip to Holland, an indication of the high position he held at court.

Bull's name figured infrequently in legal squabbles, but on 23 April 1694 he petitioned against kettledrummer Robert Mawgridge for using "scandalous words"; the details of the case are not known, however. Bull was occasionally cited in the Lord Chamberlain's accounts in connection with finances, so we know his salary in 1697 was £91 5*s.* annually, over twice that of most other instrumentalists, for trumpeters were highly valued. His salary plus his flourishing business must have given Bull a handsome income, and that may have led him, on 5 January 1700, to surrender his post at court to John Conrad Richter.

William Bull's place of business shifted from time to time. In 1681 his shop, "The Trumpet and Horn," was in Salisbury Street, near the Strand, but in that year he moved to the lower end of the Haymarket, near Pall Mall, where he stayed until 1700. After the turn of the century he had his shop in Castle Street by Leicester Fields, "near the Muyse." Some of his musical instruments have been preserved at the London and Horniman Museums, and they demonstrate how advanced over the French and German trumpet makers William Bull was.

A William Bull, possibly the trumpeter, was from the parish of St Margaret, Westminster; he had three sons by his wife Elizabeth: George, baptized on 26 October 1671; William, baptized on 22 August 1673, who died in infancy; and a second William, baptized on 28 January 1675.

Bullard, John [*fl.* 1690–1692], *kettledrummer.*

In a 9 March 1690 livery warrant, John Bullard was mentioned as a kettledrummer in the troop of Lord Overkirke; he was granted livery again on 19 May 1692. Bullard's service was as a member of the King's Musick.

Bullbrick, George [*fl.* 1750–1757],
actor, dancer.

The first mention of George Bullbrick
in the playbills was on 13 December 1750
when he played Scarlett in *Robin Hood* at
Drury Lane. He was not noticed again until 13 May 1751 when he acted Mat-o-Mint
in *The Beggar's Opera*, a performance for
which he was granted benefit tickets to sell.
His 1751–52 season is a blank, but on 11
May 1753 he shared a benefit with three
others; again in 1753–54 no mention was
made of him, but on 5 May 1755 he was
granted another shared benefit. When Noverre's *Chinese Festival* was produced on
8 November 1755 Bullbrick was named
among the dancers, but his part was omitted
a week later. The last notice of him was on
10 May 1757 when *Henry VIII* was presented; he shared a benefit this date but was
no more than a supernumerary in the production.

Bullock, Miss [*fl.* 1777–1778],
dancer.

A Miss Bullock, possibly related to the
large family of Bullocks, performers of the
first half of the eighteenth century, danced
at Covent Garden during the 1777–78 season.

Bullock, Christopher *c.* 1690–1722,
actor, playwright.

Christopher Bullock was born about
1690, the first son of the elder William
Bullock, actor and booth operator. To distinguish him from his father during his
early years, he was usually noted as Bullock
Junior or Young Bullock. It was under this
latter billing that he made what was probably his first stage appearance on 31 December 1707 at the Queen's Theatre in the
Haymarket playing Appletree in *The Recruiting Officer*. On this same date the acting of straight plays was restricted to Drury
Lane and operas to the Queen's so Christopher and his father switched houses, and it
was at Drury Lane in July 1708 that Christopher was billed again, this time as Posa

in *Don Carlos* and Hypolito in *The Tempest*. In 1709–10 the rules changed again
and Bullock went back to the Queen's Theatre, adding to his repertory such roles as
Antonio in *The Rover*, Young Bellair in
The Man of Mode, King Edward in *Edward III*, and Statira in a burlesque of *The
Rival Queens* (skirts parts were played by
all the male Bullocks). At Greenwich on
1 July 1710 he acted Horatio in *Hamlet*,
and on the twelfth he was Purser in *The
Fair Quaker of Deal*.

Back at Drury Lane the next season
(after another managerial shuffling) Bullock acted Dorilant in *The Country Wife*
on 29 April 1709 and Whisper in *The
Busy Body* on 12 May. Though his name
had not appeared in the bills with great
frequency up to this time, beginning with
the 1710–11 season he was much more active and his popularity was growing. For
four more seasons he remained at Drury
Lane, playing such roles as Edgeworth in
Bartholomew Fair, Sylla in *Caius Marius*,
Vernon in *1 Henry IV*, Shamwell in *The
Squire of Alsatia*, Tranio in *Sauny the Scot*,
Clerimont in *Philaster*, Lovewell in *Love
and a Bottle*, Malcolm in *Macbeth*, the title
role in *The Pilgrim*, and Antonio in *The
Tempest*.

In the summer of 1714 Bullock and a
collection of other actors calling themselves the Duke of Southampton and
Cleaveland's Servants acted *Injured Virtue*
at a playhouse in Richmond; he may have
performed with the group when the play
was revived on 1 November at the King's
Arms Tavern in Southwark. Bullock's association with Drury Lane was nearing an
end, for he and his father were lured by
John Rich to the new Lincoln's Inn Fields
Theatre in late 1714; on 27 November
Christopher played Young Bellair at Drury
Lane, but by 4 January 1715 he was working at Rich's house. With the new troupe
he was able to play a considerable number
of roles which had been unavailable to him
before, among which were Fondlewife in

CHRISTOPHER BULLOCK

engraved by Charles Hall, after Hogarth

The Old Bachelor, Trapland in *Love for Love*, Stanmore in *Oroonoko*, Brazen in *The Recruiting Officer*, Novel in *The Plain Dealer*, Lord Rake in *The Provoked Wife*, Antonio in *Don Sebastian*, Sir Novelty in *Love's Last Shift*, and Balderdash in *The Twin Rivals*. His range was wide, encompassing fops and comic servants, as well as handsome lovers and, occasionally, serious roles in tragedies. His forte was comedy, though, and the *Poetical Register* described him as "sprightly on the Stage" and the counterpart at Lincoln's Inn Fields of Colley Cibber at the rival house.

During these years Christopher Bullock expanded his activities into the field of playwriting. His first attempt was an afterpiece, *The Slip*, first given on 3 February 1715; the work was based on Middleton's *A Mad World My Masters*, and Bullock wrote the role of Trickwell for himself. His other works, chiefly farces, came out within the next three years: *A Woman's Revenge* (adapted from Behn) in 1715;

The Cobler of Preston (original but based on *The Taming of the Shrew*), *The Adventures of Half an Hour* (original), and *Woman's a Riddle* (adapted from *La Dama Duende*) in 1716; *The Per-Juror* (original) in 1717; and his revision of *The Traytor* on 1718. Though Bullock wrote nothing of great significance, many of his works remained popular for years and were splendid vehicles for his own lively acting talent.

A promising young actress, Jane Rogers, the natural daughter of Robert Wilks and the elder Jane Rogers, had joined John Rich's company at the same time as Bullock, and on 23 May 1717 they were married. By this time Christopher had gained a position of considerable importance in the troupe, and when Rich completed the 1716–17 season "almost broke," the management was taken over by Bullock and Theophilus Keene. He had to curtail his acting during his first season as co-manager, though on 3 February 1718 he was a triumph as Colonel Fainwell in *A Bold Stroke for a Wife*, a role remembered four decades later as the one which established the reputation of "Kit Bullock, a smart sprightly actor." In 1718–19 he had more time for acting and played such roles as Brisk in *The Double Dealer*, Obadiah in *The Committee*, Constant in *The Provoked Wife*, Prig in *The Royal Merchant*, Gripe in *The City Wives' Conspiracy*, Poins in *1 Henry IV*, Young Woudbe in *The Twin Rivals*, and Osric in *Hamlet*.

There seems to be only one record of Christopher Bullock's being in a scrape with the law, and the details of the case are a mystery: on 22 May 1719 he was to play the Doctor in *Harlequin Hydaspes*, but the premier performance had to be postponed because of his "unexpected arrest." His record otherwise appears remarkably clean, and one might guess that he was too busy working to get himself into trouble.

During the 1719–20 season at Lincoln's Inn Fields Bullock added still more new roles to his expanding repertory, among which were Decius Brutus in *Julius Caesar*, Truman in *The Squire of Alsatia*, The Bishop of Carlisle in *Richard II*, Shattilion in *Cymbeline*, Gratiano in *The Merchant of Venice*, and Gripe in *The Confederacy*. In 1720–21 he was plagued off and on by illness and apparently in financial difficulties because of it. He received, according to Latreille, four benefits. As the season began he acted regularly, playing, among other roles, Slender in *The Merry Wives of Windsor*; on 27 October 1720 he played Osric for his own benefit, but the receipts were only £76 15s. In November and December he played a busy schedule, and on 24 January 1721 *King Lear* was done for his benefit, the receipts being £72 12s. He continued acting in January and February, adding Lucio in *Measure for Measure* to his parts, and on 14 March he was granted a third benefit, this time taking in £98. 6d. On 26 April he had his fourth benefit, the receipts for which were £98 18s. The strain of trying to perform despite his deteriorating physical condition finally caught up with him on 17 May 1721 when the play had to be changed because he was too sick to go on.

By the fall of 1721 Bullock was sufficiently recovered to act frequently through the end of the year, and he even had strength to add such roles as the Chaplain in *The Orphan*, Scrub in *The Stratagem*, Renault in *Venice Preserved*, and Snuffle in *Injured Love*. He did his last acting in January 1722, playing Slender, Gratiano, Brisk, and a comic role in *Coriolanus*. He was scheduled to play Sir Davy in *The Soldier's Fortune* on 9 January, and though dangerously ill, he "chose to rise [from his bed] and perform his Part; rather than disappoint the Audience, but was not able to finish it; therefore his Part in the last Act was read by another." In the cast that day were his father, playing Sir Jolly, and his wife Jane, playing Sylvia. For the next two months his fellow actors took

his parts for him: Aston played Scrub on 17 January, and Kit's brother William played Slender for him at his benefit on 26 March. The benefit bill said that Christopher was "in great Distress" and had "kept his Chamber these Two Months, under a Severe and Expensive Sickness." The receipts were £117 14s., but he did not live long enough to enjoy his profit.

On Thursday morning 5 April 1722 Christopher Bullock died "of a Fistula and a Consumption." He was buried on 8 April at Hampstead, "his corpse . . . attended from his father's house at North End in this parish to the place of interment by a great number of theatrical gentlemen" from both major playhouses. One report'had it that he had languished for a long time "under the concern of very bad circumstances & a much worse wife." He and Jane had at least three children: Robert (named after Robert Wilks?), baptized at St Clement Danes on 11 June 1718 when the Bullocks were living in Hollis Street; James, baptized on 30 July 1719 at the same church; and, probably, Harriet, born in late February or March 1721.

Christopher Bullock was looked upon in his time as the only possible successor to Colley Cibber in fop roles, and he seemed to have held the respect of both his colleagues and his competitors—if not his wife. The *London Chronicle* in 1758 remembered him as "tall, agreeable in his person," with "a comic kind of voice, which vented itself in a shrillness of tone, but never sunk into meanness."

The Garrick Club has an oil sketch attributed to Hogarth which is now called Christopher Bullock but was once identified as his father William. The Huntington Library has an uncatalogued portrait of the actor.

Bullock, Mrs Christopher, Jane, née Rogers *d. 1739, actress.*

Mrs Christopher Bullock was born Jane Rogers, the natural daughter of actors Robert Wilks and Jane Rogers. Since she first appeared on 14 March 1715 billed as Miss Rogers (playing Morena in *Ibrahim*, a role her mother had "created" in May 1696), young Jane was probably born around the turn of the century. Robert Wilks had been in London from 1699–1700 on, but he had also been there in 1693–94, so another possible birthdate for his daughter might be about 1694–95; in either case, young Jane could have been styled "Miss" in 1715, and the size of some of her early roles might argue for the earlier birthdate.

During the rest of the 1714–15 season Miss Rogers played Athenais in *Theodosius*, Rosalinda in *Sophonisba*, Amintia in *The Sea Voyage*, Selima in *Tamerlane*, and the title role in *The Fair Quaker of Deal*. Considering the importance of these parts, she may have come to the Lincoln's Inn Fields Theatre with some experience behind her, though her debut bill on 14 March called her "Mrs Rogers' Daughter, who never yet appear'd upon any Stage." In 1715–16 she added such parts as Rutland in *The Unhappy Favorite*, Fidelia in *The Plain Dealer*, Selinda in *The Perfidious Brothers*, and Indamora in *Aurengzebe*; and the following season saw her play Aurelia in *The Twin Rivals*, Angelina in *Love Makes a Man*, Parisatis in *The Rival Queens*, and Isabella in *The Squire of Alsatia*.

On 23 May 1717 she married Christopher Bullock, actor, playwright, and member of a large family of performers. Since Bullock became for a few years a manager of Lincoln's Inn Fields, Jane was in a favorable position to get several new and important roles, though, to be sure, her own talent also helped her to them. During 1718–19 she was given Morayma in *Don Sebastian*, Kate in *1 Henry IV*, Elvira in *The Spanish Friar*, Marcia in *Cato*, Lady Froth in *The Double Dealer*, Lady Macduff in *Macbeth*, Portia in *Julius Caesar*, Quisara in *The Island Princess*, and Belinda in *The Provoked Wife*. Between this season and her husband's death in 1722 she added

Lady Macbeth, Aurelia in *The Twin Rivals*, the Queen in *Richard II*, Angelica in *Love for Love*, Eugenia in *Cymbeline*, Imoinda in *Oroonoko*, Nerissa in *The Jew of Venice*, Clarissa in *The Confederacy*, Andromache in *Troilus and Cressida*, Dorinda in *The Stratagem*, Lady Anne in *Richard III*, Ruth in *The Committee*, and Lady Truman in *The Drummer*. Her range was remarkable, and she seems to have been able to handle comedy and tragedy equally well.

On 31 January 1721 *Friendship Betrayed* was deferred "on Account of Mrs Bullock's hourly Expectation of being brought to Bed, she having the Principal Part in the Play." She had acted regularly through 28 January, missed 31 January, and was scheduled to perform on 1, 4, and 14 February (and may have done so); but beginning on 18 February her parts were taken by others. Jane Bullock did not appear on stage again until the following 17 April. It seems very likely that she gave birth in late February or March and that the child was probably Harriet, who performed in the 1730's and became Mrs Michael Dyer on 26 December 1744.

Jane's husband Christopher died on 5 April 1722, the day on which she acted Silvia in *The Soldier's Fortune* at Lincoln's Inn Fields; one report stated that he had been languishing for some time from "very bad circumstances & a much worse wife" —which may well have been true in view of the fact that she performed the day of his death and again on 9 April, the day following his funeral.

During the next ten years Jane Bullock continued acting regularly for Rich's company at a salary (in 1724–25 at least) of about £100 annually, the highest in the troupe. She kept most of her old roles and added several important new ones: Melinda in *The Recruiting Officer*, Euridice in *Oedipus*, Statira in *The Rival Queens*, Belinda in *The Old Bachelor*, Charlotte in *Oroonoko*, Mrs Page in *The Merry Wives of Windsor*, Mrs Sullen in *The Stratagem*,

Hellena and Angelica in *The Rover*, Lady Fidget in *The Country Wife*, the title role in *Sophonisba*, Anne Bullen in *Henry VIII*, the Wanton Wife and Lady Brittle in *The Amorous Widow*, Celia in *Volpone*, and Alinda in *The Pilgrim*. Though she gradually moved into more mature roles, she was apparently capable of playing young coquettes, sweet young ladies, sophisticated women of fashion, and tragic heroines of the pathetic variety.

After Covent Garden opened in December 1732, Mrs Bullock continued expanding her repertory with such parts as Lady Townly in *The Provoked Husband*, Cressida in *Troilus and Cressida*, Lady Sadlife in *The Double Gallant*, Mrs Sealand in *The Conscious Lovers*, and Lady Harriet in *The Funeral*. But by 1735–36 she was nearing the end of her career at Covent Garden, and her popularity may have been waning. She was earning 16s. 8d. daily at this time, and when *The Double Dealer* was done for her benefit on 13 April 1736 it took in only £10 11s. in money and £55 in tickets. Jane had advertised an apology in advance: "The severe Affliction of Sciatica in my Hyp which I have labour'd under for near Six Weeks past . . . [has] render'd me incapable of paying my Duty to and soliciting the Interest of those Persons of Quality and Fashion who were used to honour me with their Presence." At her benefit she played Lady Froth, and in May and June she acted her old roles of Isabinda in *The Busy Body*, Isabella in *Wit Without Money*, Laetitia in *The Old Bachelor*, and the Queen in *The Unhappy Favorite*. This last role she played on 14 June 1736, after which she left for Dublin with her daughter Harriet, never to return. Whether the two sons known to have been born to Christopher and Jane Bullock were still alive is not known. Robert, possibly named after Jane's father, was born in Hollis Street and baptized at St Clement Danes on 11 June 1718; James was baptized at the same church on 30 July 1719. The three children were apparently alive in 1727, for the Lincoln's Inn Fields Theatre free list for 21 October includes "Mrs Bullock and 3 Children"—though this may have referred to Ann Russell Bullock the dancer.

On 28 January 1737 Jane Bullock was given a benefit at the Smock Alley Theatre in Dublin, though whether or not she participated in the performance of *The Careless Husband* is not known. On 7 February she played the youthful Angelica in *Love for Love*, which may have been her last stage appearance. On 11 March 1739 she died in Ireland, and on 18 March she was buried in Glasneven churchyard. The *Dublin Journal* noted only that she was "formerly a very noted actress." Chetwood later said she "pleas'd in several dramatic characters, assisted by a graceful Form and Figure." It is odd that an actress who played so many important parts should have received so little critical comment.

Bullock, Harriet. *See* DYER, MRS MICHAEL.

Bullock, Henrietta Maria, later Mrs John Ogden [fl. 1719–1748?], *dancer, actress.*

Henrietta Maria Bullock, who was presumably the daughter of the veteran actor William Bullock, made her first appearance on 5 October 1719 at Lincoln's Inn Fields Theatre, dancing between the acts of *The Busy Body*. In the play her father played Traffick, Jane Rogers Bullock (the wife of her brother Christopher) played Isabinda, and John Ogden (her future husband) played Charles. Henrietta Maria was billed as Miss Bullock and so continued until the 1720–21 season, which suggests she was probably near 20 at her first appearance and was born about the turn of the century. She was remarkably active from the start, though only occasionally did she do a specialty dance important enough to be described in the bills, as, for examples, the *Burgomaster and His Frow*, which she danced with Newhouse on 27 February 1720, or the *Dutch Skipper*, which she and Pelling performed on 14 May of the same year. She was a significant enough young member of the company to receive a benefit on 12 May 1720 shared with only one other performer.

Beginning in 1720–21 she was billed as Mrs Bullock—an indication of her maturity, not her marital status. Though she was hired as a dancer, on 7 November 1722 she tried her hand at acting, apparently for the first time, playing the one-line role of Belinda in *The Old Bachelor*. Her billing for this was, curiously, as "Miss Bullock," though the bill was probably in error; in her notices as a dancer she was occasionally called "Miss" as late as May 1723, and there is no evidence, incidentally, of these references being to a second person. On 20 December 1723 she was given what was apparently her first role in a pantomime, the Scaramouch Woman in *The Necromancer*.

On 16 February 1724 Henrietta Maria Bullock, spinster, married the bachelor actor John Ogden at St Benet, Paul's Wharf, and on 14 March she was billed as Mrs Ogden. By September 1724 she was receiving 6s. 8d. daily wages at Lincoln's Inn Fields, and, beginning this season, she was more frequently used in pantomimes and given such roles as Clotho in *Harlequin Sorcerer* (21 January 1725) and one of the Graces in *Mars and Venus* (17 April 1725). The following season she played a Nymph and a Bacchante in *Apollo and Daphne* (14 January 1726), Colombine in *The Jealous Doctor* (19 July), and the small servant's role of Peg in *Epsom Wells* (22 July). During the next few years she continued her dancing chores and again occasionally played a small role in a play: on 8 May 1727 she acted the Mad Lady in *The Pilgrim*, and on 25 August 1729 at her father's booth at Bartholomew Fair she played Betty in the ballad opera *Flora*. Though her summers at this point in her career were

usually spent at Bullock's fair booth, in July 1730 she performed at the Richmond theatre, where her husband acted.

John Ogden died on 3 July 1732 at their lodgings in Richmond and was buried on 8 July. Despite this, Mrs Ogden performed with the Richmond troupe in August, doing a "Fingalian" dance and a hornpipe with Smith on 17 August; and in September she was back on duty at Lincoln's Inn Fields. Certain pantomime roles appear to have become her property: a Nymph and a Polonese Woman in *Apollo and Daphne*, the Scaramouch Woman in *The Necromancer*, a Sylvan in *The Rape of Proserpine*, and an Amazon in *Perseus and Andromeda*. These, plus a few specialty dances, she continued performing at Lincoln's Inn Fields and, after it opened in 1732, Covent Garden, but she now seldom made summer appearances at Bartholomew Fair. By the 1735–36 season she was being paid £43 for 172 nights, and she received no benefits —a straight salary arrangement which apparently held true throughout most of her career. After 19 May 1737, her name dropped from the bills; on that date she danced again a Fingalian with Smith. She seems not to have made a great deal of progress in her career, and perhaps at this point she decided to retire.

On 24 August 1748 a Mrs Ogden danced between the acts of *The Unnatural Parents* at the Lee and Yeates booth at Bartholomew Fair. It would have been strange for her to dance again after so many years, and by this time Henrietta Maria would have been in her late forties, so perhaps the notice refers to a different person—possibly a daughter.

Bullock, Hildebrand *d. 1733, actor.*

Hildebrand Bullock was the second son of actor and booth manager William Bullock the elder. The first record of his appearance on stage was as Bonniface in *The Stratagem* at the playhouse in St Martin's Lane on 11 June 1712; the company consisted of sons and daughters of performers at the major theatres, and Bullock was identified as "Bullock's youngest son," which Hildebrand was if the phrase meant the youngest son on stage; he had a younger brother William; an older brother Christopher, known as Bullock Junior, was then about 22. Hildebrand acted the Companion in *The Slip*, an afterpiece by Christopher, on 3 February 1715 at Lincoln's Inn Fields, and by this time he had apparently joined his brother and father in Rich's company there. On 3 May 1715 at St Benet, Paul's Wharf, he married Ann Russell, a dancer in the Lincoln's Inn Fields troupe, so one may guess that he may have been born in the early 1690's. Though Hildebrand remained affiliated with Lincoln's Inn Fields (and Covent Garden, after it opened) for the rest of his career, his wife Ann changed companies frequently and seems not to have geared her career to his.

Most of the roles Bullock played before 1723–24 were small comic parts, such as the servant Spatterdash in *The Fond Husband*, Flute and Crotchet in the afterpiece *Pyramus and Thisbe*, a sailor in *The Fair Quaker of Deal*, Snap in *The Royal Merchant*, the Irish servant Teague in *The Twin Rivals*, Cloten in *Cymbeline*, MacMorris (another dialect role) in *The Half Pay Officers*, a recruit in *The Recruiting Officer*, and Barnardine in *Measure for Measure*. But as he matured in the early 1720's he added other, more significant parts, such as Teague in *The Committee*, Sir Amorous in *Woman's a Riddle*, Manuel in *Don Quixote*, and (replacing James Spiller) Snap in *Love's Last Shift*. He sometimes played the second Gravedigger in *Hamlet* to his father's first, and, like the elder Bullock, Hildebrand seems sometimes to have played citizens in such plays as *Oedipus* and *Julius Caesar*.

Beginning in 1723–24—the season after his talented brother Christopher died— Hildebrand's name was more frequently noted in the bills; this was not because he took over his brother's roles but probably because the Bullock name was good publicity for the company, and Hildebrand was a willing and energetic actor. He played Mrs Trudge in *Love and a Bottle*, a skirts role similar to those his father and his younger brother William frequently acted. He also was given Tom in *A Woman's Revenge*, Curtis in *Sauny the Scot*, Sancho in *Love Makes a Man*, Clodpate in *Epsom Wells*, Friar Andrew in *The Spanish Wives*, Sir Toby in *Love's Contrivances*, Saygrace in *The Double Dealer*, Jemmy Twitcher in *The Beggar's Opera*, Foigard in *The Stratagem*, one of the witches in *Macbeth*, Whisper in *The Busy Body*, and Isadore in *Timon of Athens*.

On 24 May 1733 at Covent Garden he was given a benefit and described as "under Misfortunes," and the following fall, on 25 September 1733, he played Foigard in *The Stratagem*, his last appearance on the stage. In October 1733 Hildebrand Bullock died, and he was buried at Hampstead on the twenty-first of that month. His younger brother William had died only four months before. Hildebrand never gained the prominence that his brother Christopher and father William achieved, but he was apparently a responsible and dependable actor, useful in comic servants' roles, occasional dialect characters, and small parts in crowd scenes. Even at the end of his career he was earning only 15s. daily, but he was a Bullock, and the Bullocks were good troupers. At the time of his death his wife Ann Russell Bullock was performing with the Goodman's Fields company, pursuing a stage career no more illustrious than his had been. She continued acting there and at other theatres, possibly until 1748.

Bullock, Mrs Hildebrand, Ann, née Russell [fl. 1714–1748], dancer.

Ann Russell's first appearance on stage seems to have been on 22 December 1714 at the Lincoln's Inn Fields Theatre where she danced between the acts of *The Busy*

Body. She was usually billed as Miss Russell, and this would have meant that she was probably still a minor. She had studied dancing under Delagarde and sometimes performed with her master. On 3 May 1715 she was granted a solo benefit, which suggests a high standing in the troupe and probably more public appearances than the bills of the time indicate. She celebrated her benefit day by marrying Hildebrand Bullock at St Benet, Paul's Wharf, and on 9 May, after precious little honeymooning, she danced as Mrs Bullock. Just before her marriage the bills had called her variously Miss and Mrs Russell, so she was probably about 20 or 21 in the spring of 1715 and thus, we conjecture, born about 1695.

Through 2 October 1719 Ann Russell Bullock danced regularly at Lincoln's Inn Fields, often doing such specialties as *The Dutch Skipper* or *A Burgomaster and his Frow* with Delagarde; most of the time, however, the bills give no clue as to the type of dance she offered but only indicate that she performed. She seems to have done mostly specialty work, not dances within plays, in both the comic and serious veins. On 2 October 1719 she apparently gave her last performance at John Rich's playhouse before transferring to Drury Lane, and, interestingly, on 5 October at Lincoln's Inn Fields a Miss Bullock (presumably Hildebrand's sister Henrietta Maria) made her first appearance as a dancer. There may have been a connection between this debut and Ann Russell Bullock's desertion, but there are no details to clarify the matter, just as there is no explanation in the records for Ann's husband's remaining behind at Lincoln's Inn Fields.

At Drury Lane Mrs Bullock again danced specialties at performances of regular plays, one being *The Dutch Skipper*, but this time with Thurmond Junior as her partner. She also paired off with John Weaver on occasion, one of her numbers with him being *The Sailor and his Lass*. Alone she frequently offered a Scotch dance, and with the younger Thurmond she sometimes did Delagarde's *Burgomaster* which she had previously performed with her teacher. About 1723–24 she began appearing in pantomimes, one of the first being *The Escapes of Harlequin* in which she was one of two Punch women, this being performed possibly as early as 9 October 1723. Toward the end of the season, on 4 May 1724, she and Topham danced *The Venetians* at Drury Lane, and she appeared the next day at Lincoln's Inn Fields, dancing a *Chacone* and billed as "Mrs Bullock from Drury Lane, being the first Time of her appearing on the [*recte* this] Stage these 5 Years." It was for her husband Hildebrand's benefit and a special occasion, for she was back at Drury Lane by the end of the week. If there had been any estrangement between the two during these years, it seems to have ended in 1724, for Ann completed the season at Drury Lane and went back to Lincoln's Inn Fields in the fall.

John Rich paid Mrs Bullock a daily salary of £1 13s. 4d. as of 25 September 1724 when she began dancing for him again, and she remained with his troupe for the next eight seasons. It may have been her husband who lured her back, but it may have been another consideration: if she hoped to get more assignments in pantomimes, Lincoln's Inn Fields might have appeared to be a better house, for at Drury Lane her competition would have been Hester Santlow Booth, one of the pillars of the troupe. Her first season back at Lincoln's Inn Fields was not auspicious, but in 1725–26, in addition to her occasional specialty dances, she was assigned some pantomime roles: the Pierrot Woman in *The Necromancer*, Clotho in *Harlequin Sorcerer*, and a Nymph and a Spanish Woman in *Apollo and Daphne*. On 2 May 1726 she shared a benefit with "W. Bullock"—her brother-in-law William; this has led some historians to suppose that she may have been the second wife of the elder William Bullock, but such is clearly not the case.

During the next several seasons Mrs Bullock danced regularly in John Rich's pantomimes, though she never achieved top billing; her competition at Lincoln's Inn Fields turned out to be as stiff as that at Drury Lane, for her rivals Mrs Younger, Mrs Barbier, and Mrs Chambers were all good singers, and Mrs Younger, at least, was an accomplished actress as well. Ann Bullock seems to have been only a dancer, and this may have restricted her opportunities. Perhaps the disappointment in not making any more progress at Lincoln's Inn Fields than she had made at the rival house led her to make, in the late 1720's and after, some appearances at the summer fairs. On 25 August 1729, for example, she danced at her father-in-law's booth at Bartholomew Fair, and she continued, though not regularly, to extend her activities this way. By May 1732 she was searching for other opportunities, and though Rich was planning to open the new Covent Garden Theatre the next season, Mrs Bullock shifted companies once again.

After appearing on 23 August 1732 at her father-in-law's booth at Bartholomew Fair, she moved to the Goodman's Fields Theatre and Giffard's troupe, billed as "Mrs Bullock from Lincoln's Inn Fields." During her first season there she danced the first Nymph in *The Amorous Sportsman* and Mademoiselle in a *Masquerade* composed by Thurmond, and did a number of specialty dances; on 18 April 1733 she shared a benefit with Norris—an indication that her position in the company was high, but no higher than it had been at Rich's house. In October 1733 her husband Hildebrand died, but how this affected her is far from clear; of their relationship virtually nothing is known beyond what can be guessed from her pattern of changing company affiliations —and that may have had no bearing on her home life. She and Hildebrand had at least one child, but when is not known. On the free list at Lincoln's Inn Fields on 8 January 1729 was "Mrs Bullock Dancer and Daugh-

ter"; this surely must have referred to Ann Bullock and her child.

Over the next few years at Goodman's Fields Mrs Bullock's roles were somewhat more significant than previously: she was the first Nymph in *Britannia,* Diana in *Diana and Acteon,* the Demon in *The Necromancer*, and Laverna in *Jupiter and Io*. But for the 1738–39 season Ann switched companies again, joining Rich's troupe at Covent Garden for nine months; there she danced a Mezzetin Woman in *The Necromancer,* a Grace in the *Royal Chace,* a Sylvan in *The Rape of Proserpine,* and an Amazon in *Perseus and Andromeda.* Then, in 1740–41, she went back to Goodman's Fields. During this season she played Betty Doxey, one of the Ladies of the Town, in *The Beggar's Opera,* one of her rare appearances in something other than a pantomime or *entr'acte* dance. She remained at Goodman's Fields in 1741–42 but also danced at Sadler's Wells, one of her appearances at the latter being on 19 June 1742. When the Goodman's Fields venture collapsed, Mrs Bullock, instead of again changing companies, apparently decided to be a free-lance performer. By this time she was probably in her late forties, and perhaps she reconciled herself to the fact that she was not star material.

From 1743 onward her appearances were infrequent. She was in a pantomime at Sadler's Wells on 4 April 1743; in September 1747 a Mrs Bullock, probably Ann, danced at the Yeates and Lee booth at Southwark Fair; in 1747–48 she performed occasionally at minor theatres; and with Smith as her partner she danced on 7 September 1748 at Yeates and Lee's booth again. The appearances, especially in 1747 and 1748 of a Mrs Bullock, dancer, might not refer to Ann; yet there seems to be no other candidate. By this time the daughter of Christopher and Jane Bullock had become Mrs Dyer, Henrietta Maria Bullock had long since married John Ogden, and the other known Bullock performers were dead. Perhaps Ann and Hildebrand's daughter grew up to be a dancer and billed herself as Mrs Bullock, but there is no evidence to support such a conjecture.

Ann Russell Bullock's stage career had been undistinguished, and quietly, after 1748, her name disappeared from the records.

Bullock, William *c. 1667–1742, actor, booth manager.*

William Bullock, the patriarch of the family of Bullocks who were performers, was born, probably about 1667, perhaps at York. Before coming to London in 1695 he married, but the background of his wife Margaret is obscure; it is said that he married twice before he died, but this appears to be incorrect, an error caused by a confusion of Bullock and his youngest son. William and Margaret had four children: Christopher, born about 1690; Hildebrand, born in the early 1690's; Henrietta Maria, born about 1700; and William, born probably a year or so later.

On 15 April 1695 Bullock contracted with Christopher Rich to act for the remainder of the 1694–95 season at Drury Lane for £1 weekly; Thomas Betterton and his followers had seceded from Rich's troupe just before this, and the manager included in Bullock's contract an agreement that the actor would play only with the Drury Lane company and that neither party would terminate the contract without a nine-months' notice. Whether or not Bullock arrived in London with some acting experience behind him is not known, but he may have had some, for his salary placed him in the middle rank of the company.

Though he probably acted in April and May, Bullock's first recorded performance was in September 1695 when he played "Landlady &c." in *The Mock-Marriage*; this penchant for skirts roles he bequeathed to all his sons. From the start his specialty was comedy and farce, as a sampling of his roles before the turn of the century indicates: Sly

in *Love's Last Shift*, Sir Morgan in *The Younger Brother*, Shuffle in *The Cornish Comedy*, Sir Tunbelly Clumsey in *The Relapse*, Frowzy in *A Plot and No Plot*, the title role in *Sauny the Scot* (dialect roles also ran in the family), Mockmode in *Love and a Bottle*, Sir Fickle Cheat in *Love Without Interest*, and Clincher Junior in *The Constant Couple*. Fops, country bumpkins, coarse fathers, comic Irishmen and Scots, hotheads, and old ladies seem to have been his favorites during these early years. He established himself very quickly, for *A Comparison Between the Two Stages* of 1702 called Bullock "the best Comedian that has trod the Stage since *Nokes* and *Lee,* and a fellow that has a very humble Opinion of himself"—which, in a work full of caustic comments on many actors and plays, was high praise indeed.

During the first five years of the eighteenth century, Bullock acted a number of new and typical roles which he continued playing for the next 40 years: Kate Matchlock in *The Funeral*, the Host in *The Merry Wives of Windsor*, Vandunck in *The Royal Merchant*, and, appropriately, Bullock in *The Recruiting Officer*. His name began to appear in other connections as well. In early June 1701 he was one of several players tried (but acquitted) in connection with a performance of Thomas Baker's *The Fox*, a work judged obscene by the authorities. And in August 1703 he joined with Simpson and Pinkethman to operate a Bartholomew Fair booth, a sideline which he continued for the rest of his career.

In 1705 Owen Swiney recruited a number of Drury Lane actors to perform at the Queen's Theatre in the Haymarket, and Bullock was among them. With this group during the 1706–7 and 1707–8 seasons he acted, among other characters, Friar Dominic in *The Spanish Friar*, Hothead in *Sir Courtly Nice*, Abel in *The Committee*, Sir Amorous LaFool in *The Silent Woman*, Bonniface in *The Stratagem*, Lopez in *The Pilgrim*, Teague in *The Lancashire*

Harvard Theatre Collection

WILLIAM BULLOCK

by T. Johnson

Witches, Cokes in *Bartholomew Fair*, and one of the witches in *Macbeth*. Several of these roles, and others that he played, he passed on in time to his sons.

By this time Bullock was probably receiving a salary of £50 annually—a rather low base pay; but, along with such other favorite comedians as Doggett, Underhill, and Pinkethman, he received also one guinea whenever he acted. Since Bullock performed with great frequency, his yearly income may well have been at least triple his base salary. But, though popular, Bullock ranked fifth in the list of 10 comedians in the company, and Doggett, for example, received twice the annual fee that Bullock was granted.

The companies had rearranged themselves by February 1708, and Bullock was back at Drury Lane through the end of the 1708–9 season. To his line he added Trinculo in *The Tempest*, Belfond Senior in *The Squire of Alsatia*, Biskett in *Epsom Wells*, Sir Joseph in *The Old Bachelor*, Sir Humphrey in *The Tender Husband*, and Sir Jealous in *The Busy Body*. His fame was growing, and one of his most enthusiastic fans was Sir Richard Steele. In the *Tatler* of 25 April 1709 Steele wrote:

This evening the comedy, called "Epsom Wells," was acted for the benefit of Mr. Bullock, who, though he is a person of much wit and ingenuity, has a peculiar talent of looking like a fool, and therefore excellently well qualified for the part of Bisket in this play. I cannot indeed sufficiently admire his way of bearing a beating, as he does in this drama, and that with such a natural air and propriety of folly, that one cannot help wishing the whip in one's own hand: so richly does he seem to deserve his chastisement. Skilful actors think it a very peculiar happiness to play in a scene with such as top their parts. Therefore I cannot but say, when the judgment of any good author directs him to write a beating for Mr. Bullock from Mr. William Pinkethman, or for Mr. William Pinkethman from Mr. Bullock, those excellent players seem to be in their most shining circumstances, and please me more, but with a different sort of delight, than that which I receive from those grave scenes of Brutus and Cassius, or Antony and Ventidius.

The next day Steele jokingly described how he would like to have his own funeral managed. He wanted Elizabeth Barry to play his widow in order to get all the ladies weeping, and in the funeral procession he wanted "Mr. Pinkethman to follow in the habit of a Cardinal and Mr. Bullock in that of a privy-counsellor."

Pinkethman and Bullock were often paired, both onstage and in the press. In June 1709 the *Female Tatler* described something of the foolery of the two: " 'Tis very rare that a Comedy succeeds from Mr. Wilks's inimitable bright Air, without a little of Pinkethman's—Alackaday—and Bullock's—O Lamentable."

After a season and a half at Drury Lane Bullock signed again with Owen Swiney at the Queen's Theatre, this time for five years starting July 1709 at a salary of £80 yearly, a benefit in April with £50 charges, and a vacation from 10 June to 10 September. Under this agreement he played such roles as Trapland in *Love for Love*, Kastril in *The Alchemist*, the King of Brentford in *The Rehearsal*, the second carrier in *1 Henry IV*, and Roxana in a burlesque of *The Rival Queens*. He occasionally participated in serious works, but usually in small roles like the Chancellor in *Edward III* or Bedamar in *Venice Preserved*. His stay at the Queen's, despite the long-term contract, lasted only until the end of January 1710, but through no fault of his own. The companies reorganized yet again, and Bullock found himself, temporarily, without a theatrical home. When Pinkethman opened his theatre at Greenwich in the summer of 1710, Bullock joined him, but by January 1711 he was back at Drury Lane.

There he played for the first time Gratiano in *The Jew of Venice*, Licinius in *Valentinian*, a Senator in *Timon of Athens*, a citizen in *Oedipus*, and a plebeian in *Julius Caesar*; his repertory was not shifting but rather expanding, for he kept most of his old comic parts and now began adding more roles in serious plays, especially small parts in crowds, which he seemed to enjoy. On 18 May 1713 for his benefit, on the other hand, he attempted Falstaff in *1 Henry IV*; the choice was odd, for as funny as Falstaff is, one doesn't imagine a clown playing him. But Bullock apparently made a success of the part and kept it for a number of years.

Buffoonery, though, was still Bullock's trade. In the *Tatler* No 188 Steele wrote again of his favorite funnymen:

[They] are of the same age, profession, and sex. They both distinguish themselves in a very particular manner under the discipline of the crabtree, with this only difference, that Mr. Bullock has the more agreeable sqawl, and Mr. Penkethman the more graceful shrug. Penkethman devours a cold chicken with great applause; Bullock's talent lies chiefly in asparagus. Penkethman is very dexterous at conveying himself under a table; Bullock is no less active at jumping over a stick. Mr. Penkethman has a great deal of money, but Mr. Bullock is the taller man.

In the *Spectator* of 20 April 1711, however, Addison wrote of "the innumerable small shifts that small wits put in practice to raise a laugh. Bullock in a short coat, and Norris in a long one, seldom fail of this effect." Much of Bullock's humor apparently stemmed from the fact that he was tall, but, as the *Spectator* of 6 November 1712 noted, he had "height and gracefulness" too.

When the Rich family began recruiting a company for the new theatre in Lincoln's Inn Fields, they were able to lure away from Drury Lane a number of actors who, according to Colley Cibber, were irritated by Robert Wilks's bad temper. Among these were William Bullock and his son Christopher. The Lincoln's Inn Fields playhouse and manager John Rich became closely identified with the whole Bullock clan over the years, and it was probably the elder Bullock who drew in the rest of the family. He himself remained with Rich's troupe for the rest of his career, as did Christopher, his wife Jane, Hildebrand, and, when they started their careers in 1719, William and Henrietta Maria. The only wayward one was Ann Bullock, Hildebrand's wife, who played under Rich's management off and on but made a career of changing companies. For a brief period just before and after 1720 there were so many Bullocks at Lincoln's Inn Fields that it is frequently impossible to distinguish them clearly in the bills. It was, in a very real sense, Bullock's house.

The elder Bullock brought with him to Lincoln's Inn Fields most of the old parts, especially the comic ones, which he had played earlier in his career; one of them, Sir Joseph in *The Old Bachelor*, he used for his first role at the new playhouse on 4 January 1715. He acted regularly there during the winter months and continued his fair activity in the summers. During the next five years he added to his repertory such parts as Mufti in *Don Sebastian*, Scaramouch in *The Emperor of the Moon*, the first Gravedigger in *Hamlet* (which he played first on 17 October 1719 and kept acting for many years), and Thersites in *Troilus and Cressida*. He seems also to have given his son Christopher a helping hand during the 1718–20 period when the burden of management fell to his lot. In December 1718, for example, he seems to have aided in the arrangements for a French company which played an engagement at Lincoln's Inn Fields, and he may have served as their producer; on 30 December the foreigners performed for Bullock's benefit.

In 1722 his son Christopher died, and it is significant that after his death the elder Bullock added only a few new roles to his line and began to act somewhat less frequently. He was now about 55, and the loss of his most talented child must have been a terrible blow. Yet he continued working. He played small comic parts in *Coriolanus*, *The Island Princess*, and *Massaniello*; he took on Sir Jolly in *The Soldier's Fortune*, Roger in *Aesop*, and the lead in *The Fond Husband*. His salary in the mid-1720's was 13*s.* 4*d.* per acting day (or possibly £1 6*s.* 8*d.* daily; the accounts for the theatre do not always indicate which Bullock received what salary, and there were three Bullocks there in 1724–25). He was still popular, but he was not the favorite he had been ten years earlier, and living in the North End, Hampstead, he was not as intimately involved with theatre life now as the performers who chose to live near the playhouses. Another blow came in 1729 when his wife Margaret

died; she was buried at Hampstead on 15 November.

After Rich opened Covent Garden Theatre in 1732, Bullock remained faithful; though he did not act a heavy schedule, still he kept up with his favorite old roles: the first Gravedigger, Bonniface, the Host, the carrier, the title role in *The Spanish Friar*, and several others. But the 1733–34 season was his last really active one, and little wonder. His son William died on 18 June 1733, and four months later, in October, Hildebrand Bullock died. How the elder Bullock managed to struggle through the 1733–34 season is a mystery; after that, however, he did very little acting. At Richmond on 26 September 1734 he played another of his favorite parts, the Coachman in *The Drummer*, and then he went into semi-retirement. Covent Garden kept him on the roster, probably as a pensioner; in 1735–36 he received £57 6*s.* 8*d.* for 172 days (at 6*s.* 8*d.* daily) but this was clearly not for performing. He came back to play his old role of the Gravedigger on 16 April 1736 at Lincoln's Inn Fields, and the bill noted that he had "not acted these three years." At Covent Garden on 6 January 1739 he played the Spanish Friar for his benefit, and the playbill advertised him as not having appeared on the stage (of Covent Garden, that is) for six years. "Mr Bullock," the plaintive bill read, "hopes his great Age, upwards of Threescore and Twelve, will plead his Excuse, that he cannot pay his Duty to his Acquaintances and Friends, whose Good Nature may engage them to assist him in this decline of Life, in order to make the Remainder of his Days easy and comfortable to him."

The hardy old trouper played the Host in *The Merry Wives of Windsor* on 25 April 1739 and ran what was advertised as the largest booth at Bartholomew Fair that August. In 1740–41 Covent Garden still carried him on the books, but he is not known to have acted. In January 1742 he died, having outlived his sons, his wife, and possibly his daughter Henrietta Maria Bullock Ogden, whose career after 1737 is obscure. Davies wrote of him in later years: "Bullock was an actor of great glee and much comic vivacity. . . . The comic ability of Bullock was confirmed to me by Mr Macklin, who assured me, very lately, that he was, in his department, a true genius of the stage."

One Bullock certainly survived old William: Harriet, the daughter of Christopher and Jane. She was probably the one referred to in the Lincoln's Inn Fields free list on 29 October 1728 as "Mr Bullocks Grand Daughter." With her mother she went to Ireland in 1736, had a brief performing career as Miss Bullock, and on 26 December 1744 married Michael Dyer and continued acting under her married name.

References to the Bullocks in the records are frequently ambiguous and sometimes probably in error, examples being those to a Mrs Bullock playing Leucippe in *The Humorous Lieutenant* at Drury Lane in late July 1697 and Phaeax in *Timon of Athens* at the same house on 30 October 1711. These parts were doubtless acted by William Bullock in skirts.

Bullock was supposedly painted by Hogarth, and an engraving of the portrait was made by Charles Hall. But the "Hogarth" may not have been done by the master, and the work has sometimes been identified as a picture of William's son Christopher. The National Portrait Gallery has a water color of William Bullock attributed to Sylvester Harding, after a mezzotint by Thomas Johnson; five engravings of the watercolor are at the British Museum. The Garrick Club owns a similar picture.

Bullock, William *d. 1733, actor.*

William Bullock the younger was apparently the third son of William Bullock, actor and booth operator; to distinguish him from his father he was usually designated in playbills of the 1720's not as "Junior"— a distinction given to his eldest brother Christopher—but as W. Bullock. The date of his birth is uncertain, but on 28 February 1719 at Lincoln's Inn Fields he played a boy in *'Tis Well If It Takes*, billed as "Billy Bullock," and his roles in 1722 suggest that he was at least out of his minority by then. This would lead one to guess a birthdate just after the turn of the century. In addition to Christopher, he had an elder brother Hildebrand, probably born in the early 1690's. Billy Bullock in February 1719, then, was probably in his 'teens, and at this first appearance on stage he was supported by his father, his brother Christopher, and Christopher's wife Jane.

On 19 January 1722 the younger William Bullock was again named in the bills, this time replacing his ailing brother Christopher as Slender in *The Merry Wives of Windsor*. William also played another of his brother's parts, Osric in *Hamlet*, on 29 January. Two months later Christopher died of consumption. After his two January appearances at Lincoln's Inn Fields, William, on 28 June 1722, joined a new group at the Haymarket Theatre, acting Gloster in *Jane Shore*; the venture there came to nothing, but it was doubtless good experience for the fledgling actor.

William seems to have become a regular member of the Lincoln's Inn Fields troupe during the 1722–23 season, but if so he played little that was noted in the playbills: Slender again, and three roles his father had played in previous seasons, Belfond Senior in *The Squire of Alsatia*, Sir Joseph in *The Old Bachelor*, and Mockmode in *Love and a Bottle*. All of these roles were tried in May and June of 1724. Though one might wonder whether the last three assignments might be errors for the elder Bullock, young William seems to have played them all; in *Love and a Bottle* both father and son were in the cast. Despite his youth, the younger Bullock must have had a knack for older roles, and his father may have encouraged him to try them during the benefit period when actors often attempted parts outside their line.

Bullock returned to play at Lincoln's

Inn Fields for the 1724–25 season, and, again, he partly followed in his father's footsteps by playing Sir Joseph once more, Stephen in *Every Man In His Humour*, Abel in *The Committee*, and a role in *Masaniello*. The next season he came more into his own, acting Cuff in *Epsom Wells*, the Marquis of Hazard in *The Gamester*, a Maiden in *Tunbridge Wells* (skirts roles ran in the family), and Clodio in *Love Makes a Man* (for his benefit on 2 May 1726, shared with his sister-in-law Ann Russell Bullock, Hildebrand's wife).

Up to this point most of Bullock's roles that were large enough to be mentioned in the bills were scheduled at the end of the season. Starting in 1726–27, however, he was apparently no longer considered such a risk, and his named roles were distributed throughout the theatrical year. He played, among other new parts, Prig in *The Royal Merchant*, Brazen in *The Recruiting Officer*, Brisk in *The Double Dealer*, Dorilant in *The Country Wife*, and Gibbet in *The Stratagem*. These were all roles of some importance and far different from his earlier parts, for all were young fops (which had been a specialty of his deceased brother Christopher). He developed this line further as time went on, playing Tattle in *Love for Love*, Marplot in *The Busy Body*, Young Clincher in *The Constant Couple*, Foppington in *The Careless Husband*, Sir Novelty in *Love's Last Shift*, the Gentleman Usher in *King Lear*, Tinsel in *The Drummer*, and Roderigo in *Othello*.

By 15 November 1729 he switched his affiliation to the Goodman's Fields Theatre, and there he spent the rest of his career. He had acquired, in the late 1720's, a coffee house near that theatre, and at his death on 18 June 1733 he was remembered by the *Daily Advertiser* both as a comedian and the master of the coffee house. His last performance had been on 9 May, as Young Clincher.

It is not known whether or not William Bullock ever married or had any offspring. If he had a son, perhaps that was the Mr Bullock who was given a benefit at the Haymarket Theatre on 26 October 1749 to help "procure his Enlargement" from Fleet Prison. No other male Bullocks are known to have been alive at that time, and whoever the imprisoned Bullock was, he had theatrical connections.

Bulls, Mr [*fl.* 1782], *actor.*
Mr Bulls played an unspecified role in *The Taylors* at the Haymarket Theatre on 25 November 1782.

Bulmer, Mr [*fl.* 1772–1774], *scourer.*
The Covent Garden account books contain two references to Mr Bulmer, one of the "Scowerers": on 29 December 1772 he was paid £5 11s. and on 14 February 1774 £3 13s. 6d. In neither of these instances do the books indicate how many days of work the payments covered.

Buononcini. *See* BONONCINI.

Bur, Mr [*fl.* 1742], *actor.*
On 8 November 1742 Mr Bur played George Barnwell in *The London Merchant* at the James Street Theatre.

Burbage, Mr [*fl.* 1794], *singer.*
Mr Burbage sang at Drury Lane on 31 October 1794 as one of the chorus of guards in *The Mountaineers*.

Burch, Mr [*fl.* 1708], *dresser.*
One Burch was listed as a dresser at the Queen's Theatre in the Haymarket in a Harvard document dated 8 March 1708; Burch's salary was 1s. 6d. per day.

Burchall or **Burchell, Miss.** *See* VINCENT, MRS RICHARD, ISABELLA.

Burchett, Mr [*fl.* 1794], *singer?*
Doane's *Musical Directory* of 1794 listed Mr Burchett, of Ball's Pond, Newington, as a bass (singer, presumably, but possibly a bass viol player) who participated in Handelian performances at Westminster Abbey

and concerts by the Cecilian Society. There is a possibility that Burchett should be identified as Thomas Burkitt, who sang in the 1780's.

Burchinshaw. Birchensha.

Burden. *See also* BURDON and BOURDON.

Burden, Jahaziel [*fl.* 1794], *singer.*

In 1794 Doane listed Jahaziel Burden, of No 46, Longacre, as a tenor who participated in performances by the Handelian Society at Westminster Abbey, in oratorios at Covent Garden, and in concerts presented by the Choral Fund. He was doubtless related to the other singing Burdens of the time.

Burden, John Jabez [*fl.* 1794], *singer.*

In 1794 Doane listed John Jabez Burden, of Edgeware Road, as an alto who participated in concerts presented by the Choral Fund and the Portland Chapel Society. He was doubtless related to the other singing Burdens of this time.

Burden, Kitty, née White [*fl.* 1757–1783], *actress, singer.*

Miss Kitty White made her first appearance on any stage at Covent Garden on 2 November 1757 as Sylvia in *The Recruiting Officer.* She may have been the daughter of the Mr White who acted at Covent Garden at this time and the Mrs White who performed later in the 1750's and 1760's. On 8 April 1758 Kitty's benefit tickets were accepted, but she sold only £24 6s. worth and received only half value; for her audience she played Cherry in *The Stratagem.* The following season she spent most of her time in unnamed roles, but on 29 January 1759 she played Melissa in *The Lying Valet* and on 30 May she shared a benefit with two others and then played at Portsmouth for the summer. Her 1759–60

season was similarly undistinguished; a Mrs White, chiefly a dancer in the Covent Garden troupe, seems to have performed named roles occasionally, but Miss White was not cited in a bill until her benefit (with two others) on 3 May 1760; again she did not do well, selling £12 6s. worth of tickets but getting only half value from the management; *The Country Lasses* was performed; and the Mrs White who acted Aura for the first time may well have been Kitty. During these seasons at Covent Garden Kitty White is said to have been a pupil of Mr Rich and Mr O'Brien.

In the summer of 1760, when she was playing at Portsmouth, Kitty married a Mr Burden; this may have been after she played Lucy in *The Minor* as a member of Foote's Haymarket company on 28 June, yet she was billed as "Miss Burden" on that date. In any case, in the fall of 1760 she was back at Covent Garden as Mrs Burden and was frequently named in the bills. Her salary was 3s. 4d. daily at the beginning of the season, but she was given a 1s. 8d. raise on 3 January 1761, doubtless due to her increased activity. During the season she played, among other roles, Mrs Vixen in *The Beggar's Opera*, Lucinda in *The Englishman Returned from Paris*, Anne Page in *The Merry Wives of Windsor*, Lucy in *The Minor*, Jessica in *The Merchant of Venice*, Isabella in *The Wonder*, Parisatis in *The Rival Queens*, Charlotte in *Love à la Mode*, Isabella in *Wit Without Women* (for her benefit), and Lady Weldon in *Oroonoko.* Though her activity was impressive, her 17 April 1761 benefit was shared with three others and she ended up making only £7 11s. profit. On that occasion, in addition to acting Isabella, she made her first attempt at playing the Fine Gentleman in *Lethe.*

Her 1761–62 Covent Garden season was almost a carbon copy of the previous one, with only a few new parts listed for her; among them were Serina in *The Orphan*, Lucinda in *The Conscious Lovers*, Miranda in *The Busy Body*, and Jilt All in *The Counterfeit Heiress*. She had a good talent for comedy, but apparently she longed to play tragedy, and *The Rosciad of C—v—nt G—rd—n* (1762) poked fun at her for it:

> THEN *B—RD—EN* comes, cursing her
>   lowly state;
> No guards attend her, and no laquies
>   wait:
> 'And shall I ne'er the heroine act? (she
>   cries)
> 'Ne'er to so great a dignity arise!
> 'Shall I to third-rate parts be still con-
>   fin'd?
> 'Still with my worth obscurely lag be-
>   hind?
> 'Still shall my genius in the farce be
>   seen;
> 'Which might, with grace adorn the
>   Tragic Queen.'
> AH! *B—RD—N*, to the farce thyself
>   confine;
> 'Tis there you please us, and 'tis there
>   you shine. . . .

In 1762 Mrs Burden was in Dublin, acting at the Smock Alley Theatre, and though Mr and Mrs White, possibly her parents, both worked at Covent Garden during the early 1760's, Kitty did not reappear in London until the summer of 1765. She joined Foote's summer troupe at the Haymarket Theatre, acting a role in *The Lyar* on 15 July 1765 and then Polly in *Polly Honeycombe*, Isabinda in *The Busy Body*, and Amaryllis in *The Rehearsal*. In the fall she rejoined the Covent Garden company, opening her season with Louisa in *Love Makes a Man*, billed as making her first appearance there in three years. Her salary was now 5s. daily and her parts more considerable: Lady Macduff in *Macbeth*, Mrs Foresight in *Love for Love*, and Teresa in *The Squire of Alsatia* are typical.

In the summer of 1766 she divided her time between Foote's company at the Haymarket and Barry's at the King's Theatre; at the former she acted Melissa in *The Lying Valet*, Mrs Sneak in *The Mayor of Garratt*, and Mrs Sullen in *The Beaux' Stratagem*, and at the latter she was Emilia in *Othello* and Lady Capulet in *Romeo and Juliet*. After this productive sequence, she returned to Covent Garden in the fall to her usual line but added Lucilla in *The Fair Penitent* and Marwood in *The Way of the World*. Her last Covent Garden appearance was as Louisa in *Love Makes a Man* on 21 May 1767.

Mrs Burden joined Foote's company again at the Haymarket for the summer of 1767, repeating some of her earlier roles but adding such significant new ones as Pulcheria in *Theodosius*, Goneril in *King Lear*, and Roxana in *Alexander* (*The Rival Queens*). After this she was off to Ireland again, this time for a lengthy stay that took her to Limerick in 1768, Cork in 1769 and 1770, and Belfast, Limerick, and Cork in 1772. In 1773 she acted with Macklin at the Crow Street Theatre in Dublin.

She reappeared in London for the first time in eight years, the bill said, playing her old role of Mrs Sneak in *The Mayor of Garratt* on 17, 18, and 19 September 1777. The following spring she joined a troupe at the China Hall Theatre in Rotherhithe, where she made the biggest splash of her London career. In May and June 1778 she played, in quick sequence, Violante in *The Wonder*, Lady Randolph in *Douglas*, Mrs Sneak, Miss Hardcastle in *She Stoops to Conquer*, Alicia in *Jane Shore*, Maria in *The Citizen*, Miranda in *The Busy Body*, Miss Sterling in *The Clandestine Marriage*, Millwood in *The London Merchant*, Mrs Harlow in *The Old Maid*, Anne Lovely in *A Bold Stroke for a Wife*, Queen Elizabeth in *The Earl of Essex*, Miss Aubrey in *The Fashionable Lover*, and Marianna in *The Miser*. Whether she was suited to playing tragedy or not, she finally had her chance before London audiences.

Mrs Burden did not appear again in London until 25 November 1782, when she was one of the wives in *The Taylors*. She is also supposed to have acted in Edinburgh in 1782–83. After that season, the records show no further stage activity for her.

The "Mrs Burdan" who was listed for several weekly payments of £2 each during the 1778–79 season at Drury Lane seems not to have been the actress Kitty, but a supplier of some kind of materials. She may well have been related to Mrs Burden the actress through her husband.

Burden, W. [fl. 1768–1794], *actor, singer.*

The Mr Burden who acted at Limerick on 13 October 1768 was possibly, though not certainly, the *basso* W. Burden of the 1790's. Burden was busy at several Irish theatres during the early 1770's: Cork and Dublin (Capel Street) in 1770, Belfast and Newry in 1771, and Belfast and Cork again in 1772. He was probably the Mr Burden who appeared at the Haymarket Theatre in London on 23 February 1784 as part of the cast for the single performance of *The Reprisal,* and he may have been the Mr Burden who was a Brideman in *Royal Clemency* at the same playhouse on 10 October 1793 and sang in the production of *The Tempest* on 19 November. In 1794 Doane listed *basso* W. Burden of No 10, Blue Cross Street, Leicester Square, as a participant in Covent Garden oratorios and performances by the Handelian Society at Westminster Abbey. The other singing Burdens of this period were probably related to him, but in what way is not known.

Burdett, Anne. *See* BELFILLE, ANNE.

Burdett, James [fl. 1794], *instrumentalist, singer?*

Doane's *Musical Directory* of 1794 listed James Burdett of Cannon Row, Westminster, as a player on the piano, violin, and tenor (viola) and a participant in oratorio performances at Covent Garden and Westminster Abbey. He was also connected with the Westminster Abbey Choir, which indi-

cates that he was probably a singer as well as an instrumentalist.

Burdon. *See also* BURDEN *and* BOURDON.

Burdon, Mr [fl. 1795–1806?], *singer.*

Mr Burdon sang in the oratorios at Covent Garden in the Lenten period of 1795, 1796, and 1797; when he was first engaged (starting 20 February 1795) he was billed as from Salisbury. Though he may be one of the three "Burdens" who sang in London about this time, the information that he was from out of London would suggest he was not. He may have been the Burdon who performed at Sadler's Wells on 25 June 1806.

Bureau, Joseph Grégoir [fl. 1749], *musician.*

When the French impresario Jean Louis Monnet brought over a troupe of comedians for a series of performances at the Haymarket Theatre in the winter of 1749, Joseph Grégoir Bureau was a member of the company. His position must have been an important one, for his contract with Monnet was for £257 8s. 7d., the second highest individual figure in the group; this sum may have been meant to cover Bureau's wife, the actress Marie Jeanne le Maignan, called "Brillant," who accompanied him to London, but she is not known to have performed there. The playbills for the troupe's performances carried no casts, so it is difficult to be certain about Bureau's specialty; in his *Lexique* of French performers, however, Fuchs identifies Bureau as a musician.

The company's stay in England was a stormy one, marked by riots at the playhouse caused by anti-French feeling, and the group was able to perform only from 14 November to 16 December 1749. Sometime after this the actors apparently returned to France, leaving their manager behind to settle the debts. Bureau and his wife are known to have had two children—Marie, baptized on 20 April 1746, and Louis, baptized on 15 May 1747.

Burford, Mr [fl. 1670–1672], *actor, dancer.*

A minor member of the Duke's Company, Mr Burford, about 1670–71, danced in a production of *The Lady-Errant*, possibly at the Dorset Garden Theatre. The next season he acted Gonsalvo in *Charles VIII* in late November 1671 and Pedro in *The Fatal Jealousy* on 3 August 1672 at that playhouse.

Burgani, Mr [fl. 1786–1787], *house servant?*

The Covent Garden accounts list a Mr Burgani on 25 November 1786 and 14 June 1787; at the beginning of the season he was being paid a constant salary of 12s. for six nights, and at the end he received 8s. for four nights—a slight raise in salary. He was probably a house servant.

Burgen, Henry [fl. 1667–1670] *scenekeeper.*

Henry Burgen was a scenekeeper in the King's Company at the Bridges Street Theatre on 25 October 1667 when he was named in a Lord Chamberlain's warrant. He was mentioned as serving the company in 1669–70 as well, and it is likely that his employment had been continuous for at least three seasons.

Burges. *See* **Burgess, Burgesse** and **Burgis.**

Burgess. *See also* **BURGESSE** and **BURGIS.**

Burgess, Master [fl. 1738–1739], *actor.*

A Master Burgess, possibly related to the actress Miss Burgess, was cited three times in the Drury Lane bills: as Moth in *Robin Goodfellow* on 30 November 1738 and 7 February 1739 and as Cobweb in the same

work on 10 October 1739. There is a possibility also that these citations are errors for Miss Burgess.

Burgess, Master [fl. 1789–1790], *house servant.*

Though the Covent Garden accounts are somewhat unclear, it would seem that for the 1789–90 season a boy named Burgess was serving as the lampman's helper at 1s. daily; entries in the books concerning him are sometimes confused with those concerning Henry Burgess Junior, who was, apparently, the theatre's solicitor.

Burgess, [Elizabeth?] [fl. 1735–1742], *actress.*

Miss Burgess, who played during the late 1730's and early 1740's, may have been the Elizabeth Burgess who subscribed to Henry Ward's *Works* in 1746, but there is not sufficient evidence to be certain. Her first recorded appearance, probably as a young girl, was as Leander in *The Mock Doctor* on 10 March 1735 at York Buildings. She was given a benefit there on 12 March as one of the "Lilliputians." On 19 May at the same place she was Lucy in *The Beggar's Opera* and Lady Lace in *The Lottery*, and at the Haymarket Theatre on 4 August of this year she played a traditional role for young girls, the page Cordelio in *The Orphan.*

She spent most of the early part of 1736 at the Haymarket, playing, among other roles, Molly Wheedle in *The Rival Milliners*, Edging in *The Careless Husband*, Miss Stitch in *Pasquin*, and Terra in *Tumble Down Dick*. She had a benefit on 12 May at which she spoke a new epilogue to *Pasquin* and was lauded in the bill for having "so zealously espoused the Country-Interest." She acted in early 1737, playing on 4 March Prince Arthur in *King John* for her benefit, again at the Haymarket. During these seasons she seems not to have acted a full season schedule, but starting in 1739–40 she associated herself with Covent Garden and acted regularly and frequently all season.

Her first appearance at Covent Garden was on 5 September 1739 when she played Dorcas in *The Mock Doctor*. Thereafter she was Busy in *The Man of Mode*, Eurydice in *Oedipus*, Mustacha in *The Tragedy of Tragedies*, and Philadelphia in *The Amorous Widow*. Though she had no regular benefit, on 7 May 1740 tickets delivered by her were accepted. The season of 1740–41 at Covent Garden was her last full one, during which she added such parts as Lettice in *The Constant Couple*, Situp in *The Double Gallant*, Regan in *King Lear*, and an Amazon in *Perseus and Andromeda*. In 1741–42 she seems to have played only two billed roles: Honoria in *Love Makes a Man* (2 October and 4 December 1741 and 27 January 1742) and Teresa in *The Spanish Friar* (27 October 1741 and 15 March 1742). She may have left the company before the end of the season.

The Master Burgess who appeared briefly in 1738 and 1739 may have been related to Miss Burgess or, indeed, the few references to him may be errors for her.

Burgess, Henry *d. 1765, musician.*

On 28 August 1739 Henry Burgess the elder became one of the founding members and governors of the Royal Society of Musicians. His talented son Henry also subscribed to the Society. Burgess was a professional musician at this time, but nothing is known of his activities; in 1763 when Mortimer's *London Directory* was published Burgess was listed as one of his Majesty's band, and he may have held this position during the previous years. Mortimer noted his address as being in Brownlow Street, and it was presumably there that he died, in early 1765.

Burgess had made his will on 7 March 1764, describing himself as a musician from the parish of St Martin-in-the-Fields. To his son Henry he left all his music, printed or in manuscript; to a son Thomas

he bequeathed one shilling and a pair of buttons; to his daughter Isabella Burgess Wilcox, wife of a bookseller, he gave one shilling and a gold ring; and to his wife Mary, daughter of Thomas Wamsley, he left the rest of his estate. Sarah Reina and Jacob Kirkman (the harpsichord maker) witnessed the will. Mary Burgess proved the will on 19 March 1765.

Burgess, Henry *[fl. 1738–1765], harpsichordist, organist, composer.*

Henry Burgess the younger was already recognized as a composer by 26 January 1738 when two of his songs were sung at Drury Lane. A year later, on 17 and 19 January 1739 at the same playhouse, he performed a new concerto of his own composition, and the Drury Lane bills for 3, 5, and 22 May list performances of his music, perhaps again played by him. On 28 August he became one of the original subscribers, along with his musical father, to the Royal Society of Musicians.

In the summer of 1741 Henry played an organ concerto of his own composition at Cuper's Gardens, and the bills in May and June gave him a puff: "it may be said without ostentation that he is of as promising a genius and as neat a performer as any of the age." In 1744 he apparently performed on the harpsichord again at Drury Lane, and when Mortimer's *London Directory* came out in 1763 he was still listed as an active London musician, then living in Great Queen Street, Lincoln's Inn Fields.

When his father died in 1765 he left Henry all his music, printed or in manuscript. We learn from the elder Burgess's will that the younger Henry had a brother Thomas and a sister Isabella; his mother was Mary Burgess, daughter of Thomas Wamsley.

Burgess, John *[fl. 1794], singer.*

Doane in 1794 listed John Burgess, of Bird's Buildings, St George's Fields, as a singer who participated in concerts presented by the Academy of Ancient Music, the St Paul's Choir, and the Handelian Society (at Westminster Abbey).

Burgesse. *See also* **BURGESS** and **BURGIS.**

Burgesse, Charles [*fl. 1686*], *trumpeter.*

The only notice of Charles Burgesse appears to be a warrant of 12 October 1686 which directed that he be delivered a silver trumpet; he was, presumably, a member of the King's Musick.

Burgesse, Robert [*fl. 1662–1669*], *trumpeter.*

Robert Burgesse was appointed on 6 June 1662 to attend the Duke of Ormonde in Ireland, and on 3 February 1669 he was replaced by Bryan Quinne. It is not known whether Burgesse spent his entire musical career in Ireland, but the implication of the initial warrant is that he had been serving in London.

Burghall, J. E. [*fl. 1778–1797*], *actor, fencing master, dancing master.*

J. E. Burghall was billed as making his first appearance on any stage on 5 October 1778 when he played Tressel in *Richard III*; he was advertised only as "A Gentleman," but a manuscript note on a British Museum playbill identified him as Mr Burghall. He played, for that night only, at Covent Garden; and on 8 February 1779, again for a single performance, he was the Officer in *The Law of Lombardy* at Drury Lane.

These were probably his only London appearances. From July to 1 November 1779 Burghall was with Joseph Austin's troupe at Chester, and on 9 November he made his Hull debut. For the 1780–81 season he was at York, and on 22 August 1781 he received a benefit at Richmond.

After this wandering, Burghall settled at London as a master of dancing and fencing. He became involved in a domestic crisis brought on by Mrs John Booth, the actress, who encouraged him in an affair with her granddaughter, Miss Julia Granger, at the expense of Burghall's wife Sally, who was niece to Mrs Booth. Burghall recounted the circumstances in a sixteen-page pamphlet which he published in 1797 entitled *A Statement of Facts*. On the last page is the note, "Copy of a Deposition made at the Sessions-House, Clerkenwell, Feb. 17, 1797." The short introduction states, "The Meaning of this is not entirely to exculpate Mr. Burghall from Error, or the just Imputation of Folly:—but to prove, that the Person [Mrs Booth] who has dared to be loudest in Complaint and Virulence, was the *Encourager*, and *abetting* Instrument to every past Circumstance, wherein the Parties stand condemned."

In the form of numbered paragraphs addressed to Mrs Booth of Drury Lane, the story emerges that she had alienated Burghall from his wife Sally by criticising her for "painting" and of being more attentive to her own person and dress than to her husband, while at the same time Mrs Booth encouraged his attentions to her granddaughter and ward. Burghall entered into "numberless Expences, in Wearing Apparel, &c. &c. for Miss Granger," and was led by Mrs Booth to believe that Miss Granger loved him. In the presence of Miss Granger, Mrs Booth told Burghall, "if Sally were to die, I should glory in you for a Husband to *my* Julia." Although she encouraged him to make a will almost entirely excluding his wife in favor of Miss Granger, Burghall's will, which was witnessed by Mr Card, Mrs Booth's landlord, was not so unfair to his wife as the old woman wished.

Burghall and his wife separated, but only after some physical violence had ensued among all parties. When Mrs Booth received an anonymous letter threatening to expose her in the newspapers, she changed sides, took the public view, and attacked Miss Granger, forcing her to flee from her house. Mrs Booth then spread the libel that Burghall had thrown out his wife Sally without a penny or any spare clothing. But he had actually behaved properly, he claims, having signed proper articles of separation with his wife and having sent her quarterly payments as well as a gift of £20. Moreover, Mrs Booth had asked him to invest some of her money in consolidated annuities, which he had done in strict honesty, though she spread the report that he meant to defraud her.

When Burghall attempted to reach a reconciliation with his wife, again Mrs Booth intervened by sending Sally some letters which Burghall had written in the earlier times of stress and which contained remarks about Sally which destroyed all hopes of reunion.

In the conclusion of his pamphlet Burghall urged Mrs Booth to repent, she being "an Old Woman, verging on the Grave." He also hinted that Mrs Booth had similarly duped "poor Sinclair"—another performer? —by falsely encouraging his attentions to Miss Granger. In 1800 Miss Granger married a Mr Jones and went off to act in America. Burghall's pamphlet is our last notice of him.

Burghi. *See* BORGHI.

Burgin. *See* BURGEN.

Burgis. *See also* BURGESS *and* BURGESSE.

Burgis, Mrs [*fl.* 1740–1747?], *house servant?*

The Covent Garden accounts mention a Mrs Burgis who served the theatre in some capacity in the 1740–41 season at 3s. 4d. daily. On 23 February 1747 a "Mrs Burges," perhaps the same woman, was paid £14 15s. 6d. for "Mrs Cooke's board etc"— which suggests the possibility that she may

have been operating a theatrical boarding house.

Burk. *See also* BOURK.

Burke of Thumond. *See* THUMOTH, BURKE.

Burke, Mr [*fl.* 1751–1752], *house servant?*

Mr Burke shared benefits at Drury Lane on 8 May 1751 and 2 May 1752, but his function in the theatre is not known.

Burke, Mr [1765–1777], *dresser.*

Mr Burke was working at Drury Lane as a dresser on 9 February 1765 at a salary of 1s. 6d. daily or 9s. per week; the accounts show that in the 1776–77 season he was still in the same position at the same wage.

Burke, Mr [*fl.* 1797–1807], *house servant?*

One Burke (or Bourke) was mentioned in the Drury Lane accounts on 24 February 1797 and again on 26 September 1807, but his function at the playhouse was not noted. Burke was apparently earning 1s. daily, which suggests that he was a minor house servant.

Burkett or **Burkhead.** *See* BURKITT, BIRKHEAD, and KNIGHT, MARY.

Burkitt, Thomas [*fl.* 1776–1790], *singer.*

Thomas Burkitt (or Birkett, Burkett) made his first stage appearance on 23 March 1776 at Drury Lane, billed as a "Young Gentleman," playing Frederick in the musical drama *Valentine's Day*. Sometime during the next four years he performed at the Crow Street playhouse in Dublin and then returned to England. At Covent Garden he was the "Gentleman" who played Bacchanal in *Comus* on 17

February 1780, billed as making his initial appearance on that stage.

On 9 October 1784 he sang "Blue-Ey'd Patty" as an interpolation in the burletta *The Jovial Cobler* at the Royal Circus, and from 1785 to about 1788 he made singing appearances at Ranelagh and Bermondsey Gardens. During this same period he also performed occasionally at Astley's Amphitheatre in musical productions. On 24 July 1786, for instance, he was the King of Hearts in *The Marriage of the Knave of Hearts* and a clown in *The Two Nannys*; on 4 September he played Theodore in the new musical spectacle, *Love from the Heart*; he participated in *A Sale of English Beauties at Grand Cairo* on 17 September; and several years later, on 4 September 1789, he returned to Astley's to be one of the pilots in *The Royal Naval Review at Plymouth*. Burkitt made another appearance at one of the regular playhouses on 30 October 1788 when he sang two songs at the Haymarket Theatre. The last notice of him is at the Royal Circus: about 1790 he sang "As when some Maiden in her Teens" in *The Lover's Device*.

Burleigh, John ₁*fl. 1729₁, *performer?*
On 23 May 1729 at the Lincoln's Inn Fields Theatre, John Burleigh was given a benefit which took in £84 17*s*. Burleigh's function in the theatre, if any, was not noted in the bill, and there seems to be no other record of him. At the Haymarket Theatre on 9 February 1737 a Widow Burley and her three small children were given a benefit; she could have been Burleigh's widow, though she, too, is otherwise unrecorded.

Burling, Mr ₁*fl. 1785–1788₁, *singer.*
Mr Burling (or Birling) sang at Bermondsey Spa Gardens during the period 1785–1788; the *Catalogue of Printed Music* at the British Museum cites several popular songs he offered there, all of them by composer Jonas Blewitt.

Burlington, Mr ₁*fl. 1784₁, *singer.*
Mr Burlington, a tenor, sang at the Handel Memorial Concerts at Westminster Abbey and the Pantheon on 26, 27, 29 May and 3, 5 June 1784.

Burn. *See also* **Burns**, **Byrn** and **Byrne.**

Burn, Miss ₁*fl. 1759₁, *actress, dancer.*
On 18 April 1759 Miss Burn played Young Sifroy in *Cleone* at the Haymarket Theatre. The performance was for the benefit of Miss Burn and Miss Valois who had, on 20 March 1759, received a license from the Lord Chamberlain to perform the work. There may have been others involved in preparing *Cleone*, though the records suggest that the two young ladies were their own producers; they were both under 13 years of age, as were all the members of their cast.

On 21 April at the King's Theatre in the Haymarket Miss Burn acted the Young Prince in *Farnace*, and she doubtless participated in other performances of this opera during the season. Though their license had specified only a single performance of *Cleone*, the work was done again by the children on 10 May at the Haymarket, and this time Miss Burn also performed a solo dance for the audience. On 9 August at Marylebone Gardens she offered a comic dance, and on the sixteenth she danced again, this time adding a hornpipe, in sailor's garb. The last notice of her, again as a dancer at Marylebone Gardens, was on 6 September 1759.

Burnaby. *See* **Burnley.**

Burnard, Joseph ₁*fl. 1794₁, *singer?*
Doane's *Musical Directory* of 1794 listed Joseph Burnard, of No 5, Star Court, Great Eastcheap, as a bass (singer, presumably, though he may have been a bass viol player) who participated in concerts given by the Handelian Society.

Burnard, Thomas ₍fl. 1739₎, musician.

Thomas Burnard was one of the original subscribers ("being musicians") to the Royal Society of Musicians on 28 August 1739.

Burnat. See BURNETT.

Burnell, Mr ₍fl. 1719₎, boxkeeper.

On 19 May 1719 at Lincoln's Inn Fields the boxkeeper Burnell shared a benefit with the numberer Abbott.

Burnet. See also BURNETT.

Burnet, Mrs ₍fl. 1749₎, actress.

A Mrs Burnet was in the summer companies at Richmond and Twickenham in 1749.

Burnet, ₍Richard?₎ ₍fl. 1728–1755?₎, actor, dancer.

Mr Burnet, who may have been the dancing master Richard Burney of the 1750's, was first mentioned in theatrical bills as one of the sailors in *Perseus and Andromeda* at Drury Lane on 15 November 1728. He was a minor member of the corps of dancers, and though he was probably kept busy throughout the season, he was not mentioned in the bills again until June 1729, when he played some minor roles. In August he acted the Merchant in *Maudlin* at the Hall-Oates booth at Bartholomew Fair. His 1729–30 season followed a similar pattern: he was named in the Drury Lane bills on 23 April 1730 when he danced a small part in *Diana and Acteon*, and in August and September at the Fielding-Oates booth at Bartholomew and Southwark fairs he played Sir Jasper in *The Generous Free Mason*.

He continued dancing small roles in afterpieces at Drury Lane through the 1732–33 season, seldom receiving particular notice; but when Theophilus Cibber deserted the theatre in the fall of 1733, Burnet remained loyal and consequently received more frequent billing through 15 May 1734. On that date he danced as a Chinese Guard in *Cephalus and Procris*, a role he had done frequently over the years, after which he joined the troupe at the Haymarket Theatre and played Industrious Jenny in *The Covent Garden Tragedy* on 27 May 1734. The work was given only once, and after this Burnet's name dropped from the theatrical records.

A newspaper notice of 31 March 1755 cited a Richard Burney, dancing master; if a spelling error was made, perhaps this was the dancer Burnet who had been active earlier at Drury Lane.

Burnett. See also BURNET.

Burnett, Mr ₍fl. 1772–1781₎, actor.

Mr Burnett played Mause in *The Gentle Shepherd* at the Haymarket Theatre on 21 December 1772; in the cast was a Mrs Burnett; probably his wife, and since the group doing the Scottish play seems to have come down to London just for the occasion, the Burnetts were doubtless Scots. Though Mrs Burnett seems not to have appeared again in London, references to a Mr "Burnat" or Mr Burnett at minor houses in the city probably point to the actor who played Mause in 1772. On 7 October 1776 a Mr "Burnat" acted Roger in *The Gentle Shepherd* at the Haymarket, and in June 1778 at the China Hall, Rotherhithe, a Mr Burnett played a number of roles: Sterling in *The Clandestine Marriage,* Friar Laurence in *Romeo and Juliet,* Pierre in *Venice Preserved,* Robert in *High Life Below Stairs,* Burleigh in *The Earl of Essex,* and the Lieutenant of the Tower in *Richard III.* At the Crown Inn, Islington, a Mr "Burnat" was Bullock in *The Recruiting Officer* on 15 March 1781, Horatio in *The Fair Penitent* on 27 March, King Henry in *Richard III* on 30 March, and the Chaplain in *The Orphan* on 5 April.

Burnett, Mrs [fl. 1772], actress.

Mrs Burnett played Peggy in *The Gentle Shepherd* at the Haymarket Theatre on 21 December 1772. The Mr Burnett who flourished from 1772 to 1781 and was also in this performance was probably her husband.

Burnett, Miss [fl. 1783–1822], singer, actress.

Miss Burnett was very likely the daughter of Mr and Mrs William Burnett. She was first noticed in the bills on 14 May 1783 at Sadler's Wells when she joined her mother as one of the singers there; she and her mother were paired off again, as "treebles" at the Handel Memorial Concerts in May and June 1784 at Westminster Abbey and the Pantheon. In 1784–85 the two joined the Drury Lane company, and for a few seasons swelled the choruses there. Miss Burnett seems to have been more talented than her mother, for in addition to choral work in such pieces as *Harlequin Junior, The Tempest, Macbeth,* and *The Cauldron,* she was occasionally given named roles when she moved with many of the actors to the Haymarket during the summers.

Her first acting assignment there was Leonora in *The Padlock* on 8 August 1785, billed not as from Drury Lane, where she had been a nobody, but from Sadler's Wells, where she must have gained some popularity. The following Haymarket summer, after again getting lost in the crowds at Drury Lane during the winter, Miss Burnett played Theodosia in *The Maid of the Mill,* Lucinda in *Love in a Village,* Maria "(with a song in character)" in *Fatal Curiosity,* a Pastoral Nymph in *Comus,* Penelope in *The Romp,* and Miss Di in *Seeing is Believing.*

When the new Royalty Theatre opened on 20 June 1787 she was part of the venture, playing Phoebe in *As You Like It.* She was there again on 31 October 1787 to sing a principal role in *The Birthday,* and

sometime in 1787 at the Royalty she was Venus in *Apollo Turned Stroller.* She sang again at the Royalty on 29 September 1788, was at Sadler's Wells on 9 April 1792 as a singer in the spectacle *Maedea's Kettle,* and sang again at Sadler's Wells on 4 October 1793; one may assume from these samples of her activity that have survived that she was probably busy throughout the early 1790's.

Beginning in 1796–97 Miss Burnett was a member of the Covent Garden company at a salary of £1 weekly. The bills and accounts show her active there, chiefly as a singer in the chorus, from 19 September 1796 when she was in the *Romeo and Juliet* procession through 1802–3 when the accounts show her to have stayed at exactly the same salary through the years. At Covent Garden she was occasionally in named roles, as on 16 March 1797 when she was Annette in *Raymond,* but most of the time she was submerged in the choruses in such works as *Ramah Droog, Albert and Adelaide, The Death of Captain Cook,* and *The Intriguing Chambermaid.* She may have continued to be affiliated with Covent Garden as late as 1814–15, for the accounts seem to cite her that season, but detailed information on her theatrical activity ceases after 1802–3. The last mention of her was in an entry of 3 February 1822 to the Minute Books of the Royal Society of Musicians when she applied for expenses to cover her mother's funeral.

Burnett, William c. 1742–c. 1797, kettledrummer.

Since William Burnett was bound apprentice to the musician John Ward the elder on 26 October 1756, it is likely that he was born about 1742. He became a freeman on 26 October 1763 and was admitted to livery in the Worshipful Company of Musicians, giving his address as No 16, New Exeter Court, the Strand. He was probably the Burnet listed in the Covent Garden accounts in 1766–67 at 5s. daily, but he also served as a teacher. On 23 February 1774, for example, when he was living at No 4, Hyde Street, Bloomsbury, his ex-master's son John was bound apprentice to him, and on 18 September 1776 young Martin Platts, son of a blacksmith, became apprenticed to Burnett.

By 27 November 1778 he was on the staff of Drury Lane, apparently serving as an extra instrumentalist; the accounts cite him twice for "extra music," and on the date noted he was paid £28 10s. for 11 nights. By 1783 he was attached to the King's Theatre in the Haymarket, playing in the operas there, and his service continued at least through the 1784–85 season. By this time he had moved to No 18, Harford, Longacre. In May and June of 1784 he was probably the Mr "Burnet" who played kettledrums at the Handel Memorial Concerts at Westminster Abbey and the Pantheon. At some point before 6 March 1785 Burnett was elected to the Royal Society of Musicians, for on that date he attended a meeting as a member of the Court of Assistants.

On 6 June 1790 his wife petitioned the Society for financial aid, but her plea was rejected on the grounds that William was still alive; had he been ill he could have petitioned in his name; therefore doubtless he and his wife were separated. On 5 February 1797 a Mr Connell of Dublin reported to the Society that Burnett had died (apparently in Ireland), and he asked for £26 to cover the late musician's illness and funeral expenses. Burnett's widow was reported dead on 3 February 1822 when her daughter asked for Society funds to pay her mother's funeral costs.

Burnett, Mrs ₁William?, née Goodman? *d. c. 1822?*₁, *singer, actress.*

Though proof is lacking, it is likely that the Mrs Burnett who performed at Sadler's Wells and Drury Lane during the 1770's and 1780's was the daughter of Ann Goodman and wife of the musician William Bur-

nett; the Miss Burnett who performed in the 1780's and 1790's was evidently William's daughter. The Burnetts probably married in the 1760's, in view of their daughter's activity from 1783 onward. Mrs Burnett's first stage appearances seem to have been in 1773 at Sadler's Wells; she sang there at least occasionally through 1783. A benefit bill, undated but from the year 1776, gave her address as No 117, Longacre.

This Mrs Burnett may have been the "Mrs Burnet" who acted at York in August 1777, billed as from the Norwich theatre; if so, she was engaged at Bath the ensuing winter as a principal actress. By 5 April 1779, however, she was singing again at Sadler's Wells, and on 14 May 1783 she was joined there by Miss Burnett, also a singer. The pair moved to Drury Lane starting in the fall of 1783, and through the 1785–86 season Mrs Burnett was part of the singing chorus in such works as *The Triumph of Mirth, Harlequin Junior, The Cauldron, Macbeth, Arthur and Emmeline,* and *Hurly Burly.* Her chores may have involved some acting, though she seems to have been a singer primarily, which fact casts doubt upon her being the Norwich-York-Bath actress.

In May and June of 1784 Mrs Burnett was one of the "treebles" at the Handel Memorial Concerts at Westminster Abbey and the Pantheon (William Burnett also participated, beating out rhythms on the kettledrums). A Mrs Burnett was recorded as in the company acting at Brighton in October 1786, and she played Mysis in *Apollo Turned Stroller* at the Royalty Theatre, probably late in 1787.

Though her daughter continued performing, Mrs Burnett's activity apparently stopped before the 1790's and, indeed, may have ended with her brief appearance at the Royalty in 1787. After this, records of a different sort concern her. William Burnett had become a member of the Royal Society of Musicians, probably in the

1780's. Starting on 6 June 1790 a series of entries in the Society Minute Books concern the Burnetts—assuming we have identified the people correctly. On that date Mrs Burnett petitioned for aid, stating that she was in extreme distress. Her plea was denied on the grounds that her husband was still alive; the Burnetts must have been estranged, a fact borne out by an entry in the books on 3 February 1793 concerning Mrs Ann Goodman, Mrs Burnett's mother. Mrs Goodman presented evidence to support a claim she was making, and it included a will of her sister, Mrs Harris of Exeter; Mrs Harris had left a £1000 trust to Mrs Goodman which, upon Mrs Goodman's death would pass on to "M.ʳˢ Burnet the daughter of the said Ann Goodman for her seperate use apart from Her Husband."

Indeed, the Burnetts were so far estranged that William, at some point, went off to Ireland, where he died shortly before 5 February 1797, not attended by his wife. Hard upon his death, Mrs Burnett was importuning the Society for financial relief; on 4 June 1797 she explained that due to a suit in Chancery her annuity had been stopped (her mother must by now have died), and she needed help. The Society gave her an allowance, which continued at least through 4 April 1802. Mrs Burnett apparently managed without the Society's help after that, though when she died, her daughter (on 3 February 1822) requested money to cover her mother's funeral expenses.

Burney, Mr ₁*fl. 1718–1731*₁, *actor.*
Though it is often difficult to discriminate between the two Burneys who performed at Goodman's Fields in the late 1720's and early 1730's, one was an actor (frequently called Burney Senior) and the other a dancer (named Thomas Burney and called Burney Junior). They may have been father and son, but there is no certain evidence of this.

The senior Burney made what was advertised as his first appearance on that stage at Lincoln's Inn Fields on 30 October 1718 playing Ben in *Love for Love*; he had, it would seem, previous theatrical experience and may have come from a provincial company. Since his name disappeared from London bills for 11 years, he may well have left the city. On 5 November 1729 at Goodman's Fields he appeared again as Ben, billed as Burney Senior to distinguish him from the dancer who was also in the troupe. Burney Senior's roles during the 1729–30 season were fairly important: Obadiah in *The Committee*, Fondlewife in *The Old Bachelor*, and Purser in *The Fair Quaker of Deal* were among them, and his 3 June 1730 benefit was shared with only one other actor.

In 1730–31 he played Modely in *The Fashionable Lady*, Dorcas in *The Cobler of Preston*, and, on 18 March 1731, Obadiah again for his last appearance. After this he may have returned to the provinces. Hogan, in *Shakespeare in the Theatre*, calls this Burney "Richard," apparently on the basis of a 31 March 1755 *Daily Advertiser* notice of a Richard Burney, dancing master; but Burney Senior was not a dancer, and the newspaper notice may instead refer to the Drury Lane dancer Burnet.

Burney, Mr ₁*fl. 1730*₁, *harpsichordist.*
Mr Burney performed a lesson on the harpsichord at the Goodman's Fields Theatre on 12 May 1730, being billed as from Oxford.

Burney, Charles *1726–1814, organist, composer, music historian.*
Charles Burney was born at Shrewsbury on 7 April 1726, the youngest of the many children of James Burney, a portrait painter by his second wife Ann Burney, née Cooper.

Elected Fellow of the Royal Society of Arts in 1764, made Doctor of Music at Oxford in 1769, and elected Fellow of the Royal Society in 1773, Charles Burney was one of the great personalities of eighteenth-century London social life. He enjoyed a large circle of friends among the famous, including George III and Queen Charlotte, Burke, the younger Pitt, Rousseau, Diderot, Reynolds, Captain Cook, Haydn, Handel, and Garrick. Dr Johnson wrote of him, "I must question if there is in the world such another man, for mind intelligence and manners, as Dr Burney."

As a young man Burney served as apprentice to the eminent musician Thomas A. Arne, living in his house for two years and assisting him with musical assignments at the playhouses and pleasure gardens. In September 1745, Burney made a choral and orchestral arrangement of "God Save the King" at Covent Garden while his master furnished an arrangement of the same air to Drury Lane. During this period Burney played the violin and viola in Handel's orchestra for musical evenings at Handel's house in Lower Brook Street and at Carlton House, the residence of the Prince of

Harvard Theatre Collection
CHARLES BURNEY
by Reynolds

Wales. Appointed organist of St Dionis Backchurch in 1748, he also was harpsichordist to several concert organizations at the King's Arms, Cornhill, and elsewhere. On 3 July 1749 he was made a freeman of the Worshipful Company of Musicians in the City (and was admitted to its livery on 29 March 1759). In the same year he was admitted to the Royal Society of Musicians.

Burney's first composition for the theatre was the music for *Robin Hood*, a new entertainment written by Moses Mendez and produced by Garrick at Drury Lane on 13 December 1750. The piece had little success, but several weeks later at the same theatre Burney provided music for Henry Woodward's entertainment *Queen Mab*, which opened on 29 December, became an immediate popular success, and remained a favorite in the repertory for some years. Some of Burney's music to both pieces was published in 1750. According to a fragment of a manuscript autobiography in Burney's hand at the British Museum, there being no vacancy in the Drury Lane band during this period, he was occasionally employed there as a supernumerary violin or tenor for pantomimes or musical pieces, at a salary of 5s. each time he played.

In 1759 he set the music for Bonnell Thornton's humorous "Ode on St Cecilia's Day," which was performed in costume at Ranelagh Gardens with great success and in which Burney employed such instruments as the salt-box, the jew's-harp, and bladder-and-string. His other work for the theatre included the music for *The Cunning Man*, adapted from Rousseau's pastoral *Le Devin du village*, at Drury Lane on 21 November 1766 and seven more nights that season. On 11 June 1767, Burney's man was paid £2 5s. by Drury Lane for copying music.

Dr Burney made an appearance at the Haymarket Theatre on 18 February 1774, when he played a concerto on the organ at the end of part 1 of the *Messiah*. According to Wroth, he had also played the organ at Ranelagh in 1770. Towards the end of his career, Burney wrote the music for "A new Loyal Song and Chorus, which recounts all the recent victories of our Naval Heroes," sung by Incledon, Johnstone, Townsend, and Hill at Covent Garden on 7 November 1798.

Dr Burney, of course, is best remembered for his publications on musical history which included *The Present State of Music in France and Italy* (1771), *The Present State of Music in Germany* (1773), *A General History of Music* (1776, 1782, 1789), *Account of the Infant Musician, Crotch* (1779), *Memoirs of the Letters and Writings of the Abate Metastasio* (1796), and numerous contributions to the *Monthly Review* (1785–1802), and to Rees's *Cyclopaedia.*

Burney was much involved in the organization and presentation of the great Handel Commemoration in Westminster Abbey and the Pantheon in 1784, and in the following year he gave an account of the event in a book commissioned and supported by the Royal Society of Musicians; the account was prefaced by a life of Handel and was illustrated by Dr Burney's artist-nephew, Edward Francis Burney. Many other literary and musical works by Burney are listed in the *Cambridge Bibliography of English Literature*, the *Catalogue of Printed Music in the British Museum*, and *Grove's Dictionary of Music and Musicians.*

Dr Burney died at Chelsea on 12 April 1814 and was buried on 20 April in the burial grounds of Chelsea Hospital, where he had occupied rooms during his last years. His children erected a tablet to his memory in the north choir aisle of Westminster Abbey. By his long will, dated 12 January 1807 and proved 30 April 1814, Dr Burney made specific bequests of his many pictures and extensive properties to his children and relatives, but his immense musical library of printed and manuscript music was sold in an auction which took nine days. The books on music were bought separately by the British Museum. His son, Rev Charles Burney, Jr (1757–1817), a famous Greek scholar, made a comprehensive file of playbills and presscuttings which now forms the basis of the extraordinary Burney collection of theatrical materials at the British Museum. Dr Burney was painted by Joshua Reynolds and by his sister Frances Reynolds; his bust was done by Nollekens in 1805.

In the words of Hazlitt, "There are whole families who are born classical, and are entered in the herald's college of reputation by the right of consanguinity." Such was the Burney family—it produced wits, scholars, novelists, musicians, artists. Hazlitt thought that "The name alone is a passport to the Temple of Fame" and that Dr Burney, himself, sat on its throne.

For the many details of Burney's life, ancestry, progeny, will, and the extensive accomplishments and history of the enormous family, see Percy Scholes's authoritative *The Great Dr. Burney* (Oxford, 1948) and Annie Ellis's *The Early Diary of Frances Burney* (London, 1889). Brief accounts of the events of Dr Burney's non-theatrical activities can be found in Grove and in the *Dictionary of National Biography.*

Burney, Charles Rousseau 1747–1819, *harpsichordist.*

Charles Rousseau Burney was born in 1747 at Worcester, the son of Richard Burney of Barborne Lodge in that city, who was the eldest brother of the great musician and musical historian Dr Charles Burney (1726–1814). C. R. Burney made his first appearance on the London stage, billed as "Mr Burney Jr from Worcester," on 3 December 1766 at Drury Lane when he played a concerto on the harpsichord at the seventh performance of *The Cunning Man*, for the benefit of that piece's composer, his uncle Dr Burney. He played the following night before the King and Queen and again on 1 January. Although his name did not reappear in the bills, he seems to have continued as a Drury Lane musician for that season, for on 7 April 1767 he was paid a salary of £1 13*s.* 4*d.* for eight days. In 1767 and 1770 he performed at the Worcester Festival.

Playing at various musical evenings sponsored by his uncle at St Martin's Street, and later at his own house in Great Titchfield Street, Charles Rousseau Burney became known as a virtuoso on the harpsichord. He was also excellent on the violin. Frances Burney made numerous references to his playing in her diary and letters which testify that on such occasions he was "the King of the evening" and that his playing "raised a general astonishment." She described the admiration expressed by the fashionable Italian musician Millico for Burney's playing:

It is impossible to express the delight which his performance gave to Millico. His amazing execution really excited in him the most hearty laughs. The Italians cultivate harpsichord-playing so little, giving all their time to the voice, that execution such as Mr.

Burney's appeared miraculous, and when Millico saw him make a fine and long shake with his fourth and little fingers, and then change from finger to finger, while his left hand kept on the subject, he was really almost convulsed . . . and when it was over, rising from his seat, he clapt his hands and cried with emphasis and in a very droll accent, "It is terrible, I really tink."

On 20 September 1770 at St Paul, Covent Garden, Charles Rousseau Burney married his cousin Esther Burney (1749–1832), also a distinguished harpsichordist and the eldest daughter of Dr Burney. Their duet playing at their house in Great Titchfield Street attracted many distinguished guests, including Prince Orloff of Russia. Charles also gave unusual private performances for the sole enjoyment of the historian William Beckford (d. 1799), Dr Burney's friend who was confined in the Fleet Prison in 1791. Dr Burney wrote to Beckford's daughter Frances on 8 October 1791: "My most worthy and good nephew Charles, of Titchfield Street, goes to him generally once a week, and dines, and plays to him on a miserable pianoforte for five or six hours at a time."

Charles Rosseau Burney died at Bath in 1819. By his wife Esther, who died in 1832, he had ten children. A portrait of him playing the violin, painted by his brother Edward F. Burney, is in the National Portrait Gallery. A portrait of him by Gainsborough, sold at Christie's in June 1930, is now in New York at the Metropolitan Museum. A third painting of him, with his wife and father, is described in the entry of Mrs Charles Rousseau Burney.

National Portrait Gallery

CHARLES ROUSSEAU BURNEY
by E. F. Burney

Burney, Mrs Charles Rousseau, Esther, née Burney *1749–1832, harpsichordist.*

Esther Burney was born in 1749, the eldest child of the great Dr Charles Burney (1726–1814) and his first wife Esther, née Sleepe (d. 1761). In the tradition of the accomplished and prodigious Burney family, at the age of nine Esther played "a Lesson on the Harpsichord" in a concert of instrumental music presented at the Haymarket Theatre on 23 April 1760, with "The Solos by young Performers who never appeared in Public." The other young musicians included Master Barron, age 13, on the violin, Master James Cervetto, age 11, on the violoncello, and Miss Schmelling (later Madame Mara), age 11, on the violin. Between 1764 and 1767 Esther traveled with her father in France and also attended a convent school at Paris. Upon her return, recognized as a prodigy, she often played for the entertainment of her father's distinguished friends at musical parties.

On 20 September 1770 at St Paul, Covent Garden, she married her cousin Charles Rousseau Burney, also a very capable harpsichordist. They lived for some time in

ESTHER, CHARLES ROUSSEAU, and RICHARD BURNEY

by Hudson

Great Titchfield Street and gave frequent musical parties there, their duet playing becoming famous and attracting great vocal performers, such as Pacchierotti, to come sing for their guests. The Burneys had ten children, two of whom died in infancy. In 1814, when living at Turnham Green, Esther inherited £1000 in Navy Bonds from her father's will. In 1817 she and her husband moved to Bath, where he died in 1819. Esther died there also 13 years later.

Esther was painted by Hudson in a threesome which also included her husband and his father, Richard Burney (the brother of Dr Burney); in 1948 the painting was in the possession of the Misses Burney of Wandsworth, and it has been reproduced in Percy Scholes's *The Great Dr. Burney* (Oxford, 1948). Professor Scholes and the edition of Annie Raine Ellis, *The Early Diary of Frances Burney* (London, 1889), should be consulted for details of Esther Burney's non-professional life and for information about her immediate family.

Burney, Thomas *fl. 1726–1732*, *dancer, dancing master.*

Thomas Burney was first mentioned in the Lincoln's Inn Fields bills on 9 May 1726 when he and Mrs Anderson, both students of Essex, performed a pastoral and a Venetian dance. He continued performing at this theatre through October 1726, after which he may have left London for a year, for his name did not appear again in the theatrical records until 6 October 1727 when he played Punch in *Harlequin Doctor Faustus* at Drury Lane. He danced at this playhouse through the 1728–29 season, doing *entr'acte* numbers and pantomime roles, and he concluded his engagement with a benefit on 8 May 1729 shared with two others.

On 25 November 1729 he made his first appearance at the Goodman's Fields Theatre, dancing *The Shepherd's Holiday*. His position with the company was apparently that of leading dancer, and for his benefit on 16 April 1730 he styled himself "T. Burney, Dancing-Master." At Goodman's Fields he was frequently called "Burney Junior" to distinguish him from the actor Burney who was also in the troupe, but whether or not they were father and son is not certain. Thomas Burney worked at Goodman's Fields through the 1731–32 season, but after his appearance as Pierrot in *Harlequin's Contrivance* at his benefit on 21 April 1732 his London activity apparently ended.

Burnitt. *See* **BURNET** and **BURNETT**.

Burnley, Mr [*fl.* 1725–1732], *house servant?*

The Lincoln's Inn Fields Theatre accounts in 1725 and 1726 show payments to one Burnley (or Burnaby) "for properties," and a Burnley shared a benefit with two others there on 18 May 1732. It is not clear whether Burnley was on the theatre staff or was an outside supplier.

Burns. *See also* **BURN**, **BYRN** and **BYRNE**.

Burns, James *d. 1796, ventriloquist.*

All that seems to be known of James Burns the ventriloquist is that an etching of him was published by R. S. Kirby (engraver unknown) and that he died in 1796.

Burnum, Mr [*fl.* 1729], *actor.*

Mr Burnum played Priuli in *Venice Preserved* at the Haymarket Theatre on 10 January 1729.

Burny. *See* **BURNEY**.

Buroni, Signora [*fl.* 1777], *singer.*

Signora Buroni sang Donna Isabella in two performances of *Vittorina* at the King's Theatre in the Haymarket—on 16 and 23 December 1777.

Harvard Theatre Collection

JAMES BURNS
artist unknown

Burr, Mrs [*fl.* 1694], *singer.*

Mrs Burr sang in a production of *The Lancashire Witches* at either Drury Lane or Dorset Garden in February 1694 as a member of the United Company.

Burr, Simon [*fl.* 1654–1671], *musician.*

Simon Burr was a musician in London before the Restoration, but no details of his early activity have come to light. He lived in Robinhood Court, Shoe Lane, and on 6 August 1654 his son Humphrey was buried at St Andrew, Holborn. His wife, Anne, was buried at the same church on 13 December 1662. The parish registers in both cases identify Burr as a "Musitioner." On 31 March 1671 Burr and three other musicians were ordered to be apprehended for playing, teaching, and practising the profession of music without a license.

Burell, Mr *[fl. 1778]*, *pit and box officekeeper.*

Mr Burell was the pit and box office-keeper at Sadler's Wells in 1778 and was then living at No 41, Rosoman Street.

Burroughs. *See also* BURROWS.

Burroughs, Mr *[fl. 1771–1781]*, *house servant.*

Though there may have been two house servants named Burroughs (or Boroughs, Borroughs, Burrows, Borrows) working at Drury Lane in the 1770's, it is probable that there was only one. He was in the company from 1771–72 through 1780–81 and was identified as a second gallery cheque-taker in 1775–76 and a dresser in 1776–77; his salary in the latter capacity was 9s. weekly.

Burroughs, Mrs *[fl. 1671–1673]*, *actress.*

A member of the Duke's Company, Mrs Burroughs was first mentioned in the records as playing Marina, a major role, in *The Citizen Turned Gentleman* at Dorset Garden on 4 July 1672. Marina is rather specifically described in the text as short, well shaped, with a wide mouth, black eyes, and dimples—characteristics which the author Ravenscroft may have given Marina in view of the actress who would play her. Mrs Burroughs also played the lead, Jacinta, in another Ravenscroft play, *The Careless Lovers*, at Dorset Garden on 12 March 1673, but no other roles are known for her. One might guess that she was a personal friend of the playwright.

Burrows. *See also* BURROUGHS.

Burrows, Mr *[fl. 1746]*, *house servant?*

A Mr Burrows, otherwise unrecorded, shared a benefit with Mr Toole at Goodman's Fields on 20 February 1746; he may have been a house servant with Hallam's troupe.

Burrows, James *[fl. 1796–1825]*, *singer, actor, instrumentalist?*

James Burrows made his first appearance as Jack Junk "(with a new sea song)" in the afterpiece *The Married Un-Married* on 1 September 1796 at the Haymarket Theatre. During the 1796–97 season he was with the Covent Garden company, probably in the singing chorus, and sometime in 1797 he sang "In vain we fill the Sparkling Bowl" at Freemason's Hall. He seems to have stayed with the Covent Garden troupe at a salary of £2 weekly over the years, but not until 7 June 1799 did his presence there receive recognition in the bills; on that date he sang "Flow thou regal purple stream" in *The Brilliants* and was billed, strangely, as making his first appearance.

After the turn of the century Burrows sang at the Royal Circus. His roles were not leads, but they were significant enough to be mentioned in the bills; among them were the Priest of Fo in *The Eclipse; or, Harlequin in China* on 17 August 1801, Old Timbertoe in *The Golden Farmer* on 28 June 1802, a vassal in *Halloween* (a "Scotch Spectacle") on 27 September 1802, the Genius of Adventure in *The Rival Statues* on 11 April 1803, and the peasant Ricardo in *Louisa of Lombardy* (a serious musical spectacle) on 25 April 1803.

For the 1803–4 season he was at Drury Lane, sharing a benefit there on 6 June 1804 and earning a weekly salary of £6. At some point he performed at the Royalty Theatre, but his career was undistinguished, and the *Thespian Dictionary* of 1805 could only describe him as "a good bass singer and useful in choruses."

He was probably the same James Burrows who was cited several times from 1812 to 1825 in the Minute Books of the Royal Society of Musicians. He was appointed to perform at the annual St Paul's concert in 1812, was elected a new governor in the Society for 1815, an old governor for 1816, and a member of the Court of Assistants in 1825. In 1815, 1820, and 1821 he asked permission to send a deputy to perform at the St Paul's concerts, so he may have been past his prime and no longer singing.

When the singer John Friend died on 25 December 1798, he left bequests to John Freckleton Burrows (then a boy) and to his brother William; both were sons of Grace Burrows of the Haymarket, stationer. James Burrows the singer may have been related to this family in some way. He may also have been the James Burrows who married Louisa Ann Sword at St Paul, Covent Garden, on 24 December 1806, but the marriage register indicates considerable illiteracy in the Sword family, and the educated singer might have disdained such a match.

Burrows, Robert ₁fl. 1794₁, singer?

Doane listed Robert Burrows, of No 54, Great Marylebone Street, as a tenor (singer, presumably, though he could have been a viola player) who participated in the Handelian concerts at Westminster Abbey in 1794. He may have been the Robert Burrows who married Eleanor Collins at St George, Hanover Square, on 25 April 1799, or the Robert Burrows who married Elizabeth Howlett at St Paul, Covent Garden, on 6 December 1808.

Burt. See also **BIRT.**

Burt, Mr ₁fl. 1745₁, actor.

Mr Burt played "Rochfacalt" in The Massacre at Paris on 28 October 1745 at Goodman's Fields.

Burt, Mr ₁fl. 1777–1785₁, clown.

Mr Burt (or Birt) was a clown at Astley's Amphitheatre, perhaps as early as 1772, but certainly by 19 September 1777 when he shared a benefit with Mr Taylor. Burt was a tumbling specialist, and he used his talent in an exhibition called "Theatre of Florence" which Astley presented in July, September, and October 1780. The last mention of Burt was on 7 April 1785 when he was still tumbling at the Amphitheatre.

Burt, Nicholas ₁fl. c. 1635–1690₁, actor.

Nicholas Burt was one of the handful of actors from Caroline times who reappeared on the stage after the Restoration. Since he is said to have been a boy actor under Shank, who died in January 1636, Burt was probably born about 1624 – possibly earlier but surely not much later. It seems likely that after Shank died, young Nicholas transferred to the King's and Queen's Company, familiarly known as Beeston's Boys, to play female roles under Christopher Beeston. With him were other boy actors who continued into the Restoration period, including Michael Mohun and Robert Shatterell. One of Burt's known roles from this period was Clariana in Love's Cruelty.

In 1642 Burt enlisted in the King's army as a cornet under Sir Thomas Dallison in Prince Rupert's regiment, a group in which his fellow actors Shatterell and Charles Hart also served. By the winter of 1648 he and some of his fellows formed an acting company and tried to play at the Cockpit in Drury Lane, but they were raided by soldiers as they were acting The Bloody Brother (also known as Rollo), with Burt playing Latorch. The performers were temporarily imprisoned and their habits confiscated, but they were finally released. Burt may have engaged in other illegal theatrical activity at this time, but the next certain record of his performing is not until 1660.

With a company headed by Mohun at the old Red Bull playhouse, Burt played Hubert in The Beggar's Bush in 1659–60, and in the transitional month of October 1660 he acted with the mixed company at the Cockpit in Drury Lane. There, on 11 October 1660, he played Othello, a role which was to become one of his favorites. By early November the two major Restoration companies had been established, the Duke's under Sir William Davenant and the King's under Thomas Killigrew. With most of the older players, Burt allied himself with the latter troupe and played at the converted tennis court in Vere Street. Hubert in *The Beggar's Bush* was again one of his parts, played there on 7 November 1660; he also acted Surly in *The Alchemist* in December, Tygranes in *A King and No King* on 3 December, and his pre-Restoration role of Latorch in *The Bloody Brother* on 6 December. Burt's position in the company was a strong one, yet his talent was clearly not equal to that of his colleagues Hart and Mohun, who shared the leading roles in most of the plays Killigrew's group was permitted to act. As one of the old timers, however, Burt was a chief signer on 20 December 1661 of an agreement with the Earl of Bedford concerning the construction of a new playhouse in Bridges Street. He held two shares in the building, as many as any of the other players except John Lacy. That he could afford this investment is evidence that at this time he was reasonably well off.

Sometime in 1661–62 Burt played the King of England in *The Royall King*; on 28 January 1662 he acted Don Decastrio in *Rule a Wife and Have a Wife*; and he was probably Ferentes in *Love's Sacrifice*, perhaps this season or later. By 10 January 1662 Burt, in addition to his two shares in the projected Bridges Street playhouse, held one share in the acting company, thus enjoying income from daily profits while the troupe played at Vere Street. By the 1662–63 season the new house was under construction, and as early as 28 January 1662 Burt had agreed with his fellow actors to perform there. When the new playhouse opened in 7 May 1663, Burt acted Seleucus in *The Humorous Lieutenant*, a great success that ran for 12 performances.

Between the opening of the Bridges Street Theatre and its destruction by fire nine years later, Burt continued acting secondary roles for the most part. He played Corvino in *Volpone* (14 January 1665), Vasquez in *The Indian Emperor* (April 1665), Cleremont in *The Silent Woman* (10 December 1666), and Lysimantes in *Secret Love* (late February 1667). On 11 December 1667 Pepys reported that Burt would act Cicero in *Catiline* presently, "which they all conclude he will not be able to do well." Pepys got his information from one of the leading players in the rival Duke's Company, Henry Harris, and though Harris was a rather conceited fellow and prone to denigrate his colleagues, there may have been some truth in his opinion of Burt. Burt was certainly not given many leading parts by his company; he played Othello regularly, to be sure, but on 6 February 1669 Pepys saw him play the Moor and felt he did not do as well in the role as he once had. Prince Hal in *1 Henry IV* was another of his major parts (first recorded for him on 2 November 1668), but such a role was the exception, not the rule; more typical, and perhaps just his type, was Surly in *The Alchemist*.

But it may not have been entirely due to a second-rate talent that Burt had to settle for secondary roles. In 1669–70 he was treated for a "lyngring disease" of some kind by Dr John Archer; he may have been afflicted for some time before this, and the cost to him in money was more than he could afford. On 10 June 1670 Dr Archer was in the process of going to court against Burt to collect his fee.

The last recorded role for Burt at the Bridges Street playhouse before it burned down was Ligarius in *Julius Caesar*, performed about 1670–71. After the disaster, the King's Company moved to the old Lincoln's Inn Fields Theatre which the Duke's Company had abandoned, and there Burt played Camillo in *The Assignation* (November 1672) and Perez in *Amboyna* (May 1673) while the new Drury Lane

Theatre was under construction on the old site. On 17 December 1673 Burt agreed to perform at the new house, and his finances were now sufficiently improved that he was able to become one of the sharers in it. On 16 May 1674, after the new theatre opened, Burt played Petronius in *Nero*, but records of his acting during the 1670's are far fewer than those concerning his off-stage theatrical work.

Burt had funds enough on 20 March 1674 to put up £160 toward the construction of a scene house to augment the new Drury Lane, yet at this same time the troupe was in serious financial trouble, some of the actors threatened to quit, and manager Thomas Killigrew was having increasing difficulty keeping his theatrical venture from foundering. Finally he turned over much of his power to his son Charles, who on 1 May 1676 entered into a new sharing agreement with the major company members, including Burt. During the ensuing few years Burt figured frequently in King's Company financial dealings and often served as the troupe's representative in controversies or law suits. On 20 March 1677, for instance, Joseph Bowles and Elizabeth Sutton sued the King's Company for the rent of their cellar (for storage perhaps), and Burt was one of the representative members named; and on 16 January 1678 Burt was arrested by Robert Baden for a company debt—and bailed. But other members named were not taken into custody, so Burt was serving as the official scapegoat.

It was at this time that Burt apparently withdrew from acting. In March 1678 he played Maldrin in *The Men of Newmarket*, the last acting assignment recorded for him. He would now have been in his mid-fifties, and perhaps he decided to give up any pretensions to acting and devote his time to administration instead. The last notice of a great role for him was back in February 1669 when he acted Othello, and as late as about 1684 he was remembered as "strutting Burt" in a *Satyr on the Players*. But he

was apparently of value to the company in its financial dealings, and he had enough invested in it to be more than casually interested. Consequently, the records show him regularly involved in legal and financial matters. On 19 April 1678 he, Shatterell, and Mohun posted a £500 bond in connection with costumes the players had spirited out of the theatre; he figured in the contractual arrangements with Dryden for plays; and on 29 January 1680 he was named in a suit brought against the company by Will West the embroiderer for an unpaid debt.

The financial condition of the troupe was so poor by 1680 that it is not surprising that at about this time Burt retired. He still held a financial interest in the company, but now he was on the other end of the litigation: on 23 February 1681 he had to sue his ex-colleagues for his share of the profits. After the King's troupe merged with their rivals to form the United Company, Nicholas and Richard Burt (probably a relative) held a share each in the new group. The last notice of Nicholas Burt is on 10 February 1690 when he charged Charles Killigrew with detaining his share in the clothes, scenes, and books belonging to the theatre.

Burtoft, [William?] [*fl.* 1781–1787], *housekeeper, box bookkeeper.*

Mr Burtoft the theatre employee was probably the William Burtoft, haberdasher of King Street, who was named in his mother Sarah's will dated 5 January 1781 and proved on the following 8 March. At the time the will was drawn, Sarah Burtoft was a widow. A memorandum concerning the operation of the Royalty Theatre was witnessed by a William Burtoft on 5 May 1786, and this was very likely Sarah's son, now turned to a career in the theatre. He was housekeeper at John Palmer's Royalty Theatre when it opened (and closed) on 20 June 1787, and when the playhouse later reopened to provide non-dramatic entertainments, Burtoft remained on the staff in the same position and also served as box bookkeeper.

Burton. *See also* **BLURTON** and **JEFFERSON, THOMAS**

Burton, Mr [*fl. 1722–1727*], *numberer.*

Mr Burton is said to have been a numberer at Drury Lane in November 1722 when, according to W. J. Lawrence, he was in charge of the center middle gallery box still referred to 20 years later in Fielding's *The Miser* as "Burton's box." This may have been so, and there certainly was a Mr Burton active in the theatres in the 1720's, but the middle gallery boxkeeper at Drury Lane at this time was *Mrs* Burton, who served Drury Lane in that capacity at least from 1722 to 1730, receiving annual benefits (unshared).

On 27 May 1725 a Mr Burton was paid £1 15s. at Lincoln's Inn Fields for oil, and was on that theatre's free list in 1726–27. He may have been a Drury Lane numberer (not boxkeeper) earlier in the 1720's and switched to Lincoln's Inn Fields after a few years. It is very likely that Mr and Mrs Burton were related, perhaps as man and wife.

Burton, Mrs [*fl. 1722–1730*], *boxkeeper. See* **BURTON, MR** [*fl. 1722–1727*].

Burton, Mr [*fl. 1792–1794*], *singer.*

A Mr Burton sang at Bermondsey Spa Gardens in 1792. According to Doane, a Mr Burton of No 7, China Row, Lambeth, was a tenor singer at Drury Lane in 1794. The only Burton to be found in the bills of that theatre at this time was John Burton, the actor, not known as a singer. The tenor was no doubt a member of the chorus and may have been the Burton whose name was on the pay list for £1 per week at a time when John Burton was being paid at least £3.

Burton, Miss *d. 1771? actress.*

On 27 March 1770 "a young Gentlewoman, first appearance on any stage" played the part of Lady Townly in *The Provok'd Husband* at Drury Lane. James Winston in a Folger manuscript tentatively identified her: "Query: Lady Townly a Miss Burton who [died] the following year at Bath."

Burton, Edmund *d. 1772, actor.*

Edmund Burton, who acted for 27 years on the London stage, may have originally been intended for a career as a musician. According to the registers of the Worshipful Company of Musicians, an "Edmond" Burton, of Bow Street, Covent Garden, became a freeman on 11 March 1730 and was admitted to livery on 9 March 1743. He or his father may have been the "Edm^d Burton" who witnessed the will of the musician William Turner on 4 January 1728.

Billed as making "his first appearance on the stage," Burton acted Sir Friendly in *The Lady's Last Stake* at Covent Garden on 30 April 1746, when he also shared a benefit with Delagarde and Thompson. On the previous day his full name was listed by the *General Advertiser* in an advance notice. He played no other roles during the remainder of that season but was a member of a company which acted at Twickenham and Richmond the summer following. That fall he joined Hallam's company at the theatre in New Wells, Lemon Street, Goodman's Fields, where he acted Zanga in *The Revenge* on 27 October 1746, Tamerlane on 4 and 5 November, Oroonoko on 16 December, and Carlos in *The Fatal Marriage* on 19 March 1747. Burton then joined the Hallams, Shuter, Lee, and Foote in some 28 performances of Foote's *The Diversions of the Morning, or, a Dish of Chocolate* at the Haymarket between 22 April and 1 June 1747, after which he again played during the summer at Twickenham and Richmond.

In the fall of 1747 Burton joined Drury

Harvard Theatre Collection

EDMUND BURTON as Subtle, WILLIAM PARSONS as Face, and DAVID GARRICK
as Abel Drugger

in *The Alchemist*

by Zoffany

Lane, which that season came under the management of Garrick, where Burton was to be engaged for the remainder of his career. He made his first appearance there as Blunt in *Richard III* on 6 November 1747, and in that season he also played Salisbury in *Henry V*, Darby in *Jane Shore*, and Gonzalo in *The Tempest*. For his benefit on 2 May 1748, in which he shared net receipts of £117 with Raftor and Isaac Sparks, Burton played the Beggar in *The Beggar's Opera* and the King in *The King and the Miller of Mansfield*. His address given on the benefit bill was at Mr Thacker's in Three-King's Court, King Street. In the summer of 1748 he operated a booth with Bridges, Cross, and Vaughan at Bartholomew Fair.

During his 24 years at Drury Lane Burton continued in a line of small supporting roles, usually in comedy and often as a good lord or a secondary king. In 1766 Kelly praised his conscientiousness but described him as "one of those unnoticed things" with a "wond'rous weight of lead" for a head. "Yoked" with Bransby, wrote Gentleman in *The Theatres* (1772), Burton was as "Dull, heavy, cold as dark November weather." Perhaps his most important roles were Gloster in *King Lear*, which he first played on 31 December 1762, and Subtle in *The Alchymist*, which he first played on 20 March 1753. Woodward played the latter role for the next five years but when he went off to Dublin to take up management, the role fell back to Burton.

In addition to those mentioned above, among Burton's roles in the repertory were: a witch and the doctor in *Macbeth*, Alvarez in *The Revenge*, Capulet in *Romeo and Juliet*, Sir William in *All in the Wrong*, Northumberland in *1 Henry IV*, the uncle in *The London Merchant*, Don Pedro in *The Wonder*, Russet in *The Jealous Wife*, Chatillion in *Zara*, Old Willful in *The Double Gallant*, Norbal in *Herod and Mariamne*, Enox in *Merope*, Richard Wealthy in *The Minor*, Sullen in *The Stratagem*, the player king in *Hamlet*, the governor in *Oroonoko*, Balance in *The Recruiting Officer*, Oliver in *As You Like It*, Don Lopez in *Marplot in Lisbon*, the shoemaker in *The Man of Mode*, Lord Grizzle in *The Tragedy of Tragedies*, and Morat in *The Orphan of China*, which he played in the first performance on 21 April 1758. He also played again at Richmond in the summers of 1752, 1753, 1760, and 1765. Between 1750 and 1756 his London address was at the Lock and Key in Brownlow Street, Longacre. His salary at Drury Lane in 1764–65 was £3 per week.

Burton was the victim of an on-stage accident on 13 October 1755, when Holland made his debut as Oroonoko. On that night the prompter Richard Cross wrote in his diary "[Holland] in stabbing the Governor (Mr Burton) in the last Scene, he struck him on the Cheek, & upon hearing him cry O God! was so shocked that he did not die so well as was expected—Burton was taken off, & dress'd by Mr Bromfield, [who] was accidentally behind the Scenes."

Burton's last performance was as Brabantio in *Othello* on 7 January 1772. He died on 3 May 1772, and on 11 May the "Widow Burton" was given a benefit in which she shared profits of £100 19 *s.* with Bransby. When *Cymbeline* was performed

in the following fall on 19 September 1772, with the Queen being played by Mrs Hopkins instead of Mrs Reddish and Bellarius by J. Aickin in place of the late Burton, the press remarked that both changes "were much for the better, particularly the last."

Edmund Burton's son John made his debut 28 November 1762 as the page in *Love Makes a Man*, in which the father played Antonio. John Burton then acted for many years at Drury Lane. Possibly Edmund Burton was the father of another actor named Burton who played at the Haymarket in the 1790's.

Burton appears as Subtle, with Palmer as Face and Garrick as Drugger, in a magnificent painting by Zoffany of a scene in *The Alchymist*, which was exhibited at the Royal Academy in 1770. It was purchased by Sir Joshua Reynolds for £100 and then sold by him to the Earl of Carlisle for £150. The picture has been engraved by numerous engravers and published many times.

Burton, Elizabeth *1751–1771, actress.*

Elizabeth Burton was born in 1751, the daughter of Thomas Burton, an ostler at the Ship Inn, Feversham, who, according to Winston, used to snuff candles when William Smith's circuit company performed there, and of Mary Burton (1733–1770). When in 1768 Smith relinquished the management of the eastern part of the Kent circuit (which included Canterbury, Dover, Deal, Maidstone, Rochester, and Feversham), Thomas Burton took over his interests. In May 1769 the *Kent Gazette* announced that Mr Burton was "fitting up" the theatre at Margate. He died at Margate on 17 July 1771. His wife, who had acted with him, had died on 10 November 1770 and had been buried in St John's, Margate, on 14 November, at the age of 37.

Elizabeth Burton was acting on the east Kent circuit before her father became manager, and she was deemed, according to James Winston in *The Theatric Tourist*, "in these parts a star of considerable magnitude." Announced as "A young Gentlewoman," she made her first appearance at Drury Lane on 1 December 1768 in the title role of *The Country Girl*, at which time the prompter William Hopkins wrote in his diary, "She is a pretty, genteel figure. Played the part well, and was much applauded." Miss Burton repeated the role on 10 and 27 December (when she was named in the bills) and on 18 January and 10 and 29 May 1769. These seven performances were the only ones she gave that season. On 30 September 1769 she again played the Country Girl, she then appeared as a shepherdess in *Cymon* (4 October 1769), a character in *A Trip to Scotland* (6 January and for a benefit she shared with Hartry on 15 May), and Miss Fuz in *A Peep Behind the Curtain* (22 March 1770). During her last season at Drury Lane, 1770–71, she played Miss Flack in *A Trip to Scotland* five times, Arabella in *The Author* twice, a role in *The Rehearsal* once (6 April), and Isabel in *The Double Disappointment* once (30 April). Her last performance was as Miss Fuz in *A Peep Behind the Curtain* on 7 May 1770. In the summer of 1771 she went to act at Exeter, Plymouth, and Barnstable.

Winston states that Miss Burton died at Poole, in Dorsetshire, but we believe he has confused her with Mrs Philippina Burton who, according to a manuscript notation at the British Museum, reputedly died on 29 October 1771. Elizabeth Burton died at Barnstable or Exeter on 2 November 1771, according to her epitaph in the Barnstable Church written and placed there by J. Foote, manager of the theatre at Exeter:

UNDERNEATH
THE LIBRARY OF THIS CHURCH
RESTETH
UNTIL THE ARCHANGEL'S TRUMP
SHALL SUMMON HER TO APPEAR

ON AN IMMORTAL STAGE,
THE BODY OF
ELIZABETH BURTON, COMEDIAN;
FORMERLY OF DRURY-LANE
BUT LATE OF THE EXETER THEATRE;
WHO CHANGED TIME FOR ETERNITY
ON ALL SOULS DAY, 1771,
AGED 20 YEARS
LIFE'S BUT A WALKING SHADOW,
A POOR PLAYER,
WHO STRUTS ITS HOUR OR TWO
UPON THE STAGE,
AND THEN IS HEARD NO MORE.
THIS SMALL TRIBUTE,
TO THE MEMORY OF
AN AMIABLE YOUNG WOMAN,
AN INNOCENT CHEARFUL COMPANION,
AND MOST EXCELLENT ACTRESS,
WAS PLACED HERE BY J. FOOTE,
MANAGER OF THE THEATRE.

Doggerel verses "On the death of Miss Burton, who lately performed at the Plymouth Theatre with great applause" were published in the *Gentleman's Magazine*, November 1771.

From the testimony of the epitaph it seems that the intelligence in the *St James's Chronicle* 23–25 January 1772 – "Miss Burton, late of Drury Lane Theatre, who was supposed to have died at Exeter, we are informed is now in good Health at Bristol" – was as confused as Winston. Again, this must be a reference to Mrs Philippina Burton.

Burton, George *d. 1784, singer.*

According to the bills, George Burton made his first appearance on the Drury Lane stage on 29 April 1749, when he sang unspecified songs on a benefit night which he shared with the prompter Richard Cross. Burton continued as an occasional chorus singer at that theatre, usually at 5s. per performance, until he was discharged in November 1776. On 30 April 1750 he shared benefit receipts of £150 (less charges) with Ray, W. Vaughan, and Cross; and on 4 May 1753, he shared £140 (less charges) with

Raftor and Boucher. On 11 February 1756 (and five more times that season), Burton played an unspecified role, conjectured by Hogan as Antonio, in John C. Smith's operatic setting of *The Tempest*.

Probably he was the Burton who performed at Marylebone Gardens in the summer of 1773. About this time he became the earliest music teacher of Samuel Harrison. In May and June of 1784, Burton was among the bass singers in the Handel Memorial Concerts at Westminster Abbey and the Pantheon.

During the late 1770's and early 1780's Burton was engaged as a singer for the summer seasons at the Haymarket, where he usually performed in unspecified chorus roles. On 7 and 9 September 1778 he sang in *Macbeth*, and he was a singing anchorsmith in the pantomime *Harlequin Teague* which was performed 23 times in 1782 and was revived in 1783. No doubt he was the chorus singer who, according to an entry in Reed's "Notitia Dramatica," was one of six people of the Haymarket Theatre who died during the summer of 1784. A Mary Burton, "wife of George Burton," was buried at St Paul, Covent Garden, on 16 December 1770.

Burton, John 1730–1782, *harpsichordist, organist, composer.*

The musician John Burton, born in Yorkshire in 1730 and a pupil of John Keeble, became one of the foremost harpsichord players and organists of his day. In 1754 he gave very successful concerts in Germany. No doubt he was the Mr Burton who played a concerto on the organ at the end of the oratorio *I pellegrini* at Drury Lane on 25 March 1757.

In 1782 Burton was a guest at the casino of Sir William Hamilton at Portici, near Naples, and was music master to the Gothic novelist William Beckford, then resident at Naples. On 27 August Lady Hamilton suddenly died, and on 1 September John Burton also succumbed, probably of the same ailment, "during the Delerium of a Fever."

John Burton may have been the father of the John Burton, harpsichordist, listed by Doane as living at No 45, Holborn, in 1794 (who may have been the John Burton, aged 53, who was buried at St Paul, Covent Garden, on 6 May 1798). A Miss Burton, organist of Piercey Chapel, Rathbone Place, resident in 1794 at No 26, Windmill Street, Tottenham Court Road, may have been the daughter of the subject of this entry.

Burney wrote of Burton that he was "an enthusiast in his art,"

but having in his youth exercised his hand more than his head, he was not a deep or correct contrapuntist. He had, however, in his pieces and manner of playing them a style of his own, to which, from his having been one of the first harpsichord players in our country who attempted expression and light and shade, he excited an interest and attention, which would now [1789] perhaps be much more difficult to obtain.

Burton composed three concertos for harpsichord, one for organ and harpsichord, ten sonatas for keyboard, six sonatas for keyboard with accompaniments for the violin, and 12 Italian canzonets for the voice and harpsichord. On occasion, he also served as a music copyist for the theatres. On 24 November 1749 he received £1 2s. 3d. for writing out parts. A manuscript in his hand of the opera *Attilio Regolo*, music by Jomelli and text by Metastasio, which was performed at the King's Theatre on 23 April 1754, is at the British Museum.

Burton, John d. 1797?, *actor.*

John Burton was born in London about 1749, the son of the Drury Lane actor Edmund Burton (d. 1772). As Master Burton he was first brought on the stage of Drury Lane on 28 October 1762 in the role of the page in *Love Makes a Man*, in which his father acted Antonio. On 17 January 1763

Harvard Theatre Collection

A Landscape Water-color done by the actor JOHN BURTON

he played Fleance in *Macbeth*, a play in which his father regularly performed as one of the witches and in which they both shared a benefit on 13 April 1763. When Miss Rogers was taken ill on 20 February 1764, Master Burton was sent on to read the role of the page in *The Orphan*. That season he also played Donalbain in *Macbeth* and Squire Richard in *The Provok'd Husband*.

For several years Master Burton continued in similar roles, such as Prince Edward in *Richard III* and Prince Henry in *King John*. He was earning 15s. per week in 1764–65 and £1 per week by 1766–67. He also acted with his father at Richmond in the summer of 1765.

In the season of 1767–68, apparently now having reached his maturity, he began to be billed as "J. Burton"; and he acted a

number of roles which reflected his more mature status, including Fribble in *The Hermit*, Dick in *Flora*, the tailor in *Catherine and Petruchio*, Tester in *The Suspicious Husband*, Peter in *Romeo and Juliet*, and unspecified parts in *Fortunatus* and *The Absent Man*. For his father's benefit on 29 April 1768 he played Drawer in *The Beggar's Opera*. During his remaining 28 years, roles of only slightly greater significance came to him, and he performed throughout his long career a variety of numerous minor supporting characters with little distinction or notice. After his father's death in 1772, John was billed as "Mr Burton." In addition to the above-mentioned parts, his repertory included: Cymon in *All the World's a Stage*, the watchman in *The Apprentice*, Papillion in *The Lyar*, Sir Benjamin Backbite in *The School for Scandal*, Kastril in

The Alchymist, Quildrive in *The Citizen,* Printer's Devil in *The Fair Quaker,* Dick in *Hob in the Well,* Jessamin in *The Confederacy,* Dick in *The Minor,* Tom in *The Funeral,* Jasper in *Miss in her Teens,* Daniel in *The Conscious Lovers,* and Davy in *Variety.* Among his many Shakespearean parts were the gravedigger and Rosencrantz in *Hamlet,* Shadow in *2 Henry IV,* Nym in *Henry V,* Titus in *Timon,* the watchman in *Much Ado about Nothing,* and, following his father, one of the witches in *Macbeth.*

On 7 May 1773, when he played Charles Dudley in *The West Indian* and Abram in *Harlequin's Invasion,* both for the first time, he shared benefit profits of £85 4*s.* with Bransby. On 1 May 1776, playing Thomas in *The Irish Widow* for the first time, he took on a benefit deficit of £9 19*s.* 6*d.* with the same actor. Later with Hurst he shared benefit profits of £144 12*s.* on 5 May 1778 and £127 on 4 May 1779. Burton's salary by 1774–75 was £1 15*s.* per week and by 1789–90 it was £3. Between 1777 and 1779 he lived at Duke's Court, Bow Street, and in 1780 he was at No 149, Fleet Street; by 1786 he had moved to No 8, Clement's Inn.

In the 1780's and 1790's, Burton also acted at the Haymarket during the summers, in a similar line of roles, and it is difficult at times to distinguish him from several other performers named Burton who also performed on occasion at this theatre during the period. John Burton seems to have been at the Haymarket, in any event, in 1774, 1776, from 1781 to 1783, from 1785 to 1795, and possibly in 1796. He also acted at Richmond in 1781.

On 10 September 1796, the periodical *How Do You Do?* reported that the comedian Burton was confined at Newgate, not through extravagance and dishonesty, but "from over care to a sister." The editor expressed hope that one of the managers would hire him, for though he was not first rate, he was "a useful performer." In some

Harvard Theatre Collection

JOHN BURTON, as Heartwell
artist unknown

manuscript notes in the British Museum, Reed confused him with William Burton (d. 1813?) by claiming he was bred as a painter but stated he died at Newgate about August 1797—"His creditors would have released [him] on almost any terms but he obstinately rejected every proposal." The Burney notes at the British Museum state Burton died in April 1797, and the Winston Fundbook at the Folger states that Burton, having neglected payment in 1796, died in April of that year, an obvious error since according to the *How Do You Do?,* he was still in prison in September 1796 and had played at Drury Lane until 15 June of that year.

The *Thespian Dictionary* in 1805 wrote of Burton the "son of an old performer at Drury Lane, who was greatly befriended by Mrs Abington"—meaning John Burton, son of Edmund Burton—but then continued, stating that "he supported little comic parts at the Haymarket Theatre, and died in great distress in Newgate, 1797."

Up to his last season on the Drury Lane stage, 1795–96, John Burton had been a reliable utility actor of whom T. Bellamy wrote in *The London Theatres* (1797):

> BURTON, *in humble station, ne'er offends,*
> *Burton is modest, there his virtue lies;*
> *Burton be modest still, and keep thy friends.*

Hawkins considered him "A useful stopgap." The author of *The Secret History of the Green Room* (1792) was disappointed that Burton, who had grown up in the theatre of Weston, Shuter, Yates, and Garrick, had not developed into a comedian of repute. He described Burton as an inoffensive "bottle muser"—being so fond of the cup that it "obliterates" all other vices—and one who had not been involved in scandalous amours or quarrels; and he stated that Burton was worthy in a few little parts, notably Thomas in *The Irish Widow* and Daniel in *The Conscious Lovers*. He said John Burton was a "time-server" in his profession. That he served with honor and enjoyed the respect of his colleagues, at any rate, is perhaps suggested by the fact that he was an original member of the so-called "School of Garrick," a society formed by some notable Drury Lane actors after Garrick's death in 1779.

An anonymous engraving of John Burton and William Parsons as the carpenters in *The Surrender of Calais* (first performed at the Haymarket, 30 July 1791) was published by E. Lay in 1793. An anonymous engraving of him as Heartwell in *The Old Bachelor* (a role he never played in London, although he acted Barnaby in that play on 11 February 1777) was published by Harrison in 1781. A portrait of John Burton, artist unknown, is in the Garrick Club

and is listed in the catalogue as being William Burton, an error carried over from the catalogue of the Mathews Collection. A small water color by W. Loftis of Burton as Nym in *Henry V*, 1789, is in the Folger Library. The Harvard Theatre Collection hold a water color of a rural landscape titled "Cottages from Nature by John Burton Comedian"; it was published as a print on 1 March 1794 by Darling and Thompson, booksellers, of Great Newport Street.

Burton, Lancelot   [fl. 1776–1786?], actor?, house servant?

In a manuscript list of actors of the "late 18th Century," in the Folger Library, is the name of Lancelot Burton, about whose career nothing is known. He may have been a supernumerary or house servant, without his name ever appearing on the bills.

On 7 September 1774 administration of the effects of a Lancelot Burton was granted to his widow, Hannah Burton, of the parish of St Clement Danes. A year later on 16 November 1775, administration of the effects of Hannah Burton, widow, was granted to Lancelot Burton, lawful son and only child, of the same parish. The actor was no doubt the second Lancelot Burton. In a British Museum manuscript pertaining to the Covent Garden accounts is the obscure notation for 12 December 1785, "L Burton draft on Thos Harris £34. 14. 4." The name of Lancelot Burton is found on an early nineteenth-century list of payments, in Winston's hand, probably for the Haymarket.

Burton, Philippina, later Mrs Hill?   [fl. 1770–1788?], actress, dramatist.

Mrs Philippina Burton acted a principal unnamed character in a comedy of her own authorship, *Fashion Display'd*, at the Haymarket on 27 April 1770 and delivered the epilogue. (The play, never published, is found in Larpent MS 10. M. in the Huntington Library.) She played Constance in *King John* at the Haymarket on 13 August

1770 and again on 30 August, announced on the latter date as making "her second appearance on any stage, except in a piece of her own." She was probably the Mrs Burton who acted the title role of *Jane Shore* and Maria in *The Citizen* at the same theatre on 14 November 1770.

According to a notation on a manuscript in the British Museum, she died 29 October 1771. In the *Theatric Tourist* Winston confused her with Miss Elizabeth Burton, who died on 2 November 1771, but perhaps the place of death, which he gave as Poole, Dorsetshire, is the correct one for Philippina Burton. A report in the *St James's Chronicle* January 23–25, 1772, while perpetuating the confusion with Elizabeth Burton, who surely had died, suggested that Philippina had not died: "Miss Burton, late of Drury Lane Theatre, who was supposed to have died at Exeter, we are informed is now in good Health at Bristol." In his *Biographia Dramatica*, David E. Baker stated that Philippina was probably still alive in 1782. Six years later, on 29 March 1788, the *World* reported that a Mrs Hill, "alias Philippina Burton," had lately acted Scrub at Brighton and had written a pamphlet about it.

Burton, Robert *[fl. 1784–1800]*, *proprietor*.

A Robert Burton was named with many others in a cause in Chancery in 1784 respecting a suit brought by Thomas Harris and John Gallini against the Opera House. His name was listed with such known proprietors as Richard Yates, Peter Crawford, and Mrs John Brooke. In 1800 a license was granted to Lord Kinnaird, William Sheldon, and Robert Burton for Italian opera at the King's Theatre from 6 June to 29 September.

Burton, William *d. 1813?*, *actor*, *scene painter*.

William Burton was born in London, the son of Allen Burton, who was a builder at Marylebone and later at Brompton, where once he sold a house to the actress Mrs Billington for £800. After serving seven years as an apprentice to a coach herald painter in Longacre, Burton joined Strictland's company in the provinces. According to the *Authentic Memoirs of the Green Room* (1804), Burton's first appearance on the stage was as David in *The Rivals*, and his second was as Snake in *School for Scandal*; in both instances he was struck dumb with stage fright. When his expectations of a legacy were lost as a result of his father's going bankrupt, Burton continued as a strolling player during the early 1790's. While at Shaftesbury under Shalford's management, he turned some of his early training to advantage and was employed as a scene painter. (Among his productions was the stump of a tree for the pantomime *William Tell* which without alteration afterwards on the same night was suspended as a Flitch of Bacon, in the farce of that name.) Burton was a member of the Norwich company in 1793.

Burton obtained a situation at Covent Garden for the season 1794–95 at £1 per week, making his first appearance as Tester in *The Suspicious Husband* on 15 September 1794. He also acted Diggory in *She Stoops to Conquer*, Squire Richard in *The Provok'd Husband*, Peter in *Romeo and Juliet*, the waiter in *Arrived at Portsmouth*, the constable in *Life's Vagaries*, Robin in *The Absent Man*, and Vasquez in *A Bold Stroke for a Wife*. On 30 June 1795 he shared benefit tickets with a number of minor performers and house servants. Before the beginning of the next season Burton was discharged.

On leaving Covent Garden, Burton returned to the provincial theatres. In 1799 he was announced to play at York — "Burton, of comical-face memory, who played one season at Covent Garden, is among the recent engagements." He remained at York through the season of 1801, when he wrote his twenty-four-page pamphlet, *A*

Pasquinade Upon the Performers of the York Company (published at Leeds, 1801). In a *Retort Courteous*, published in the same year, George Wilson wrote of him:

His face is by nature for Comedy *fram'd,*
But how can he help that his Bufflehead's *maim'd?*
I'd advise him again to return to Long-Acre,
Bid Thalia *good bye, and for ever forsake her.*

According to the York company lists a Mrs Burton was a member of that company from July 1799 and acted there in 1800 and 1801. Perhaps she was related in some way (she may even have been his first wife) but the *Monthly Mirror* announced the marriage of "Mr Burton, of the York Theatre, to Miss Close of Northallerton" in June 1801. The Burtons went to play at Belfast in the season 1801–2. On their first benefit night on 1 February 1802 the response was indifferent, so they were given a second night, on 26 February, which was well patronized. In a dispatch to the *Monthly Mirror*, dated 26 March 1802, it was reported that Burton and his wife, "from York," were playing with the Belfast company at Derry. The correspondent identified him as the Mr Burton who played Master Richard in *The Provok'd Husband* "a few seasons back" at Covent Garden. "He now ranks high in his profession, and is a very great favourite here. His Solus, Ollapod, Crack, &c. present a rich display of comic humour." Mrs Burton was described as a "lovely person" with "vocal abilities, superior to any we have witnessed for a long time."

In 1803 Burton was engaged by Elliston to act at the Haymarket, where he played Sir Felix Friendly in *The Agreeable Surprise*. He was discharged in 1804. Perhaps William Burton was the actor who, according to the *Gentleman's Magazine* of July

1813, died at his mother's home at Hans Place, London, on 13 July 1813.

Burtt, Mr [*fl.* 1784], *actor.*
Mr Burtt played at least once in London, as Conolly in *The School for Wives* on 16 November 1784 at the Haymarket Theatre.

Bury, Mons [*fl.* 1675], *musician.*
Monsieur Bury performed in the masque *Calisto* at court on 15 February 1675.

Bury, Mr [*fl.* 1720–1721], *performer?*
On 1 June 1720 and again on 29 May 1721 at Drury Lane, one Bury shared benefits; his function in the theatre, if any, is not known.

Bury, Miss [*fl.* 1783–1789], *dancer.*
On 18 October 1783 Miss Bury played a principal role in a pantomime *Harlequin: The Phantom of a Day*, at the Royal Circus. She was probably the same Miss Bury who danced *The Graces* with Menage and the two Miss Simonets at the Haymarket Theatre on 22 May 1789.

Bus, Gabriel-Éléanor-Hervé du. *See* CHAMPVILLE.

Busby, Thomas 1755–1838, *composer, pianist, organist, singer, author.*
Thomas Busby was born in December 1755 in Westminster, the son of a coach painter. As a boy he was unable to get an appointment in the Westminster Choir, which would have provided him with schooling and musical training, so he studied singing under Champness and harpsichord under Knyvett. He performed as a boy singer in 1769 at Vauxhall, but his voice finally broke, and for the following three years he was apprenticed to Jonathan Battishill (probably in composition).

After this early training he turned to writing for a period: he was a parliamentary reporter for the *London Courant* and wrote

THOMAS BUSBY
by R. White

musical pieces for the *European Review.* He began composing music, too, and if the Mr Busby, tenor, who sang in the Handel Memorial Concerts at Westminster Abbey and the Pantheon in May and June of 1784 was Thomas, then he also returned to singing. In 1786 he was set up as a teacher, one of his students being young Thomas Adams, the future organist and composer. In this same year, probably, he was made organist at St Mary, Stoke Newington, and began his collaboration with Thomas Arnold on a *Musical Dictionary* (which never reached completion but ran to 197 numbers). To make this eventful year complete, Busby married the eldest daughter of Charles Angier of Kensington.

From this time forward Busby was constantly at work composing, writing, and performing. His *The Divine Harmonist* was published in 1788, running for 12 numbers, and two years later *Melodia Britannica, or the Beauties of British Song* came out. In 1798 he was appointed organist at St Mary Woolnoth. For some years he had been working on an oratorio based on Pope's "Messiah," and on 29 April 1799 at the Haymarket Theatre it received its first performance, billed as the only oratorio composed in England in 30 years; Busby called it *The Prophecy* and at its premiere played piano in the band. As Public Record Office documents show, Busby (or "Bosbery," as one account called him) was granted a special license for this performance and apparently served as his own producer. He also wrote the music for Richard Cumberland's *Joanna,* which was first performed at Covent Garden on 16 January 1800.

A new Busby oratorio, *Britannia,* was given on 16 June 1800, again with the composer at the keyboard. Busby made tickets for it available at his house, No 9, China Terrace, Vauxhall Road. The *Monthly Mirror* of June 1800 found the work full of grandeur and solemnity, "much (perhaps too much for theatrical music) in the style of Handel. The overture is bold and masterly."

In 1800 Busby entered himself in Magdalen College, Cambridge, and became a candidate for a doctor's degree in music; this was granted him in June of the following year. In 1801 he also published *A Complete Dictionary of Music* and four issues of the *Monthly Musical Journal,* in addition to composing a funeral service for his old teacher Jonathan Battishill and presenting a concert at the Haymarket Theatre, probably in May. In 1802 he composed the music for *A Tale of Mystery,* for which he was paid by Covent Garden Theatre £31 10s., and the next year he wrote music for *The Fair Fugitives.* In 1805 his music for *Rugantino* was first heard, and in 1809 he provided a new overture and other musical selections for a spectacle production of

Macbeth at the Royal Circus on 30 August. His association with the Circus was revived in April 1810 when he wrote an address for Elliston to deliver at the opening of the revamped building, now called the Surrey Theatre.

After the first decade of the new century, Busby devoted most of his time to writing. In 1813 he made a translation of Lucretius; in 1818 *A Grammar of Music* was published; the following year *A History of Music* came out; in 1825 he wrote the three-volume *Concert Room and Orchestra Anecdotes*; and in 1828 he published *A Musical Manual*. Dr Busby died in London on 28 May 1838.

The British Museum has an unpublished engraving of Busby by R. White.

Bush. *See also* **BOSCH.**

Bush, Mr [*fl.* 1779], *actor, singer.*

Mr Bush played only one known role in London: Byron (with songs) in *The Students* at the Haymarket Theatre on 11 January 1779, as an afterpiece to the popular Scottish pastoral *The Gentle Shepherd.*

Bushby, Mr [*fl.* 1784], *singer.*

A Mr Bushby (which apparently is not an error for Busby, since a singer named Busby was cited on the same document) sang countertenor in the Handel Memorial Concerts at Westminster Abbey and the Pantheon on 26, 27, 29 May and 3, 5 June 1784.

Bushel, Robert [*fl.* 1766–1794], *gallerykeeper, treasurer.*

On 3 October 1766 Robert Bushel (or Bushell) was paid £4 4*s.* for 42 nights as gallerykeeper at Covent Garden. He may at this time have been married, for a Phillis Bushel was paid on 6 October of this same year for mending lace for the theatre, and she may well have been Robert's wife, doing work at home. Robert Bushel continued at Covent Garden at a salary of 2*s.* per

night through the 1769–70 season, by which time he was apparently the second gallery officekeeper. In 1794 a Mr Bushell, probably Robert, was serving as treasurer at Astley's Amphitheatre.

Bussart, Alexandre. *See* **PLACIDE, ALEXANDRE.**

Bustler, Mr [*fl.* 1742–1743], *actor.*

The London Stage lists Mr Bustler as an actor in Giffard's troupe at Lincoln's Inn Fields in 1742–43, but no roles seem to be recorded for him, and his name could be a scribal error, perhaps for Mrs Butler, who was quite active in the company that season.

Buswell, John *1733–1763, musician, composer.*

John Buswell was born in 1733, became a Gentleman of the Chapel Royal and of Windsor Chapel, and received his Bachelor of Music degree at Cambridge in 1757 and his Doctor of Music degree in 1758. By this last date he had already published a number of light songs, and he was clearly a young man of considerable ability. His career was cut short, however, on 14 November 1763, when he died at the age of 30. He was buried in the North Cloister of Westminster Abbey on 18 November. One might guess that Buswell was not in good health even in his twenties, for he made his will on 25 November 1758 at New Windsor, Berkshire; it was proved on 20 December 1763 by his widow and executrix, Elizabeth Buswell, born Fullerton. The Buswells had not yet married when John made his will, though he called Elizabeth his intended wife and described her (in 1758) as of the parish of St Botolph, Aldgate.

Butcher. *See also* **BOUCHER, BOUCHIER, BOUTCHER,** and **BOWCHER.**

Butcher, Mr [*fl.* 1724–1728], *actor.*

Mr Butcher played Gudgeon in *The Blind Beggar* at Pinkethman's booth at

Bartholomew Fair on 22 August 1724; he appeared at the same manager's Southwark Fair booth as Peter Pitiful in *Valentine and Orson* on 5 September. He was probably the Butcher who had a minor role in *Massaniello* on 21 May 1725 and was one of the recruits in *The Recruiting Officer* on 13 October 1725 at Lincoln's Inn Fields. The accounts for this playhouse indicate that he had participated in *The Recruiting Officer* earlier, though the calendar of events in *The London Stage* does not show it; on 2 October 1724 he was paid £1 1s. for acting in the play. It was probably he who was given £3 3s. on account for himself and his daughters on 11 June 1725, though a tinman named Butcher was also named in the accounts this year, and this reference could be to him. Perhaps the Mr Boucher who played the Earl of Essex in *Bateman* at the Hall-Miller booth at Bartholomew Fair on 24 August 1728 was the actor Butcher, and it is possible that Butcher was related to the Mrs Butcher who played at Lincoln's Inn Fields at about this time.

Butcher, Mrs *[fl. 1724–1725]*, actress.

Mrs Butcher, possibly the wife of the Mr Butcher who performed from 1724 to 1728, was first noticed in the bills on 11 August 1724 at Lincoln's Inn Fields when she played Lucilla in *The Roman Maid*. On 5 September of this same summer she acted Cleora in *Valentine and Orson* at Pinkethman's booth at Southwark Fair. At a daily salary of 10s. she played with the Lincoln's Inn Fields company under John Rich, and in the early months of 1725 she acted a number of sizeable roles, most of them young women: Lucinda in the alteration of *Every Man In His Humour* (11 January), Alinda in *The Pilgrim* (15 January), Hillaria in *Love's Last Shift* (13 March), Valeria in *The Rover* (5 April), Arabella in *The Committee* (26 April), and Charlotte in *Oroonoko* (6 May). On 17 May she received a benefit, shared with two others,

and, oddly, chose to play the bit part of Belinda in *The Old Bachelor*. Her last recorded role was Mrs Squeamish in *The Country Wife* on 4 October 1725; Mrs Smythies replaced her in this role on 27 November, and after this brief but promising career, Mrs Butcher seems to have left the stage.

Latreille guessed that Mrs Butcher might have been, before her marriage, the Miss Purden who acted during the four years immediately preceding the first notice of Mrs Butcher in the bills, but the roles assigned to these two names do not match, and a Mrs Purden (who was clearly the same person as the earlier Miss Purden, playing the same roles) acted from October 1728 into the 1740's.

Butcher, Mrs *[fl. 1746–1748]*, house servant?

A Mrs Butcher received regular payments, amounts unspecified, at Covent Garden from 1746 through January 1748; her duties in the company are not known, but she may have been a house servant and possibly related to the Master Butcher who sang at Southwark in 1746.

Butcher, Master *[fl. 1746]*, singer.

Master Butcher, possibly related to the Mrs Butcher who was connected with Covent Garden from 1746 to 1748, sang "In Praise of their Wives" at Southwark on 27 October 1746.

Butcher, Sarah. *See* WARD, MRS JOHN.

Butler. *See also* BUCKLER.

Butler, Mr *[fl. 1720]*, house servant?

A Mr Butler shared a benefit on 27 May 1720 at Lincoln's Inn Fields Theatre, but his function, if any, was not mentioned in the playbill.

Butler, Mr [*fl. 1734–1748*], *actor.*

A Mr Butler, possibly to be identified as James the singer, played Polydor in *The Orphan* on 28 August 1734 at York Buildings; he was billed as making his first appearance on the stage, and the place would suggest the possibility of his being an amateur. Chetwood reported him at Aungier Street, Dublin, in 1734, after his London appearance. On 26 December 1748 at the New Wells, Shepherd's Market, one Butler was granted a benefit; *The Orphan* and *Chrononhotonthologos* were given, and it seems likely that this was the same Butler who had been active in 1734.

Butler, Mr [*fl. 1770–1779*], *actor.*

A person (or persons) named Butler acted Lord Randolph in *Douglas* on 21 November 1770, Quildrive in *The Citizen* on 24 January 1774, and Tradelove in *A Bold Stroke for a Wife* on 13 October 1779, all out-of-season at the Haymarket.

Butler, Mr [*fl. c. 1772*], *organist.*

According to Burney, a Mr Butler was organist at Ranelagh Gardens and at St Margaret's, and St Anne's, Westminster, about 1772, when he married the painter of miniatures Miss Penelope Carwardine (1730?–1800). She was a close friend of Gainsborough and she exhibited at the Society of Artists. Mr Butler predeceased his wife, who died about 1800, without issue.

Butler, Mrs [*fl. 1746–1750*], *actress, singer.*

There are several references in the records to a Mrs Butler who played at various minor theatres and fair booths between 1746 and 1750, and it is likely that they all concern the same woman. When Hallam opened his 1746–47 season at the theatre in Lemon Street, Goodman's Fields, Mrs Butler played Isabella in *The Revenge* and Melissa in *The Lying Valet* on 27 October 1746. From this date through 14 November she acted such other roles as Sylvia in

The Recruiting Officer, Dorinda in *The Stratagem*, Selima in *Tamerlane*, Mrs Frail in *Love for Love*, Ann Lovely in *A Bold Stroke for a Wife*, Maria in *The London Merchant*, and Jaqueline in *The Royal Merchant.*

During the 1747–48 season Mrs Butler made some appearances, but not at the major playhouses, and in August 1748 she played at Mr and Mrs Phillips's booth at Southwark Fair. The 1748–49 season was similar, her most noteworthy appearance being as Madame Grandant in *L'Opéra du gueux,* the French version of *The Beggar's Opera,* which was presented at the Haymarket Theatre. In August 1749 she was at Yates's booth at Bartholomew Fair. She appeared again in *L'Opéra du gueux* when it was revived on 16 and 21 February 1750, but after that she seems to have dropped from sight.

Butler, Charlotte [*fl. 1673–1695*], *actress, singer, dancer.*

According to Colley Cibber, Charlotte Butler (or Boteler) was the daughter of a "decay'd Knight" and was given the name Charlotte by Charles II; it was the King himself, said Cibber, who recommended her to the Duke's Company at the Dorset Garden Theatre. This, he noted, was "a provident Restitution, giving to the Stage in kind what he had sometimes taken from it: The Publick at least was oblig'd by it; for she prov'd not only a good Actress, but was allow'd in those Days to sing and dance to great perfection."

Mrs Butler may have become a member of the Duke's players in 1673–74, and possibly it was she who sang Plenty and played an African Woman and a Shepherdess in the court masque *Calisto* on 15 February 1675, a production which made use of both professionals and amateurs. Her first recorded appearance on the public stage was in late February 1680 at Dorset Garden when she played Serina and spoke the epilogue to *The Orphan*. In late June she acted Marinda in *The Revenge*, after which there are no more notices of her in the bills until March 1682 when she spoke the prologue to *Like Father, Like Son* (in which she may also have played a role). Her early popularity is indicated by her frequent presentations of prologues and epilogues.

The next season, in July 1683, she played her first recorded breeches part, Lucretia in *The Atheist* at Dorset Garden with the newly formed United Company. After the 1683–84 season she may have left the stage temporarily, or toured, for the next certain role for her was Sophia in *The Fortune Hunters* at Drury Lane in March 1689, though a manuscript cast of uncertain date, but probably about 1686–87, shows her playing Flavia in *The Libertine*. In April 1689 at Drury Lane she was in another breeches part, Philadelphia in *Bury Fair*; in January 1690 she danced in *The Successful Strangers* and played the breeches part of Statilia in *The Treacherous Brothers*—and spoke the epilogue; in mid-March 1690 she acted the courtesan Airy in *The English Friar*; and in late March 1690 she was Levia, another breeches-part courtesan, in *The Amorous Bigot*—and spoke the prologue.

During the following two seasons she sang more frequently, though she continued building her repertory of roles, her most significant being Belinda in *The Man of Mode* which she apparently played sometime between 1690 and 1692. She also acted the second Constantia in *The Chances* during the 1691–92 season. Her singing assignments were in *Dioclesian*, *Amphitryon*, *Sir Anthony Love*, *The Prophetess*, *King Arthur*, *The Wives' Excuse*, *Cleomenes*, and, most importantly, *The Fairy Queen*. She sang in this last work on 2 May and 13 June 1692. Charlotte Butler was clearly a popular attraction, yet when she asked the United Company for a raise from 40s. to 50s. per week, they refused to grant it; it was apparently this rebuff which

caused her to accept Dublin manager Joseph Ashbury's offer to play at Smock Alley for the 1694–95 season. She seems not to have returned to the London stage, and of her work in Dublin, nothing specific is known.

Like many Restoration performers, Charlotte Butler had a spotty reputation. One satire of about 1684 said that

> *Fam'd Butlers Wiles are now so common*
> *   grown*
> *That by each Feather'd Cully, she is*
> *   known*
> *So that at last to save her Tott'ring Fame*
> *At Music Club she strives to get a Name*
> *But mony is the Syren's cheifest Aym.*
> *At Treats her squeamish Stomach cannot*
> *   bear*
> *What Amorous Spark Provides with*
> *   Cost & Care*
> *But if She's hungry, faith I must be blunt*
> *She'l for a Dish of Cutlets shew her*
> *   C——t.*

Another satire of 1683 is just as disparaging:

> *Whorwood, whom Butler clapt & made*
> *   a Chiaux,*
> *To save his Stake, marry'd, & clapt his*
> *   Spouse . . .*

A third, written in 1689, goes on in a similar vein:

> *But Butler oh thou Strumpet Termagant*
> *Durst thou pretend to husband or gallant*
> *Ev'n to thy owne Profession a disgrace*
> *To sett up for a Whore with such a face*
> *Who but an Irish Fool would make this*
> *   Choice?*

It is not known whether the references to "Whorwood" and "an Irish Fool" were to a specific lover of Charlotte Butler's, but they probably were.

On the other hand, Colley Cibber, whose theatrical career was beginning when Charlotte Butler was at the peak of her powers, had high praise for her performing talent:

In the Dramatick Operas of *Dioclesian* and that of *King Arthur*, she was a capital and admired Performer. In speaking, too, she had a sweet-ton'd Voice, which, with her naturally genteel Air and sensible Pronunciation, render'd her wholly Mistress of the Amiable in many serious Characters. In Parts of Humour, too, she had a manner of blending her assuasive Softness even with the Gay, and Lively, and the Alluring. Of this she gave an agreeable Instance in her Action of the . . . second *Constantia* in the *Chances*.

Roger North, who knew his music, was delighted with her singing and amusingly wrote of her vanity:

I remember in Purcell's excellent opera of *King Arthur* [May 1691], when Mrs Butler, in the person of Cupid, was to call up Genius, she had the liberty to turne her face to the scean, and her back to the theater. She was in no concerne for her face, but sang a recitative of calling towards the place where Genius was to rise, and performed it admirably, even beyond any thing I ever heard upon the English stage. . . . And I could ascribe it to nothing so much as the liberty she had of concealing her face, which she could not endure should be so contorted as is necessary to sound well, before her gallants, or at least her envious sex.

If D'Urfey had her in mind when he wrote the part of Betty Jiltall in *Love for Money*, Charlotte Butler was a dark-eyed brunette and very handsome.

Butler, Elizabeth *d. 1748, actress.*

Davies reported that Elizabeth Butler was "said to be an illegitimate daughter of a noble duke whose monument is erected in Westminster-abbey," but beyond this vague rumor nothing seems to be known of her early years. Her first recorded appearance on stage was on 24 March 1726 at Drury Lane as the Widow in *The Scornful Lady*. Before this season was finished she also played Emilia in *The Man of Mode*

(15 April), Emilia in *Othello* (27 April), Lucinda in *The Conscious Lovers* (29 April), Julia in *The Fatal Marriage* (11 May), and Violante in *Sir Courtly Nice* (25 May); the two Emilia characters became her property for the next 15 years.

During the ensuing six seasons, before she inherited some of Mary Porter's starring roles, she added a number of important parts to her repertory on the basis of her own talent: Araminta in *The Old Bachelor*, Dame Pliant in *The Alchemist*, Regan in *King Lear*, Calphurnia in *Julius Caesar*, Lavinia in *The Fair Penitent*, the Duchess of York in *Richard III*, Alithea in *The Country Wife*, Zayda in *Aureng-Zebe* and on 22 June 1731, the important role of Millwood in the premiere of *The London Merchant*.

During the 1731–32 season at Drury Lane she was Doll Mavis in *The Silent Woman*, Melissa in *Timon of Athens*, Anna Bullen in *Henry VIII*, Lady Macduff in *Macbeth*, and the lead in *Jane Shore*. By 1733 she was earning £3 weekly as one of the more important members of the Drury Lane troupe. When Theophilus Cibber and most of the best performers from Drury Lane seceded and played for the first half of the 1733–34 season at the Haymarket Theatre, Mrs Butler joined them to play Mrs Frail in *Love for Love*, Amanda in *The Relapse*, Gertrude in *Hamlet*, Belvidera in *Venice Preserved*, Marwood in *The Way of the World*, Alcmena in *Amphitryon*, Celia in *Volpone*, and Epicoene in *The Silent Woman*. When the seceders returned to Drury Lane, she kept most of these important roles and added to them a number of other significant ones: Zara in *The Mourning Bride* (28 September 1734), Lady Macbeth (21 October 1735), Melinda in *The Recruiting Officer* (30 October 1735), Mrs Page in *The Merry Wives of Windsor* (21 November 1735), Lady Brute in *The Provoked Wife* (17 November 1737), and Evandra in *Timon of Athens* (20 March 1740).

During this same period in the last half of the 1730's Mrs Butler was involved in the finances and management of Drury Lane. A proposal was made in 1735 which would have placed more control in the hands of the actors by having Mills, Johnson, Miller, Theophilus Cibber, Mrs Heron, and Mrs Butler rent Drury Lane from patentee Fleetwood for 15 years at an annual fee of £920. This arrangement did not immediately materialize, but by late 1742 something very like it had been worked out. The details are incomplete and the reports of the situation are conflicting, but what seems to have happened is that Mills, Cibber, and Mrs Butler became lessees of Drury Lane in 1742 or perhaps earlier. Fleetwood had agreed with them to pay a £1000 company debt which was in arrears, but, according to one report, when the creditors could not get at Fleetwood, they sued the trio of actors. Mrs Butler claimed that she was "forc'd to keep her chamber for four months, for fear of being arrested." Fleetwood published a denial, saying that her confinement was a pretense and that the money for the debt was in the hands of bankers who would pay it. Mills, Cibber, and Mrs Butler tried to make over their lease to Fleetwood in order to retain their "easy Situation" in the Drury Lane company, but Fleetwood banished them— or at least Cibber and Mrs Butler—for the 1742–43 season. One report had it that Mills was arrested, but this would have been for a very short spell, since he acted regularly at Drury Lane despite the squabble; the same report had Mrs Butler locking herself for six months in her own house in King Street (to which she had moved from Leicester Fields in 1740–41), but six weeks may have been closer to the truth. In any case, Cibber and Mrs Butler went to Lincoln's Inn Fields to act with Giffard's troupe in 1742–43, Mills stayed at Drury Lane, and the debt apparently got settled.

With Giffard's players Mrs Butler had an opportunity to add some new roles to her comic line, including Arbella in *The Committee*, Amanda in *The Relapse*, Melinda in *The Recruiting Officer*, Lady Woodvil in *The Non Juror*, and Clarissa in *The Confederacy*. She also acted Queen Elizabeth in *Richard III* and the Countess in *All's Well that Ends Well*. On 11 April 1743 she played Mrs Frail in *Love for Love* and then gave up acting. The Giffard venture at Lincoln's Inn Fields had collapsed, and her opportunities back at Drury Lane were now probably nil. Times were changing, too, and the rising stars of Garrick, Macklin, Mrs Cibber, Mrs Pritchard, and Mrs Woffington may have persuaded Mrs Butler to leave the stage to the new generation. She was probably wealthy enough to retire, for she would have needed capital to become involved in the Drury Lane finances in the first place. Her talent, though adequate, was apparently not great; she played a number of significant roles, though many of them fell to her by default, and she was probably considered a second lady. The only critical comment on her ability is a rather left-handed one in *An Impartial Examen* in 1744: "Mrs Butler was receiv'd, on Mrs. Porters' Misfortune, in many of her Parts; and, without paying her any Compliment, supported herself in them, to the Satisfaction of most People."

In William Kent's will of 1748 an Elizabeth Butler of St Paul, Covent Garden, was left £600; her son George and daughter Elizabeth received £300 each. If the ex-actress was concerned, the will gives us all we know of her family plus an indication of the wealthy circles in which she apparently moved. But if this was she, she did not live to enjoy the legacy. Elizabeth Butler died on 16 September 1748, apparently forgotten by the theatre-going public.

Butler, James *fl.* 1732–1739, *singer*.

James Butler, probably a *basso*, sang Ahasuerus and the First Israelite in Handel's *Esther* when it was given a private performance at the Crown and Anchor Tavern in the Strand on 23 February 1732. He was very likely a Gentleman of the Chapel Royal. The Mr Butler who sang Doeg in *Saul* at the King's Theatre in the Haymarket on 16 January 1739 may have been James, though there is a possibility that this was the music teacher John Butler. A singer named James Butler performed at Smock Alley in the winter of 1753–54 in *Lethe*, *Macbeth*, *Romeo and Juliet*, and *The Tempest*, but there is no certainty that he was the London singer of the 1730's.

Butler, John [fl. 1773–1788], *gallery office keeper.*

By his own petition, signed by him on 30 September 1784, John Butler stated he had been ticket seller at the "Crown Gallery" of the King's Theatre for the past 11 years. The petition, sent from his address at Bread Street, Golden Square, to the Earl of Salisbury, Lord Chamberlain, was occasioned by the fact that Butler had "without any provocation" been discharged at the end of the 1783–84 season "by the People who assum'd the power of carrying on the Operas." Butler claimed he was a creditor for about £30 for salary due to him under the management of Taylor, who had gone bankrupt, and he considered it very unjust that he should be discharged "to make room for One who had sustain'd no Loss." The petition evidently succeeded and Butler was at his situation of first gallery money taker in 1784–85, in which he remained at least through 1787–88.

Butler, Philip d. 1786, *master carpenter.*

Philip Butler was described by Winston as having been the builder of the Richmond Theatre in 1764–65, assisted by a bricklayer of Richmond named Adler. At the time, Butler was also "architect and principal machinist" of Drury Lane Theatre. Butler's position at Drury Lane, which

he held until his death in 1786, actually was that of master carpenter. Butler frequently shared his benefits with Wright or Fawcett. On 11 May 1778, he and Wright shared net benefit receipts of £209 1s. His benefits with Fawcett on 18 May 1784 and 17 May 1785 resulted in deficits of £73 15s. and £69 1s. 7d. respectively. At the funeral of David Garrick in 1779, Butler and the bookkeeper Fosbrook rode in the tenth coach of the processional. During his career at London, he lived in Russell Street, next door to the theatre.

Butler died on 16 February 1786. In his will, made on 22 March 1782 and proved on 4 March 1786, he left most of his estate, including leasehold properties in Reading, to his widow Hannah Frances Butler and three children, William, Hannah Frances, and Elizabeth Maria. Two other children had died earlier and were buried at St Paul, Covent Garden: a son Philip on 7 November 1775 and a daughter Anne Isabella on 22 March 1778. On 23 May 1786 the widow Butler shared net benefit receipts of £136 3s. 8d. with Fawcett, but according to a notation in Fawcett's notebook at the Folger Library Mrs Butler had died the day before. William Butler, their son, danced at Drury Lane from 1780 to at least 1801.

Butler, William [fl. 1780–1817?], *dancer, house servant?*

William Butler was born the son of Philip Butler, the Drury Lane carpenter, and his wife Hannah Frances Butler. Announced as Master Butler, the scholar of the dancer Miller, he made his first appearance dancing a hornpipe on 5 May 1780, a benefit night of his father. Over the next five years his appearances, still as Master Butler, were limited to one each year, always for his father's benefit, and always in a hornpipe. On 17 May 1785 he danced with an unidentified "Young Lady," also a scholar of Miller, in a double hornpipe.

Butler's father, Philip Butler, died on 16

February 1786 and left William and his sisters Hannah Frances and Elizabeth Maria some properties in Reading, through their mother, who died only a few months later on 22 May 1786. William Butler seems to have continued working at Drury Lane and in 1791–92 was dancing at 5s. per day. In 1793–94 his name reappeared in the bills, now as "Mr" Butler, in very minor roles in the dancing choruses for such spectacles as *Lodoiska*, which played at Drury Lane on 9 June 1794 and 19 other times that summer and then was performed another 34 times in the regular season of 1794–95. Butler danced an Indian warrior in *Cherokee* and a waiter in *Harlequin Captive* in 1795–96, a shepherd in *The Triumph of Love*, and a warrior in *Robinson Crusoe* in 1796–97. In May 1799 he shared £192 11s. 6d. in benefit receipts with Wright.

Butler continued at the salary of 5s. per day until at least 1801–2. In 1802–3 a Mr Butler, perhaps William Butler, either injured or too old to continue dancing, appeared on the Drury Lane pay list for ticket-taking at £1 10s. per week. Butler, the house servant, was there at least through 1816–17. According to a notation in the Drury Lane Fundbook, a Mr Butler's claim for benefits was rejected on 21 May 1808.

The Mrs Butler who sang in the chorus at Drury Lane from 1789 until about 1809 was doubtless William Butler's wife. A Miss Butler, who began to perform at Drury Lane in 1805–6, was probably their daughter.

Butler, Mrs William [fl. 1789–1812], singer.

The Mrs Butler who sang at Drury Lane in the 1790's was doubtless the wife of William Butler, dancer at the same theatre during this period. She made her first billed appearance as Mrs Butler on 24 September 1789 playing Molly Brazen in *The Beggar's Opera*. That season, 1789–90, in which she was paid £1 5s. per week, she also had singing roles in *The Tempest* and *The Island of St Marguerite*. Mrs Butler continued at Drury Lane at the same salary of £1 5s. per week at least through 1808–9, singing minor chorus roles in such pieces as *Poor Old Drury*, *The Cave of Trophonius*, and *Dido, Queen of Carthage* (all in 1791–92), *Lodoiska*, *The Pirates*, *The Mountaineers*, and *Harlequin Captive* (all 1794–95), and *Blue-Beard* (1799–1800). Between 1794 and 1801 she also sang regularly in summers at the Haymarket. A Mrs Butler sang at the Lyceum in 1811–12, at 10s. per week.

Doane's *Musical Directory* of 1794 listed Mrs "Butter," of Prospect Row, Lambeth, as a singer at the Drury Lane Theatre; she was probably our subject.

Her husband, William Butler, ceased dancing in 1801–2. He perhaps was the Mr Butler who was a house servant at Drury Lane from 1802 through 1817. A Miss Butler, probably their daughter, performed at Drury Lane beginning in 1805–6.

Butterton. See BETTERTON, THOMAS WILLIAM.

Buttery, Miss. See CLELAND, MISS.

Buttler. See BUTLER and BUCKLER.

Buxton, Mr [fl. 1782], actor.

On 4 March 1782 a Mr Buxton played Norfolk in *Richard III* and the Mayor in *Don Quixote in England* at the Haymarket Theatre. He may have been the John Buxton who worked in the early nineteenth century, apparently at the Haymarket; or he may have been George Buxton, apparently a copyist and actor at Drury Lane from at least 1811 through 1819.

Buzaglo. See BUZARGLO.

Buzarglo, Mr [fl. 1792–1797], scene painter. See BUZARGLO, LOUIS.

Buzarglo, Louis [fl. 1793–1795], scene painter.

The theatre playbills and accounts for the 1790's at Covent Garden and Drury Lane play havoc with Louis Buzarglo's name and seldom differentiate him from his brother (who may have had a first name that so baffled the scribes that they never used it). One finds the brothers' surname spelled Buzarglo, Balzago, Barzago, Bazago, and Buzaglo, and it is anyone's guess which is correct, if any. The brothers may have been related to Abraham (William) Buzaglo (1716–1788) who invented a heating device for large buildings and apparently provided the Covent Garden playhouse with one in 1767. It was probably Abraham who did some work at Drury Lane as a smith in 1776 and again in 1780.

At least one of the Buzarglo brothers served as a scene painter at Covent Garden in 1792–93, receiving £10 on the fifth night of the season and £100 on the sixty-sixth night; his daily salary by the end of the season was £2 2s. This painter was probably Louis's brother, for Louis, though he is known to have worked at both patent houses, was most closely associated with Drury Lane.

Louis worked under Henry Holland during the rebuilding of Drury Lane in 1793–94, his chief responsibilities being "scene painting and stage decoration." He had been recommended to Holland as having studied and worked under Messrs Galliari, painters and architects of Milan. It was probably Louis, then, who was one of the painters who prepared the scenic embellishment for the production of *Macbeth* with which John Philip Kemble opened the new Drury Lane on 21 April 1794. Buzarglo was noted in the theatre accounts as receiving £50 "on account" on 20 April 1794, another £50 "on account" on 20 September, and £19 14s. 6d. on 16 October.

During the 1794–95 season at Drury Lane both brothers were on the staff, for the 28 October 1794 playbill for *Emilia Galotti* noted that "Signor Barzago and his brother" did the scenery for the first four acts; the chief scene painter, Greenwood, did the last act and the frontispiece. The Covent Garden accounts show a payment on 29 May 1795 to a Balzago (Louis's brother, probably) for £111 (or £114 as reported in *Theatre Notebook*, Autumn 1964).

Sometime during 1795 at Drury Lane one of the brothers, probably Louis, was paid £543 13s. for scene painting, a sum which either must have covered an extended period of time or included fees for Buzarglo's helpers, or both.

The last reference to a Buzarglo seems to be on 4 April 1797 when the Covent Garden accounts show a payment of £31 11s., probably to Louis's brother.

Buzilarico, Signor [fl. 1786], ventriloquist.

Signor Buzilarico (or Bouzilarico) performed on 26 August, 4 September, and 9 October 1786 at Astley's Amphitheatre, pleasing his auditors with such delights as an imitation of "the assembling of the fox hounds, in full cry, with the French horn" and "the General alarm of Horse and Foot; with Trumpet and Drum." His imitation of a Savoyard with an organ was billed as "truly laughable" and, "in a most extraordinary manner," he created the sound of a trumpet. He ended his part of the programs with "the Chase and Death of the Wild Boar."

Bym. See BYRNE.

Bynam, Mr J. [fl. 1797–1820], house servant.

Mr Bynam was a house servant at Drury Lane as early as 1797, though no salary is known for him for that year, nor do the accounts mention his duties. On 13 October 1798, however, he was noted as an office keeper at a salary of £1 1s.—probably per week. Bynam continued his service at Drury

Lane through 1804–5, occasionally varying his duty: he was apparently a doorkeeper or boxkeeper for a while in 1801; in 1803–4 he was taking money in the upper gallery; and in 1805 he was serving again as a doorkeeper. His salary was not always cited in the books, but the £1 10s. per week he received in 1801 was probably about what he was getting in the four years that followed.

His name disappeared from the Drury Lane account books from 1805 to 1811, when he turned up again working for £1 per week. In 1812–13 he was serving as a messenger at £1 4s. weekly, but the next season he dropped to sweeper at 9s. per week. He seems to have remained a sweeper for the rest of his career, though his salary oddly rose and fell over the years, sometimes getting as high as £1 5s. weekly (in 1813–14) and at other times dropping as low as 9s. per week (in 1818–19). In 1815 and 1816 he seems to have served as a call boy at the Haymarket Theatre while holding his place at Drury Lane. In 1819–20 he was still a Drury Lane sweeper, earning 2s. a day. There is a possibility that some of the Bynam references in the account books refer to a second person of that name.

Bynion. *See* **BENION.**

Byrd. *See* **BIRD.**

Byrn. *See also* **BURN, BURNS** and **BYRNE.**

Byrn, [Mrs?] [fl. 1760–1766], *char-woman.*

The Covent Garden accounts in 1760 and 1766 list one Byrn (or possibly Byrne) as a charwoman receiving 1s. daily in the former year and 1s. 2d. daily in the latter.

Byrn, Eleanor. *See* **GOODWIN, MRS THOMAS.**

Byrn, James *1756–1845, dancer, choreographer.*

James Byrn was born in 1756, his mother's name being Ann. His father's first name is not known. It is probable, since his mother's burial notice on 8 February 1793 specified her parish as St Martin-in-the-Fields, that James was born in that parish; the spelling of his name was certainly "Byrn," for he took the pains to have the parish-register error of "Byrne" at the notation of his mother's death altered. He had a sister Eleanor who danced with him in the early part of his stage career and who became Mrs Thomas Goodwin.

His first appearance was on 5 May 1772 at Drury Lane with Eleanor and Miss Wilkinson; all three young people were billed as scholars of Signor Giorgi. Young James danced at the Haymarket Theatre during the following summer as a feature of Foote's presentations, appeared with his sister in minuets and allemandes at Drury Lane in the winter season, and rejoined Foote during the summer of 1774. In 1775 and 1776 he danced at Sadler's Wells, and he appeared regularly at the Haymarket each summer from 1778 through 1791, at Bristol in 1779–80, at Cambridge sometime during 1780, and at Covent Garden during the winters from 1782–83 through 1795–96. Until the summer of 1782 he was billed as Master Byrn, and his appearances consisted of frequent dances where he was paired off with his sister (a *Provençalle Dance, The Merry Lasses, The Gardeners,* a *Tambourine Dance, The Italian Peasants,* a *Minuet à la cour,* and an *allemande*), occasional participation in afterpieces (*The Genius of Nonsense,* for example), and solo hornpipes, sometimes in girls' clothes.

After joining the Covent Garden company in 1782–83 his billing changed to "Mr" Byrn. His salary was £1 10s. weekly, and, though he eventually became far more famous than his sister Eleanor, she was earning £2 weekly at this time. The pair danced together as before (her name changing to Mrs Goodwin in the bills in the winter of 1783–84), but James was not frequently cited. He began, however, to participate in ballets, as for example on 26 August 1784 when he was the Prince de la Cour "(as a Running Footman)" in *Medea and Jason*; he also danced more in afterpieces, as on 31 August 1785 when he was the Abbé in *Here and There and Every Where*. Most important, he appears to have started his career as a choreographer in 1785; on 7 October at Covent Garden *The Recruiting Serjeant*, a new dance composed by Byrn, was presented, and on 10 October another, called *Leap Year*, was given its premier performance. By 1786–87, in consequence, Byrn's salary was up to £3 weekly, yet the bills show hardly any further choreographic work by him for several years thereafter. He was, however, the official ballet master at Covent Garden, at least from 1788–89, danced frequently in group dance specialties, and soloed in afterpieces and mainpieces (he danced in Act II of *The Beggar's Opera*, for instance: a hornpipe in character).

In 1789–90 he was raised to £3 10s. weekly, and the following season his income jumped to £4. It was on 4 October 1790 that his ballet pantomime *The Provocation* was first done, the earliest of his more extensive compositions. The *Biographical and Imperial Magazine* commented that "The Provocation is an interesting Pantomime, on the subject of Spanish indignities; in which Byrne displays much talent for dumb expression; and from which we were glad to see Harlequin and his mummy companions excluded." After this, Byrn's compositions appeared fairly regularly. Sometimes he devised spectacles for afterpieces, as on 20 December 1790 when he choreographed dances in *The Picture of Paris*; on 20 October 1791 his *Oscar and Malvina* was danced; and on 28 February 1792 he composed dances for *Orpheus and Euridice*. Byrn danced in many of his works, and when he was dancing Oscar

in *Oscar and Malvina* on 28 October 1791 he missed his guard in a fencing sequence and was wounded, quite seriously, in the arm. On 21 November he was still performing with his arm in a sling. His compensation for *Oscar and Malvina* was £50.

Byrn was accident-prone this season, for the *Public Advertiser* noted on 31 December 1791 that he could not play Harlequin in *Blue Beard* because he "had again unfortunately broken his right arm." The "again" doubtless referred to the sword wound. By 25 October 1792 his *Oscar and Malvina* had reached its fortieth performance. Two days after this Byrn danced with Signora Rossi, perhaps for the first time, and their association was eventually to develop into a love affair.

At some point Byrn had married, but all that is known of his wife we learn from the St Paul, Covent Garden, parish registers; she was buried on 26 January 1792, and James altered the incorrect "Isabella" to "Arabella Maria" in the register. By her, James had had at least two sons, Charles Edward, baptized at the same church on 7 September 1791, and James, buried there on 16 November 1791 and incorrectly called Mark Byrne. James had this error corrected, too, saying that "Mark, Son of James Burn" should read "James, Son of James Byrn." A year after James's wife died, his mother Ann was buried, on 8 February 1793, at St Paul, Covent Garden.

On 20 December 1792 Byrn composed dances for *Harlequin's Museum*, in which he introduced a *Burlesque Pas de Russe*; on 11 March 1793 his pantomime ballet *The Governor* was first done, with Byrn dancing the title role; and on 27 May *The Shipwreck* was given its premier performance, with the choreographer as Captain Briton. By 1793–94 Byrn was being paid £6 weekly, dancing regularly, and bringing out still more new works. His dances for *Harlequin's Chaplet* were done on 2 October 1793, for *Harlequin and Faustus* on 19 December, and for *The Travellers in Swit-*

zerland on 22 February 1794; and during this season his ballet *Dermot and Kathlane* was first performed, on 18 October 1793.

On 26 May 1794 Byrn was involved in another stage accident, this time wounding his fellow dancer Rochford when, by mistake, the property man handed Byrn a sword instead of a foil; the occasion was a performance of *The Shipwreck*, a pantomime about Captain Cook.

Byrn had declared himself to be living in Great Russell Street, Bloomsbury, in 1791; Doane in 1794 listed him as then at No 15, Bow Street, Covent Garden. Doane also noted that Byrn was not only the Covent Garden ballet master but also a violinist and a performer at concerts sponsored by the New Musical Fund. This may have been a confusion with the violinist Felix Byrne, though as a dancing master James would surely have been a violinist and may well have been proficient enough to perform in concerts.

On 17 November 1794 another Byrn afterpiece was performed, *Hercules and Omphale* ("the most magnificent exhibited on the English stage for many years," said the *Universal Magazine*), and he composed dances for *Mago and Dago*, which was performed on 26 December with Byrn dancing Harlequin. On 12 May 1795 his *The Tythe Pig* came out, with the choreographer dancing Countryman in it, and on 6 June dances which he composed for *The Poor Soldier* were first seen. On 12 June Byrn was paid £152 10s. for *Hercules and Omphale* and for his "music performance of Harlequin" (he probably played the violin in the character of Harlequin during the season) in lieu of a benefit. During the 1795 summer the Mr Byrn who performed at Birmingham was probably James, though the identification is not certain.

In Byrn's 1795–96 season at Covent Garden he danced as usual in a number of specialty dances and afterpieces, and he composed the dances for *Merry Sherwood*, *Harlequin's Treasure*, and *The Point at*

Herqui. On 8 April 1796 Byrn was performing with Signora Rossi (who by now was his mistress and mother of his son Oscar, born about 1795), when, according to a newspaper,

a young lady with a party hissed and hooted Byrn and Rossi in a way so marked as to breed a riot—a boxing match took place & Byrn leaped into the pit to take part in the fray. The lady's name was Pomfret & on her being brought before the magistrate next day it seemed that she had formerly been kept by Byrne who had forsaken her for Rossi—hence the affray.

By this time Byrn had made a contract with Wignell to go to America, and he proposed taking Signora Rossi with him. Whether or not they legalized their relationship before they left is not clear, for the reports speak of Byrn as going with Rossi, but in Birmingham in the summer of 1796 and in America they were billed as "Mr and Mrs Byrn."

Byrn was apparently reluctant to leave England, but his contract with Wignell was binding, and on 7 December 1796 he and "Mrs Byrn" appeared at the Chestnut Street Theatre in Philadelphia in Byrn's *Dermot and Kathlane*. The Byrns may have appeared prior to this in Baltimore, and they certainly appeared afterwards in New York. Their son Oscar danced at the Chestnut Street Theatre on 14 April 1798. The Byrns were not happy in America, though they performed at Philadelphia at least through 27 May 1799; but, according to John Bernard, Byrn longed to try his fortune in Jamaica and then return home to England. Bernard called Byrn "a most worthy and talented little fellow." Upon their arrival in Jamaica, Byrn was so terrified at the sight of so many hearses and the stories of how slim the chances were of survival in the tropics, that he gave up the idea of hunting a fortune and headed home to England.

Back in London, Byrn became attached to the Royal Circus, his ballet *Jockey and*

Jeny being performed there in April 1800. On 27 May the three Byrns—James, Lucy, and Master Oscar—appeared at Covent Garden but met with a most unfavorable response. The *Dramatic Censor* reported that "The Play was succeeded by a silly dance, transplanted to Covent Garden, for that night only, from the Circus, in which the family of the vamper-up of the dance, Mr. BYRNE, made their appearance. It was intolerably long, and . . . met with considerable opposition." In May at the Royal Circus a new "Grand Ballet Dance, produced under the Direction of Mr. Byrne" called *The Nuptials* was performed, and in June he composed marches and dances for *The Magic Flute; or, Harlequin Champion.* On 13 June 1800 at Covent Garden he transplanted his new ballet, *The Animated Statue* from the Royal Circus, for a single performance; Mr, Mrs, and Master Byrn all participated. In July his new *Blue Bells of Scotland* was added to the bills at the Royal Circus, and on 4 August he composed the dances for *Sir Francis Drake and the Iron Arm.*

In 1800–1801 Mr and Mrs Byrn were engaged by Drury Lane, James serving as ballet master there; he still kept his connection with the Royal Circus, however, through 1803. His first appearance at Drury Lane was as Actaeon in his own ballet *Actaeon and Diana.* The account books do not always distinguish clearly amongst the various Byrns (of several spellings), but James seems to have been paid a salary of £10 weekly. During the next few years he brought out a number of new works, among them *Lasses,* the dances in *Harlequin Amulet,* a festive war dance in *Gonsalvo de Cordova, Zamor and Ramora,* and *The True Lover's Knot.* On 4 January 1802 a Master Byrne, apparently another son of James and Lucy, made his first appearance at Drury Lane. Who this may have been is not clear; James and Lucy (according to Lucy's will of 1845) had sons Oscar, Edmond, Nelson, and James, and a daughter Malvina.

The last record of Byrn at Drury Lane is at the end of the 1804–5 season when he was still paid £10 per week; he may have retired after this, though he lived on to 4 December 1845, when he died at the age of 89, two months after the death of his wife.

Byrn, Mrs James. *See* Rossi, Signora Joseph.

Byrn, John [*fl.* 1794], *singer?*
Doane listed John Byrn, of No 15, Bow Street, Covent Garden, as a tenor (singer, probably, though he may have been an instrumentalist) who participated in performances sponsored by the New Musical Fund in 1794.

Byrn, Oscar *c. 1795–1867, dancer.*
Oscar Byrn was the natural son of dancer and choreographer James Byrn by Signora Lucy Rossi, and though his precise birth date is not known, he was probably born about 1795. He made his first appearance on the stage on 14 April 1798 at the Chestnut Street Theatre in Philadelphia where his parents were under contract to the American manager Wignell. The Byrns returned to England by way of Jamaica in 1799, and on 27 May 1800 Oscar made his London debut at Covent Garden in a dance composed by his father and featuring Mr and Mrs Byrn, the three Misses Adams, and young Oscar. Oscar appeared at Covent Garden again on 13 June in his father's *The Animated Statue*, a work transplanted from the Royal Circus where the Byrns also performed. (His first appearance often has been recorded as 1803, and another Master Byrn made his first appearance at Drury Lane on 4 January 1802; it is possible that these nineteenth century debuts concern Oscar's brothers, for they seem not to point to Oscar himself.)

Master Byrn appeared regularly at the Royal Circus in the fall of 1802, occasionally doing solos or taking roles in his father's ballets, as, for example, Zarai the Peruvian boy in *Zamor and Ramora* on 27 September. He continued appearing at the Circus in 1803, but he also danced at Drury Lane from 1802–3 through at least 1816–17, at Covent Garden from 1803–4 sporadically through 1808–9, at the King's Theatre in the Haymarket from 1809 to at least 1820, and at the Haymarket Theatre in the summers from 1804 to 1810. The bills are sometimes not careful to distinguish Oscar from his father, especially after Oscar ceased being called Master, but it would appear that even as early as 1801 he was paid £1 5s. weekly; by 1805 his salary had risen to £2, and by 1815 he was being paid £10.

As a ballet master in 1850 at the Princess's Theatre he choreographed many of the revivals staged by Charles Kean, and in 1862 he joined the Drury Lane company under Falconer and Chatterton. His last contract was at Her Majesty's Theatre. Byrn died on 4 September 1867, aged about 72, at Islip Street, Kentish Town Road. His will described him as previously successively of No 2, Wellesley Road, Maldon Road, and Upper Newbury Place, Haverstock Hill. The will was proved on 28 September 1867 by his widow Abigail; his estate was valued at under £8000. Seven children, along with his widow, survived him.

Oscar Byrn had figured prominently in his mother's will when it was proved by him as one of the executors on 3 October 1845. She left her moveables to Oscar, his brother Edmond, and his sister Malvina equally, and to Oscar she left also £1000. In her will she furnished us the name of one of Oscar's children: Andrew Walter, to whom she bequeathed £200.

Byrne. *See also* **BURN, BURNS** and **BYRN.**

Byrne, Mr *d. 1780, dancer.*

A Mr Byrne was Pantaloon in *The Elopement* on 10 November 1777, again on 11 May 1779 for a single performance, and again on 21 September 1779. No other roles are known for him, though the accounts indicate that he was a member of the company as early as the 1774–75 season. His salary was £1 5s. weekly, and in 1775 he contributed 10s. 6d. to the Drury Lane pension fund. He may have been the Mr "Burn" who performed at Kilkenny, Ireland, in July 1769, and he may have been related to James Byrn the dancer-choreographer; he was certainly the husband of the dancer Mrs Byrne who worked at Drury Lane in the late 1770's and died in 1782. Mr Byrne died on 30 January 1780.

Byrne, Mr [*fl. 1783–1790*], *boxkeeper, lobby keeper.*

A Mr Byrne (or Bym, Byrn) was a boxkeeper at the King's Theatre in the Haymarket in 1783, a box and lobby keeper there in 1784–85, and a house servant at Covent Garden from 23 September 1786 through 8 June 1790 at 12s. weekly. He was probably the husband of the Mrs Byrne who sang, danced, and acted from about 1785 to 1800; both she and he were sometimes cited in contemporary sources as "Bym."

Byrne, Mrs *d. 1782, dancer.*

Mrs Byrne, the wife of the Drury Lane dancer who died in 1780, was a member of that troupe, too, as early as 1774–75. She paid 10s. 6d. to the theatre's pension fund in 1775 and was given a salary of £1 10s. per week. Her name appeared rarely in the bills, the last mention of her being on 16 May 1782 when her benefit tickets were announced as acceptable at the theatre door. No roles are known for her, and she was probably only a member of the dancing chorus. She died in September 1782.

Byrne, Mrs [*fl. c. 1785–1800*], *singer, dancer, actress.*

Mrs Byrne sang at the Spa Gardens, Bermondsey, probably in 1785, three of her songs being works of Jonas Blewitt: "Had I the Pinions of a Dove," "What raptures ring around," and "When skipping round the May-pole gay." From 1786–87 through 1791–92 she was at Covent Garden, at a steady salary of £1 5s. weekly. Her chores there were in the singing chorus, and over the years she was in *The Roman Father*, *A King and No King*, *Romeo and Juliet*, *Macbeth*, *The Woodman*, and *The Crusade*. At least twice she was singled out: on 13 November 1786 she was Lucia in *The Cheats of Scapin*, and on 23 January 1790 she played a Shepherdess "(with 'Cast, my Love, thine Eyes around')" and a principal witch in *Harlequin's Chaplet*.

Her husband was probably the box-keeper who was active during these years. Both were sometimes cited as "Bym."

After disappearing from the notices for a few years, she was engaged at Drury Lane for the seasons 1796–97 through 1799–1800. Her salary was again £1 5s. and her duties this time chiefly dancing in the choruses of such works as *The Triumph of Love*, *Robinson Crusoe*, *Blue Beard*, and *Feudal Times*. Her last appearance was on 11 March 1800 as a slave in *The Egyptian Festival*. The gap between Mrs Byrne's work at Covent Garden and Drury Lane, plus the change from singing to dancing chores, suggests the possibility that two different women were referred to in the bills and accounts. There were so many different performers named Byrne, Byrn, Burn, and Burns during these years that it is difficult to be certain which was which; one thing seems clear, however: this Mrs Byrne was not Mrs James Byrn, though she may have been related to the Byrn family.

Byrne, Miss [*fl.* 1784–1787], *dancer.*
Miss Byrne, not to be confused with Eleanor Byrn the sister of the choreographer James, was possibly the daughter of the Mr and Mrs Byrne (or Burn) who danced at Drury Lane in the late 1770's. Miss Byrne's first notice was on 28 May 1784 when she danced in *The Medley* with Master Giorgi at the Haymarket Theatre.

She appeared at that playhouse every summer thereafter through 23 May 1787, when once again she and Master Giorgi were paired off in a dance called *The Shepherds*. In April 1787 she was also one of the minor dancers at the Royal Circus.

Byrne, Charles *1761–1783, giant.*
Charles Byrne was born in 1761. By the time he was exhibited in London in July 1782 he stood over eight feet tall. He was said to have grown two inches since August 1780 and was still growing. Sylas Neville recorded his impressions of Byrne in his *Diary* on 4 July 1782:

Saw Byrne, the famous Irish giant, in whose person nature has exceeded her usual limits in a most astonishing degree. Even the great

By Permission of the Folger Shakespeare Library
CHARLES BYRNE (center)
by John Kay

Patagonians are nothing to this—8 feet 2 inches. Tall men walk considerably under his arm, but he stoops, is not well shaped, his flesh loose & his appearance far from wholesome. His voice sounds like thunder & he is an ill bred disagreeable beast, tho' very young —only in his 22nd year.

Byrne lost all his savings in a single £700 bank note, and it is said he died in Cockspur Street on 1 June 1783 from overdrinking. By this time he had grown to eight feet four inches, and because of his fear that surgeons would anatomize him, he requested burial at sea off Margate. His body is said to have been conveyed to Margate, but his last wishes were not carried out, for his skeleton was, in 1904, still preserved at the Royal College of Surgeons.

At Covent Garden Theatre on 23 May 1783 as part of the afterpiece *The Royal Chace*, an "exact Representation of the Irish Giant" was shown, an indication of London's curiosity about Byrne just before he died. Kay made two sketches of Byrne for the first volume of *Original Etchings*.

Byrne, Eleanor. *See* **GOODWIN, MRS THOMAS.**

Byrne, Mr [**William?**] [*1743–1805?*], *scene painter.*

Mr Byrne, possibly a relative of the dancing Byrnes of the eighteenth and nine-teenth centuries, became an assistant scene painter under Whitmore in Sir Vere Hunt's company at Limerick in 1790 at 10*s. 6d.* daily. By 6 May 1791 he had come to London and, again with Whitmore, was painting scenery for productions at Astley's Amphitheatre; on that date *The King and the Cobbler* was performed, and the bill mentioned Byrne as one of the painters. He became affiliated with Covent Garden by 1792–93 and apparently remained there through 1797–98, still at 10*s. 6d.* daily. The bills over the years cited him as having helped with the scenery for *Hercules and Omphale* (17 November 1794), *Harlequin and Oberon* (19 December 1796), and *Raymond and Agnes* (16 March 1797). The theatre accounts sometimes called him Biron or Byron, the last mention of him in the books being on 15 January 1798.

The final volume of *The London Stage* identifies Byrne as the landscape engraver William Byrne (1743–1805) who has a short entry in the *Dictionary of National Biography*, but there seem to be too few facts about the scene painter to be certain of the identification.

Byron. *See also* **BYRN** and **BYRNE.**

Byzand. *See* **BAYZAND.**

Illustrations

THEATRE EXTERIORS AND INTERIORS

465

Folger Shakespeare Library
Goodman's Fields Theatre, c. 1730s

Haymarket Theatre, Mid-Eighteenth Century
from Wilkinson's *Londina Illustrata*, 1819–25

Harvard Theatre Collection
Drury Lane Theatre, 1775

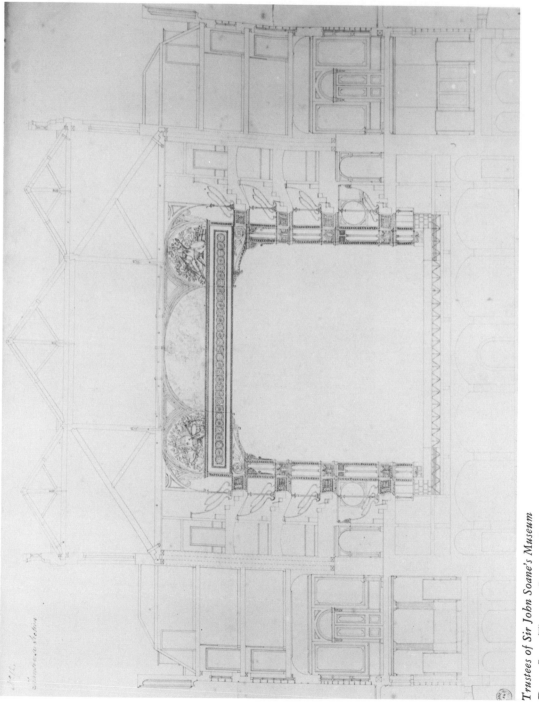

Drury Lane Theatre, Cross-section at the Proscenium Arch
by Henry Holland, 1793

Drury Lane Theatre After the 1797 Alterations
from Wilkinson's *Londina Illustrata*, 1819–25

Trustees of the British Museum

Drury Lane Theatre, 1791–94
drawing by William Capon

Huntington Library
Bagnigge Wells, 1788

Folger Shakespeare Library
Surrey Theatre, 1828

473

Lincoln's Inn Fields Theatre Building After It Became a Warehouse
painted by an unknown artist in 1805

Sadler's Wells, 1792
from Wilkinson's *Londina Illustrata*, 1819–25

Warden and Fellows of All Souls College, Oxford

Sir Christopher Wren's Section View of a Restoration Playhouse, c. 1672–74

Probably a preliminary Design for the Drury Lane Theatre

Front of Astley's Amphitheatre, c. 1780(?)
from Wilkinson's *Londina Illustrata,* 1819–25

Arena of Astley's Amphitheatre, c. 1780(?)
from Wilkinson's *Londina Illustrata*, 1819–25

THEATRE ROYAL COVENT GARDEN, as altered previous to the opening on 15th. Sep. 1794. Destroyed by Fire *Sept. 20th 1808.*

Engraved from an Original Drawing   *by &c. in the Possession of John Winston Esqr.*

The Original Entrance from the Piazza to the late   *Covent Garden Theatre destroyed by Fire Sep. 20. 1808.*

London, Published 1st Jan. 1809 by Robert Wilkinson, No. 125 Fenchurch Street.

Huntington Library
Covent Garden Theatre Auditorium and Entrance
from the Piazza, before 1794

479

Dorset Garden Theatre, 1673
from Wilkinson's *Londina Illustrata*, 1819–25

Stage of Dorset Garden Theatre
engraved by Dolle for the 1673 edition of Settle's *The Empress of Morocco*

Harvard Theatre Collection
King's Theatre in the Haymarket, c. 1780
published by Harrison in 1795

Pantheon Theatre, 1795
from Wilkinson's *Londina Illustrata*, 1819–25

Orchard Street Theatre in Bath
from a watercolor by Nixon, reproduced in Mowbray Green's
The Eighteenth Century Architecture of Bath, 1902

King's Theatre in the Haymarket, 1780s (?)
from Wilkinson's *Londina Illustrata,* 1819–25

Sybil Rosenfeld and Cambridge University Press
A Country Fair Booth, Probably Late Eighteenth Century
engraved by Thomas Tegg after Rowlandson

Harvard Theatre Collection
A Provincial Theatre, 1788
from an aquatint by J. Wright after W. R. Pyne